De Gaulle ⚜ ⚜

Brian Crozier

De Gaulle

Charles Scribner's Sons · New York

Contents

Author's Note and Acknowledgements   ix

PART I: THE ENIGMA OF DE GAULLE
1   The Man   3
2   Historical Prologue   10

PART II: HISTORIAN AND THINKER 1890–1939
1   Pupil of the Jesuits (1890–1909)   17
2   The Young Officer (1909–1918)   23
3   The Historian (1919–1924)   32
4   Pétain's Protégé (1924–1932)   41
5   A Prophet Ignored (1932–1939)   57

PART II: FREE FRANCE 1939–1945
1   The Defeat (1939–1940)   83
2   The Challenge   109
3   The Free French   119
4   Divided They Fall   134
5   De Gaulle versus his Allies: 1   144
6   De Gaulle versus his Allies: 2   165
7   Roosevelt in the Ascendant   183
8   "Torch" and After   195
9   Casablanca   207
10   Algiers   222
11   The Resistance   235
12   Roots of the Fourth Republic   246
13   The Agony of France   259

PART IV: THE LIBERATION AND AFTER 1944–1946

1 Jostling for Position 273
2 De Gaulle's Parisian Triumph 295
3 Trial of Strength 317
4 Foreign Disappointments 329
5 International Discords 349
6 Vichy on Trial 368
7 The Patient Stirs 375
8 De Gaulle Steps Down 385

PART V: THE FOURTH REPUBLIC 1946–1958

1 Birth and Challenge 399
2 Triumph and Collapse 419
3 In the Wilderness 441
4 De Gaulle Returns 453

PART VI: THE FIFTH REPUBLIC

1 De Gaulle breaks the Opposition (1958–1962) 481
2 The Atlantic Directorate Affair 520
3 Europe and the World 545
4 The Pressure Mounts 569
5 The Roots of Discontent 590
6 Storm and Aftermath 616
7 Exit and Death 646

PART VII: DE GAULLE IN HISTORY

1 Man and Showman 663
2 Soldier and Writer 666
3 Politician and Statesman 672

Bibliographical Note 687

Index 705

Author's Note
and Acknowledgements

To claim a love-hate relationship with the French is not unusual, but the phrase does apply to me. I spent seven years of my childhood in France, six of them at school in the Lycée at Montpellier. At twelve, I spoke English badly and with a strong French accent. Now I am bilingual enough to be taken for French in France and to use occasional Gallicisms in English. Some of my best friends are French, and so are some of the people I have most cordially detested. This alone gives me something in common with the subject of this book.

My attitude towards General de Gaulle is, perhaps, similarly ambivalent. In common with most people of the British Isles who lived through the Second World War, I was emotionally stirred by de Gaulle's decision to fight on after France's stunning defeat. I remained, broadly speaking, a "Gaullist" throughout the war, and was intolerant of Roosevelt's doubts, and of his obtuseness in preferring Giraud: I never doubted that de Gaulle would come out on top in Algiers, and of course he did.

My admiration for de Gaulle did not, however, extend to his followers, whom I found irritatingly self-righteous. In recent years, and with honourable exceptions, I have found self-righteousness to be a continuing characteristic of the Gaullist movement. To claim superiority over that vast majority of the French people who initially sided with Marshal Pétain was, of course, a pardonable conceit in men who took pride in upholding France's honour; but I have always been less tolerant of the assumption that Gaullists are superior to non-Frenchmen as well.

As for General de Gaulle himself, my experience in writing his biography has been the opposite of that of writing Franco's life. With Franco, I started from a point of hostility, discovered how profoundly he had been misrepresented and reached the stage of "grudging admiration". With de Gaulle, while my admiration for the man of June 1940 remains, to compile the inventory of his later aberrations is to be deeply disillusioned.

The personality, the will and the skill, the erudition and the self-discipline, the memory and the courage: these things still kindle the admiration. But the harm he did the West, and therefore France, outlives him. I hope this book makes it clear that it is possible to admire the man and to deplore much of what he did or failed to do. To those of my French friends who are also Gaullists, I tender my apologies. I hope only that they will recognise the care I have taken to be objective.

Although no other study of de Gaulle's entire life had appeared when this book was completed, his career is richly documented. Some entirely new material did, however, come my way, both in the form of documents and in that of personal reminiscences, orally expressed.

Many of the well-placed people who told me what they knew, especially about Franco-German, Franco-British and Franco-American relations during de Gaulle's second period of power, asked to remain anonymous. I have respected their wishes, and simply attributed the relevant matter to "private source" or "private information". I wish to emphasise that these anonymous informants are of several nationalities.

Among those who did not ask me to conceal their names are the following, to whom I express my thanks: MM. Jacques Baumel, Roger Frey, Louis Joxe, Pierre Mendès France, Gaston Palewski, Jean Sainteny, Jacques Soustelle and Louis Vallon. I am grateful to Major-General Sir Edward Spears for his kind permission to quote from a wartime report of his on de Gaulle and the Free French. And I owe a special debt of gratitude to Mrs A. D. Lacy, who kindly gave me access to the papers of her late husband, Commander A. D. Lacy, relating to his service as naval liaison officer to the then commander of the Free French naval forces, Admiral Muselier. This important collection, of which I have made a selective use, throws a new light on the successive "Muselier affairs".

Thanks are also due to my research assistant, Judith Miller, without whose help I would not have been able to complete the copy on time; and to Mrs Dorothy Pickles, who took on the daunting task of reading the entire typescript and commenting on it in detail. I owe much to her knowledge and advice; any remaining errors or oddities of judgment are, of course, entirely my own responsibility. As always, the staff of the London Library and of Chatham House were admirably cooperative. The Quai d'Orsay was courteous but unwilling to depart from its fifty-year rule of official secrecy. The French official historian, M. Henri Michel, was courteously helpful and kindly gave me access to his material on Free France and the Resistance. My thanks are due to him, as they are to the staffs of the Association Nationale pour le Soutien à l'Action du Général de Gaulle, and of the Photothèque of the French Armed Forces at Ivry.

I did not meet General de Gaulle. I had been promised an audience in May 1969, on the assumption that he would have won the referendum of April and would still be in power. He lost, and was not. In our subsequent exchanges of letters, he agreed to answer any questions I might send him at Colombey-les-Deux-Eglises. Not wishing to importune him, I saved them up until the collection was of decent length, and posted them at the beginning of November 1970. He died, however, a week later.

Although I regret, on personal grounds, not having met de Gaulle my regret is mitigated by the thought that personal acquaintance, and exposure to the force of his personality, might have interfered with my purpose, which was to treat him as a figure in history, as one would write a biography of, say, Cromwell or Richelieu.

My thanks are also due to M. Georges Albertini for kindly sending me much current material of interest, and especially for introducing me to a number of leading Gaullists; and to M. Boris Souvarine, who kindly sent me the typescript of the late General Odic's unpublished memoirs.

The bulk of the British official documents relating to the Second World War was only made available at the Public Records Office, London, about the time this work was being completed. I do not believe they would have affected my interpretation of events.

Finally, I must record my thanks to Mr Frank Shakespeare, formerly head of the United States Information Agency, and Mr Eugene Rosenfeld, of the American Embassy in London, for procuring State Department publications relating to wartime meetings in which General de Gaulle was involved.

Brian Crozier

1973

Part I ⚜ The Enigma of De Gaulle

Chapter 1 ❧ The Man

The presence was crushing. The ruin of a military face, laden with years, wisdom, cunning and rancour, was perched almost incongruously on a massive pear-shaped body. The eyes, which but for vanity would have been hidden behind thick lenses, peered disconcertingly at the visitor. The voice, though old, was a noble compound of the Paris *faubourgs*, the barrack square and the lecture room. Everything about him was beyond the normal measure – his height, his intellect, his memory. When he fixed you, in the flesh or on the little screen – even through the printed word – there was no god in sight but Charles de Gaulle.

This hyperbolic personage twice flashed across French history, casting a gigantic shadow in which lesser figures were at times only faintly visible. Although always known as *mon Général*, even in the highest civilian office of the French Republic, his military career was honourable rather than distinguished, the fortunes of war having denied him the opportunities of ultimate fame. He spent much of the Great War in a German prison camp, having been left for dead on the battlefield after a desperate wound. The Second World War brought him rapid battle promotion, but only to a temporary rank in the lowest grade of general officer, and after the fall of France, he fought the remainder of the war as a politician and statesman, not as a soldier. In earlier military life, much of it on boring garrison duties, he had achieved distinction as an intellectual: a writer and an historian. A prophet also, as events were to show.

This was a man of heroic stature and the adulation or hatred he provoked was of appropriate scale. In a permanent sense, de Gaulle was a hero to millions of ordinary Frenchmen (and, even more, to French women) who had tired of the antics of politicians and who longed for a leader who would tell foreigners where they might no longer trespass. He was also a hero to the "unconditional" Gaullists – that is, to those who, for opportunistic or idealistic motives, would say that the general was right whatever he said or did. At various times, he was also a hero to followers who later turned against him because he disappointed their particular hopes.

To these, and to those who were against him anyway, he was a monster. Among the former were many supporters of *Algérie Française;* among the latter, many supporters of Vichy and much of the French *Patronat.* For the extremes of contradictory passion which his name aroused, and in certain other obvious respects, his career invites comparison with that of General Franco. But there was a deep and significant difference between Franco Spain and Gaullist France. Franco came to power as the outcome of a bloody civil war, after which his opponents were either exiled or liquidated. France avoided a civil war, but only just; for paying off old scores between resisters and collaborators after the Second World War approximated to one. Indeed there were liquidations in France and some famous trials – of which those of Pétain and Laval were the most notorious – but the shedding of compatriots' blood was on a far smaller scale than in Spain. Apart from some collaborators and some "French Algeria" politicians and army officers, most of de Gaulle's antagonists remained in France. For that reason, opposition to him was always stronger at home than opposition to Franco in Spain.

His appeal, however, was always immense, and in 1945 and 1958 overwhelming. He had to an extraordinary degree the capacity to transcend individual groups by stirring up patriotic sentiments among people to whom patriotism meant different things. Many Vichyists rallied round him (and showed it by supporting his rally of the French people), partly through love of the paternalistic authority which Pétain had represented for them, and which they now sought in the younger man. Although the monarchists shunned him, he strongly appealed to residual royalist sentiment among Republicans, since he was so clearly an uncrowned monarch. At the same time, he could be seen as the "defender" and "saviour" of the Republic. Although a section of the army rebelled against him, the bulk of it remained faithful: another source of appeal was to those who were nostalgic for another Bonaparte. Among the many paradoxes of de Gaulle is that he symbolised, for some, authority and legitimacy, for others, glory and adventure.

Another paradox was this. On the one hand, de Gaulle, who came of a line of minor aristocrats and *bourgeois,* and was a practising Catholic, appealed to the *bien-pensants* of conservative France; on the other hand, his family was poor and he despised the *bourgeoisie* and the bosses of the *Patronat,* so that he was able to compete with the Communist party for the voters of the left. In this respect, too, he was a "bridge", for the French are both conservative and revolutionary: their conservatism delays necessary reforms, so that revolution becomes inevitable.

The popular image of him abroad, to which his enemies at home contributed, was that of a dictator. But this was misleading. His claim to be the defender of the legitimacy of the Republic inhibited him from asserting, in the full and formal sense, a dictatorship. Other inhibiting factors were the French tradition of liberty and the relative weakness of the authoritarian tradition in comparison with, say, Spain or Germany. He was an autocrat by disposition and character, who exercised his authority through a compelling personality and a uniquely subtle political skill. He was, too, an illusionist or magician, adept at creating a sense of achievement when nothing, in fact, had been done. And with all that, he was of course a consummate actor, and an orator of unusual power and nobility of style.

As long ago as 1932, de Gaulle set out his master-ideas on the requirements of leadership in the most important of his shorter works, *Le Fil de l'Epée* – "The Edge of the Sword". (It is a linguistic irony, by the way, that the French language, de Gaulle's vehicle for this richly subtle and allusive study of the qualities of a leader, lacks a word for "leadership".) Literally translated, these requirements sound strangely alien, though intelligible, in English: the magnetism of confidence, and even of illusion; the elevation of the leader's aims and his contempt for contingencies, leaving to the mass the care of details; the isolation of grandeur[1] and renunciation of happiness. The young de Gaulle knew of course, or felt in his bones, that a time would come when he would act out the part he then wrote. Men of destiny, as we know to our cost, have this habit of writing well in advance the history they plan to make. When Charles de Gaulle was young, his intelligence did not go unnoticed, but his fixed ideas of grandeur were generally ascribed to an overweening vanity. Undeflected from a chosen course, he carried his ideas with him through two wars, the London period, the Algiers period, the Fighting French triumph, the sudden resignation, the years in the wilderness of Colombey-les-Deux-Eglises and the return to power (though he disguised the fact) on the back of a higher-ranking general – Salan – who looked to him to do things he had no intention of doing.

When the second call came in 1958, those who facilitated his return to power were soon to learn the meaning of some of the more devastating notions of *Le Fil de l'Epée*, such as his contemptuous dismissal of "the walkers-on of the hierarchy, parasites who absorb everything and give nothing in return ... safeguarding their careers as civil servants, their promotion as soldiers or their ministers' portfolios". To de Gaulle, in

---

[1] The French word *grandeur* comprehends the English "greatness" and "grandeur"; the English word "grandeur" is mostly used in this double sense throughout this work.

1958 as in 1932, there was no prestige for such as these, but only "the deference that comes with custom". When de Gaulle reigned in the Elysée Palace those dismissive words were still true, in his eyes, of his ministers and even of his soldiers. But it was hardly true or just to call his higher civil servants parasites, for it was they – the hard-worked men in the shadows – who really governed France from the confines of de Gaulle's Elyseum.

For all its frivolous associations, there was a certain aptness in this choice of a dwelling place for an uncrowned monarch. Beyond the little gates and the watchful *gardes Républicains* lies a gravel quadrangle, and beyond that, not the world of Watteau and Fragonard appropriate to the rococo interior (except for visiting dignitaries), but the austere cerebral world of the technocrats – the *Polytechniciens* and *Normaliens*, the *hauts fonctionnaires* who gave Gaullism its underlying structure. For the Elysée has in its day been the home not only of an emperor, a courtesan – Madame de Pompadour – and foreign kings, but of that technocrat of the pretechnocratic age, the financier Beaujon, who lived there in 1773.

It was said, and not untruly, that de Gaulle's technocrats constituted a parallel government. The essence of the Fifth Republic, tailored to the measurements of this exceptional man, lay in the fact that the Prime Minister was not the president of the Council of Ministers. The president of de Gaulle's Republic also presided over the Council of Ministers – and in a dominant way not matched by the weaker presidents of earlier republics when chairing such occasions. Nor was the large and unwieldy *Conseil des Ministres* in the British sense, a cabinet. When the ministers met in council, they were there *en masse*, not at the Hôtel Matignon, where the Prime Minister worked, but at the Elysée.

The agenda would have been decided in advance – by General de Gaulle. The decisions would have been taken in advance – by General de Gaulle. And the real purpose of the gathering of the council was not to thrash out a policy that had already been determined, but to discuss and report on problems and policies, then take note of policy decisions, the better to execute them. In effect, the visible government executed the orders of the invisible one.

This was what happened, yet in a sense it *is* an exaggeration to say that there was a parallel government. For visible or invisible, the men who helped de Gaulle reach decisions or carry out his orders owed their positions entirely to the president of the Fifth Republic. In that sense, all were equal in their inequality, and only one was more equal than the others. In that sense, too, there was only one man in de Gaulle's government: the presiding president.

6

De Gaulle did not of course invent the Elysée system. Some of it he inherited from the long line of under-powered presidents of the Third and Fourth Republics, notably the departments charged with protocol and other ceremonial matters. But the machinery that had been geared to the needs of ornamental presidents was inadequate for those of a man who wanted to rule as well as symbolise. The new Elysée was expanded to meet those wider needs. Under de Gaulle, the Elysée's staff comprised four organs: the *cabinet* (in the French sense of the term, meaning a private secretariat for the president): the secretariat-general; the department for African and Malagasy affairs; and the private general staff.

The *cabinet* regulated the general's personal life, his appointments, the audiences he granted (to which great importance was attached), receptions, dinners and lunches, and journeys. The department for African and Malagasy affairs, in effect, maintained the personal and public links between the general and the African empire he had emancipated, originally known as the Community, and later – when all its African members opted for independence – more realistically as the *ex*-Community. There was nevertheless a strangeness about the presence of this department at the Elysée, and the incumbent in General de Gaulle's time, Jacques Foccart, a much parachuted ex-Resistance man and an old faithful, was also – and primarily – in charge of secret departments covering intelligence and security. Algerian affairs were handled outside the Elysée, by a special office.

The real parallel government was the secretariat-general, whose personnel comprised some fifteen high officials, each of whom had charge of one or more departments corresponding to ministries. The most important dealt with finance, the interior, foreign affairs, education, scientific research and information. Unusual qualities were required of the scarcely known technocrats who manned the secretariat-general. They had to be prepared to work long hours, to produce in written form with unerring accuracy and sometimes at an almost impossible speed the facts, figures, and arguments with which General de Gaulle would later confront the responsible ministers; and of course to bear the brunt of ministerial ire or envy when criticisms or suggestions were resented.

Although de Gaulle valued the *tête-à-tête* over lunch or dinner (a rarely accorded honour) and the small, informal discussion, he wanted everything of importance in writing. To be a Gaullist functionary was thus an exacting occupation for which only a physically fit intellectual *élite* need apply. The most impressive holder of the key office of secretary-general was Etienne Burin des Roziers, an Oxonian ex-ambassador who had belonged to de Gaulle's innermost circle from 1945. It was a punishing job, with an awe-inspiring daily dosage of reading, embracing all the diplomatic telegrams and all the Bills; all the notes, reports and dossiers prepared by the high officials under him. At the Elysée, under the shadow of the president himself, he was the biggest of the "big four" – the others were the head of the *cabinet*, who, besides arranging the general's appointments, had his remaining time full listening to those whom the general declined to receive; the head of the department of African and Malagasy affairs; and the head of the private general staff, once called the *maison militaire*, and later restyled the *état-major particulier*. Everything military, including relations with NATO, nuclear research for military ends, and the transmission of orders to the general's aides-de-camp, came under the head of the private general staff.

These, then, were the organs, but how did they pulsate, gestate, digest, or otherwise function? The secret was known, at least to a few, but shrouded in mystery. It consisted of a procedure evolved for de Gaulle's purposes and known as "restricted councils". Nobody but the participants knew what went on at these meetings which, by definition, were small. The written word, essential to de Gaulle in other respects, was out of its element in this context: there was no agenda for the restricted councils, and no record was kept either of the proceedings or of the identities of participants. The high officials and their departmental chiefs were constantly producing memoranda for de Gaulle. Whenever the general felt a question had ripened sufficiently, he called a restricted council.

Strictly, the system did exist before de Gaulle, in the form of *Conseils interministériels*; but de Gaulle included civil servants and indeed anybody he chose, as well as ministers, in his *conseils restreints*. The originality of the system as revised under General de Gaulle lay in its expansion to duplicate and anticipate the work of the ministries. Regular restricted councils were held on military, African and Malagasy, and Algerian affairs; and less frequent ones on economic and financial affairs, education, scientific research, public works, radio and television, agriculture, and foreign policy.

On paper, the system looked a perfect recipe for secret and absolute rule, and the high officials like overworked men at the beck and call of a tyrant. But de Gaulle was *sui generis* and made short shrift of preconceived notions. Though an exacting taskmaster who made a fetish of punctuality, he did not expect his advisers to be yes-men. By definition, indeed, they were not: he hand picked the best administrative brains, then expected them to argue with him if need be, knowing always that in the end he would make the decisions alone. Nor was it always as militarily efficient as it looked. Too often, the ageing man at the helm merely read a report, endorsed it as "seen" and took no action; and just as often, a decision was taken, but somewhere between the thrusting high official and a more devious minister, the decision trickled out into a dry creek of immobility. "It is as though," a prominent Gaullist told me, "you were on a ship sailing for the North Pole and an officer put a piece of paper before the captain proposing a change of direction to the South Pole. The captain reads it, marks it 'seen', and the ship sails on heading north."

For de Gaulle, who was already fifty when he achieved national and world fame, was an old man when he returned to power; and therein lay his tragedy. A tragedy of hopes deferred and belated opportunities, of obsolete visions and frustrating realities. In his relatively short period of supreme office, de Gaulle consolidated the claim to immortality he had already staked in 1940 as an unknown junior general, but he achieved less than he had hoped or than had been expected of him. Like Bonaparte, de Gaulle came to fame and power as the consequence of a great national upheaval. But Bonaparte was in his twenties when opportunity knocked; de Gaulle was well into middle age. Nor was history kind to de Gaulle in its gift of a century in which to operate.

It was given to de Gaulle to revitalise France; but the France he revitalised was dwarfed by two super-powers in a bi-polar world. Napoleonic France could dominate Europe as Gaullist France could not. Nor was the divided and demoralised people whom de Gaulle to some extent regenerated and united, a match for his dreams of grandeur. All his life, as the general himself put it, he had a "certain idea of France"; but he could never hide his contempt for the French people, who perennially disappointed him by their patent unworthiness of the country of his vision. Nothing written today can diminish the aura of General de Gaulle's wartime exploit. But history may well record the verdict that as a writer, he wrote too little; as a soldier, he fought too little; and as a statesman, he came too late.

When a man has become a living legend, when he has deliberately chosen the solitary path to greatness, when every word and gesture is weighed and calculated in advance for its effect upon others, it becomes difficult indeed to pierce the public armour to reach the flesh and blood beneath. De Gaulle had a few intimates but no friends. Even the earliest Gaullist memoirs are suspect, since they were written by followers who hoped to create a legend and succeeded. As with other great names, many of the anecdotes about him are apocryphal. But all, whether true or false, are consistent. His language in private, generously laced with barrack-square coarseness, was marked by an abrasive and sardonic wit. His sufferance of fools was short-lived. As a schoolboy and a subaltern, he was liked, but usually at a distance: already, his height, the singularity of his mind, and his vocation of solitude set him apart from the others. His character training began early, under the fond but professorial sternness of his father; and he consciously trained himself for greatness. Adversity completed the process, with his wartime captivity in Germany and later, the death of his handicapped daughter Anne. His marriage was felicitous, his private life untouched by scandal.

Perhaps, after all, there was no enigma – except in the minds of lesser men who found it hard to conceive such tenacity of purpose, such apparent perverseness in the pursuit of the unattainable, such constancy in striving to reproduce in real life the plans so carefully described in a literary youth. To such as these, de Gaulle was frequently disconcerting. But he was so only to those who expected him to behave as timidly or inconsistently as lesser men might. To those who knew him best, or studied him most assiduously, there was no enigma: very early in life, Charles de Gaulle knew where he wanted to go, and in later life, he did or attempted to do what he had always said he would do.

Chapter 2 ✤ Historical Prologue

Charles de Gaulle was born in 1890 at the height of the Panama scandal, and in the wake of the Boulanger crisis and the Wilson affair.

The common background to these events was the Bonapartist experiment of Prince Louis-Napoleon, who became Napoleon III and as such a precursor of the twentieth-century dictators. Tiny in stature and pompous in appearance, Napoleon III owed his success in gaining power at least as much to the magic of his name and the nostalgia for recent imperial glory as to his talent as a conspirator and self-propagandist. The people of France undoubtedly wanted him to be, first, their prince-president and later, their emperor. There was no need for him to fake the plebiscite by which they overwhelmingly approved of the *coup d'état* he had carried out in December 1851. For eight years or so, he gave them sound, authoritarian government, economic expansion and even foreign successes – in particular, the defeat of Russia, in alliance with England, in the Crimean War. He also gave them, as had the first Napoleon, a stifling of political liberty. The splendour of his court, however, contributed to his popularity, as it had to that of the first Napoleon. Certainly, the initial stability of the Second Empire contributed to its economic successes. A depression in 1846, aggravated by revolutionary violence in 1848, turned into a surge of expansion. King Louis-Philippe (1830–48) had given France a railway system; Napoleon III trebled it and more, making of Paris more than ever the scintillating capital of France. Credit institutions and joint stock banks, such as the Société Générale, were founded and flourished. Small investors proliferated. By 1870 France was a notable industrial power.

It was in foreign affairs that Napoleon III's judgment was most deficient. His interventions in Italy, Austria and Mexico were ill-judged and costly adventures. The dominant political and military reality of Europe after the seven weeks' war of 1866 was the emergence of Prussia as a great power. Napoleon III allowed himself to be goaded by Bismarck into a disastrous declaration of war on 19 July 1870. The outcome was the invasion of France, the capitulation of the French army and the collapse of the Second Empire. Thus, for the second time in less than a century, a Napoleon had brought both grandeur and humiliation to France.

This second disaster, worse even than 1815 in its consequences for France, might have seemed enough. But it did not deter yet another Bonapartist adventure – that of General Boulanger. General Boulanger was popular on a number of counts, none of them historically impressive. On the positive side, he had fought bravely in Africa, in Italy and in Cochin-China. As minister of War in 1886 under the Third Republic, he cut a dashing figure that endeared him to women, and made speeches that flattered the crowd. There was a negative asset as well: one of his wounds was received as fighting began in Paris in the wake of defeat in the Franco-Prussian war. This circumstance saved him from involvement in repressing the revolutionary Communards. He was thus acceptable to the mob as well as to the military hierarchy.

Boulanger's Bonapartist moment came, however, on the crest of the wave of anti-Prussian patriotic sentiment. Boulanger crystallised the popular mood of *revanchisme*. The instrument of France's revenge against the Germans was to be Boulanger's "republicanised" army. Overnight, Boulanger became "General Revanche", when Bismarck, in a *Reichstag* speech in January 1887, named him as the greatest obstacle

11

to good relations between France and Germany. In May, however, the ministry fell. Instantly, Boulanger turned to conspiracy. The Wilson affair – one of the juicy scandals so characteristic of French republics – gave him his chance. President Grévy's son-in-law, Daniel Wilson, was found to have been conducting a thriving traffic in honours and decorations, which he sold from the Elysée Palace itself, thus economising on office space. High personages were implicated, and the long crisis that followed this discovery forced the resignation of the President and his government.

The Royalists and Bonapartists decided that only Boulanger could save France. In January 1889, Boulanger was elected to parliament with a big majority. The *coup d'état* that was to bring him to power was prepared. Had Boulanger been as resolute as his oratory indicated, it might have succeeded. Instead, his essential frivolity and laziness came uppermost. Losing his nerve, he walked out on his followers. Not long after, threatened with prosecution, Boulanger fled to Brussels. Appropriately, it was All Fools' day. Thirty months later, he committed suicide on the grave of his mistress.

In 1889, at the height of the Boulangist crisis, the Panama Canal Company crashed spectacularly. The panic-stricken shareholders appealed to the government to protect their interests. The director, Ferdinand de Lesseps, of Suez Canal fame, was charged with corruption, along with some of his colleagues. The charges remained unproven, but rumours that deputies had been bribed by Jewish financiers persisted. One of the financiers, Baron de Reinach, was found dead; and another, Cornelius Hertz, fled to England, lending apparent substance to the allegations. The scandal, on top of Boulanger's disastrous failure and the earlier Wilson scandal, drove many Frenchmen to the political extremes. On the right, there was a wave of virulent anti-Semitism, echoed some years later in the notorious Dreyfus affair; on the left, especially in the provinces – ever distrustful of Paris – many voters took the view that the Republic's politicians were incurably corrupt.

The most important fact of European history at the time when de Gaulle entered it, however, was the emergence of Prussia as the dominant land power in Europe. *Revanchisme* was in the air in his boyhood and youth (significantly, the penultimate chapter of his *La France et son Armée* is entitled "*Vers la Revanche*") and the concept of a permanent see-saw struggle for European hegemony between Germany and France permeates General de Gaulle's early writings. The history of de Gaulle's middle and later years is marked by his stubborn resistance to the changed realities of power politics after 1940: the emergence of Russia and America as the overwhelming powers, the traumatic paradox of a defeated France with a place among the victors (itself one of de Gaulle's greatest achievements), and the consequent moral ascendancy of France over an economically resurgent but truncated Germany; and the enfeeblement of Great Britain.

Part II ⚜ Historian and Thinker
1890–1939

Chapter 1 ✤ Pupil of the Jesuits 1890–1909

Aged ten, Charles de Gaulle had already formed his "certain idea of France"; at thirteen, he had chosen a military calling.

The family background of his childhood was itself, of course, the product of a long heredity of solid northern burghers and petty nobility with a tradition of duty and service to the State. His nearest forbears included a literary grandmother and a scientific uncle. His father, a teacher, presided over an austere but loving household, in which money, it is said, was held in quiet contempt.[1]

But liberalism, in this unostentatious home, went hand in hand with propriety and Catholic observance. It was at first considered normal to defend the accusers of Dreyfus, the Jewish officer condemned for alleged treason; but Charles de Gaulle's father valued justice above class solidarity, and soon started defending the accused.[2]

The de Gaulles came from Flanders, Champagne and Burgundy. A fifteenth-century de Gaulle fought against the king of England; an eighteenth-century descendant was Prosecutor to the parliament of Paris.[3]

In 1835 the de Gaulles of Burgundy renewed their ancestral links with French Flanders, when Julien-Philippe de Gaulle married Joséphine-Anne-Marie Maillot, whose family came from Lille, though it owned tobacco factory at Dunkirk. It was an interesting union. Socially, it united a Burgundian family of nobles and civil servants with a *bourgeois* family of the industrious Flemish north. Personally, it joined a historian and a writer. For it was Julien-Philippe de Gaulle who was the author of the *Nouvelle Histoire de Paris et de ses Environs*. A palaeographer, Julien-Philippe had compiled an elaborate history of the de Gaulle family, which remains unpublished. His wife Joséphine, General de Gaulle's paternal

---

[1] Pierre Galante, *Le Général* (Paris, 1968), p. 47 (henceforth, Galante).
[2] J. R. Tournoux, *Pétain and de Gaulle* (Paris, 1964), p. 39n. (henceforth, Tournoux, *Pétain*).
[3] For a fuller account of de Gaulle's genealogy, *see* Georges Cattaui, *Charles de Gaulle* (l'*Homme et son Destin*) (Paris, 1960), pp. 11–17, (henceforth, Cattaui).

grandmother, was, however, a more distinguished literary figure. Intellectually emancipated at a time when women of good family were not encouraged to do anything more ambitious than dabble in the arts, she became the editor of a review entitled *Correspondance des Familles* in which she was bold enough to publish essays by the revolutionary socialist Jules Vallès. She herself wrote eulogies of a more serious socialist, the philosopher Proudhon. Yet Joséphine Maillot was far from being a socialist. A fervent Catholic, she wrote more than a dozen works of piety, whose high moral tone was much praised at the time. Her versatility was indeed remarkable, for she made her name with a novel that still finds interested readers: *Adhémar de Belcastel*. Moreover, her works include a life of Chateaubriand and another of *O'Connell, Libérateur de l'Irlande*. Both biographies have a curious bearing on the taste and achievements of her grandson, for Charles de Gaulle became a great admirer of Chateaubriand, while the thesis of her book on O'Connell provides a parallel with de Gaulle's life. In it, she praised the Irish patriot for having made a revolution without bloodshed, and a settlement that respected law and order.

Three sons were born of the marriage, and each in his way was remarkable. The eldest, Charles, was a chronic invalid who found relief in a life-long study of the Celts. He learned Welsh and Breton, published poems in the latter under the name of *Barz Bro-C'hall* – Breton for "the Bard de Gaulle", and wrote a work on the Celts of the nineteenth century. A visionary as well as a scholar, he dreamed of forming a union of the Celts of all the world, associating the Bretons with the Welsh, the Irish and the Scots.

His brother Jules was to become France's foremost entomologist, and catalogued 5,000 varieties of French bees and wasps. The third brother, Henri, born in 1848, married a cousin, Jeanne Maillot-Delannoy, in her native town of Lille on 2 August 1886. A pious young woman, two of whose sisters were nuns, Jeanne had a recent Irish and Scottish ancestry. A tall, distinguished-looking man with a slight stoop, Henri de Gaulle had chosen a military career and had passed the entrance examination to the Polytechnique, but changed his plans when his father died suddenly, leaving him in charge of the family. He was twenty-two, and it was 1870. France faced defeat, and Henri de Gaulle answered Gambetta's call for volunteers. Since the Germans did not recognise them, they were publicly called "sharpshooters". Young Henri was wounded, and a medal – later treasured by his son – marked the occasion.

When peace returned in 1870, Henri de Gaulle would have liked to resume his studies. But necessity made him earn his living as a teacher.

He was thirty-eight before he felt sufficiently established to take on the responsibility of marriage. Madame de Gaulle chose to have her babies, as she had chosen to get married, at Lille. The first was a son, Xavier, named after the Jesuit saint of the parish. Henri's brother Charles – the Celtic visionary – died shortly after, at barely thirty. And the second son was named after him. Charles de Gaulle was born on 22 November 1890, in the house of his maternal grandparents, 9 Rue Princesse. Next day, he was baptised in the austere Carmelite church of St André, with the Christian names Charles André Joseph Marie. Though Charles de Gaulle was thus by birth a Lillois, he was given a Parisian upbringing.

When Charles was born, his father was teaching philosophy, mathematics and literature in the College of the Immaculate Conception, founded by the Jesuit fathers at 389 Rue de Vaugirard. And a year later, he was appointed director (*préfet*) of studies. It was a bad time to be teaching for the Jesuits. In the wake of the Dreyfus scandal, a wave of anti-militarism and anti-clericalism swept the Third Republic, whose leaders linked the army and the Church as symbols of reaction. The Premier, Emile Combes, a prominent freemason, was determined to end the privileges of the religious orders and transform the Concordat with the Vatican into a "Discordat". On 9 December 1905, on the eve of his fall from office, a law he had sponsored severed all ties between Church and State. From that day, the Republic would no longer pay priests and bishops; nor was the Church allowed to own property, which the State seized as its own. Lay committees were set up to administer church affairs in every parish. The Combes law was denounced in the papal encyclical *Vehementor Nos,* and in the more pious regions of France – in Brittany, in Auvergne and in Flanders – defiant Catholics barricaded themselves in the churches to prevent inventories by the hated fiscal agents of the State. In several places, troops had to be used to evict them.

The Jesuit fathers had to abandon the College of the Immaculate Conception, and took refuge in Belgium. One day, the police commissioner of the Vaugirard district, with the authority of the tricolour sash of office, called at the college and asked to see "Father" de Gaulle, who, as director of studies, was in charge of the diminished establishment. M. de Gaulle received him in his normal garb – frock-coat and pale yellow gloves. "I am not 'Father de Gaulle'," he said with his usual dignity. "You have no business here."

"Not at all," said the policeman, vaguely disconcerted, "you are a Jesuit in civilian clothes."

M. de Gaulle was not a man to lose his temper or equanimity. With patient courtesy, he enquired: "Would you like me to introduce you to my wife and five children?"[4]

There was a cruel irony in Henri de Gaulle's minor confrontation with the police. The Radicals were out to punish the military and Catholic establishment, which they blamed for the mad adventures of Napoleon III, the defeat of France by the Prussians and the Dreyfus affair. But Henri de Gaulle was a nationalist and a practising Christian through passionate moral conviction, and not because those were the views of the class into which he was born. Above all, he was a man of justice who became convinced of the innocence of Dreyfus. The *affaire* had split France. For two years, from 1894, a French staff officer and playboy, Major Esterhazy, had been selling information to the Germans. French counter-intelligence accused the young Jewish officer Captain Alfred Dreyfus of the crime, but would probably have dropped the charge for lack of evidence if a vicious anti-Semite, Edouard Drumont, author of the explosive best-seller *La France juive*, had not got wind of the affair and published a charge that wealthy Jews were trying to protect a traitor. Forged documents sent Dreyfus to Devil's Island for life (though he was later vindicated). One of his staunchest defenders was the nationalist poet Charles Péguy – one of the major influences in Charles de Gaulle's life. The Dreyfus affair was a table topic in the de Gaulle household, and years later Charles de Gaulle was to write this passage about it in his book on the French army:

> By a kind of fatality, at the very moment when the spirit of the public is tending to take its distance from the army, there bursts the crisis that is most likely to magnify evil intentions. In this lamentable trial, nothing that could poison the passions was to be lacking. The probability of a judicial error, supported by forgeries, irresponsibilities, abuses on the part of the prosecution, but rejected with horror by those who, by faith or for reasons of State, are determined to maintain the infallibility of a hierarchy devoted to the service of the fatherland; an exasperating obscurity, in which a thousand muddled incidents, intrigues, confessions, retractions, duels, suicides, subsidiary trials, enrage and constantly throw off the scent the two rival packs; an unhealthy frenzy, where that elementary respect for the symbol of their power in which the divided French manage to unite, sinks helter-skelter along with mutual respect, convictions, friendships.[5]

Charles de Gaulle was too young by a few years to understand what

---

[4] Galante, p. 41.
[5] *La France et son Armée* (Paris, 1938, 1965), pp. 243–4 (henceforth, De Gaulle, *France*).

was going on at the time, but old enough to realise later what the Dreyfus affair meant to his father's generation. Shame and defeat; patriotism and the nation; faith and religion – these were the themes of Professor de Gaulle's paternal guidance. The affair had tarnished the army's prestige: many officers resigned their commissions, and applications for entrance into the Saint-Cyr Military Academy fell by half.[6]

The Radicals, who in Gambetta's day had been fiercely patriotic, turned anti-militaristic. The Waldeck–Rousseau government (1899–1902) – though relatively mild in comparison with the successor government of Emile Combes – brought in legislation depriving the officer corps of the power to make its own promotions, and anti-clerical laws that forced thousands of monks and nuns into exile.

It was against this background that Charles de Gaulle heard his father's story of the wound he had sustained when the Germans were besieging Paris, and his mother's talk of her parents in tears at the news that the vainglorious Marshal Bazaine had capitulated with all his forces. That stern moralist, Henri de Gaulle, never failed to point the contrast between the ideal of a grave and faithful Christian France, and the unworthiness of the citizens who fell short of it – a theme that was to dominate General de Gaulle's nationalist thinking. Shame and honour, indeed, alternated in France at large and at the de Gaulle table. There was Sedan, and Dreyfus; there was also, in a relatively minor vein, Fashoda, where a bold but unfortunate young French officer, Captain Marchand, had been forced to turn tail when leading an expedition to challenge Britain's hold on the Upper Nile in 1899.[7] But against these symbols of national shame were names that spelt France's honour. One, much talked about at home, was that of General Faidherbe, a Lillois like de Gaulle's mother, and the conqueror of Senegal. Others held to have brought honour to the French name were thinkers and writers: the philosopher Henri Bergson, and his teacher Boutroux; the Dreyfusard journalist Bernard Lazare; the Dreyfusard poet Péguy; Péguy's friend, the officer and writer Ernest Psichari; the poet and playwright Edmond Rostand; and that wild and unpredictable romantic, the ex-Boulangiste, Maurice Barrès, whose shattering novel, *Du sang, de la volupté, et de la mort* ('Blood, Sensuality and Death'), was published when Charles de Gaulle was four, and who lived on to campaign passionately for the restoration of Alsace and Lorraine and to write a chronicle of the First World War.

[6] Gordon Wright, *France in Modern Times* (London, 1962) (henceforth, Wright).
[7] De Gaulle, père, thought "perfidious" too mild a word for Queen Victoria's Albion (Tournoux, *Pétain*, p. 39).

21

As a boy, Charles de Gaulle's favourite poet was Rostand. On his tenth birthday, his father took him to see Rostand's *l'Aiglon*, a patriotic play which so fascinated the boy that on coming home he announced he would become a soldier.[8] Later, he learned the same writer's *Cyrano de Bergerac* by heart. Péguy was a literary and patriotic love of later adolescence, and lasted all de Gaulle's life. This austere and mystical figure, deeply influenced by Bergson, from whom he derived a distaste for ready-made thinking, wrote intricately skilful verse, much of it on the Joan of Arc theme, in which he expressed his vision of France as the symbol of Christian virtues. His view of a mother France, the duty of whose sons was to serve her, was a lasting influence on de Gaulle.

Charles had three brothers and a sister. Xavier was the eldest, Charles the second; his sister was named Marie-Agnès; the youngest boy was Pierre, and Jacques came between Charles and Pierre. To accommodate this large family, Henri de Gaulle had bought an austere but impressive property called La Ligerie, in the Dordogne valley, and there they spent their summer holidays. The children were given the option of one book each to take away, and Charles, on the first journey south, chose a history of France.[9]

Though affectionate toward his parents, Charles had an aggressive temper, and his father often chastised him physically.[10] He appears to have taken the warlike games natural to boys of their ages more seriously than the others. One day Pierre, the youngest, came in tears to his mother, who asked him what was the matter. The boy replied, "Charles has beaten me." Asked why, he explained, "We were at war. I was the secret agent. I was captured. I had a message. Instead of carrying out the orders of the commanding general . . ."

"What general?"

"Charles! Instead of swallowing the message, I gave it to the enemy."[11]

On another occasion, Charles refused to surrender the crown of France to Xavier who had tired of always being the emperor of Germany, exclaiming indignantly, "Never! France belongs to me."

Apocryphal or not, these stories are in character. Galante, who records the second anecdote, goes on to say that when de Gaulle was in the second form (equivalent to the British upper fifth) he came home one day to announce that he was indeed determined to be a soldier: "I have taken my decision. I shall prepare for Saint-Cyr, I shall become a soldier." Until then, de Gaulle appears to have given unexpectedly little attention

---

8 Cattaui, p. 20. 9 Galante, p. 47. 10 Tournoux, *Pétain*, p. 25.
11 Galante's version of a story also recounted by other biographers. A different version appears in Cattaui, p. 31.

to his formal studies. Absorbed by his martial games, by adventure stories, and by his beloved poets and writers, he spent more time writing verses of his own than studying. His mother thought piano lessons would encourage a more studious discipline, but was soon disappointed by his lack of interest (although he loved to listen to music). His astonishing memory – which he had already begun to train by speaking words spelt backwards – usually carried him through. But his father was obliged to warn him that if he did not settle down to serious work, he could not hope to pass the entrance examination to Saint-Cyr.

Charles was fourteen. He listened to the warning, set to work and came top of his class. But at fifteen he allowed himself a last poetic fling. Working in secret, he wrote a sketch in verse, *An Ill-fated Meeting*, recording the misfortunes of a naïve passer-by, deprived of his possessions by a clever rogue.[12] He sent the playlet to a literary review, which offered him a choice between a fee of twenty-five francs and publication of his work. Characteristically, he chose publication.

He was growing fast and already towered above his classmates. Though quarrelsome and a natural leader, he was not without a sense of humour. Taking advantage of the fact he was already as tall as an adult, he chose a suitable disguise, and knocked at the door of his own home one day, announcing himself as "General Faidherbe". The choice of identification with this conquering general was perhaps significant.

In 1907, he was sent to the Belgian side of the frontier to finish his secondary studies in the Antoine College, which the exiled French Jesuits had set up there. But he returned to Paris after a year to attend Stanislas College, where he prepared for the entrance examination to Saint-Cyr. And in August 1909, he learned that he had been accepted. His military life was about to begin.

[12] The text is reproduced in full in Tournoux, *Pétain*, pp. 29 *et seq.*

Chapter 2 ⚜ The Young Officer 1909–1918

Charles de Gaulle became a soldier at a time of industrial unrest, rising nationalism and a philosophical cult of the irrational. Those were his years of maximum awareness. The cloud beyond the horizon was war

– a war yet unnamed, which de Gaulle was not alone in sensing and which many of his elders anticipated with patriotic expectancy.

With marked reluctance, French society was moving into the modern age. An increasingly literate peasantry was beginning to take an interest in the political process, and becoming aware of the power of the peasant vote. Much of French industry retained its artisan character; and the urban workers clung to the right to remain ununionised. One-fifth of them – about a million – had, however, joined the Confédération Générale du Travail (CGT), and thereby opted for syndicalism – that is, for revolutionary militancy. In 1909, the year de Gaulle entered Saint-Cyr, there were more than one thousand strikes throughout the country.[1] France had not yet ceased to be a traditional society, but parts of her were already touched by the twentieth century.

More directly inspired by Marx than by the French Socialist philosophers, the organised workers were in the vanguard of the anti-militarists. In 1906 the CGT adopted a marching order that was to become famous: "Anti-militarist and anti-patriotic propaganda must become ever more intense and even bolder." Commenting later on this period in *La France et son Armée* Charles de Gaulle noted disdainfully that "the active wing of the Social Movement", scorning Fourier, Proudhon and other French philosophers, had enrolled itself under the banner of Karl Marx. In the next paragraph, he notes sorrowfully that the working masses were repudiating the warlike sentiment previously associated with the Revolution. "A considerable fraction of the people joins the International. No enemies, other than the enemies of the proletariat!"[2]

Nor were the organised workers alone in the wave of anti-militarism that swept France in the first years of the century. A schoolmaster named Gustave Hervé launched a vitriolic campaign against the army in the trade union press. Denigrating patriotism, pouring scorn on the officers, he called on army recruits to tear down the flag and plant it on a dung heap. On the military issue, as on so many others, however, the French were deeply divided; nor was Marx the only important German influence upon French thought. In the wake of the disasters of 1870, the national mood of introspection turned to the study of German political organisation and German culture in a search for causes and possible remedies. As de Gaulle put it, Kant, Fichte, Hegel and Nietzsche were being taught in the Sorbonne through third parties. One of the foremost French thinkers of the dying quarter of the nineteenth century, Ernest Renan, cam-

[1] P.-M. de la Gorce, *De Gaulle entre Deux Mondes* (Paris, 1964), p. 35 (henceforth, Gorce).
[2] De Gaulle, *France*, pp. 242–3.

paigned for years for the introduction of German scientific methods into French education.

The State too looked to Germany for a military model to emulate. In the late nineteenth century the official wisdom was that France must have as many men under arms as Germany – neither more nor less. For a while, parity was indeed achieved. But the demographic facts made the struggle unequal: the birth rate was rising in Germany and falling in France. The anti-militarist wave that followed the Dreyfus scandal made it difficult to find enough officers to command the conscripts.

By 1906, however, the anti-militarist wave had largely spent itself; and so too had the slavish adulation of science. A new wind of nationalism was blowing, and it sought its strength not in facts, science and organisation so much as in instinct, intuition and mysticism. Reason was yielding to the irrational. In the contest between science and the irrational, Charles de Gaulle consciously opted for the latter, as emerges from an interminable sentence about French national recovery on page 259 of *La France et Son Armée*:

> ... in the domain of thought the advent of people like Boutroux or Bergson, who reawaken French spirituality, the secret radiance of a Péguy, the precocious maturity of youth which feels the coming of the harvester, in literature the influence of a Barrès, reviving in the élite an awareness of national permanency by uncovering the links that attach it to its ancestors, are at once effects and causes of this recovery. . . .

Those were the writers whose books Charles de Gaulle took with him into the Army.[3] Under a new regulation successful candidates for Saint-Cyr were required to serve one full year in the ranks before admission. De Gaulle spent his year with the 9th Company of the 33rd Infantry Regiment at Arras. He did not enjoy it, and found his only consolation from the deadening routine of barrack-square drill and potato peeling in the municipal library of Arras, housed in an ancient abbey where the monks had lovingly collected the books. When somebody asked his

[3] At this time, de Gaulle also read the works of the ultra-right wing monarchist writer, Charles Maurras, founder of *L'Action française*. As the French political scientist Pierre Hassner pointed out in the New York magazine *Interplay* (vol. 1, No. 7, February 1968), there are interesting parallels between the expansionist outlook of Maurras and de Gaulle's later foreign policy. De Gaulle, however, could never swallow Maurras whole. He might approve Maurras's view of France's national grandeur and his advocacy of national unity. But *L'Action française* was the organ of the anti-Dreyfusards, and Maurras the leader of the anti-Semites of France. With his family background of support for Dreyfus, de Gaulle could hardly be a *Maurrassien* in the full sense.

company commander, Captain de Tugny, why he did not promote de Gaulle to sergeant, the reply was: "How can I make this boy a sergeant when he would only feel at his ease as High Constable?"[4]

The studious young man did not begin to feel at home in his chosen career until he entered Saint-Cyr itself. He did not go unnoticed, not only because of his exceptional height, but because of his character and his memory. As in other military institutions, ragging was customary, and his surname was rarely used. Instead, it was "Big Charles", "The Cock", "The Asparagus", "Double Metre" and similar nicknames. De Gaulle seems to have taken these pleasantries in reasonably good part. If this was the game, he reasoned, then he would play it; much as, forty-eight years later, he condescended to play the parliamentary game, in a scene of suitable brevity, before sweeping the Fourth Republic into limbo. Apart from the nicknames attributable to his stature, there was another that referred to the length of his nose: "Cyrano". Since Rostand was one of his favourite writers, this did not annoy him; and for a rag, he was made to stand up on a table and recite a passage from *Cyrano de Bergerac*. In 1912, dressed as a clown, he performed an acrobatic number. On another occasion, he played the role of "the village fiancé", in a Vaudeville organised on the occasion of the "Triumph" of Saint-Cyr.

While nobody could complain of his inability to take a joke, his companions seemed to have found him cold and aloof. And indeed, he was already cultivating the aloofness of the future leader he was later to describe and advocate in *Le Fil de l'Epée*. By all accounts, his conversation consisted largely of impromptu lessons by Charles de Gaulle on the history of France – in which he dazzled his listeners with his prodigious recollection of facts and dates. Inside his exercise book he wrote a quotation from Victor Hugo which he evidently took seriously as a guide to his own conduct: "Concision in style. Precision in thought. Decision in life."

On 1 October 1912, Charles de Gaulle left Saint-Cyr with the rank of second-lieutenant. His place in the final exams was number 13. An unperceptive instructor is said to have noted that he was "average in everything, except height".[5] Top of the class was Alphonse Juin, a future marshal of France.[6]

Having graduated, Charles de Gaulle was offered a choice of regiment. He opted for the 33rd Infantry, where he had served his painful and humble apprenticeship. He therefore returned to Arras. In the mean-

[4] Gaston Bonheur, *Charles de Gaulle* (Paris, 1946, 1958), p. 30 (henceforth, Bonheur).
[5] Jean Lacouture, *De Gaulle* (Paris, 1965), p. 13 (henceforth, Lacouture, *De Gaulle*).
[6] Lucien Nachin, *Charles de Gaulle, Général de France* (Paris, 1944), p. 20n. (henceforth, Nachin).

time, there had been a change at the top, and the new colonel of the regiment was Philippe Pétain.

One day, on the banks of the river Scarpe, Colonel Pétain was lecturing his officers on the importance of fire-power – a view then considered "advanced" at General Staff Headquarters, where the bayonet still tended to be rated superior to the barrel of the gun. A remark of his on a manoeuvre by the Prince de Condé prompted an interruption by the young de Gaulle, who pointed out that Marshal Turenne had silenced Condé with cannon power and saved Arras.

The colonel was favourably impressed by this junior intervention. Taking de Gaulle by the arm, he walked away from the group, deep in discussion upon the respective merits of Condé and Turenne. It was the first mark of Pétain's favour,[7] and the first stage of an acquaintanceship that was to ripen into the friendship of a senior officer for a brilliant young protégé, before degenerating into a clash of dissimilar temperaments and, at length, a confrontation between two outstanding men, each of whom was convinced that he stood for France.

Discipline, however, came first. On Bastille Day, 1913, Pétain had de Gaulle placed under arrest for allowing his troops to break ranks while the colonel, on horseback, was inspecting them. De Gaulle thought he had been wrongly blamed for somebody else's mistake, but there was nothing he could do about it and he faced the prospect of failing to get to Paris the following Sunday, as he usually did. At the last moment, however, Pétain cancelled all punishments. De Gaulle ran all the way to the station and jumped on the train as it was pulling out. He stepped into a carriage already occupied by a middle-aged man in civilian clothes. It was Pétain.

"So, young man," said the colonel, "you almost missed the train?"

"Yes, mon Colonel," said the young man, "but I was sure I would catch it."

"But you were under arrest!"

"That's true, but since the penalty was unjust, I was sure you would lift it!"[8]

Promotion to lieutenant came in October 1913. His companions and the good people of Arras did not know quite what to make of this austere young man of twenty-three who read that dull and excessively Republican newspaper, Le Temps.[9] Nor perhaps did the men under de Gaulle's orders, who were mostly northern Frenchmen, miners from the Pas-de-Calais, peasants from the Tardenois, Thiérarche and Valenciennois districts. They were rough and hardy men, with a sense of their own

[7] Bonheur, pp. 34–5.   [8] Cattaui, p. 30.   [9] Lacouture, De Gaulle, p. 16.

dignity, hardworking but capable of sudden explosions of joy or wrath. They were men after de Gaulle's own heart, however, and (says de la Gorce) when de Gaulle in later life talked about the French people, it was always men like these he had in mind: the people of northern France.[10]

Inexorably, Europe was drawing near to war. For twenty years or so after 1871, defeated France had lived in humiliating isolation. Frustrated at home and hemmed in by her powerful neighbour, she sought compensation in imperial expansion. Though public opinion was deeply divided on this issue as on others, this was the most intensive period of empire building. Although Jules Ferry, who managed the colonial drive during his two periods as Prime Minister (1880–1 and 1883–5), saw Indo-China as a new outlet for French industry, it would be a mistake to think of French imperialism purely in economic terms. To carry the gospel to pagan peoples and civilise them, to absorb the frustrated energies of a virile people – these were, above all, the motivations of the period. Tunisia and the Congolese equator, Djibouti and Madagascar came under French rule before the century was out, as did Tonking in the Far East.

In foreign affairs, in the more restricted sense, the French Republic hesitated between Russia and England as potential allies of isolated France. Both had their advocates, and in the end, France secured the friendship, or at any rate the goodwill, of both. In 1891, a pact with Russia ended France's isolation; and a military pact followed in 1894. The *rapprochement* with England was delayed by Anglo-French rivalries along the Nile, but these resolved themselves into the Entente Cordiale in 1904. Among the politicians in Paris, there could also be found a group that advocated at least an exploration of the possibilities of a settlement with Germany. They included the patriotic firebrand of 1871, Gambetta, who in 1878 toyed with the idea of a secret meeting with Bismarck. But the price of a deal with Germany, which would have included the permanent surrender of Alsace and Lorraine, was too high: few Frenchmen would have contemplated it, and any politician willing to pay it would have found himself out of office. In the 1870s and 1880s, the French mood was of *revanchisme* and at the turn of the century, following the Dreyfus scandal, it turned to anti-militarism; in the wave of nationalism that followed, the mood changed again – less to thoughts of revenge than to resigned acceptance of the probability that a further war with Germany was in prospect, and a determination that this time, come what might, France would be victorious.

[10] Gorce, p. 40.

The roots of the painful cleavage within the French nation during the Second World War, between collaborators and resisters, may be found in the early years of this century. The Monarchist historian Jacques Bainville divided the politicians of the Third Republic into patriots and appeasers. Three men, in particular, qualified for his patriotic accolade: Delcassé, the foreign minister who had negotiated the Entente Cordial; Clemenceau, known as the "Tiger", who had ruthlessly suppressed the workers during his first premiership (1906-9) and who was later to become an inspiring leader during the war he had foreseen; and Raymond Poincaré, a Lorrainer who came to power for one year in 1912 and became the foremost spokesman of the Nationalist revival. Among the defeatists, Bainville placed Gambetta, Ferry, Thiers and others whom he found guilty of being contented with a second-class status for France.

The Germans lost no occasion to confront the French. The Moroccan crises of 1905 and 1911 are cases in point. When the French took steps to absorb Morocco in 1905, the Germans retaliated by sending the Kaiser on a State visit to that country. On the second occasion, the Germans sent a gunboat, the *Panther*, to Agadir to protect German nationals, although there were none in that area. The French premier, Joseph Caillaux, tried to appease Germany by offering her a slice of the Congo in return for a free hand in Morocco.[11] He was overthrown for his pains, and in the ensuing wave of anti-German feelings, Poincaré came to power. Although Franco-German differences were not the only cause of the Great War, they were beginning to make a new conflict look inevitable.

When it came, in August 1914, Lieutenant Charles de Gaulle was not quite twenty-four. His political hero was Clemenceau, both because of his authoritarian and indomitable character, and because he had had the sense – as the young de Gaulle saw it – to understand that France's overseas adventures were a kind of high treason at a time when all forces were needed to defend the mother country from attack across the Rhine.[12] In the post-war years, writing of Clemenceau's wartime leadership, de Gaulle saw him as France's "fury", while Poincaré was France's "reason". At times, he wrote, France had to pay for Clemenceau's excesses; but his fierce drive was indispensable for the ultimate efforts that were needed.[13]

De Gaulle – serving in the 1st Battalion, 33rd Regiment, 2nd Infantry Division – had recently been posted to the northern frontier, close to his birthplace of Lille. Nine years earlier, aged fifteen, he had been haunted by a strange dream – that war would break out between France and

[11] Wright, p. 390.   [12] Tournoux, *Pétain*, p. 43.   [13] De Gaulle, *France*, p. 308.

Germany in 1914, that he would take part in a battle and would be killed in action on 15 August.[14] And so, apart from the fateful end of his dream, it turned out. On 15 August, Charles de Gaulle was in action for the first time, near Dinant, on the Belgian Meuse, and was wounded. Having expected death that day, since his premotion as an adolescent, he now felt (according to his early biographers) that his life was no longer his own, that his remaining days belonged to some destiny yet to be uncovered.

He was out of action for three months, when he rejoined his 33rd regiment, by that time sadly depleted after heavy fighting. On 20 January 1915 an order of the day of the 2nd Division mentioned him in these words: "Carried out a series of reconnaissances of enemy positions in perilous conditions and brought back valuable information."

Two more battle wounds awaited him. The first was on 15 March 1915, at Mesnil-les-Hurlus, on the Champagne front. On 4 September, barely recovered, de Gaulle was promoted captain. On 30 October, he was given the command of the 10th Company – still in his 33rd regiment. Under him were miners from the north; above him was Colonel Boudhors, who was much impressed with his assistant, both for his bravery and his memory. Years later, Boudhors recalled that de Gaulle was always ready to correct the chaplain in a quotation from St Augustine, and knew by heart the military record of every man in the regiment. Less than three months later, Captain de Gaulle asked to be sent to the Verdun front, and Colonel Boudhors agreed, recording his decision in these words: "In view of the gravity of the situation, and of the importance I attach to this mission, I believe that Captain de Gaulle alone is capable of accomplishing it."[15]

On 2 March 1916, a murderous German bombardment hit the French at Douaumont. Captain de Gaulle, encouraged by a cry of "Reinforcements!" turned around to see a group of men wearing the blue helmet of the French forces. Not long before, however, the helmets had been on the heads of French soldiers killed by the Germans, who now wore them. Realising what had happened, de Gaulle ordered his men to fix their bayonets and charge. Almost instantly, a bullet pierced his thigh. He fell unconscious, and Boudhors, who had seen him fall, covered in blood, thought him dead, and wrote to his parents to tell them Charles had died in action. In later years Boudhors liked to say: "I have been a Gaullist since 1916." General Pétain conferred a "posthumous" Cross of the Legion of Honour upon the young captain, with the following mention:

14 Cattaui, p. 26.   15 ibid. p. 32.

Captain de Gaulle, commanding the company, reputed for his intellectual and moral work of high quality, while his battalion, undergoing a frightful bombardment, was decimated and while the enemies were pressing on the company on all sides, led his men in a furious assault and fierce hand-to-hand fighting, the only solution he considered compatible with his sentiment of military honour. Fell in the fray. A peerless officer in all respects.

Captain de Gaulle, however, was not dead. He had been rescued by a German who, moments before the bullet had hit him was fighting him hand-to-hand. Now de Gaulle was a prisoner, with thirty-two months of captivity before him. His first detention camp was at Friedberg. As soon as he was fit, he started digging a tunnel, through which he escaped into open country. But his great height made concealment difficult: he was recaptured. A second attempt misfired because the German uniform he had stolen scarcely covered his elbows and his knees. There was yet a third unsuccessful attempt at escape, after which de Gaulle was transferred to the punishment camp of Ingolstadt. There, he was greeted by other bold and unsuccessful spirits, such as Rémy Roure, later to become his champion in the column of the newspaper Le Temps, and by his future publisher, Berger-Levrault; and by Major Catroux, who in 1940, as Governor-General of French Indo-China, was one of the first to rally to General de Gaulle's call to all Frenchmen. There were two hundred officers in Fort IX, and they included Russians and British as well as French. Among the Russians was a handsome, stocky, insolent young man of twenty-three, called Tukhachevsky, later a marshal of the Red Army.

For Captain de Gaulle, the enforced leisure of Ingolstadt, though frustrating, was not wasted. With the German newspapers as raw material, he perfected his German. As self-appointed lecturer to his companions, he gave them courses in military strategy, in which he hailed the advent of the tank as a decisive development.[16] Meantime, he was taking extensive notes, which were later to form the basis of his first book, La Discorde chez l'Ennemi. He confided to a fellow-prisoner that if he – de Gaulle – were not a soldier, he would go in for politics.[17]

The character later familiar to his subordinates and the world at large was hardening fast. De Gaulle wanted to learn, to know, to teach; and he was determined always to be right. When he clashed with the commander of Fort IX, he landed in the punishment cell. When he clashed with his companions, they tended to give way. A new nickname, echoing

[16] Bonheur, p. 55.　　　　[17] Lacouture, De Gaulle, p. 18.

his captain's summing up at Arras, was coined for him: "The High Constable." Years later, Winston Churchill hit on the same name for him; it always did seem appropriate.

Two other camps harboured Captain de Gaulle during the Great War: Magdeburg and Ludwigshafen; and two prisons: Szutzyn and Rosenburg. It was at Ludwigshafen (writes Gaston Bonheur) that he began to write *La Discorde:*[18] and his first reader was Major Catroux.

At length, the armistice of 11 November 1918 brought back his freedom.

[18] Bonheur, p. 54.

Chapter 3 ❧ The Historian 1919–1924

Peace deepened the frustration of Charles de Gaulle as a career soldier who had spent much of his war inactive. A grand family reunion awaited him at La Ligerie, but the joys and comforts of home were insufficient compensation for lost opportunities. Together with his three brothers Charles was photographed in the family grounds. The four young men all wore uniform, and all four displayed the Croix de Guerre; Charles alone wore the Legion of Honour. Haughtiness may be found in all four faces. Charles stands slightly apart from the others, inches taller than his neighbour Xavier, his eyes hard with ambition.

Though France and the West were at peace, fighting of a kind had resumed in Eastern Europe. In Russia, the Tsarist regime had collapsed under the strains of war. Lenin and his Bolsheviks had returned from exile in the famous sealed train provided by the German High Command in the expectation that they would undermine the pro-Allied provisional government. Their calculation was vindicated when the revolutionary Bolsheviks concluded the Treaty of Brest-Litovsk with the Germans, buying external peace at the price of Poland, the Ukraine and the non-Russian borderlands. Emboldened, the Poles sought to re-conquer the territories that had been theirs at the time of the first partition of Poland in 1772. Soon, the Polish armies clashed with the Bolsheviks in

White Russia and Lithuania. On 5 January 1919, Vilna fell to the Bolsheviks; and on 19 April, the Poles recaptured the city and moved into White Russia. In this unexpected war, de Gaulle found his chance to make up for lost fighting time.

For the best part of a year, the Polish General Joseph Haller, who had commanded the Polish army on the French front during the late war, had been recruiting French volunteers to fight against the Russian Red Army. Captain de Gaulle was among those who signed on. Under the orders of Colonel Mercier, he disembarked on 19 May at Modlin (Novo-Georgiewsk) with the 5th Polish Light Infantry – just in time to take part in the operations in Volhynia.[1] On 28 June, the Treaty of Versailles gave the Poles much of, though not all, the land to which they aspired.

There was a coincidental irony in Captain de Gaulle's first Polish operation: in command of the Red Army was the young Russian officer with whom he had spent many hours in conversation in the fortress of Ingoldstadt – Tukhachevsky. However, de Gaulle was still a captain, while Tukhachevsky, making full use of his revolutionary opportunities, had already been promoted by Trotsky to the command of the 4th Red Army. (The two men were to meet once again, in Paris in 1936. The previous year, Tukhachevsky had become one of the five marshals of the Soviet Union; the following year, aged forty-three, he was executed on Stalin's orders.)

Now Captain de Gaulle and his companions moved to a former camp of the Imperial Russian Guard, at Rembertow, six miles from the centre of Warsaw, which had been converted into a military college. It was his duty to teach military tactics. At first, says Galante,[2] he made an effort to teach in Polish, but soon gave up the struggle, and was given an interpreter. Rembertow being with easy reach of Warsaw, De Gaulle lived for a while in the Bristol Hotel on the Capital's central square, graced by the statue of Marshal Poniatowski, near the Saxe Gardens. Later, he rented a tiny bachelor flat in Warecka Street.

To the extent that Captain de Gaulle had any wild oats to sow, it was here that he sowed them. Though conscientious as ever in his teaching, de Gaulle enjoyed the freedom of Warsaw, far from the constraints of his own country. For the first two weeks of each month, his officer's pay enabled him to live the life of a *grand seigneur*. He was seen at the best restaurants, especially the Liewski – much frequented by poets and intellectuals – and in the best of Polish society's salons.[3] He was often a

[1] Bonheur, p. 64; Nachin, p. 33. Other biographers, however, say he did not take part in any fighting until 1920; Gorce (p. 48) gives the regiment as the 4th Polish Light Infantry.
[2] Galante, p. 104.   [3] ibid. p. 106.

guest in the sumptuous town residence of the beautiful Countess Rose Tyszkiewicz, née Branicka, where he acquired a reputation for Gallic charm. Another Polish lady, Countess Czetwertynska, as lively as she was tiny, was often seen in his company in the café Blikle, where they consumed quantities of jam fritters.

On 27 March 1920, the Poles, dissatisfied with the "Curzon Line" offered to them under the Versailles treaty as their eastern boundary, called on the Russians to restore the frontiers of 1772. Predictably, the Bolsheviks refused, and on 25 April the Russian–Polish war began. Soon the Poles were in difficulties. The dashing Colonel Budenny, commander of the First Cavalry army of the Red Army, led his horses and men swiftly from the Caucasus and soon pressed hard on the approaches to Warsaw.

General Weygand, in charge of the French Mission in the Polish capital, lent his talent and experience to Marshal Pilsudski and his staff. Captain de Gaulle, given the temporary rank of major in the Polish army, was in action as commander of a battalion of light infantry. For his successful defence of the river Zbrucz, he was awarded the highest Polish decoration, for "Military virtue", and commended by Weygand in a special Order of the Day. The Russians were thrown back, and under the Treaty of Riga, on 18 March 1921, conceded most of, though not all, the Polish claims to the east.

Having taken part in the Polish counter-offensive, de Gaulle now wrote about it, in the form of a campaign journal which appeared some months later in La Revue de Paris, under the necessary cloak of anonymity. As a writer, he had not yet found himself, and the journal is not one of de Gaulle's literary masterpieces: as Jean Lacouture puts it, it consists of verbal drum-rolls, interspersed with thoughts on the Slavonic soul.[4]

By October, the fighting was over on the Polish front, and Charles de Gaulle went to Paris on leave. It was, for his private life, a more fateful furlough than he could have expected. Without his knowledge, the matchmakers were at work. The chief matchmaker, by her own claim, was a Mme Denquin, who had known Charles de Gaulle and his family when both were children. Later, moving to Calais, she had met the Vendroux, who were locally well-known biscuit manufacturers. The daughter of the house, Yvonne, had turned down a marriage proposal from a young officer, the son of a general, on the ground that she had no wish to be married to a military man, but would prefer to raise a family in her home town rather than be transferred at short notice from one garrison to another.

[4] Lacouture, De Gaulle, p. 22.

Mme Denquin, however, on a visit to her parents' home, met Captain de Gaulle, who was lunching there. A thought struck her: this impressive young officer, whom she had often teased when both were younger, could well change Yvonne Vendroux's reservations about military suitors. She mentioned her thought to Mme Vendroux, whose curiosity was aroused. And it was decided that a "chance" meeting should be elaborately planned. It was to take place in the Salon d'Automne in Paris, which the Vendroux family were planning to visit a fortnight later. As though by accident, the two families crossed in the Salon and Mme Denquin introduced them. Soon Charles and Yvonne were walking ahead of the others. They came to a picture representing the poet and playwright Maurice Rostand as a child. Seizing the occasion to demonstrate his knowledge of the work of one of his favourite poets, and his dazzling memory, Charles de Gaulle proceeded to quote at length. Yvonne listened fascinated.[5]

Back with her family, Yvonne did not hide her interest but said to her mother: "I think he found me too small for him."

After the meeting at the Salon d'Automne, the Vendroux invited the de Gaulles to tea. De Gaulle had his *képi*, his gloves and his stick on his knees. But when he tried to add a cup of tea to the clutter, he fumbled and spilt the tea over Yvonne's dress. But she was already in love, and put the blushing soldier at his ease by laughing.[6]

Next week the pair met again at Versailles, where the Ecole Polytechnique was holding a gala evening. Yvonne was with her brother, who had gone to Paris to take part in a fencing contest. Seeing them, Captain de Gaulle went up to her brother, Jacques, and asked permission to dance with his sister. When the sixth waltz was over, Charles proposed to Yvonne, and was accepted.

Back on leave from Poland some months later, Charles de Gaulle married Yvonne Vendroux in the church of Notre-Dame de Calais, between the statues of Charlemagne and St Louis. It was 7 April 1921.

Captain de Gaulle's Polish freedom had ended, but not his Polish servitude. According to Gaston Bonheur,[7] it was during this period that Charles de Gaulle first developed his then revolutionary theories about the use of infantry and tanks in close contact with the air force. His

[5] This account of de Gaulle meeting his future wife is drawn mainly from Galante, pp. 64–5.

[6] Several early biographers recount this anecdote, which Galante's informant denies. In context, however, Galante's informant appears to be denying that tea was spilt on another occasion.

[7] Bonheur, p. 65.

lectures on the subject deeply impressed the Poles. And after one of them, General Stanislaw Haller, chief of Staff of the Polish army and a cousin of Joseph Haller, and Marshal Pilsudski, president of the Republic, came to the podium to be introduced to the French captain. They brought an offer of a lectureship in tactics in the Polish School of War Studies. De Gaulle was considering his reply when his immediate superior, Colonel Mercier, told him that under a decision of the French minister of war he had just received, de Gaulle was transferred, as from 1 October 1921, to the Special Military School of Saint-Cyr, as a lecturer in military history.

Charles de Gaulle was thirty-one. Up to this point, there had been nothing remarkable about his military career. At that age, Alexander of Macedonia had conquered half the ancient world; Bonaparte had been a general for several years, and his compatriot Hoche could look back on four years as generalissimo; the Spaniard, Franco, two years younger than de Gaulle, was promoted from major to lieutenant-colonel in 1923, aged thirty-one. So far, opportunities for military prowess had been scarce. De Gaulle's absolute self-confidence, his sentiment of a beckoning fate, were unshaken, however; in the absence of historic opportunities, they were expressed in his aloofness, in the cutting abruptness of his manner, his unvarying conviction of personal rightness, and his total refusal ever to lose or admit to being in the wrong. (On a visit to Calais during his engagement Charles de Gaulle had shocked the Vendroux family by losing his temper during a game of bridge. His fiancée was the only one who thought his conduct pardonable.)[8]

It was at Saint-Cyr, and later at the Ecole de Guerre, that de Gaulle's character – indomitable but "impossible" and a trial to those around him – settled into its familiar mould. It was there in particular that his talent as an orator crystallised. His assets were learning, memory and a mastery of language. His height, his ungainly figure and his stiffness of gesture were disadvantages. So was his curious voice, issuing from the pit of his stomach, but liable to crack and sound like a prematurely senile cackle. His new job at Saint-Cyr, however, gave him all the practice he needed to turn his awkwardness into an asset, by the cultivation of idiosyncrasies of gesture, and to tame and master his voice, transforming it into an irresistible organ of command, persuasion and sarcasm. Essentially, the oratorical de Gaulle of the BBC broadcasts, and the visual de Gaulle of French television, were born during that year at Saint-Cyr.[9]

On 8 December 1921, a slightly premature baby boy was born to the

8 Galante, p. 66.   9 Lacouture, De Gaulle, pp. 23–4.

younger de Gaulles: he was named Philippe, after Marshal Pétain. There were to be two more children. Yvonne de Gaulle, who had declared her lack of taste for military life, had begun to accustom herself to the thought that Versailles was only the first of many dwelling places.

It was expected of the young teaching staff at Saint-Cyr that they should prepare the entrance examination for the Ecole Supérieure de Guerre. The teacher was therefore expected to become a pupil again, the better to serve the State. Charles de Gaulle did what was expected of him, and entered the Ecole de Guerre in November 1922.

While at the Ecole de Guerre, de Gaulle made several friendships which later failed to withstand the strains of the fall of France. One of his companions was Georges-Picot, who was to oppose him in Syria in 1940; and later at Algiers and Paris. Another, Bridoux, was to become war minister of the Vichy regime, and was condemned to death *in absentia* by de Gaulle's government in 1945, eventually becoming a military adviser to General Franco. Yet another was Loustaunau-Lacau, an adventurer born, who sided with Vichy, then with de Gaulle, was deported and died a general and a right-wing deputy.[10]

From the start, de Gaulle was in conflict with the principal of the school, a Colonel Moyrand, whose concept of tactics was essentially static and formalistic. As far as Moyrand was concerned, a commander made his plan, in the most minute detail, and stuck to it, regardless of circumstances. De Gaulle, as a good disciple of Bergson, rejected this kind of *a priori* reasoning. Moyrand had, or thought he had, digested the lessons of the Great War: fire power favoured defence and made attack exorbitantly costly. De Gaulle, however, was already convinced that the real lessons of the Great War were that the next war would be fought with tanks and that increasing mechanisation would mean a war of movement. At the end of the course, having sat for his written examination, de Gaulle had to pass his practical test in the tactical field. He resolved to turn it into a demonstration that he was right and Moyrand wrong. It was a rash decision on his part. Appointed to command the "Blue Uniforms" in this final exercise, on 17 June 1924, de Gaulle led his cavalry in a lightning manoeuvre which caught the "enemy" off balance and knocked Moyand's theories of static defence to the ground.[11] To make matters worse, de Gaulle declined to answer a question put to him by Colonel Moyrand, delegating it to his subordinate in the tactical exercise. Irritated, Moyrand exclaimed: "But I put the question to *you*, de Gaulle!"

Unabashed, de Gaulle replied: "*Mon Colonel* you have entrusted me

10 ibid. p. 26.   11 Bonheur, pp. 68–9.

with the responsibilities of the commander of an army corps. If in addition I have to take on those of my subordinates, my mind would no longer be free to carry out my mission. *De minimis non curat praetor.* ....[12] Chateauieux [the name of the subordinate], please answer the colonel."[13]

Not unexpectedly, a furious row over de Gaulle's final grading followed this incident. Departing students were divided into three groups, graded respectively: *Très bien, Bien,* and *Assez bien* ("very good", "good" and "fair"). The *Assez bien* grading implied a bare pass. The assistant commandant, General Dufieux, presided over the examining board.[14] De Gaulle had opposed him on mechanised war, but thought as he did on the need to deal with situations as they arose and not by preconceived notions.

Everyone agreed that de Gaulle was an exceptionally gifted officer: his extraordinary memory, his "vast culture", his decisiveness and his capacity for instantly summing up a situation, all attracted praise. But in the eyes of most of the members of the board, these qualities were outweighed by his impossible character, his conceit, his unwillingness to submit to criticism or even discussion. The question was not whether to place him in the top grade, but whether he should be graded *Bien* or *Assez bien.* General Dufieux, an unvindictive man, insisted on second-class grading, against the forcefully expressed majority view that he deserved no more than a third-class grade.

Marshal Pétain, who was on a tour of inspection at the time of de Gaulle's final examination, had heard the story of his clash with Moyrand – the leader of the majority in favour of the lowest grading – and had declared the younger man to be in the right. Now he was alerted about the squabble over his protégé's grading, and forcefully intervened, in favour of a *Très bien,* declaring de Gaulle to be the hope of his generation. Dufieux, however, was within his rights in merely taking the Marshal's views into account, without yielding completely. That is, instead of bowing before the majority, he apparently used Pétain's authority to insist on a *Bien* instead of an *Assez bien.*

The captain's report, signed by Colonel Moyrand, concluded with the following observations: "An intelligent, cultured and serious-minded soldier, has brilliance and facility; good material. Unfortunately spoils his undeniable qualities by his excessive self-assurance, his severity for other people's opinions and his attitude of a King-in-exile." Such qualities, which Moyrand was not alone in attributing to de Gaulle, were

---

[12] "The law does not concern itself with small matters."
[13] Lacouture, *De Gaulle,* pp. 26–7.   [14] Tournoux, *Pétain,* pp. 99 *et seq.*

of course well suited to the man who was later to occupy the Elysée Palace; they were less happily indicated for an impatient and ambitious young soldier.

The news was brought to de Gaulle in the courtyard of honour of the Palais Gabriel. He exploded. Gesticulating (says Tournoux) and in a loud, clear voice, he exclaimed: "Those c...s of the Ecole de Guerre! I shall only come back to this dirty hole [*sale boîte*] as Commandant of the Ecole! And you'll see how everything will change!"

Had Charles de Gaulle been awarded a *Très bien*, he would have been transferred to the coveted Third Bureau (Planning) of the General Staff, to try out in practice his theoretical notions of tactics and strategy. But the displeasure he had incurred meant a second setback to his career – the first being his involuntary inaction in Germany. Instead of the Third Bureau, he was posted to the Fourth (Transport and Supply), first at Army Headquarters, and some months later, at Mayence, headquarters of the French army of the Rhine. Bonheur, one of the early hagiographers, writes that he was delighted with "this apparent disgrace",[15] but this is undoubtedly untrue. Indeed, for a soldier with his innate conviction of intellectual superiority, the choice of a department concerned with such routine matters as transport and supplies was humiliating. At Mayence, in fact, he was put in charge of *refrigeration*, which must have seemed an insulting punishment for an unwelcome independence of spirit.[16]

Before going, he called on Pétain at General Headquarters in the Boulevard des Invalides. The marshal did not hide the displeasure which the verdict of the examiners had caused him. He promised the captain that he would find him a job on his own staff, and that the time would come when he would get his own back on the establishment of the Ecole de Guerre.

Although the verdict of the Ecole was wounding to de Gaulle's pride and his posting to Mayence a setback in his career, it offered two compensations: it gave him a chance to study the German people again, in conditions of freedom; and to create mobile armoured units in accordance with the views on mechanised war which General Estienne had initially expounded, but which de Gaulle himself had independently developed while in captivity. For months past, he had been working in his spare time, collating and rewriting his prison notes. The outcome was to be his first book, *La Discorde chez l'Ennemi*.

Published in 1924, *La Discorde* was de Gaulle's first memorable achievement. He was not a man of precocious destiny. Had he died before

---

[15] Bonheur, p. 70.   [16] Tournoux, *Pétain*, p. 133n.

writing this first book, he would have lingered in the memory of family and friends as a strange young man with eccentric views who might or might not have had a future. Had death claimed him after publication, his name would have been that of an acute and penetrating military thinker who could have expected a distinguished future as an historian. To read it in 1924 was to be enlightened about the causes of Germany's defeat in the late war. To read it at any time after 1940 was to be struck by its prophetic insight and the glow it cast upon fundamental elements in the author's character and thoughts. Everything – his captivity in Germany, his service in Poland, his observation of the Slavs, his experience of the behaviour of the Russians, even under Bolshevism, and his more mature reflections on the German collapse – strengthened his fundamental view that history was the study of peoples and nations, each of which had its own characteristics that would never, so he believed, be altered by ideology.

In Germany's case, especially, he singled out the Nietzschean cult:

> . . . the Superman with his exceptional character, the will to power, the taste for risk, the contempt for others which Zarathustra wants to see in him, appeared to these passionate and vicious men as the ideal they ought to attain; they freely opted to belong to this formidable Nietzschean élite which, while pursuing its own glory, is convinced that it is serving the general interst, which constrains "the mass of slaves" while contemptuous of it, and which does not stop before human suffering, except to salute it as necessary and as desirable.

Within a few years, the emergence of Hitler was to show yet again and in a more paroxysmal form, the validity of the cult of Superman. The spirit of reconciliation between France and Germany, which de Gaulle was to practise in the Adenauer era more than thirty years later, was, however, also manifest, especially in his foreword:

> . . . The sudden and complete moral collapse of a valiant people, a decadence the more grandiose in that this people had, until then, known how to display a collective will to vanquish, an obstinacy of endurance, a capacity to suffer that merited, from the first day of the war, the astonishment and admiration of its enemies and will assuredly obtain the homage of History.

> The German military leaders, who had as their task to orientate and coordinate such efforts, displayed a boldness, a spirit of enterprise, a will to succeed, a vigour in the handling of the means, the fame of which their final failure has not diminished.

De Gaulle must have found a bitter irony in the recollection of these passages at the time of France's moral collapse in the Second World War. In 1924, however, he wished to dwell on the contrast – a favourable one to France, in his view – between the German and French peoples. On the German side, he found "the characteristic taste for disproportionate enterprises, the passion to extend, whatever the cost, their personal power, the contempt for the limits traced by human experience, common sense and the law". But France was the ideal vision he had always nurtured, in this characteristic passage which concludes the foreword:

> In the French-style garden, no tree seeks to stifle the others with its shade, the flowerbeds put up with being geometrically designed, the pond has no ambition to have a waterfall, the statues do not pretend to monopolise one's admiration. At times a noble melancholy emanates from it. Perhaps this comes from the feeling that each element, in isolation, might cast a brighter glow. But this would have been to the detriment of the whole, and the stroller is thankful for the rules that impress upon the garden its magnificent harmony.

This was the idealised French garden of de Gaulle's dreams. It held disappointments in store for him, however, and he was to discover that its fruits, though enticing to the eye, were sometimes bitter to the taste.

Chapter 4 ⚜ Pétain's Protégé 1924–1932

While Charles de Gaulle was serving in Poland, teaching at Saint-Cyr and learning at the Ecole de Guerre, France was trying to preserve the fruits of her exhausting victory over Germany. At Versailles, where the peacemakers met, the woolly idealism of President Woodrow Wilson clashed with the vengeful realism of M. Clemenceau. The idealism took the form of faith in collective security; and the realism was of the kind that saw in a permanently weakened Germany the only real guarantee of French security. Both were represented in the post-war governments in Paris. At the outset, the hard-headed school triumphed, under the Aristide Briand cabinet of 1921–2 and the Poincaré government that succeeded Briand's and lasted until June 1924. Thereafter, Briand dominated French foreign policy in a succession of short-lived governments, four of which he himself headed; and it was a policy of peace, largely based, as it now seems with the wisdom of hindsight, upon wishful illusions about the nature of men and international organisations.

Although much folly marked this first decade of the precarious peace, it is not easy to apportion praise and blame. The politicians of the French Republic were vulnerable men. It was open to John Maynard Keynes, writing from across the English Channel, to deplore the economic consequences of a peace settlement dominated by France's lust for reparative revenge. But in the eyes of the French electorate, the peace terms were excessively lenient and Clemenceau – paying for his failure to secure a harsher treaty in accordance with his own views as well as those of the public – fell from office in January 1920. Briand and Poincaré were soon, in their turn, to experience the precarious nature of political power, when the elected representatives of the people turned against the policies advocated by these men of goodwill. Under the Versailles treaty, France's security appeared to be guaranteed by the return of Alsace and Lorraine; the occupation and demilitarisation of the Rhineland; the drastic reduction of the German armed forces; and the maintenance of a French army of vastly superior size. But these terms presupposed certain conditions, such as the maintenance of the wartime alliance between France, Britain and the United States; and the stability of the French franc. The first of these collapsed with almost indecent suddenness, and the second was soon under pressure from the guarantees France herself had written into the peace treaty.

On 28 June 1919, the day the Versailles treaty was signed, defensive treaties between France, Britain and the United States were also concluded. In the event of aggression by Germany, Britain and the United States were to come to France's assistance. The American Senate, however, not only rejected the Versailles treaty wholesale, but also declined to ratify the tripartite defence treaties. Thereupon, the British government withdrew its own guarantee to France. Thus at one blow the Versailles settlement lost one of its major props (and the League of Nations, which was created by the Versailles treaty, its principal sponsor), and the Entente Cordiale was shown to be a fragile basis for European security. Frustrated, the French looked elsewhere, and over the next few years built up a system of defensive alliances with Belgium, and the smaller countries of eastern Europe. But these arrangements were not a true substitute for the support of Britain and America, and the French were aware of it. Briand, who in his first post-war premier-ship was a partisan of toughness towards the defeated enemy, tried to do something about it. Closeted with Lloyd George, he extracted a British guarantee of military help for France in the event of aggression, and agreed in return to cut German reparations. But (as Gordon Wright puts it[1]) "the news leaked out before Briand had time to charm parliament into accepting his policy". He then paid the usual penalty when he was overthrown.

It was now January 1922, and the French parliament looked to Briand's successor, Raymond Poincaré – the arch-advocate of rigour towards Germany, the upholder of France's legal rights under Versailles, and the champion of an independent French policy – to carry out its will. Poincaré's clear mandate was to force reparation payments from the Germans, who had shown themselves unwilling to pay for their defeat, to meet the expense of rehabilitating the devastated regions of France. Since France's major erstwhile allies refused to take action, the French decided to go it alone; or more accurately, to accept the military support of Belgium and the moral support of Italy. On 11 January 1923, French and Belgian troops invaded the Ruhr valley. On legal grounds, Poincaré felt himself to be in the right, although the British government declared some months later (on 11 August) that the "Franco-Belgian action . . . was not a sanction authorised by the treaty". As an exercise in power politics, the occupation of the Ruhr was an instructive blend of failure and success, in which the first predominated. Nothing had been able to stop the French military machine: neither the disapproval of Britain, nor the outrage of the embattled French left, nor the dissuasive advice of Marshal Foch.

The ostensible purpose of the occupation failed dismally. In 1923, the French collected barely any more in reparations than they had the previous year, and the cost of the occupation considerably exceeded the value of the goods delivered. Nor was the unstated objective of encouraging a separatist movement in the Ruhr and Rhineland more than marginally successful. True, by the end of 1923 the Stresemann cabinet, newly in office in Berlin, stopped trying to avoid reparation payments, and indeed agreed to resume them. But by then the German mark was worth less than the paper it was printed on. The financial contagion, indeed, spread to France, where the franc fell by about 25 per cent. But what stuck still more persistently in French gullets was the fact that the Poincaré government had had to raise taxes by 20 per cent to cover the costs of the Ruhr expedition. The Dawes Plan of April 1924, though

[1] Wright, p. 441.

it insisted on the resumption of reparation payments, gave the Germans a massive gold loan to help them pay. In these circumstances, Poincaré could hardly claim that his policy of unilateral action had succeeded. And on 1 June, it was his turn to pay the usual penalty of failure under the Third Republic, by resigning.

On 14 June, three days before de Gaulle's unfortunate final confrontation with the examiners at the Ecole de Guerre, the Radical leader Edouard Herriot became Prime Minister for the first time. It was the culmination of the crisis that had followed the fall of Poincaré, and Herriot's reward for having provoked the resignation of President Millerand by accusing him of abandoning the neutrality that becomes a head of State by siding with the right. Charles de Gaulle and his contemporaries were discussing these changes, which foreshadowed a period of anti-clerical government, the closing down of the French embassy to the Vatican, and an assault on what Herriot and his *Cartel des Gauches* picturesquely called "the wall of money" – *le mur d'argent*. "As for me," said de Gaulle calmly, "by family tradition I can only be a monarchist."[2]

One day, the young "king-in-exile" was talking about life in general with a Captain Chauvin, who said to him after a silence: "My dear chap, I'm going to say something to you that will probably make you smile. I have this curious feeling that you are heading for a very great destiny."

To his surprise, de Gaulle did not contradict him. Looking into the distance, he said in a toneless voice: "Yes . . . me too."[3]

Before this manifest destiny could be fulfilled, however, many obstacles would need to be scaled. One of these was the grading of *Bien* at the Ecole de Guerre. At one time, de Gaulle had dreamt of being offered a Chair at the Ecole; but professorships were reserved for students who had been graded *Très bien*. Now, having published his first book, he was seriously thinking of resigning his commission and abandoning his military career. But Marshal Pétain had not forgotten his promises to the younger soldier. In October 1925 he had de Gaulle appointed to his personal staff. By this time, Pétain was vice-president of the Superior Council of War and inspector-general of the army, and in the latter capacity the head of all the armed forces.

In retrospect, there was a certain irony in the first task that was assigned to him as a member of Pétain's staff. It was to write a study on fortifications and strongpoints in the defence of France. Some months earlier, de Gaulle had expressed himself with relative freedom in an article on "The Orientation of our War Doctrines" in the *Revue mili-*

---

[2] Tournoux, *Pétain*, p. 98.   [3] Loc. cit.

taire française. Now, as an official headquarters theoretician, he was required to find an historic justification for the theories of static defence which – as an exponent of mechanised war – he abhorred, and which were to lead to the construction of the Maginot Line. Though he had little relish for the assignment, he completed it with his usual brisk efficiency, in one month, and the study appeared in the same publication under the title, "The Historic Role of the French Fortified Towns".[4] The date was 1 December 1925. Although de Gaulle considered it consistent with his duty to draw attention to the vulnerable gaps in France's frontier defences, he saw evident dangers in the War Council's view that the construction of a permanent line of fortifications along the border would provide a permanent solution to the problem of defence against invasion. The purpose of his article was indeed to alert public opinion to the need for such a line.[5] About this time, Captain de Gaulle began to write regularly to Captain Nachin, the only friend in whom he confided his deepest misgivings and highest ambitions. In January 1926, apparently taken aback by the attention and approval which his article had aroused, he wrote to Nachin:

> In my humble opinion, the defensive organisation must not be – as many wish – part of the operational plan. The necessary and permanent defensive organisation, which is related to the geographical, political and even moral conditions in which the country finds itself, is a question for the government. The operational plan is a question for the command. The latter takes account of the strongholds (whatever their form) in its projects, as one of its means, exactly as it takes account of its forces, of the *matériel* and of economic power.[6]

A year later, having discussed the matter with Nachin, de Gaulle wrote to him again, to say: "To bar the way: that is what Vauban wanted. . . . I have read with much satisfaction the phrase of Vauban's which you quote concerning the number of strongholds. Yes, there must be few of them, but good ones."[7]

Satisfied with Captain de Gaulle's work, Pétain now thought the time had come to fulfil his second promise, and give the younger man a chance to get his own back on the Ecole de Guerre. It was not simply to please de Gaulle that Pétain wished to humiliate the military establishment at the war school. He had his own earlier disappointments to avenge. In his day, a quarter of a century earlier – in 1900 – he had been

---

[4] Capitaine de Gaulle, "Rôle historique des places françaises", *Revue militaire française*, No. 5, 1 December 1925 (Berger-Lévrault).
[5] Cattaui, pp. 44–5.   [6] Nachin, pp. 47–8.   [7] ibid. p. 48.

dismissed as instructor at the National Firing School for advocating doctrines then considered heretical. Later, as assistant professor of infantry tactics at the war school, graduating to the Chair, he had affronted the orthodox tacticians of the day, who put their trust in the incomparable virtues of the bayonet charge. Pétain, for his part, knew that fire power would be the decisive element in the forthcoming war. He also knew that the Germans would heavily outgun the French. He had been derided, but had lived to see his ideas vindicated during the first two years of the Great War. Remembering all this, and spurred by this new example of the incomprehension of the military teachers, he resolved to teach them, in their turn, a lesson.

"The more I think about it, the more I think this de Gaulle affair is as monstrous as a judicial error," the marshal said one day to General Hering, who had just become the commandant of the Ecole de Guerre.[8] The new commandant, an Alsatian of forward-looking ideas, was, like de Gaulle, a disciple of General Jean-Baptiste Estienne, the first French officer of importance to have discerned the tremendous potential of mechanised war.

Pétain gave his orders: "Hering, you are going to organise at the school a cycle of lectures, to be given by de Gaulle. His grading is a scandal. I shall be in the chair. I want to teach a lesson to some of these professors. They will get the point!"

The circumstances were indeed unprecedented, and the intent unmistakable. That a mere captain, awarded a secondary grade, should be called upon to address the war school, was in itself extraordinary. But that he should choose as his theme the qualities of leadership was surely at best an impertinence, at worst a calculated insult. That Marshal Pétain, inspector-general of the army, should choose to be present and to preside over the whole occasion gave it a stamp of authority that made the forthcoming humiliation even more distasteful to those affected by it, while the marshal's presence precluded indiscipline.

The first lecture fell – as a blow falls – on 7 April 1927. The professors gathered in an office near the amphitheatre. The marshal arrived, flanked by General Hering. De Gaulle was there too, aloof and apart. When the professors pulled back to let Marshal Pétain through, the marshal himself made way for de Gaulle. It was all a little theatrical. De Gaulle was in full dress uniform. The amphitheatre was full. De Gaulle climbed on to the platform. Slowly, he placed his *képi* upon the table, and next to it his sword. And then, with deliberation, he removed his white gloves.

[8] The ensuing account of de Gaulle's relationship with Pétain draws heavily upon Tournoux, *Pétain*.

Pétain, never a man to waste words, rose and declared: "*Messieurs*, Captain de Gaulle is about to set forth his ideas, which I ask you to listen to attentively."[9]

The subject of this first lecture was "Action in War and the Leader". Straight as a ramrod, and in perfect control of his nerves, Captain de Gaulle gave a dazzling display. Speaking without notes, he quoted an astonishing selection of philosophers, statesmen, soldiers and writers of the past. He irritated quite as many listeners as he dazzled. For who, in reality, was the subject of this elaborate description of the virtues of the ideal leader? Was it Pétain, who sat in the front row, a contented smile on his lips? Or was it de Gaulle himself, as many seemed to think, when they expressed their views later in the electric turmoil that followed the lecture? Or was it, more subtly still, a composite portrait – a Charles Pétain, a Philippe de Gaulle?

At different times, each of these answers seemed applicable. In one passage that aroused the deep hostility of those who felt themselves obscurely criticised, he had declared: "Strong characters are usually harsh, difficult, even fierce. If most people agree privately about their superiority and so implicitly do them justice, they are rarely liked or, in later life, looked on with favour. The choice of those who determine careers is more likely to fall upon those who please than those who are deserving." Who was this supposed to be, the outraged listeners asked themselves? The words could aptly apply to Pétain, whose non-conformist views had retarded his promotion before 1914. But they could equally apply to de Gaulle himself, whose outstanding gifts had brought him no more than a secondary grading at the war school.

For his part, General Hering was certain de Gaulle's references were to Pétain. This was at least what de Gaulle wished people to believe. But today, re-reading the passages in his lectures – gathered together later, polished and expanded in *Le Fil de l'Epée* – it is impossible not to see that he himself was the unnamed hero of his short thesis on leadership. For *Le Fil de l'Epée*, like Colonel Nasser's *Philosophy of the Revolution* and Hitler's *Mein Kampf*, was the prophetic book of a future leader who sensed his own destiny.

However much one may disapprove of rigidly conservative military hierarchies, it is hard to withhold all sympathy from the professors and students of the Ecole Supérieure de Guerre. A snub may have been deserved, but this was a snub in three instalments: an irritation that

[9] Tournoux discounts further words attributed to Pétain by Nachin and other hagiographers, who embellished the story by adding a prophetic note: "for the day will come when a grateful France will call upon him".

became a torture and then an outrage to those who had to sit through it. And there was no escape. Twice more, in successive weeks, those who taught and those who learned had to turn up. Whatever the reservations about the propriety of more or less compulsory attendance at lectures by a captain with an inferior grade, whatever the disapproval of de Gaulle's evident vanity, all agreed that as a performer he was spellbinding. Not a vacant seat was to be found on the second and third occasions.

The *mise-en-scène* was invariably the same. The professorial corps, led by the marshal, occupied the front benches. The tall and glacial captain climbed on to the platform in full dress uniform, and removed his *képi*, his sword and his white gloves. And the show began. The second time, his theme was the "character of the leader", and the "meaning of discipline". Here came a passage which many thought particularly out of place in a military college. For they heard de Gaulle singing the praises of men like General Pélissier, who put Napoleon III's despatches in his pocket unread during the siege of Sebastopol (in the process of disobedience, helping to win a war for France, and for himself a dukedom and a marshal's baton); and Lyautey, who kept Morocco for France in 1914, despite instructions that would have lost it. They heard him, too, quoting Lord Fisher's comment on Admiral Jellicoe: "He has all Nelson's qualities except one: he doesn't know how to disobey."[10]

"Prestige" was the theme of the third and final ordeal. And, once again, came references to qualities which those present attributed to Pétain and which posterity applies to de Gaulle himself: "That fact is that some men cast around them, almost from the moment they are born, an aura of authority the essence of which is not precisely discernible, while its effects are sometimes surprising." There followed a famous passage that found its way unchanged into Le Fil de l'Epée:

> And, first of all, there can be no prestige without mystery, for what is too well known evokes little reverence. All faiths have their tabernacles and no man is a hero to his valet. In plans, methods and ways of thought, there must therefore be something that others cannot grasp and that intrigues them, moves them, keeps them on their toes. Not that one should shut oneself up in an ivory tower, take no notice of subordinates, remain inaccessible. On the contrary, to gain

---

[10] See de Gaulle, Le Fil de l'Epée (henceforth De Gaulle, l'Epée), p. 59. De Gaulle says this was Lord Fisher's exclamation on Jellicoe's report to the Admiralty after failing to destroy the German fleet at Jutland. A more literary version is recorded by Fisher himself in his Memories of Admiral of the Fleet Lord Fisher (London, 1919), p. 38. Writing to a privy councillor on 27 December 1916 he put it this way: "I told the Dardanelles Commission . . . that Jellicoe had all the Nelsonic attributes save one – he was totally wanting in the great gift of insubordination."

a hold on men's minds one must observe men and everyone must feel that he has been singled out. But in trying to do this, it is essential not to go too far to meet people, to keep in reserve some surprising secret that may emerge at any time. The latent confidence of the masses does the rest.

The third lecture, and consequently the trilogy as a whole, fell rather flat. Indignant after the first, angry after the second, the captive audience now affected to be bored by the whole performance. A small minority nodded approvingly when de Gaulle's friend Captain Chauvin said he would like to see the lectures gathered together and put into the hands of young men choosing the calling of arms. His confidant, Lucien Nachin, wrote later that de Gaulle had met with "a veritable incomprehension, and even a sort of latent hostility, a state of resistance, an inhibition against his teaching". And he commented in loyal indignation, "Really, de Gaulle and they are not on the same plane!"[11]

Now, more than ever, frustration constricted Charles de Gaulle. For twelve years, since March 1915, he had stayed frozen in his early rank of captain. While he was learning German and plotting his abortive escape, others with battle opportunities had soared ahead of him. He felt himself born to serve France and to lead others in her service. And the years were passing in obscurity or misunderstanding. He had tried to attract attention, and had merely aroused hostility. His months in charge of refrigeration with the army of the Rhine still rankled. Short of dramatic events, which he confusedly hoped for but could not precisely forecast, his future seemed not dishonourable but worse by far: undistinguished. Nothing that he had written until then had aroused attention or admiration beyond a very limited circle. This was true of *La Discorde chez l'Ennemi*, and equally of a story he published in April 1927 – the month of his lectures at the war school – under the title of *Le Flambeau* ("The Torch"). It was a work of little distinction – an imaginary dialogue between a sergeant, a grenadier and a captain, spanning the period between the French Revolution and the Restoration, and built upon the theme of eternal France.

One hope of promotion and wider advancement remained, however: Marshal Pétain. For the admiration which the ageing hero of Verdun felt for Captain de Gaulle had not yet begun to cool off. His own memory had begun to falter, and he was dazzled by de Gaulle's extraordinary mastery of facts, dates and quotations. He had taken a mischievous pleasure in giving the younger man a chance to snub the military

[11] Nachin, pp. 51–2.

establishment. And when de Gaulle put it to him that he would like to test the impact of his three lectures before a less specialised audience than that of the Ecole de Guerre, Pétain nodded benignly. The outcome was that permission was granted to Captain de Gaulle to deliver three lectures at the Sorbonne.

De Gaulle's intermediary in the arrangements was a right-wing group known as the Cercle Fustel de Coulanges, which had links with (though it was not controlled by) the extreme monarchist organisation, Action française. Politicians and intellectuals, writers and fashionable ladies, gathered in the amphitheatre of the Collège de France to hear the captain. Once again, however, Charles de Gaulle was disappointed. True, the audience was distinguished and numerous. A virtuoso had been applauded, but there were doubts about the composition. And those who had listened were left wondering what it was they had admired.

And now at last, promotion came. At the end of 1926, his name had been put forward for promotion, but ten more months had elapsed before action was taken. At the time, de Gaulle had written to Nachin: "It is nice to be promoted, but the real question is different: the important thing is to make one's mark."[12] When advancement came the following year, however, de Gaulle could not yet claim to have made his mark. He was promoted to major, and appointed to command the 19th Battalion of Light Infantry, in occupation of Trêves (Trier). Nachin records that General Matter, director of infantry at General Headquarters, had told him when discussing de Gaulle's new appointment: "The man I am posting there is a future generalissimo of the French army."[13]

On arriving at Trier, on the banks of the Moselle, in December 1927, Major de Gaulle's pessimism was at its deepest. French history, as usual, dominated his thoughts, as he showed in a letter to Nachin with a reference to the minister who had reorganised the French army under Louis XIV: "We still have all the elements we need to rebuild the army, but we no longer have an army. Who will provide the Republic with a Louvois?"[14]

In the wider sense of the word, de Gaulle may have failed to make his mark. But he was determined to make it upon the battalion under his orders. Gaston Bonheur draws attention to the fact that de Gaulle's appointment was itself an exception to the general rule that only a former *chasseur* should be given the command of a battalion of Alpine light infantry, which he explains by General Matter's eulogistic view of de Gaulle. Within a few days, says Bonheur, de Gaulle was the idol of his 721 men, and was given the title of "*Chasseur d'Honneur*".[15] Tour-

[12] ibid. p. 48.   [13] ibid. p. 54.   [14] ibid. p. 55.   [15] Bonheur, p. 30.

noux, on the other hand, while granting that de Gaulle aroused admiration, records that his men soon nicknamed him "the statue of the Virgin" – a reference to an oversized statue, called the Mariensaule, which dominated the Sidi-Brahim barracks on the left bank of the Moselle, not far from the road to Cologne. And some said, "No, he seems to think he is God the Father."[16]

Once again, his character and behaviour recalled those of General Franco at a corresponding stage. For Major de Gaulle was a stern and austere disciplinarian. Manoeuvres and alerts alternated with parades, target practice and competition of all kinds. When they were not on forced marches or in other ways kept up to the mark, the soldiers were required to take part in athletic contests, stage plays or organise festivities. Nor was the intellectual side of the battalion's needs neglected by its philosopher commander. At Trier, Mayence and other places in the area, the garrisons were often called upon to listen to a lecture by Major de Gaulle.

The white gloves, which de Gaulle had insisted on wearing ever since his passage through Saint-Cyr, had become a peculiarity in his dress. They were not required by the regulations of the light infantry. At home, scorning the services of his batman, which he reserved for the normal chores incumbent upon an officer's servant, Yvonne de Gaulle kept an ample supply of her husband's gloves, which she washed out, pair by pair, each evening. By now, she was the mother of two, for a girl, Elizabeth, had been born while the couple were living in the Boulevard des Invalides.

In various ways, Major de Gaulle created new conventions. Traditionally, the *chasseurs* wore their berets inclined to the left. De Gaulle preferred to wear his leaning to the right; and the 700 men under his command had to do likewise.

One day, says Tournoux, de Gaulle decided, in defiance of orders, to make the battalion carry out a double forced march, returning to Trier that evening, without permission. This deliberate breach of discipline made him liable to a penalty of a fortnight's close arrest. To the officers who warned him of this possible consequence, the major answered, "You will see. Everything will die down, for I belong to the *maison* Pétain."

And that was indeed the way things worked out. The commanding general made discreet enquiries and decided, against all precedent, not to take action against his headstrong major.[17]

A terrible winter gripped occupied Germany in 1928–9. The thermometer dropped to below 25 degrees centigrade. The worst epidemic of

[16] Tournoux, *Pétain*, p. 123.   [17] ibid. pp. 126–7.

influenza since 1918 swept the region. The French army of the Rhine alone had 143 dead. Public opinion was alarmed, and an indignant parliament called for an enquiry.

As ill luck would have it, Major de Gaulle's 19th Battalion had suffered the heaviest mortality of all. But the army's commission of enquiry was swiftly reassured. The 19th, indeed, emerged with top marks for care of the soldiers, despite the harshness of the major's discipline. A member of the parliamentary commission, Colonel Picot, reported: "There have been a large number of deaths in the 19th Battalion of Light Infantry. But these are certainly not due to the way in which the men have been treated. This battalion is admirably commanded." And he went on to tell the hushed politicians that Major de Gaulle, on learning of the death of a *chasseur* who had no next of kin, had insisted on going into mourning for the boy himself.

Normally, de Gaulle was not averse from publicity, but on this occasion the limelight appears to have irritated him. He wrote to Nachin: "The 19th Battalion has not, by a long way, been as badly hit by the epidemic as Colonel Picot pretended it was to bring out something else. This whole story is lamentable, in itself and for its consequences."[18]

For de Gaulle, and for his wife, this had been the second winter of bitterness. A shadow of pain had fallen over the household. By the time the de Gaulles reached Trier, a third baby was on the way. One day, some weeks before the expected date of birth, Madame de Gaulle was knocked over by a car. Though unwounded, she was badly shocked. When her time came, Yvonne de Gaulle gave birth to a subnormal baby girl, a Mongol. They called her Anne. Madame de Gaulle wrote to a friend: "Charles and I would give everything, everything, health, fortune, promotion, career, if only Anne were a little girl like the others."[19]

Two further letters to Nachin deserve to be quoted for the light they throw upon Charles de Gaulle's prescience, his character and the nature of his preoccupations. In the first, written at the end of 1928, de Gaulle depicted an unusually precise likeness of the crisis that was to afflict Europe ten years later. "The force of circumstance," he wrote, "is tearing down what is left of Europe's agreed and precious barriers. It seems obvious that the *Anschluss* is near, then the recapture by Germany, by force or by agreement, of what was torn away from her and given to Poland. After that, they will claim Alsace from us. This seems to me to be written in the stars."[20]

The second letter, dated 20 June 1929, has been more often quoted and has aroused more controversy, than any other letter in de Gaulle's

[18] Nachin, p. 57.   [19] Galante, p. 68.   [20] Nachin, pp. 56–7.

voluminous correspondence. "Ah!" he lamented in one version of it, "what bitterness nowadays to be in uniform! One must be, however. Within a few years, they will be hanging on to our coat tails to save the country . . . and the riff-raff will be to the fore."

But what did he mean about hanging on to coat tails, and whose coat tails did he mean? In his book, *Pétain et de Gaulle*, Tournoux reproduces the original letter in de Gaulle's difficult handwriting. The scrawl that precedes the word "coat tails" (*basques*) could be *mes* or *nos*. Tournoux, and most other commentators, have assumed that de Gaulle wrote "my coat tails". This interpretation does strain credibility, but is consistent with de Gaulle's monstrous ego and ambition. In 1929, Charles de Gaulle was still a major, not long promoted after twelve years as a mere captain, and – on paper – a relatively undistinguished record in the field and even at the desk. By what presumption would he have seen himself as the saviour of his country in a hypothetical crisis? This interpretation has seemed to some excessively fanciful. Lacouture opts for the view that the scrawled word was "*nos*". In context, "our coat tails" certainly makes sense if it refers to the French army. I think that predominant weight must be given to Nachin's interpretation. The letter was, after all, sent to him; he knew de Gaulle's writing better than most and had ample opportunity to check the wording with the writer. And he quotes the words as "*mes basques*". Curiously, Nachin omits the ensuing reference to "riff-raff" (*canaille*), presumably because it is incompatible with the "hero" image he tries to build.[21] The reference is, however, entirely typical of, and personal to, de Gaulle. How many times through the decades did he make clear his sweeping contempt for ordinary people! That he had a vision of forthcoming catastrophe cannot be doubted.

Once more, but once only, de Gaulle was to need – and be given – the powerful protection of Marshal Pétain. It was a question of discipline and influence in high places. Marshal Pétain had visited Trier, seen de Gaulle, inspected the 19th Battalion, and returned to Paris declaring himself satisfied with what he had seen. No sooner was he back than Major de Gaulle was in trouble. For the conscripts, service in Germany and in particular at Trier was unpopular. It was cold, foreign, and rigorous. Some of the young men had well-placed relatives or approachable deputies in parliament. So many of them managed to get themselves transferred to more congenial places in France that de Gaulle's anger was aroused;

---

[21] ibid. p. 12. In November 1970, I wrote to de Gaulle, to ask him, among other things, whether the key word was *mes* or *nos*; but he died before he could reply. It was typical of him, as Lacouture noted, that he never troubled to dispel the mystery.

and he announced that any *chasseur* who attempted to have himself posted elsewhere would be punished. Every man in the battalion was ordered to read his battalion commander's notice to this effect every day.

Shortly after this decision, an official telegram reached de Gaulle ordering the transfer of one of his men. Instead of complying with the telegram, de Gaulle gaoled the young man for a fortnight.[22] (It turned out later that the unfortunate *chasseur* had approached his deputy before de Gaulle had posted his order. But de Gaulle did not know this at the time, and it may be supposed that he would not have allowed the knowledge to influence him, had he known.)

Predictably, a row ensued. The deputy complained to the Ministry of War, which ordered an enquiry. The commander of the army of the Rhine, General Guillaumat, carpeted de Gaulle and reminded him that his refusal to carry out an order from the minister made him liable to a minimum penalty of sixty days under close arrest, and perhaps, if the minister took a grave view of the matter, of suspension.

De Gaulle immediately took the train for Paris and turned up at Marshal Pétain's office at general headquarters in the Boulevard des Invalides. To the staff officers, who well knew why he had come, de Gaulle declared: "I have had a bad blow. I have a dirty business on my hands. I have come to see the boss." Pétain received him and heard his version of the story. Fortunately for de Gaulle, Pétain was not only still disposed to help him, but on excellent terms with the war minister, M. Paul Painlevé. On hearing the marshal's special plea for de Gaulle, Painlevé decided to take no action. "That was quite a thorn I pulled out of his side," said the marshal to his *entourage*.

The major's statutory two years on the Rhine were drawing to a close towards the end of 1929. Disillusioned with the army, dreading a possible return to general headquarters (for which he felt an enduring contempt) Charles de Gaulle sought the distraction of distance. He applied for a transfer to the army of the Levant, which was granted without argument. He was transferred directly from Trier to Beirut without stopping in Paris. He was to spend nearly two years in the Near East, visiting Cairo, Baghdad, Damascus, Aleppo and Jerusalem. Although the experience would be useful to him in his later years of power during the Algerian crisis, the places he saw seem to have made relatively little impression upon him. He found the Arab world alien, un-French. This was not, of course, an ethnic view of things, but a cultural one. In de Gaulle's eyes alien peoples who accept French civilisation thereby acquired an aura of civilisation for themselves and the right,

22 Tournoux, *Pétain*, p. 131.

in certain circumstances, to be considered as part of the great French family. This was not, he discovered, the case of the Near East at that time, predominant though the French cultural influence was, among other alien influences. If these people rejected France, then (he argued) they did not deserve France, and France should retire. He was to use much the same arguments when presenting the case for an "Algerian Algeria", more than thirty years later.

This was how he expressed himself in a letter to the faithful Colonel Nachin six months after his arrival in Beirut:

> My impression is that we haven't really made much impact here, and that the people are as alien to us – and we to them – as they ever were. It is true that as a course of action, we have adopted the worst possible system in this country, that is to try to get the people to do things for themselves . . . whereas nothing has ever been achieved here, neither the canals of the Nile, nor the aqueduct of Palmyra, nor a Roman road, nor an olive grove, without compulsion. As far as I can see, our fate will be to go as far as that or to get out.[23]

De Gaulle had other things to interest him beside the people of the Middle East and France's attempts at penetration. He had brought some personal homework with him: the texts of the three lectures he had delivered in 1927 at the Ecole de Guerre. And he spent his leisure hours revising and polishing them, with a view to publishing them in book form. To add substance to the publication, he wrote two additional chapters, entitled "On Doctrine" and "Politics and the Soldier". About this time, writes Tournoux,[24] he became acquainted with a work lately published by a retired artillery officer, Lieutenant-Colonel René Quinton, much praised by Marshal Foch, and entitled *Maxims on War*. In it, de Gaulle found much that was in harmony with his war school lectures, for instance these passages quoted by Tournoux:

"The hero is a predestined man. He obeys a mission."

"Heroes are crucified in advance; they march to ultimate risks, unto death; they are the aspirants of death."

"What constitutes the hero? The joy of hurting the adversary. The joy of imposing a will upon him."

"The tragic is the natural element of the hero."

"There is a gambling-table of destiny; whoever places big bets on it never does so in vain."

And last, but not least appropriate: "The hero does not want to be the first, but the only one."

[23] Nachin, pp. 58–9.   [24] Tournoux, *Pétain*, pp. 138–9.

Towards the end of 1931, de Gaulle returned to Paris and, during his leave, prepared his book for the press. Le Fil de l'Epée was published in 1932. This strange and striking little work – a bare 160 pages in small format and large type – is both de Gaulle's philosophy and his self-projection as a hero. It is not fanciful to discover a parallel with The Prince and even with Mein Kampf; although it is closer to the first in concision. The resemblance to Machiavelli's little work is enhanced by the printed dedication on the fly-leaf of the special copy, No. 1, on vellum, which he presented to its subject, and which reads:

TO MARSHAL PÉTAIN
This essay, Monsieur le Maréchal,
could be dedicated only to you,
for nothing shows better than your
glory, the virtue which action may
derive from the glow of thought.

To this, the author added a handwritten dedication: "With my very respectful and deepest devotion – C. de Gaulle."

But that was not all. In the first of his two additional chapters, de Gaulle found three occasions to praise Pétain, first as a colonel, then as a general, while omitting any mention of his superior, Marshal Foch. In the second extra chapter, mindful of the fact that more than one "prince" had saved him from punishment for indiscipline, he quoted an opinion of Paul Painlevé, the former Minister of War.

If sycophancy were the only point of Le Fil de l'Epée its interest would have palled before now. But there is more to it than that. Packed with allusions, some of them beyond the reach of men less erudite in French history than de Gaulle himself, and couched in a style of great nobility, it is a definition of the qualities of leadership, of the circumstances in which duty must be exercised, and of the limits to individual military ambition. De Gaulle places the army firmly in its non-political place, subordinate in all respects to the authority of the State. But he envisages a national crisis in which it would be the duty of the military leader to take over control of policy. And he quotes the case of Marshal Foch, who went so far as to defy the civil power of Clemenceau. When the time came, de Gaulle acted on his own advice.

In terms of his search for fame and influence, Le Fil de l'Epée disappointed de Gaulle's hopes. It fell flat and sold only modestly. Its readers did, however, include influential men who remembered de Gaulle when the crisis came some years later.

Chapter 5 ✤ A Prophet Ignored 1932—1939

When de Gaulle returned from the Near East in 1931, Pierre Laval was premier and the ripples of the world economic depression were only just beginning to reach the rich and sheltered land that was France. True, the franc had continued to disappoint all hopes misguidedly vested in it, dropping from 70 to the £1 to 240 to the £1 in the two years from 1924 to 1926. But Poincaré, called back to power, had administered the drastic medicine his wizardry suggested; and the decline was sharply arrested, then reversed. For this service to the country's stability and the purses of its citizens, he was dubbed "the well-beloved" by the Paris daily, Le Temps, and the legend of his success hardened into a stubborn refusal to abandon the "Poincaré franc" even when world economic conditions made revision inevitable. By 1929, when the Wall Street crash touched off the great depression, France's recovery from the World War was virtually complete. The systematic anti-Americanism of later years had not yet made its appearance. Men like André Citroën and André Tardieu went to the United States to learn the secrets of American dynamism.

At about the same time as Tardieu was seeking public support for his plan for the economic regeneration of the Republic through the adoption of an Anglo-American electoral system, Charles de Gaulle was thinking along parallel lines, for he was engaged on a study of the correlation between economics and politics in the creation of a defence system. On his return from the Levant, a desk had been found for him in the secretariat of the Higher Council of National Defence – an organisation created on the initiative of Marshal Pétain. His first job, in collaboration with a Major Yvon, was to write a "History of the Troops of the Levant". Now he was entrusted with a study on the mobilisation of national resources and the organisation of the country in the event of war. This was not the first time this subject had been studied. A bill had been drafted in 1923, but it was buried five years later after protracted verbal warfare.[1]

As de Gaulle's critics have often noted, economics was neither his strongest point nor his major interest. Indeed, he often indicated his contempt for, or at any rate his reluctant tolerance of, a field that appeared to bore him; as did everything connected with what the French call *l'intendance*, which covers supplies and administration. It must be said in his defence, however, that his study of the 1930s, executed on orders from above, is not lacking in insight. It appeared on 1 January 1934, in the *Revue militaire française*, under the title, "Economic mobilisation abroad". It is rich in passages that can be used to attribute various opinions to de Gaulle, according to the taste and degree of hostility towards the author, of each particular reader. Was he, for instance, pro-Facist? A passage on the usefulness of coercive measures in Mussolini's regime, if torn from its context, could be said to justify it:

> The Fascist regime allows the authorities to draw from existing resources, without reservations or consideration, everything they are capable of yielding. The imperative subordination of private interests to those of the State, the discipline demanded and obtained from all, the coordination imposed on the various departments by the personal action of the Duce, and finally that sort of latent exaltation maintained among the people . . . are extremely favourable to measures of national defence.

Those reading the article in full, however, would have found a passage that could be held to imply approval of American capitalism. What struck Major de Gaulle was the close cooperation between the leaders of State and industry in the United States.

There was also a passage contrasting the Belgian example with the Italian: "A very interesting study published in the *Bulletin Belge des Sciences militaires* by Lieutenant-Colonel Giron, head of the mobilisation services of the nation, shows us that the efforts made in a free country can also prove not to have been made in vain."

At this stage, de Gaulle seems to have been attracted by the idea that American methods, adapted to French conditions, might provide the answer to the problems of a country threatened, as France was, by a potential external enemy. The machinery of government was, however, dangerously slow and ponderous. He had written his article in the *Revue militaire française* to stimulate a public discussion, and possibly

[1] Gorce, p. 62.

arouse public opinion, in favour of the adoption of a law on economic mobilisation in wartime. The article was the outward reflection of the more formal task he had completed for the Higher Council of National Defence, which was a draft programme for application in the event of the adoption of such a law. More than eighteen months, however, elapsed before a new bill was presented to the Chamber of Deputies. The bill passed what in Britain would be called the committee stage in March 1936; but it was not put to the vote until 22 March 1938, and became law, after receiving Senate approval, only on 11 July in the year of Munich. By this time, Hitler had been in power for more than five years, and the Second World War was only thirteen months away.

Those five years were disillusioning ones for de Gaulle, and disastrous ones for his country. In France, a mood of weariness and disillusion had succeeded the three years of euphoria known as *Poincarisme*. The country, it seemed, was again becoming ungovernable. Laval's governments in 1931 and 1932 were the seventy-ninth and eightieth of the Third Republic; when Edouard Daladier came to "power" in January 1934, his was the eighty-seventh – and it lasted only nine days. There would be eleven more governments before the collapse of France in 1940. Marshal Pétain, brought back to bury the Republic after France's defeat, sent the score up to ninety-nine.

Beyond the Rhine, the German giant was shaking off the shackles of Versailles without, it is true, much resistance on the part of former foes. Under the treaty, the Allies were supposed to withdraw their troops from the Rhineland in 1935; but they anticipated the deadline by five years. With a worthless currency and an army of unemployed, the Weimar Republic was collapsing under the weight of its own incompetence. In the second round of the presidential elections of 1932, in April, the rough and determined National Socialists polled thirteen million votes, paving Adolf Hitler's rise to power, which he achieved the following January.

On the French side, as indeed elsewhere in western Europe, the despair of the workless and the frustrations of the ruling few translated themselves into movements dedicated to violent, and in some cases revolutionary, solutions. It has become fashionable to lump them all under the universal description of "Fascist", but the label does not fit them all. For Fascism was a revolutionary movement. Among those which the label fitted, however, were Pierre Taittinger's Jeunesses patriotes, Marcel Bucard's Francistes and Major Jean Renaud's Solidarité française. To this list could be added the murderous gang of hooded men known as the Cagoule, whose real name was the Secret Committee of Revolutionary

Action; and above all Jacques Doriot's Parti populaire français (PPF), whose founder had been a leading Communist but turned to the extreme right on his expulsion from the party in 1934. But this list did not exhaust the militant movement of the extreme right. Apart from the durable and authoritarian Monarchist Action française of Murras, there was the populist – and popular – Croix de Feu created by Colonel de la Rocque in 1928 and originally restricted to decorated war veterans. But neither Action française nor the Croix de Feu was Fascist except in the loosest sense: both were fundamentally traditional. And many who joined the Croix de Feu for revolutionary purposes left on discovering that fact and joined Doriot's PPF.

Typically, perhaps, in a country that had known great scandals in the recent past, a sordid swindle was the spark that ignited the politically explosive mixture then at hand. A shady Russian-born financier, Stavisky, committed suicide when the police closed in on him in a villa in Chamonix. Or did he? Some said the police had killed him on orders from very high, to protect the prominent people who, it was alleged, had themselves protected him from arrest for a long series of fraudulent transactions. Now an odour of corruption and discredit hung over the regime. The discovery of the mutilated body of a prosecuting counsel in the case fed the rumours. The explosion came on 6 February 1934, when rival mobs of demonstrators clashed on the Place de la Concorde in the heart of Paris. It was, in retrospect, a mini-Commune, with fifteen dead and one hundred times that number hurt to show for it. But it was not a revolution; nor even, probably, a right-wing plot to seize power, as the left had alleged.

Just over a week before the riot, the Radical leader Daladier had come to power with an assured parliamentary majority. Now, yielding before the Paris mob, he resigned. The veteran Gaston Doumergue came back from the country house of his retirement to form a government of National Union – from which the Royalists, Socialists, and Communists stayed aloof – to avert civil war. For good measure, a general strike paralysed French industry from the 12th to the 13th.

Against this background, worthy but impotent men struggled to give France a foreign policy.

One of them was Louis Barthou, formerly a close associate of Poincaré's, who came to office as foreign minister early in 1934. Between April and June that year, Barthou made a grand tour of European capitals, east and west, to encircle Germany with a military and diplomatic ring. But on 9 October, he was assassinated at Marseilles, together with King Alexander of Yugoslavia. Thereafter, French foreign policy was increasingly at the mercy of the extremist factions that mirrored the discords of Europe at large.

It was against this background, too, that Major de Gaulle – and others of like mind – strove to alert French public opinion to the mounting dangers outside, and to create the military weapon that might withstand the expected onslaught from across the Rhine. It was a disillusioning task. "In the army, you know as well as I do," he wrote to Colonel Bouvard, "people find ideas burdensome."[2]

While working at the Higher Council of National Defence, however, he had found new friends and formed new habits. Every Monday, on leaving his desk in the evening, he went to the Brasserie Dumesnil, off the Boulevard Montparnasse. There, he dined with a number of friends, not all of them military men. The natural chairman of the little dinner group was Colonel Emile Mayer who, when de Gaulle first met him in 1932, was already over eighty, but still sparkling with wit and vitality. It was the faithful Lucien Nachin who introduced the two men, and despite the great age gap between them, an instant affinity asserted itself. The careers of both had been retarded by the incomprehension of the less gifted; in Mayer's case by his rashness, as a Jewish officer, in announcing his belief in the innocence of Dreyfus,[3] and by expressing his admiration for the German people in 1917. Nachin introduced de Gaulle to Mayer in the flat of the old colonel's son-in-law, Paul Grunebaum-Ballin. After that, the two men usually met either alone or with others in the flat on Sunday mornings, or at the Brasserie Dumesnil. One Monday (writes Gaston Bonheur[4]), on being reminded that it was closing time, de Gaulle prepared himself to leave, but changed his mind, searched his desk, then dealt a kick at the overflowing wastepaper basket, fishing out from the scattered mound a crumpled publication, which he smoothed out and folded into his pocket. At the restaurant, taking his place next to Mayer, he asked nobody in particular: "Have you read the *Journal des anciens Enfants de Troupe?*"

"Yes," said Nachin, "and I think what they say about your book is very good."

De Gaulle knew what he meant, clearly a reference to an unsigned article in the review – which Lacouture tentatively attributes to Nachin himself – which had lavished praise on de Gaulle's book *Le Fil de l'Epée.*[5] But this was not the reason why de Gaulle had sought to retrieve the review. It was for the sake of another article, also anonymous, but

[2] Tournoux, *Pétain*, p. 149.   [3] Lacouture, *De Gaulle*, p. 38.
[4] Bonheur, pp. 86 *et seq.*
[5] Lacouture, *De Gaulle*, p. 40. Nachin himself (p. 65) quotes from this article, in deprecatory terms suggesting the modesty that becomes an author.

61

attributed to "an amateur", which stated, in terms with which de Gaulle was bound to agree, the case for armoured divisions. Impatiently, then, de Gaulle answered: "No, that's not it. I mean an article entitled 'Reflections of an Amateur'."

And he launched into a speech, eloquently advocating his army of the future, which he thought need not exceed 100,000 men.

An animated debate ensued, which Colonel Mayer closed with the suggestion that de Gaulle should write an article exposing his ideas. Several of the guests proposed that de Gaulle should put his theory in the form of a book, but Mayer interposed: "No! That would take too long. The book can come later. For the time being, let us be content with an article, but an explosive article! As for the title, de Gaulle has already mentioned it this evening: 'Towards the professional army'."

De Gaulle had relatively little time of his own. Besides, he needed to think his ideas through and organise them. His article did not appear until 10 May 1933, in the *Revue politique et parlementaire*. By that time, Hitler had been in power for more than three months. The article disappointed the hopes vested in it by de Gaulle and his small circle of friends. Its impact was negligible, except within the military hierarchy, whom it irritated. De Gaulle was given to understand that the time had come for him to choose between his career and his self-imposed mission.[6] His reply is not recorded, but he made it clear by his subsequent actions that he rated the importance of his mission of enlightening the French public above his military career. It was now obvious to de Gaulle that something more than a mere article would be needed to shake the rigid men who controlled France's military machine: a book and a personal campaign of persuasion. For the rest of that year, de Gaulle's leisure energies were spent improving and expanding the ideas in his article. The book appeared one year later, in May 1934, under the same title as the article: *Vers l'Armée de Métier*. Like his preceding works, it was a short book, scarcely more than an expanded essay, indeed, at some 200 sparse pages, not much longer than *Le Fil de l'Epée*. And it made no more impact – in France, at any rate – than the article or than his previous works. No more than 750 copies were sold in France; although the subsequent German and Russian publishers appear to have found more buyers.[7]

It is not easy today, even for those with vivid memories of the prevailing apathy of that period of French history, to account for this indifference on the part of the public, although the character of some of the personalities involved on the official side helps to explain the hostility it aroused in those quarters. Hindsight, at any rate, suggests that the

[6] Bonheur, p. 96.   [7] ibid. p. 98. Tournoux, *Pétain*, p. 158n.

essential truth of de Gaulle's thesis should have been blindingly obvious. He begins eloquently with a description of France's topography, the aim of which is to point out the glaring vulnerability of France's frontier on the Belgian side. As he puts it, Britain and the United States are protected by the oceans; Germany by the dispersion of her centres of power and industry; Spain by the Pyrenees and Italy by the Alps. In contrast, the heart of France – Paris – lies wide open to an enemy advancing across a broad but shallow plain that is almost impossible to defend. And in these circumstances, de Gaulle argued, the only defence lay, not in fortification, but in the creation of a small professional army of 100,000 men grouped in six mobile armoured divisions. Six years later, the German army was to demonstrate that it understood and was ready to grasp the opportunities offered by France's geography, to which the French High Command had shown itself so blind.

The presentation of de Gaulle's thesis appeared in two respects to come at a propitious moment. For one thing, in 1933, while de Gaulle was writing his book, the Disarmament Conference had been meeting in London. Although Nazi Germany's insistence on her immediate need for weapons was one of the concerns of the conference, the prevailing climate favoured the reduction of military numbers. The British, in particular, were putting pressure on the French to reduce their enormous army. So in these circumstances, what could be more logical than de Gaulle's proposal to create a much smaller professional army, which would increase French defensive fire power, while meeting the hope of the disarmers? This seemed all the more self-evident for the fact that in any competition in numbers alone, France was bound to be outstripped by Germany. The other factor that apparently favoured de Gaulle was the appointment of his old protector, Marshal Pétain, as war minister in the Doumergue government after the February riots in 1934. In practice, however, neither the logic of the situation nor Pétain's presence in the government sufficed to overcome the weight of prejudice against new ideas and hostility towards de Gaulle himself.

On the left, de Gaulle's L'Armée de Métier was naturally regarded as a potential Praetorian guard with a vocation for seizing power; and on the right, as a potential "hotbed of Communism".[8] In parliament, the view that France could not afford to create a mechanised army carried much weight. And at General Headquarters, the official view was that France already had as many tanks as she needed – a reference to France's single armoured division.

[8] Alistair Horne, in To Lose a Battle (London, 1969), p. 64 (henceforth, Horne), attributes this remark to General Weygand.

To understand de Gaulle's contribution to the theory of mechanised warfare and to see it in proportion, the first essential is to clear one's mind of the legend carefully manufactured by the Gaullist myth-making machine during the Second World War. The early hagiographers, such as Bonheur and Cattaui, added glosses of their own to the legend. Bonheur for instance, claimed that the German Panzer General Guderian learned *L'Armée de Métier* by heart, and quoted a Frenchman as telling the Germans after the armistice that followed the defeat of France that their victory had cost them fifteen francs – the price of de Gaulle's book.[9] Cattaui's contribution was the astonishing statement that "once more, by virtue of the 'stick-in-the-mud' spirit, the invention of a Frenchman was to benefit only the adversaries of France".[10]

The facts are more prosaic. De Gaulle was in no sense an innovator. He did not invent the armoured division, nor the theory of mechanised war; nor did the Germans acquire their own knowledge from reading his work. The tank was a British invention. The Royal Tank Corps first went into action as an autonomous force in March 1917, in the battle of Cambrai. On the British side, the theorists of mechanised war were Generals Fuller and Morell and, of course, Captain Liddell Hart. In France General Estienne had himself commanded French tanks in units created on his recommendation, in support of Infantry battalions in action at Corbeny on 17 April 1917. And on 15 February 1920, the same general gave a lecture at the Conservatoire national des Arts et Métiers, in which he called for a mechanised army of 100,000 men – the same figure advocated thirteen years later by de Gaulle – supported by 8,000 lorries or motor-tractors and 4,000 tanks. Two years later, General Estienne, by now known in army circles as the "Father of the Tank", published a study urging the creation of armoured divisions. In 1928 General Doumenc submitted to the General Headquarters a plan for a modern armoured division.[11]

Moreover, the Gaullist claim that the Germans had got their ideas of armoured war from de Gaulle are without foundation. Limited to an army of 100,000 men (again, de Gaulle's proposed figure) under the Versailles treaty, the Germans had every incentive to compensate for their lack of military numbers by greater fire power and mobility. The organiser of the pre-Hitlerian Reichswehr, Colonel-General Hans von Seeckt, knew he had to create an "army of captains", and indeed created very much what de Gaulle had in mind when he called for an *armée de métier*. But the real pioneer was the man who later emerged as the master of Blitzkrieg, Heinz Guderian, who in 1931 became the commander of

[9] Bonheur, p. 98.   [10] Cattaui, p. 69.   [11] Gorce, pp. 93–4.

Germany's first motorised battalion. At that time it had to be a "toy" battalion, since Germany was disarmed and could supply him only with wooden cannon and plywood armour.

When the time came for Guderian to create the armoured divisions that won the Blitzkrieg, his inspirer was not de Gaulle but an Austrian general, Ritter von Eimmansberger, whose book, *Kampfwagenkrieg* ("Tank War"), appeared in 1934.[12] True, this was the year de Gaulle's own book appeared, but (as Lacouture noted) the German High Command would have been able to read von Eimmansberger's manuscript months before publication. There is no evidence that the Germans took any notice of de Gaulle's article of May 1933. Between 1932 and 1937, the German military attachés in Paris never once mentioned de Gaulle or his work in their reports. In his own memoirs, Guderian does mention de Gaulle before reaching the battles of 1940, but only once and simply as the propagator of "such ideas" in France.[13] Indeed, in 1933, before Hitler had decided to defy the Versailles treaty, the German military publication, *Militär-Wochenblatt*, had published a tactical article on the use of large-scale tank formations. German thinking on armoured warfare was, in fact, well known to the French and formed the subject of various official reports; though they did not influence the people in power or the establishment of the army.

De Gaulle himself never claimed to have invented mechanised war. On the other hand, he is not known to have discouraged his followers when they were creating a legend that undoubtedly enhanced the attractive power of the Free French forces. Moreover, he was not above attempting, long after the event, to improve his reputation for pre-war prescience.[14] When *L'Armée de Métier* was republished after the war, he inserted an important passage on the role of air power in support of armoured divisions. It is clear, however, that he had not given much thought to the relationship between air power and tanks.

The considerable credit that is due to de Gaulle is not for having invented a method which others had pioneered, but to have had the vision to be converted, to see that the forthcoming war would be won by the side that had the best armoured formations, and to have pressed the case for a mechanised army with unrelenting courage in the face of incomprehension or hostility. Some writers have further criticised him for the

[12] Lacouture, *De Gaulle*, pp. 41–2.
[13] Tournoux notes (*Pétain*, p. 154) that de Gaulle on a number of occasions wrote dedications in his book to various people, with a reference to "these ideas which are not new but which are renewed".
[14] Horne, p. 62; and Tournoux, *Pétain*, p. 157. De Gaulle himself, in the first volume of his war memoirs (*L'Appel*, pp. 10–12) gives full credit to the British and German pioneers of mechanised war.

relative imprecision of his book, compared with the technically detailed work of his British and German precursors. This criticism seems to me misplaced. It is true that General de Gaulle did not bother himself with details: it always was true. His role in the 1930s was as a writer, a philosopher, a poet even, of the military role in society. It was also the role of a special advocate, in which language and rhetoric were perhaps more important than the most detailed technical blueprints. In a more receptive climate of opinon, he might well have succeeded; and in that event, the ensuing history of France might have been different and happier. That is his claim to fame in the pre-war years.

The terrible history of France during the next decade might conceivably have been different if the Pétain who was war minister in 1934 had been the same Pétain who had clashed with the military establishment less than a generation before on the respective merits of bayonet charges and artillery fire power. The younger Pétain was a man of independent character, with a mind receptive to new propositions and the courage to express them. The Pétain of 1934 was seventy-eight. Though physically vigorous, and impressive to those who met him only occasionally, his mind had been deteriorating for some time. His powers of concentration were waning, and he was decreasingly receptive to new ideas. De Gaulle had been a great admirer of the earlier Pétain. In those days, it was de Gaulle's habit, when referring to the older man, to say, "He is a great man." But for some years now, he had been using the past tense: "He was a great man."[15]

De Gaulle's declining admiration for his protector was only one of the factors in their cooling relationship. De Gaulle had tried Pétain's patience to excess by relying on his support at difficult times. De Gaulle boasted to friends that Pétain would turn to him to draft the old man's speech on his reception into the French Academy.[16] This was undoubtedly unwise on de Gaulle's part, for the word was carried to the marshal's ear, together with uncomplimentary opinions about de Gaulle's indiscretion. It was argued (writes Tournoux) that a man as proud of his literary talent as de Gaulle would never keep to himself the fact that he had drafted Pétain's speech. Though Pétain wrote little, he had views of his own on what constitutes good French. He therefore drafted a summary of what he wanted to say, and entrusted two members of his staff with the task of putting it into speech form. De Gaulle resented this literary snub, and although he continued to attend Pétain's annual dinner for friends past and present, his visits to the marshal's home became more infrequent.

[15] Tournoux, *Pétain*, p. 133.　　　　[16] ibid. pp. 133 and 145.

How closed, in fact, was Pétain's mind? Alistair Horne, in his remarkable book on the fall of France, rightly defends Pétain against the sweeping disparagement of the Gaullists.[17] He points out that Pétain's term of office under the Doumergue government was largely occupied with a frustrating struggle to obtain military credits from reluctant politicians. He even quotes from a 1936 speech tending to show that Pétain was aware of the possibilities of modern offensive techniques when used by ground and air forces.

Against this, there is no shortage of texts showing the limits of Pétain's military imagination. On 7 March 1934, for instance, in a statement to the army's Senatorial Commission, the marshal derided the ability of the tank to shorten wars, and declared that any German tanks that reached the Parisian region would soon be rounded up. In 1938, in an article in *La Revue des deux Mondes* of 1 March, he declared his faith in the Maginot Line which, he said, meant there was no need to worry about armour.[18] And in the same year, in a preface to General de Chauvineau's book, *Is an Invasion still possible?*, Pétain declared himself satisfied with the French army's ability to stop any invader.

Pétain did nothing, while he was minister of war, to improve France's capacity to resist a German army that was preparing for modernisation and offence. He did think at the outset of including de Gaulle in his staff, but yielded to counsel from those around him.[19] With Pétain's prestige, and de Gaulle's talent, energy and far-sightedness, much might have been accomplished during the Doumergue government. But this was not the way things worked out.

Lacking a position of power, and even influence, Colonel de Gaulle did what he could within his limits: he lobbied incessantly. He talked to whomsoever would listen to him. In May 1934, he delivered a lecture at the Maurrassian Cercle Fustel de Coulanges. At that time (writes Lacouture)[20] de Gaulle still read *L'Action française* every day; indeed twenty years earlier, he had sent his first book, *La Discorde chez l'Ennemi*, to Charles Maurras himself, with a personal dedication.[21] But he was by no means an unconditional *Maurrassien*, and he took great care not to be used by the extreme Royalists.

In June 1934, he met one of Colonel Mayer's innumerable friends, a young man called Jean Auburtin who had influential connections, and who in turn introduced him to two politicians called Gaston Palewski and Paul Reynaud. Palewski was to become a loyal and devoted Gaullist

[17] Horne, pp. 61–2.
[18] Quoted in Cattaui, pp. 67–8.
[19] ibid. p. 63; Nachin, p. 83.
[20] Lacouture, *De Gaulle*, p. 46.
[21] Tournoux, *Pétain*, p. 164n.

"of the first hour". Reynaud was to prove a determined and eloquent defender of de Gaulle's ideas in the Chamber of Deputies, before becoming premier of France at the time of the collapse. As de Gaulle put it in his memoirs:

> M. Paul Reynaud seemed to me, *par excellence*, qualified for this enterprise. His intelligence was of the calibre to understand the reasons; his talent, to make them understood; his courage, to sustain them. In addition, well known as he was, M. Paul Reynaud gave the impression of being a man whose future was before him. I saw him, convinced him and, from then on, worked with him.[22]

The prevailing parliamentary climate was defensive, complacent and apathetic; and consequently, hostile to de Gaulle's ideas. On 15 June 1934 – about the time de Gaulle was meeting Auburtin and Reynaud – the chamber held a debate on defence. Inevitably, although his government had fallen after the February riots that year, the debate was dominated by Edouard Daladier, who had already been war minister four times, and was again to occupy that ministry from 1936 to 1940. The "Bull of Vaucluse", as his Radical Socialist followers liked to call him, looked like a strong man and delighted in the role. But his strength was at the service of a weak policy. He advocated a defensive strategy of fortification: the Maginot Line.

Reynaud did not get his chance to defend the Gaullist thesis until nearly a year later, during the debate of 15 March 1935 on a bill extending military service to two years. Reynaud, a former finance minister, declared that he would vote in favour of the Bill, if the chamber, on its side, would approve an amendment he had drafted, proposing the creation of an armoured corps, not later than 15 April 1940 – a deadline which, if reached, might have faced the invading Germans, that year, with something more solid than they encountered as they drove down France's northern plain.

Reynaud, a small man with curiously oriental eyes, was a compelling orator. But he was swimming against the tide. Daladier stuck to the views he had expressed in June 1934. To his right, the ultra-conservative General Maurin, who had succeeded Marshal Pétain as war minister, represented all those whose careers and interests were well served by the prevailing state of affairs and might be threatened by any change. To the left, Léon Blum, the Socialist leader, had already, in an article in *Le Populaire* six months earlier, declared his opposition to de Gaulle's

---

[22] C. de Gaulle, *Mémoires de Guerre*, vol. I, *L'Appel* (Paris, 1954), p. 13 (henceforth, De Gaulle, *L'Appel*).

professional army. As he recorded later, in his memoirs, however, Blum was shaken and almost convinced by Reynaud's speech. Whether or not the speech was largely drafted by de Gaulle (as Lacouture declares[23]), it rang with a prophetic note which those whom it disturbed would have preferred not to hear.

> Let us [said Reynaud] make a hypothesis. War is declared tomorrow and Belgium is invaded. Such a fact is not without precedent. If we lack the means to go immediately to her rescue and to help her cover her Eastern frontier what will happen? What will happen is perhaps what has already happened. It is possible that the Belgian army may be thrown back towards the sea. For us, that means 350 kilometres of open frontier to the north of France, to be defended. Is there anybody here who, in advance, accepts the idea of seeing the richest provinces of France once again invaded and torn from the Motherland?

He concluded with these words: "If we do not get the armoured corps everything is lost."

In a striking description of the scene in the Chamber of Deputies on that day, Blum records in his memoirs that when Reynaud, addressing himself to the Socialists, attacked reliance upon the Maginot Line to the exclusion of other measures, he exclaimed to his colleagues: "On that point, he is right!"[24] Although shaken, however, Blum was not entirely convinced. Strong though the arguments were in favour of the armoured corps, he found himself unable to dismiss those against.

Although de Gaulle's parliamentary friends included a protégé of Blum's, Léo Lagrange, a future Socialist minister of Leisure, the left-wing journalist Philippe Serre of the *Jeune République*, and the right-wing deputy Le Cour-Grandmaison, his friends did not constitute a majority, but merely a kernel of influence. One of his strangest allies at that time was Marcel Déat, who left the Socialist party in 1933 and was trying to make up his mind which way to jump next. In time, he opted for Hitler and the Germans briefly forced him on Vichy as a minister in 1944.

Europe, meanwhile, was moving ever faster towards war. The Saar returned to Germany after a referendum held in January 1935 in accordance with the Versailles treaty. Emboldened, Hitler now formally denounced the treaty clauses restricting German armaments. Conscription was reintroduced and it was announced that the German army would be increased to thirty-six divisions. This was in March. In the

---

[23] Lacouture, *De Gaulle*, p. 46.
[24] Léon Blum, *L'Oeuvre*, vol. 5 (1955), p. 111 (henceforth, Blum, vol. 5).

autumn, Mussolini's invasion of Ethiopia shook the League of Nations and exposed the weakness of the British and French. Now there was no stopping the European dictators. On 7 March 1936, Hitler finally tore up the treaties of Versailles and Locarno when he ordered the reoccupation of the Rhineland. This was a fatal date in contemporary European history. By almost unanimous consent, the Western allies, by failing to intervene, lost their last chance of stopping Hitler while there was yet time. The British could not act without the French, and the French, faced with the need to mobilise five million men for the sake of a local action, flinched and did nothing. Had France possessed the armoured division advocated by de Gaulle and Reynaud, immediate action would have been possible. The German Panzer general, Guderian, interrogated after the Second World War by officers of the historical department of the French army, declared his view that had the French intervened in the Rhineland in 1936, German resistance would have collapsed and Hitler would have fallen.[25] In his intellectual solitude, Colonel de Gaulle felt this deeply. He wrote to his young friend Auburtin the next day: "We should have acted with surprise, brutality, speed."

It was easy, in the late 1930s, to condemn the vacillating men in power in Paris and London. But the passage of time may be allowed to soften the harsher judgment of three decades ago. In both countries, but especially perhaps in France, the men in power had lived through a world war fought largely on French soil. French political leaders and soldiers were deeply conscious of the heaviness of French losses which, relative to France's population, were far greater than Germany's. Equally, they were painfully aware of the disparity between France and Germany, not only in population, but also in war industry. Essentially, they were men of peace – even the soldiers among them. To plan for offensive action seemed to them morally wrong, or politically undesirable. Tanks spelt offence in their eyes. In contrast, to build thick fortifications was morally unassailable, even if the gap at the Belgian end of the frontier stood as an open invitation to invaders. It was their misfortune, at this moment in history, that beyond the Rhine, and to a lesser degree, beyond the Alps, the new leaders in power had aggressive designs and the self-confidence of fanaticism. Not only were technical decisions difficult to make in the prevailing climate: political courses were no less onerous. This was the age of burgeoning totalitarian ideologies. Later, when the relentless conflict broke out, the democracies were to show the latent power held in reserve by their peoples. But they were also to expose the

<hr>

[25] Tournoux, *Pétain*, p. 159n. Guderian's view, however, has been contested: some believe the German army would have resisted. But the matter was not put to the test.

dangerous weakness of the French, which the small minority who thought as Colonel de Gaulle thought were powerless to remedy, and of which the appeasers and defeatists were symptoms as well as causes.

It was harder in France than in England to resist the fateful polarisation of politics. The Nazi menace was real, precise and proximate; if Stalin's empire presented a threat, it was a vague, contingent and remote one. Less was known about what went on in the Soviet Union. In any event, Russia had been an ally of France since 2 May 1935: even a right-wing politician like Reynaud regarded her as such. Among men of goodwill, even those to whom Nazism held no attraction, there were many to whom the concept of an alliance with the French Communists ceased to be repugnant. Those to whom Bolshevism was the ultimate enemy tended to group themselves on the extreme right, while on the left the radical Socialists grouped themselves with those who called themselves just Socialists to form Blum's Popular Front, accepting Communist support.

Apart from certain social reforms that were probably overdue and that might, in more favourable circumstances, have contributed to stability, the Popular Front experiment was an almost unmitigated disaster, not least from the point of view of the anti-Fascists who had turned to it for salvation. The necessary reforms included the forty-hour week in industry, paid holidays for workers and compulsory arbitration for labour disputes. Many other measures paid tribute to left-wing mythology and contributed nothing to the stability of the State or the productivity of industry: these included the extension of State control over the Bank of France and the nationalisation of some aircraft plants. A tremendous wave of sit-down strikes accompanied the advent of the Popular Front government in May and June 1936. Alarmed by the militancy of the atmosphere and of the politicians' oratory, many businessmen and investors placed their capital outside France. The franc fell and prices rose. Many less affluent members of the French middle classes turned for protection to the extreme right-wing group, which had been suppressed by decree shortly after Blum came to power but almost immediately reappeared under different names. At home, therefore, one of the paradoxical consequences of this anti-Fascist regime was the strengthening of the Fascist groups.

Until 1936, broadly speaking, the right-wing parties in France had had a better record than the left in standing up to Germany, though not to Italy, which was seen as a possible ally) – by voting, for instance, in favour of military credit which the Socialists opposed for traditional pacifist reasons. The political alliance with communism, however, scared

them, and many right-wing Frenchmen saw much virtue in the appeasement policy of the Chamberlain government a year or two later; some
indeed went further still, by conceding defeat before the battle had begun
and seeking a place for France (and, in particular, themselves) in Hitler's
New Order.

In foreign affairs, the Popular Front had been much criticised, not least
by its own supporters, for cutting off French military aid to the Spanish
Republic within a few weeks of the outbreak of the Civil War in Spain
in mid-July 1936, under pressure from Britain within the Non-Intervention Committee. But to have allowed France to be drawn into the
Spanish War would have played into Hitler's hands by freeing him for
action in eastern Europe. Moreover, if by chance French intervention had
contributed to a Republican victory in Spain, France would almost certainly have had a Communist State as a neighbour to the south-west. In
that event, it seems highly probable that Hitler would have taken over
Spain as well as most of France during the Second World War, and
denied the western Allies their Mediterranean victories.[26] Still, the
popular Front government did nothing, and this inaction demonstrated
the growing impotence of the French Republic. France, indeed, had
ceased to be, or wish to be, a great power: the Versailles policy was in
ruins; Locarno was an unhappy and illusory memory; Italy had proved
unamenable to friendly overtures; and in all foreign policy matters,
France deferred to Britain, herself bent on appeasement. Deprived of
Communist support and driven out of office by Radical votes in the
senate in June 1937, the Popular Front scarcely existed a year later.

De Gaulle was to be given a chance to explain his military ideas to
Léon Blum, and this was yet another of the missed opportunities of this
period of French history. Colonel Mayer, who had known Blum for
many years, persuaded the Socialist premier to send for de Gaulle. Both
men have left accounts of their meeting, in their memoirs. Both are worth
quoting for the light they throw on the characters of the two men.

I saw enter [wrote Blum] with a calm, and even placid ease, a man
whose height, breadth and frame had something gigantic about them
... One felt in him, at the first contact, a man "all of one piece"....
The man who thus presented himself, who looked at me so calmly,
who spoke to me with his slow and measured voice, could only, by all
the evidence, be occupied at any one time but by one idea, one design,

---

[26] These arguments are more fully developed in the author's *Franco – A Biographical
History* (1967) (henceforth, Crozier, *Franco*).

one belief, but then he had to give himself up to it absolutely so that nothing else should enter into consideration. He was probably hardly capable of conceiving that his own convictions should not be fully shared by everybody else. . . . He in no way resembled the inspired inventor fascinated by his own idea. Neither chimera nor illusions; rather a shade, I shall not say of discouragement, nor even of lassitude, but of disenchantment. Certainly, he was determined to persevere in the path which he had undertaken nearly two years earlier, because his nature included neither readiness to yield nor compromise, but he did not seem to believe that his efforts would be successful. . . . Clemenceau is the extreme type of those temperaments which a misanthropy, often contemptuous, prevents from believing that any action can have useful results and yet which nothing can turn away from action, because action for them is a vital necessity. Colonel de Gaulle gave me the impression of being in that category. . . . I gave him to understand, before he left me, that I should be very interested in having him in the immediate *entourage* of the war minister. The colonel avoided this opening even before I had had time to make my meaning clear. He declared, in his level tone, that he had been appointed to give the opening courses of the Centre of Higher Military Studies and that, during his stay there, he could not take on another job.[27]

As might be expected, de Gaulle's account of the same conversation is deeply tinged with the disdain he felt for political animals such as Blum. He shocked the Socialist leader with his suggestion that if the Germans marched into Austria, Czechoslavakia or Poland, the French should enter the Ruhr. And he depressed Blum with his visions of a military collapse in France should the Germans break through French defences. When Blum protested that he was proposing a massive increase in military credits, and that these were, in large measure, to be devoted to the provision of tanks and aircraft, de Gaulle countered by pointing out that both the planes and the tanks were of the wrong type. " 'The use of credits allocated to the war department,' the president observed, 'is the business of M. Daladier and of General Gamelin [the then chief of the army, General Staff].'

" 'Doubtless,' I answered. 'Allow me, however, to believe that national defence is the responsibility of the government.' " De Gaulle went on to mention that during their conversation, the telephone had rung ten times, and that the premier had complained of the difficulty of concentrating on any idea for even five minutes. In fact although Blum was

[27] Blum, vol. 5, pp. 114–15.

impressed by this curious personage, he was also permeated by doubts.[28] And in the end, he did nothing.

De Gaulle, meanwhile, settled down to his duties at the Centre for Higher Military Studies, which had lately been created and was soon to be known as the "School for marshals". In fact, de Gaulle was at that time never so far from being in the running as a future marshal of France (a rank which, of course, he never did reach). For he had just been struck off the 1936 promotions list on direct orders from General Maurin, the war minister, to signify displeasure not only with his theories, but with the political lobbying by which he attempted to further them.[29] He had now been a lieutenant-colonel for four years, and would have to wait another year before becoming a full colonel.

The great debate on mechanisation went on. The arch-conservative General Weygand attacked de Gaulle's doctrines, though without naming him directly, in an article in *La Revue des Deux Mondes* on 15 October 1936. The following month a former chief of the General Staff of the army, General Debeney, wrote an equally hostile article in the same publication. But the *Revue* was not necessarily antagonistic towards Colonel de Gaulle, for it also carried a favourable article by Daniel Halévy. Another defender was Rémy Roure, who had shared de Gaulle's wartime captivity in Germany, and who wrote an article in *Le Temps* warmly praising his friend's ideas, under the pseudonym of Paul Ervacque.[30] Gamelin's attitude was ambiguous. On 14 October 1936, before the Higher War Council, he argued the case for an offensive arm that would be stronger than the German Panzer division. But faced with the almost unanimous hostility of his colleagues, he contented himself with grumbling, "Whatever one thinks, the use of a heavy mechanised division ought to be studied."[31] General Gamelin brought the question up again on 15 December 1937, and was again outweighed. Against the evidences of open-mindedness should be set the fact that Gamelin evidently did not wish to be seen as a supporter of the eccentric Colonel de Gaulle. Tournoux quotes him as saying to the parliamentary delegate who visited him to sound him out on the increasing mechanisation of the German army, that he did not believe in Colonel de Gaulle's theories.[32] Of course, tanks and planes were important. But the tank could not be autonomous since it depended on fuel supplies; as for the air force, it could cause much damage but would not be decisive.

[28] De Gaulle, *L'Appel*, p. 20.
[29] Cattaui, p. 67; Horne, p. 60. Nachin (p. 85) attributes the omission of de Gaulle from the promotions list to General Gamelin, chief of the General Staff, who, he says, was trying to curry favour with the war minister.
[30] Cattaui, p. 67.   [31] Gorce, pp. 106–7.   [32] Tournoux, *Pétain*, p. 185.

In fact, towards the end of the inter-war period, the conservatism of the French army had gradually given ground. The Higher War Council, debating the Munich settlement on 2 December 1938, finally decided to create two armoured divisions, consisting of four battalions of tanks. The actual creation of these units was, however, to be deferred until further study had taken place.

Disillusioning though Colonel de Gaulle's contacts with the politicians were, it was during this phase that he acquired a life-long taste for politics as well as a contempt for those who practised them. His own ideas were changing. When in March 1936 the leader of Action française, Charles Maurras, whom de Gaulle had fervently admired, began to take up positions which he considered contrary to France's national interest, de Gaulle decisively broke with him. Though reluctant, even in those days, to identify himself too closely with any political group, de Gaulle began to read the Christian Democrats' weekly, *Temps présent*, and frequent the moderate anti-Fascists who ran it.[33] Towards the end of 1937 de Gaulle, whose name had been put back on to the promotions list by Daladier as war minister and despite the opposition of General Gamelin, was appointed colonel of the 507th Tank Regiment at Metz.[34] This promotion was also, in a sense, an exile, for the war ministry had long tired of de Gaulle's presence in Paris, whether or not the remark Tournoux attributes to the war ministry is authentic: "You have given us enough trouble with paper tanks. Now we shall see what you can do with a metal tank."[35]

For a while, de Gaulle was indeed in his element, to the extent that his enthusiasm for tank manoeuvres, rapid actions and the chance he now had to test out his theories in action, caused him to be nicknamed, half in fun, half in admiration, "Colonel Motor". Still wearing his non-regulation white gloves, despite the constant hazard of grease from his mechanical surroundings, de Gaulle was adding a new facet to his minor legend. On 14 July 1938, on the occasion of Bastille Day, the white-gloved colonel displayed his tanks in all their unorthodox fury. The military governor of Metz was present. He congratulated de Gaulle, to whom he had not taken a liking, upon the remarkable discipline of his regiment, but made it clear that he had no time for the doctrinal de Gaulle, with these cutting words: "So long as I am alive, my dear de Gaulle, you shall not make people put your theories into practice here."

The man who spoke those words was himself tall in stature, though not as tall as de Gaulle, whom he was to meet again in dramatic

[33] Lacouture, *De Gaulle*, pp. 50–51. [34] Nachin, pp. 86–7.
[35] Tournoux, *Pétain*, p. 182.

circumstances. His name was General Giraud. (In 1939, however, Giraud, despite his personal antipathy for de Gaulle, allowed himself to be persuaded to put de Gaulle's name on the list of "fitness" for the rank of general. The man who did the persuading was General de la Porte du Theil, who was in command of the Bastille Day manoeuvres in which de Gaulle had taken part.)[36]

Scarcely had Colonel de Gaulle arrived at Metz in November 1937, than the hooded men of the Fascist Cagoule, led by an ambitious engineer called Eugène Deloncle, attempted a putsch in Paris. Deloncle had worked hard within the army General Staff and (writes Tournoux) had enrolled a marshal of France and three regional generals in his "secret committee of revolutionary action".[37] It was a near thing, but the Cagoulards had underestimated the capacity of the Republic to defend itself. Their coup collapsed the night they had launched it, 15 to 16 November.

From Metz, Colonel de Gaulle was transferred to Lower Alsace, to take command of the tanks of the 5th Army, the chief of whose General Staff was to become one of the relatively few French higher officers to distinguish themselves in the Second World War: General de Lattre de Tassigny.[38]

About this time, the de Gaulles bought a large property with extensive grounds in the village of Colombey-les-Deux-Eglises, whose wooded climate had been recommended for their Mongol daughter Anne, then aged ten. The colonel and his wife had resisted all suggestions that they should send their handicapped daughter to a special home: "She did not ask to come into the world," de Gaulle used to say, "we shall do everything to make her happy." For Anne, and for her alone, the stiff and disdainful officer would forget his dignity: dancing and slapping his thighs, singing popular songs and allowing her to play with his *képi*.[39]

De Gaulle's Christian Democrat friends were to bring him new literary opportunities, and unwittingly cause his final break with Marshal Pétain.

---

[36] ibid. p. 184.   [37] ibid. p. 163.

[38] An interesting, but unfortunately apocryphal, de Gaulle story originated at this time. One day General de Lattre is said to have had an appointment with de Gaulle. He knocked on the door of de Gaulle's office. There was no answer, but the door being open, he walked in. On de Gaulle's desk, he found a much thumbed and annotated copy of Machiavelli's *The Prince*. Idly, de Lattre picked it up. It was open at a page which contained the following passage, marked by triple underlining. "Watch your military commanders very closely. If they become too successful and popular, remove them before they remove you." There is only one thing wrong with the story: the passage, though in character with Machiavelli, does not occur in *The Prince*. I have been unable to find it in other works either, although it may well exist somewhere. I heard the anecdote, which I believe to be unpublished hitherto, from Mr P. J. Honey, of the School of Oriental and African Studies, London. He himself heard it in Indo-China during de Lattre's passage there as French commander-in-chief.

[39] Tournoux, *Pétain*, p. 167.

One of the *Temps présent* journalists who encouraged him at that time was later to become famous as a broadcaster from wartime London, and in 1969, after de Gaulle's departure from the political scene, to be made foreign minister. His name was Maurice Schumann, but he wrote under the name of André Sidobre. His young friend, the lawyer Jean Auburtin, had given the publisher Daniel-Rops *Le Fil de l'Epée* to read. Daniel-Rops, who published the series known as *Présences*, asked de Gaulle to contribute a title to it.[40] De Gaulle thought about it, and decided to gather together the notes he had taken in 1925, when he was working on Marshal Pétain's staff, on a projected history of the French army.

He had already completely rewritten the first five chapters, and he now added two further ones. He wrote to the ageing marshal to ask his permission to publish the book under his own (de Gaulle's) name. But the marshal had other views; he himself had kept the notes of the original study, which he was proposing, at some future unstated time, to publish under his own illustrious name. In time, he did yield to de Gaulle's insistence, but on condition that the book should carry a dedication which he himself had drafted. The text, however, appeared with a dedication of de Gaulle's own drafting, which had displeased the marshal, flattering though it was: "To *Monsieur le Maréchal* Pétain, who wanted this book to be written, who directed with his advice the drafting of the first five chapters and thanks to whom the last two are the story of our victory."

In a temper, the marshal wrote to the publisher on 6 October 1938, to complain that "this officer" had made use, without his prior authority, of work carried out while he was under Pétain's orders between 1925 and 1927. He agreed that he had finally, out of goodwill, given his permission for the book to be published, but only on condition that the dedication he himself had drafted should precede the text. But the printed dedication was quite different and inaccurate in two particulars: in the first place because he had not wished the book to be published; and in the second, because he had had nothing to do with the first chapter. The publication of Colonel de Gaulle's dedication thus constituted "a veritable abuse of confidence". He therefore demanded the suppression of the de Gaulle dedication, and its substitution by the following: "To *Monsieur le Maréchal* Pétain – who was good enough, during the years 1925 to 1927, to help me with his advice for the preparation of chapters II to IV of this volume [*"Ancien régime"*, *"Revolution"*, *"Napoleon, from one Disaster to Another"*] – I address the

40 Cattaui, p. 72n.

77

homage of my gratitude."[41] As Tournoux records, the first impression had still not sold out by 1940, and the text with the revised dedication was never printed.

Some weeks later, Charles de Gaulle lost his father, and his old friend, supporter and confidant, Colonel Emile Mayer. That day, 28 November 1938, Mayer had noted in his diary: "Today, my death."[42]

Despite its official beginning under Marshal Pétain's direction, La France et son Armée is unmistakably the work of Charles de Gaulle. Though often informative and even precise, it is in no sense a military text book. There is an epic sweep about it, a patriotic surge, that are quintessentially Gaullist. Of all de Gaulle's works, it is possibly the one most likely to be read for pleasure, even by those without any special interest in the subject. Though full of psychological clues about the character of its author it does not, however, compare in importance with de Gaulle's other shorter works.

A few days before the publication of his controversial book, de Gaulle wrote to Paul Reynaud, to tell him that La France et son Armée was about to appear, and to ask him to find a few moments to read it. He added: "As for me, I see ahead without the slightest surprise the greatest events in the history of France, and I am sure that you are marked out to play a predominant role in them. Let me tell you that in any case I shall be – unless I am dead – resolved to serve you if it should please you."[43]

The letter was dated 24 September 1938, and written from Metz. Five days later, Hitler, Mussolini, Chamberlain and Daladier signed the Munich agreement. For the West, it was the ignominious culmination of a dreadful year. In March, Hitler had annexed Austria, in the Anschluss which he had planned for many years. That month, the short-lived Radical ministry of Camille Chautemps fell after two months in office. Blum had another attempt at a Popular Front government, but lasted only one month. Then in April, Daladier, the disillusioned heir to the appeasement policy and to conservative military doctrine, formed the Radical ministry that still held power when the Second World War broke out seventeen months later. Although the Radicals had taken part in the Popular Front government, Daladier himself was no sympathiser with communism. When the trade union organisation, the CGT, in

41 For full text, see Tournoux, Pétain, pp. 174–5.
42 Lacouture, De Gaulle, p. 50, says Mayer died while correcting the proofs of La France et son Armée, but the book appeared in September, so the story is without foundation. That he did correct the proofs is not in doubt, however. De Gaulle, on duty at Mailly camp, was unable to attend the funeral (Nachin, p. 93n.).
43 Tournoux, Pétain, p. 179.

which the communists were strong, attempted a general strike in November 1938, Daladier took energetic action against its leaders. And when war came, he arrested the leaders of the French Communist party, as Blum during his first Popular Front government had taken corresponding action against the extremist movement of the right. History, however, and the fate of France itself as well as of Europe, were being decided outside France, by Hitler himself. Under the Munich agreement, he had imposed his will on Czechoslovakia. And on 15 March 1939 he delivered the *coup de grâce* to that unfortune country, by provoking the abdication of President Hacha and entering Prague.

In these distressing events, Colonel de Gaulle himself, from his military post at Metz, was powerless to intervene. As he records, his political friend Reynaud was in office in Daladier's government, but was fully occupied with his successive portfolios of Justice and Finance; and frustrated in any event by cabinet solidarity.[44] De Gaulle and Reynaud, Daladier and Chamberlain, were impotent and inactive spectators when, on 1 September 1939, Hitler's Panzers crossed the Polish frontier.

[44] De Gaulle, *L'Appel*, pp. 21–2.

Part III ⚜ Free France 1939–1945

Les armes de Jésus c'est la croix de Lorraine,
Et le sang dans l'artère et le sang dans la veine,
Et la source de grâce et la claire fontaine;

Les armes de Satan c'est la croix de Lorraine,
Et c'est la même artère et c'est la même veine
Et c'est le même sang et la trouble fontaine . . .

The weapons of Jesus are the Cross of Lorraine,
And the blood in the artery and the blood in the vein,
And the source of grace and the clear fountain;

The weapons of Satan are the Cross of Lorraine,
And the same artery and the same vein,
And the same blood and the cloudy fountain . . .

CHARLES PÉGUY, "*La Tapisserie de Sainte Geneviève*",
from *Oeuvres Poétiques Complètes* (La Pléiade, 1957), p. 849

Chapter 1 ⚜ The Defeat 1939–1940

The great confrontation, when it came, was rudely unequal. On one side stood an assertive and self-contained Germany, led by a madman of genius whose intuition, until then, had never failed. On the other, a weak and divided France, with an army whose strength was illusory, led by men who had no stomach for a fight and who rejected the technical challenge of modern warfare; and beyond the Channel, a Britain weakened by years of complacency and falsely secure behind her moat of water. The distant giants stood immobile – Russia, neutralised for the time being by the Stalin-Hitler pact, and America hopeful of non-involvement.

The diplomacy of the Entente Cordiale reflected the lack of will, as much as the military unpreparedness, of France and Britain. The two governments' acquiescence in the Munich pact had shattered their credibility as great powers. Hitler was unimpressed when, on 31 March 1939, Chamberlain told parliament that his government would defend Polish independence; and remained unmoved when the French, who themselves had guaranteed Poland's integrity under the Locarno pact, made precise military commitments to Poland on 19 May. Stalin was equally unimpressed by British and French diplomatic efforts to bring the Soviet Union into an East-West pact against aggression. Instead, he stunned the world in August 1939 with the news of his pact with Hitler. Now the Fuehrer knew he could attack Poland with impunity.

In the preciseness of its military guarantees to Poland, the French High Command had shown itself consistent with its own proclaimed disbelief in the efficacy of mechanised war. General Gamelin, chief of the National General Staff, had promised the Polish war minister, General Kasprzycki, limited French assistance on the third day of a war, and a general offensive on the fifteenth.[1] What this diminutive, ineffectual, intellectual officer had not foreseen was that it would all be over in sixteen days. By that time, Hitler's invading forces of 1,700,000

[1] Gorce, pp. 124–5.

men, spearheaded by armoured divisions and with overwhelming air support, had overrun half Poland. The following day, 17 September, Stalin's forces invaded from the east. And ten days after that, all Polish resistance was at an end. On the British and French sides, the only response to the devastating Nazi onslaught on Poland was the joint declaration of war on Germany on 3 September. In military terms, no action was deemed possible.

The French were still obsessed with their relative weakness and memories of the great blood-letting thirty years earlier. At the outbreak of war, they could put fewer than 500 aircraft in the air, against Germany's 4,000. The land army, with sixty-seven divisions mobilised, was impressive on paper – but fell short of Germany's mobilised strength by some forty divisions. On 3 December 1938, the Higher War Council had at last decided to create two armoured divisions. But this was not the mechanised army Colonel de Gaulle had envisaged. Not only was it terribly late in the day, since the first of these new units was not to be ready until January 1940; but in total numbers, they were to fall far short of the needs de Gaulle had estimated. De Gaulle had called for 500 tanks; each of the new divisions was limited to 120.[2] Worse still, from the standpoint of the minority that understood the character of mechanised warfare, the new armoured divisions were not to be allowed to function as autonomous forces: instead, their tanks were to be scattered throughout the army, in support of individual infantry units.

When the clash came in the spring of 1940, the French army was to show that it was simply not a match for the Wehrmacht. Nor was it merely a matter of numbers and organisation: it was, perhaps above all, a question of offensive spirit. The German High Command, indeed, feared a French offensive on the western front while the bulk of the German forces were engaged in Poland. At the Nuremberg War Crimes trials after the war, General Jodl of the Wehrmacht General Staff was to declare: "In 1939 catastrophe was avoided only because the 110 French and British divisions remained inactive against our 25 divisions in the West." Field-Marshal Keitel, chief of the General Staff, confirmed this view, and General Hadler, chief of the General Staff of the Land Forces, went further still: "The victory in Poland was possible for us only through uncovering almost completely our western frontier. The French could have crossed the Rhine without our being able to stop them and

[2] De Gaulle, *L'Appel*, p. 24. Benoist-Méchin says, however, that the 2nd division was to comprise 169 tanks. *See* J. Benoist-Méchin, *Soixante Jours qui Ebranlèrant l'Occident*, Vol. 1, pp. 48–9 (henceforth Benoist-Méchin).

they would have threatened the Ruhr zone which was for Germany the most decisive factor in the conduct of the war."[3]

The "phoney" war had begun. Watching the Siegfried Line (or, in the words of a briefly popular British song that now brings blushes to the cheeks, "Hanging out our washing" on it) became the primary occupation of the French and British forces. Discipline was lax in the concrete fool's paradise of the Maginot Line. Paul Reynaud, who probably knew better, declared on the radio on 10 September: "We shall win because we are the stronger side." At that stage of the game, Reynaud was the energetic finance minister who was exhorting the workers to work longer hours. Soon, he was to take over as premier at a time of impending disaster.

The allies were floundering. Instead of making plans, they nursed hopes; especially the hope that the war could be kept far from the western front. Very soon, events did seem to justify their hopes that the German forces would be kept employed far from the nerve centres of the Franco-British alliance. In November 1939, the Russians, having imposed treaties on the three Baltic States, presented similar demands to the Finns. The Finnish government rejected the demands and on 30 November the Soviet armies attacked Finland on three fronts. In France, and to a lesser degree in Britain, the news was received in a mood of mingled indignation and self-congratulation. The spirit of Munich brooded heavily over the French conduct of the phoney war. In both countries, the men in supreme office were those who had signed a pact with Hitler. Did they still nurse the illusion that a further understanding might yet be possible? Probably not; but in France, at all events, it was clear that the Soviet Union was then regarded as the main enemy, with Hitler's Germany less a foe than a headstrong member of the Western family, whose pact with Stalin was an aberration that did not affect her fundamental anti-Bolshevism; to be treated in any case with kid gloves, so that her attention might be diverted to other places. This is the only interpretation that accounts for the vastly different treatments meted out to the two fifth columns at that time operating in France: the Commu-

[3] Quoted by Gorce, p. 126. At that time, however, nothing was further from the minds of the French High Command – and indeed from those of the British – than an offensive against Germany. There was indeed a token offensive – not with the intention of risking a clash with the German forces, but with the aim of being able to say that something at least had been attempted to relieve the hard-pressed Poles. Between 4 and 7 September, French forces advanced and penetrated into German territory in the Saar. Nine divisions were involved, and the territory they overran had been abandoned by the Germans. By the 12th, their advance extended fully five miles on a sixteen-mile front. Now they were within sight of the Siegfried Line; and they went no further. This was Gamelin's idea of an "offensive". (See Horne, pp. 83–4.)

nists and the Fascists. The Communist party was declared dissolved on 27 September. Thirty-five Communist deputies were arrested and *L'Humanité* was closed down. The party boss, Maurice Thorez, who knew he was down for arrest, deserted from the army and was deprived of his citizenship. Later, thousands of Communists, and many who were not Communist but were labelled as such, were thrown into concentration camps. It was noticeable that the right-wing groups were left unmolested; indeed, among the many interned on the left were staunch anti-Nazis, including refugees from Hitler's concentration camps.[4]

When the Russians invaded Finland, the government thought itself vindicated in its anti-Communist policy. Soon, in London as well as in Paris, when the ill-equipped Russian troops ran into initially successful counter-attacks from the better clad Finns, in the intense cold of the frozen Finnish forests, the mood turned to elation. "The conclusion was drawn too hastily," wrote Churchill, "that the Russian army had been ruined by the purge, and that the inherent rottenness and degradation of their system of government and society was now proved."[5]

Churchill himself sympathised deeply with the Finns and thought that, by establishing an allied supply base at Narvik in northern Norway, it would be possible both to supply the Finnish forces and to impede the flow of iron ore bought by the Germans in Sweden.[6] The French had already decided to send material aid to Finland, and 175 planes, 500 cannon, 5,000 machine-guns and other automatic weapons were despatched; the British having sent about 100 aircraft and 200 guns.[7] On 8 January, Daladier ordered the equipment of a mixed brigade of Alpine troops for the Finnish front and on the 19th, the British war cabinet agreed "that the basis of all help [*secours*] to Finland is the effective support of Norway and Sweden against a German reaction".[8]

On 17 February 1940, British naval forces rescued 326 prisoners of war from the German ship *Altmark* in Norwegian waters. Some weeks later, the British and French governments announced that these waters had now been mined to prevent the passage of German ships. Next day, 9 April, the German land forces overran Denmark without meeting any resistance; simultaneously sea- and airborne divisions descended on Norway. The determined resistance of the Norwegians encouraged the allies to go ahead with their plan to establish a base at Narvik. On the 13th, British naval units attacked the Germans, sinking all ships in Narvik harbour. On the 20th an Anglo-French expeditionary force landed in

[4] Horne, pp. 96–7.
[5] Winston S. Churchill, *The Second World War*, Vol. I, p. 429 (henceforth Churchill).
[6] Churchill, Vol. I, p. 430 *et seq.*   [7] Gorce, p. 130.   [8] ibid. p. 131.

southern Norway. It was, however, a short-lived success. Narvik was held only until 9 June; and the expeditionary troops in the south were compelled to leave after two weeks.

The western allies already had some knowledge of German plans for a forthcoming invasion of France through Holland and Belgium, full documents having been found on a German staff major intercepted in Belgium. Churchill thought these plans rang true, but the argument that the documents were planted found many supporters.[9] The British expeditionary force was being built up in France and was training itself to a fair degree of efficiency. It was, however, badly equipped and, as Churchill wryly notes, it lacked even one armoured division. The British, though they had invented the tank, were thus even less well prepared in this domain than the French. But among the French troops idleness and demoralisation were taking their toll. By all accounts, the skilful propaganda of Dr Goebbels was proving poisonously successful in its intended object of driving a wedge between the French and British. The French "Lord Haw-Haw", Paul Ferdonnet, coined telling slogans, such as "English weapons, French casualties".[10]

From his command in Alsace, frustratingly distant from the centres of decision, Colonel de Gaulle watched events with deepening dismay. A stream of distinguished visitors passed through, watched the tanks he commanded for the 5th Army, and expressed their scepticism or complacency before his warnings. One of them was the president of the Republic, M. Lebrun, who said amiably: "Your ideas are known to me. But for the enemy to apply them, it does seem that it is too late."[11]

In de Gaulle's eyes, neither Finland nor Norway was of more than marginal significance. Two things obsessed him: the devastating speed of Germany's armoured *Blitzkrieg* against Poland, and on the western side, the vulnerability of the Belgian front – unprotected even by the Maginot Line – the complacency of the politicians and the technical backwardness and lack of fighting spirit of the armed forces. In January 1940 he made a last attempt to force the French leaders to grasp and face the lessons of the *Blitzkrieg* in Poland. In November 1939 he sent a note to the General Staff in which he expressed himself with his usual clarity and vigour about the effectiveness of an armoured force and the vulnerability of a lengthy and continuous front line.[12]

---

[9] Churchill. Vol. I, pp. 440–1. [10] Horne, pp. 94–5.
[11] De Gaulle, *L'Appel*, pp. 22–3.
[12] Gorce, p. 133. De Gaulle makes no mention of this note in his own memoirs. Horne (pp. 113–14) records that General Armengaud, an air force general who had observed events in Poland, delivered a memorandum on German methods to General Gamelin in the autumn of 1939. He argued that the Germans, having succeeded in Poland, would

The note was read, but no action taken. General Dufieux, at that time inspector-general of infantry and tanks, declared that "these conclusions, in the present state of the question, are to be rejected".

In January 1940 Colonel de Gaulle, who continued to cultivate his friendship with Paul Reynaud, dined with the finance minister in his Rue de Rivoli flat. Another guest was the socialist leader, Léon Blum. Both Blum and de Gaulle have left accounts of the dinner conversation that evening. Blum's version is the more interesting.[13] Before taking his leave, and after a gloomy discourse on the war situation, de Gaulle disclosed that he had written a short report on the state of the army and on immediate measures that needed to be taken. He offered to send it to Blum, and did so a few days later.

De Gaulle's memorandum, dated 26 January 1940, was entitled, "The Advent of Mechanical Force". It was never set up in type, but was duplicated from an original typescript, and despatched to some eighty leading politicians. Essentially, the new memorandum was a sort of additional chapter to Vers l'Armée de Métier. After contrasting Germany's frightening striking power with France's relative impotence, and attributing the former to Germany's mechanised strength, de Gaulle dismissed the current defensive strategy as useless. "Any defender who limited himself to static resistance by old-fashioned elements would be doomed to disaster," he wrote. "To smash mechanical force only mechanical force carries certain effectiveness. A massive counter-attack of air and ground squadrons . . . that is therefore the indispensable resort of modern defence." Thus de Gaulle demonstrated that he had at last grasped the fact that tank power needs to be supplemented by air power – a point he had ignored in his earlier book. For good measure, he added: "In the present conflict, as in those that preceded it, to be inert is to be beaten." There was only one remedy: to create a new military instrument. He called for a "vast programme", in cooperation with Britain and America, for the construction of an autonomous mechanised force. He dismissed the existing programme aimed at the creation of light mechanised divisions as in itself inadequate, unless those divisions

---

attempt a similar breakthrough in the west. "For his pains," writes Horne, "Armengaud was relegated to an administrative post, as commander of the Paris air region." The second bureau chief, Colonel Gauche, also delivered a telling report on the effectiveness of German tank warfare; but this warning was likewise ignored by the French High Command. It is interesting to note that neither General de Gaulle nor his French biographers mentioned these competitive warnings, presumably because they detract from the claim of unique prescience.

[13] De Gaulle, L'Appel, p. 23. Blum, in L'Oeuvre, Vol. 5, pp. 115–17, agrees with de Gaulle's version on essentials, but dates the dinner as having taken place "in the last weeks of autumn 1939".

were used to support more powerful ones. He envisaged combined air-sea-ground operations.[14] In an eloquent peroration, he foresaw a world-wide extension of the conflict, and called on France to draw the right conclusions.

He might as well not have written a word. General Keller, inspector-general of tanks, wrote the following comment:

> Even supposing that the present fortified line were breached or out-flanked, it does not appear that our opponents will find a combination of circumstances as favourable for a *Blitzkrieg* as in Poland. One can see, then, that in future operations, the primary role of the tank will be the same as in the past: to assist the infantry in reaching successive objectives.[15]

The collapse of the western intervention in Norway brought down the Dalaidier government on 21 March; and shortly afterwards, the Chamberlain government in London. A painful demonstration of the incapacity of the French party system to cope with a national emergency now followed. Daladier had fallen, but he was not out. President Lebrun called on Reynaud to form a government; but he could not do without the support of the Radical-Socialist group in parliament, which made the retention of Daladier in the war cabinet a condition of its goodwill. Reynaud therefore had no option but to appoint Daladier, yet again, minister for National Defence and War. On first hearing of Reynaud's advent to power, Colonel de Gaulle had been elated. At last, the one politician who had enthusiastically supported his ideas on mechanised warfare had reached supreme office. His elation increased when Reynaud immediately invited him to Paris, and it was in a mood of hopeful ex-pectancy that de Gaulle left his post at Wangenbourg. As soon as he reached Paris, he reported to the Prime Minister, who called on him to draft his first statement to parliament. It was 23 March. Reynaud read the statement exactly as de Gaulle had written it.

Disillusion, however, was immediate and brutal. De Gaulle attended a "ghastly" session in a dull and sceptical Chamber of Deputies, in which the politicians showed that behind their patriotic phrases, their only true preoccupations were with their own political fortunes or those of their parties. Only Blum, although he had not been offered a job in the Reynaud government, seemed to rise above the general level of

[14] Nachin (p. 105) records that Colonel de Gaulle was deeply impressed by Colonel Rougeron's *Air Lessons of the Spanish War*, published by Berger-Levrault in 1939. Nachin was the first biographer to quote extensively from the de Gaulle memorandum of 26 January 1940. De Gaulle himself (*L'Appel*, pp. 23-4) gives a more concise account.
[15] Quoted by Horne, p. 115.

self-centred mediocrity. Reynaud had hoped to have de Gaulle in his new War Council, with the title of Under-Secretary of State.[16] But he had counted without Daladier and the Radicals. On hearing of this proposal, Daladier sent word that if Reynaud went ahead, he would suggest that de Gaulle might as well take over as war minister, leaving Daladier to resign from the cabinet. Unwilling to risk the collapse of his new government, Reynaud regretfully withdrew his offer to de Gaulle, who returned to Wangenbourg. Instead, Reynaud gave the job to the director-general of the Bank of Indo-China, Paul Baudouin, who was publicly on record with a foreign policy the opposite of Reynaud's own.

The painful exigencies of party politics had indeed obliged Reynaud to bring in men whose policies differed radically from his own. His vice-premier, Camille Chautemps, one of the leading Radicals and himself an ex-premier, was an appeaser; his war minister, Daladier, was the man who stood for the defensive military policy Reynaud had attacked; and his under-secretary of State was also a man who had opposed him. Reynaud was in "power"; but in reality, he was paralysed. Combative though he was, he was surrounded by pessimism and defeatism. From Madrid, where Marshal Pétain was France's ambassador, came insistent rumours that the Germans would be ready to make an "arrangement" with the French, with Laval in power and Pétain at his side to guarantee that the High Command would accept an armistice. Thousands of printed folders – presumably drafted by the Germans – showed three pictures of Pétain, the first as the victorious soldier of the First World War and the second as ambassador, while the third was an indistinct image with the caption, "Tomorrow? . . ."[17]

On his way from Paris to Wangenbourg, de Gaulle was called to General Gamelin's headquarters in the château of Vincennes. The tiny supreme commander, in his abstracted way, announced that the armoured divisions were about to be doubled in number: from two to four. De Gaulle, though still a colonel, was to be given the command of the Fourth, to be formed on 15 May. De Gaulle declared himself honoured, but could not refrain from expressing his gloom at the prevailing situation. Gamelin's reply was: "I understand your satisfaction. As for your worries, I don't believe they are justified."

It was now desperately late. On 3 May, deeply disappointed at Reynaud's failure to initiate any of the policies he had been advocating, de Gaulle sent him the following letter:

16 De Gaulle, L'Appel, p. 26.
17 ibid. pp. 25–6.

Monsieur Le Président,
The events of Norway, after those of Poland, prove that today no military enterprise is possible, except in function, and on the scale, of the mechanical force available. If tomorrow operations extend to Swedish territory, the day after tomorrow to the Balkans, later still to the Ukraine, after that to Belgium, and finally to the West, either against the Siegfried or against the Maginot Line, the same evident truth will stand out.

Now the French military system is conceived, organised, armed, commanded on the opposite principle to this law of modern warfare. There is no necessity more absolute, or more urgent, than radically to reform this system. For us, the capital problem of the war is today, will be tomorrow, as it was yesterday, "the French military problem". But the reform and, in consequence, the victory, are becoming more difficult, the longer decision and action are postponed.

We must repeat that the military body, through a conformism inherent in its nature, will not reform itself on its own. This is an affair of State, above all others. A statesman is needed. In France, the great man of this war will be Carnot,[18] or will not exist at all.

You alone . . . by reason of your job, your personality, the position you have taken in this business – and taken alone – for the past six years, can and must see the task through. I take the liberty of adding that in making this question the great concern of your government, you would change the atmosphere within and without, and you would bring into play trump cards that are not yet in use. From this moment, each day that passes, each event that happens, helps our doctrine, but also, alas, the enemy, which is putting it into practice.

I need hardly say that I have no greater ambition than the honour to serve you in this capital undertaking, as soon as you should judge that the moment has come for it.[19]

Yours, etc.,

Ch. de Gaulle

Exactly a week later, on 10 May 1940, the German army, without prior warning, invaded Holland, Belgium and Luxembourg. That day in London, Winston Churchill took Neville Chamberlain's place as British Prime Minister. Events now moved with crushing speed and force. The direst possibilities foreseen by Charles de Gaulle and the minority who thought as he did now came to pass. On the 11th, the French

[18] Lazare Carnot (1752–1823) created the armies of the French Revolutionary Republic. Known as "the organiser of victory".
[19] Tournoux, *Pétain*, pp. 196–7.

and British governments sent expeditionary forces into Belgium. There were too few of them, and they arrived too late. On the 12th, the Germans crossed the Meuse at Sedan, scene of the decisive defeat of Napoleon III's forces in 1870. Next day Rotterdam surrendered; and on the 14th the Netherlands army capitulated, Queen Wilhelmina and her government having escaped to London the day before. By then, de Gaulle's brief but courageous military involvement in the war had begun. On the 11th, he was ordered to take command of the 4th Armoured Division; which, as he noted later, did not yet exist, but was to consist of men and tanks drawn from scattered places, to be gathered and placed under his orders. On the 15th, General Doumenc summoned him to General Headquarters to explain what was expected of him.[20] A defensive front was to be established on the Aisne and the Ailette to bar the way to Paris. The new division was to operate alone in the Laon region, and it was thought that there would be time to put it together. He was to be directly responsible to General Georges, the commander-in-chief on the north-eastern front.

"Calm, cordial, but visibly overcome", General Georges received de Gaulle. His parting words were: "Now go, de Gaulle! For a long time, you have held the concepts which the enemy is applying. Here is your chance to do something." Despite the shock of surprise and the suddenness of its new burdens, the general staff seemed to be working fairly well. But hope was on its way out, and all resiliency had gone.

On reaching Laon, Colonel de Gaulle set up his command post at Bruyères, to the south-east, and had himself driven in all directions. There was an air of desperate improvisation about everything. All the roads were choked with convoys of refugees finding their way south as best they could. Among them were many disarmed soldiers. Caught by surprise by the speed of the advancing Panzers, they had been told by the Germans to throw down their rifles and walk or drive southward, so that the German advance should not be impeded. "We have no time," the Germans shouted, "to take you prisoner."

On hearing this proof of the enemy's contempt for the bewildered French defenders, de Gaulle's mood changed from sadness to uncontrolled fury. The French army had 3,000 modern tanks and 800 machine-guns – as many of the one and the other as the Germans disposed of on the western front. But the French armour was scattered and useless; the Germans, concentrated and irresistible. It was too silly. That day, de Gaulle noted, he resolved to fight wherever possible and

[20] De Gaulle, L'Appel, p. 30.

however long it might take, until the stain on the national honour should be washed out and the enemy defeated.[21]

At dawn on the 17th, three tank battalions reached de Gaulle. At first light, he threw them into action, and, sweeping aside the enemy formations encountered, they soon reached Montcornet. It was a brief, exhilarating but short-lived success. On reaching the river Serre, the tanks were unable to cross, for lack of support in the rear. During the day, the 4th Battalion Light Infantry arrived, and General de Gaulle immediately used them to wipe out a German pocket of resistance left behind after his first advance. Then the German artillery massed to the north of the Serre opened up. The French guns were not yet in position. In the afternoon the Stukas dive-bombed the French tanks and lorries. When night fell, de Gaulle had the satisfaction to note that 130 German prisoners had been captured and hundreds of enemy dead were counted; on the French side losses were fewer than 200. Behind them the rush of refugees had halted.

The situation, however, was hopeless. The French were inexperienced, many of the tank crews having spent no more than four hours in all in their machines. In many cases, the officers had first met their men on this local battlefield. The French lacked even such elementary amenities as radio sets, and de Gaulle later recorded that motorcycle despatch riders were his only means of communication. On the 19th, nevertheless, de Gaulle decided to resume his advance, or more accurately, his attempt to delay the advancing Germans. Tournoux's picture of him in battle, though based upon quotations that cannot be verified, has the ring of truth. He was tireless, icy, contemptuous of personal risk. Deeply aware, too, of the prestige of his new rank, and ready to rebuke those who questioned his orders with some such phrase as "One's divisional general is always right".[22]

General Georges had, in fact, ordered him not to attempt any further advance. The main object of de Gaulle's action had been achieved: it had enabled Georges's 6th Army to deploy. But success was bound to be localised and short-lived. There was no way in which the Germans could be more than temporarily frustrated. Already, they had decided to finish off the Allied Army of the north before dealing with the centre

---

[21] ibid. pp. 29–31.
[22] Tournoux, *Pétain*, p. 195. As Tournoux notes, de Gaulle instinctively gave himself a further promotion. He was not a divisional general – and indeed never became one – but a temporary brigadier in command of a division. Tournoux (ibid. p. 197) gives 15 May as the date of his promotion; Gorce (p. 150) gives the 23rd, and Cattaui the 28th, adding that at forty-nine, de Gaulle was the youngest general in the French army. The discrepancies are apparent only, as a promotion is decided (and communicated to the man concerned), then promulgated, and finally published.

and east. One German column, starting from St Quentin, drove towards Dunkirk, and a second proceeded up the coast, via Etaples and Boulogne. Meantime, two Panzer divisions seized Amiens and Abbeville, setting up bridgeheads south of the Somme.

Now 20 May dawned. That day, General Gamelin was removed and General Weygand took his place as commander-in-chief. The change brought no benefit to the defenders. Gamelin was a philosopher in uniform whose interest lay in speculative analysis, and who lacked the gift or taste for leadership. Weygand was seventy-three, fighting fit, but intellectually convinced that victory was not merely impossible, but probably undesirable. His political views were of the extreme right. It is generally agreed that faced with a revolution in the hour of defeat, he would have chosen to fight the revolutionaries rather than the invaders.[28] He was, moreover, a convinced Anglophobe. In at least one other respect, he was a curious choice for a commander-in-chief: he had never commanded troops in action. He had indeed been a staff officer – albeit a successful one – all his life. De Gaulle felt a residual admiration and respect for him for his part in planning the Polish campaign of 1920 which had blunted the Soviet invasion. But Weygand, though ready to recognise de Gaulle's battle prowess, had no time for his theories. Nor did he, incidentallly, for the views of the politician who had supported de Gaulle, and happened to be the Prime Minister of France: Paul Reynaud.

Reynaud was indeed gradually being surrounded by men who lacked his will to fight. One of them was Marshal Pétain, who, on that same day, had joined his cabinet as vice-premier. Optimistically, Reynaud declared on the radio: "Marshal Pétain will remain at my side till victory is won." But the aged marshal was not thinking in terms of victory. Indeed, for long periods, he gave no evidence of any remaining capacity to think at all. He was eighty-four – eleven years older than Weygand. With advancing years, he was living increasingly in his glorious past, the past of Verdun. He saw himself as the potential father of a defeated people. Reynaud had called on him because he was thought to stand for the victorious France of 1918, and he was the man who had restored morale among the mutinous French troops in 1917. When appointed, he was still in Spain as France's ambassador, and General Franco had tried to persuade him not to go, on the ground that there was no need for him to allow his name to be linked with a defeat for which other people were responsible. "I know, General," the old man said. "But my

[23] Horne, pp. 422 *et seq.*; De Gaulle, *L'Appel*, pp. 40–1; and Major-General Sir Edward Spears, *Assignment to Catastrophe*, Vol. I, pp. 149–50 (henceforth, Spears).

country is calling me and it is my duty to go. It will perhaps be the last service I can render."[24]

A week later, General de Gaulle's second and last action of the Second World War began. The day before his removal, General Gamelin was planning to join together the sundered allied armies of Belgium and Flanders at one end, and of the Somme and the Aisne at the other. Weygand thought this made sense, but forty-eight hours were lost while he prepared for action. Contradictory orders reached de Gaulle: to attack to the north; to hit at the German bridgehead at Amiens. At last, he was ordered to attack the enemy at Abbeville. It was now the 27th, and his 4th Armoured Division had been fighting continuously. Again, however, he was successful within his unavoidable limitations of time and space. In three days, he drove the enemy back about nine miles and captured 500 prisoners and considerable booty.[25] At the height of the fighting, de Gaulle was sustained by anger no less than courage. He found time, while the shells were flying, to write to a friend, "I hope now you will have the same contempt as I for the intelligence and character of Dufieux."[26] This reference to the former inspector-general of infantry and tanks was eloquent.

By the 30th, de Gaulle had exhausted his limited possibilities. Four days earlier, Boulogne had fallen to the Germans; and Leopold III of the Belgians had ordered his army to capitulate, leaving the British expeditionary force exposed before the German onslaught. A quarter of a million British soldiers and about half that number of Frenchmen gathered on the beach at Dunkirk, awaiting the flotilla of little boats that was to evacuate them to England.

General Weygand had already decided that further fighting was useless. On 26 May, he had told a minister: "I have thought a great deal. . . . The government must stay in Paris and allow itself to be taken prisoner . . . there is no other attitude to take." Pétain, the new vice-premier, supported him.

On 1 June, General Weygand summoned de Gaulle to his headquarters in the château of Montry. Although the commander-in-chief had no personal sympathy towards de Gaulle, he was in a congratulatory mood. He had in fact just mentioned the younger general in a eulogistic citation, in the following words:

> Admirable leader, bold and energetic, on 30 and 31 May attacked an enemy bridgehead, penetrating 14 kilometres in his line and capturing several hundred prisoners and considerable war material.[27]

---

[24] Crozier, *Franco*, p. 313.
[26] Tournoux, *Pétain*, pp. 198-9.
[25] Gorce, pp. 145-6; De Gaulle, *L'Appel*, p. 38.
[27] Bonheur (p. 132) dates the citation 2 June.

Having congratulated de Gaulle, Weygand sought his advice. How, he asked, could the 1,200 modern tanks still in combat be used to best advantage? But he showed little interest in de Gaulle's detailed plan to save Paris and bar the way to the south. Instead, he enumerated the conditions of victory, as he saw them:

> If things don't go too fast; if I can recuperate, in time, the French troops that have escaped from Dunkirk; if I had arms to give them; if the British army comes back to play a part in the struggle, after re-equipping itself; if the Royal Air Force consents to play its part unreservedly in the fight on the continent; if all these things happen, we have a chance left.

And he added: "If not . . ."[28]

Heavy in heart, de Gaulle took his leave.

On the 4th, 215,000 British and 120,000 French troops were rescued at Dunkirk; but nearly all their equipment was lost and 30,000 British troops were taken prisoner. Next day, the Germans attacked the French on an arc from Sedan to Abbeville. That night, General de Gaulle learned that Reynaud had appointed him under-secretary for war. It was his first political post. He took leave of his division and went to Paris.

He found Reynaud assured and incisive; but increasingly isolated within his own cabinet. On hearing of his appointment, Marshal Pétain had tried to dissuade the Prime Minister from making it, recounting at length the story of de Gaulle's publication of *La France et son Armée* against his wishes and without proper acknowledgement.[29]

At his first interview with Reynaud, de Gaulle warned him that he would probably regret having included the defeatist marshal in his team. He conceded that "the war of '40" was probably lost, but added that it was still possible to win another war.

> Without giving up the fight on European soil as long as possible, we must decide and prepare to continue the struggle in the Empire. That implies an adequate policy: the means to fight must be transported towards North Africa, leaders qualified to direct the operations must be chosen, close contact with the British must be maintained, whatever grievances we may have against them.

And he asked for instructions to carry out this plan.

The Prime Minister agreed.

---

[28] De Gaulle, *L'Appel*, p. 40.
[29] Pétain also told Spears of this incident, in full detail, commenting, "Not only is he vain, he is ungrateful." *See* Spears, Vol. II, p. 85.

I ask you to go to London as soon as possible. During the conversations I had on 26 and 31 May with the British government, I may have given the impression that we did not rule out the prospect of an armistice. But at present, we need on the contrary to convince the British that we shall stand firm, whatever happens, even overseas if need be. You will see Mr Churchill and you will tell him that my cabinet reshuffle and your presence at my side are the signs of our resolve.[30]

This was a general directive; but there was a particular one as well. De Gaulle was to try to obtain a firm commitment from London that the RAF – especially fighter planes – should continue to be available for operations in France. He was also instructed to find out how long it would take for the British units evacuated at Dunkirk to be re-equipped and rearmed, and sent back to the continent.

While arrangements for his visit were being made, de Gaulle called upon General Weygand. It was now the 8th. He found the commander-in-chief calm, self-assured and irreversibly fatalistic. The Germans were crossing the Somme; they would soon cross the Seine and the Marne. After that, it would all be over.

"What do you mean? Over? What about the world? And the Empire?"

Weygand gave a desperate laugh; "The Empire? Childish fantasies! As for the world, when I have been beaten here, England will not wait a week before negotiating with the Reich." And his next remarks betrayed his overriding fear – not of defeat but of revolution. "Ah! if only I could be sure the Germans would leave me the necessary forces to maintain order!"

Defeatism surrounded de Gaulle and weighed heavily upon him: in the army, in the country and in the government. Before going to London, he had another interview with Reynaud and immediately proposed the removal of General Weygand from his command. The man for the job, said de Gaulle, was General Huntziger, an intellectually brilliant soldier of Alsatian and Breton parentage who, in de Gaulle's view, was capable of rising to the heights of a world strategy. Reynaud's reply was evasive: he agreed *en principe*, but it was not possible to make a change at that time.[31]

Isolated though he now felt, General de Gaulle sat down to work out

---

[30] De Gaulle, *L'Appel*, p. 44.
[31] Huntziger was not, in fact, given his chance of rising to strategic heights. He had commanded the French in their second defeat at Sedan, and was to lead the Armistice delegation; he was killed in a plane crash in 1941.

precise plans to continue the war from North Africa. It meant evacuating about half a million men, consisting of new recruits under training in the west and south and the survivors of the northern disaster. Aircraft of the right range could cross the Mediterranean; but for the men and material, naval transport was required, and the French navy fell short of the space needed by some 500,000 tons of shipping. Only the British could close the gap.

Early on 9 June, de Gaulle flew to London for the first time. With him in the plane were his aide-de-camp, Geoffroy de Courcel – later France's ambassador in London – and the head of the diplomatic secretariat of the French Prime Minister's office, Roland de Margerie. After the turmoil of Paris, London struck de Gaulle as inordinately calm, even allowing for the fact that it was Sunday. "In the eyes of the English," he noted, "the Channel was still wide."

Churchill, who received de Gaulle at 10 Downing Street, made an immediate and lasting impression upon him – as the indomitable fighter, with his poetic and moving eloquence, ever the master of events and "the great artist of a great history"[32] – a view that survived their later clashes.

De Gaulle, speaking perhaps more on his own behalf than Reynaud's, said in the French Prime Minister's name that the government was determined to carry on the struggle, if necessary in the French Empire. Churchill heard him with mingled delight and scepticism. He made it clear that he no longer believed in the possibility of a French military recovery, at least in metropolitan France. For the French, and for the British from a different standpoint, the crucial question was the use and location of the Royal Air Force. Operating as they were, from British soil, the RAF planes were less and less useful to the French forces as the battle moved southward. When de Gaulle requested that RAF squadrons should be transferred to bases south of the Loire, Churchill categorically refused. He was, however, ready to promise the despatch to Normandy of a Canadian division now arriving in England, and to maintain the 51st Highland Division in France, as well as the remnants of the armoured brigade.

De Gaulle spent the rest of that day in conversations with Anthony Eden, at that time Churchill's war minister, A. V. Alexander, first lord of the Admiralty, Sir Archibald Sinclair, the air minister, and General Sir John Dill, chief of the Imperial General Staff. He had also met the French ambassador, M. Corbin, and Jean Monnet, chairman of the Franco-British Coordinating Committee for purchases of war material, together with the chiefs of the French service liaison missions in London.

[32] De Gaulle, *L'Appel*, pp. 46–8. Most of the account that follows is based on *L'Appel*. Curiously, Winston Churchill made no mention of this meeting in his war memoirs.

From his meeting with Churchill and his other talks, de Gaulle formed the clear impression that the British were calm and resolute, but that his own resolution had not sufficed to convince them that France would fight on. That evening he flew back to France, landing with difficulty at Le Bourget airport, which had just been bombed by the Germans.

Now the pace of events quickened still further. As soon as General de Gaulle had reached Paris, Reynaud sent for him at home. The Seine had been crossed downstream from Paris and a decisive German attack in the Champagne region was expected any hour. From Rome the French ambassador, François-Poncet, telegraphed to say that he expected the Italian government to declare war at any moment. What should be done in this catastrophic situation, asked Reynaud? All de Gaulle could think of was his previous plan: go to Africa forthwith and carry on the war with France's allies.

The 10th dawned – "a day of agony," wrote de Gaulle. As foreshadowed, Mussolini declared war against France and Britain, and Italian forces invaded southern France. The German tide was lapping at the feet of the capital. The cabinet had, indeed, decided to evacuate Paris that night. Reynaud was fast losing control over his government, having already lost control over events. While de Gaulle was drafting a statement Reynaud intended to make over the radio, General Weygand entered his office unannounced. He immediately embarked on an exposition of the situation as he saw it: his conclusion was firm in its pessimism – there was now nothing to be done except to ask for an armistice. When de Gaulle objected that other courses were still open, Weygand asked him mockingly: "Have you something to propose?"

"The government," answered de Gaulle, "has no proposals to make, but orders to give. I count upon it to give them." When Weygand left, the atmosphere was tense.

What was to happen to Paris? De Gaulle was in favour of defending it, if need be, street by street. As soon as he had joined the government, he had requested Reynaud in his capacity as president of the Council, minister of National Defence and of War, to name a determined man as governor of the French capital. His man for the job was General de Lattre, who had lately distinguished himself in the fighting around Rethel. But he had counted without General Weygand, who took it upon himself to declare Paris an open city; and the Council of Ministers endorsed his decision, although it flew in the face of repeated previous declarations that Paris would be defended. Amidst wildly ringing telephones and a flurry of last-minute visits, de Gaulle supervised the packing of furniture, cases and belongings.

Towards midnight, he and Reynaud climbed into an official car and started on a desperately slow journey along cluttered roads. They reached Orleans at dawn and entered the Prefecture building. The military, under General Weygand, had set up headquarters at Briare. The first news of importance came from the commander-in-chief in a personal call to the Prime Minister announcing the arrival – that afternoon – of Winston Churchill. It was Weygand himself, he revealed, who had invited the British Prime Minister to come to Briare as soon as possible. "Mr Churchill must be informed directly about the real situation on the front," added General Weygand.

When Reynaud had put the receiver down and passed on Weygand's message, General de Gaulle indignantly taxed the commander-in-chief with playing politics by his improper invitations to the British Prime Minister. "Don't you see," he asked, "that what General Weygand is doing is not carrying out a plan of operations but executing a policy, and that this policy is not yours? Is the government going to let him carry on in his job?"

"You are right!" answered Reynaud. "This situation must stop. We have mentioned General Huntziger as a possible successor to Weygand. Let us go and see Huntziger straight away!"

But on his way, the French Prime Minister's resolution faltered once again. As he was about to step into the car, he said: "On reflection, it would be better if you alone went to see Huntziger. As for me, I am going to prepare for the meeting with Churchill and the British. You will find me later at Briare."

As General de Gaulle reached General Huntziger's command post at Arcis-sur-Aube, news had just come that Guderian's Panzers had pierced the Champagne front under Huntziger's command. The general, however, remained cool. "The government," said de Gaulle, using the collective noun with a confidence that was hard to justify, "can see that the battle of France is virtually lost, but it wants to continue the war by transporting itself to Africa with all the means it is possible to take along. This implies a complete change of strategy and organisation. The present Generalissimo is no longer the man who can do this. Would you be that man?"

"Yes," said Huntziger with soldierly simplicity.

"Well," said de Gaulle, "you will be getting the government's instructions."

At Briare, de Gaulle conveyed Huntziger's reply to Reynaud. But it was immediately clear from Reynaud's lack of interest that he had given up the idea of dismissing Weygand. On his way through the gallery of the headquarters building, de Gaulle caught sight of Pétain, whom he had not seen since 1938. "So you're a general!" exclaimed the marshal. "I don't congratulate you. What's the use of high ranks in defeat?"

"But you yourself, *Monsieur le Maréchal*, you yourself got your first stars during the retreat of 1914. A few days later the battle of the Marne began."

"No connection!" grumbled Pétain. On this point, commented de Gaulle in his memoirs, Pétain was right. Thereafter, Pétain affected not to notice de Gaulle's presence.

But Churchill and his ministers were arriving. And the conference began.[33] With Churchill were Mr Eden, General Dill, the new C.I.G.S., and General Sir Hastings Ismay, secretary to the Imperial Defence Council. General Spears was also present. It was the first time he had seen de Gaulle, and his striking description of the Frenchman is worth requoting:

> For relief I turned to de Gaulle, whose bearing alone among his compatriots matched the calm, healthy phlegm of the British. A strange-looking man, enormously tall; sitting at the table he dominated everyone else by his height, as he had done when walking into the room. No chin, a long, drooping, elephantine nose over a closely-cut moustache, a shadow over a small mouth whose thick lips tended to protrude as if in a pout before speaking, a high, receding forehead and pointed head surmounted by sparse black hair lying flat and neatly parted. His heavily-hooded eyes were very shrewd. When about to speak he oscillated his head slightly like a pendulum, while searching for words. I at once remembered and understood the nickname of *"Le Connétable"* which Pétain said had been given him at Saint-Cyr. It was easy to imagine that head on a ruff, that secret face at Catherine de Medici's Council Chamber.

It was a dismal occasion. Weygand, aggressive in his pessimism, explained in detail why an armistice was the only course left. Short of an ordered capitulation, the armed forces might fall apart, bringing revolution and anarchy. Marshal Pétain intervened in support. Striving to lighten the atmosphere, Churchill reminded the marshal about the battle of Amiens in March 1918, when all had seemed lost yet the front had been restored. Within a few days of Churchill's visit to him Pétain commented harshly, "Yes, the front was restored. You British were bogged down. As for me, I sent forty divisions to get you out of your mess. To-

[33] The best account of what followed is neither de Gaulle's nor Churchill's, but that of Spears (Vol. II, pp. 138 *et seq.*).

day we are the ones who are being torn to pieces. Where are your forty divisions?"

With all his moving eloquence, Churchill tried to instil some fight into the defeated French leaders. But his argument that the French should at least hold out until re-equipped British divisions could come back to resume the fight fell on dejected ears. De Gaulle sensed Churchill's private elation at the thought that England would soon stand alone. Three hours of discussion ended inconclusively.

At dinner that evening, de Gaulle sat next to Churchill and his conviction that the British Prime Minister's will would never weaken was confirmed. "He himself," wrote de Gaulle, "doubtless concluded that de Gaulle, though without means, was not less resolute."

Next day, the conference was resumed. When Reynaud and Weygand appealed for British fighters and day bombers, Churchill assured them that the whole question of increased air support for France "would be examined carefully and sympathetically by the war cabinet" immediately on his return to London.[34] But he again emphasised that the United Kingdom must not be denuded of its own defences. Churchill, in fact, had two priorities in mind: the defence of the British Isles, and the future of the French fleet. On taking leave of his French hosts, the Prime Minister took Admiral Darlan apart and said: "Darlan, you must never let them get the French fleet." Darlan gave him a solemn promise that this would never happen.

During 12 June, while the British were returning to London, de Gaulle, who was staying in the stately home of M. le Provost de Launay, worked with General Colson on a detailed plan for transporting the armed forces to North Africa. Bearing with the plan, he called on Reynaud. It was late. The Prime Minister had just closed a session of his cabinet, to which de Gaulle had not been invited. As Reynaud consumed a late meal, de Gaulle sat near him and broached the question of North Africa. But North Africa was far from the minds of the Prime Minister and those who were with him. The question that concerned them was where to move the seat of the government. Two alternative destinations were under discussion – Quimper in Brittany or Bordeaux on the Atlantic coast. The place chosen would in itself indicate the government's true strategic intentions.

When de Gaulle had joined Reynaud's government, the Prime Minister had told him of the plan for a "Breton redoubt". The idea was that should Paris fall, a last desperate stand would be made in the peninsula of Brittany. De Gaulle eagerly espoused this concept. And now, he hoped

[34] Churchill, Vol. I, pp. 139–40.

Quimper would be chosen – not that he believed in the Breton redoubt plan any longer, but because he knew that if the Germans intended to strike at England, they would have to occupy Brittany, and in that event the French government, if installed at Quimper, would have no option but to embark – perhaps for Africa, perhaps for England – on their way to another place.

The debate was resumed early on the 13th. But by now, de Gaulle's arguments weighed but little against the combined counsels of the defeatists, Pétain, Weygand, and Paul Baudouin, secretary to the war cabinet and the War Council. And the defeatists' choice was, of course, Bordeaux. Overruled, General de Gaulle insisted that Reynaud should sign an order to the commander-in-chief to prepare for the move to Africa. Towards midday, Reynaud did indeed write a letter to General Weygand, in which he stated that the government expected a stand to be made as long as possible in the Massif Central and in Brittany. "Should we fail," the letter went on, "we are to install ourselves and organise the struggle in the Empire by utilising the freedom of the seas." The letter, however, was not delivered until the following day. By then – on the 13th – Paris had been evacuated before the continuing German advance.

At Beauvais early on the afternoon of the 13th, a telephone call warned de Gaulle that Churchill had just returned to France with several ministers and was about to attend a conference at the Prefecture of Tours with the French Prime Minister. Depressed and indignant at not having heard from Reynaud himself of this plan for talks with the British, de Gaulle hurried to the scene. Roland de Margerie, who had made the telephone call, told him quickly that the reason for the meeting was to consider whether Britain was prepared to release France from the Ghent agreement of 28 March 1940, which ruled out any separate cessation of hostilities. "Baudouin is at work," he added, "and I don't like the way things are going."[35]

With Churchill were Lord Halifax, Lord Beaverbrook and Sir Alexander Cadogan, together with General Spears. In his inimitable French, the British Prime Minister, lighting one of his famous cigars, commiserated with France in her plight. But whatever happened to France, he said, England would fight on; she would consider neither terms nor surrender. The alternatives were death or victory. To de Gaulle's astonishment, however, he showed himself quite willing to give sympathetic consideration to the French request to be released from the agreement of 28 March. A deal, indeed, was possible. The British would not object to

[35] Cattaui, pp. 86–8.

a French armistice with Germany, if on their side, the French would undertake not to deliver their fleet into German hands. Moreover, Churchill insisted, if France should cease the combat, she should – before deposing her arms – hand over to Britain the 400 German airmen captured on French soil. Both promises were forthcoming.

Seizing an opportunity, de Gaulle asked Reynaud if he really meant to request an armistice. "Of course not!" was the reply. "But one must make an impression on the English in order to obtain from them a wider cooperation." Deeply depressed, de Gaulle went back to Beauvais. Reynaud, on his side, telegraphed to President Roosevelt, appealing for an American intervention if all was not to be lost.

Now General de Gaulle had but one thought: to resign from this defeated government. He drafted a letter of resignation, but before he could deliver it, a message came from the French minister of the Interior, Georges Mandel – one of the few remaining politicians who wanted to fight on, and who had heard of de Gaulle's intended resignation. Gravely, Mandel reasoned with de Gaulle. If he resigned, the minister argued, he would be losing his last chance of serving France. Even now, perhaps, it was not too late, and the government might yet decide to go to Algiers. Impressed, de Gaulle agreed to wait a little longer. He was later to recognise the value of Mandel's advice.

While the French and British statesmen were meeting, the president of the Chamber of Deputies, Edouard Herriot, and the president of the Senate, M. Jeanneney, were waiting in an adjoining ante-room. Churchill and his companions were shown through it and heard the two parliamentary chairmen declaring their passionate conviction that France should fight unto death. The passage into the courtyard was crowded, but the huge figure of General de Gaulle stood out. Greeting him, Churchill said in a low tone and in French, "l'homme du destin". He remained impassive, records Churchill.[36]

On 14 June, another journey – more depressing still than the previous one, with the roads even more crowded – faced the French leaders. The destination was Bordeaux. What was left of Reynaud's authority was dwindling fast. Among his senior ministers, only Mandel supported him wholeheartedly. Pétain's massive presence cast a pall of gloom on the demoralised ministry. Weygand's only wish was to cease fighting: and Baudouin's influence was pervasively defeatist.

Moreover, the Prime Minister's private life was now intruding into French history. His mistress, Mme de Portes, never ceased to badger him on the urgent need, as she saw it, to bring the fighting to an end. "If I

[36] Churchill, Vol. I, p. 162.

have ever seen hate in a woman's eyes," wrote Spears, "it was in her glances as they swept across us like the stroke of a scythe. What a very unattractive woman, I thought, apart from the ugly expression the presence of Englishmen called forth."

On arriving at Bordeaux, however, de Gaulle made a last attempt to wring from Reynaud a promise of executive action in favour of continuing the war from overseas. "I gave you my modest help," he told the premier, "but this was to make war. I refuse to submit to an armistice. If you stay here, you will be submerged by defeat. We must go to Algiers as quickly as possible. Are you, or are you not, resolved to do so?"

"Yes!" answered Reynaud.

"In that case," said de Gaulle, "I myself must go straight away to London to arrange the help of the British in transporting us. I shall go tomorrow. Where shall I find you?"

The president of the Council's answer was: "You will find me in Algiers."[37] The general left during the night, stopping briefly in Brittany on his way. During a hasty dinner in the Hotel Splendide with Geoffroy de Courcel, one of the ministers of State, Jean Ybarnégaray, dropped in to see him. Until then, the minister had been among the fighters. Now, however, he told de Gaulle that the only important thing left was to obey his leaders – Pétain and Weygand. De Gaulle's answer was: "Perhaps you will see one day that for a minister the fate of the State must take priority over all other sentiments."

As de Gaulle walked out of the dining-room, he saw Marshal Pétain still at his table. In silence, he went up to the old man and saluted him. Pétain extended his hand without a word. "I was never to see him again, ever," wrote de Gaulle.

De Gaulle spent most of 15 June in Brittany, first at Rennes, then at Brest, where he embarked in the destroyer *Milan*. He slept that night in the Hyde Park Hotel in London. There, early next morning, the French ambassador, Corbin, and the president of the Franco-British Purchasing Commission, Jean Monnet, brought him unwelcome news. The French government, in an official telegram, had just confirmed its demand to be relieved of the obligations of the 28 March agreement. Clearly, the Bordeaux government was seeking to remove the last formal impediment in the way of an armistice. They also brought in news of a more optimistic, and indeed sensational kind: a proposal for an "indissoluble Franco-British union". The permanent under-secretary at the Foreign Office, Sir Robert Vansittart, had helped Monnet and other

[37] De Gaulle, *L'Appel*, p. 59.

105

French high officials to draft an appropriate text, which they now showed de Gaulle.[38]

The General's reactions were, not unnaturally, ambivalent. Intellectually as well as emotionally, he was convinced of the particularity of nations: to propose what, in effect, would be a "merger" between two ancient nations, each with its own history, language and culture, was to him an illogical aberration. At that time, however, he was obsessed by the need to fight on, and therefore to prop up the flagging capacity of the French Prime Minister to lend his authority to continued war. If this project for an "indissoluble union" would serve this end, then de Gaulle would support it. The Frenchmen had told him that he only could persuade Churchill to accept the draft. And he agreed to try.

At the Carlton Club, de Gaulle, Corbin and Monnet met the British Prime Minister for lunch. With Churchill were Lord Halifax and the Prime Minister's private secretary, Major Desmond Morton. De Gaulle chose an attacking gambit. He assured Churchill that whatever happened, the French fleet would not be surrendered to the Germans. Not even Pétain would do that; not even Darlan who controlled the fleet. But it was essential that France should stay in the war. Churchill's attitude of resignation at Tours had come as a disagreeable surprise to de Gaulle and encouraged those who favoured capitulation. After that, the defeatists were able to argue that no other course was open to them since even the British consented to it. These powerful arguments seemed to shake Churchill. A reply to the French telegram had already been drafted, in which Churchill pledged his government to accept a separate armistice for France, on condition that the French fleet should sail for British harbours pending negotiations. After his talk with de Gaulle, Churchill decided to hold up the British reply – in case the offer of union deflected the French government from its defeatist course. While the British cabinet met to endorse this decision, de Gaulle telephoned Reynaud to say that he would be in touch again later that day with a very important communication. On hearing this, Reynaud agreed to postpone his own cabinet meeting until 5 p.m.

De Gaulle had made his telephone call from an ante-room at 10 Downing Street. After two hours, Churchill entered, rosy-faced and beaming to say there had been complete agreement about the offer of union. Immediately, de Gaulle put through a second telephone call to

[38] In an interesting monograph, "The Anglo-French Union Project of June 1940", Professor Max Beloff ascribes the authorship of the project thus: "although very largely French in inspiration [it] was translated into positive terms by British civil servants and endorsed by the war cabinet". Max Beloff, *The Intellectual in Politics* (1970).

Reynaud, to whom he dictated the document. Seizing the instrument from the general, Churchill exclaimed, "Hello! Reynaud! De Gaulle is right! Our proposal may have great consequences. You must hold on." It is fruitless, today, to speculate what the "great consequences" of the offer might have been, had it been accepted. Although necessarily vague about practical details, it could not have been more sweeping. Under a joint union constitution, every citizen of France was to enjoy immediate citizenship of Great Britain; and *vice versa*. There was to be a single war cabinet and all forces of both countries were to be placed under a single

The Fall of France 1940

107

command. The two parliaments were to be formally associated. But all this was to remain no more than the documentary record of an offer of unprecedented generosity.

In a stormy final session of his cabinet, Reynaud had read out the British offer of union, which had fallen in stony silence. The British acceptance of a conditional separate armistice for France had at first been delivered by the British ambassador, then withdrawn on urgent instructions from London. Though assured of the continuing support of the presidents of the Chamber and the Senate, Reynaud knew that he had lost the confidence of his ministerial colleagues. It remained only for him to lay down a burden that had become excessively heavy.

When de Gaulle, who had flown in a British plane, landed at Bordeaux airport at 9.30 p.m., it was already too late. The general's aides told him that Reynaud had resigned, and that President Lebrun had called on Marshal Pétain to form a government. This could only mean capitulation. De Gaulle took his final decision to leave France the following morning. He had already, in fact, taken a slightly irregular executive decision that implied an irrevocable commitment to fight on. While in London, in his inadequate capacity as under-secretary for war, he had telegraphed orders to the French ship *Pasteur*, diverting her from her prescribed destination of Bordeaux to a British port. On board were a thousand 75 cannon, thousands of machine-guns and a heavy load of ammunition from the United States. Instead of falling into German hands, this important cargo served to rearm the British Expeditionary Force from Dunkirk.

And now, de Gaulle went to see his defeated Prime Minister, whom he found wretched from desperation and loss of sleep. Intelligent and initially resolute as he had been, Paul Reynaud had no fight left in him: the enormity of recent events, and the disloyalty of his more pusillanimous colleagues, had sapped his will. Nothing more was to be expected from that quarter.

Late that evening, de Gaulle went to the hotel at which the British ambassador, Sir Ronald Campbell, was staying, and told him of his intention to go to London next day.

General Spears, who entered the room while this conversation was in progress, offered to accompany de Gaulle.

One last service, despite everything, remained in the gift of the French Prime Minister. On hearing of de Gaulle's decision, he raided the secret fund to send the general 100,000 francs.[39] Bidding farewell to his faithful de Margerie, de Gaulle asked him without delay to send to his wife

[39] De Gaulle, *L'Appel*, p. 67.

and children, who were then at Carantec in Brittany, the passports they would need to travel to England. They caught the last ship leaving Brest.

At 9 a.m. on 17 June, accompanied by General Spears and Lieutenant de Courcel,[40] Charles de Gaulle flew to England.

[40] I regret to say that when I saw M. de Courcel, by then ambassador in London, in search of reminiscences, he was uncommunicative.

Chapter 2 ✤ The Challenge

De Gaulle had crossed his Rubicon. He now knew there could be no return — save in defeat or victory. He knew, in broad terms, what his aims were; but he had little idea how to fulfil them. That he wanted to fight on was obvious. But on whose behalf?

Many thought that the handful of Frenchmen who crossed the Channel in those days simply wished to offer their services as auxiliary troops to support the fighting British Empire. To people with a less exalted sense of national destiny than Charles de Gaulle, this seemed a worthy thing to do. But not for a moment did de Gaulle think of his choice in such humdrum terms. The State had crumbled and the nation was in danger: in his eyes, the need of the hour was to serve and save them both. To him, it was intolerable that France, alone among the powers, should capitulate and simply opt out of the world war. The thought that a definitely beaten France should in time be saved by foreign arms alone was deeply repugnant to him. It was not sufficient that some Frenchmen should fight on; France herself should be brought back into the conflict.[1]

It was a tall order, and de Gaulle — despite his astonishing self-confidence, his vision and his courage — was aware of it. The enemy was powerful and would soon dispose of the willing help of the official apparatus of occupied France. The French people were deeply divided, and many of them had lost the will to fight. He himself, at this stage, was unknown and virtually alone. He had no following and no organisation. He lacked all prestige. Indeed, apart from his will and his character,

[1] De Gaulle, L'Appel, p. 69.

his only assets lay in the receptiveness of his British hosts to the improbable proposition that France, in his person, should be given an opportunity to fight on.

With a realistic sense of priorities, de Gaulle set out to proclaim a cause, to secure arms and to build up a following – in that order. It was his great good fortune to have found in Winston Churchill a kindred spirit. Churchill too was battling against fearful odds. With the rump of a defeated army and a handful of aircraft, with his principal ally prostrate, he was preparing to defend his islands against an expected German onslaught. But his assets were incomparably greater than de Gaulle's. Britain's national territory was intact, and the will of her people unbroken. The full machinery and powers of the State were at Churchill's disposal, whereas de Gaulle had nothing. This evident disparity was a powerful factor in their relationship. In de Gaulle's eyes, British actions frequently looked high-handed; in Churchill's eyes, de Gaulle's attitude, touchy and haughty, often seemed unrealistic to the point of absurdity. It was a question of power: Churchill had it, and de Gaulle, lacking it, made up for it with a rigid pride to match his idea of the dignity of France.

At all events, Churchill immediately recognised the potential value of de Gaulle. A few days earlier, at Tours, Churchill had murmured half to himself that here was a man of destiny. Later, when describing de Gaulle's escape from France – stepping into the small aircraft and slamming the door after ostensibly bidding farewell to the returning General Spears – Churchill was to write that "de Gaulle carried with him, in this small aeroplane, the honour of France".

But this was long after the event. Now, on the afternoon of 17 June, de Gaulle stood before the Prime Minister and asked him to make the BBC available to him; and Churchill did not hesitate. The two men agreed, however, that de Gaulle would not broadcast until Pétain had asked the Germans for an armistice. News came that evening that Pétain had already done so, and next evening, at six o'clock, accompanied by Geoffroy de Courcel, de Gaulle seated himself before a microphone in Studio B2 at Bush House, and began his first broadcast to France. It was an historic occasion, and indeed ever since – especially in France – de Gaulle has been known as "the man of 18 June". But a sense of occasion was entirely lacking – to the extent that the broadcast was left unrecorded.

"Has the last word been spoken? Must hope disappear? Is the defeat definitive? No!

"Believe me, who speak to you in full knowledge of the facts and who say to you that nothing is lost for France. The same means that have defeated us can one day bring victory.

"For France is not alone! She is not alone! She is not alone! She has a vast empire behind her. She can form a bloc with the British Empire which holds the sea and continues the struggle. She can, like England, use without limit the tremendous industry of the United States. . . .

"I, General de Gaulle, at present in London, invite the French officers and men who are in British territory or who might find themselves there, with their arms or without their arms, I invite the engineers and skilled workers of the arms industries who are in British territory or who might find themselves there, to get in touch with me.

"Whatever happens, the flame of French resistance must not be extinguished and shall not be extinguished."[2]

That day, Winston Churchill himself made one of his most famous speeches. Evoking the battle of France, he foreshadowed the battle of Britain, and exclaimed, "Let us therefore brace ourselves to our duties, and so bear ourselves that, if the British Empire and its Commonwealth last for a thousand years, men will still say: 'This was their finest hour'."

To read again, in French or in English, words that stirred the listeners or readers of a generation ago, is to be struck by the similarity of spirit between the two speakers. As Churchill well knew, his own rhetoric alone would not suffice to withstand a German invasion. In his memoirs, however, he emphatically rejects the suggestion – widespread at the time – that rhetoric and bluff were indeed all he had to offer. His confidence, he says, was based in equal measure upon the united and indomitable spirit of the nation and upon a cool calculation of the advantages of Britain's insular position and the technical resources that had been carefully husbanded for this final defence.

De Gaulle's position was infinitely weaker, and his impassioned words correspondingly less convincing to those who heard them. Still, he had proclaimed his cause; and he now made a last attempt to see whether the slightest flame of resistance still burned in the hearts of the men he had left behind, and to sound out the high dignitaries of France overseas. As soon as he had arrived in London, on the 17th, he had telegraphed the government at Bordeaux to offer to carry on the negotiations already initiated concerning the use of war material from the United States, German prisoners and transport facilities for Africa. The response, two days later, was a peremptory summons to the general to return forthwith.

On the 19th, de Gaulle telegraphed General Noguès, the French

[2] Churchill, Vol. I, p. 192, states in error that this first broadcast took place on 17 June.

commander-in-chief in North Africa and resident-general in Morocco, offering to serve under him should Noguès reject the armistice.[3] That evening, he launched his second radio appeal "in the name of France". "Every Frenchman who still carries arms," he cried, "has the absolute duty to continue to resist. To lay down arms, to evacuate a military position, to accept to surrender any piece of French territory whatever to the control of the enemy, would be a crime against the motherland."

On the 20th, de Gaulle decided to respond to the impersonal official summons to return to France with a personal letter to General Weygand. He declared his readiness to return within twenty-four hours, but only if the act of capitulation had not been signed. If it had been, he would join any French resistance movement, wherever it might be. And he expressed the wish, for France and for Weygand himself, that the senior general should escape from metropolitan territory and continue the struggle overseas.

Needless to say, this last appeal to the defeatist general, who had now – to de Gaulle's indignation – assumed the title of "Minister of National Defence" – fell on stony ground. There was no immediate answer. Months later – in September – de Gaulle's letter was returned to him with a typewritten note attached, which read: "If the retired Colonel de Gaulle wants to enter into communication with General Weygand, he must do so through the regular channels."[4]

Long before this, de Gaulle's letter to Weygand had lost all possible interest. On 30 June, the French Embassy had notified him of the order that he should surrender himself to the prison of St Michel at Toulouse to be court-martialled. In time, he was sentenced *in absentia*, first to four years' imprisonment, and then, on Weygand's intervention, to death.

The goodwill of Marshal Pétain's government was not, however, one of de Gaulle's major preoccupations. On 24 June he renewed his appeal to Noguès and combined it with similar telegraphed appeals to the commander-in-chief in the Levant, General Mittelhauser, and the high commissioner, M. Puaux; and to the governor-general of Indo-China, General Catroux. The unifying theme of these messages was the news that de Gaulle was setting up a French national committee to coordinate all resistance groups; each of the recipients was asked to join the committee. Three days later, on detecting a note of defiance in a speech by the French resident-general in Tunisia, M. Peyrouton, de Gaulle telegraphed him as well, inviting him to join the proposed committee. And

[3] De Gaulle's account (on p. 71 of *L'Appel*) of his telegram to Noguès does not, however, correspond with the text given in the appendices (p. 268), which makes no mention of the armistice.
[4] De Gaulle, *L'Appel*, p. 269.

he renewed his offer to General Mittelhauser and M. Puaux. To be ready for all eventualities, he reserved a place for himself and his military subordinates on a French merchantman bound for Morocco.

Not one of the French proconsuls replied to any of de Gaulle's appeals, although Catroux did in time come to London to place himself under the orders of the relatively junior General de Gaulle. The reasons for this disappointing silence are perhaps not hard to find. For was it not evident that France was utterly defeated? And who was this "general" de Gaulle but an ambitious, self-seeking colonel lately and temporarily promoted, whose only claim to official status was the fact that he had been under-secretary for war in Reynaud's cabinet, itself no longer in power? Nor should it be overlooked that in those anxious days, the legality of the Pétain government had not been seriously questioned except by the handful of people who shared de Gaulle's view that a government that surrendered thereby forfeited all rights. Even General Noguès, who wanted to go on fighting and had telegraphed Bordeaux on the 25th to say so, saw no compelling reason to rally to de Gaulle's appeal. Indeed, on grounds of hierarchy as well as legality, the high dignitaries who kept their silence felt themselves to be on firm ground.

In these exceptional circumstances, concepts of duty varied in striking fashion. General Noguès, for instance, evidently thought it his duty to detain Georges Mandel, lately minister of the Interior, who had arrived in Casablanca on the evening of 24 June in the armed auxiliary cruiser *Massilia*, together with about thirty other parliamentarians whose journey plainly signified that they favoured the formation of an anti-armistice government in French North Africa. The truth about the *Massilia* incident may never be known. The question of setting up a potential centre of resistance in North Africa had been discussed at a meeting of Pétain's new cabinet on the 18th. At that stage, with the armistice still some days away, even Pétain was not against the scheme. Although he himself intended to stay in France, he saw no reason why he should not be represented in North Africa by the vice-premier, Camille Chautemps.[5]

As Minister of the Fleet, Admiral Darlan offered room on the *Massilia* to politicians who wished to go to Africa. In the end, however, only a few decided to go: they included Mandel and Mendès France. Mandel attempted to proclaim himself Prime Minister, but his announcement was intercepted by General Noguès, who had him arrested. And when the local magistrate freed him on the ground that there was no case to answer, the governor-general had him re-arrested and detained on the

[5] Churchill, Vol. I, pp. 192–3.

Massilia. A few days later, Mandel was returned to France, where a long internment ended with his death at the end of 1944 after tortures inflicted by the Gestapo.

Mandel's return in captivity marked the collapse of all remaining hopes of French official resistance to the Germans. Unknown to General de Gaulle, indeed, the future "men of Vichy" were preparing to set up a totalitarian State acceptable to the German invaders. Three men in particular – two of them already well known, and the third relatively obscure – played a crucial part in the week that followed Pétain's assumption of the premiership. The little known one was Raphael Alibert, a jurist who had become a junior minister in Pétain's first cabinet on 17 June and was later to be his minister of Justice; the well-known ones were Pierre Laval and Admiral Darlan.

All three were able and ambitious men. All three were guilty of giant miscalculations in the service of their ambitions. Alibert had been described as the evil genius of Pétain's national revolution.[6] He was also described – by Marshal Pétain's physician, Ménetrel – as "suffering from megalomania, with a certain tendency to mental unbalance, characterised by periods of excitement alternating with periods of mental depression". Within a few hours of joining Pétain's cabinet, he had ordered Mandel's arrest. This was on 17 June, and on this occasion Mandel was only held for a few hours. When the then President Lebrun asked Alibert why he had ordered the arrest, Alibert could only say that a journalist – whom he did not name – had denounced Mandel, for allegedly collecting arms with which to assassinate leading ministers. His part in the *Massilia* affair was outrageous. By falsely pretending he had news that the Germans had not crossed the Loire, he dissuaded Pétain's ministers from embarking for North Africa; and he supplemented his lie by forging the marshal's signature on a document ordering the ministers and various parliamentarians to stay at home and await further instructions.[7]

In all his actions at this time, Alibert had one thought only – to make sure that Pétain, whom he had met in 1917 and tutored in politics, should be made chief of State. A fanatical monarchist of the Action française group, Alibert was determined to destroy the Third Republic, and looked to Pétain to create the kind of State in which his own ambitions would flourish. To fulfil these plans, however, it was essential to prevent the formation of a centre of French resistance in North Africa, which would have denied Pétain any chance of becoming chief of State.

[6] Robert Aron, *Histoire de Vichy*, pp. 52 *et seq.* (henceforth, Rob. Aron, *Vichy*).
[7] Robert Aron (*Vichy*, pp. 69–71) does, however, raise doubts about the evidence for these charges against Alibert.

Laval was, of course, a man of much greater calibre. A strange figure, repulsive and sinister to many, but curiously attractive to others, he was born in Auvergne in 1883. His dark skin and heavy-lidded eyes gave him an oriental appearance. As a boy and a young man, he had a violent temper and all his life carried the scars of early fist fights. A practising lawyer at twenty-four, and initially a socialist, he had a peasant's sense of the value of money, and an extraordinary gift for making it. Whether he was corrupt in the strict sense of the word is open to doubt; but it is certain that he used his official posts to good effect, buying poverty-stricken businesses and turning all he touched into gold.

The effect of Alibert's manoeuvres had been to delay any decision on whether to embark for North Africa. Laval did not mind if the ex-ministers – those, such as Mandel, who opposed the armistice – should depart. But he was determined to prevent the departure of President Lebrun. Although on 21 June he had not yet joined Pétain's government, he already had a detailed programme for his own future and that of France. In an extraordinary scene, he stormed into the president's office, unannounced and without going through the usual formalities. There, accompanied by a handful of deputies, he harangued Lebrun with unprecedented violence, threatening him that should he leave, he would never again set foot on French soil. The president's departure now, he shouted, would amount to defection and treason. These bullying tactics succeeded. Lebrun, near to tears, agreed to stay.

Darlan's attitude was somewhat different. A highly professional sailor, he was deeply anti-British; and although perhaps equally anti-German, he saw his own future and that of his country in terms of preserving what could be preserved of French independence after Germany's victory – not in fighting on to the probable benefit of Britain alone. As far as he was concerned, any deputies and senators who wished to go to North Africa would by definition be men he wished to be rid of. He therefore raised no objection to the *Massilia* plan.[8]

It was against this troubled background of intrigue, invective and despair, which General de Gaulle had no means of knowing at the time, that he pursued his apparently unavailing efforts. Even Jean Monnet, although determined that resistance to the Germans should continue, wrote to de Gaulle on 23 June to dissociate himself from the whole idea of setting up a French movement in London, where it could only appear as a movement protected by Britain, "inspired by her interests and,

[8] Churchill, Vol. II, pp. 192–3.

115

because of that, condemned to a failure that would render more difficult later efforts at recovery".[9]

The British too were trying to revive the spirit of French resistance, but with no more success than de Gaulle. On the 25th, Churchill sent the Information minister, Duff Cooper, to Rabat, in the hope of making contact with Mandel and perhaps of influencing General Noguès to throw in his lot with the Frenchmen of London.[10] But all contact with Mandel was denied them, and Noguès refused to see them. General Dillon, head of the British Military liaison mission in North Africa, was asked to leave Algiers. Any hopes the British may have entertained of persuading a better known or more representative French personality to take over the cause of French resistance to the Germans were now dying. And on the 28th, it was officially announced that His Majesty's government recognised General de Gaulle as leader of all the Free French, wherever they might be. In one sense, this was a victory for de Gaulle; but in another sense, as a French historian later remarked, it was the acknowledgment of a failure.[11]

In the face of these successive discouragements, de Gaulle pressed on with his attempts to build an armed following. About 100,000 tons of French shipping had taken refuge in British harbours, and manning the ships were no fewer than 10,000 sailors. In addition, several thousand soldiers wounded in Belgium were recovering in British hospitals. Most of these men – soldiers and sailors – thought only of returning home, the war having ended for them. Such were the orders of Pétain's government, and the majority were inclined to obey. The British authorities had placed the White City stadium at de Gaulle's disposal, as a rallying centre for volunteers. But a week after his appeal of 18 June, only a few hundred had flocked to the Free French colours. In any event, apart from Churchill himself and General Spears, most of the people de Gaulle approached on the British side were sceptical and un-cooperative. With a general shortage of arms after the Dunkirk disaster, there were few weapons to spare for the French, and it was thought simpler to allow them to return to France. On 29 June, however, de Gaulle went to Trentham Park, near Liverpool, where the French Light Alpine Division was encamped. With the permission of the General Officer Commanding, de Gaulle recruited the bulk of two battalions of the 13th half-brigade of the Foreign Legion, 200 Alpine troops, two-thirds of a tank company, some artillery men, some sappers and com-

[9] De Gaulle, L'Appel, pp. 270–1.
[10] Churchill, Vol. I, p. 194; De Gaulle, L'Appel, p. 72.
[11] Henri Michel, Histoire de la France Libre, p. 9 (henceforth Michel, France Libre).

munications personnel.[12] Among them were men who were later to rise to prominence in the Free French movement, such as Captain Koenig and Captain Dewavrin (better known under his code name of "Passy").[13] De Gaulle's attempt to visit the camps at Aintree and Haydock was, however, frustrated by the British admiral in charge at Liverpool, who objected to the proposed visits on the grounds that they might affect law and order. At Harrow Park, some days later, he was more successful. Several naval commanders, including d'Argenlieu, joined the Free French. Two submarines and a patrol boat declared themselves for de Gaulle; and a few dozen airmen camped at St Athan were to form the nucleus of the Free French air force.

At the end of June, therefore, de Gaulle's recruiting campaign – though not overwhelmingly successful – was beginning to gather momentum. And on the last day of the month, the first personality of high rank declared himself for de Gaulle on his arrival in London. This was Vice-Admiral Muselier, a controversial figure whose career had been stormy in earlier life and was to run into further bad weather during his stay in London. At the time, however, his arrival and his decision greatly encouraged de Gaulle. So, too, did the continuous arrival of isolated volunteers. In total, they were few, but their importance could not be measured by numbers alone. Some came from Spain, whither they had escaped from France; others from North Africa via Gibraltar; of 2,000 Dunkirk wounded, gathered in the White City, 200 opted for Free France; a colonial battalion, detached from the army of the Levant and stationed in Cyprus, rallied to the Free French banner; and at the end of June, a flotilla of fishing boats landed on the Cornish coast, bearing all able-bodied men from the Isle of Sein, off the Breton coast.

At the beginning of July, the atmosphere around de Gaulle was thus one of buoyant hope. Almost immediately, however, this hope was severely dented by one of the more unfortunate Franco-British incidents of the war: the British naval bombardment of Mers-el-Kébir.

No problem haunted Winston Churchill more deeply on the morrow of France's fall than the fate of the French Fleet. Article 8 of the Franco-German armistice provided for the demobilising and disarming of French warships under German or Italian control. In the light of Hitler's record, there could be no faith or security in the accompanying German declaration that they would not be used for Germany's own purposes during

---

[12] De Gaulle, L'Appel, p. 75.
[13] "Passy" is the name of a station on the Paris métro. Others who later worked under Dewavrin in the Free French intelligence service likewise assumed métro station names.

the war. In those circumstances, Churchill did not hesitate: the French fleet must be destroyed, seized or incapacitated.[14] At that time, this powerful instrument of war was scattered in British, Mediterranean, African and Martinique harbours. Early on 3 July, an overwhelming British force swooped on the French ships at Portsmouth and Plymouth, seizing two battleships, four light cruisers, eight destroyers, some submarines and about 200 smaller craft. The crew of the large submarine *Surcouf* was the only one to offer resistance, one man losing his life on either side, with three British wounded.

That day at Oran, near the naval base of Mers-el-Kébir, the French Admiral Gensoul turned down a British ultimatum, undertaking not to allow French warships to fall intact into German or Italian hands, but threatening to meet British force with force. In the ensuing action, the battleship *Bretagne* was blown up by aircraft from the *Ark Royal*; the *Dunkerque* ran aground, as did the battleship *Provence*. The *Strasbourg*, though damaged, escaped to Toulon, together with the cruisers from Algiers.

At Alexandria, Admiral Godfroy, yielding before Admiral Cunningham's threats, agreed to dismantle certain gun mechanisms, repatriate some crew, and discharge oil fuel. At Dakar, on 8 July, the battleship *Richelieu* was severely damaged by a British air torpedo. The warships in the French West Indies were immobilised under an agreement with the United States.

Reporting on the Mers-el-Kébir action to the House of Commons on 4 July, Churchill received a standing ovation from all sides of the House. Though clearly proud of this demonstration of ruthlessness, Churchill described the decision to attack Britain's "dearest friends" as "hateful" and "the most unnatural and painful in which I have ever been concerned".

For de Gaulle, however, the news, which he first learned from the press and radio, came as a traumatic shock. He found in it not only motives of legitimate security, but "the musty odours of an old maritime rivalry, the grievances accumulated since the start of the battle of France and brought to a paroxysm by the armistice concluded by Vichy".[15] After adducing various reasons – such as Darlan's word of honour and Pétain's formal commitment – for presuming that the fleet would have stayed out of German hands, the general conceded, however, that in the face of the capitulation and the prospect of future defaults, Britain might well fear the worst, in which event, she would have been "mortally threatened". He therefore swallowed his pain and anger –

[14] Churchill, Vol. I, pp. 205 *et seq.*   [15] De Gaulle, *L'Appel*, pp. 77–8.

not merely over what had happened but at the way the British were glorying in it – and decided that the fight must go on, since the fate of France herself must be rated more highly than that of her ships.

In his memoirs, de Gaulle praises the Information minister, Duff Cooper, for his "elegant cleverness" in allowing him to speak his mind, as he did in a broadcast to the French people on 8 July 1940, when he denounced this "deplorable and detestable" action, but appealed for the understanding of the British. He steeled himself to say that without doubt the Germans would one day have used the French ships against Britain and the French Empire, and added, "I say without beating about the bush that it was best that they should have been destroyed."

The whole episode was nevertheless a grave blow to the nascent hopes of the Free French. Recruitment fell off drastically (although some hundreds of French sailors opted for service with the British navy).

The French government, which on 1 July had moved to Vichy, reacted on the 5th by breaking off relations with Great Britain. Six days later, Marshal Pétain was voted chief of State, in succession to President Lebrun. His overwhelming majority in the Assembly – 569 to 80, with seventeen abstentions and many absences – undoubtedly reflected the vacant will of the French people. Few believed in the cause for which de Gaulle stood, and fewer still were prepared to acknowledge his leadership.

Chapter 3 ⚜ The Free French

The story of the Free French in London is both heroic and sordid, pitiful and tragi-comic. This dualism, which was perhaps inherent in the circumstances of de Gaulle's enterprise, needs to be understood. De Gaulle himself was at once noble, romantic and Machiavellian. There was something quixotic as well as a touch of mysticism about his conceit that he incarnated France. But the dispositions he made to create and consolidate a personal power base were systematic and hard-headed. In sober fact, he was not at all representative of the spirit of the French people in the summer and autumn of 1940. By his own admission, a clear majority of the French supported Pétain. The achievement of his gradual rise to influence and power is all the more remarkable, though no one can tell what might have happened if a more senior personality – such as General Noguès – had declared himself the leader of the Free French.

As for the Free French, they were but a small minority even among those Frenchmen in exile who disapproved of their government's surrender. Of those in England, whether on active service or on civilian missions, most chose repatriation. Some, like Monnet, declined to serve under de Gaulle. Others came through London only as a first stepping stone on the way to a more comfortable American exile: one such was the famous French writer André Maurois. Of him, Churchill was to say, "We thought we had a friend: we found we had a customer." Few personalities of high rank, or even of more than average ability, joined de Gaulle in the early days. Not surprisingly, the talented few who loyally served the general were later recompensed by high office. Among these were Gaston Palewski, Maurice Dejean, Hervé Alphand, Jacques Soustelle (a later arrival, from Canada), Professor René Cassin and René Pleven. Some Frenchmen, wishing to continue the fight but disinclined to serve under a dissident French officer, chose to enlist in the British forces. Finally, many of those who did join the Free French were adventurers, intriguers, or power-seekers. In consequence, the atmosphere at Free French headquarters, at least during the early period, was not harmonious. Where de Gaulle had hoped for unity and devotion to duty, there prevailed the petty quarrels of the ambitious and the envious, tittle-tattle, smear campaigns and false accusations.

De Gaulle's first abode in London was a modest three-room flat at Seymour Place, near the Connaught Hotel. His possessions were few: two pairs of trousers, four shirts and a photograph of his family were the most important items.[1] The first headquarters of the Free French were at St Stephen's House on the embankment, with a view of Westminster Bridge and the Houses of Parliament. The two storeys provided by the British soon proved insufficient, and in August 1940 de Gaulle's administration was removed to the relatively spacious house at 4 Carlton Gardens. The general's office at St Stephen's House was on the third floor, overlooking the Thames. The furniture was austere. Adjoining it were the offices of his *chef de cabinet*, Hettier de Boislambert, a small, red-faced, fat man with an authoritative manner; and of his secretary, Lieutenant Geoffroy de Courcel who, in startling contrast, was tall and

[1] Henri Amouroux, Le 18 juin 1940, p. 358 (henceforth, Amouroux). Amouroux's spelling, evidently borrowed from de Gaulle's, is "Seamore".

thin, with a small head dominated by an eagle's nose.[2] Other offices were occupied by civilians, such as René Pleven and Professor Cassin; by Admiral Muselier and military men. On the ground floor were less senior people, including Georges Boris, a former assistant to Léon Blum and editor of a left-wing weekly, *La Lumière*.

In those early days, the general, although aware that he was embarking on an essentially political career, still retained his cutting military manner. Though capable, when relaxed and off duty, of a temporary charm, his greeting for new recruits was discouragingly icy – a fact which those well disposed towards him attributed to his natural shyness and reserve. Passy's account of his first meeting with de Gaulle is typical. A formal military introduction of himself by Captain Dewavrin (Passy's real name); a series of brief questions in de Gaulle's "clear, incisive, rather brutal voice", eliciting the information that the younger man had a law degree and spoke English fluently; a sudden decision that he was thereby appointed chief of the Second and Third bureaux of de Gaulle's staff; and an abrupt dismissal. In this glacial welcome, Passy noticed especially the general's "grey and piercing look, his tenacious will, still more apparent in word than in gestures; also perhaps a touch of pride and scorn, but it could just as well have been a form of shyness".

Passy's appointment was a key one, closely affecting the course of relations between the Free French and their British hosts. On the military side, the Free French contribution was at that time derisory; but it was soon evident to Passy – although he came to his job without the slightest previous experience of such work – that in the field of Intelligence, the British could not do without them. So precipitate had been the fall of France and the evacuation of the British Expeditionary Force, that the Secret Intelligence Service had virtually no agents in France. Frenchmen reaching England and wishing to serve General de Gaulle were first interrogated by the British (wrote Passy).[3] Soon a special centre, called the "Patriotic School", was set up in a London suburb. Every effort was made to persuade the new arrivals to serve as agents directly under British orders. Appeals to honour and patriotism were combined with subtle denigration of the rather amateurish organisation under Passy.[4] Some Frenchmen did indeed join the British service, but rather more

[2] Colonel Passy, *Souvenirs*, Vol. I, pp. 32–5 (henceforth, Passy).
[3] ibid. Vol. I, pp. 75 *et seq.*
[4] Passy soon handed over the Third Bureau to Captain de Hautecloque, better known as Leclerc. He kept the Second Bureau, which in theory was supposed to be a centre for processing intelligence prior to military operations; but owing to the feebleness of the Free French forces, operations were of secondary importance, and Passy's Second Bureau became essentially an intelligence service, which was successively known by the initials BCRAM and BCRA.

opted to serve under de Gaulle. Passy was thus able to set up a network of informants in occupied France that was to be of increasing benefit to the British and allied cause; and by the same token, a strong card for the Free French in their unequal dealings with the British.

In this atmosphere of feverish improvisation, internecine intrigues and Anglo-French rivalries, de Gaulle set about creating not only a movement loyal to his person and faithful to his concept of France, but the embryo of a new French State. On Bastille day – 14 July 1940 – de Gaulle made a symbolic public gesture, taking the salute, under the approving gaze of a London crowd, whilst the first Free French detachments marched past in Whitehall. Later, he placed a red, white and blue bouquet on the statue of Marshal Foch. A week later, the first Free French airmen took part in a bombing raid on the Ruhr, and the news of their action was published. About this time, at Admiral d'Argenlieu's suggestion, the Cross of Lorraine was adopted as the insignia of the Free French Forces. At the end of the month, some 7,000 men were under arms for de Gaulle and France.[5] And on 24 August, King George VI honoured them with an inspection.

This was a form of recognition. But recognition had already come in a form more useful to de Gaulle. In his first contacts with Churchill, the general had disclosed his intention of forming a "National Committee" as soon as possible, to direct the Free French war effort. As early as 23 June, two British official announcements respectively denied the independence of the French government at Bordeaux and foreshadowed recognition for the proposed French National Committee, while taking note that a number of high representatives of the French Empire had manifested their desire to continue the struggle. The further announcement on 28 June, recognising de Gaulle as leader of all the Free French forces, was in a sense anticlimactic, since it implicitly recognised the failure of any more senior personality to accept British offers of help in the event of their further resistance. It remained for the general to consolidate the position that was his by default. To this end, he outlined his suggestions in a memorandum sent to Churchill and to his Foreign Secretary Lord Halifax, on 26 June. Close negotiations followed, between William Strang,[6] the permanent under-secretary at the Foreign Office, and Professor Cassin, the distinguished jurist who had been one of the first to join General de Gaulle. The outcome was a formal agreement announced on 7 August 1940.

The Churchill-de Gaulle agreement, as it is usually known, was the foundation stone of the edifice he was trying to construct. But it was not

[5] De Gaulle, L'Appel, pp. 78–9.　　　　　[6] Later Lord Strang.

in all respects satisfactory to de Gaulle. He had tried to persuade the British to guarantee to restore not only the frontiers of metropolitan France, but also those of the French Empire. This was his way of legally removing any adventurous temptation the British might feel to grab French territory and add it to their own empire. But this was more than Churchill was prepared to promise. Instead, the British undertook to seek "the integral restoration of the independence and greatness of France". Tortuous semantic arguments attended the drafting of the articles defining the general's own authority, and the use of the Free French forces. Realism forced General de Gaulle to recognise that in any joint operations, the supreme authority could only be British. But he was eager for firm recognition of his own authority over the Free French and for a formula that would establish their national character and limit the power of the British to use them in operations of which he might not approve. The outcome was stated in two elaborately worded articles. Article I, 2, declared that the Free French forces would *never* be required "to bear arms against France". This did not, as de Gaulle explains in his memoirs, mean that they could never fight against other Frenchmen, given the character of the Vichy regime, as it was to be. France, at all times, was what de Gaulle defined it to be. Article II, 6, described de Gaulle as supreme commander of the French force, but recorded his acceptance of "the general directives of the British command" and his readiness to delegate part of his force to British officers – but without prejudice to the provisions of Article I, 2.

Another clause – a most humiliating one because it underlined the feebleness and dependence of the Free French – was Article IV, 1, which stipulated that all expenditures of the French force would be provisionally chargeable to the relevant British ministries. The second part of Article IV, however, preserved French honour by providing that all such charges would be separately accounted and in time reimbursed (in fact, reimbursement was made in full before the end of the war, as de Gaulle proudly records). In a secret letter to General de Gaulle, Churchill explained that the expression in the agreement concerning "the integral restoration of the independence and greatness of France" did not amount to a precise guarantee of territorial frontiers – a guarantee which the British had felt unable to extend to any of the nations fighting at their side. "But we shall, of course," he added, "do our best." The Prime Minister went on to say that the articles stipulating that de Gaulle's troops would not have to bear arms against France must be interpreted as referring to "a France free to choose a road and not subject to the direct or indirect constraint of Germany". In other words, it excluded

Vichy France, should Pétain's government declare war against the United Kingdom.

Replying in equal secrecy, de Gaulle took note of these interpretations, but expressed the hope that the day might come when the British government would "consider" these questions with less reserve.[7]

The Churchill-de Gaulle agreement marked the highest point in relations between the two leaders. Vichy having broken off relations with Britain after the destruction of the French fleet at Mers-el-Kébir, Churchill had in effect extended recognition to de Gaulle's embryonic State. True, he had not altogether given up hope of influencing Vichy in an anti-German sense; but of this, at the time, de Gaulle was unaware. There is a rare serenity about his account of this period. Touching demonstrations of the kindness of the British people, high and low, towards the Free French were happening constantly. When the London press reported the general's condemnation to death by Vichy, and the confiscation of his property, unknown British sympathisers deposited jewels and wedding rings at Carlton Gardens as a contribution to his effort. He writes with admiration of the "vibrant atmosphere" in England at a time when the expectation of a German invasion was universal. "It was a truly admirable spectacle," he wrote, "to see each Englishman behave as if his country's salvation depended on his own behaviour." The young men of the RAF were preparing for the German assault; and air raid shelters were being built. One day in August, at Chequers, de Gaulle saw Churchill, his fists clasped and brandished skywards, exclaiming, "Will they never come?" In the discussion that followed, Churchill remarked that de Gaulle could now see why he had refused to leave the British fighter planes in France. But de Gaulle refused to concede this point, which he countered with the view that if the British planes had stayed on, French resistance might have been sustained, and the fight continued from the Mediterranean. Churchill, however, had his eyes on more distant objectives: his hope at that time was that once the Germans began bombarding British cities, the United States would be shaken out of its neutrality.

Writing of this incident years later, de Gaulle appended a "banal but definitive conclusion", which does much to explain his later foreign policy: "When all is said, England is an island; France, the cape of a continent; America, another world."

Assured now of British support, dependent still but autonomous, and relieved of financial stringency, de Gaulle turned his thoughts towards Africa. His earlier hopes of a general anti-German uprising in the French

[7] De Gaulle, L'Appel, pp. 80–1, 279–83.

Empire had been disappointed – but by a remarkably small margin. In
North Africa, Noguès resisted the armistice for three days, then accepted
it on 25 June. In Indo-China, Catroux maintained his opposition, but
allowed himself to be replaced by a Vichy nominee. In the Levant,
Puaux, the resident-general, and General Mittelhauser remained opposed
to the armistice until the 26th. More determined was Colonel de Larminat, Mittelhauser's chief of staff, who made it possible for the Polish
brigade of General Kopansky to cross the border into British-mandated
Palestine. De Larminat wanted to go further and raise a force of French

De Gaulle and Leclerc 1940–43

volunteers; but General Wavell, apparently afraid that such dissidence might bring more trouble than it was worth, refused him the use of facilities in Cairo. In the end, of the 70,000 French troops in the Levant, only a few hundred crossed to the Free French side. As for the fleet anchored at Alexandria under Admiral Godfroy, only six officers and a couple of dozen warrant officers and sailors opted for de Gaulle.

In the Horn of Africa, on the French Somali coast, General Legentil-homme, with only a handful of followers, crossed the border into British Somaliland on 2 August.[8]

In North Africa, then, and in the more distant parts of the French Empire, the overwhelming majority of armed Frenchmen and of the civilian administrators had in the end taken refuge in the comforting thought that Pétain and Weygand themselves favoured surrender. In Africa, both West and Equatorial, however, the outlook seemed more promising to de Gaulle. From many of these vast but sparsely populated territories, encouraging messages were reaching the general.

The strongest ripples of dissidence came from Cameroun and Tchad. In the former, a French-mandated territory, there was instant awareness that a German victory would mean the reversion of the colony to Germany. Although the governor-general, Brunot, declined to declare himself, an action committee had been formed under the director of Public Works, Mauclère, who declared himself for de Gaulle. In Tchad, the governor, Félix Eboué, "that ardently French black man", in de Gaulle's phrase, had many reasons for being anti-Hitler, not least his disgust at the racialist theories of the Nazis. Eboué declared his readiness to make a public announcement of support.

Elsewhere in French Africa, the indications were either equivocal or discouraging. In the French Congo the governor-general, Boisson, was initially defiant; but on being transferred from Brazzaville to Dakar and promoted to High Commissioner of the more important group of territories comprising French West Africa, his attitude had changed in Vichy's favour. His successor in Brazzaville, General Husson, was obedient to France's generally recognised government. In Oubangui,[9] the mood was in favour of resistance, but the territory was unlikely to move without approval from Brazzaville. In Gabon, there was an enigmatic but probably hostile silence.

General de Gaulle decided to strike immediately in the apparently favourable territories – Tchad, Cameroun and the Congo, leaving until later the trickier operation of Dakar. Lord Lloyd, the colonial secretary,

[8] Michel, *France Libre*, pp. 14–15.
[9] Oubangui, or Oubangui-Chari, now styles itself the Central African Republic.

immediately grasped the importance of de Gaulle's plans for the security of Nigeria, the Gold Coast, Sierra Leone and Gambia. He put a plane at the general's disposal, to carry from London to Lagos a team of Free French "missionaries".[10] Initially there were to be three of them: Pleven, Major Parant, Hettier de Boislambert (de Gaulle's *chef de cabinet*). Their first destination was to be Fort Lamy, in Tchad, where they were to see Governor Eboué, make sure of Tchad's adherence, and go to Doualla to support Mauclère and his committee in the proposed Cameroun "*coup d'état*" in de Gaulle's favour. At the last minute, a fourth "missionary" joined the group, Leclerc.

De Gaulle now felt confident that Tchad and Cameroun would come over. But what of Equatorial Africa? The man for the job, he thought, would be Colonel de Larminat, then in Cairo after his Levantine escapade. His mission was to seize Brazzaville, capital of the administrative region and seat of authority not only over the French Congo but over the neighbouring colonies of Lower Congo, Oubangui, and Gabon. All five of de Gaulle's young men were brilliantly and bloodlessly successful. By the end of August, Tchad, Cameroun, the Congo and Oubangui had rallied. Even Gabon had temporarily rallied, but had changed course on the arrival of a Vichy general with military means. About that time, de Gaulle learned with elation of the impending arrival of General Catroux from Indo-China. Since he himself was planning to leave for Africa, he wrote Catroux a letter dated 29 August 1940, to be read on the latter's arrival in London. In it, he told Catroux of his plan to set up a defence council for France Overseas, and invited the senior general to take over responsibility for Morocco, Algeria and Tunisia.

The leader of the Free French had hoped that a successful expedition to Dakar would bring Senegal and the rest of French West Africa flocking to his colours, but circumstances conspired to frustrate him. Although painfully and realistically aware that it would not always be possible to avoid clashes between Frenchmen, de Gaulle was determined to avoid anything like a major battle. His original plan was to land a small Free French force at Conakry, in French Guinea, and to approach Dakar gradually from the rear, gaining adherents and general support on the way. For such an operation to succeed, however, it would be necessary to provide naval support: otherwise, the Vichy navy might annihilate the expeditionary force. Already, towards the end of July, de Gaulle had exposed his project to Churchill, who, at the time, made no commitment. On 6 August, the Prime Minister summoned de Gaulle to 10 Downing Street. Maps of Africa were deployed over the vast Cabinet

[10] De Gaulle, *L'Appel*, pp. 92–3.

table. Churchill was in animated and eloquent form. He ruled out the Conakry project on the grounds that it would mean keeping a British naval force off the coast of Africa for months. Instead, he proposed a swifter and more imaginative programme, which he described to de Gaulle with Churchillian gusto.[11]

In sparkling mood, the Prime Minister painted a picture of Dakar at dawn, sad and uncertain, awakening to a sea covered with ships. A hundred vessels slowly draw closer, and as they move in, broadcast messages of friendship. Some would have the French tricolour, others would be flying British, Dutch, Polish or Belgian colours. From this allied squadron, an inoffensive little boat would detach itself, flying a white flag. Entering harbour, it would carry General de Gaulle's personal envoys, who would be taken to the governor. Friendly but determined pressure would ensue: cooperate, or face an unequal combat. Meanwhile, Free French and British planes would be flying over the city, dropping persuasive leaflets. At most, the governor might discharge a blast or two, for form's sake. But he would not go beyond that: that night, he would dine with de Gaulle and drink to final victory.

Even allowing for the special effects of Churchill's enthusiasm, de Gaulle saw much sense in this plan. And indeed, it *could* have worked. The fiasco that followed is, however, notorious; and it is fair after the lapse of time to blame it less upon Churchill's optimism and de Gaulle's acquiescence than upon sheer ill-luck and the incompetence of subordinates.

De Gaulle accepted Churchill's proposals. Next, the general elaborated a plan of action with Admiral John Cunningham. Inevitably, the expedition was overwhelmingly British, even though Admiral Cunningham found he could spare fewer ships than Churchill had envisaged on 6 August. The Free French naval contribution was feeble: three despatch-boats – *Savorgnan de Brazza, Commandant Duboc, Commandant Dominé*; and two armed trawlers – *Vaillant* and *Viking*. No passenger transports were available to the Free French at that time, and on board two Dutch ships, *Pennland* and *Westerland*, were a battalion of the Foreign Legion, a company of recruits, a company of marines, enough manpower for a tank company and for an artillery battery. In all, 2,000 men. Four French cargo ships – *Anadyr, Casamance, Fort Lamy, Nevada* – carried the heavy war material – tanks, cannon, and Lysander, Hurricane and Blenheim planes – not ready for action but packed in their

---

[11] That is, according to de Gaulle's account which begins on p. 97 of *L'Appel*. Churchill's own account (chapter XXIV of Volume I) is more sober. My own account draws from both.

cases, together with various vehicles and food supplies. On the British side, were two old battleships, *Barham* and *Resolution*, four cruisers, the aircraft-carrier *Ark Royal*, a few destroyers and a tanker. In addition, three transport vessels were to carry two battalions of marine infantry, commanded by Major-General N. M. S. Irwin, together with landing gear.

On the eve of departure, allied harmony was marred by an acrimonious dispute. At issue was a large stock of gold deposited at Bamako in the French Sudan by the Bank of France, for its own use and for the State banks of Belgium and Poland. The British, while making no proprietary claims on the gold, wished to use it to finance their purchases of war material in the United States which, as they pointed out, were for the common good of the Western allies. General de Gaulle called in M. Spaak of Belgium and Mr Zaleski of Poland, to reassure them that their countries' interests would be looked after, although he refused to permit the British to use the gold as they pleased. And he held firm, even when General Spears threatened that the British would withdraw from the Dakar expedition. The British gave in.

The expedition set off from Liverpool on 31 August 1940. General de Gaulle himself was on board the *Westerland*, which was flying the French flag; and with him was Spears – "as Churchill's liaison officer, diplomatist and informant" (wrote de Gaulle). The chapter of woe was just beginning. After a long and devious journey, the Anglo-French armada reached Freetown on 17 September. A few days earlier, alarming news had come: a powerful Vichy fleet, consisting of three large modern cruisers – *Georges Leygues*, *Gloire*, *Montcalm* – and three light cruisers – *Audacieux*, *Fantasque* and *Malin* – leaving Toulon, had steamed past Gibraltar unmolested and were heading south along the coast of West Africa. By the time the British and Free French ships reached Freetown, the Vichy fleet, having reached Dakar and been reinforced by the cruiser *Primauget*, was steaming south. Three ciphered telegrams – from Tangier and Madrid – had given the news; but owing in part to the interruptions of normal work due to the continuous bombardment of London, and in part to two separate failures to see that the messages were passed on urgently, they did not reach the sea lords until the 14th.

De Gaulle was determined to push on with the Dakar enterprise. His fear was that the Vichy ships would intimidate the coastal areas of Equatorial Africa. In London, Churchill "had no doubt whatever that the enterprise should be abandoned". The expedition, he said, should be diverted to Douala and should cover de Gaulle's operations against Cameroun. Orders to this effect were telegraphed from London. On the spot, however, Admiral Cunningham agreed with de Gaulle that the operation must go on, and they telegraphed this view to Churchill. Reassured – and, says de Gaulle, "surprised and charmed by this insistence" – Churchill concurred.

The fleet sailed on the 21st, and reached Dakar two days later at dawn.

Now came the second stroke of ill-luck. For Churchill's theatrical effect to succeed, perfect visibility was necessary; but, exceptionally for this area at that time of the year, an impenetrable fog separated the Anglo-French armada from those who were supposed to see and be intimidated by it. De Gaulle's emissaries were fired upon and two of them seriously wounded. After an exchange of fire betwen the shore batteries and the British warships, it was decided that de Gaulle should attempt a landing at the small port of Rufisque, near Dakar. But in fog and confusion, and in the face of some resistance from land, the attempt was abandoned. Sadly, de Gaulle, Cunningham and Irwin agreed that the operation must be called off, despite a further telegram from Churchill inviting them insistently to continue.

For de Gaulle, the disappointment was cruel. He felt, he wrote later, like a man whose house has been shaken by an earthquake and who gets a shower of roof tiles on his head. For Churchill, too it had been a humiliating blow. The battleship *Resolution* was disabled for months, and two destroyers were severely damaged. On the other hand, two Vichy submarines had been sunk, two destroyers burnt out and the battleship *Richelieu* badly damaged and out of action owing to the lack of repair facilities at Dakar. An angry press in London blamed de Gaulle for the fiasco. As for Vichy, it gloated over his discomfiture, and sent planes from Morocco to bomb Gibraltar.

And yet, all was not lost. In London, Churchill told the House of Commons that de Gaulle's conduct and bearing had made his confidence in the general greater than ever. And the loyalty of General de Gaulle's small band of followers remained unshaken. Affirmations of loyalty came in warm telegrams from Larminat and Leclerc. The latter was at Douala, where he greeted the general on his arrival on 8 October, amid scenes of euphoric enthusiasm for the Free French cause. This enthusiasm seems, paradoxically, to have been an embarrassment to de Gaulle. Henceforth, he felt himself bound to live up to the new image of himself as the symbol of an indomitable France. This was, he records, a heavy burden for him.[12]

Burdensome or not, the enthusiastic welcome that awaited de Gaulle at Yaoundé and Fort Lamy must have brought him much comfort after

[12] De Gaulle, *L'Appel*, p. 111.

the painful reverse of Dakar. His trip to Tchad, incidentally, almost ended in disaster, for the Potez 540 in which he was travelling made a forced landing in marshes after engine trouble.

Given the paucity of means at his disposal, the general's strategy was little short of grandiose. In the cruel and remote desert in which Tchad meets Libya he planned to set up a base for Saharan operations so that, in time, a French force might capture the Fezzan and reach the Mediterranean. At the same time, he wanted to send a Free French expeditionary corps to the Middle East, to join forces with the British. The ultimate prize of these manoeuvres was French North Africa. Accordingly, after a heart-warming welcome from Governor Eboué, and in the company of Colonel Marchand, the commander in Tchad, de Gaulle flew to Faya, and the desert outposts of the north. The poorly supplied troops there greeted him with unfurled Crosses of Lorraine, but were deeply sceptical about his Fezzan plans.

Back at Fort Lamy, he found awaiting him the man who was by far the biggest "catch" his movement had made to date – General Catroux. This intelligent and highly literate five-star general had reached London during de Gaulle's absence, and been received with flattering attention by Churchill who, if de Gaulle's speculation is to be believed, had gone so far as to propose that Catroux should take over from de Gaulle. On 22 September the Prime Minister had telegraphed de Gaulle to say that he had taken the responsibility "in your name" of inviting General Catroux to go to Syria.[13] And now, Catroux, having gone to Cairo, had thought it right to break his journey to consult with General de Gaulle at Fort Lamy. At dinner that night, de Gaulle toasted "this great leader, for whom I had always felt a deferential friendship". Catroux's impressive response was to say that he placed himself under de Gaulle's own leadership. Those present, including Governor Eboué, realised that, in Catroux's eyes, de Gaulle's importance now transcended his military rank. With de Gaulle's blessing, Catroux returned to Cairo.

On 24 October 1940, de Gaulle arrived at Brazzaville, where he found the main problem to be economic: he therefore appointed Pleven as secretary-general of the administration, under de Larminat. He went on to Oubangui, where he was greeted by the governor, de Saint-Mart, who took him to the French Congo port of Pointe-Noire. On the 27th he visited Leopoldville, across the river from Brazzaville, where the Belgian authorities and the local French colony gave him a "very moving reception".

There remained one major African problem for de Gaulle to liquidate

13 Churchill, Vol. I, p. 596.

– that of Gabon. The Vichy General Têtu had orders to fight, and four battalions, plus artillery and other means to do so. Larminat had already been preparing for the inevitable but fratricidal operation; and de Gaulle announced that, whatever the outcome, there would be no citations. Between 27 October and 12 November, at the cost of twenty lives, Leclerc's troops and Koenig's had occupied the main centres. De Gaulle, having named Parant governor, went to Libreville on 15 November. The Vichy governor, Masson, who had initially announced Gabon's support for de Gaulle then changed his mind, hanged himself. This touch of grimness was characteristic of a distasteful success.

Vichy's radio stations in Vichy itself and in Dakar, together with Radio Paris, immediately accused de Gaulle's troops of various atrocities, such as the burning and pillage of Libreville, and the shooting of notables, including the bishop, Monseigneur Tardy. Alarmed lest these false charges should foreshadow Vichy reprisals against Free French prisoners, de Gaulle warned the High Commissioner in Dakar that enough of his friends were held by the Free French to answer for the lives of those in Vichy hands. The tone of the radio war dropped immediately. Less satisfactory was the fact that once again only a small minority of the local forces (in Gabon) decided to join the Free French forces; most preferred to express their passive loyalty to Marshal Pétain by opting for internment.

More worrying, from de Gaulle's viewpoint, was the news that reached him in telegrams from Churchill and Eden, of conversations in Madrid between the Vichy and British ambassadors, M. de la Baume and Sir Samuel Hoare. De la Baume was asking for a British guarantee that French supplies from North Africa would not be impeded, the Germans having "guaranteed" that they themselves would not touch them. If, however, the Germans broke their word, de la Baume had added, the Vichy administration would transfer itself to North Africa and resume the fight at Britain's side.

De Gaulle put the British on their guard against such blandishments. In any event, Pétain's meeting with Hitler at Montoire on 24 October soon made it clear that Vichy would actively collaborate with the Nazis. Indeed, Vichy halted the Madrid talks early in November.

For de Gaulle, the logic of the situation was inescapable, and it coincided with his own ambitions. It was not sufficient to denounce Vichy and deny its legitimacy; he himself must be the guardian of the nation's interests and exercise the attributes of a sovereign government in the liberated territories. In this context, 27 October 1940 was an important, as well as a busy day. The fight for Gabon was beginning and de Gaulle went to Leopoldville that day; and in Brazzaville, he published a manifesto denouncing the Vichy "organism" as "unconstitutional and subservient to the invader". He solemnly undertook to account for his actions to the representatives of the French people as soon as it should be possible to appoint them freely – an undertaking which he fulfilled, in effect, five years later on handing over his powers to the French Provisional Assembly. Still on the 27th, he issued two ordinances. The first announced the creation of a Defence Council of the Empire, with the powers and attributes of a government. In effect, however, the ordinance amounted to notice of a personal dictatorship, "for the duration", for Article 3 read: "Decisions will be taken by the Leader of the Free French, after consultations, *if the need arises*, with the Defence Council." (Italics added.)

The second ordinance appointed the following as members of the council: General Catroux, Vice-Admiral Muselier, General de Larminat, Governor Eboué, Governor Sautot, Médecin-Général Sicé, Professor Cassin, Reverend Father d'Argenlieu, Colonel Leclerc. De Gaulle followed these actions with a long telegram to Churchill, dated 2 November,[14] in which he gave warning against any facile optimism concerning the chances of winning over to the allied cause such men as Noguès and Weygand.

It remained for de Gaulle to warn all Frenchmen of the significance of the Brazzaville manifesto and the accompanying ordinances. To this end, on 16 November, while still in Brazzaville, he issued a solemn "Organic Declaration", which announced the aim of his assumption of power as the liberation of the whole of France; and denounced Vichy's creation of a "French State" as unconstitutional under the law of 1884.

In the manifesto of 27 October, de Gaulle still referred to himself as "I"; but in the ordinances, he used the royal "we" for the first time, as he did in the Organic Declaration. For now, in his own eyes, he represented the French State.

On 17 November, de Gaulle left Free French Africa for England, via Lagos, Freetown, Bathurst and Gibraltar. He left behind him something more solid than the fading humiliation of the Dakar fiasco: an extensive base of operations and an efficient administration. More, a Free French State had been created, with de Gaulle as its unquestioned leader.

---

[14] De Gaulle, *L'Appel*, pp. 309–10; but his account in the narrative section (p. 119) dates the telegram 5 November and calls it a "note" to the British government.

Chapter 4 ✤ Divided They Fall

While de Gaulle was in Africa, the resentments, jealousies and rivalries of his followers were boiling over in London. In his war memoirs, the general dismisses most of them in a short paragraph.[1] This unwillingness to dwell upon the fragility of his following and the self-seeking motives of some of his followers is understandable. But the squabbles of the Free French deserve more space than de Gaulle accords them; for while they diminish the epic side of the movement, they enhance the achievement of his bid for power.

There were three main groups of dissidents: the ideological, the disgruntled and the hierarchical. In other words, there were those who thought of the general as a potential military dictator, and his movement as a refuge for Fascists; the adventurers, whose motivation of personal advancement was frustrated; and those who thought De Gaulle too junior in rank to lead a movement with national pretensions and would have preferred to follow a more senior man, such as Admiral Muselier. Within each category, there were further sub-divisions.

The first "ideological" dissidents consisted of left-wingers from the *Front Populaire*, of whom the best known were Pierre Comert, former head of the press department at the Quai d'Orsay, and Georges Gombault, who had worked with Georges Boris on the Socialist weekly *La Lumière*. These men and their friends were "old Republicans", with the emphasis on the "old".[2] With the Third Republic in ruins, their thought processes continued blissfully unimpeded. A soldier could only be a "reactionary". Moreover, were there not Cagoulards and other Fascists in his *entourage*? There were indeed; and the fact that there were also Socialists like Boris (Gombault's colleague of *La Lumière*), and André Philip, and anti-Fascists such as Professor Cassin and Jacques Soustelle, left them unmoved. The Comert-Gombault group founded the French-language daily, *France*, with subsidies from the British ministry of Information, and adopted an attitude towards the Free French movement

[1] De Gaulle, *L'Appel*, pp. 123–4.
[2] Jacques Soustelle, *Envers et Contre Tout*, Vol. I, pp. 48–9 (henceforth, Soustelle, *Envers*).

134

that could be described as "non-recognition". Any information from Free French sources was labelled "official communiqués" and published with dissociative brevity. Though disowned in due course by Léon Blum and the official French Socialist party (*Section Française Internationale Ouvrière*), operating clandestinely in France, the *France* group had the ear of the British Labour party.[3] Its aloofness towards de Gaulle turned into outright hostility when de Gaulle was fighting for his political future in Algiers from 1943 on.

Nor was *France* the only non-Gaullist information or propaganda venture in which the Frenchmen of London were involved. One was a miniature newspaper called *Le Courrier de l'Air*, which the Royal Air Force dropped over France.[4] Then there was the BBC French service. Many, perhaps nearly all, of its listeners in France, must have assumed that it was the voice of the Free French, but it was not. The able and enthusiastic team of Frenchmen talking to their captive countrymen – men like Pierre Bourdan, Jacques Duchesne[5] and Jean Marin – were employees of the BBC. The Free French made use of the BBC by invitation and sometimes on sufferance. In any event, their radio time was severely rationed: of the daily five and a half hours of French language broadcasts, only ten minutes were available to the Free French. And even this modest period was sometimes disdained for reasons of offended national dignity. For the Free French were not represented (until as late as May 1944) in the weekly conference of the Political Information Department (later the Political Warfare Executive) which decided the "line" to adopt in broadcasts to France. The Free French messages were sometimes cut, and sometimes cut out; and de Gaulle and Maurice Schumann took it in turns to boycott the BBC. It was not until June 1943 that radio relations improved; and not until May 1944 – on the eve of the Normandy landings – that the Free French were invited to the discussions of the Political Warfare Executive.[6]

Against this massive British-controlled propaganda effort, the Free French disposed, in the early days, of very modest means. One outlet was the review, *France Libre*, whose editor was André Labarthe, but whose high literary and intellectual merit was mostly attributable to his assistant, Raymond Aron. But Labarthe later joined Giraud, for he was one of the disgruntled adventurers in the second group of dissidents. Later – from July 1942 – a Free French information department was set

[3] Michel, *France Libre*, p. 31.
[4] Robert Mengin – who, in his book *No Laurels for de Gaulle* (henceforth, Mengin), gives subjectively valid reasons for his denying the general's leadership – worked on *Le Courrier de l'Air*.
[5] The late Michel St Denis, the theatrical producer.   [6] Michel, *France Libre*, pp. 32–3.

up, under Soustelle, and its publications greatly increased the communicative power of the Gaullists.

Who, then, were the "Cagoulards" and "Fascists" of diverse hues? One of those most persistently labelled a Cagoulard was Passy of the Deuxième Bureau. The motives of the labellers were, however, open to question. One was Henri de Kérillis, who in his bitterly anti-Gaullist memoirs, *I Accuse de Gaulle*, makes the charge repeatedly, but without offering supporting evidence. Another was Labarthe of the *Revue de la France Libre*, who was to give Passy himself an elaborately fanciful account of how the rumour must have started. This Labarthe, swarthy, thin, fortyish, animated and unfailingly imaginative – a Don Juan, moreover, says Passy[7] – had scientific pretensions. Explaining the theories of the chemist Mendeleieff to a receptive audience, he mentioned "element 93", the existence of which could be presumed, although it still eluded discovery. The subject changed to de Gaulle and his *entourage*. De Gaulle, said Labarthe, was all right, but some very dubious people were in his movement, including inveterate Cagoulards. "And what do you think of Passy?" he was asked.

"Oh, Passy," replied Labarthe, "he's 'element 93'." Thus, said Labarthe, did the whole of London come to "know" that Passy held card No. 93 in the Cagoule secret society.

Passy, however, strenuously denies that he was ever a Cagoulard. But his staff did include two ex-Cagoulards: Captain Fourcaud, an effervescent and quixotic adventurer, whose talent as a raconteur rivalled that of Labarthe, whom he destested; and Duclos, a jovial giant, with a huge appetite for food, drink and women, whose reasons for having, at one time, joined the Cagoule were opaque, his bent (says Passy) being commercial not political.

In this atmosphere of rancorous intrigue, dissension flourished. It was to affect Labarthe and, in time, Fourcaud. The Labarthe "rebellion" was, however, overshadowed by the Muselier affair, in which he played an undistinguished part.

It is not possible to write with assurance about this curious business. Not unexpectedly, the accounts of the two leading personages – Vice-Admiral Muselier and General de Gaulle – are strikingly at variance. And there are many other versions of the facts: those of Passy, Soustelle, Mengin, for instance. To these should be added the unpublished archives of the British Security Service (M.I.5), and the long report – also unpublished – which the French agent Howard wrote after his Isle of Man internment for the French Sûreté. Published or not, each account must be

[7] Passy, Vol. I, pp. 48 *et seq.*

presumed to suffer from the need of each actor to present his role in the most favourable light. My own account attempts to establish a balance of probability between conflicting claims, including those of Admiral Muselier himself, who was, after all, the aggrieved party, but whose testimony has been too sweepingly discounted by the Gaullists.

Like de Gaulle, but in quite different ways, Muselier had a "difficult" character. He was about sixty when he reached London. With his jaunty manner, his black moustache (which, says Passy, looked as if it had been dyed, and his sparkling eyes, he had the air of a great corsair. It is generally agreed that he had a "terrible" or "frightful" reputation in the French navy, but nobody seemed to know why.[8] De Gaulle, who had heard of his "reputation", and worried on account of it, went to see the head of the French Naval Mission in London, Admiral Odend'hal, and asked him whether, to his knowledge, Muselier had ever, in his career, done anything dishonourable. The admiral's "No" was categorical and de Gaulle, reassured, decided to appoint Muselier head of the Free French naval forces.

Muselier, however, did not like the idea of being "appointed" by de Gaulle. After all, he (Muselier) was a three-star admiral, whereas de Gaulle was only a two-star general, and a temporary one at that. There was the rub. Almost immediately, he began to give orders outside the duties de Gaulle had defined for him, or to frustrate the execution of de Gaulle's orders. De Gaulle had no wish to leave the direction of the Free French movement in Muselier's hands during his own absence in Africa in the autumn of 1940. Instead, in an internal memorandum dated 27 August, he divided interim authority as follows:[9]

> Muselier to be superior commander of all Free French forces in Britain.
>
> General direction of civilian departments to be under M. Fontaine, who, four days after his arrival in London on 15 August, had been appointed director of Economic Affairs.[10]
>
> Lieutenant Serreules to be in charge of the military secretariat, and Major Passy to be General de Gaulle's chief of staff.
>
> All promotions and appointments, both civil and military, to be reserved for de Gaulle himself.

[8] Whatever the reason, hundreds of French naval officers, on hearing of his appointment as head of the Free French navy, decided not to join de Gaulle; though whether their decision would have been different if somebody else had been appointed cannot be said with any confidence. See Passy, Vol. I, p. 83 and n.
[9] ibid. Vol. I, p. 81; De Gaulle, L'Appel, p. 101, summarises these arrangements, avoiding details.
[10] Vice-Admiral Muselier, De Gaulle contre le Gaullisme, p. 23 (henceforth, Muselier).

Friction was virtually built into this elaborate machinery. Passy, we have already met. Fontaine was a businessman whose real name was Antoine. Aged about fifty, he was short, emaciated, lively and intelligent. He had managed several electric power companies, some of which were controlled by the Belgian financier, Baron Empain, whose collaborationist zeal splashed Antoine with the mud of suspicions that he might be a planted Vichy spy. The arch-adventurer of the Free French movement, Labarthe, hardly gave Antoine time to unpack before launching a vituperative campaign against him, as Empain's personal representative for pro-German deals, or a Vichy agent, or both. Muselier, irked by the division of authority between himself and Antoine, joined in the campaign with his customary gusto.

Muselier had grounds for considering himself aggrieved. As the most senior of the servicemen who had rallied to the Free French movement, he naturally expected to be appointed as de Gaulle's deputy in his absence. In a bitter mood, he protested, in a letter to de Gaulle dated 28 August, against the temporary arrangements.[11]

Muselier does seem to have suspected Antoine, but he also resented the fact that the man was only a reserve officer, with the rank of major. More wounding still to his pride was the fact that Passy and Serreulles, who was to run de Gaulle's military secretariat, were young men of thirty, the first a captain and the second a lieutenant in the Reserves.

On his side, Antoine had no tolerance towards the men who were spreading calumny about him. He had left his lucrative job to come to London with patriotic intent – and perhaps to escape from Baron Empain, rather than to do the baron's bidding – and moreover, he was desperately worried about the fate of his wife. One of his first executive actions was to dismiss Labarthe. Since de Gaulle had reserved all promotions and appointments to himself, Muselier felt on strong ground in cabling the general to protest against Antoine's presumption. But de Gaulle, who had other worries, did not reply.

Muselier thereupon appointed Labarthe as a professor at the naval school he had just created, and caused him to be awarded a sinecure in the French Institute in London. The stormy atmosphere resulting from such moves, and the rows they generated, were not improved by Muselier's attempts to establish an intelligence service of his own without reference to the one Passy was trying to set up at de Gaulle's behest and with the help of the British. Exasperated in his turn, Passy sent de Gaulle a long memorandum, dated 16 October 1940, in which he complained bitterly of the admiral's interference, and proposed the appoint-

11 ibid. pp. 93–4.

ment of General Catroux (who had just arrived in London) as the sole authority in General de Gaulle's absence. Failing that, he thought it would be better for Muselier to be named the sole representative than for the "frightful dualism that was paralysing everything" to continue.[12] He did not, of course, tell Muselier of his representations to General de Gaulle. Later, Muselier learned that Passy had indeed recommended that he should be made de Gaulle's sole representative, and – evidently flattered – twice mentioned the fact in his memoirs, but without reference to the uncomplimentary arguments that had led Passy to this desperate conclusion.[13]

A week earlier (on 9 October), de Gaulle had cabled Muselier instructing him to send as many Free French ships as he could to Pointe-Noire, in French Equatorial Africa, where he proposed to establish a naval base. Muselier's reply, on the 12th, listing technical reasons why de Gaulle's order could not be complied with, seems to have infuriated the general who, in the meantime, must have received complaints against the admiral. And on 20 October, he sent a new and peremptory telegram, of which these are typical extracts:

> Your present attitude does not give me any satisfaction. For a month after my departure, you gave proper service. This is no longer the case. I instruct you to deal only with military questions. I invite you not to make sudden staff appointments that cause disorder and discontent. . . . I will not allow you to promote officers; I reserve such promotions entirely to myself.

In his reply, Muselier said he had to appeal to his own patriotism to keep the debate on a higher plane. "You will learn soon enough about the intrigues that have been conducted in your absence, and in which the navy has avoided taking part," he added rather primly.

De Gaulle, then, did not trust Muselier sufficiently to leave him in full charge in his absence; the "triumvirate" did not work (in this respect, Muselier, who made sure that it did not, was right); and de Gaulle sided with his junior civilian assistants in their quarrel with the admiral.

At this stage in the little drama, a major actor, a minor one and several supporting characters enter the scene. The major actor was a man called Meffre, whose *nom de guerre* was Howard. Towards the end of September 1940 Passy, worried by the growing influx of French volunteers – many of whom might easily be planted Vichy spies – had successfully proposed to Admiral Muselier that a security service should be set up.

---

[12] Passy, Vol. I, pp. 102–6.   [13] Muselier, pp. 96 n. and 102.

For obvious reasons, this could only be done with the help of the British. Passy set to work. The first need was a reliable man who could run the security service under Passy's supervision. On paper, the man was Meffre, who had been introduced to Passy by a member of the Spears liaison mission, with a warm recommendation. Little, however, seemed to be known about Captain Meffre, except that he had left France at the height of the *débâcle*, in company with Lord Suffolk – at that time a high official in the Ministry of Supply. (Suffolk, who wore two huge revolvers attached to his braces at chest level, used to defuse time bombs as a hobby – until one of them blew him up.[14]) His lordship's recommendation was without reserve, and Passy proposed to Muselier that the job should be given to Captain Meffre. At that time, says Passy, Muselier made no objections to this appointment. Both were aware that Meffre would probably act as a British informer, but they did not see how this could be avoided, nor did they think it mattered. At all events, Meffre moved into Carlton Gardens, under his new name of Howard, and in the company of the minor "actor", a "faceless" young man named Colin, and a pretty young British secretary.

To complicate matters, the admiral had set up a naval security service of his own, under a certain Legrain. Both Legrain and Howard were soon to prove, however, that their concept of a security service was the purveying of low-level tittle-tattle. Muselier lost his temper on learning that Howard had several times visited Antoine. Moreover, Howard disliked Labarthe and Muselier, who already considered Howard a dangerous competitor to his own Legrain, and tried to persuade Passy to get rid of him. Passy himself was soon exasperated by Howard, but refused to sack him on Muselier's demand.

Some weeks after his return from Africa, General de Gaulle spent New Year's day 1941 with his wife and children, who had moved into a cottage in Shropshire. That evening, Anthony Eden, who had lately replaced Lord Halifax as foreign secretary, sent word to the general to return urgently to London. Next morning, Eden greeted him with every sign of extreme agitation.[15] "A lamentable thing had happened," said the foreign secretary. "We have just had proof that Admiral Muselier is secretly in contact with Vichy, that he tried to transmit to Darlan the plan for the Dakar expedition at the time when it was being prepared and that he intends to hand over the *Surcouf*. As soon as the Prime Minister was informed, he ordered the admiral's arrest. The order was immediately approved by the cabinet. Muselier is therefore incarcerated. We are aware of the impression this horrible story is going to make on

[14] Passy, Vol. I, pp. 90–1.   [15] De Gaulle, *L'Appel*, pp. 124 *et seq.*

your side and on ours. But it was impossible for us not to act without delay."

The "proof", which Eden immediately produced, consisted of type-written notes stamped with the seal of the French Consulate in London and containing reports on information said to have been furnished by Admiral Muselier to General Rozoy, the former head of the French Air Mission who had lately been repatriated. At that time, the consulate was still controlled by a Vichy official. They had been intercepted, said Eden, by the British intelligence service, and after a careful enquiry, the British authorities were convinced they were authentic.

Taken aback, de Gaulle immediately felt that there must have been a ghastly mistake, and said so to Eden. He wished to place on record his own reservations on this extraordinary story. He did not, however, insist upon the immediate release of the admiral – a fact which Muselier was understandably to hold against him. Instead, he allowed himself forty-eight hours of enquiry and reflection; at the end of which he returned to Eden's office and declared: "The documents are highly suspect, both by their context and by their supposed source. In any case, they do not constitute proof. Nothing justifies the outrageous arrest of a French vice-admiral. Moreover, he has not been heard. I myself have not had a chance to see him. All that is unjustifiable. For the moment, and for a start Admiral Muselier must come out of prison and be honourably treated until this obscure story is cleared up."

Though puzzled, Eden declined to give the general satisfaction, on the grounds that the British enquiry had indeed been thorough. Having belatedly decided that Muselier must be released, de Gaulle sent a letter and a memorandum to confirm his protests. He intervened with Admiral Sir Dudley Pound, the first sea lord, and went to see Muselier at Scotland Yard. At the general's insistence, Muselier was brought from his cell into an office, where de Gaulle was able to see him without witnesses and to assure him that he rejected the charges against him. Finally, having got wind of the appointment of Howard and Colin – "on the insistence of the English" – he summoned the two men (whom he does not name in his memoirs) and, on seeing their confusion, decided that the whole thing had been cooked up by the British intelligence service.

On 8 January, he summoned General Spears and declared that he gave the British government twenty-four hours to free the admiral and make amends; failing that, all relations would be broken between Free France and Great Britain, whatever the consequences. Later that day, a crestfallen Spears came back to tell him that there had indeed been a mistake, that the "documents" were forgeries, the culprits had confessed and Muselier was being released. Next afternoon, at 10 Downing Street, Churchill and Eden expressed their deep apologies and promised to repair the insult to Muselier. Essentially, this was de Gaulle's account of this strange incident. For further details, one must turn to Passy and Muselier himself. As Passy pointed out at the time, the accusations were absurd in the first place. However unbearable Muselier was, there could be no doubt about his patriotism. Nor did Vichy need Muselier to learn about the Dakar operation, which had been the subject of careless talk wherever Free Frenchmen gathered. Again, if Muselier had been an agent of General Rozoy, the latter would hardly have left incriminating papers in his office.

Soustelle, in his account – a hostile one for Muselier – gives General de Gaulle the entire credit for having demonstrated that the "documents" were forgeries.[16] In his meeting with Sir Edward Spears, on 7 January 1941, de Gaulle had handed over his "observations on the documents that brought about the arrest of Vice-Admiral Muselier". With pitiless logic (says Soustelle) he pointed out the absurdity of supposing that General Rozoy would himself sign letters on official paper and mention Muselier by name. Moreover, one of the letters was dated 5 August, but must have been written later, since the Dakar plan had not been elaborated at that time.

Who was to blame for the "Muselier affair"? It must be assumed that neither Howard nor Colin would have taken it upon himself to try to prove charges against Muselier. They must therefore have been acting on somebody else's behalf. De Gaulle himself, and his supporters (especially Soustelle), assumed that the blame rested with the British intelligence service, since it was on their recommendation that Howard and Colin had been appointed. But in this, as in other cases of the kind, the question must be asked: Who was likely to benefit from Muselier's arrest and disgrace? Since Churchill had decided to give General de Gaulle his unqualified support, the attempt to discredit Muselier – which was bound to damage the Free French movement as a whole – clearly went against official policy.

It may be objected, of course, that secret services sometimes act against official policy for long-term reasons of their own. The only conceivable reason, in this instance, would have been a desire to please the Vichy regime, and thus facilitate an eventual reconciliation. But the grim winter of 1940–1 was hardly the time for a sinister operation of this kind. Indeed, the presumptive beneficiaries of the whole affair could only be the Vichy regime and its German masters. Howard and Colin

16 Soustelle, Vol. I, pp. 44–5.

could only have been Vichy agents planted on the British intelligence service. It was not the British intelligence service that "insisted" on foisting Howard and Colin upon the Free French; as Passy recalls, it was he himself who asked the British to recommend a man to head his proposed security service. True, the British recommended Howard, and the least that can be said of this recommendation was that it was an unfortunate error of judgment.

At all events, when de Gaulle had disowned Howard and Colin, and dismissed them from the Free French forces, the British tried both men. Colin was jailed for one year for forgery, and Howard deported to the Isle of Man for the duration of the war.

General de Gaulle's own part in this unsalubrious episode remains questionable. One cannot lightly dismiss Muselier's complaint that the general did not immediately seek his release, nor his account of certain details left unmentioned in de Gaulle's account and in the version presented by his followers. For instance, Muselier alleges that de Gaulle received Howard on 27 December 1940 and learned that grave charges were pending against Muselier. Without telling the admiral, de Gaulle is said to have let events take their course and – in the knowledge that Muselier was in grave trouble – left London on 31 December for a forty-eight-hour stay in the country. Moreover, if Muselier is to be believed, Captain Moret, his chief of staff, had gone to see de Gaulle on 2 January and been greeted by the general with a contemptuous exclamation, "Well, well, I hear some fine things about your Admiral!" Recalled next day, Moret found the general considerably sweeter in temper and now convinced that the letters were forgeries. Moret (says Muselier) replied, "You have taken fifteen hours to convince yourself. That was on the long side!"[17]

Understandably, Muselier was also outraged that no officers of the Free French naval forces were called upon to give evidence at the trial of Howard and Colin. He was also resentful of the fact that General de Gaulle had washed his hands of the two men, handing them over to British justice. At that time, however, de Gaulle had not yet reached agreement with the British about the establishment of special tribunals to try Free Frenchmen under his orders. There was therefore a certain logic about his exclamation to Churchill: "I shall hand over your agents so that you may punish them yourself."[18] Was the general secretly pleased that Muselier was in trouble? Did he, however, change his mind on studying the "evidence" produced by Eden and finding it consisted of clumsy forgeries? Certainly this would be consistent with Muselier's evidence – as distinct from his theories.

[17] Muselier, pp. 146–7.   [18] Passy, Vol. I, p. 132 n.

Muselier himself, though ill with a pleurisy contracted in the first of his prison cells, was mollified by an apologetic letter from Eden, a luncheon at 10 Downing Street and an audience with the king. And the British, anxious to make amends to the Free French as a whole, were temporarily disposed to concede most of General de Gaulle's requests. On the surface, then, all was well that ended well.[19]

[19] The whole episode, however, was a further blow to the morale of the Free French navy, which had already been affected by the attack on the French fleet at Mers-el-Kébir and the Dakar fiasco, as well as by rumours of continuing dissension among the Gaullists. Muselier's colleagues in the Royal Navy remained loyal to him and were indignant at the injustice he had suffered. They, too, had been affected by the unfavourable rumours that accompanied him on his arrival in England at the end of June 1940. But those who knew him best came to like and admire him. One of them, in a memorandum to Admiral Sir Gerald Dickens at the time of his release, wrote: "I learnt that I was wrong. He has a strong character and a heart of gold. His methods are sometimes not identical with ours, but that is a feature rather of his countrymen than of himself. He is extremely sympathetic towards the Admiralty and the Royal Navy. . . . His courage is outstanding and he would prefer to be leading some daring exploit against the enemy, than sitting in an office." Shortly afterwards, a "MOST SECRET AND PERSONAL" report from the same source complained that the Admiralty was being denied access to a Scotland Yard report on the case to the attorney-general. The naval report pleaded in favour of Muselier's being invited to meet the Prime Minister; which, of course, was soon to happen. The Lacy Papers (henceforth, Lacy).

Chapter 5 ✤ De Gaulle versus his Allies: 1

The war continued to spread. On 27 September 1940, the Germans, Italians and Japanese, meeting in Berlin, concluded a ten-year military and economic alliance. The Axis had become a triangle. With this new security, both the Italians and the Japanese went into action. On 4 October, Hitler and Mussolini conferred at the Brenner Pass. Four days later, German troops entered Rumania to "protect" the oil fields. A further Hitler-Mussolini meeting took place in Florence on the 28th; and that day the Italians invaded Greece from Albania.

In the Far East, the Japanese had poured into the breach caused by the fall of France. The governor-general of French Indo-China, General Catroux, had been replaced by Vichy's man, Admiral Decoux, and Japan was given the use of three airfields and several harbours. On 26

September, the Japanese forces began to occupy the peninsula and crossed into China 120 miles from Hanoi. Now, in January 1941, the Siamese, egged on by Japan, crossed the Mekong in Laos and Cambodia, to reclaim territory they had ceded to the French half a century earlier. In May, under a treaty signed in Tokyo, the Vichy authorities gave the Siamese what they wanted: Laotian territories on the right bank of the Mekong and two Cambodian provinces.

To de Gaulle, in London, these events merely confirmed the degradation which the Vichy government had inflicted upon France. But this fact, though self-evident, had no effect whatever, at this stage, on Marshal Pétain's standing with the French people. As de Gaulle himself noted, the marshal was still very popular.[1] De Gaulle sought to explain this unwelcome popularity with the theory that the great majority of the French were convinced that Pétain was dissembling, and that he was in secret agreement with de Gaulle. But this was almost certainly wishful thinking: the French had shown they had no desire to fight.

Occasional straws of comfort were, however, blown in de Gaulle's direction. On armistice day 1940, for instance, Parisian students had gathered in procession before the Arc de Triomphe bearing two fishing-rods symbolising their attachment to de Gaulle – the two fishing-rods being, in French, *deux gaules*. And on 1 January, as the general had requested them by radio, a large part of the population, especially in the occupied zone, had left all public places empty, staying at home for a symbolic "hour of hope".

The harsh reality, however, was the emergence of Vichy's new *Etat français*, dedicated to collaboration with the German occupying authorities. Although Laval had not been a member of the government that signed the armistice, he joined it the following day. At the village of Montoire in October 1940, Laval had a personal meeting with Hitler, at which he convinced the Fuehrer of the advantages to Germany of a collaborating France. A few days later, Laval arranged for Pétain to meet Hitler, with the aim of endorsing his new policy.

The next step was to be a meeting between Laval and the German foreign minister, von Ribbentrop, in the hope of securing the release of most of the French prisoners-of-war in Germany, and the reduction by half of German occupation charges.[2] But Laval was overplaying his hand. The Vichyists, though relieved to be out of the fight, drew the line at a declaration of war on Britain, which they saw as Laval's secret aim. Those who thought this gained the marshal's ear, and in December Pétain abruptly dismissed Laval, who was placed under house arrest;

[1] De Gaulle, *L'Appel*, p. 132. [2] Wright, pp. 514–15.

though not for long. Briefly, Pierre-Etienne Flandin, who had partnered Laval in the appeasement of Italy some years earlier, stepped into his shoes. Laval went to Paris, where he established close relations with the Germans; and Admiral Darlan replaced Flandin as head of a government determined to help Hitler's war effort by all means short of war.

In the face of Vichy's challenge, General de Gaulle pushed on with the creation of the State of Free France.[3] In January 1941 the Free French began to issue their own *Journal Officiel*. The first issue recorded the text of the Churchill-de Gaulle agreement, the manifesto of 27 October 1940 and the Brazzaville declaration of 16 November. The second, dated 10 February 1941, published the texts of various decrees relating to the organisation of discipline within the Free French forces, of which the first gave General de Gaulle, and him alone, the right of pardon. Under complementary decrees, permanent Free French military and naval tribunals, together with courts of appeal, were set up in London. March brought the organisation of a justice department of Free France.

Already, in the scattered territories of this State-in-exile, de Gaulle was the uncrowned monarch. He could defend, prosecute and judge his "subjects". And equally he could reward them, through the Order of Liberation, created at the end of January 1941, whose green and black ribbon symbolised "the mourning and hope of the motherland". While in France itself, Pétain and Darlan were setting up their authoritarian State in which the new slogan was "Work, Family, Fatherland" (sweeping away the familiar Republican banner of "Liberty, Equality, Fraternity"), de Gaulle in London was setting up what, in all but name, was the first government of the Free French State, which consisted of commissioners appointed by decree and responsible to de Gaulle as president of the committee. It had taken de Gaulle, in fact, just over a year to transform his initially meagre following into a power base, with himself as an already potent contender for the political succession in a liberated France.[4]

[3] No such State was ever proclaimed; I use the term, as other writers have used it, to express a reality. Cf. Michel, *France Libre*, especially chapter 1.
[4] The texts of the relevant decrees will be found in the *Journal Officiel de la France Libre* (published at 4 Carlton Gardens, London), Nos 1 (20 January 1941), 2 (10 February 1941), 3 (25 February 1941), 4 (25 March 1941), 9 (26 August 1941) and 11 (14 October 1941). The first commissioners (i.e. ministers) of the National Committee were:
Economy, Finance and Colonies: M. Pleven
Foreign Affairs: M. Dejean
War: General Legentilhomme
Navy and Merchant Navy: Vice-Admiral Muselier
Justice and Education: Professor Cassin
Interior, Labour and Information: M. Diethelm
Air: General Valin
Without Portfolio: Captain Thierry d'Argenlieu
n addition, Pleven was charged with coordinating several administrative departments.

Clearly, de Gaulle could not have got far with his Free French arrangements without the tacit approval of the British government; and he was greatly helped in the early stages of his administrative expansion by the atmosphere of penitent amiability that prevailed on the British side after the Muselier fiasco.

One of the outstanding problems was the need for a machinery of payments, to enable the distant parts of the Free French empire, from Africa to Oceania, to receive supplies and pay for them. Lacking banking facilities of his own, and aware of the problems that would inevitably arise if local authorities in remote territories were to make their own arrangements, de Gaulle realised that in this as in most things he was dependent upon the British. It was therefore agreed, on 19 March 1941, after difficult negotiations, that all payments would be settled in London between de Gaulle and the British government. The exchange rate was fixed at 176 francs to the pound – the rate prevailing when France fell. Later, a "Central Coffer of Free France" was instituted in London. In effect, this became the central bank of issue of the Free French State. Three aims were thus accomplished: the rise of local financial "satrapies" was avoided, financial unity over a vast but scattered area was estab-lished, and the independence of Free France, vis-à-vis the British, was safeguarded.[5]

The financial agreement of 19 March was, in fact, concluded in General de Gaulle's absence, the negotiators on the Free French side being Cassin, Pleven and Denis. For a few days earlier, on 14 March, de Gaulle had left London on a journey to Africa and the Middle East. Before leaving, he spent the weekend at Chequers as Winston Churchill's guest. On 9 March at dawn, Churchill woke him up. "Literally dancing with joy", he announced that the American Congress had voted the Lend-Lease Bill. Seeing that this good news – both for Britain and for Free France – had put the general in good humour, Churchill revealed that he had decided to ask General Spears to accompany him on his trip to Cairo. He knew, he said, that de Gaulle had grievances against Spears, but he asked de Gaulle to accept, as a personal service to him. In the circumstances, the general could scarcely refuse.

The purposes of his journey were, as always, both military and political; and to understand them, they must be placed in the context of Free French military actions and of international rivalries and machinations affecting the future of French territories. If de Gaulle's movement was

[5] The main source for this and ensuing passages is de Gaulle, *L'Appel*, pp. 127, 375 and 947 (in that order).

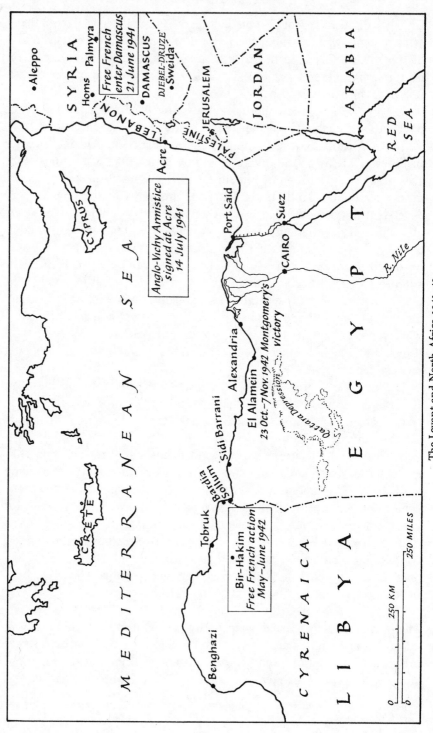

The Levant and North Africa 1941–42

to be taken seriously and carry weight in allied counsels, it was necessary for the Free French forces to fight and distinguish themselves; and equally that their numbers should grow. But they could grow only if more Frenchmen joined them, bearing arms. And the glittering prizes that pulled de Gaulle eastward were the Vichy garrisons in French Somaliland and the Levant – 10,000 and 45,000 strong, respectively. These were his latent reservoirs of manpower.

Already, there were indeed some successes to show, in Eritrea, Ethiopia and the Sahara – but they were inevitably on a small scale. In Eritrea and Ethiopia, the Free French had been in action since December 1940. A battalion of colonial infantry, which had come from Cyprus, fought at Sidi Barrani during the British push towards the Italian positions at Tobruk. Before leaving London, the general had decided to make a final appeal to General Weygand in Algiers. His letter, dated 24 February 1941, was obviously sent more for the historical record than in any spirit of expectation. There was, of course, no answer.

As de Gaulle put it: "Towards the complicated east, I flew with simple ideas." For him, it was sufficient that important events were about to take place, and that France should take part in them. The key to the Middle East on one side and the Mediterranean on the other – and therefore of Africa – was the Suez Canal, and de Gaulle's first objectives were the garrison of French Somaliland and the equally idle naval force at Alexandria. He landed at Khartoum, the operational base for the campaigns of the Sudan and Eritrea. Shortly afterwards, the new Free French brigade, fighting with an Indian division, and commanded by Colonel Monclar, helped to defeat the Italians at Keren. Almost immediately afterwards, however, the Free French force – now called the First Free French Division – was sent to Egypt.

Politically, alas, de Gaulle made virtually no headway. French Somaliland, under a ruthless Vichy governor, Noailhetas, had decreed the death penalty for servicemen combative enough to attempt to join the Free French movement. De Gaulle had instructed General Legentilhomme to make contact with volunteers; but few were so foolhardy as to disobey the governor's orders. The British were blockading French Somaliland, and de Gaulle hoped that this alone would force the Vichy authorities to give in. But in this he was disillusioned: General Catroux, his man in Cairo, warned him that the British, far from maintaining the blockade, were making their own contacts with the Vichy authorities, proposing that the blockade should be lifted and the Vichy administration recognised, in return for the use of the port of Djibouti and of the Djibouti–Addis Ababa railway. When de Gaulle protested, Churchill telegraphed General Wavell, the British commander-in-chief in Egypt, to restore the blockade and support the Free French,[6] but neither instruction was carried out – at least not to de Gaulle's satisfaction.

In his memoirs, de Gaulle attributes the British attitude to post-war imperial ambitions. There is no real evidence, however, that Churchill, at that time obsessed by the need to attack his German and Italian enemies, was thinking on such lines. The explanation offered by Churchill himself is more convincing. General Wavell feared that a strict blockade of Djibouti would merely stiffen its resistance. At home, added Churchill, they took a different view, and Churchill's telegram to Wavell reminded him of His Majesty's government's solemn engagements to General de Gaulle.

But Wavell had other things to think about, and on 15 May 1941, Catroux wrote to him in these terms: "Either Free France will grow with the support of her English friends and the Djibouti affair provides an occasion to make her grow without risk; or else she will not grow because of a too frequent British obstruction. In the latter event, she will die."[7]

In the meantime, General de Gaulle had gone to Brazzaville. The most successful of his commanders, Colonel Leclerc, was becoming legendary. Though combative and a born leader, Leclerc was handicapped by feeble equipment. The Tchad Regiment was being mechanised when war broke out, but the process had not gone far, and only eighty lorries were at his disposal. In January 1941 he sent a diversionary column towards Mourzouk, but the real objective was the oasis of Koufra, more than a thousand miles from Fort Lamy, most of it roadless. By judicious requisitioning, Leclerc brought his vehicles to about 100 in number. In them were a few hundred men, with a single 75 cannon, smaller 37 guns, and a few machine-guns in indifferent working order. Leclerc forced the Italian garrison of Koufra to surrender on 1 March. It was only after their capitulation that the Italians found out how small was the force that had defeated them.

On 4 April, General de Gaulle – back in Cairo – read with pleasure a telegram from Winston Churchill congratulating him on the Free French contribution to recent victories in Africa. A week later, de Gaulle wrote to General Wavell, formally offering the services of the Free French First Division, under General Legentilhomme, for use in the Cyrenaica-Egypt theatre. He wanted, however, to make it clear that he considered it essential that the division should remain whole and under the orders of its commander. And he reminded Wavell how important

[6] Churchill, Vol. III, pp. 77–8.　　　　　[7] Gorce, p. 189.

he thought it was to persuade the garrison at Djibouti to change sides, requesting Wavell to ensure that the blockade should be total, and to give every facility to the Free French in such matters as contacts with Djibouti, the dropping of leaflets and other forms of propaganda.[8]

But despite their successes, the Free French still counted for little in Allied calculations. Frustratingly, the warships of the French navy, anchored in Alexandria harbour, symbolised the impotence of defeat. De Gaulle saw them, "with anguish", one day in April 1941, when crossing the bay to visit Admiral Cunningham; and noted the contrast between the somnolent French and the fighting briskness of the British.

There was, indeed, little that de Gaulle could do in Cairo, and he soon decided to return to the main centre of Free French power overseas, in West and Equatorial Africa. From Brazzaville he cabled Churchill with an account of the situation as he saw it, and returned to the charge about the capital importance of Djibouti. As he moved round his vast African territories de Gaulle's thoughts increasingly dwelt on the Levant. The problem was complex, for it involved no fewer than five distinct sets of interests: those of the Germans, the Vichy French, the Free French, the British and the Arabs. To these should perhaps be added the Americans, for although the United States was not yet at war, American dealings with Vichy played a not unimportant part of the events of this period.

The Germans, however, held the initiative, and the German forces still seemed invincible. Wavell's successes against the Italians were spectacular but short-lived, and the Germans could take the credit for a dramatic change of fortune. By mid-February, Wavell had smashed the Italian army in Libya; but on 3 April, General Rommel, who had arrived in North Africa, struck against the imperial outposts. On 20 April the Germans laid siege on Tobruk. Earlier – on 6 April – Hitler, having flattened Belgrade with bombs, sent his forces into Yugoslavia and Greece. Strained though they were, the British had no option but to intervene in force. Meanwhile, Hitler's agents had been busy in Iraq, where, on 2 May, Rashid Ali – stiffened by German gold and promises – proclaimed a pro-Axis government and invited German aid.

These circumstances involved Vichy France and Free France in their rival ways. In Vichy, Admiral Darlan was now the foreign minister. Though not initially pro-German,[9] Darlan was undoubtedly anti-British – and bitterly so since Mers-el-Kébir. He was moreover convinced (as

[8] De Gaulle, L'Appel, pp. 385–6; see also pp. 150 and 389–90.
[9] Tournoux, Pétain, p. 255.

Pétain no longer was) that the Germans were bound to win the war; and he cherished the fancy that the French, with their superior cleverness, were bound to emerge as the leading nation in Hitler's New Order.[10] This impelled him to seek to collaborate in ways that went beyond the provisions of the armistice and which the marshal considered dishonourable. During the early spring of 1941, however, the Germans seemed quite uninterested in Darlan's overtures, if collaboration meant giving Vichy France something to look forward to. But the Rashid Ali affair provoked a sudden change. On 3 May Hitler's representative in Paris, Otto Abetz, summoned Darlan to Paris, to tell him that in return for military facilities in Syria, the Vichy regime could expect certain concessions from the Germans, and he himself would be granted an audience with the Fuehrer. Three days later, Admiral Darlan and General Vogl, for the Germans, concluded an agreement. The French government was to provide Rashid Ali's forces with armaments and landing rights. In return, the Germans promised freer trade across the occupation line, the rearmament of six French destroyers and seven torpedo-boats, a cut in occupation charges from 400 to 300 million francs a day, and the liberation of 83,000 prisoners of war.

Three days later, the first German planes arrived at Aleppo. On 11 and 12 May, Darlan conferred with Hitler and his foreign minister, Ribbentrop, at Berchtesgaden. Back at Vichy, Darlan advocated collaboration. And on 27 May, after exchanges of some vehemence, Darlan concluded three military protocols with the German General Warlimont.[11] In distant Brazzaville, General de Gaulle was suffering all the frustrations inherent in his inadequate power base. His relations with the British were going through a painful phase. In February, before his departure from London, the British Admiralty had ignored his warnings and allowed the liner *Providence* to sail from Beirut to Marseille, repatriating Frenchmen from the Levant whom the Vichy authorities had declared to be "Gaullists", without giving the Free French representatives in the Middle East a chance to talk to them and persuade them to join the Free French forces.[12] Then there were the differences over French Somaliland. And now, there was total disagreement about Syria. From Cairo on 9 May, General Spears cabled de Gaulle to say that no further need for the Free French forces in the area semed likely to arise for the time being, and to add that although General Wavell was always

[10] Rob. Aron, *Vichy*, p. 424; for ensuing matter, *see also* pp. 427 *et seq.*
[11] The Paris protocols, which were to be matched by political concessions, were in fact never ratified, for Darlan, in the face of opposition from Marshal Weygand, hesitated to go still further along the road to collaboration.
[12] De Gaulle, *L'Appel*, pp. 153 and 371; *see also* pp. 154 and 396–7.

personally happy to see him, he saw no need for de Gaulle to come to Cairo either then or in the near future.

Coldly furious, de Gaulle cabled back the following day to say that he had no intention of returning to Cairo in view of the unilateral decisions affecting Syria and Djibouti. He might of course decide later to inspect the French troops in the Near East, but in that event he would see them alone; apart from that, he had no intention of going back to London. He found it particularly regrettable that the concentration of the Legentilhomme division had been delayed, since this would prevent any action by the Free French in Syria, should the Germans land there as now seemed probable. Referring to the Vichy High Commissioner and commander-in-chief, General Dentz, de Gaulle added that it was a pure illusion to imagine that he would give orders to resist the Germans. In any event, de Gaulle thought that current developments in the East would enhance the strategic importance of the Free French forces in Africa, especially in Tchad, and he had therefore decided to concentrate his effort and the means at his disposal on the defence of these territories. If, however, General Wavell needed French troops in the near future, he would gladly place General Legentilhomme's forces at Wavell's disposition.

On the 13th he telegraphed General Catroux to come to Brazzaville to see him. He was to tell the British in Cairo of this decision. Meantime, he was appointing Gaston Palewski as his political representative in the Near East, and General Legentilhomme as superior commander. A week later, on the 18th, having learned of Darlan's visit to Berchtesgaden, de Gaulle broadcast his wrath and indignation at the "infamous deal concluded between the enemy and his collaborators".

In his memoirs, de Gaulle attributes the British attitude to pressure from President Roosevelt who, he argues, was impressed by the messages reaching him from Admiral Leahy, the American ambassador in Vichy, who had shown himself obligingly susceptible to the blandishments of Pétain and Darlan.[13] But this argument ignores the fact that there was at this time a strong, and obviously sincere, difference of opinion between Churchill and Wavell about the conduct of military and political operations in the Near East.

It was a difficult time for the British. From bases in the Dodecanese, the Luftwaffe was attacking the Suez Canal, and it was within its power to land airborne troops in Syria. Should this happen, Egypt, the canal zone and the oil refineries at Abadan would be directly threatened.[14] Meanwhile, Greece had been evacuated, Crete needed to be defended,

---

[13] ibid. p. 153.   [14] Churchill, Vol. III, pp. 287 et seq.

Malta needed support and Iraq called for troops. Churchill, in London, saw all this very clearly. He sympathised with General de Gaulle's call for prompt military action in Syria by the Free French forces. But the disastrous experience of Dakar was too recent to be forgotten, and London agreed with Wavell that it was inadvisable to use the Free French alone.

Weighing up all these factors, Churchill telegraphed to General Wavell on 9 May to say that in view of Darlan's deal with the Germans and the lack of available British forces, the only course now open was to give General Catroux the necessary transport and "let him and his Free French do their best at the moment they deem suitable, the RAF acting against German landings". Irked by what he interpreted as a sign of declining confidence in him, Wavell cabled to the chief of the Imperial General Staff to say that if the British leaders were now relying on the advice of the Free French instead of his own, he would like to be relieved of his command.

But Wavell climbed down, with a grumble about the "proved inaccuracy of Free French information about the position in Syria".

De Gaulle was about to get his own way, although in circumstances that fell far short of his highest hopes. With his usual percipience, he had understood that no lasting or valid agreement could be reached over the future of Syria and Lebanon without taking account of Arab nationalism. On 23 April, in a telegram to the Free French delegation in London, he had declared his readiness to recognise the independence and sovereignty of both countries. The British government was to be informed, and asked in return for a public affirmation of its respect for French rights in the Levant.[15] He had followed this up two days later with detailed instructions to General Catroux for military operations in Syria.

It was not, however, till 6 June 1941, on the eve of the Franco-British operations, that Churchill cabled de Gaulle to welcome his decision to promise independence to Syria and the Lebanon.[16] But the Prime Minister refrained from making a formal statement of respect for French rights. Instead, he called for a parallel Franco-British policy towards the Arabs. "You know," he said, "that we have sought no special advantages in the French Empire, and have no intention of exploiting the tragic position of France for our own gain." And he ended with an entreaty to de Gaulle, "in this grave hour not to insist on declaring Catroux High Commissioner for Syria".

In Damascus, General Dentz watched events in an agony of indecision.

[15] De Gaulle, L'Appel, pp. 391–2.   [16] Churchill, Vol. III, p. 294.

His parents had left Alsace to stay French. He was bewildered by Vichy's instructions, explaining the Darlan-Hitler agreements and ordering him to stand firm in Syria (against the British) and in so doing, avert a probable occupation of North Africa by the Germans. In the end, as de Gaulle had foreseen, Dentz, though unhappy, decided to obey Marshal Pétain. His earlier hope that the local French would turn against the Germans when they started landing in Syria on their way to Iraq remained unfulfilled.[17]

Churchill's message to de Gaulle merely confirmed what he already knew from Catroux – that his own display of firmness had caused the British to counter General Wavell's veto on the use of Free French forces. On the 15th a delighted de Gaulle sent Churchill a telegram that was notable both for its brevity and the fact that it was couched in English. It read: "1. Thank you. 2. Catroux remains in Palestine. 3. I shall go to Cairo soon. 4. You will win the war."[18]

On 25 May de Gaulle at last returned to Cairo where he found Wavell resigned to carry out the order to launch a joint expedition. Since the Free French division at that time numbered no more than 6,000 infantry men, with eight cannon and ten tanks, and with a couple of dozen aircraft, unilateral action seemed out of the question in the face of General Dentz's 30,000 men (plus half that number of Syrian and Lebanese forces), adequately armoured and covered in the air. Whatever de Gaulle's inclinations, he could not do without British help.

Morale was high, and de Gaulle sought to improve it further by handing out the first Crosses of Liberation, won by his troops in Eritrea and Libya.

In the event, the joint force was barely adequate. The expedition crossed the border on 8 June 1941, with the allied banners flying, and with orders from Wavell and Catroux to fire only in self-defence. There was a heavy reliance on psychological warfare. For weeks French voices, from a radio base in Palestine, had been calling on their compatriots inside Syria to greet them as friends not enemies. Nor were the Arabs neglected; on de Gaulle's instructions, General Catroux had drafted a proclamation to the local population.[19]

Despite all these precautions, they met fierce resistance from the Vichy garrison. While this bitter news of fratricidal fighting reached him in Cairo, de Gaulle faced new and unwelcome worries. Unwelcome, but not exactly unforeseen: on 5 June, he had handed to the American

[17] Tournoux, *Pétain*, pp. 256–61.
[18] De Gaulle, *L'Appel*, p. 408; *see also* pp. 155 *et seq.*
[19] Gorce, p. 193.

minister a memorandum arguing that Africa would one day be a base for the United States in the forthcoming liberation of Europe, and proposing that the Americans should, without delay, send air forces to Cameroun, Tchad and the Congo. Now, on 9 June (the day after the joint invasion of Syria), two telegrams from Eden informed de Gaulle of Admiral Darlan's deal with the Germans offering military facilities in North Africa; of General Weygand's determined opposition to it within the Vichy cabinet. Two days later, there was a further telegram from Eden that Weygand had persuaded Pétain to limit Vichy's collaboration with Germany to Syria alone, and resist any encroachments on North Africa. Weygand (said Eden) had told Murphy of the U.S. State Department on 8 June that Vichy would resist any attack on North Africa; and that Weygand, for his part, had no intention to attack the Free French colonies.

On the 13th, de Gaulle cabled his representative at Brazzaville, General de Larminat, relaying Eden's information about Darlan, Weygand and Vichy's intentions, and instructing him to prepare to repulse any attacks, especially in Dahomey, Togoland and Niger. He followed this up next day with a telegram from Jerusalem to Pleven, the delegate of Free France in Washington, informing him that Larminat had given the American consul a list of Free French military requirements, and instructing him to pursue the matter with President Roosevelt's administration, and in consultation with the British ambassador, Lord Halifax.[20]

The vague but worrying threat of German action against the major Free French bases in Africa impelled de Gaulle, more than ever, to seek a swift solution of the Syrian problem. But this was to prove even harder than de Gaulle had expected, for the Vichy French and the Germans were not his only opponents in the Near East: the British too – or so he supposed – had aims of their own, which were certainly incompatible with his own conception of France's interests. Britain was a great power still, and France merely a defeated one. From many sources, hints that Britain was deploying a vast but hidden legion of Intelligence servicemen reached de Gaulle. He heard or saw his evidence in the conversations of allied staff officers, in the reported machinations of the British ambassador in Cairo and the High Commissioner's office in Jerusalem, in the confidences of the British Foreign Office to his representative in London, and in the articles – inspired, he was certain, by the British – in the newspapers, in particular the *Palestine Post*.

On his side, it was plain that France's promise of independence for Syria and the Lebanon must be fulfilled, once the war was over. But

20 De Gaulle, *L'Appel*, pp. 416–21.

whatever had to be done would be done by France and France alone; and France would retain her mandate in the Levant. De Gaulle was not, in other words, prepared to delegate either authority or sovereignty to Britain.

Ever suspicious of British intentions, de Gaulle had ignored Churchill's suggestion for a British guarantee of the Free French promise of independence. Likewise, he turned down a proposal by the British ambassador in Cairo, Sir Miles Lampson (later Lord Killearn), that General Catroux's proclamation of independence should be in the name of Britain as well as of Free France. When Sir Miles said that the least he could do would be to mention the British guarantee, de Gaulle countered that France's word did not need a foreign guarantee. Beneath this outward show of touchy pride was a more practical consideration: de Gaulle feared that the British were trying to create the impression that the Syrians and Lebanese would owe their independence to Britain not France; and that they had set themselves up as arbiters between the Free French and the States of the Levant. So he went ahead with General Catroux's proclamation; which, to his annoyance, the British government duplicated in its own name.

Against this background, the resistance his forces met in Syria was humiliating to de Gaulle. If the Vichy soldiers and civil servants had crossed to his side *en masse*, his position and prestige would have been immeasurably strengthened. But this was not the way it worked out. On 18 June 1941, in a doleful celebration of his call to resistance one year earlier, de Gaulle told his assembled followers in Cairo that the resistance of the Vichy forces in Syria carried the diabolical signature of Hitler.[21] But this was mere rhetoric. Next day, in the British Embassy and in the presence of Sir Miles Lampson, Wavell and Catroux, he drafted conditions for a cessation of hostilities in Syria, word having reached Cairo that General Dentz now realised resistance was hopeless. He proposed the following bases for a surrender of the Vichy garrison: all soldiers and civil servants to be honourably treated; the rights and interests of France in the Levant to be respected, under the British guarantee; France to be represented by the Free French authorities. He wished to make it clear that all French personnel, together with their families, should be given the freedom to choose whether to stay or to be repatriated later. And he sought to dispel Vichy rumours of Free French reprisals by stating that he had no intention of bringing to trial any Frenchmen who had fought against him on orders from above.

[21] De Gaulle, *Discours et Messages* (henceforth, De Gaulle, *Discours*), Vol. I. pp. 89–90.

Sir Miles transmitted General de Gaulle's draft faithfully enough to London, but the general was furious to learn that the British foreign secretary had followed up with a cable to Lord Halifax in Washington, in which the proposed arrangements for Syria were set out under the authority of the British government alone. In a telegram to Eden from Cairo on 20 June 1941, de Gaulle expressed his astonishment at this unilateral approach in a matter of direct concern to Free France. He reminded Eden that Vichy's High Commissioner in Beirut had specifically asked the American representative to find out the Free French as well as the British terms for a cease-fire. And yet, he complained, Eden had telegraphed Washington as though his government only were qualified to answer. He considered himself in no way bound by the telegram's arguments and conclusions and would respect only the terms of Sir Miles Lampson's telegram of the 19th, which he had agreed with the British ambassador and military commanders.[22]

After two days for reflection, Eden cabled Sir Miles Lampson expressing his regret that General de Gaulle should have been dissatisfied. He hoped de Gaulle would trust in Britain's good faith.

Disappointingly, three more weeks elapsed before the Vichy authorities accepted the British and Free French terms, which had been presented by the American consul in Beirut on 21 June. Why the delay? De Gaulle finds the explanation in the fact that next day, 22 June, Hitler's armies invaded Russia. The Germans, he surmised, must have put pressure on Vichy to continue their resistance, while in the North African desert Rommel was doing the same. Nevertheless, on 21 June, the Free French forces entered Damascus, and Catroux went there immediately. De Gaulle himself arrived in the Syrian capital on the 23rd. That night the Germans demonstrated their solidarity with the Vichy authority by bombing the city.

But de Gaulle was less worried by the Vichy French or the Germans, at that moment, than by the British. From various places came reports that they were behaving as though Free France did not exist. On 24 June, therefore, de Gaulle formally appointed General Catroux as his delegate-general and plenipotentiary in the Levant, instructing him to negotiate the independence and sovereignty of the States of the Levant and their alliance with France; and to ensure the defence of the territory against the enemy, while cooperating with the Allies in the war operations in the Near East. Meanwhile, Catroux was to assume "all the powers and all the responsibilities of the High Commissioner of France in the Levant". Thus, he added, "a mandate entrusted to France

22 De Gaulle, L'Appel, pp. 162 and 428–9.

in the Levant will be brought to its term and the work of France continued."

On 10 July General Dentz was ready to surrender. He sent his warships and planes to Turkey, where they were interned, and requested a cease-fire. The surrender terms were to be discussed three days later at Acre. But the military crisis was about to yield to a political one, the gravest so far in de Gaulle's stormy relations with his British allies. On 28 June, the general had warned Churchill that England's behaviour towards the Free French in the Near East would be of "extreme importance" to the alliance between the two sides.[23]

But Churchill, who admittedly had other things to think about, does not seem to have heeded this warning. Towards the end of June 1941, following Rommel's successes in the western desert, he had decided to relieve General Wavell of his command and send him to India as commander-in-chief, where he would succeed General Auchinleck. The latter was to replace Wavell in the Middle East. At the same time, Churchill decided to appoint Captain Oliver Lyttelton as minister of State in that area. At the time of the Acre negotiations, Lyttelton had arrived in Cairo, but Auchinleck had not. De Gaulle thought these circumstances particularly unfavourable from the Free French standpoint. Despite his earlier disagreements with Wavell, he was convinced of his fairness and loyalty. His departure left a gap, which the arrival of Lyttelton, fresh from London, did not quite fill. De Gaulle sensed that the British Intelligence Service would take advantage of this *de facto* vacuum to plot against him. And events seemed to confirm his worst apprehensions. General Catroux was present at the British negotiations with the Vichy French, but was virtually ignored. In the end, the armistice was signed by General Maitland-Wilson (later Field-Marshal Sir Henry Maitland-Wilson) on the British side and General de Verdilhac for Vichy.

De Gaulle was in Brazzaville during the negotiations, and the BBC's report of the agreement, which was signed on 14 July (France's National Day) plunged him into fury. As he saw it, the agreement simply meant the transfer of Syria and the Lebanon to the British. There was no mention of the rights of France, or of the States of the Levant. Nor was there any question of a free choice for the French military personnel in the area. Indeed, the Free French were forbidden to make contact with them and try to persuade them to join de Gaulle. Instead, they were

[23] My account of the political crisis that followed the military victory in Syria is based, in the main, on General de Gaulle's memoirs; Churchill himself, though he covers events in some detail up to the armistice, has nothing to say about his relations with Free France after that time. De Gaulle's charges against the British are therefore left unanswered at that level.

to be sent straight to France, and their equipment was to be handed over to the British. As for the Syrian and Lebanese forces, they were simply to be placed under British command. Determined to wreck the agreement if possible, de Gaulle left for Cairo, making sure that at each stopping point his views were made known in no uncertain terms, so that alarming telegrams should precede him. On 21 July, he met Captain Lyttelton for the first time. He found the British minister of State pleasant, thoughtful, lively – and embarrassed. Having just arrived, he had no desire for a row. De Gaulle, on his side, wanted a row, but not a violent one. So, "wrapping myself in ice", he protested in strong but controlled language against the exclusion of the Free French from the arrangements for Damascus and Beirut.

Soothingly, Captain Lyttelton explained that the arrangements had been made with the aim of maintaining law and order and avoiding domestic disturbances. The States of the Levant had to be given the independence which Britain had guaranteed. As for the technical conditions agreed between Generals Wilson and de Verdilhac about the concentration and repatriation of the French troops, these too concerned the maintenance of order. He appealed for General de Gaulle's trust.

Inflexible, the General replied that France, not Britain, was the mandatory power in the Levant. As for public order in Syria and the Lebanon, it was the business of the French not the British.

When Lyttelton countered that the Free French had recognised the authority of the British command, under the agreement of 7 August 1940, de Gaulle declared that this agreement applied only to strategic matters and against the common enemy. It had never been his understanding that such arrangements should extend to French territories. He asked rhetorically whether the British would invoke the August 1940 agreement to govern France herself in the event of a future landing. Moreover, it was essential for the Free French to make contact with the Vichy troops who, otherwise, would later face them in battle in Africa or elsewhere. Finally, the French equipment and control of the local forces must be handed over to Free France.

This, observed Lyttelton, was all very well, but the Armistice was already signed, and had to be observed.

Still coldly in control of himself, de Gaulle declared that he had not ratified the armistice and would not consider himself bound by it. Moreover, as from 24 July, three days hence, the Free French forces in Syria and the Lebanon would cease to be responsible to the British command. He was instructing General Catroux to take over responsibility for the whole territory. Meanwhile the Free French forces would make contact on their own with the French and local personnel.

Handing Lyttelton a note prepared in advance, General de Gaulle took his leave. In any event, he declared, the Free French would continue to fight against the common enemy. But he was ready for any further negotiation with the British.

As usual, when Franco-British relations threatened to get out of hand, General de Gaulle cabled Churchill. The armistice of Acre, he said, was contrary to the military and political interests of France.

Churchill did not reply directly, but as usual, de Gaulle's intransigence paid off. That evening, Captain Lyttelton asked to see him again. Disclaiming any intentions of usurping France's place in the Levant, he declared himself ready to write de Gaulle a letter guaranteeing Britain's complete disinterest in the political and administrative spheres. But this was not enough to satisfy de Gaulle, who pointed out that the Armistice Convention would remain in force, and would give rise to serious incidents between the British, who upheld it, and the French, who did not accept it. Moreover, British plans to extend the authority of the British military command were incompatible with the Free French position. He proposed an immediate agreement between the British minister of State and himself, concerning the "application" of the Armistice Convention, and a firm British undertaking to limit the functions of the British command in Syrian and Lebanese territory to military operations against the common enemy.

"Allow me to think it over," said Lyttelton.

De Gaulle was winning. On 24 July, an "interpretative" agreement on the Armistice Convention was reached. De Gaulle interpreted this supplementary agreement as meaning that the whole question of the destination of the Vichy forces would now be reconsidered, and Captain Lyttelton assured him that this was so.

De Gaulle trusted Lyttelton, but his trust did not extend to General "Jumbo" Wilson and his pro-Arab advisers. How would they behave on the ground? Once again, de Gaulle had recourse to Churchill, whom he abjured by cable not to allow an entire army to be sent back to Vichy.

Next day, on the 25th, Captain Lyttelton wrote to de Gaulle in the name of his government, to recognise the "historic interests" of France in the Levant. On paper, then, de Gaulle's triumph was complete. But he was soon to discover yet again how great the gap can be between a formal agreement and its observance. That day he left for Damascus and Beirut, where once again – as in French Africa – he tasted the delights of popular acclaim. Overnight, the loyal functionaries of the Vichy administration had transferred their allegiance to Free France. De Gaulle certainly needed all the loyalties he could muster, for he found, as he had suspected, that as far as General Wilson and his advisers were concerned, his agreements with Lyttelton might as well never have been concluded. Not only had General Dentz sent his ships and planes to Turkey, but he had been allowed to regroup his forces near Tripoli, where they lived in a little Vichy of their own, under the approving eyes of the British. They were forbidden all contact with the Free French; and, loaded with battle honours conferred by Marshal Pétain's government, their one thought was repatriation. Indeed Admiral Darlan had already let it be known that the warships that would bring them home were gathering at Marseille.

As for respecting French sovereignty, British army officers were giving the orders in many parts of Syria and Lebanon, and British agents were, or General de Gaulle thought they were, subverting the local tribes. The worst case of all, from de Gaulle's point of view, was the situation at Sweida, where the local British Commander, ignoring the presence of a Free French delegate, had set up headquarters in the local Maison de France, pulling down the tricolour flag and hoisting the Union Jack.

This was too much. Without hesitating, de Gaulle instructed General Catroux to send a column to Sweida, regain possession of the Maison de France, and restore authority over the local Druzes who, de Gaulle was persuaded, had been bribed by the British to reject French authority.

Hearing of this, General Wilson, who was in Jerusalem, sent a coldly threatening letter to de Gaulle, dated 30 July 1941 and couched in the third person. The arrival of Free French forces in Djebel-Druze, he said, could well cause disorders that would affect security throughout the country. He must request an immediate halt to Free French troop movements, pending a meeting between General Wilson and General Catroux. Meanwhile, he reminded de Gaulle that under Article 1 of the interpretative agreement between de Gaulle and Lyttelton, the last word rested with General Wilson, unless de Gaulle intervened personally with the British government. A very grave situation could result from a failure to meet his request. As a gesture of goodwill, however, General Wilson agreed to turn over the Maison de France to the French representative.

In the same impersonal style, General de Gaulle, from Beirut, rejected Wilson's request, on the ground that the French battalion had already reached Sweida when Wilson's note had arrived. He declared that his interpretation of Article 1 of the supplementary agreement did not coincide with General Wilson's. In fact, said General de Gaulle (rightly), this article applied only to defensive measures against the common enemy. He noted with satisfaction that the Maison de France was going to be returned to the French, but regretted that General Wilson should have thought it necessary to threaten him with a "grave situation". He remained ready for a frank military cooperation with the British, but only on condition that France's sovereignty in Syria and the dignity of the French army should be beyond all question.

Still on 30 July came another blow to General de Gaulle's jealously guarded sovereignty. Captain Lyttelton wrote directly to General Catroux, merely sending a copy of the letter to de Gaulle, to request him to include General Spears in the proposed treaty negotiations with Syria and Lebanon. Catroux, in agreement with de Gaulle, turned down this request out of hand, and a furious de Gaulle telegraphed his delegation in London with instructions to see Anthony Eden and tell him that the continued ignoring of French rights by the British could result only in a disagreement which could bring major disadvantages to both sides.

Once again, the British side climbed down, at least in appearance. On 7 August, Oliver Lyttelton spent a day with de Gaulle in Beirut. While accepting his apologies, de Gaulle was not going to allow the minister of State to escape so lightly. The Free French, said de Gaulle, were exasperated by the way their allies practised cooperation. "Rather than go on like this," he said, "we prefer to go our own way, while you go yours." It would be wise to meet the contingency of a future renewed Axis threat to the region with a common defence plan, but not through British political encroachments in the French domain.

Seeking a way out with evident relief, Captain Lyttelton proposed a meeting with General Wilson to discuss a common defence plan. But de Gaulle had no desire to meet Wilson, and proposed instead that Wilson and Catroux should confer on this question.

Throughout this prolonged crisis, General de Gaulle alarmed his London representatives by his unbending refusal to compromise and his sublime indifference to the weakness of his own position. In a telegram to him on 25 July, they complained that General de Gaulle was taking decisions in the name of the Defence Council of the French Empire without adequate consultation of its members. They appealed to him not to push his quarrel with the British to the point of an actual breach, in which they saw incalculable risks. In a further telegram on 10 August, they lamented the probable consequences of Darlan's apparent readiness to give the Germans bases in North Africa and Dakar. This, they thought, would create fresh difficulties for Free France. "To be frank," they added, "it seems to us inconceivable that one should be able to speak of a rupture with Great Britain. Militarily and financially, we cannot exist without the support of England. Indeed, a break would mean the end of Free France, that is, of the last hope of saving France."

But de Gaulle, with his rock-like conviction of righteousness, was immovable. Replying on 13 August to the London telegrams of 25 July and 10 August, he rejected the points made, one by one. He knew better than anybody how grave the consequences would be, both nationally and internationally, if there were a break between Free France and Britain. That was why he had faced the British with these consequences, thus saving the situation. British irritation weighed for little in comparison with duties towards France. He was sure the crisis would be salutary for fair relations with Britain, and that Mr Churchill himself would understand. He disagreed with his representatives about the effect of the Vichy's further capitulation to Germany in Africa. The consequence would be to make Free France greater both in the nation itself and abroad, especially from the American point of view. He neither needed nor recognised the British guarantee of independence of Syria and Lebanon. The participation of General Spears in negotiations with Damascus and Beirut was inadmissible. And de Gaulle ended with a rebuke. He invited his representatives to stiffen their resolution and stop giving the impression that his representatives did not follow his policy faithfully. "Our greatness and our strength," he ended, "consist solely of intransigence as far as the rights of France are concerned. We shall need this intransigence up to the Rhine inclusively."

In the end, for all his intransigence and Catroux's talent, the Levant was at best a half-success for de Gaulle, if not quite a total failure. Yielding before his insistence, and his appeals to Churchill and Lyttelton, the British did finally allow him to make contact with the Vichy French soldiers; but this delayed concession came too late to be really effective. Only 127 officers and about 6,000 NCOs and other ranks came over to the Free French forces. True, they were joined by 290 Syrian and Lebanese officers, and 14,000 local troops; but the bulk of the French army of the Levant – 25,000 officers and men – opted for repatriation. Thus, more than a year after his famous appeal from London, de Gaulle found himself snubbed once again by his military compatriots. It was a humiliating reverse that confirmed the widespread view among the British (and even more among the Americans) that de Gaulle and his movement were a tiresome thing of little consequence, while Vichy continued to represent the reality of a defeated nation. There were, however, compensations from General de Gaulle's standpoint. Despite General Wilson's proclamation of martial law, and the irritating presence of General Spears with all the panoply of British power and prestige as minister plenipotentiary with the Syrian and Lebanese governments; despite the intrigues, as he saw them, of Glubb Pasha, of Transjordan; despite all these things, de Gaulle had succeeded in restoring France's mandatory sovereignty in the Levant and in negotiating with the Arab authorities. He had indeed proved to himself, and possibly to his London followers, that in a situation of acute weakness, *intransigence is inescapable.*

At all events, the arrival on the Free French side of some thousands of local and French troops did enable him to create two new brigades and an armoured group. In Cairo, de Gaulle called on the new British commander-in-chief, General Auchinleck, and offered his forces, on condition that they should be used in combat. Rommel, said "the Auk", was certain to give him a chance to use them.

But it was in politics and diplomacy that General de Gaulle saw his opportunities. And it was in London, not in the Middle East, that he could best exploit them. On 1 September he was back in Churchill's capital.

Chapter 6 ⚜ De Gaulle versus his Allies: 2

Back in London, General de Gaulle faced complex problems. Handicapped though he was by his limited achievements in the Near East, he had to restore his good relations with Churchill, while never conceding a point on the substance of his claim. At the same time, he needed to make his mark with President Roosevelt's administration, and to exploit the new opportunities created by Hitler's invasion of the Soviet Union. In domestic affairs – that is, within the Free French movement – he had to ensure that the differences of opinion about his conduct of foreign policy had not dented his authority or weakened the loyalty of his followers. And he knew the time had come when the need of the Free French State, and

165

of his own parallel ambitions, would best be served by the creation of a "government".

Seriously irked by the Franco-British quarrels in the Levant, the Prime Minister wrote to de Gaulle on 2 September 1941 to say that in view of the general's attitude, he did not think a meeting between them would serve any useful purpose. And a week later, in the House of Commons, he declared that though Britain recognised the privileged position of France in Syria and the Lebanon, there was no question of a simple substitution of Free French interests for those of Vichy. For days, the British government declined all contact with the Free French; and de Gaulle retaliated by forbidding his followers to broadcast on the BBC. On the 15th, however, Churchill consented to see de Gaulle.[1] The interview began badly, but ended amicably, with an assurance from the Prime Minister that Britain's policy was to respect the agreements General de Gaulle had concluded in Cairo.

Almost immediately, de Gaulle had a second Muselier affair on his hands (there was to be a third and last). The admiral still nursed the resentment he had felt from the time of his arrival in London at the fact that he was politically and militarily subordinate to General de Gaulle, while outranking him in the hierarchy of the French forces. As far as de Gaulle was concerned, Muselier was just one of the Frenchmen who had joined him in London – not the most important, and not the least troublesome. As a sailor, he had proved his competence and the tiny Free French navy was an efficient force within its limits. When it came to distributing jobs in his proposed National Committee, the obvious one for Muselier was the Department of the Navy. But the admiral had other ideas. De Gaulle thought intrigue held a fatal attraction for him and saw him as an instrument, conscious or otherwise, of the little political cliques who continued in exile the wrangles and accommodations of the regime which de Gaulle held largely responsible for the collapse of France. Another, cast in the same mould, was André Labarthe, whom de Gaulle proposed to appoint as Commissioner for Information – another natural choice, it seemed, since he was editor of France Libre. But Labarthe made common cause with Muselier, and in a joint interview with General de Gaulle both men told him that they declined his suggestions. Instead, said Muselier, he had proposals of his own to make. On 18 September, the admiral sent General de Gaulle a letter proposing the creation of an "Executive Committee" in which he – Admiral Muselier – would be chairman, and responsible for national defence, the Merchant Navy and armaments. Labarthe was to be in charge of

[1] De Gaulle, L'Appel, pp. 200–1.

political action in France and the empire, and of propaganda. As for General de Gaulle, he would become the president of the Free French movement, but with purely ornamental functions.

Expecting a clash, Muselier sought British support. On the 19th, Lord Bessborough gave a lunch for him in a private room at the Savoy. Other guests were one Englishman – Major Morton – and four Frenchmen: Captain Moret (whom Muselier wanted as Free French intelligence chief), Commander Schaeffer, Labarthe and the diplomat Dejean. Muselier explained his proposals, and said he was prepared to allow General Legentilhomme to attend meetings of the Executive Committee as an observer, if de Gaulle thought the army should be represented. He argued that as the British government had been responsible for launching the Free French movement, it could not dissociate itself from such grave developments within the movement. It was essential, he added, that the new committee should be housed away from the contaminating influence of Carlton Gardens.[2]

Apparently in the belief that he could count on British support, Muselier called on de Gaulle, learned that he did indeed insist on the inclusion of Legentilhomme – and Captain d'Argenlieu – in the committee. He learned little else, however, about the general's reactions, and went away under the impression that de Gaulle was giving in. Dejean then drafted a modified proposal, which Muselier revised. It took the form of a draft decree for the general's signature, which the admiral sent him, with a covering letter, on 20 September. This time, the committee was to be styled "Executive Committee of Liberation". The chairman would be de Gaulle, but only in plenary session; and Admiral Muselier, as vice-chairman, would have executive powers and determine when plenary sessions were to be called.[3]

But the confrontation between Muselier and de Gaulle was, by the nature of the contestants, an unequal combat. On the evening of the 21st, the two men met again, Muselier being accompanied by Labarthe. This time, there was nothing conciliatory about de Gaulle. He declared that under his own scheme for an executive committee, he himself would be the executive chairman; nor could he accept Moret as head of intelligence: Passy would carry on in that post.

Next day, Muselier telephoned Dejean to ask for news, and learned that de Gaulle was about to announce his executive committee, which would exclude the admiral, Labarthe and Moret. Furious, Muselier said that if that was how things were the navy would keep out of politics altogether and concentrate on the war, in close liaison with the British.

[2] *Lacy.*   [3] Muselier, pp. 229–31; *see also* p. 239.

As relayed by Dejean to de Gaulle, Muselier's outburst came out as a declaration of the Free French navy's independence of de Gaulle's political control.

Furious in his turn, but better controlled than Muselier, de Gaulle responded on the 23rd with a letter to the admiral, accusing him of "an intolerable abuse" of his command and giving him twenty-four hours to come back into line, failing which he would be "rendered harmless" and publicly stigmatised. He added that he had assured himself of the support of his British allies.

In his memoirs, the indignant Muselier describes this letter (which de Gaulle does not mention) as a form of blackmail and denies that de Gaulle had consulted the British in this matter. In this, however, the admiral was mistaken. At 1 p.m. that day, General de Gaulle had called on Churchill and informed him that he proposed announcing to the press in the afternoon the creation of a National Committee. He would not include Admiral Muselier in it. Indeed, he intended to relieve the admiral of his command on the grounds of his disloyalty through personal ambition. The Prime Minister, however, requested de Gaulle to postpone any final action for at least another twenty-four hours.[4]

Later that day, General de Gaulle called in the press to announce the formation of a National Committee, the membership of which would be published next day. At 11 p.m., Churchill discussed the latest Free French storm with Eden, the First Lord of the Admiralty (Alexander), and Major Morton. It was agreed that the admiral should put his case to de Gaulle in writing, and in such a way that the general would not be able to sustain his charge of disloyalty through personal ambition.

Acting on British advice, Muselier duly wrote, on the 24th, to explain that his remarks to Dejean had been misrepresented; there was no question of disloyalty, and he had merely desired to express a wish to get on with the war and have nothing to do with politics. The general summoned him at 4 p.m. An hour later, he saw the foreign secretary and declared that he had composed his differences with Muselier. But this was not the way the admiral saw it: at a party given by Lord Bessborough he complained that de Gaulle had renewed his accusation of disloyalty and said he could not longer work with him.

Once again, the British intervened. Both de Gaulle and Muselier were summoned to the Foreign Office, and at 11 p.m. the First Lord – whose feelings for Muselier were friendly – suggested that he should give way to de Gaulle in the interests of the general war effort. Reluctantly,

[4] *Lacy.*

Muselier complied.[5] De Gaulle withdrew his charges, and Muselier was duly appointed Commissioner for the Navy and Merchant Navy. Labarthe was out altogether; instead, information was given to Diethelm.

Not long after de Gaulle had disposed of the second Muselier affair, he faced the relatively minor Odic affair. General Odic, of the French air force, first rallied to General de Gaulle, then changed his mind. Aged fifty-four in 1941, he was in North Africa, and increasingly out of harmony with the Vichy authorities. He made his way to Washington, where he wrote a declaration condemning the Vichy government and announcing his decision to offer his services to General de Gaulle. The Gaullist propaganda organisation in Washington gave his statement top publicity. De Gaulle personally cabled his thanks, and on arriving in England on 12 December 1941, Odic was immediately taken to Carlton Gardens, where the Free French leader awaited him. Photographers were present, to record the Free French leader's embrace. "For me," Odic wrote later, "he was the ambassador of silent France."

General de Gaulle's first words came as a shock to him, however, and disillusion soon followed.

"I am making you commander-in-chief of my land, sea and air forces in Africa, at Brazzaville," said de Gaulle.[6]

Not wanting to be made a commander without troops in a fictitious theatre of operations, Odic reminded de Gaulle that he had come to London to help counter the Franco-German military alliance apparently accepted by Vichy.

De Gaulle's answer shook the honest but naïve general to the core: "On the contrary, France must be in the war by Germany's side, in order to prove the guilt of the men of Vichy."

Here was a clash of incompatible attitudes. De Gaulle wanted Germany to be defeated but realised that the Free French contribution to victory was unlikely to be decisive. His real interest was in the position of France after the war. France's interests, as he saw them, could be defended only by an organisation that remained untainted by defeat and collaboration. He had cast the Free French organisation for this role, but it could be satisfactorily fulfilled only if Vichy were totally discredited.

Odic, for his part, saw the question in simple military terms, without political considerations. The one essential thing was to fight the enemy.

[5] De Gaulle's brief account of the crisis (*L'Appel*, pp. 219–21) makes no mention of British arbitration, ascribing Muselier's compliance to his own authority alone.
[6] This account of Odic's relations with General de Gaulle is based on the unpublished typescript of his memoirs, which was made available to me by M. Boris Souvarine, with the consent of the late General Odic's family.

If Vichy resisted the Germans, it should be helped and encouraged. If it collaborated, it should be opposed. If there were guilty men in the regime, they should be brought to justice after the war.

Fighting his distaste for the Free French set-up, which he found shallow and artificial, reeking of show-business and the advertising world, Odic stayed about four months. At his second meeting with de Gaulle, Odic defended Weygand. Icily, de Gaulle countered, "Marshal Pétain is a traitor and I shall have him shot. General Weygand is a traitor and I shall have him shot. I shall do the same with the others."

The final break came during a stormy interview on 3 February 1942.

"It seems incredible to me," said Odic, "that anybody should actually try to cultivate hatred between Frenchmen. The culprits are not numerous, and we demand that they should be punished." And he pleaded for contacts with the French in North Africa.

De Gaulle's reply had a chill finality about it: "If that's the way you think, just go back to North Africa, and I shall make war on you."

Full of indignation, Odic informed the British government that his honour forbade him to associate himself with the Free French organisation, just as it had forbidden him to work with Vichy.[7]

These domestic pinpricks from de Gaulle's turbulent *entourage* were, at the most, temporary diversions. They did not seriously interfere with General de Gaulle's exploitation of the ever-widening international opportunities that were coming his way. Although his dependence on British goodwill was inescapable, he sought to reduce it as far as possible by cultivating other allied friendships. The one that proved most elusive, throughout the war, was that of the Americans. Although he did not know it at the time of his return to London from the Middle East, President Roosevelt had an instinctive antipathy for de Gaulle, both as a personality and for his national pretensions. This sentiment was formed before their first meeting, and personal contact did not diminish it. The president saw in the general an upstart and a potential dictator. Until Pearl Harbor, and indeed for some time after, Roosevelt's French policy consisted of maintaining good relations with Vichy, in the hope of countering the German influence. In Gaullist eyes this amounted to self-defeating appeasement; and it became clearer as time went on that the United States, rich and powerful though it was, was too distant to compete with the Nazis who were occupying France. President Roosevelt's

[7] Tournoux, *Pétain* (p. 259), quotes Odic's views, attributing them to Kenneth Pendar (formerly Robert Murphy's assistant in North Africa): *Le dilemme France-Etats-Unis* (Beauchemin, Montreal). The English title of Pendar's book is *Adventure in Diplomacy: the Emergence of General de Gaulle in North Africa*. See also Muselier, pp. 318–20; Muselier quotes Pendar in another context on p. 337.

ambassador to Vichy, Admiral Leahy, unfortunately showed little discernment in his relations with Marshal Pétain and it never occurred to him to question Pétain's view of de Gaulle as a traitor to his country. Roosevelt was strengthened in his views by the reports from his representative in North Africa, Robert Murphy, and cherished for some time the illusion that Nazi plans could be frustrated through General Weygand, whose anti-German attitude was clear, but who was, in the final analysis, powerless to oppose Pétain. Both in his Vichy policy and in his antipathy towards de Gaulle, Roosevelt was strongly supported by his secretary of State, Cordell Hull, who saw the general as a Fascist and an enemy of the United States.

Against this unpromising background, not all of which was known to him at the time, de Gaulle did nevertheless make considerable headway in 1941. From Brazzaville, on 19 May, he had cabled René Pleven, instructing him to proceed from London to Washington and stay as many weeks as necessary in the United States to carry out six essential tasks: to set up permanent relations with the Department of State; to organise economic and financial relations between Free French Africa and Oceania and the United States; to purchase war material; to create or re-create Free French committees; to set up an information and propaganda organisation; and to make contact with influential private Americans who might be disposed to help Free France.[8] De Gaulle's reference to the need to re-create the Free French committees was a reminder that in the early, "heroic" days of his movement, committees had in fact been set up. But they had tended to die from neglect, and when Pleven arrived in America early in June 1941 he found that little was known about the Free French, and that mostly unfavourable. He did not, however, arrive entirely empty-handed. His assets were France's possessions in the Pacific and Africa, over which the Free French movement exercised *de facto* control; and de Gaulle instructed him to offer the Americans facilities for air bases in Cameroun, Tchad and the Congo, as well as in the Pacific Islands. The bait was the probability that the Americans would eventually need such bases in Africa for action in Europe, since North Africa was under Vichy control; while in the Pacific, the threat of further Japanese action seemed evident. In fact, the American government soon requested the use of facilities both in Africa and in the New Hebrides and New Caledonia. Since the United States, at that time, was still not a belligerent power, the request was in the name of Pan-American Airways, but its ultimate purpose could hardly be doubted.

[8] De Gaulle, *L'Appel*, p. 471; for sources of the ensuing matter, *see also* ibid. pp. 182–4, 477, 485.

Much as he wanted American support and recognition (in a practical not a formal sense), de Gaulle was not prepared to compromise on his claim to represent France as a whole. When Pleven informed him that the State Department had invited him to attend conversations with the British Embassy, "not as a representative but as an expert", de Gaulle called him to order. In a cable from Aleppo on 9 August, he set out a reminder of his unshakable position:

> In a general way, you do understand that we do not ask any alms of the United States, but only means of fighting. I see that, for the moment, the Department of State is offering us medicaments but not arms. We refuse the medicaments without the arms. The illusions of conformism prevail, evidently, in Washington and favour Vichy, that is to say Hitler who created Vichy.
>
> I do not accept that you, representing France, should take part as an expert only in a tripartite conference. You will take part on equal terms with the other participants or you will not take part at all.

That month, the Americans sent a military liaison mission to Tchad, and in September Cordell Hull publicly declared that a community of interests existed between the American government and Free France. Answering a question at a press conference, the secretary of State mentioned that "our relations – in all respects – with this group are of the most cordial". On 1 October, Pleven was received at the State Department by the assistant secretary, Sumner Welles, but recognition was still far off. Indeed, Pleven found Wells "very cold", and still deeply convinced, on the basis of Admiral Leahy's reports, that America's influence and Weygand's goodwill were causing the Vichy government as a whole to resist Darlan's plans for collaboration with the Germans. But at the end of November, Weygand was recalled from Algiers, carrying with him one of Washington's more persistent illusions. On the 11th of that month the benefits of lend-lease had been extended to Free France by President Roosevelt, in a letter to Mr Stettinius, on grounds of national self-interest which de Gaulle could not but approve. "The defence of territories that have rallied to Free France," wrote the president, "is vital for the defence of the United States."

By and large, Pleven had fulfilled the mission entrusted to him by de Gaulle. He was now brought back to London to take over the Departments of Economy, Finance and Colonies in de Gaulle's new National Committee. Before recalling him, de Gaulle had thought it useful to instruct him to enlighten Sumner Welles and Cordell Hull on the character of the Free French administration in London. ". . . General de

Gaulle," said his telegram to Pleven on 22 September 1941, "has always solemnly proclaimed that he would exercise these responsibilities only on an essentially provisional basis, as manager of the French patrimony, and that he submitted himself in advance to national representatives as soon as it would be possible for them to meet freely." To take Pleven's place, as a kind of unrecognised ambassador, de Gaulle appointed the French director of the International Labour Office, Adrien Tixier; while in London regular Free French contacts were taking place with Drexel Biddle, the American ambassador with the foreign governments-in-exile.

In various ways, then, de Gaulle had reason to suppose that the basis of a continuing working relationship with the United States had now been firmly laid. And on 7 December, when the Japanese air force struck with lethal suddenness at the American fleet in Pearl Harbor, he assumed that from that point forward, any remaining American coolness would be dispelled, in the interests of joint action against the common enemy. But in this he was soon to be disillusioned. In the eyes of Roosevelt and Cordell Hull, the Gaullist movement continued to be an illegitimate and potentially dangerous group, with which limited agreements might be negotiated on matters of self-interest, but which was in no way representative and did not have to be consulted when French interests were at stake. On 13 December, the American government requisitioned fourteen French ships, including the passenger liner *Normandie*, that happened to be in American ports, declining absolutely to consult the Free French or listen to their representations. That month, Free France was unrepresented among the twenty-seven governments that signed the new pact of the United Nations.

All this was bad enough from de Gaulle's point of view, but there was worse to come with the serio-comic incident of Saint-Pierre and Miquelon, the two French island dependencies near Newfoundland. Rarely can such an essentially marginal problem have been vested with such inflated importance. For reasons of naval duty and not, this time, of political intrigue, Admiral Muselier was the centre of this storm in a teacup.

These tiny islands had been French since the sixteenth century, and their population – largely of Breton and Norman origin – was thought to be favourable to the Free French movement, but was firmly held under the authority of the Vichy High Commissioner, Admiral Robert. The radio station on the archipelago was a vehicle for pro-German Vichy propaganda, and while the islands remained under Vichy rule, there was always a danger that they might be used by the Germans as a submarine base with which to threaten the allied Atlantic convoys. In these circumstances, de Gaulle thought it sensible to liberate them. But there was no reason to suppose that the operation would be difficult, given the reported feelings of the local population. As it happened, Admiral Muselier was about to go to Canada to inspect the French submarine cruiser *Surcouf*, then anchored in Halifax Harbour, as well as the Free French corvettes that were helping to escort the allied convoys. It would be a simple matter for him to occupy Saint-Pierre and Miquelon from Halifax.

The British were consulted and raised no objections, subject only to Washington's agreement. De Gaulle himself regarded American approval as desirable but not indispensable, since this was, as he saw it, a purely French internal matter. Having learnt in December that the American Admiral Horne had been sent by Roosevelt to Fort-de-France, apparently to discuss with Admiral Robert the conditions for neutralising the French possessions in America, and the warships in American waters, de Gaulle decided to act without delay. He had intended to keep his decision secret, but Muselier, having gathered three corvettes around the *Surcouf*, thought it wise to request the approval of the Canadians, and through them, the Americans. The secret was out, and de Gaulle felt obliged to tell the British. Washington sent word to Muselier through its minister in Ottawa, and the word was "No". Thereupon, the admiral proposed to abandon the expedition. The British asked de Gaulle to desist, and he said he would.

An unexpected development, offensive to his Free French pride, made him change his mind, however. He learned from the British Foreign Office that the Canadian government, by agreement with the United States, had decided to land at Saint-Pierre and seize the radio station. The French National Committee immediately protested to London and Washington, and de Gaulle – without informing his allies – decided to reactivate his plans.[9]

As de Gaulle reasoned, since the prospect now was of a foreign intervention in French territory, no further hesitation was possible. He ordered Admiral Muselier to proceed immediately to Saint-Pierre and Miquelon. Arriving on Christmas Eve, the admiral was greeted with delirious enthusiasm, and did not need to use force. In the plebiscite

---

[9] De Gaulle's account differs from Winston Churchill's, as regards the sequence of events. In Churchill, Vol. III, pp. 590–1, the British asked de Gaulle to refrain from occupying the islands, on learning that the American State Department wished the occupation to be made by a Canadian expedition; and the general "certainly said he would do so". In de Gaulle's account, however, the general reversed his decision to cancel the expedition on learning that the Canadians were planning to intervene.

that followed, an enormous majority declared themselves in favour of Free France. The young men began to enlist in the Free French forces, and the older men to form a local defence force. De Gaulle's envoy, Savary, was appointed administrator in place of the Vichy High Commissioner.

A small matter, one might think, successfully carried out and satisfactory to all; at most, the occasion for raised eyebrows and diplomatic noises of disapproval from the State Department. This was not, however, the way the Americans saw it. The president himself seems to have been reasonably philosophical about the whole affair, but Cordell Hull's indignation knew no bounds. As Churchill put it, "Mr Hull . . . in my opinion pushed what was little more than a departmental point far beyond its proportions." Deeply affronted, he issued a statement on Christmas Day castigating the action of the "so-called Free French ships" as "an arbitrary action contrary to the agreement of all parties concerned". Indeed, so serious a view had he taken of the matter, that he had interrupted his Christmas holidays to return urgently to Washington. He called upon the Canadian government to announce the measures it proposed to take to restore the *status quo ante* in the islands.

For three weeks, the storm raged. Churchill had gone to Quebec to confer with President Roosevelt and de Gaulle telegraphed him to warn him of the deplorable effect on French public opinion of the State Department's attitude. The phrase "so-called Free French", as Churchill and de Gaulle both noted, had certainly aroused widespread resentment, and not among the Free French alone. With strong backing from the Foreign Office, Churchill defended de Gaulle. But Cordell Hull, despite the British intervention and a spate of soothing messages and *démarches* from the Free French, was attached to his disapproval. On 14 January, the British foreign secretary, Anthony Eden, called on de Gaulle – apparently under pressure from the Americans – and tried, but not very hard, to persuade him to agree to the neutralisation of the islands, their independence of the Free French National Committee, and joint allied control. Predictably, de Gaulle declined, and Eden asked what would happen if the Americans sent a cruiser and two destoyers to Saint-Pierre, as was apparently their intention. In high good humour, de Gaulle answered: "The allied ships will stop at the limit of French territorial waters and the American admiral will have lunch with Muselier who will certainly be delighted."

"But what if the cruiser goes beyond the limit?" asked Eden.

"Our people will issue the customary challenge."

"And if the cruiser still advances?"

"That would be a great shame," said de Gaulle, "for in that event our people would have to fire."

And seeing the alarm on Eden's face, he added with a smile that he had confidence in the democracies.

Exaggerated though the American fury was, it should be remembered that the U.S. government had just concluded an agreement with Admiral Robert which involved the maintenance of the *status quo* in all French possessions in the western hemisphere. Admiral Robert himself, although he had authority over the tiny islands of Saint-Pierre and Miquelon, was stationed on the French West Indian island of Martinique, some 2,000 miles to the south, which together with French Guiana, was covered by the agreement. Moreover, on 13 December 1941, Roosevelt had assured Pétain that the United States intended to stand by the Havana Convention of 1940, guaranteeing the *status quo* in the western hemisphere. De Gaulle's unilateral action was interpreted as a flagrant violation of the Monroe doctrine of 1823 ruling out European encroachments on the hemisphere as a whole.

Not only did the Americans feel outraged on all these grounds, but they considered de Gaulle's action as a breach of his word. Small though the incident was, it festered in Cordell Hull's mind. And on 30 December, speaking at Ottawa, Churchill publicly poured scorn on Pétain, Darlan and other Vichy leaders, while heaping praise on de Gaulle and his followers. This drove Cordell Hull into a renewed frenzy. The president himself, though initially inclined to dismiss the whole thing as of little importance, was gradually influenced by his secretary of State into revising his opinion.[10] In the end, the occupation of two small islands poisoned General de Gaulle's chances of achieving a good relationship with Roosevelt.

By the end of January, however, the Americans had decided with reasonably good grace to accept the accomplished fact of the Free French seizure of the islands. For some weeks, Admiral Muselier stayed there, and rumours reached him that he was to be made a scapegoat for de Gaulle's quarrel with the Americans. There was no substance to these reports, but the admiral, still smarting from his clash with de Gaulle in September, was receptive to such poison. To his surprise, General de Gaulle himself and all his fellow members of the National Committee were there to greet him when he returned to London on 28 February.[11]

[10] Robert E. Sherwood, *The White House Papers of Harry L. Hopkins* (henceforth, Sherwood, *Hopkins*), Vol. I, pp. 456 *et seq.*; and A. L. Funk, *Charles de Gaulle – the Crucial Years 1943–4* (henceforth, Funk), pp. 17 *et seq. See also* Charles de Gaulle, *Memoires de Guerre: L'Unité 1942–4* (henceforth, De Gaulle, *L'Unité*), pp. 128–31.
[11] Soustelle, *Envers*, Vol. I, pp. 281–2.

Muselier had worked himself up into a rage during his absence, and a few days of talks with Labarthe and Moret, those other opponents of de Gaulle's, added fuel to the fire. On 3 March, at a meeting of the National Committee, he exploded with a list of his grievances and announced his resignation, to be conveyed to General de Gaulle in a letter.

De Gaulle immediately named Admiral Auboyneau (at that time at sea on board the *Triomphant*) to replace Muselier both as national commissioner for the navy and as commander-in-chief of the Free French naval forces. (Ortoli was to replace Moret as chief of staff to the naval c.-in-c.) But this was not the way Admiral Muselier conceived of his resignation. He had not, he declared, resigned as commander-in-chief – only as a member of the National Committee. Lobbying furiously among the British, the admiral secured their powerful support. A. V. Alexander, first lord of the Admiralty, and one of the Labour politicians who accepted the view that de Gaulle had "Fascist leanings", intervened to request that Muselier should remain commander-in-chief. On 5 and 6 March 1942 Eden accompanied Alexander on visits to de Gaulle to press this point of view.

By now, de Gaulle's concept of national sovereignty and honour was involved, and on the 8th he wrote to Eden turning down flat any British interference in the decision of the National Committee removing Muselier from his command. A curious and typical test of wills followed. De Gaulle sentenced Admiral Muselier and Commander Moret to thirty days house arrest, and requested the British to enforce this sentence under the juridical agreement of 15 January 1941, since the arrest was to take place on British territory. As for him, he retired to the country, leaving his assistants a secret testament containing a message to the French people in the event of his being unable to continue his mission. And he allowed it to be known that, to his deep regret, he was unable to resume relations with his allies until they had applied the juridical agreement.

On 12 March, Admiral Muselier and Capitaine de Vaisseau Moret called on Charles Peake, Britain's representative with the National Committee, to complain that the general was acting illegally in sentencing him to detention. He claimed also that de Gaulle's staff had suborned Moret's cipher officer. The British, however, were anxious to avoid further trouble with de Gaulle and unwilling to meet the general in head-on collision. They therefore persuaded Muselier to go on leave in the country.[12] On the 23rd, they duly capitulated when Peake called on de Gaulle

---

12 Muselier gives supporting evidence on the bribery of Moret's cipher officer, but does not mention his meeting with Peake on 12 March, which is documented in

with a note conceding that Admiral Muselier would not remain commander-in-chief of the Free French naval forces and undertaking to deprive him of any contact with those forces for one month. The British, however, asked General de Gaulle to be kind enough to find the admiral a new post consistent with his services.

Having won his victory, de Gaulle was ready to oblige, and invited Admiral Muselier to visit him on 5 May to discuss a proposed mission as inspector-general of the naval forces. Stubbornly, the admiral wrote back to say he still considered himself commander-in-chief as of right and wanted an assurance that he would be received in that capacity. Patiently, de Gaulle explained to him that nobody had a prescriptive right to any position or command: Muselier could come as inspector-general or not at all. Muselier thereupon notified de Gaulle that he was severing all connections with Free France. "I was sorry for his sake," the general commented laconically in his memoirs.[13] Both Muselier and Labarthe were later to join General Giraud in North Africa.

Throughout 1941, then, de Gaulle continued to have stormy relations not only with his British allies and Britain's American allies, but also with his own followers. Storms and pressures seemed inherent in his position, the intransigence of his character and the grandeur of his pretensions. In one direction only did he meet with diplomatic success and an apparently unalloyed welcome: Russia. When Hitler's armies invaded the Soviet Union on 22 June 1941, de Gaulle's reaction was similar to Churchill's and almost as spontaneous. Churchill had attempted to strangle the Soviet Republic at birth; de Gaulle had fought the Soviet armies in Poland. Neither had any love for communism. But both decided that since the Russians were now fighting the common enemy, they too were allies – even though Stalin had signed a pact with Hitler and refused to believe that the Fuehrer had aggressive intentions towards Russia.

Lacy. About this time, the British Naval Liaison Office, in a secret memorandum, drew up a list of measures that might be taken "to avoid constant upheavals with General de Gaulle" by limiting his "autocratic power". These were: (1) no interference from him on naval matters; (2) de Gaulle to be excluded from the National Committee, the members of which should be denied diplomatic privileges; (3) close scrutiny of the Free French budget; (4) de Gaulle to be forbidden to use secret ciphers; (5) the *Journal Officiel* to be closed down; (6) de Gaulle to be denied direct access to the Prime Minister; (7) reduction of Free French staffs in London; (8) de Gaulle to be forbidden to make press announcements unless previously passed by British censorship; and (9) no written agreements to be made with General de Gaulle: "They only limit our action and not his." Although these suggestions were turned down, they reflect the tensions of the time.

[13] De Gaulle, *L'Appel*, p. 223; *see also* pp. 193 *et seq.*, and 620–5.

General de Gaulle was in Damascus when the news reached him on the 23rd. Next day, he cabled his delegation in London:

> Without wishing to discuss at present the vices and even the crimes of the Soviet regime, we must proclaim – like Churchill – that we are very frankly with the Russians, they are fighting the Germans. . . . It is not the Russians who are crushing France, who occupy Paris, Rheims, Bordeaux, Strasbourg. . . . The German planes, tanks and soldiers which the Russians are destroying and will destroy will no longer be there to prevent us from liberating France.

This was henceforth to be the keynote of Free French propaganda.

De Gaulle followed up his message immediately with diplomatic action. On his instructions, Cassin and Dejean called to see the Soviet ambassador in London, Ivan Maisky, to bring assurances of Free French support and request the organisation of military relations with Moscow. Whereas de Gaulle's attempts to draw closer to Washington were impeded at every step by American recognition of Vichy and President Roosevelt's Vichy policy, no such obstacle stood in the way of his search for Russian friends. Indeed, Hitler soon insisted that the Vichy government should break off diplomatic relations with the Soviet Union.

From Beirut on 2 August, de Gaulle instructed Cassin and Dejean to ask Maisky whether Moscow would be prepared to enter into direct relations with the Free French movement, and make a declaration of their intention to restore the independence and greatness of France, and if possible her integrity. With his goatee beard, his twinkling eyes and his engaging personality, Maisky gave the visiting Free Frenchmen a first welcome that was cordial but reserved, and a second one that was unreservedly warm. Stalin's totalitarian propaganda machine had gone into reverse gear overnight. Before the German attack, there had been daily diatribes from Moscow Radio against British imperialism and its "Gaullist mercenaries". Now the praise was switched on. Moreover, between the first Free French visit to the ambassador at the end of June, and the second early in August, Maisky had evidently received an explicit green light from the Kremlin.

It was not, however, till 26 September, that the Soviet ambassador complied with his formal request, by writing to the general to declare the Soviet government's recognition of the general as the leader of all the Free French, and its readiness to enter into relations with the Defence Council of the French Empire. Moscow was, moreover, ready to help the Free French in the common fight against Hitler's Germany and her allies. As for France, the Soviet government underlined its firm resolve to ensure the full and entire restoration of the independence and greatness of France, once victory over the common enemy had been achieved. As in the corresponding declaration by the British government on 7 August 1940, however, there was no mention of France's territorial integrity.

For de Gaulle, this encouragement from a great power could not have come at a more opportune moment. For it happened when his relations with Churchill's government were going through the sour phase that followed the events in Syria and the Lebanon, and when he was facing open rebellion from Admiral Muselier on the eve of the formation of the Free French National Committee. Shortly afterwards, the Soviet government appointed Mr Bogomolov as its representative with the National Committee. As if to underline the dramatic nature of the change in Moscow's foreign relations, Bogomolov had until lately been Moscow's ambassador at Vichy. De Gaulle was soon on cordial terms with him and finding him, to his surprise, both cultured and human – indeed humorous enough to allow himself an occasional smile – he concluded that for all the rigidity of the conformist strait jacket imposed upon its servants by the Soviet system, they remained men underneath.

After that, de Gaulle never lost an opportunity to try, within his painful limitations, to be helpful to the Russians. One element that entered into his thinking was his enduring conviction, as an historian, that regardless of ideologies, Russia's interests as a nation were eternal, as France's were. As his own military representative in Moscow, de Gaulle sent General Petit, who was immediately treated, by the Russians with all the signs of friendly consideration, such as staff briefings, a visit to the front and a personal visit to Stalin. So assiduous indeed were the Russian advances, that General de Gaulle came to wonder whether their interest in Petit was more than professional.

What could de Gaulle do to help the Russians and impress them with his goodwill? Free French corvettes and merchant ships were indeed taking part in the allied convoys to Murmansk through the Arctic route, the coldest and toughest of all. But this contribution was overshadowed by the much greater British help in the vital convoys. The autumn brought the opportunity he was seeking. It was clear to General de Gaulle, although his allies kept him inadequately informed, that the British forces in the Middle East were planning to launch a major offensive against the Germans and Italians in North Africa; and he was determined that the new Free French forces should play their part in it. This was important to him, on grounds of prestige and political effectiveness as well as of military utility and honour. On 7 October, he pressed the Free French claims to participate in the offensive in letters to General Ismay, chief of staff to the war cabinet, and to General Auchinleck at British Middle East headquarters.

A long and at times acrimonious correspondence followed. The offensive began, in fact, on 18 November 1941, *without* Free French participation. On the 27th, General Ismay wrote to de Gaulle to say that it was impossible to assemble, equip and train the Free French forces which were scattered throughout Syria, in time for the current operations in Cyrenaica. Next day, de Gaulle replied, withdrawing the offer of Free French participation in all actions in the Near East, Libya and even, when the time came, in West Africa; although he maintained his plans for an attack from the Free French base in Tchad against Mourzouk, reserving for himself the right to decide when it should be launched.

Now de Gaulle played his Russian card. He called in Bogomolov and offered to transfer to the Russian front the two Free French divisions in the Levant.[14]

The general's intransigence produced its usual effect. On 7 December 1941 – the day the Japanese attacked Pearl Harbor – Churchill wrote to him on a cordial note to say that General Auchinleck was now anxious to use immediately a Free French brigade in the Cyrenaica operations. He added that he and his wife were looking forward to seeing the general and Mme de Gaulle at lunch the following Wednesday. The incident was not yet closed, however, for the British let it be known that they could not equip and use more than one of the two Free French light divisions. On the 29th, de Gaulle wrote to Ismay to say that the Soviet government welcomed the offer of Free French help, and he therefore proposed to send to Russia the other Free French light division now idle in Syria. He thought the Free French troops could leave for the Caucasus about mid-March. Catroux was instructed to this effect on 12 January 1942.[15] In the end, de Gaulle got his way, for Auchinleck agreed to use all the available Free French forces. The Russians therefore had to content themselves with a group of well-trained Free French fighter pilots.

De Gaulle's relations with the Russians remained warm, despite this apparent withdrawal of a promise. Some two hundred French soldiers with fifteen officers under Captain Billotte, who had been interned in Russia after escaping from a German prisoner-of-war camp, were sent to London to join the Free French. On 20 January 1942, in a radio speech,

[14] Gorce, pp. 200–1.
[15] The text of de Gaulle's letter to Catroux of 12 January 1942 appears on pp. 650–1 of de Gaulle, *L'Appel*; on p. 196, in the course of his narrative, however, de Gaulle gives February as the date of the instructions.

de Gaulle gave eloquent praise to Russian military prowess, and re-affirmed his faith in the new French alliance with Russia. The following month, he sent Roger Garreau, formerly the French minister in Bangkok, to Moscow as delegate of the National Committee – in effect, as ambassador. And in May, when the Soviet foreign minister, Molotov, came to London, de Gaulle had a long talk with him. It was the 24th; Bogomolov was with his diplomatic chief, and Dejean, who looked after foreign affairs for the Free French, accompanied de Gaulle. De Gaulle saw in Molotov a perfectly oiled piece of machinery in a totalitarian system.

In a curious way, the giant Soviet Union and the tiny Free French movement needed each other at that time. Although Marshal Zhukov's counter-blow in December had relieved Moscow, the Russians were still very hard pressed by the German invaders. Molotov had come to London to extend the mutual aid pact between Great Britain and Russia into a twenty-year treaty, but in their life-and-death struggle, the Russians were keenly conscious of their years of diplomatic isolation, and disinclined to spurn friendships, however weak. De Gaulle's diplomatic isolation, though due to quite different causes, was even more acute. Each side had diplomatic objectives which it felt the other could help to achieve. So de Gaulle undertook to put pressure upon the British and Americans for the rapid opening of a second front in Europe. In return, Molotov undertook to support the Free French in their resistance to American and British encroachments upon the unity of France and the French empire. Wherever this unity might be threatened, for instance at Madagascar, the Russians would uphold France's rights. It was agreed, moreover, that Franco-Soviet collaboration should not cease with the end of hostilities but extend to the construction of a just peace. With evident satisfaction, General de Gaulle heard Molotov declare, "My government is the ally of the governments of London and Washington. It is essential for the war that we should closely collaborate with them. But with France Russia desires to have an independent alliance."

Although de Gaulle was later to have his own clashes with Stalin, there is no doubt that he drew conclusions of lasting importance from his ability to use his Russian connections to get his own way in dealings with the British and Americans, and was deeply impressed by the contrast between Russia's apparently genuine desire to help, and the obstructiveness and interferences (as he saw it) of the "Anglo-Saxons". Indeed, he was to show during his second period in power, from 1958 on, that his appreciation of the situation in 1941 and 1942 continued to be valid in his eyes.

Chapter 7 ⚜ Roosevelt in the Ascendant

After his return from the Middle East in September 1941, General de Gaulle spent ten months in London. He lived at the Connaught Hotel, and his family stayed in the country, first in a cottage at Ellesmere in Shropshire, later at Berkhamsted. There, at the weekend, Charles de Gaulle visited his wife and their ailing daughter Anne. Later, they all moved into a house in Hampstead. De Gaulle's son, Philippe, was serving at sea in the Free French navy, and Elisabeth was boarding with the Daughters of Zion, while preparing for Oxford.[1] Whatever the state of his official relations with the British authorities, de Gaulle had nothing but praise for the behaviour of the people of England. Always ready to cheer him when he appeared in public, they treated de Gaulle and his family with self-effacing courtesy when the general was off duty.

His working days were spent at Free French headquarters at Carlton Gardens, and working lunches and dinners were frequent. Though always busy with his inter-allied wrangles, and his instructions to the scattered centres of Free France overseas, he always found time to keep in touch with the various organisations of Franco-British friendship and to administer his own turbulent staff. In the evenings when alone, or at home at the weekends, he wrote his many speeches and radio addresses. He chain-smoked, but remained fighting fit.

His character had become, if possible, more uncompromising than ever. Though always capable of sardonic humour, his outward behaviour was normally of glacial self-possession, punctuated occasionally by spontaneous rages, and more often by carefully calculated ones. For in his case, as with most outstanding public leaders, acting played its part in the total effect he tried to create. Many years before, in Le Fil de L'Epée, he had noted and admired the acting talents of Caesar and Napoleon. His own role, the great role brought within his reach by history, was France herself. One cannot doubt the sincerity of his conviction that he not only represented, but *was* France. But, like other great actors, he both lived

[1] De Gaulle, L'Appel, p. 239.

the part and believed in it. It was a superb performance always, convincing to many who saw it at close quarters.

Roosevelt, who had to wait for the benefit of a private performance, never understood or accepted de Gaulle's pretensions. Churchill, who had as it were a seat in the front stalls, was perhaps too close to be entirely convinced.

"You say you are France! You are not France! I do not recognise you as France!" the Prime Minister once shouted to him in a growing rage. "France! Where is she? I agree, of course, that General de Gaulle and those who follow him are an important and respectable part of that people. But we may, doubtless, find outside them another authority which might also have its value." And de Gaulle cut in, "If in your eyes I am not the representative of France, why and by what right do you negotiate with me about her world interests?" Churchill stayed silent.[2]

In private, Churchill compared de Gaulle to the Frankenstein monster.[3] Frankenstein? Or Joan of Arc? The rumour that de Gaulle, like Joan of Arc, heard "voices", duly went the rounds in London and Washington. Roosevelt delighted in repeating it. But when the rumour came back to de Gaulle, he saw in it only one more proof of the stupidity of ordinary people. At all events, his visitors tended to fall into two categories: those who thought him a genius, and those who thought him a megalomaniac. Then there were those who thought he was both. When Charles Peake represented the Foreign Office with the National Committee, he used to gauge de Gaulle's temper by his initial greeting when he entered the general's office. If he said: "Ah! My dear Peake, do come in!" all was well. But if he started: "Well, Monsieur Peake, do you want something?" the outlook was poor.[4]

Given de Gaulle's intransigence, and Churchill's overwhelming need to get on with the war regardless of the general's susceptibilities, relations between the two men were bound to be normally bad and only intermittently better. The wonder is not that there was so much acrimony, but that matters were never pushed to a final break. The two men held each other in mutual esteem. Relations, however, inevitably grew even worse when Roosevelt came on to the scene. Almost immediately, Churchill – while always ready to press his own point of view – tacitly accepted the role of junior partner in the new Grand Alliance. Since Roosevelt had no time for the Free French, and Churchill was committed to support them, the Prime Minister went through a difficult

[2] De Gaulle, *L'Unité*, p. 33.　　　　[3] Tournoux, *Pétain*, p. 278.
[4] Galante, p. 123.

phase, which de Gaulle's constant pressing of his claims sometimes made worse than it need have been. Not that Churchill was ever disloyal to de Gaulle, though exasperation often tempted him to be, but in any clash between de Gaulle and Roosevelt, Churchill was bound to support the American president. The winter of 1941–2 was, of course, one of the darkest periods of the war, and the Prime Minister was under serious strain. The Japanese attack on the American fleet at Pearl Harbor, though in itself a naval disaster, had at least brought the good news of America's entry into the conflict. But three days later, the British warships *Prince of Wales* and *Repulse* were sunk by Japanese planes off the coast of Malaya. And on 15 February 1942, a large British army surrendered to the invading Japanese in fortress Singapore. Moreover, Auchinleck's North African successes were proving short-lived, and Rommel's counter-offensive was soon to smash the British front in the desert for the second time. As de Gaulle noted, the fall of Tobruk on 21 June 1942 completed a six months' story of disasters, at the close of which, Churchill – though still undeniably in control of cabinet, parliament and people – was in a shakier position in public esteem than at any time since he had come to power. None of this was calculated to improve the temper of his relations with de Gaulle.[5]

During the whole of the difficult period that spanned General de Gaulle's renewed stay in London, Franco-British relations in the Levant continued to break out into repeated crises; while in the Horn of Africa, de Gaulle's representative, Gaston Palewski, frequently clashed with the British authorities over relations with the emperor of Ethiopia and the railway from Addis Ababa to Djibouti.[6] But there was worse to come. The new crisis broke on 5 May 1942, with a news agency telephone call to de Gaulle at 3 a.m., informing him that a British task force was landing troops at Diego Suarez, the strategic harbour on the north-eastern coast of Madagascar.[7] Since de Gaulle had not even been consulted about this landing in a French possession, his indignation immediately rose to boiling point. The general had, in fact, been urging a Free French operation against Madagascar since Japan's entry into the war. He had first written to Churchill about it on 16 December 1941; and on 19 February 1942, he had written again, to press for a decision and to submit a detailed plan to the British chief of staff.[8] He had followed this up on 9 April with a pressing note to Anthony Eden.

[5] Churchill, Vol. IV, pp. 343–4.
[6] There is no space, in this general biography of de Gaulle, to consider in any detail Franco-British relations in the Levant and the Horn of Africa. De Gaulle's version of these events is given in the first two volumes of his War Memoirs.
[7] De Gaulle, *L'Appel*, pp. 204 *et seq.*   [8] Churchill, Vol. IV, pp. 198 *et seq.*

It was indeed obvious that the island would come to be of great strategic importance, with a possible threat of occupation by Japan. At the time of de Gaulle's first proposal, however, Churchill gave Madagascar a relatively low priority rating. But the rapid Japanese military successes in south-east Asia, and the consequent threat to the Bay of Bengal, Ceylon and the Indian ocean, caused the Prime Minister to revise his views. The question was whether the Free French should or should not take part in any landing. On their own, they clearly lacked the means. British naval and air support would therefore be needed. But with memories of the fiasco at Dakar, and of the monumental Free French indiscretions that had jeopardised that operation, Churchill and his military advisers, in consultation with the United States, decided to do the job themselves and to keep it secret from de Gaulle.

In context, this made much sense, but the decision was bound to inflame the general. His gall was thickened by a communiqué from Washington on the day of the British landing, declaring that the United States and Great Britain agreed that Madagascar should be restored to France as soon as the occupation of the island should cease to be necessary for the common cause. The thought that, in the meantime, France should be deprived of one of her possessions, was intolerable to General de Gaulle. When Eden asked to see him, de Gaulle kept him waiting for six days. When they met on 11 May, he found the foreign secretary somewhat embarrassed. "I guarantee," said Eden, "that we have no claims on Madagascar. We wish the French administration to continue to function."

"Which French administration?" asked de Gaulle. On learning that the British proposed to negotiate with the Vichy governor-general Annet, to establish a *modus vivendi*, confining themselves to Diego Suarez and leaving the rest of the island under Vichy administration, de Gaulle immediately rejected the plan. If the operation succeeded, he said, the result would be the neutralisation of a French territory under an Allied guarantee, and this he would never admit. Failing that, however, there was the greater likelihood that the Germans would force Vichy to fight. Eden countered by saying that he realised the help of the Free French would be needed. The British government was ready to declare publicly that the authority of the Free French would be established. And on 14 May it was announced that the French National Committee was to play its proper part in the administration of the liberated territory.

De Gaulle immediately ordered the assembling in Equatorial Africa of a mixed brigade, to be sent to Madagascar at the earliest opportunity. Once again, however, de Gaulle was about to be frustrated by the gap that always seemed to exist between British official declarations and the actions of the service men and special agents who executed the government's policy. In this case, as he recalls the facts in his memoirs, an intelligence service group from East Africa, led by a certain Mr Lush, was sent to Madagascar. When de Gaulle wanted to send his own envoy, Colonel Pechkoff, to Diego Suarez to keep an eye on developments, the British refused to allow him to leave. De Gaulle himself, having decided to fly to Libya to inspect the French forces there, was urgently requested to postpone his trip; which he interpreted, doubtless rightly, to mean that no transport would be available for him if he did decide to go.

Once again, as in all the previous crises of the kind, de Gaulle resorted to maximum intransigence. On 6 June, he instructed Charles Peake to explain his position to Churchill and Eden. "If it happened," he said, "that in Madagascar, in Syria or elsewhere, France should, through her Allies, lose anything that belongs to her, our direct cooperation with Great Britain and even with the United States, would no longer be justified." And he went on to threaten to withdraw to territories under Free French authority and carry on the struggle alone. He followed these unbending words with telegrams to his military and civil representatives in Africa and the Middle East.

As usual, his methods worked. On 10 June, Churchill invited him to drop in. An amiable conversation of about an hour followed. The Prime Minister congratulated him warmly upon the valiant resistance of the French troops then under German pressure at Bir-Hakim, then broached the subject of Madagascar. The British, he assured de Gaulle, had no designs on Madagascar. "I am the friend of France!" he exclaimed.

When de Gaulle raised the question of Roosevelt's attitude, the Prime Minister advised him, "Don't rush things! Look at me, how I yield and reassert myself in turn."

"You can do that," de Gaulle observed, "because you are based on a strong State, a unified nation, a united empire, great armies. As for me! What means have I got? And yet, as you know, I am responsible for the interests and destiny of France. The burden is too heavy and I'm too poor to afford to yield."

"I shall not let you down," said Churchill in farewell, "you can count on me."[9]

Three days later, Eden told him that Lush was being recalled and Pechkoff could now go.

*   *   *

9 De Gaulle, *L'Appel*, p. 209.

The widely praised behaviour of the Free French forces at Bir-Hakim had given de Gaulle his first unambiguous military asset in his relations with his Allies. Dakar had been a flop, and Syria a humiliating half-success; while Leclerc's advances in the Sahara were on too small a scale to fire the imagination. The Bir-Hakim action, too, was small, but it took place in a spotlight of tense awareness. Rommel was attacking in the direction of Tobruk. Under the command of General Koenig, the first Free French brigade was charged with holding a crossing of desert tracks, thirty-five miles from the coast, waterless and treeless, and absent from most maps: Bir-Hakim. Koenig had fortified this inhospitable place, and 3,500 men defended it. The British needed time to regroup further east. Rejecting Rommel's ultimatum, Koenig and his men held out, in intense heat and with a miserable water ration, well beyond the six days the British had asked him to delay the German advance. On 10 June, the British sent word that the strongpoint could now be evacuated. Having lost ninety-six men and destroyed all equipment that could not be carried, Koenig ordered his men to leave on the night of the 11th. On their way to the British lines, however, some nine hundred more were killed or wounded, or disappeared.[10]

Small though the action was, Bir-Hakim had shown that the Free French were capable of fighting heroically and dying for the allied cause. The news came as a stimulant to the Resistance inside France, and boosted the standing of the Free French movement at large, with corresponding damage to Vichy's prestige. Alone in his office, after hearing the news, de Gaulle wept tears of pride and joy and relief that most of Koenig's men were safe.[11]

For a brief moment, indeed, de Gaulle's relations with Washington improved at such speed that a real understanding began to look possible. The new American ambassador in London, John Winant, had met him in London on 21 May 1942 and listened with respect to his views on the opening of a second front in Europe. A further meeting, with Eden present, followed on 1 June, and de Gaulle cabled his representative in Washington, Adrien Tixier, to say that it now seemed as if Cordell Hull and Sumner Welles of the State Department were beginning to realise that their attitude towards the Free French was unrealistic. On the 29th, the British foreign Secretary told the general that the United States government was thinking of changing its policy towards the French National Committee. Next evening, Winant dined with de Gaulle, expressed his sympathy for the general, and undertook to do his best to present the general's personality in a favourable light at home.

[10] Michel, *France Libre*, pp. 51 et seq. [11] De Gaulle, *L'Appel*, p. 258.

Churchill, at this time, was in Washington, and trying to persuade President Roosevelt to soften his attitude towards the Free French leader. The outcome was the publication in Washington on 9 July of a communiqué, the text of which had been submitted to de Gaulle for his approval, which conferred recognition of a kind upon his movement. Admiral Stark and General Bolte were appointed as representatives of the American government, to confer with the French National Committee in London on all questions relating to the conduct of the war. The Americans recognised the contribution of General de Gaulle and the efforts of the National Committee to keep alive the traditional spirit and the institutions of France. All possible assistance was to be given to the National Committee "as a symbol of French resistance in general against the powers of the Axis". A veiled reminder that President Roosevelt suspected General de Gaulle of pursuing private political ambitions followed, however, for the communiqué recorded that the United States government shared with the British government the view – "which it knows to be also that of the French National Committee – that the political future of France could only be decided in freedom and without coercion".

De Gaulle was pleased enough with this statement, and wrote to Tixier to tell him so. But he was soon to discover that its practical value was limited. The statement declared that the United States would deal with Free French officials in their respective territories, wherever they exercised effective authority. But it said nothing about the very important remaining territories – especially those of French North Africa – where Vichy continued to exercise control. When General de Gaulle, on 23 July, met the American army and navy leaders – General Marshall, chief of the General Staff, Admiral King, commander-in-chief of the naval forces, and Lieutenant-General Eisenhower, commander-in-chief of the American land forces in Europe – and told them what contribution Free France could make in the event of a landing in French territory, he found them reticent and "embarrassed by that new and enormous thing for the United States which is called a world war".[12]

In fact, neither the British nor the Americans were yet prepared – either mentally or militarily – for a second front in Europe, much less for an invasion of France. Their thoughts were turning towards French North Africa, and they had no intention of confiding in General de Gaulle. His success in Washington was indeed ephemeral and illusory. Cordell Hull had never really forgotten or forgiven his anger over the Free French "liberation" of Saint-Pierre and Miquelon. A subsequent

[12] De Gaulle, L'Unité, p. 347; see also pp. 5–9, 327–9, 330–1, 333–5 and 337–9.

incident in New Caledonia had arisen when General Patch, the American commander in the Pacific, had turned up on the island. Taking advantage of the American presence, native politicians had attempted to assert themselves, and de Gaulle's governor, Admiral d'Argenlieu, had been forced, humiliatingly, to take temporary refuge in the jungle. The whole thing had ended satisfactorily on 28 February 1942 with an American declaration recognising that the island territories in the Pacific "are under the effective control of the French National Committee established in London".[13]

But the Americans dealt with the Free French only when they could not do otherwise. In Washington, Tixier had failed to see either President Roosevelt or the secretary of State. He had been equally unsuccessful in his attempts to bring some of the distinguished French exiles into the Gaullist movement. Apart from Jean Monnet, the former French premier Camille Chautemps, the philosopher Jacques Maritain and the former secretary-general in the French Foreign ministry, Alexis Léger, were among those who stood aloof from the Free French.[14] This reticence among French exiles strengthened American official doubts on the standing of General de Gaulle among his compatriots. The Americans continued to believe that in France itself de Gaulle's name carried little weight; and this was of course the strongly held view of the American ambassador in Vichy, Admiral Leahy.

De Gaulle, however, now had heartening evidence that the French Resistance groups in France were beginning to look to him for overall leadership. Several of their leaders came to London to see him.[15] One of them was Emmanuel d'Astier de la Vigerie, who met de Gaulle in London in April 1942, and de Gaulle decided to send him to Washington on a semi-secret mission to explain and interpret the state of mind of the French people. One of his instructions was to reassure Tixier himself that the labour groups in France stood behind the National Committee; another was to persuade Léger to join the National Committee and take the portfolio of foreign affairs. Léger, however, remained to the end unable to concede any legitimacy to General de Gaulle though he retained anti-Vichy views. Tixier, on the other hand, was duly reassured; and d'Astier could claim some of the credit for the American communiqué of 9 July. Even d'Astier, however, was unable to see President Roosevelt, although he did have a talk with the president's personal assistant, Harry Hopkins. In May, Admiral Leahy returned to America.

[13] Funk, pp. 25–7. [14] Léger is perhaps better known as the poet, St John Perse.
[15] De Gaulle's relations with the French internal Resistance are dealt with in detail in Part III, chapter 11.

He was given an office in the old State Department building next to the White House, and was thus in easy reach of the president, who continued to consult him.[16]

As the summer of 1942 wore on, General de Gaulle's thoughts were increasingly on the Middle East. Catroux's reports told him of continuing difficulties between the French and British in Syria and the Lebanon, and de Gaulle decided to go and see for himself and bring whatever comfort his presence might mean to his fighting troops. In mid-July he had renamed his movement "Fighting France" instead of "Free France", to mark the fact that he now commanded the allegiance of resisters inside as well as outside France. Towards the end of July, de Gaulle did indeed summon to London the leaders of the three main Resistance groups. On the 27th, he reshuffled his National Committee. The French Socialist leader, André Philip, who had reached England, was given charge of the Interior; and Jacques Soustelle, who had been successful on missions in Mexico and elsewhere in Spanish America, was made commissioner for Information. The National Committee's affairs now being in order, de Gaulle felt he could leave London. On the 29th he called on the Prime Minister to take his leave.

"So?" said Churchill, "You're off to Africa and the Levant!"

"I'm not displeased to go to the Levant," the general replied. "Spears is agitating. He is making trouble for us."

"Spears," commented Winston Churchill, "has many enemies. But he has one friend: the Prime Minister."

An inconclusive argument followed, about Dakar and Madagascar. The Prime Minister taxed de Gaulle with reports that Syria and the Lebanon were not truly independent, and the general countered by saying that the local people were at least as happy as those in the territories under British tutelage, in Iraq, Palestine or Egypt.[17]

The heart of the Franco-British dispute in the Levant was the fact that the Free French were mainly concerned to preserve French authority over the territories, whereas the British were mainly interested in fighting the war. This, however, was not quite the way de Gaulle saw it. For him, the real problem was that he suspected the British of having designs on the territories under French mandate. Each time the British put pressure on him to hold free elections in Syria and the Lebanon, he thought of the consequences: the two countries would become independent

[16] Fleet Admiral William D. Leahy, I Was There (henceforth, Leahy), pp. 116 and 119–120.
[17] De Gaulle, L'Unité, p. 346; for ensuing matter, see also pp. 13–15, 20–5, 35 and 381–5.

before the right moment had come, and the British would simply take over. He sensed, moreover, from a certain embarrassment in the manner of Churchill and Eden, that something important was being concealed from him. His suspicions were confirmed during his flight to Cairo on 5 August. In the plane with him was President Roosevelt's new ambassador to Moscow, Averell Harriman. Normally open and communicative, Harriman was silent and withdrawn. In Gibraltar, de Gaulle could see that vast preparations were in progress, but the governor, General Mason MacFarlane, normally so relaxed, was putting on a mysterious air.

Reaching Cairo on 7 August, General de Gaulle lunched with the Prime Minister and heard about his three dominant worries at that time: the reorganisation of the British High Command, the Syrian dispute with the French, and his forthcoming trip to Moscow. "As you say," said de Gaulle, "those are three grave subjects. The first is your business. As for the second, which is mine, and the third, which particularly affects Stalin to whom you are probably going to announce that the second front will not be opened this year, I can understand your apprehensions. But you will overcome them easily, so long as your conscience has nothing to reproach you with."

"My conscience," Churchill grumbled, "is a good girl with whom I always reach an understanding."

The latest military reverses had brought Rommel to El Alamein, only two hours' drive from Alexandria. Only the Free French, whom de Gaulle inspected on the 8th and 11th, were buoyant with the valour of their resistance at Bir-Hakim. From his point of view, news from the Levant continued to be bad: not only were the British insisting on elections which he considered premature, but they were attempting to close down French installations at the receiving end of the Iraq Petroleum Company's pipeline and thus make the Free French administration entirely dependent on British goodwill. Faced with this situation, de Gaulle decided quite deliberately to create a mounting crisis by carefully organised stages. It was an effective piece of political orchestration. He began with the new British minister of State in the Middle East, the Australian Richard Casey,[18] to whom he expressed Free French displeasure on 8 August. On the 14th, having spent two days in Beirut and Damascus, he cabled a formal protest to Churchill. He called for an end to "the constant interventions of the representatives of the British government" which he found incompatible with Franco-British agreements.

The Prime Minister, who read de Gaulle's message while in Moscow,

[18] Later Sir Richard, and later still, Lord Casey.

replied on the 23rd, from Cairo, on his way back to London. But his carefully worded and soothing phrases did not mollify the general, who immediately cabled a second protest in stronger terms: "It is not possible for me to accept your conception according to which the political interference of British representatives in the Levant is compatible with the commitments entered into by the British government concerning the respect for the position of France and her mandate." For good measure de Gaulle informed both the Russians and the Americans of the stand he was making. As he saw it, the stake was not simply Syria and the Lebanon, but Madagascar as well, and French North Africa.

Although London and Washington continued to keep the Free French representatives in the dark, the signs that some important military action was being planned were becoming unmistakable. While in Cairo, Churchill had appointed General Alexander as commander-in-chief; not long after General Montgomery had taken over as commander of the 8th army. The build up of tanks and aircraft continued. On 27 August, de Gaulle cabled his London committee to announce his conclusion that the United States had decided to land troops in French North Africa, in conjunction with a British offensive from Egypt.

In the meantime, on the 16th, the American consul-general, Mr Gwyn, had called on de Gaulle, obviously worried by the deterioration in Franco-British relations. "I did nothing to reassure him," wrote de Gaulle in his memoirs. It was one more note in de Gaulle's orchestrated crisis.

When Richard Casey, on 29 August, suggested a "frank discussion" in Cairo, threatening in its absence that he would report the situation as he saw it to the Prime Minister, de Gaulle countered by suggesting that the meeting should take place in Beirut.

Now the crisis, from de Gaulle's point of view, was boiling up nicely. On the 31st, Churchill cabled from London to say he agreed that the situation was serious, and to invite him to hasten his return to England. With maddening calm, de Gaulle replied to say that he could not return just yet. And on 7 September he brought tension to its highest point (as he records in his memoirs) with a memorandum to Casey, setting out his grievances in detail. That day in London, Eden told Pleven of the British government's extreme irritation over de Gaulle's attitude in the Levant. Over the next few days, however, the Foreign Office notified the French National Committee of its intention to resume military operations in Madagascar, all attempts at reaching an agreement with the Vichy authorities having failed; and let it be known that it was intended to establish a Free French administration on the island. The action began at dawn on 10 September. Things were now going his way, de Gaulle concluded, and he sent Eden a message of goodwill saying he hoped soon to be able to discuss with him and the Prime Minister both Franco-British relations in the Levant and the future civil administration of Madagascar.

But de Gaulle was still not ready to return to London. Instead he spent ten days in French Africa, where he briefed General Leclerc on future Free French military operations in the Fezzan, which were to culminate in a drive on Tripoli. Only when the Free French had reached that point were they to come under the command of Alexander and Montgomery.

De Gaulle, then, was not back in London until the 25th. As if to confirm him in his resistance to the "Anglo-Saxons", Bogomolov brought him a message from the Soviet government pointing out that in her present death-struggle with the invader, Russia could do little to help, but that she would, when the time came, be prepared to intervene to defend the Free French against excessive American pressure. And on 28 September, a Soviet communiqué announced that the USSR recognised the French National Committee as "the controlling organ of fighting France, being alone qualified to organise the participation of French citizens and territories in the war".

By now, as he had calculated, Winston Churchill had had ample time to work himself up into a monumental rage. The full force of it hit de Gaulle and Pleven when they called at 10 Downing Street on 29 September to see Churchill and Eden. When de Gaulle had flatly refused to hold elections in Syria and Lebanon that year, Churchill said that in that event, he saw no reason why the British should help set up a Gaullist command in Madagascar. It was in the clash of words that followed that Churchill exclaimed, "You are not France!" The foreign secretary joined in to support the Prime Minister, and the French leaders took their leave in an acrimonious atmosphere.

The usual pressures followed. For eleven days, the British suspended the despatch of Gaullist telegrams to Free French centres in Africa, the Levant and the Pacific. Maurice Dejean, de Gaulle's commissioner for Foreign Affairs, pleaded with him to make concessions to the British, to avoid the complete rupture which the Foreign Office was now threatening. But as usual, de Gaulle said, No concessions. Dejean thereupon resigned, though without quarrelling with de Gaulle who, some weeks later, put him in charge of relations with the Allied refugee governments in Britain. Pleven took over Foreign Affairs, handing Finance to Diethelm, pending the arrival in London of Massigli from France itself.

As always, de Gaulle's intransigence brought results. The telegrams started humming again, and on 23 October Churchill sent his private secretary, Major Desmond Morton, to congratulate de Gaulle on the exploit of the Free French submarine *Junon*, which had lately sunk two large enemy ships off the coast of Norway. Cordiality itself, Morton expressed British thanks for the French contribution to the great battle of El Alamein which had just begun. Negotiations then opened over the future administration of Madagascar. De Gaulle's plans were ready. He had already decided to appoint General Legentilhomme as high commissioner for the Indian Ocean, and Pierre de Saint-Mart, at that time governor of Oubangui, as governor-general of Madagascar.

General de Gaulle had reasoned that the British were now bound to make concessions to him in compensation for their exclusion of the Free French from the pending operations in North Africa. And when, on 6 November, Anthony Eden, "all sugar and honey", proposed the publication of a joint communiqué announcing the appointment of Legentilhomme, de Gaulle concluded that the North African landings were about to take place. He learned next day that he was right.

Chapter 8 ❀ "Torch" and After

De Gaulle was about to be drawn into one of the most astonishingly complicated situations of the entire war in which, with all the odds initially against him, he would score the most audacious of his political triumphs. The scene of the imbroglio was that pirate's nest of old, Algiers. The main personages involved on the French side were General Giraud, Admiral Darlan and himself. Overcoming all local opposition, cutting his way through divided loyalties, brushing aside the diplomatic interventions and stratagems of the American representative, Robert Murphy, de Gaulle was to emerge as the unassailable representative of France, despite his failure – which persisted to the end – to win over President Roosevelt. Roosevelt, in fact, was playing a Machiavellian game, based on a cold and calculating appraisal of the political forces then in play. There was only one thing wrong in his calculation: a total failure to understand the character and strength of Charles de Gaulle.

In this autumn of 1942, however, de Gaulle knew nothing of the plans and plots of his allies, though he guessed their military intentions. He could sense that the key to the isolation in which he was being kept was Roosevelt. He had already sent his emissary d'Astier to Washington, with limited results. And he now decided to send a second envoy, André Philip, the Socialist Resistance leader who had joined him in London, with a personal letter to the president of the United States. The letter started with fundamentals. France had borne the main burden of the 1914–18 war, from which she had emerged victorious but exhausted.[1] French errors of strategy and policy, together with lack of Allied support, had caused her defeat in the Second World War. It was essential to bring back France into the war. He had taken this upon himself. He was not a politician, and indeed agreed that he and his followers should not meddle in politics if this meant taking part in factional political quarrels. But if it meant defending French interests and fighting for France against the enemy, then he did engage in politics. He rejected all rumours that he had personal ambitions in France after the war. It was absurd to think he wished to be a dictator, or that the French people would allow a dictatorship. The American president had an enormous and uncontested prestige in France. But which France should the American president deal with? The France of yesterday? The France of Vichy? The France of tomorrow, whose shape remained unknown? No, he argued: the only France that counted during the war was now Fighting France. De Gaulle asked Roosevelt to "accept the idea of a general and direct examination of the relations between the United States and Fighting France".

The letter was dated 26 October. It was duly delivered. But President Roosevelt did not reply.

By that time, the president's plans, both military and political, were far advanced; and de Gaulle did not figure in them. Roosevelt had already picked another man as the instrument of his policy in North Africa – Henri Giraud.

On several counts, this choice was understandable. Giraud, a five-star general, outranked de Gaulle. He had had a distinguished career as a fighting soldier, and the fact that he was known not to have political ambitions helped to commend him to the Americans; although in the event, his total lack of political sense was to prove his undoing. Tall, erect and powerfully built, he had once had de Gaulle under his orders at Metz.[2] Captured by the Germans during the First World War, he had successfully escaped. And now, he had done it again. Despite his sixty-

[1] De Gaulle, L'Unité, pp. 381–5.   [2] See above, pp. 75–6.

three years, he had thrown a rope over the wall of the prison fortress of Koenigstein, and made his way to Switzerland in April 1942. With a price of 100,000 marks on his head, he reached the unoccupied zone of France and was summoned by Marshal Pétain, with whom he had a cordial talk. The Vichy Prime Minister, Laval, later tried to persuade him to surrender himself to the Germans, but Giraud naturally refused. In the end, he was told that if he wanted the Germans to leave him alone, he would have to sign a declaration of loyalty to Marshal Pétain. This fact was not known to the Americans when they decided to make a deal with him.[3] In due course, however, Vichy broadcast the text of Giraud's letter to Pétain, which the marshal had drafted, and which read:

Monsieur le Maréchal,

Following our recent talks, and to remove all doubt on my attitude, I want to express my sentiments of perfect loyalty towards you. You have been good enough to explain to me, together with the head of the government, the policy that you intend to follow towards Germany. I am fully in agreement with you. I give you my word as an officer that I shall do nothing that might embarrass in any way your relations with the German government or impede the task with which you have charged Admiral Darlan and Prime Minister Pierre Laval to carry out under your high authority. My past is the guarantee of my loyalty. I ask you, *Monsieur le Maréchal*, to accept the assurance of my absolute devotion.

Understandably, this fulsome declaration caused deep embarrassment when its text was disclosed. Another thing the Americans knew little about was Giraud's character. Without de Gaulle's intelligence, he was very nearly as intransigent. As a young officer in Tunis, encountering a local Jew dressed in native costume and apparently determined not to give way on a narrow pavement, Giraud had lifted the unfortunate man bodily in his powerful arms and thrown him into a shop window. When reprimanded, he said he had not hesitated to impose respect for his uniform and therefore for France.

With this background, he had matured into a fairly arrogant representative of the officer class. De Gaulle, to his credit, lost no time in publicly praising Giraud and in sending emissaries to him to propose cooperation in the interests of France.[4] In fact, he was offering Giraud the prospect of commanding a unified French army in the future battle for

---

[3] Claude Paillat, *L'Echequier d'Algier* (henceforth, Paillat, *L'Echequier*, Vol. I, pp. 311 *et seq.*; for other material in this chapter, *see also* pp. 323, 330–1.
[4] De Gaulle, *L'Unité*, pp. 9–11.

the liberation of France. Giraud, however, spurned de Gaulle's advances. He let it be known that the problem, as he saw it, could simply be solved within the normal military hierarchy. All he needed to do, he thought, was to show himself in North Africa, and everybody would rally to him because of his higher rank. Doubtless, this would include General de Gaulle.

General Giraud's military plans, as relayed to de Gaulle in London, struck him as pure fantasy, and comparable in simplicity with his political ideas. As Giraud saw it, the Allies already had their bridgehead – unoccupied France. All they needed to do was to land. He would take over the command of the Armistice Army in unoccupied France and all would be well. He appeared to overlook the need for a powerful fleet and for air support, and the probability that the Wehrmacht would immediately counter any Allied landings with an irresistible drive to the Mediterranean coast.

While Giraud was elaborating his dreams of glory, Robert Murphy was organising political support for the Allied cause in North Africa. Having served the State Department, not unsuccessfully, as *chargé d'affaires* at Vichy, he had been picked by President Roosevelt as his personal envoy to French Africa. After meeting General Weygand at Dakar, Murphy had gone on to North Africa. In Algiers, he had built up a number of contacts, the most important of which was the French businessman Lemaigre-Dubreuil, who owned peanut oil factories as far apart as Dakar and Dunkirk. This gave him a perfectly legitimate excuse for wide travels through French-speaking territories, and he became an indispensable source of information to Murphy.[5] At Murphy's behest, Lemaigre-Dubreuil had several clandestine meetings with Giraud. The going was never entirely easy. Giraud's first thought had been to appeal to Weygand, whom he asked to lead a general French uprising against the Germans, whether in Europe or in Africa. The old man, however, though he listened to Giraud with sympathy, declined his proposal on the grounds of age and ill health.

Giraud pressed on the Americans, through Lemaigre-Dubreuil, his idea of landings in southern France. Then he argued his own claims to the overall command of any expeditionary force, whether in France or in North Africa. The Americans played along with him. They dared not tell him that British troops would be taking part in the North African landings, as Giraud had specifically said that he would take part in the operation only if the Americans alone took part. In the end, Murphy sent an ambiguous message asking him to accept American command

[5] Robert Murphy, *Diplomat Among Warriors* (henceforth, Murphy), pp. 115 *et seq.*

during the early stages of the operation, without explaining in detail what would happen later.[6] After strong recriminations, Giraud agreed to come to Algiers a day or two before the invasion.

A complicating factor in American and British calculations was Admiral Darlan. The admiral, at that time Vichy's foreign minister, had been on a tour of inspection in North Africa. He was back in France when news came that his son had been stricken by poliomyelitis and taken to hospital in Algiers. Darlan then decided to fly back. It was 5 November 1942, and his return meant that he would be present at the time of the projected landings three days later. What was to be done? He had shown himself uncompromisingly hostile towards Britain and ready to collaborate with Hitler. On the other hand, both by his rank and his portfolio, he was in overriding authority on the spot, and therefore able, if he so chose, to order a surrender and keep Allied casualties to a minimum. Moreover, he held in his hands the fate of the powerful French fleet at Toulon.

It was a difficult decision, and it fell to General Dwight D. Eisenhower, who had been appointed overall commander-in-chief of the expeditionary forces, to take it. Churchill had placed Gibraltar under his command, and there he went on 5 November, to meet General Giraud, and explain to him the nature of the arrangements and his part in them. The vast operation had been baptised "Torch". A joint British-American force landed outside Algiers and Oran and an American one on the Atlantic side at Casablanca in Morocco. There was fierce resistance from the Vichy French, especially in Morocco, where the governor-general, Noguès, decreed uncompromising opposition to the landing. On the morning of the 9th, General Giraud was flown to Algiers to arrange an ending to the hostilities. To his surprise, however, he met with an icy reception from the French commanders.[7] It became clear that only Darlan carried the weight to bring the fighting to an end. Eisenhower's deputy, General Mark Clark, called on Darlan and gave him half an hour to make up his mind. Bowing to superior force, Darlan ordered a general cease-fire throughout North Africa, "in the name of the marshal". He assumed complete authority throughout the French North African territories and ordered the local authorities to stay at their posts.

By political good fortune, the Germans began to invade unoccupied France two days later. This enabled Darlan to claim that Pétain was no longer a free agent.

Where was de Gaulle in all this? From daybreak on 7 November

---

[6] ibid. p. 122.   [7] Churchill, Vol. IV, pp. 556 et seq.

1942 he knew in general terms that the landings in North Africa had begun, for the British and American radio stations were clamouring, "Robert is coming! Robert is coming!" Since Robert was Murphy's Christian name, he had no doubt that this was the code name for the expeditionary force.[8] At midday, summoned by the Prime Minister, de Gaulle went to 10 Downing Street, where Churchill and Eden greeted him with embarrassed friendliness. Churchill launched into an explanation. At sea and in the air, the British share was great, but on the ground the American forces outnumbered the British. In fact, it was an American show, with Eisenhower in command. And unfortunately, the Americans had insisted that the Free French should be kept out of it. "We were obliged to do this," said Churchill. "You may rest assured, however, that we do not in any way renounce our agreements with you. You are the one to whom we have, since June 1940, promised our support." More emotionally, he added, "You were with us in the worst moments of the war. We shall not abandon you now that the horizon is becoming brighter."[9]

On hearing of the proposal that General Giraud should take command of the French forces in North Africa, de Gaulle expressed his praise and good wishes. On the military side, however, he declared himself astonished that there was to be no landing at Bizerta, the great naval base in Tunisia, which he thought the Germans and Italians were bound to use. Moreover, he could have arranged for Koenig's division to disembark there. Churchill and Eden expressed agreement with him, but reminded him that the responsibility was with the Americans.

"I can't understand," said de Gaulle, "that you British should hand over so completely in an enterprise that concerns Europe above all." This was to become a recurring theme in his dealings with Churchill at this time.

The Prime Minister did not of course tell de Gaulle of the circumstances that had led him to keep the general in the dark about the North African landings.[10] In his memoirs, he attributed the decision to "the president's prejudices against General de Gaulle, the contacts he possessed through Admiral Leahy with Vichy, and our memories of the leakage about Dakar two years before". In a letter to the president on 5 November, however, Churchill reminded Roosevelt that he had exchanged letters with de Gaulle "of a solemn kind in 1940 recognising him as the leader of free Frenchmen". He went on to say that he was arranging

---

[8] Murphy (p. 127) gives a different and more plausible quotation, from the BBC's French service: "Allo, Robert, Franklin arrive."
[9] De Gaulle, L'Unité, p. 41.   [10] Churchill, Vol. IV, pp. 542–3.

to let de Gaulle announce General Legentilhomme's appointment as governor-general of Madagascar, as "his consolation prize".

Sickened by the news of heavy French, British and American casualties in the North African fighting, General de Gaulle summoned the American representative, Admiral Stark, on the afternoon of 9 November. The admiral was pained about the fighting, having doubted that there would be any. "Eisenhower, too," he said, "is surprised and upset." De Gaulle, however, wanted action. "I should like to send a mission to Algiers," he declared. "I request the government of the United States to take the necessary measures so that this mission may reach its destination." Stark promised to do what was necessary. Next day, de Gaulle wrote asking Churchill to intervene in his support with Roosevelt, and he ordered Pleven, Billotte, d'Astier and Frénay to prepare to go. On the evening of the 11th – Armistice day – the "Frenchmen of Great Britain" gathered in their thousands in the Albert Hall to hear General de Gaulle call passionately for the national unity of France. There was one discordant voice. It belonged to an aged soldier, General Eon, who had taken refuge in London. With a piece of paper in his hand, and in a quavery voice, General Eon read out a short statement calling on de Gaulle to place himself under General Giraud's orders, the latter being of higher rank than de Gaulle, having more troops at his disposal and having led forces in victorious battles. The speaker was manhandled and ejected from the hall by zealous and exasperated Gaullists.[11]

At Algiers, in the meantime, a curious and sordid situation was developing. The Giraud plan, and the Murphy-Giraud agreements which had made it possible, assumed the general's arrival on French soil ahead of the military expedition. But his own hesitations had contributed to his arriving a day late, and the Americans had therefore felt it necessary to deal with Admiral Darlan, who happened to be present although his presence had not been envisaged. Cold-shouldered by his brother officers because he lacked a regular command, Giraud was impotent. Darlan retained his authority over the local French officers and functionaries, but lost it in France itself by virtue of his willingness to work with the Americans. Thus his order on the afternoon of 11 November that the Toulon fleet was to put to sea if in danger of capture by the Germans was ignored by the commander of the French Mediterranean fleet, Admiral de Laborde, who was, if anything, even more fanatically anti-British than Darlan himself. On the 27th the Germans started an operation to take over the fleet. Laborde and his subordinates thereupon

[11] Paillat, L'Echiquier, Vol. II, p. 77. De Gaulle mentions this incident in L'Unité (pp. 45–6), but not the old man's name.

decided on a wholesale scuttling; seventy-three ships sank in the port. They included one battleship, two battle cruisers, seven cruisers, twenty-nine destroyers and torpedo-boats and sixteen submarines.[12] In London, de Gaulle heard the news with frustrated sadness and anger. This same Laborde was the man who, on hearing the news of the Allied landings, had wished to put his fleet to sea to attack the Allied convoys.

The Germans had intercepted Darlan's message to Pétain announcing the cease-fire. Under their pressure, Pétain immediately disavowed Darlan, who thereupon told the Americans that since he had been deprived of his mandate, he regarded himself as no more than their prisoner. An ingenious solution was found on 12 November, when Noguès arrived in Algiers from Morocco with the news that Marshal Pétain had conferred full powers on him. After stormy discussions, Noguès transferred his powers to Darlan, who assumed the title of high commissioner and appointed Giraud commander-in-chief of all French forces. This agreement was obviously satisfactory to Giraud, whose aspirations were purely military, and to Darlan who may have thought that they would safeguard his future in the event of an Allied victory. And they brought temporary relief to the Americans on the spot: General Mark Clark, who took the decision to recognise Darlan, and Robert Murphy, who had done the negotiating. It was, however, frustrating to two groups of local Frenchmen: Lemaigre-Dubreuil, who had been Murphy's intermediary with Giraud, and his group, who found themselves without jobs; and the small network of semi-clandestine Gaullists, headed by Professor René Capitant, of the Resistance group known as Combat. In a wider sense, it was impossible to disguise the unsavoury character of the Darlan deal. General Eisenhower endorsed it after the event on military grounds, and was supported by Roosevelt; and the president's view, in turn, was grudgingly upheld by Winston Churchill.

General de Gaulle was of course bitterly shocked at the ease with which President Roosevelt, in Darlan's case, had discarded the democratic and juridical scruples that had prevented him from recognising de Gaulle himself. Both in Britain and in America, the press had reacted with shocked hostility. On 16 November, de Gaulle called on Churchill and Eden and told them that the decision to deal with Darlan could not be justified on strategic grounds, as was being argued. "It is a strategic error to put oneself in contradiction with the moral character of this war," said the general.

The force of de Gaulle's argument, and of the mounting wave of protests, both in the press and in private, alarmed Churchill, who cabled

[12] Churchill, Vol. IV, pp. 563–8.

Roosevelt on the 17th to remind him of Darlan's "odious record" and to urge the president to consider the deal with the admiral as only "a temporary expedient, justifiable solely by the stress of battle". Serious political injury might be done to the Allied cause, he went on, "by the feeling that we are ready to make terms with the local quislings". Next day, at his press conference, President Roosevelt adopted as his own the Prime Minister's phrase "only a temporary expedient, justified solely by the stress of battle", in an explanation of why it had been necessary to reach an arrangement with Darlan.

There is no doubt that Churchill's message to Roosevelt had reflected his genuine concern, but the Prime Minister's views on Darlan were ambivalent. He admired the admiral's strength of character and naval expertise. And he once told Eisenhower: "If I could meet Darlan, much as I hate him, I would cheerfully crawl on my hands and knees for a mile if by doing so I could get him to bring that fleet of his into the circle of Allied forces."[13]

At de Gaulle's orders, the French National Committee published a communiqué dissociating itself from the Allied arrangements in Algiers. After his meeting with Churchill and Eden, de Gaulle had stayed on to lunch. The conversation was strained, although the Prime Minister tried to placate the general by observing that events were in fact likely to turn out for the best as far as he was concerned. Giraud, he remarked, was already liquidated politically, and Darlan would be in time. "You will be the only one," he added. And he urged the general to be patient, for in time the Americans would come to him as there was no alternative.

But the general was not so easily soothed. Returning to his earlier theme, he exclaimed, "As for you, I don't understand you. You have been waging the war since the first day. One could even say that you, personally, *are* the war. Your army is advancing in Libya. There would be no Americans in Africa if, on your side, you were not beating Rommel. At this hour, no soldier of Roosevelt has yet met one of Hitler's soldiers, whereas for three years your men have been fighting everywhere. In any case, in the African affair, it is Europe that is engaged and England belongs to Europe. And yet, you allow America to take the direction of the conflict. It is up to you to exercise it, at least in the moral domain. Do it! Public opinion in Europe will follow you."

Despite Churchill's successful appeal to Roosevelt on the temporary nature of the Darlan deal, however, the BBC twice censored Free French statements over the next few days, for fear of offending the Americans. Bitterly, de Gaulle said to Churchill on the 24th, "I am aware that on

[13] Dwight D. Eisenhower, *Crusade in Europe*, p. 116 (henceforth, Eisenhower, *Crusade*).

British territory radio does not belong to me." But Churchill's behaviour, he added in his memoirs, showed that it did not belong to him either.[14]

The previous day in Washington, de Gaulle's envoys, Tixier and Philip, had protested against the Darlan deal, and the irate president had exclaimed, "Of course I shall deal with Darlan, since Darlan is giving me Algiers! Tomorrow, I shall deal with Laval if Laval gives me Paris!" He added, however, that he would very much like to see General de Gaulle in Washington, and asked the two men to convey his invitation to the general. De Gaulle had hoped that at least the Russians could support him about Darlan, but he had counted without Stalin's habitual cynicism. The Soviet dictator, in fact, told Churchill and Roosevelt that he thought it was "a great achievement" to have brought Darlan into the mainstream of the Allies fighting Hitler.[15]

Although resolved to have no dealings of his own with Admiral Darlan, de Gaulle was still anxious to send his own men to Algiers so that he could have a first-hand account of the troubled situation. Faced with a continuing British and American veto, he made a personal appeal to General Eisenhower, who said he would welcome a visit from General François d'Astier, brother of Emmanuel d'Astier, the Resistance leader whom de Gaulle had sent to Washington earlier, and of Henri d'Astier, one of the Gaullist group in Algiers. General d'Astier reached Algiers on 20 December and found all the political and military groups affected by bitterness, frustration or bewilderment. The two Vichyists were reluctant to follow Darlan, now that Pétain had denounced him. The Gaullists were plotting. The Lemaigre-Dubreuil group were deeply frustrated; and the Americans – led by Eisenhower himself – were determined that the Darlan deal should be no more than an interlude. At a stormy meeting with Darlan himself, in Giraud's presence, General d'Astier told the admiral that his presence was the main obstacle to unity, and that the best thing he could do would be to fade out. At Darlan's request, the Americans then asked d'Astier to return to London; which he did on the 24th.

But Darlan's short reign was about to end with violent suddenness. On Christmas Eve, as he was climbing the steps to his offices, he was shot down by a young man called Bonnier de la Chapelle. Within an hour, the admiral was dead. The assassin had thought it his duty to rid the French people of a dishonoured leader, but he was immediately court-martialled on General Giraud's orders, and – although only twenty – was shot on 26 December.

*   *   *

[14] De Gaulle, *L'Unité*, p. 54.   [15] Churchill, Vol. IV, p. 598.

Darlan's death removed a major obstacle in the path of General de Gaulle. But its immediate consequences were to complicate still further an already confused situation. On 27 December, de Gaulle had packed his luggage and was on his way to the airport to fly to Washington, when he was informed that Churchill and Roosevelt had decided his trip should be cancelled. The reason given was the consequences of the assassination. Recording this, Robert E. Sherwood wrote: "The beginnings of the achievement of French unity were thereby delayed for five months, during which some animosities deepened to an almost irreparable extent. It was a deplorable mischance."[16]

Back from the airport, de Gaulle immediately cabled General Giraud to say that the murder of Darlan was a warning. Now, more than ever, it was necessary that a national authority should be established. He proposed a meeting with Giraud as soon as possible in French territory, either in Algeria or in Tchad.

But the general was in no hurry to reply. The interrogation of the young assassin had disclosed some unexpected connections. The prominent Gaullist, Henri d'Astier, himself a high official in Algiers, appeared to be implicated. Some dollar notes had been found in the young man's possession, and a much larger quantity, numbered in the same series, were found in d'Astier's home. Thereupon, he was arrested. To some, including Americans, it now looked as if de Gaulle himself was implicated in the murder of Darlan. This was certainly untrue, but it was the kind of thing Roosevelt and his advisers were predisposed to believe.

On Christmas Day, Admiral Leahy had cabled Eisenhower, authorising him "to appoint Giraud" as Darlan's successor.[17] This was to overestimate Eisenhower's powers over the local French. When the French Imperial Council met the following day, however, Giraud was unanimously elected high commissioner and commander-in-chief. In these new and exalted capacities, Giraud was little disposed to listen to de Gaulle. On the 27th, Churchill warned de Gaulle that he would do nothing to oppose American policy even if Washington handed all French Africa to Giraud. On the 28th, de Gaulle paid tribute to Giraud and renewed his call for the unity of fighting Frenchmen. Next day, the 29th, Giraud at last decided to reply, but only to say that owing to the emotion aroused by Darlan's murder he thought the time was unfavourable for a meeting between them.

In a cabled reply on 1 January 1943, de Gaulle expressed his pleasure at this first exchange of views; no less ironically, he added that the complexity of the situation in Algiers did not escape him. But he could see

16 Sherwood, Hopkins, pp. 659–60.   17 Funk, p. 49.

no objections to a meeting at Fort-Lamy, Brazzaville or Beirut: "I await your reply with confidence."[18]

He followed this up with a radio speech on the 2nd, calling for the formation of a provisional central government on a broader base. This speech appears to have irritated the Americans, and in his memoirs de Gaulle attributes their irritation to the fact, as he saw it, that he had made it publicly clear he was ready to meet Giraud anywhere; since Giraud was reluctant, Murphy's advice must be to blame. In his own memoirs, Robert Murphy declared himself astonished at the attention he receives in de Gaulle's book. De Gaulle, he thought, greatly exaggerated his influence with Roosevelt, and had fallen for attempts by the Nazis to blacken his character as the exponent of a policy – the encouragement of Vichy's independence of Germany – which they feared.[19]

It is now clear that both men in their reasoning overlooked the stubbornness and limitations of General Giraud, and his rigid attachment to hierarchy. He was to say repeatedly that he had no interest in politics and that his only interest was to wage the war on Germany. De Gaulle represented politics, and therefore "trouble" and a diversion of the military effort. Moreover, he had three fewer stars than Giraud. In any case, he (Giraud) now had supreme civil and military power and, at one bound, several times the number of troops at his disposal than de Gaulle commanded in the fourth year of his lone effort. Any arrangement with de Gaulle could only dilute his own power. In these circumstances, he did not need Murphy's advice to make him resist de Gaulle's overtures.

De Gaulle was on surer ground, however, in attributing interventionist ambitions to Roosevelt. As the general surmised, it probably did suit the president that Fighting France should be kept out of Algiers, where Darlan's death had made it possible to install their own nominee after his initial failure to impose his authority.

When, on 4 January, Sumner Welles, the under-secretary of State, summoned Tixier to complain of de Gaulle's invitations to Giraud on the grounds that they were "political", de Gaulle was not surprised. Tixier, well briefed, asked why this should be unfortunate and got the usual answer: the military situation – "as though," wrote de Gaulle later, "the understanding proposed by de Gaulle threatened Eisenhower's communications in North Africa!"[20]

De Gaulle saw the proof of Roosevelt's intentions in the deferment of his own projected trip to Washington on 27 December 1942. He was, however, wrong, I believe, in blaming Roosevelt for Giraud's next mes-

[18] De Gaulle, *L'Unité*, p. 72. [19] Murphy, pp. 177–8.
[20] De Gaulle, *L'Unité*, p. 74.

sage, which reached him on 6 January. This time, Giraud said he agreed in principle to meet de Gaulle in Algiers, but regretted that "prior engagements" ruled out a meeting before the end of January. Furious, de Gaulle replied: "I must tell you frankly that the National Committee and I myself have different views as to the degree of urgency presented by the achievement of the unity of the Empire and the union of its efforts with those of the national resistance."

Despite these frustrations, de Gaulle was soon to meet Giraud, but in unforeseen circumstances and in an unexpected place.

Chapter 9 ⚜ Casablanca

In November 1942, General Montgomery's forces had broken Rommel's lines at El Alamein in one of the decisive battles of the Second World War. The road to Tripoli lay open. A month later, the German 6th Army was encircled at Stalingrad. The probability of a general Nazi retreat on the eastern front loomed ahead. What was to happen next: a second front, or an attack on Europe's "soft underbelly", via Sicily and Sardinia?

Consultation at the Summit seemed necessary. Roosevelt was not displeased at the prospect of escape from the political pressures of Washington, and Churchill was always game for a trip. Stalin, however, could not absent himself from the life-and-death struggle on Soviet soil.

But there was no reason why the British and American leaders should not meet. Iceland was considered and rejected. In the end, it was decided to meet in Casablanca, on the Atlantic coast of Morocco. Accommodation of appropriate comfort was arranged in the suburb of Anfa, where Churchill arrived on 12 January 1943. Roosevelt followed two days later. Also in attendance were Robert Murphy and Britain's new minister of State in the Middle East, Harold Macmillan.

Churchill soon persuaded Roosevelt that the situation in Algiers was serious enough for urgent action to be required. The president opted for a meeting between Giraud and de Gaulle, under the benevolent supervision of the Big Two. His attitude towards the rival French leaders was one of amused, indeed almost frivolous, superiority. "We'll call Giraud the bridegroom," he told Churchill, "and I'll produce him from Algiers, and you get the bride, de Gaulle, down from London, and we'll have a shot-gun wedding."[1]

At this supreme moment of the war, with the tide turning at last in the Allies' favour, there was remarkably little confidence between president and Prime Minister. In his memoirs, Churchill dismisses as "rubbish" the account of certain aspects of the Casablanca conference made by the president's son, Elliott Roosevelt, who was present at some of the meals with his father and the Prime Minister.[2] But there is no reason to doubt the authenticity of Elliott Roosevelt's account of his private conversations with his father, in which the president said the real reason Churchill stood by de Gaulle was that there was a community of interests between them in preserving the British and French colonial empires after the war. Roosevelt was to make it clear that he did not share these preoccupations.

At all events, the attempt to bring the two French generals together went ahead. Giraud came first, on 17 January, with a small retinue. Before he arrived, Roosevelt had heard from Murphy and Eisenhower that Giraud was proving a disappointment to the hopes the Americans had vested in him. Impulsive and overbearing, he still wanted to assume the overall Allied supreme command and lacked both knowledge of, and interest in, civil administration[3] (which came within the scope of the powers conferred upon him after Darlan's murder). The president needed only one meeting with Giraud to find himself sharing his subordinates' poor opinion of the general. It did not, however, displease him that "his" Frenchman in Algiers should have a poor grasp of administration and no political ambition. The opposite was true of de Gaulle, and this was a point against him. The president told his son he was sure de Gaulle intended to establish one-man rule in France and asked how one could have confidence in the Gaullists, whose organisation was permeated with spies and informers.[4]

Roosevelt did agree, however, that de Gaulle must be brought to Casablanca. But this, as might have been guessed, did not prove at all easy. De Gaulle had been hoping and waiting for a fresh invitation to Washington, and had no idea that Roosevelt had gone to Morocco. Instead, a telegram from Churchill was handed to him by Anthony

[1] Roosevelt press conference, 12 February 1943. Samuel I. Rosenman, compiler, *Public Papers and Addresses of Franklin D. Roosevelt, 1943*, p. 83.
[2] Churchill, Vol. IV, pp. 609–10; *see also* p. 611.
[3] Funk, pp. 65–6.
[4] Paillat, *L'Echiquier*, Vol. II, p. 182; for ensuing matter, *see also* pp. 189 and 213.

Eden on 17 January. The Prime Minister asked de Gaulle to join him in Morocco where, he said, he could meet Giraud "in conditions of complete discretion".

Eden explained that Roosevelt was in Morocco too, but this merely deepened the disfavour with which de Gaulle greeted Churchill's message. If Roosevelt was there, why hadn't Churchill said so? Why was he being invited in the Prime Minister's name alone? He had no wish to go through with the unbecoming comedy of being Churchill's fighter against Giraud in Roosevelt's corner.[5] Without consulting the National Committee, de Gaulle immediately cabled a negative reply, reminding Churchill that he had been trying unsuccessfully to arrange a meeting with Giraud. A meeting between Frenchmen would be best, he argued, and he didn't fancy the atmosphere of a "high-level Allied Aeropagus" that was proposed for a meeting that would be best arranged between Frenchmen. At the same time, he cabled Giraud to repeat that he was ready for a meeting "on French territory and between Frenchmen, wherever and whenever you should wish it".

De Gaulle's first refusal exposed Churchill to the full sting of Roosevelt's sarcasm.[6] Deeply mortified, Churchill sent a second message to de Gaulle, dated 19 January. The Prime Minister declared himself authorised to say that the invitation to Casablanca was from the president of the United States as well as himself. The tone was distinctly menacing. To refuse to come, Churchill told de Gaulle, would be to expose himself to the censure of public opinion, to the collapse of the Prime Minister's efforts to bridge the difficulties between the Gaullists and the Americans, and to a reconsideration of His Majesty's government's position towards his movement "while you remain at its head".

Unwilling to appear to be yielding before such threats, de Gaulle now decided to refer the matter to a full meeting of his committee. It was decided, after a deliberately protracted debate, that de Gaulle should go, if only for the sake of meeting Roosevelt. De Gaulle therefore told Churchill that the war situation and the state in which France found herself "provisionally" did not permit him to refuse to meet the president of the United States of America and the Prime Minister of His Britannic Majesty. This unenthusiastic formula came at the end of a fairly long cable in which General de Gaulle bitterly complained about Allied arrangements made without prior consultation and a sudden invitation to discuss vital problems without knowing the agenda of the discussions or the conditions in which they were to be held.

[5] De Gaulle, *L'Unité*, p. 75; for ensuing matter, *see also* pp. 77–96.
[6] Cordell Hull, *The Memoirs of Cordell Hull* (1948), Vol. II, p. 1207 (henceforth, Hull).

Without unseemly haste, de Gaulle picked his travelling companions: General Catroux, Admiral d'Argenlieu, Gaston Palewski, who had become his *chef de cabinet,* and his original *chef de cabinet,* Hettier de Boislambert, captured at Dakar and gaoled by Vichy but the hero of a successful escape. The party arrived at Casablanca's Fedala airport on 22 January 1943.

De Gaulle immediately found material for outrage. Here they were, on French soil, but isolated, surrounded by armed American soldiers and hemmed in by barbed wire. Giraud had invited de Gaulle and his *entourage* to lunch, and they found him similarly circumscribed. The first contact between the two men lacked cordiality. Giraud greeted him with a curt *"Bonjour, de Gaulle",* as though he were still military governor of Metz with de Gaulle his subordinate. De Gaulle embarrassed him by pointing out the "odious" conditions in which they were meeting, among strangers and surrounded by barbed wire. During the meal, de Gaulle relented sufficiently to ask Giraud to tell the story of his sensational escape. When the conversation turned to current affairs, however, the Gaullists needed all their leader's icy restraint on hearing the five-star general tell them he had nothing against Vichy: all he wanted was to fight the Germans. This they did not doubt, but they could hardly be expected to sympathise with Giraud's view that Vichy's proconsuls in North Africa – Noguès, Peyrouton, Boisson and Bergeret – should stay in their present jobs. As for the Resistance, Giraud found its revolutionary ideas incomprehensible or distasteful.

As usual in difficult inter-allied circumstances, de Gaulle had decided to go into a carefully calculated sulk. It was in this "mood" that Harold Macmillan found him that afternoon. On hearing that Macmillan and Murphy were trying to work out a formula for union that would reconcile de Gaulle and Giraud, the Free French leader tried to make him comprehend that only an understanding "between Frenchmen" could be valid. He agreed, however, to see Churchill.

A veteran, by now – and habitually a victorious one – of monumental clashes with Churchill, de Gaulle went in on the attack. He would never have come, he exclaimed, had he known he would be surrounded, on French soil, by American bayonets. Having made his point, he calmed down. Churchill then explained the "solution" the president and he had elaborated. De Gaulle and Giraud were to be joint chairmen of an executive committee. Their powers would be equal, but Giraud, in addition, would be the supreme military commander, since the Americans, who would be supplying the unified French army, insisted on it. Perhaps "my friend General Georges" could be a third co-chairman of the committee, which would include the current high officials in French North Africa – Noguès, Peyrouton, Boisson and Bergeret.

In excellent form, de Gaulle commented that these arrangements might seem adequate at the (respectable) level of American sergeant-majors, but Churchill could hardly expect him to take them seriously. He held Roosevelt and Churchill himself in the highest esteem, but did not recognise in them the slightest qualification for settling the question of powers in the French empire. Without consulting him, and indeed against him, the Allies had set up a system in Algiers and now found it did not work. They proposed therefore to drown Fighting France in it. The Fighting French would have none of it: if they had to disappear, they would do so with honour.

De Gaulle saw the problem in moral terms, Churchill in political. "Look at my own government," said the premier. "When I formed it in the first place, selected as I was for having long fought the spirit of Munich, I brought all our Municheers into it. Well, they all played the game completely, so much so that today one can't tell them apart from the others."

"I'm not a politician trying to make a cabinet and find a majority in parliament," countered de Gaulle.

In the end, Churchill undertook to reflect further on the union project. On showing de Gaulle out, he pointed out that British, not American, soldiers were on guard.

Robert Murphy had been detailed to introduce de Gaulle to President Roosevelt.[7] They talked for half an hour before going to the president's villa. Murphy appealed to him not to make legalistic conditions. If he did not, "you will have complete control of the French political situation within three months, because General Giraud is interested solely in his military command and has no political ambitions." De Gaulle, writes Murphy, "smiled thinly and replied, 'Political ambitions can develop rapidly. For example, look at me!' "

Deeply impressed by de Gaulle, Murphy noted in his memoirs that the general, having delayed his arrival, had made a grand entrance and stolen the show from the two greatest English-speaking politicians.

When the president met de Gaulle that day for the first time, his mind was made up on French affairs. It is not entirely fair, however, to attribute his attitude, as de Gaulle does, exclusively to an American thirst for domination. He regarded the sovereignty of France as resting with the French people but suspended by the German occupation, and to be

---

[7] In his memoirs, de Gaulle says the president had sent him "somebody" to arrange their meeting, which took place late in the evening (De Gaulle, *L'Unité*, p. 79).

restored only when the people should again be able to express their will freely. For this reason, he was not disposed to recognise any provisional government, whether headed by de Gaulle or anybody else. Beside these ethically valid reasons must of course be set Roosevelt's personal antipathy towards de Gaulle's public personality, for the rigidity of his pretensions and his "prima donna" behaviour, which he seems to have found irresistibly funny – a fact which he unfortunately did not trouble to hide.[8]

The president, although his mind was closed, had turned on his famous charm at this first meeting. The two men talked for an hour, seated together on a couch. But de Gaulle was conscious of unseen presences in the dim background and behind the curtains, and found them disturbing. He learned later that the moving shadows were those of Harry Hopkins, secretaries, and presidential bodyguards.

Next day, Giraud called on de Gaulle. At last, the two men were alone together. Giraud outlined his proposals, which turned out to be the same as those de Gaulle had heard from Churchill, with an interesting additional detail: de Gaulle was to be promoted to general of the army, so that he should not be outranked by the other members of the triumvirate, Giraud and Georges.[9] As for the Vichy proconsuls, they could keep their jobs, except, perhaps, Bergeret. The others could be joined by Catroux and perhaps Eboué.

This plan drew from de Gaulle a coldly devastating lecture. All Giraud was doing, he observed, was to attribute power to himself under Roosevelt's protection and with a more or less impressive supporting cast. De Gaulle went on in the kind of noble historical style he had used in his famous Saint-Cyr lectures twenty years earlier. It was as though, he explained, Giraud were setting up a Bonapartist consulate at the foreigner's discretion. But Bonaparte was almost unanimously supported. What kind of plebiscite did Giraud have in mind. If he called one, would it turn out in his favour?

With cruel logic, de Gaulle pressed on. Bonaparte could present himself as a leader who had won great victories and conquered vast provinces

[8] That these were Roosevelt's views on the eve of the Casablanca conference is strongly suggested by an unsigned memorandum, dated 24 December 1942, and found in the Harry Hopkins papers. See Sherwood, *Hopkins*, Vol. II, pp. 677–8. Roosevelt's hostility towards de Gaulle's ideas was probably deepened by personal antipathy when the two men met at Casablanca. It was during the conference that Roosevelt started telling the well-known story that he had told de Gaulle he must choose between being Joan of Arc and Clemenceau, since he couldn't be both. The anecdote, though it arose out of de Gaulle's reported remarks on different occasions, was apocryphal, says Hopkins (p. 683). But this did not prevent Roosevelt from recounting it whenever the occasion presented itself. This kind of humour did not amuse de Gaulle or his followers.
[9] Giraud does not mention this proposal in his memoirs, *Un Seul But: La Victoire* (1949), pp. 105 *et seq.* (henceforth, Giraud).

for France. He hoped, with all his soul, that Giraud would do as much. But for the time being, where were Giraud's triumphs? He added that the first consul excelled in legislative and administrative matters. Were these really Giraud's aptitudes? Moreover, he could not ignore that French public opinion now condemned Vichy. But Giraud's powers derived from Darlan, Noguès and the rest, and he had taken them over in the marshal's name. Everybody knew about his letter to Pétain giving his word that he would do nothing against the marshal's policy.[10] Did he really suppose, under these conditions, that he could hope for even elementary support from the French people or that he had any chance of preserving French sovereignty, depending, as he did, on the Anglo-Saxons?

Giraud could only reply, as he usually did, that all this was politics and he wanted no part of it. All he wanted was to rebuild the French forces. On this ground, he had advantages, which he pressed. Thanks to the agreement he had just concluded with the American president, he counted on raising twelve fully equipped divisions in six months. How many divisions did de Gaulle think he would have in that time? Where would he get the arms from?

The question of a competition in numbers did not arise, rejoined de Gaulle. The forces that happened to be in North Africa belonged to France, not to Giraud, as he would soon discover if no agreement between them was reached. The real problem was to set up a unified central power.

Giraud refused to give way. But de Gaulle, finding him "more obstinate than convinced", now hoped he would come round later. The two men did at least agree to set up a liaison group in North Africa, to be headed, on de Gaulle's side, by Catroux.

That de Gaulle was fighting with his back to the wall now became more apparent than ever. Robert Murphy called on him that afternoon to tell him about the new Anglo-American arrangements with Giraud. "In North Africa," he declared, "there are no more than ten per cent of Gaullists."[11] And he went on to confirm that arms and foodstuffs would henceforth be made available to Giraud's administration, which was formally recognised by both the American president and the British Prime Minister as "managing French military, economic and financial

[10] Giraud records bitterly that de Gaulle, at this meeting, produced a copy of his letter of loyalty to Pétain (*see above*, p. 197) but was discountenanced when Giraud asked de Gaulle if he was aware that in a further letter dated 8 November 1942, Giraud had retracted his earlier declaration.
[11] Robert Murphy, in conversation with Arthur Layton Funk, attributed the estimate of ten per cent to de Gaulle himself. See Funk, p. 74.

interests, which are associated or will be associated with the movement of national liberation now established in French North and West Africa".

De Gaulle heard Murphy with scepticism and displeasure. While approving of the supply arrangements, the point that struck him was that America and England, constituting themselves judges of French interests, were to deal with Giraud alone who, on the pretext of not dabbling in politics, would accept their authority. That French interests, thus interpreted, would not be respected, he had no doubt, and examples soon confirmed his fears. Giraud, for instance, had raised no objections when Churchill had proposed that the pound sterling should be worth 250 francs in North Africa, whereas it was worth only 176 francs according to the agreements negotiated between the British and the Free French. Similarly, Giraud had found nothing to say on learning Roosevelt had expressed his hostility to French colonialism in conversation with his dinner guest, the Sultan of Morocco, and earlier, in conversation with Vichy's representative, Noguès.[12]

The pressure on de Gaulle was kept up by Macmillan and the French-speaking American General William H. Wilbur whom de Gaulle had known in younger days when both were at the Ecole Supérieure de Guerre. Early next morning, Macmillan and Murphy brought de Gaulle the text of a proposed agreement between him and Giraud which the two diplomats had drafted during the night. An anodyne document, with a ritual reference to the United Nations, it committed the two generals to nothing more than the intention to form a joint committee to administer the French empire for the duration of the war.

Three things, however, damned it in General de Gaulle's eyes. It came from the Allies; it would oblige de Gaulle to renounce his existing administration; and it would give the impression that there was agreement where there was none. Having consulted his companions, de Gaulle therefore replied that no agreement affecting French power could come from foreign intervention, however friendly or exalted. But he declared himself ready to see the president and Prime Minister again before the conference disbanded, as it was scheduled to do that afternoon.

By de Gaulle's own account, his meeting with Churchill that day was the toughest of the series during the entire war. Bitter and vehement, the Prime Minister threatened that on his return to London, he would publicly accuse de Gaulle of having prevented an agreement, would mobilise British public opinion against him and appeal to French public

[12] For a full account of the dinner, to which neither Giraud nor de Gaulle was invited, see Elliott Roosevelt As He Saw It, pp. 109–12; for Roosevelt's conversation with Noguès, see ibid. pp. 37–9. See also Murphy, pp. 172–3.

opinion for support. De Gaulle, in return, accused Churchill of espousing a cause that was unacceptable to France, worrying for Europe and regrettable for England; and all this to give satisfaction, whatever the cost, to the Americans.

The general's second meeting with Roosevelt followed. It was doubtless a consolation to the Free French leader to know that weak as he was, and however powerful the president, he had at that moment something the president badly wanted and only he could give – consent to a French agreement. As Sherwood records, "Roosevelt knew what the criticism would be if he returned to Washington without having achieved any *rapprochement* between de Gaulle and Giraud."[13] De Gaulle was not, however, willing to give the president more than the appearance of an understanding, and even then only on his own terms.

Roosevelt's welcome, says de Gaulle, was "clever, that is, amiable and sorrowful". He was sorry to note that he had failed to persuade de Gaulle even to accept the text of a communiqué. The public, he declared, needed drama. The news that Giraud and de Gaulle had met during a conference in which he himself and Churchill had taken part, would produce the desired effect if there was some common declaration, even if the agreement reached was only theoretical.

"Leave it to me," answered de Gaulle. "There will be a communiqué, although it can't be the one you want."

He then presented his assistants to Roosevelt, who introduced his. Churchill, Giraud and their respective collaborators entered, together with Allied generals and officials. Taking advantage of this audience, Churchill launched into a fresh diatribe against de Gaulle. Murphy paints Churchill, in a white fury, shaking his finger in the general's face. "In his inimitable French, with his dentures clicking, Churchill exclaimed 'Mon Général, il ne faut pas obstacler [sic] la guerre!' " Affecting not to notice Churchill's outburst, however, the president, at his most charming, inquired whether de Gaulle would at least consent to be photographed next to him and next to the British Prime Minister, at the same time as General Giraud?

The favour asked was small, and de Gaulle conferred it with good grace: "Of course," he replied, "for I have the highest esteem for that great soldier."

"Would you," exclaimed the president, "go so far as to shake General Giraud's hand in our presence and in front of the camera lenses?"

De Gaulle replied in English: "I shall do that for you." A further invasion of the room, this time by reporters and photographers, followed.

[13] Sherwood, *Hopkins*, Vol. I, p. 677.

Twice, the two generals stiffly posed for pictures symbolising reconciliation.

Before leaving Anfa, de Gaulle drafted a brief statement, which he showed to Giraud, without "of course" making the text known to the Allies. In its final form, it read:

> We have met. We have talked. We have noted our complete agreement on the goal to be achieved, which is that of the liberation of France and the triumph of human liberties by the total defeat of the enemy.
>
> This goal will be achieved by the union in war of all Frenchmen fighting side by side with all their Allies.

In de Gaulle's draft, he had referred to the triumph of "democratic principles". At Giraud's request, he substituted "human liberties". The reference to "all" Allies was presumably intended as a reminder that France's Allies included the Russians as well as the "Anglo-Saxons".

Writing many years after the event, Robert Murphy, the principal political executant of Roosevelt's policy, thought de Gaulle had won an "unproclaimed victory" at the Casablanca conference, which he saw as "a great step forward in his plan to assure France the largest possible share in Allied conquests, including full restoration of the French empire". Too late, he realised that he, and everybody else at Casablanca, had miscalculated about de Gaulle in their belief that he gave the same priority to winning the war as they did. Hindsight had given Murphy the benefit of studying de Gaulle's own war memoirs, from which it became clear that de Gaulle's thoughts were "two jumps ahead of everybody else's". For in 1943 de Gaulle realised an Allied victory had become certain, whatever the French forces did or failed to do. His own priority was to restore France's position as a great power, by never admitting that she was anything less, and by his intuitive feeling that he could extract greater concessions while the war was on than later, even though France, at that time, was weaker than she had been for centuries.

Giraud, on his side, was plainly bewildered to learn, as Odic had been,[14] that whereas he had one enemy – the Axis – de Gaulle had two: the Axis and Vichy. Nor was his hostility towards the former necessarily the greater. As General Eisenhower shrewdly noted, de Gaulle's attitude faced his brother officers with an unsavoury choice: if *he* was right, they were cowards for obeying the orders of their government; if *they* were right, then he was no more than a deserter. For that reason, de Gaulle was widely disliked in the French army.[15]

*   *   *

[14] *See above*, pp. 169–70.   [15] Eisenhower, *Crusade*, pp. 93–4.

Having stood his ground at Casablanca, de Gaulle had to pay the usual price in Allied obstacles and difficulties of all kinds. He had planned to go from Anfa to Libya to inspect his forces, but was told the only plane available was bound for London. There, he and his four companions arrived on 26 January. And there, at a press conference on 9 February, he gave his version of what had really happened at Casablanca, which understandably contrasted with the British and American official versions. Once again, he was punished. Having let it be known that he wished to go back to the Near East, he learned from the British government on 3 March, in writing, that they would not provide transport for the journey.

Nor was the vilification of de Gaulle confined to British and American sources. The theme of his "deplorable pride" and "disappointed ambition" was taken up with gusto by French journalists and broadcasters in London and Washington; though he had some defenders, too, among the articulate French in exile. When French sailors, both naval and merchant, deserted their ships in New York harbour, asking to enlist under de Gaulle's banner, the American authorities had some of them arrested, and protested in the strongest terms to the Free French in Washington and London on the ground that de Gaulle was sabotaging the war effort by calling for volunteers.

De Gaulle, however, kept his eyes firmly on his political strategy. The power and the action were in Algiers, and he was determined to get there, but only on his terms. Tactically, his instrument was General Catroux, who was to head the liaison committee in Algiers and who had called there on his way to Beirut from Casablanca. On 18 February Catroux cabled de Gaulle a report on the situation in Algiers. Giraud, he said, seemed to be a temporiser, not the resolute man most people had thought he was. In consequence, many local Frenchmen were disappointed in him and had come to Catroux offering their services.[16] Since Giraud was on the spot, nothing could be done without him, but Catroux was confident that he could be guided in the right direction.

The essential point, from the Gaullist standpoint, was to put pressure on Giraud to cut his links with Vichy. Catroux had made it clear that the "undesirables" had to be eliminated if there was to be an understanding. On 23 February, on his instructions, the National Committee drafted a memorandum addressed to "the Civil and Military Commander-in-Chief" (Giraud), calling on him to declare the 1940 armistice null and void: remove the men of Vichy from top administrative posts; and re-establish "Republican legality" – that is, cancel the Vichy laws.

[16] De Gaulle, *L'Unité*, p. 444.

At this stage of the power game, a subtle and quietly impressive figure entered the scene – Jean Monnet. This distinguished Frenchman, whose historical influence compares with de Gaulle's, had (as we have seen) declined to join de Gaulle's movement at the outset. Instead, at Churchill's request, he had gone to Washington as a member of the British Supply Council, and served on Harry Hopkins's Combined Munitions Assignment Board. A banker and industrialist, Monnet has some claims to being regarded as an archetypal technocrat. His wide-ranging intelligence, however, was fully alive to the complexities of politics. At Harry Hopkins's suggestion, during the Casablanca conference, Roosevelt decided to send Monnet to Algiers as a semi-official political adviser to Giraud; in effect, to educate Giraud in the political game.[17]

This was a masterly appointment. The Americans had grasped Giraud's inadequacy in administrative and political affairs. In a straight contest with de Gaulle, he would not have stood a chance; nor did he, when the contest did take place. Moreover, his simplistic, right-wing views made him unacceptable to the French Resistance and to public opinion, both in France and in French North Africa, that was obviously turning away fast from the discredited Vichy regime. Monnet's mission was to give Giraud an acceptable political image. His method, which was enormously effective, was to make Giraud understand that unless he took Monnet's advice, the military supplies he needed would probably be seriously delayed.

Monnet immediately confided in Giraud that he, for his part, was a man of democratic views who leaned to the left. In contrast, he said, he had to point out that Giraud was regarded in America as a reactionary anti-Semite. There was an urgent need for him to become, at least in appearance, a good Republican.

He told Murphy, whom he had conquered along with Macmillan, that his idea in coming to Algiers was not so much to serve Giraud as to help bring the rival French factions together. In his memoirs, Murphy gives Monnet much of the credit for de Gaulle's elevation to power in Algiers later that year. Objectively this is true, but this was almost certainly not Monnet's initial object, even in private, when he went to Algiers. The

[17] A cable from Roosevelt proposing Monnet's enlistment was sent to the Secretary of State, Cordell Hull, on 16 January 1943. Hull objected on the grounds that Monnet had links with the banking firm of Lazard Frères, which had close Gaullist connections, and had seen a lot of de Gaulle's special envoy in Washington, Pleven (Sherwood, *Hopkins*, Vol. I, pp. 675–6). Roosevelt, however, listened to Hopkins, as he often did, in preference to his Secretary of State. Paillat, *L'Echiquier*, Vol. II, p. 213, states that the idea of sending Monnet to Algiers came from Giraud's industrialist friend, Lemaigre-Dubreuil. One of the consequences of Monnet's arrival in Algiers, however, was that he rapidly replaced Lemaigre-Dubreuil as Giraud's confidant.

initial impact of his advice was, in fact, harmful to de Gaulle since it improved Giraud's international standing. The truth is that, as Murphy records, Monnet was impatient with Giraud's political ineptness ("When the general looks at you with those eyes of a porcelain cat, he comprehends nothing!"). When de Gaulle came to Algiers, Monnet quickly realised that nothing could be done with Giraud and that he must therefore help de Gaulle.[18]

"Republican" measures and words soon poured out of Giraud's office. On 4 March, there was a new statute on the Legion of Fighters; on the 5th, Giraud said France had no racist prejudices; on the 8th, he banned an issue of the *Journal officiel d'Afrique du Nord* containing the texts of new Pétain decrees. And on the 14th, Giraud delivered a remarkable speech, drafted by Monnet, in which he praised de Gaulle's forces as well as his own, referred (clearly for the benefit of an American audience) to Abraham Lincoln and appealed for republican unity.[19] Four days later, many of Vichy's laws were formally repealed.

All this worked, in the sense that Giraud drew public praise in America and Britain, where Churchill told parliament that in the light of Giraud's speech and the recent National Committee statement, "it now appears that no question of principle divides these two bodies of Frenchmen". On the 15th, indeed, Giraud had written to General Catroux to say he was now ready to welcome de Gaulle in Algiers.

Next Monnet persuaded Giraud to drop a number of his Vichyist advisers, although the governors-general, Peyrouton, Boisson and Noguès, were to remain at their posts some weeks longer. Among the men who filled the new vacancies was Maurice Couve de Murville, a former Vichy official who had declared allegiance to de Gaulle, and who, in later years, was to become in turn de Gaulle's foreign minister and Prime Minister.

Things now seemed to be going de Gaulle's way. The French National Committee welcomed Giraud's speech; he himself thanked Giraud for his personal message through Catroux and said he hoped to go to North Africa soon; and he cabled Eisenhower saying he hoped to see the latter on his arrival in Algiers. Before leaving, however, he said he would await a clear reply from Algiers to the Free French memorandum of 23 February.

But de Gaulle was not quite home with his plans. The British and Americans made a supreme effort to frustrate the take-over bid he was making at long distance. On 17 March Macmillan summoned the Gaullist

[18] This was the interpretation of Jacques Soustelle, in conversation with me in Paris in 1970, long after he had broken with de Gaulle.
[19] De Gaulle, *L'Unité*, p. 93; Funk, pp. 107–8.

representative, Guy de Charbonnières, in Catroux's absence, to say that there was now no reason why French unity should not be achieved around the person of General Giraud. If de Gaulle did not take the hand that was proffered, said Macmillan threateningly, Britain and America would abandon him. On the 23rd, Cardinal Spellman of New York, who had visited Algiers, called on de Gaulle in London with a special message from President Roosevelt, appealing to the general to accept the Casablanca proposals. De Gaulle naturally rejected this appeal, but felt that his arguments had won the cardinal's sympathy.

Next, Churchill summoned de Gaulle, and, in the presence of Massigli and Sir Alexander Cadogan, the permanent secretary at the Foreign Office, painted a dire picture of the unpleasant consequences to him and to France if he persisted in refusing to accept the Casablanca proposals. The plane he had requested was ready, said the Prime Minister, but would it not be best to defer his trip until Eden, who was in Washington, had returned, and Catroux had had more time to exert his influence in Algiers?

After leaving 10 Downing Street, de Gaulle announced that he still proposed to go to Algiers, but without prior conditions. The Prime Minister thereupon let it be known that Eisenhower himself had asked the general to postpone his journey. But de Gaulle, having flown into a rage, found that Eisenhower, personally, had made no such request.[20]

On 6 April, Eden and Winant, both back from Washington, separately told de Gaulle of the benefits that would flow to Fighting France if he accepted Giraud's leadership. "I would have done this wholeheartedly," de Gaulle replied, "if Giraud had found himself in charge in North Africa on 18 June 1940 and had carried on the war by rebuffing Pétain's and Weygand's injunctions. But today the facts are accomplished."

Now de Gaulle faced opposition from his more timid collaborators as well as from his allies. Even Catroux urged him to accept Giraud's political and military predominance; and earned himself a stern rebuke from de Gaulle.

On 10 April, Giraud replied at last to the National Committee's memorandum of 23 February. His proposals were, however, unsatisfactory to de Gaulle, for he wished to establish a "Council of Overseas Territories"

---

[20] For a fuller account of the Eisenhower incident, see Funk, pp. 114–15. Macmillan merely writes, "We therefore sent on 3 April, after much discussion, a message which was a plea from General Eisenhower, from one soldier to another, not to complicate the situation until the military operations now moving rapidly to their culmination had been concluded" (Harold Macmillan, The Blast of War, p. 312 henceforth, Macmillan, War). The "military operations" were the Battle of Tunis. Eisenhower, it appears, had no prior knowledge of the message sent in his name.

in Algiers, with Giraud and de Gaulle as members, but without political powers. Giraud himself was to subordinate his command not to this body but to the Allied high command.

Under the shock of Giraud's new proposals, the French National Committee forgot its differences and, at its meeting on the 15th, unanimously supported de Gaulle in demanding the formation of an executive committee with real powers, the removal of Vichy personalities who had collaborated with the enemy, and the subordination of the French commander-in-chief – that is, Giraud – to the committee. Moreover the president of the existing National Committee – that is, de Gaulle – should have the right to go to Algiers without conditions.

Giraud's resistance was now beginning to crumble. Crosses of Lorraine were appearing in Algiers, messages of support were reaching de Gaulle, and when on 14 April, Free French and British troops entered Sfax in Tunisia, they were greeted with cries of *"Vive de Gaulle!"* On 26 April, Peyrouton offered to resign. On the 27th, Giraud wrote to de Gaulle renouncing a preponderant political position. But he repeated his proposal for a council without powers, and proposed to meet de Gaulle not in Algiers, but at Biskra or Marrakesh.

De Gaulle impatiently declared, in a public speech at Grosvenor House on 4 May, that there must be an end to delays.[21] A few days earlier, Churchill – converted by Macmillan's latest despatches from Algiers – told de Gaulle he had won the first rubber. And on the 6th, in a reply to Giraud, de Gaulle repeated the National Committee's demand for a committee with political power and declined to meet him in a distant oasis: the meeting must take place in Algiers.

A decisive accretion of strength now came to de Gaulle. His delegate to the internal Resistance, Jean Moulin,[22] in a message brought to him on 15 May, revealed the formation of a National Council of the Resistance (CNR), uniting the various groups of all political persuasions, and declared their loyalty to de Gaulle. Specifically, the Resistance ruled out the subordination of de Gaulle to Giraud and called for the rapid formation in Algiers of a provisional government under the presidency of de Gaulle, and for the appointment of Giraud as military chief.[23]

On the 17th, Giraud at last asked de Gaulle to come immediately to Algiers to form a central French administration with him. Cordially, de

---

[21] For text, see De Gaulle, Discours, Vol. I. pp. 284–90.   [22] See below, p. 142
[23] This news was even more important to de Gaulle than the occasional Free French military successes in the field such as the Bir-Hakim action and General Leclerc's spectacular dash across the desert, which on 25 and 26 January 1943 had brought his motorised columns to Tripoli and Ghadamès in Tunisia, after the Fezzan had been conquered.

Gaulle replied on the 25th, saying he would arrive at the end of the week. Two days later, the National Council of the Resistance held its first full meeting under Jean Moulin's chairmanship and confirmed the earlier message in a formal declaration that was immediately broadcast on all British, American and Free French radio stations.

De Gaulle had indeed won the "first rubber", though a further period of struggle lay ahead.

Before leaving England, de Gaulle wrote to King George VI to express his gratitude to him, to his government and to his people for their welcome and their hospitality to Free France and its leader. He had wanted to take his leave of Churchill but learned that the Prime Minister had just left for an unstated destination. Instead, he called on Eden. "Do you know," asked Eden amiably, "that you have given us more trouble than all our European allies?"

"I don't doubt it," de Gaulle replied with a smile. "France is a great power."[24]

[24] Galante (pp. 126–7) declares that de Gaulle, taking his leave of Churchill at the end of May 1943, said that, on reflection, he thought he had found the reasons for their frequent misunderstandings: "I have noticed that you were always in a bad mood when you were in the wrong... and I myself was always in a bad mood when I was in the right and could not make you accept my reasons.... So, when we meet each other, we are always both in a bad mood." Excellent though this story is, it must be apocryphal, since Churchill was not there for the leave-taking; if not, it must refer to another occasion.

Chapter 10 ✤ Algiers

When de Gaulle arrived in Algiers on 30 May 1943, he was virtually alone in largely hostile territory. True, his supporters were numerous. But General Giraud was the reigning monarch, approved by the British and Americans, and accepted by nearly all the local French officials. Yet two months later, de Gaulle was the master of Algiers and of the French. It was perhaps the most astonishing of his triumphs, and it was accomplished, against all odds, by a formidable combination of factors: a powerful personality, which won over some of those who initially opposed him; a sense of drama, in which theatrical tantrums and a gift for timing played their part; persuasive oratory; the organised support of the "mafia" of Gaullists; and, not least, the ineptitude of Giraud himself.

The British and Americans had been determined to keep de Gaulle out of North Africa while the battle of Tunis was being fought. As Macmillan put it in his memoirs, nobody wanted public demonstrations in Algiers until the battle of Tunis had been won.[1]

By mid-May, however, the battle had been gloriously won. On the 7th, the American 2nd Corps had entered the great naval base of Bizerta, and the British 1st Army occupied Tunis. Next day, the British army from the east and the American from the west had joined hands. On the 13th, General Alexander, as efficient as he was unassuming, reported to Churchill that the Tunisian campaign was over. General von Arnim himself had been captured, along with 150,000 of his German troops and about 100,000 Italians. The booty was vast and so was the rejoicing.

Only one thing marred it: the discord among the French. Giraud's numerous though ill-equipped forces had fought well; and so had de Gaulle's more modest units under General de Larminat. But when the Allied victory parade was held in Tunis on 20 May, 400 men under de Larminat's command opted to march with General Montgomery's 8th Army, to avoid association with Giraud's fighting men who were parading with General Anderson's 1st Army. And all because, at that time, de Gaulle had not yet reached agreement with Giraud.[2]

At all events, by Sunday 30 May, whatever risks the Allies had seen in de Gaulle's arrival had vanished. To guard against unexpected disorders, however, they had thought it wise to forbid the local press to report his arrival; and there was a similar silence in London and New York.[3] To his gratification, de Gaulle travelled in a Fighting French plane. With him were his nominees on the proposed joint French committee, René Massigli and André Philip, together with Palewski, Billotte, Teyssot and Charles-Roux. They landed at the military airfield of Boufarik, to the strains of the *Marseillaise*. Giraud was there to greet de Gaulle; and so was Catroux. De Gaulle was glad to note that the official cars were French, and found comfort in the contrast with the arrangements at Anfa.

De Gaulle does not record his conversation in the car with Giraud. According to a second-hand account that rings true, it was icy. Having announced the names of his team, de Gaulle asked Giraud for his

---

[1] *See above*, p. 200; Macmillan, *War*, p. 312.
[2] Paillat, *L'Echiquier*, Vol. II, p. 280; *see also* pp. 250–8.
[3] De Gaulle, *L'Unité*, pp. 103–10.

nominees to the committee. As each was named, he was ready with a cutting or derisory remark: "Monnet, that little financier on England's payroll" or "Tron, that little official of little Morocco."

In any case, he said brusquely, the men of Vichy would have to go: Noguès, Mendigal, Peyrouton and Boisson.

The journey ended on a tense but inconclusive note. A large formal lunch followed, at the Palais d'Eté. De Gaulle and Giraud faced each other, flanked by their advisers. On Giraud's side, among others, were his brother, Dr Giraud, General Odic – the man who had changed his mind about joining de Gaulle in London – and Colonel de Linarès, who years later, was to face General Giap in Tonking during the first Indo-China war.

With his habitual relish for a crisis, de Gaulle noted the disparity between the two rival teams. "On one side, everything; on the other, nothing. Here, the army, the police, the administration, the money, the press, the radio, the telecommunications . . . the power of the Allies. . . . As for me, I have, in this country, neither troops nor gendarmes, nor officials, nor a banking account, nor means of my own to make myself heard." And yet, he claimed, the attitudes of those he met made it clear that they did not doubt the outcome.

At four o'clock, when de Gaulle went to the Place de la Poste to deposit a cross on the monument to the fallen of Lorraine, thousands of supporters appeared mysteriously to cheer him. Vastly comforted, the general intoned the *Marseillaise*, which the crowd took up with enthusiasm.

How spontaneous was this demonstration? De Gaulle does not claim that it was, and merely states that it was "improvised" by the Gaullist movement, Combat. That is one way of putting it. The truth was probably more complex. Catroux, it seems, had alerted the Gaullist leaders in Algiers that General de Gaulle was about to arrive, and they had accepted his advice that there should be no demonstrations in view of the tense situation. From Gibraltar, however, Peladon, one of Passy's men in the secret Bureau Central de Renseignements et d'Action (BCRA), had ordered the "spontaneous" demonstration. In view of the local shortage of true Gaullists, Peladon's agents had rounded up as many opponents of Giraud as could be assembled at short notice, including Socialists and Communists, freemasons and trade unionists. To his astonishment, Catroux found himself being pushed unceremoniously aside so that de Gaulle could mount the steps of the monument. The whole affair was a sample of the way the Gaullists organised "public support" for their leader and hero.

De Gaulle and his suite took up residence at the Villa de Glycines, where the atmosphere was to remind Macmillan of the court of a visiting monarch. That Sunday evening, the tireless Monnet called, and had a three-hour talk with de Gaulle. Macmillan learned from him next day that de Gaulle had expressed his concern over the "mounting threat" of Anglo-Saxon domination in Europe. If it continued, said de Gaulle, France would have to lean towards Germany and Russia when the war was over.[4]

A stormy meeting of the inner groups of rivals, at the Lycée Fromentin on 31 May, was marked by de Gaulle's denunciation of the local men of Vichy – Peyrouton, the governor-general of Algeria, General Noguès, the resident-general in Morocco, and General Boisson, governor-general of French West Africa. It ended when de Gaulle abruptly decided to walk out and slammed the door behind him. At a meeting with Giraud, à deux, that afternoon, de Gaulle repeated his ultimatum: unless the three men were dismissed, he could not work with the committee.[5]

On hearing Monnet's account of the stormy meeting at the Lycée Fromentin, Macmillan said it was a pity Monnet had not formally proposed that the seven men present should constitute the proposed French committee, since de Gaulle could not have opposed a motion to this effect without appearing ridiculous.

On 1 June, with his usual sense of timing and publicity, de Gaulle summoned the French and Allied journalists to the Villa des Glycines and gave them the headlines for which they thirsted. He had come to North Africa, said de Gaulle, to set up an effective organ of French power that would direct the national war effort, and would be based on the sovereignty of France, but would exclude certain men who symbolised something else.

At noon that day, Murphy and Macmillan called on de Gaulle. Macmillan's conversion to de Gaulle may be said to date from this visit. Earlier, he had opposed the general with all the means at his power, on Churchill's instructions. As recently as 22 May, he was lamenting the "ill-timed" message to de Gaulle in which the Central Committee of the French Resistance had recognised de Gaulle as its sole leader. Now, however, with de Gaulle "at his best" and expressing "his deep feelings in a powerful and even noble way", the British minister of State was beginning to waver. Murphy, too, was "much impressed". De Gaulle requested the American diplomat to arrange for him to meet General Eisenhower, and the British politician to make appointments for him to see General Alexander and Air Chief Marshal Tedder.

[4] Macmillan, War, pp. 326–33.
[5] ibid. p. 330. De Gaulle does not mention his meeting with Giraud that afternoon.

That evening brought de Gaulle the first victory in his struggle for power in Algiers. Let us call it the "Peyrouton incident". The governor-general of Algeria was a worried man and deserving of some sympathy. Once a Vichy minister, he was bitterly opposed to Laval and had taken refuge in Argentina, until he was brought to Algiers, largely at the behest of General Eisenhower on the ground that a skilled colonial administrator was needed.[6] Echoes of de Gaulle's insistence that he should be removed, along with other Vichy high officials, had now reached him.

Peyrouton decided – misguidedly – to write two letters: one for each co-chairman of the committee. His letter to de Gaulle was a formal, dignified text. He was ready to give up his post to facilitate the union of all Frenchmen that was necessary for victory and the restoration of France's greatness. He asked only one favour: that de Gaulle should support the application he was about to make to the military authorities for service in his capacity as a colonial infantry captain on the reserve list. A friend rushed the letter to the Villa des Glycines. Peyrouton then drafted a letter to Giraud, couched in similar but not identical terms. As it was getting late, Peyrouton decided to deliver this second letter at the Summer Palace the following morning. But this, it soon turned out, was a mistake.

De Gaulle's reply to Peyrouton's first letter came within an hour, whereas Giraud had not yet received the second. De Gaulle, as might have been expected, accepted Peyrouton's resignation, and told him to consider himself mobilised for service in the army of the Levant (which, of course, was a strictly Gaullist creation).

Immediately, Peyrouton sent his second letter by messenger to the Summer Palace, with instructions to wake Giraud if necessary. But Giraud's reply, when it came, differed from de Gaulle's. Giraud accepted Peyrouton's resignation, but asked him to stay at his post until the formation of the Executive Committee before being directed to the colonial infantry (presumably in a Giraudist formation).[7]

De Gaulle records that immediately he had replied to Peyrouton, he sent copies of the governor-general's letter and his reply to Giraud, and communicated both texts to the press. His explanation that there was nothing in Peyrouton's letter to indicate that he was also writing to Giraud is valid only up to a point. It may account for de Gaulle's unilateral acceptance of the resignation, but does not atone for the gross

[6] Eisenhower, *Crusade*, p. 145.
[7] This account is based on Marcel Peyrouton, *Du Service Public à la Prison Commune* (Paris, 1950), pp. 231–5.

discourtesy to Giraud of publishing the news before he had had time to comment on the matter.

In de Gaulle's eyes, however, this was a struggle for power (and, of course, for the triumph of the Gaullist interpretation of the war), and not a time for niceties of protocol. Peyrouton's resignation addressed to de Gaulle was too important a victory to throw away: the point had to be scored immediately. Nor could the publicity value of a sensational piece of news be squandered by delays. With his usual sense of the theatre, de Gaulle turned his stroke of luck to best advantage.

What is perhaps surprising is that Peyrouton, with his experience, should have apparently been oblivious of the consequences of sending two letters of resignation to two rivals for power, without informing either that he was also writing to the other. But the man was at the end of the road and knew it; his misjudgment may be ascribed to the fact that he was under stress.

Giraud, taking cognisance of de Gaulle's actions, at about 3 a.m., promptly wrote two letters – a formally angry one expressing his astonishment at de Gaulle's handling of Peyrouton's resignation, and an informal and unbridled one accusing de Gaulle of Nazi tendencies.

Wild rumours now began to circulate. A "military *putsch*" was on the way, but on whose behalf nobody knew for certain. De Gaulle's? Giraud's? For his part, Giraud was sure the Gaullists were plotting. He appointed Admiral Muselier to maintain order in and around Algiers, sent tanks to guard the approaches to the city and the Summer Palace, and called in additional colonial troops. As one rumour had it, Roosevelt had cabled Churchill to say de Gaulle and his companions should be put on a plane forthwith and removed, no matter where.

Even in the Gaullist camp, approval of the general's behaviour was not unanimous. Catroux called at the Villa des Glycines to express his indignation at de Gaulle's "insensate" actions, and left in a huff, slamming the door behind him. Back at his own quarters, he composed a letter of resignation, but did not deliver it.[8]

At the villa, meanwhile, under the symbolic protection of ten Spahis, all was calm. The news of Giraud's panic security measures, indeed, contributed to keeping the temperature low. De Gaulle did, however, cable his London office on 3 June to complain about Giraud's actions, especially an order to arrest Gaullist soldiers on leave in Algiers. It was all, he said, a "tragi-comedy", but one that could turn nasty.[9]

On the morning of the 1st, Catroux, having decided not to resign

[8] Général Catroux, *Dans la Bataille de Mediterranée* (henceforth, Catroux), p. 369.
[9] De Gaulle, *L'Unité*, p. 488.

after all, and accompanied by Monnet, called on Giraud to smooth things over. The two men persuaded Giraud not to do anything drastic. Murphy and Macmillan also called, with further soothing words. And that afternoon, Macmillan saw de Gaulle alone at his invitation. Macmillan said he thought Peyrouton had been at fault in sending his resignation to de Gaulle, and de Gaulle in the wrong to accept it. De Gaulle replied that he had supposed, on receiving Peyrouton's letter, that the governor-general acknowledged his authority. Besides, the whole thing showed that Peyrouton was, as he had always maintained, a rascal.

Although Macmillan thought de Gaulle's explanation rather thin, and said so, he was determined to win de Gaulle's confidence and friendship. On hearing from de Gaulle that there would shortly be another meeting of "the seven" – as the rival groups were collectively known – he launched into an emotional autobiographical speech, recalling his service in France during the First World War and his stand against the Munich settlement. In a passage of interest to those who have followed the subsequent careers of both statesmen, Macmillan declared that de Gaulle's views on social matters were probably much the same as his: great wealth would pass away and property would be regarded as a trust, for the general benefit.

The Peyrouton incident was now closed. Whatever the degree of luck and the methods used by the Gaullists, whatever the part played by de Gaulle's own decision to "jump the gun", the whole thing was a major political victory for him. Giraud had been made to look a fool; and all the world learned, at the time, was that the Vichy governor-general of Algeria had made obeisance to de Gaulle by submitting his resignation to him in the first instance.

Although General Giraud, in his rage, had just accused de Gaulle of wishing to install a Nazi regime in France, he now yielded on the main stumbling-block – de Gaulle's call for the removal of the principal Vichyists. When the seven met at 10 a.m. on 3 June, they took cognisance of Peyrouton's resignation; it was agreed that Catroux, while continuing to serve on the committee, would take his place as governor-general. As for the others, General Noguès was to be removed from Morocco, Boisson would be recalled from Dakar as soon as somebody else could be found to fill his job, and General Bergeret was to be retired.

The obstacles having been removed, agreement was rapidly reached on the creation of the French Committee of National Liberation. De Gaulle and Giraud were to preside jointly. The rest of the seven – Catroux, Massigli and Philip on the Gaullist side, and Georges and

Monnet on the Giraudist – were to be the founder-members; and other members would be appointed shortly. The committee proclaimed itself the central power of France. It was to direct the French war effort everywhere, and exercise French sovereignty. Dictatorial tendencies were explicitly disclaimed: "Until such time as the Committee is able to hand over its powers to the future provisional government of the Republic, it undertakes to restore all French liberties, the laws of the Republic, the Republican regime, and entirely to destroy the arbitrary regime of personal power imposed today on the country."

Having got his way, de Gaulle warmly embraced Giraud, French style.

Although de Gaulle understandably considered the dual direction of the committee absurd, he felt confident of being able to bend it to his will. The immediate advantage – not a negligible one – was that the numerous forces and functionaries who had until then escaped his control were now, at least in part, responsible to him.[10]

As de Gaulle guessed, his major difficulties were bound to come from the Allied side. By removing the men of Vichy and assuming sovereign powers, the Liberation Committee had flouted Roosevelt's express wishes. De Gaulle was not surprised, therefore, to find that the text of the committee's first declaration was being held up by the military censors. He managed, however, to get the news out in a radio speech, the broadcasting facilities having already been largely taken over by the well-organised Gaullists. The British, however, showed their displeasure at his high-handedness by holding up for ten days transport aircraft for General de Gaulle's nominees to the committee, who were to join in from London.

And now, Churchill surfaced. He had been quietly conferring with the British and American command on the crucial question of whether and when Sicily should be invaded. He invited de Gaulle, Giraud and others to a meal which de Gaulle felt constrained to attend in view of the honours to which the Prime Minister was entitled.[11] When de Gaulle asked him, in effect, what he was doing in North Africa at such a time, Churchill protested that he had no intention of meddling in

[10] From the time of the Battle of Tunis, the Gaullist "mafia" had been at work among the Giraudist forces, making converts to Gaullism. *See* Paillat, *L'Echequier*, Vol. II, pp. 277 *et seq.*

[11] De Gaulle (*L'Unité*, p. 110) describes the occasion as a dinner and dates it 6 June; Macmillan calls it a luncheon, and says it took place on the 5th (his chronology is not, however, invariably clear, because of his habit of giving the dates of his memoranda rather than those of the events to which they refer. *See* Macmillan, *War*, p. 338) Eden was present, Churchill having summoned him to Algiers as "much better fitted than I am to be best man at the Giraud-de Gaulle wedding". Churchill, Vol. IV, p. 729.

French affairs; but the military situation obliged His Majesty's government to take account of internal developments. "We should have had to take some measures," he added, "if . . . for instance, you had gobbled up Giraud in one gulp."

De Gaulle, in his memoirs, disclaims any such intention: "I was hoping to bring General Giraud to take his place, of his own accord, on the side of public interest." But this was a euphemism: even as a military man, Giraud had his limitations, in de Gaulle's eyes, but he was welcome to take on the best jobs on offer to a French soldier in the circumstances of the moment; which could not include the Allied High Command. But it was out of the question that he should retain the power of veto over political decisions which his position as co-chairman and co-signatory of State documents gave him.

As de Gaulle knew, the isolation and removal of his rival were only a question of time. He considered the whole business a particularly painful example of the choices between personalities and personal feelings on the one hand, and the national interest on the other, that he had often faced. That, at all events, was how he put it in his memoirs.

The Liberation Committee held its second meeting on the 5th, so that its seven founder members could choose their colleagues and distribute jobs to everybody. Georges was appointed a commissioner of State; and Catroux, who already had this title, kept it. Massigli and Philip, who were already the commissioners for Foreign Affairs and the Interior, respectively, also kept their jobs. Giraud's further nominees were: Couve de Murville (Finance); René Mayer (Transport and Public Works); Abadie (Justice, Education and Health). De Gaulle proposed to bring some of his faithful supporters from London or America: Pleven, who was to deal with the Colonies, and Diethelm (Economic Affairs), both from London; Tixier from Washington (Labour); and Henri Bonnet from New York (Information). As for new proconsuls, the Vichyist Boisson was to be replaced by Pierre Cournarie from Cameroun within a fortnight; General Mast, who had de Gaulle's approval, was confirmed as governor-general in Tunisia; and two ambassadors, Puaux and Helleu, were appointed to the vacant posts in Morocco and the Levant respectively.

Not all the men appointed that day were Gaullists, but de Gaulle rightly believed that most of those who were not soon would be. The immediate prospect, however, was of a deadlocked government when important decisions had to be taken. And so it turned out three days later – on the 8th – when the committee met again to consider the crucial matter of the High Command. The new members had not yet been installed, pending the arrival of the Gaullists who were held up in London. Only the original seven met, therefore, with the Gaullists in a natural majority of one. The seven voted down a proposal of General Georges, giving full military powers to Giraud, who would remain co-chairman but would not be subject to the committee's authority in military matters.

Catroux, who had so lately slammed a door on de Gaulle, presented a plan of his own: Giraud to be commander-in-chief with de Gaulle in charge of National Defence. De Gaulle himself had a more complicated proposal. The commander-in-chief should be sent on a liaison mission with the Allied commanders. As soon as possible, he should take a field command and, by the same token, be relieved of his governmental duties. In the meantime, military affairs should be handled by a special committee, on which Giraud and de Gaulle should serve, but which would, in the last resort, be responsible to the government. But Giraud, supported by Churchill's friend, General Georges, refused to consider either Catroux's plan or de Gaulle's.

It was time for another piece of drama, and de Gaulle provided it on the 10th. Since the committee had shown itself incapable of adopting the obvious solution, said de Gaulle in a formal statement, he was unable to associate himself any longer with its work. And he shut himself up at the Villa des Glycines, letting it be known that he was thinking of moving to Brazzaville.

As de Gaulle had foreseen, a period of unutterable confusion ensued, with Monnet running in all directions on conciliatory errands, Murphy and Eisenhower at the receiving end of irate telegrams from President Roosevelt, and Macmillan similarly bombarded by Churchill. The president seemed particularly incensed by the decision to remove Boisson, whom the Americans considered helpful, from Dakar, and cabled Eisenhower on the 10th threatening to send an American task force to counter any attempt by de Gaulle to seize French West Africa.[12] A week later, Roosevelt cabled Eisenhower again, directing him to prevent de Gaulle from taking control of the French army, either "personally or through his partisans". As for Churchill, he resorted to the Bible, referring Macmillan to St Matthew, chapter vii, verse 16: "Ye shall know them by their fruits. Do men gather grapes of thorns, or figs of thistles?" This cryptic quotation was supposed to explain why Churchill had no intention, at that stage, of recognising the French National Liberation Committee.

Diligently, Macmillan and his staff searched the holy book for an answer, and found it in Revelation, chapter ii, verses 2–4, which ended:

12 Leahy, p. 200.

". . . I have somewhat against thee, because thou hast left thy first love." This reply, with its implied rebuke, reflected Macmillan's increasing admiration for de Gaulle. It left Churchill "speechless with rage".[13]

As de Gaulle had guessed, Giraud would find he could not use the committee in de Gaulle's absence. He summoned it nevertheless, probably on the 15th;[14] but when he invited those present to take cognisance of de Gaulle's resignation, the Gaullists clamoured that the union of Frenchmen was still essential, and Monnet, from his half-way position, affirmed that de Gaulle's resignation was not definitive.

By now, the Gaullist "ministers" had arrived from London. Judging that "the affair had ripened", de Gaulle summoned the full committee for that afternoon. But now it was Giraud's turn to dig his heels in: the committee, he declared, was not competent to decide the question of who was to exercise the command.

Now, under Roosevelt's pressures, Eisenhower decided to act, with an invitation to both Giraud and de Gaulle to confer with him on 19 June "on the subject of the problems relating to the command and the organisation of the French armed forces". Never one to miss the chance of an entrance, de Gaulle arrived deliberately late, and immediately began to speak, before the other generals had had a chance to collect their thoughts. There was, in fact, a fourth general present – the American Bedell Smith. But he was a silent witness. In another room, in case they should be needed, were Murphy and Macmillan.

It was the first time Eisenhower had been exposed to the full force of de Gaulle at a time of high drama. Macmillan records that he "seemed impressed by de Gaulle's powerful personality". Certainly he had no answer to de Gaulle's flood of rhetoric about French sovereign rights. The meeting broke up inconclusively.

De Gaulle, too, was impressed by Eisenhower's soldierly simplicity and the generosity of his nature. But the supreme commander had his orders, and the sympathy de Gaulle detected in him could not override military and political discipline.

At de Gaulle's request, Allied Headquarters set down its requirements on paper, which amounted to insistence that Giraud should be the French c.-in-c. and should not be subject to overriding political control. The note ended, however, with formal reassurances about French sovereignty which left de Gaulle unimpressed since they contradicted the practical requirements stated. The reason de Gaulle wanted the Allied

---

[13] Macmillan, War, pp. 343–4; see also pp. 348–52.
[14] Paillat, L'Echiquier, Vol. II, pp. 268–9. The date of this meeting is uncertain. De Gaulle mentions it but does not give the date (De Gaulle, L'Unité, p. 114).

demands in writing was so that he could have them formally rejected by the committee, which he convoked on the 21st for that purpose.

In this respect, the committee did not let de Gaulle down; indeed, it invited Giraud to decide whether to recognise the authority of the French government or to resign from it and cease to be commander-in-chief. When Giraud objected to discussing secret military matters with a council of fourteen members, de Gaulle saw his chance of pressing for the creation of a military committee under his own chairmanship. Surprisingly, Giraud accepted this proposal. It was agreed that for the time being there should be two military high commands: Giraud's in North Africa, and de Gaulle's over the rest of the French empire and the French Resistance.

At this stage, Giraud's vanity made him commit the supreme error, in any struggle for power, of absenting himself at the wrong time and for the wrong purpose. He announced that he had accepted an invitation from President Roosevelt to go to Washington to discuss arms deliveries to the French forces; and he asked the committee to defer any further discussions on the shape of the organisation and the attributions of the commander. Though irked that Giraud had not thought fit to consult his colleagues before accepting the president's invitation, de Gaulle immediately concurred. For here was a welcome chance to transform the committee into an efficient government responsive to his will.

Before Giraud departed, the Boisson crisis came to a head. Wishing, as Peyrouton had wished, to anticipate his dismissal, the governor-general of French West Africa, Boisson, wired Giraud offering to resign. Giraud, acting now as de Gaulle, to his displeasure, had acted earlier over Peyrouton, immediately accepted it, without consulting his colleagues.

Comedy was never far from the Algerian drama. When Macmillan expressed surprise at Giraud's acceptance of Boisson's resignation, Giraud inconsequentially explained that he had sent Boisson a second telegram refusing it: the first telegram was therefore unimportant. "I found myself," recorded Macmillan, "like Alice, repeating to myself: important, unimportant, refused, accepted, accepted, refused, unimportant, important." Between Giraud's two telegrams, Eisenhower, mindful of the president's threats to send a force to Dakar, had expressed his apprehensions to Giraud.

The crisis, however, was short-lived. When Murphy wisely advised the White House that it would be impolitic to try to keep Boisson in a post which he wished to quit, the president, says Macmillan, appeared to lose interest. He did not bother to reply when Murphy asked the president for his views on the appointment of the Gaullist Pierre Cournarie of Cameroun to succeed Boisson, although the Americans had insisted that any successor must be *persona grata* to them. The appointment therefore went ahead, and de Gaulle – this time without trying – had won another small victory.

On 2 July, Giraud went off to America, where he basked in well-organised official flattery and public plaudits, returning about three weeks later by way of Ottawa and London. De Gaulle, meanwhile, offered himself a share of public acclaim nearer home, with official visits to Tunisia and Morocco, in which pomp and applause mingled with a shrewd look at local situations. His real concern during Giraud's absence, however, was to get on with the organisation of an administration, which until then had been frustrated by the rivalry of its two chairmen. At the session of 10 June, a secretariat had been created, with at its head an able young journalist and historian, Louis Joxe, later to serve the Fourth Republic in high diplomatic posts, and the Fifth in ministerial capacities. One of his two assistants was a politician who later became Prime Minister under the Fourth Republic and a prominent politician under the Fifth: Edgar Faure. The other was Raymond Offroy. The secretariat transacted the day-to-day business of government. In July, still during Giraud's absence, de Gaulle set up important committees – the *Comité juridique*, under Professor Cassin, which was concerned with the drafting of laws and other official texts; and the *Comité du contentieux* under Pierre Tissier, which dealt with grievances arising out of the application of the Vichy laws. In addition, Colonel Billotte was appointed as secretary of the Military Committee, working directly under de Gaulle.

While Giraud was in America, Churchill had sent to British posts abroad, and distributed to the editors of national newspapers, a confidential memorandum in which he listed his government's grievances against General de Gaulle and his movement. Not surprisingly the text was leaked to the American press. The incident displeased de Gaulle and may have contributed to the publicity value of Giraud's trip, but it had no bearing on the realities of political power in Algiers, as Giraud was to discover on his return.

The question of the division of powers between Giraud and de Gaulle nevertheless remained unsolved until 31 July, when a compromise emerged that was satisfactory to de Gaulle. Henceforth, de Gaulle alone was to preside over the committee and direct its labours. Giraud, however, retained the right to countersign texts and decrees. While this gave him, at least in theory, a right of veto, de Gaulle was not worried, since

Giraud could no longer initiate anything in the political sphere. All French forces were now to be merged under Giraud as commander-in-chief. De Gaulle, however, was to preside over a new committee for National Defence, which replaced the short-lived Military Committee.

In all but name, the French National Liberation Committee had become the provisional government of France, with de Gaulle as its Prime Minister. Essentially, this is what he had come to Algiers to do. And it had taken him only eight weeks to achieve it, in the face of all obstacles.

Chapter 11 ✤ The Resistance

De Gaulle's victory over Giraud paved the way for the forthcoming struggle for power in France herself. The Free French leader had eliminated a contender who was not in his class and who would not have become one at all, or lasted as long as eight weeks, unless he had been sponsored by the Americans with British support. But the real struggle, the final one, could take place only in France at the time of liberation. There were two questions to be answered. Who would rule, or reign over, France? And whose concepts of the future French polity would prevail?

The two questions, though linked, were not identical. To understand why they were not, one has to retrace the history of the French Resistance. For in one sense the coming struggle for power in France was between the external Resistance – mainly the Gaullists – and the internal – the men and women who, at appalling risk and against crushing odds, banded together to fight the Nazis. By November 1942, the internal Resistance had recognised de Gaulle as its leader and as the symbol of the national will in the struggle against the oppressor. But those who saw him as such did not necessarily accept his views (to the extent that these were known) about the future of France. Many feared he would try to set up a dictatorship; and there was a widespread sentiment that the natural and honourable culmination of his struggle should be his retirement when the goal of liberation had been achieved.

In the end, however, General de Gaulle was to retire not at the

Liberation, but some nineteen months later. He had both won and lost: won by achieving power, and lost because he saw no way, short of a dictatorship, of moulding a French polity to his desires, yet did not wish to break his word by becoming a dictator. By that time, however, the unity of the Resistance was but a memory; and the Fourth Republic, which de Gaulle despised, was but a modified version – deeply marked, it is true, by the experience of the war – of the "regime of parties" whose corruption and inefficiency were major causes of the *débâcle* of 1940.

There were several Resistances. Externally, the Giraudists had their day before de Gaulle swept them away or absorbed them in his own ranks. Internally, there were those who fought with the British and under their direction, as well as the many groups that eventually united under de Gaulle, before fragmenting again under the ruthless blows of the Gestapo and its Vichy allies.

De Gaulle and Passy, his first Intelligence chief, strongly disapproved[1] of their compatriots who chose to enlist with the British instead of under the Gaullist banner, and resented British efforts to recruit French agents; although ready enough to help M.I.6 by the product of their own jealously guarded efforts. The motives on both sides – The British and Free French – were understandable, and the clash between them inevitable. The professionals of the British Secret Intelligence Service were horrified at the thought that agents, potentially useful to the Allied cause, should be responsible to the amateurish organisation created by Passy. They dreaded the insecurity of the talkative and divided French – of which the Dakar fiasco seemed such a convincing example. Nor did they automatically accept de Gaulle's national pretensions, especially in the early months, when he stood virtually alone, with his unknown or suspect band of followers, spending British money and ignored or attacked by many Frenchmen in London, from the secret Pétainists to the Republicans and Socialists who had taken refuge in London but distrusted the general and his "Fascist" retinue.

On his side, de Gaulle knew he could not surrender one iota of his claim to represent France or of his entitlement to authority over all Frenchmen. He realised, moreover, that even to secure recognition of his movement outside France was insufficient: if his wider claim was ever to be accepted, he would need to extend his authority over the internal Resistance as well. At first, this was hardly a problem, for there *was* no internal Resistance immediately after France's collapse. But if ever a Resistance movement was to be set up and flourish, it would be essen-

[1] *See above*, p. 121.

tial to make contact with it, and this could be done only through Passy's Deuxième Bureau. Passy himself did not need to have this pointed out to him.

On the British side, the relevant organisation was the Special Operations Executive (SOE), an independent secret service, formed in July 1940 – a month after de Gaulle's arrival in London – and disbanded, by an arresting coincidence, about the time when he resigned as Prime Minister of France, in January 1946. At first, SOE was instructed to operate in France without reference to de Gaulle. The executive was divided into six sections, two of which were of special importance: F section, whose agents were mostly not French and operated independently of de Gaulle; and RF section, whose agents were mostly French, and who were supposed to work in cooperation with Free French headquarters, but always under British control.[2] The functions of F and RF sections sometimes overlapped in practice, but in theory were distinct: F's agents were saboteurs, and often damagingly successful ones; the men of RF, though sabotage was among their activities, were primarily there to work up French opinion against the Germans and Vichy, and in favour of de Gaulle and the Allies.

Friction with the Free French was inherent in the independence of F section, and the initial directives of SOE as a whole. But in the view of SOE's admirable historian, Professor M. R. D. Foot, Gaullist suspicions, however understandable, would not, if the facts had been known to the Gaullists at the time, have been found justified. RF section was set up because F's initial attempts to get men into France had failed and because strong evidence came in March 1941 that de Gaulle's popularity in France was real and growing. Pursuing its independent course, F section made contact with the anti-Gaullist résistants of Giraud and of André Girard, a painter and patriot whose originality was that he "was a passionate opponent of Hitler, Pétain and de Gaulle alike";[3] but both groups proved disappointing and were dropped. Nor did F section make much headway in its dealings with the Communist Resistance (which, for ideological reasons, became active only after Hitler attacked Russia, and which, for reasons of political expediency, preferred to make its own arrangements with de Gaulle).

The Gaullist counterparts of SOE and its individual sections began with Colonel Passy's Deuxième Bureau – traditionally, in the French army, the office that filters and coordinates intelligence for the planning

---

[2] M. R. D. Foot, *History of the Second World War: SOE in France*, pp. xviii *et seq.* (henceforth, Foot).
[3] ibid. p. 204.

of military operations. But immediately after the 1940 armistice there was no intelligence to coordinate, even on the British side. Almost immediately, therefore, the Deuxième Bureau became a *Service de renseignements* (SR) – that is, an intelligence service.

Those were the days of innocence, when volunteers tended to be welcomed merely because they had volunteered. It was not long, however, before these virgin illusions were shed, when it became apparent that not everybody who joined the Gaullists acted from the highest motives, or even from mildly patriotic ones: some, indeed, were traitors. There were betrayals to the Gestapo in France, and unveilings of double agents in Britain. The time came, therefore, when the SR had to create its own counter-espionage service (CE). The date, just after Pearl Harbor, was 16 December 1941.[4] By this time, the activities of Passy's SR had so proliferated that a complete reorganisation had become necessary. With it went a further change of name, the SR being replaced by, and absorbed in, the Bureau Central de Renseignements et d'Action Militaire (BCRAM) on 17 January 1942.[5] Responsibilities within the BCRAM were divided among five sections, dealing respectively with: command matters, including liaison with Allied commands; intelligence, including liaison with the British Intelligence Service; military action, including the recruiting and placing of agents and liaison with SOE; counter-espionage, including liaison with the British security service (M.I.5); and technical matters, including secret ciphers and accounts.

At that stage, Passy's organisation had no strictly political responsibilities. These fell to the Service d'Action Politique en France (SAP), the organisation of which de Gaulle entrusted to his commissioner for the Interior, André Diethelm. Passy's BCRAM was responsible to de Gaulle's private military staff (*état-major particulier*, or EMP), itself headed, at first, by Captain Ortoli of the Free French navy who, it seems, was (if the metaphor is pardonable) completely at sea in the midst of Gaullist intrigues and proliferating paper work and asked only to be given command of a warship.

In this "vertical" command structure, Passy and Diethelm were roughly parallel, but the nature of Political Action's aims in France was such that it could not be organised without constant reference to Passy's services. Friction was probably inherent in these circumstances, and it was aggravated by incompatible temperaments. Passy

[4] Passy, Vol. II, pp. 20 *et seq.*
[5] ibid. pp. 29 *et seq.* H. Michel, in *Histoire de la Résistance en France*, p. 14 (henceforth, Michel, *Résistance*), gives October 1941 as the date when the BCRAM was formed, and dates CE from the beginning of 1942. But Passy, who created or organised both bodies, must be given precedence as a source.

passed on all he learned of a non-military nature. But he drew the line at yielding to Diethelm's repeated entreaties to hand over the full list of agents and informants in France, and delegate control over them to the commissariat for the Interior. For one thing, many of the informants' names were not known to Passy himself; for another, the organisation of the intelligence network within France was largely the creation of the Resistance, which alone could gauge its needs, and could not be handed over to a body working in London and out of touch with day-to-day problems.[6]

The initial acrimony between the two men and their services grew in bitterness and resulted in much sterile duplication of effort. In the end, Passy, with the strong support of Resistance men who came over to London for brief periods, won his point. The most eloquent of these supporters was the Socialist André Philip. As Passy notes, de Gaulle was always more inclined to show his favour to those who could marshal and present arguments than those who were merely good organisers. Professor Philip, tall, thin, his black hair in perpetual disorder, had the unattractive habit of biting off portions of his pipe and spitting out the residue with accompanying saliva. Another habit, which greatly discomfited Passy, was that of losing documents, however secret, with phenomenal rapidity. But he could talk; and de Gaulle, himself an orator, appreciated his talent. Moreover, Philip represented not only the Resistance in unoccupied France, but the reconstituted Socialist party: his words therefore carried weight. Such weight that within a few days of his arrival in London in July 1942, de Gaulle appointed him commissioner for the Interior, in succession to Diethelm, who was given Finance. Philip also persuaded de Gaulle to agree that the executive (as distinct from the policy-making) functions of Political Action should be detached from the commissariat and attached to the BCRAM. To accommodate Political Action, a new section was added to Passy's empire: the non-military section, known as NM. To mark the change, the last initial ("M" for military) was dropped from the BCRAM, which was henceforth the BCRA.

In all respects, the organisation was now stronger than it had been, for strong appointments complemented the reorganisation. Louis Vallon, a small, witty, animated Socialist, was appointed head of the NM section on 4 August 1942. Meanwhile, early in 1942, the unhappy Captain Ortoli had returned to his naval duties, and been replaced as chief of de Gaulle's military staff by a discreet and efficient soldier,

[6] Passy, Vol. II, pp. 26–9; for subsequent matter, see also (in that order) pp. 232, 25, 147, 224–5, 63–6, 81, 246.

Colonel (later General) Billotte.[7] The general's reshuffle in the summer of 1942 had also brought into his "government", as commissioner for Information, a man of high intelligence and restless energy who was later to become his greatest enemy, but who, during the whole of the war and for long after, was his most loyal supporter: Jacques Soustelle.

In other ways, too, the secret side of the Free French effort grew more effective. Relations with the British, which were bad throughout 1941, improved steadily in 1942. Generally good relations were also established between Passy's organisation and the American Office of Strategic Services (precursor of the Central Intelligence Agency), which opened an office in London early in 1942. Finally, the accommodation of the Free French secret services also improved. At first, they had been housed in cramped quarters at 3 St James's Square; at the beginning of March 1942, they moved out to spacious premises at 10 Duke Street.[8] Until Parkinson's law took effect there too, efficiency was greatly enhanced by the move.

To those who lived through the great and terrible adventure of the war in London, the intrigues and the bickerings were the shabby companions of danger and heroism. Had France not capitulated, the pettinesses and rivalries would perhaps have been less visible. De Gaulle, himself largely exempt from human weaknesses, deplored those of the men around him, the only men he had. Some of the London French were ready to give him what he most wanted; unquestioning loyalty. Others were self-seeking; and others still unwilling to follow him at all. All men were judged by their willingness or otherwise to accept his leadership and defer to his wishes. By this exalted standard, even Winston Churchill fell short. What de Gaulle expected of him – total respect for France's "independence" – was unreasonably much for the sovereign host to a group of men whose country and government had collapsed. Hence, the Free French secret services could not be otherwise than responsible to their British counterparts. And this was an added source of friction to supplement the internal divisions among the Gaullists. Nor were such divisions confined to the external Resistance;

---

[7] Billotte, whom General de Gaulle used in later years for various confidential missions, was one of a group of French officers and men who escaped from German captivity into Russia where, to their disappointment, they were immediately reinterned in conditions far worse than those they had experienced in Nazi hands (Passy, Vol. II, p. 25). They were not released until the Germans invaded Russia, and then only after two months of strong representations by the British Embassy in Moscow. Nearly all opted to serve with the British; the exceptions were French Communists, although, to the surprise of the others, they had been as badly treated as the rest while in Russian hands.

[8] Off Manchester Square, W.1, not Duke Street, St James's, S.W.1.

they existed, too, within the internal Resistance. But at least at first, the divisions in France reflected the natural pluralism of political opinion rather than the rivalries of a struggle for power.

Fractionalism was indeed inseparable from the circumstances of the occupation. At the beginning, the Resistance consisted of individuals or small groups who wanted to "do something". Soon, the groups became quite numerous, but dispersed and in total still a small minority of the population; more often than not, for fear of the Gestapo and allied Nazi services and of the Vichy security police, they worked in ignorance of similar groups, sometimes in the same neighbourhoods. Until 1943, the Resistance, though it had been growing fast, was in no sense a mass movement. Especially at the outset, when small clandestine groups sprang up in isolation, there was a bewildering profusion of names. In time, many smaller groups disappeared or merged with others. The most important organisations were Libération, Combat, Franc-Tireur and the Front National. Combat was the name adopted by two movements that merged at the end of 1941 or the beginning of 1942 – one led by Captain Henri Frénay, the other by George Bidault (later to be Foreign Minister), P.-H. Teitgen and other Christian Democrats. Franc-Tireur ("Sharpshooter"), like Combat, began in Lyon, which became in effect the capital of the Resistance in southern France. Its best known leaders were J.-P. Lévy and Claudius-Petit. Libération was the creation of that picturesque and adventurous figure, Emmanuel d'Astier de la Vigerie, a journalist and former naval officer. The important Front National was created and organised by the Communist party but, in accordance with well tested Communist precedents, was intended to be a "front organisation" representing many political tendencies. Borrowing from Fascist ideas, however, the Communist organisers set up linked "national fronts" on a corporative basis – one for the lawyers, another for shopkeepers, for peasants, for women, and so forth. Each had its newspaper. The political spectrum was remarkably wide, for it included members from Louis Marin's right-wing Fédération Républicaine, Socialists (including the scientist Joliot-Curie, later to become a Communist), Radicals and Christian Democrats. Front National was the only Resistance organisation which functioned as a coherent whole in both zones of France. Its pretension to bring all Resistance movements under its banner was, however, fiercely opposed by resisters who had not waited until Hitler's war on Russia before deciding that they were patriots. These included the OCM and Libération-Nord in the north, and the three big movements in the south. One of Front National's most unexpected successes, however, was to acquire the support of the apolitical General Giraud, who provided arms for the FN group in Corsica to such effect that it liberated the island from the Germans.[9]

Both for SOE and for the Gaullist organisation, the proliferation of Resistance groups was a real problem, for it was impossible, except by contacts and enquiries in France itself, to decide which of the groups were important and likely to grow, which were worth supporting and which would merely absorb time, money and lives without results.

Passy's job was complicated at the outset by the fact that the Resistance movements in the south were in no hurry to acknowledge de Gaulle's leadership, while in the north they were too weak, scattered and cut off from the outside world to be able to judge for themselves. Towards the end of 1941, however, a major convert placed himself under the general's orders, and the event was decisive. Jean Moulin, whose name has since become a legend and a symbol, was the prefect – that is, the representative of the central government – at Chartres, when the armistice came. He was small, slim and dark, with humorous eyes. He was intelligent, determined and fearless.

On 9 September 1941, Jean Moulin, who had been living in unoccupied France where he had made contacts with the Resistance, slipped over the border into Spain, on his way to England. The British authorities in Lisbon, instantly recognising his qualities, spent six weeks trying to recruit him for service in France. But his mind was made up: he wanted to go to London and offer to serve de Gaulle. The general, who had heard his story and realised the potential importance of the man, was furious at the delay and wrote a pressing letter to Eden, which enabled Moulin to travel from Lisbon to London, which he reached at last at the end of November.[10]

Moulin was the bearer of credentials from three of the early Resistance movements in southern France: Liberté (or Libertés), Libération Nationale and Libération. It was the first two that were about to merge to form Combat; the third was, of course, d'Astier's left-wing movement. He described them, with partial accuracy, as "the main organisations of resistance to the invader" and requested help for them from the British and Free French. His report on the situation in France, dated October 1941, which he brought with him, made the interesting point that only

[9] For a fuller account of the Resistance movements, see Michel, Résistance, chs. 2 and 3.
[10] De Gaulle, L'Appel, p. 233. Foot, pp. 180 et seq., who describes Moulin's arrival, does not directly mention the British interest in recruiting Moulin, or de Gaulle's appeal to Eden. De Gaulle himself does not reproduce his letter to the British foreign secretary.

the Communists could hope to benefit if his modest demands for money, communications, arms and moral support were not met.[11]

General de Gaulle had several long talks with Jean Moulin in December 1941, and was deeply impressed, as he often was in similar cases, by the man's natural eloquence and authority. He decided to send Moulin back to France as his sole representative in unoccupied France for all political and military action within the Resistance. On 1 January 1942, after a crash course in jumping, he was parachuted into France. For code purposes, he was first called "Rex", then "Max". His mission was to organise clandestine military cells, establish reception centres for parachuted arms, distribute funds and keep in touch with London by radio. The first subsidy of 250,000 francs changed hands in the kitchen of a modest flat in Marseille. The fact that he controlled the funds and that the Resistance groups wanted them was a master card in his hand during the ensuing months of patient organising and negotiations with men who were not as convinced as he was that de Gaulle was the only possible leader.

Over the next few months, however, other Resistance leaders went to London, to see for themselves. One of the first was Christian Pineau, the Socialist politician. Aged about forty, plumpish, thin on the cranium and with large blue eyes, Pineau was surprisingly energetic, and soon mastered the arts of clandestine action. He went back to France at the end of April, and successfully set up two secret Resistance networks.

The next arrival was Pierre Brossolette, another Socialist, who was to become one of the great inspirers and organisers of the Resistance. In his late thirties, small and thin, he made a deep impression on Passy and de Gaulle, who was delighted, among other things, by his utter readiness to accept the general as his leader and make a doctrine of "Gaullism".[12]

Shortly after Brossolette, that is, towards the end of April, the picturesque Emmanuel d'Astier, with his visions of a revolutionary France, reached London. Tall, thin, elegant, with the air of a thoroughbred, he struck Passy as a curious mixture of a *condottiere* and Machiavelli. The two men took an instant dislike to each another. De Gaulle, however, was favourably impressed, both by the man's personality, and by the fact that he was the first unquestioned leader of a big Resistance movement to reach London (Moulin being a delegate rather than a leader). He decided therefore to send d'Astier to America, where

[11] Foot reproduces the report in full in an appendix, starting on p. 489.
[12] De Gaulle, *L'Appel*, p. 237.

he was to make official contacts and rally public support for the Resistance and de Gaulle. Passy describes him, with satisfied malice, as giving a lecture in a mask or black cowl. But he achieved little, as much because of the wild exaggeration of his claims as because of the pro-Vichy advice of Admiral Leahy, the American ambassador to Pétain's government.

In France, meanwhile, Moulin was making rapid progress on the organising side of his military mission, but getting nowhere in his efforts to unite the Resistance movements, each of which was jealous of its independence and resentful of his authority as de Gaulle's "delegate-general". To settle these differences, Moulin proposed that he and the leaders of the "big three" Resistance movements should all go to London to discuss matters with de Gaulle and André Philip. They agreed; but the operation to bring Moulin himself and J.-P. Lévy (of Franc-Tireur) failed, and only Henri Frénay (of Combat) and Emmanuel d'Astier (of Libération) managed to reach London – on 17 September 1942.

Frénay had been one of the Resistance leaders most refractory to de Gaulle's leadership, partly because, in the early days of his movement, he accepted the Pétain myth and received some help from the Vichy police and from the army's Deuxième Bureau in Lyon. Passy describes him as a man of thirty-seven or thirty-eight, with a small thin body surmounted by a large and curiously shaped head, with clear and lively eyes. He had a disconcerting habit of expressing contradictory ideas in rapid succession, which Passy ironically attributes to "successive sincerities". Though not in other respects in agreement with d'Astier, he joined the leftist leader now in demanding the removal of Jean Moulin. "The Resistance doesn't need a tutor," he declared to de Gaulle.

Brossolette and Passy intervened to defend Moulin who, they thought, was doing a magnificent job. They knew the general better than the newcomers. Frénay, however, was about to learn. De Gaulle invited d'Astier and Frénay to lunch at the Savoy, along with Philip, Billotte (his personal chief of staff) and Passy. Frénay explained that the Resistance gave unquestioning obedience to the Free French National Committee in the para-military domain. As for politics, the attitude of the Resistance movements towards the committee was exactly the same as that of political parties towards a government.

"What will happen," he asked, "if we can't reach agreement with Rex [Jean Moulin]?"

"You will come here, and we shall try to find a solution," said the general.

"And if this proves impossible?"

"Well, in that case," replied de Gaulle in his best form, "France will choose between you and me!"

Frénay and d'Astier went back shaken. And in November, when the Germans occupied the "free zone" and the Vichy army refused to hand over the weapons it had hidden to the Resistance, the movements at last gave their allegiance wholeheartedly to de Gaulle.[13]

More and more, it was necessary to forge unity, or to demonstrate it where doubts had arisen. In March 1943, Passy himself went to France, accompanied by the British agent Yeo-Thomas, to prove to the Resistance that the reported gulf between the SOE and the BCRA was not as wide or deep as was alleged. Meanwhile, Moulin pushed on with his mission of unifying the Resistance movements throughout France. His triumph came on 27 May 1943, when he presided over the first plenary session of the newly constituted National Council of the Resistance (CNR), representing the main movements, the trade union groups, and the main political parties involved in the Resistance. It was a short-lived triumph. On 21 June, he was caught by the Gestapo, along with a dozen other Gaullists, as they were assembling for a meeting in a doctor's house in a suburb of Lyon. He remained silent under appalling tortures inflicted on orders from the French head of the local Gestapo, Barbié; and died from them.

The following February, Brossolette and Yeo-Thomas, the Gaullist Briton with accentless French, were captured in their turn. Brossolette jumped (or fell) to his death from the fifth storey of the Gestapo building in the Avenue Foch in Paris, having attempted to escape on arrival.[14] Yeo-Thomas suffered appalling tortures and, like Moulin, stayed silent; though, unlike Moulin, he survived his ordeal.

---

[13] Michel, *Résistance*, p. 18.
[14] Foot, p. 363. Neither Passy (Vol. II, p. 66), nor de Gaulle (*L'Appel*, p. 237) entertains the hypothesis that Brossolette may have lost his footing. The incident occurred when he was challenged on escaping through a lavatory window. That he preferred suicide to certain torture (knowing the things he knew) is, however, a likely theory.

Chapter 12 ✤ Roots of the Fourth Republic

For General de Gaulle, Jean Moulin's death was a heavy blow.[1] He had held so many of the secret threads in his own hands, if only so that they should remain secret. He had neither trained a deputy nor passed on names or arrangements. On his death, therefore, much of the machinery of the Resistance was paralysed: liaison between the groups, transport, distribution of supplies and of information. From de Gaulle's standpoint, this situation could not have come at a more difficult time, for he was in the middle of his struggle for power with Giraud in Algiers, where he had arrived only three days after the first meeting of the Conseil National de la Résistance. Away from London, where Dewavrin-Passy continued to run the clandestine network, it was doubly difficult to make another appointment.

Two of the men de Gaulle had sent to France to work with Moulin – Claude Bouchinet-Serreulles and Jacques Bingen – carried on as best they could. The first, who was in Paris, stepped into Moulin's shoes, but without any ambition to succeed him in a formal sense. It was three months before any instructions reached him from the outside.[2] The second worked in the south.

But it was the political consequences of Jean Moulin's death that were the hardest to bear, from de Gaulle's standpoint. Moulin was *his* man, and by voluntary choice. He had come to London in February 1943, to see de Gaulle and be instructed. The general had been even more deeply impressed than at their first encounter – by his conviction, his authority and his determination.[3] In a ceremony which he seems to have found more moving than others of its kind, and held in his Hampstead house, he had conferred the *Croix de la Libération* on the Resistance leader. He had then sent Moulin back to France with precise directives to set

---

[1] De Gaulle, *L'Unité*, pp. 163 *et seq.*   [2] Gorce, p. 310.
[3] De Gaulle, *L'Unité*, p. 91.

246

up the CNR unifying all the Resistance movements, with the political parties and the trade union organisations, under Moulin's own chairmanship; and defining the new body's relations with the National Committee.

As always with General de Gaulle, the purposes of his directives to Moulin were more than merely military: the CNR was to be the political instrument of Gaullism on the way to the liberation of France, and at the same time a striking demonstration to the outside world that the French people wanted de Gaulle's leadership. Moreover, by sending de Gaulle a message of loyalty in the name of the Resistance on 15 May – twelve days before the first meeting of the CNR – Moulin had given his leader powerful support when he needed it most, on the eve of his departure for Algiers. And now, the patient uphill work of Jean Moulin that was to ensure the final triumph of Gaullism lay in ruins.

The leaders of the Resistance, talked into unity and loyalty to de Gaulle by the persuasive Jean Moulin, knew as well as the general that the foundations of the future France were being laid within their ranks. To understand how precarious was the unity won by Moulin, we must now take a closer look at the politics of the Resistance.

In London first, in France later, the Resistance was at the outset apolitical. It was a patriotic reflex, and in de Gaulle's case, a military one: the idea of defeat was insupportable. But in France herself, once the resisters had emerged from the preparatory stage, political tendencies began to reveal themselves. To some extent, the political character of the Resistance was determined by the division of the French people, itself the consequence of the defeat of France. In general, the parties of the traditional right and of the extreme right supported the Vichy regime in its early days. For the traditional right, Pétain's French State, with its paternalism, its support for the Church and its theory of given authority, came as a profound relief after the traumatic period of the Popular Front. By and large the Fascist right was even more enthusiastic for the regime and saw in Hitler's triumph the vindication of the national-socialist theories it shared with the current regimes in Italy and Germany.

For many, however, this euphoria was temporary. Persons of the traditional right who were patriots as well as authoritarians began to doubt the Pétain myth and to see where collaboration with the Germans was leading the regime. Thus Louis Marin began to reconstruct his Fédération républicaine on anti-Vichy lines, and in time forged links with the Communist-controlled Front National. Again, the Reynaud fraction of the Alliance démocratique denounced its collaborationist leader, P.-E. Flandin, the former premier.[4]

Even the extreme right was split on the issue of collaboration. Charles Maurras's royalist Action française never wavered in support of Marshal Pétain; but some of its leaders, including Guillain de Benouville, joined the Resistance. Initially, Colonel de la Rocque's Parti social français (the *Croix de Feu*) had filled the ranks of the militant Vichyist Légion des Combattants, but gradually he and his followers went over to the anti-German side. Even the notorious secret organisation of the revolutionary right, the Cagoule, split into three segments. Eugène Deloncle, the Cagoulard leader, declared all-out support for the Germans, but even he broke with them later. A second group of Cagoulards supported Pétain, then turned to the anti-Gaullist Resistance, offering its services to the British or Americans or to General Giraud. Then, of course, there were Cagoulards among de Gaulle's early followers in London. Two parties of the totalitarian right did, however, stick to the Germans to the bitter end: Jacques Doriot's Parti populaire français and Marcel Bucard's Francistes.

With the right fragmented, indecisive or collaborationist, the internal Resistance was heavily weighted on the left, and as the war went on, the totalitarian left. The great Radical-Socialist party – which had dominated the Third Republic – was discredited and virtually destroyed by France's defeat. Its left-wing credentials were always open to doubt, of course, but it had supported the Popular Front and must therefore be considered left of centre. Its load of responsibility was heavy, both for the Munich settlement and for France's unreadiness for war. Most of its leaders were gaoled or closely watched after the 1940 armistice. Some joined the Resistance, as individuals; Pierre Mendès France and Henri Queuille went to London. But the Radicals, as a party, were stunned and mute until the most famous of them, Edouard Herriot, three times premier of France, wrote to de Gaulle from his prison at Evaux on 23 April 1943 to declare his readiness, at any time, "to enter a government under General de Gaulle whom I consider the only man likely to achieve the union of the immense majority of the French".

In a confused way, there was a feeling among the resisters that the old was rotten and that something new was needed. Since they were fighting against a totalitarian authority, their yearning was not for a dictatorship. To a man, the resisters wanted a republic; even the Com-

---

[4] Michel, *Résistance*, ch. IV. For a fuller understanding of the politics of the Resistance, *see* the same author's monumental *Les Courants de Pensée de la Résistance* (henceforth, Michel, *Courants*).

munists among them said they wanted one, whatever their reservations. But they did not want a return to the Third Republic. In this setting, one of the political forces that emerged from the Resistance was the Christian Left. The Catholic resisters joined together to form a Christian Democratic party, which became the Mouvement républican populaire (MRP) and as such played a major part in the politics of the Fourth Republic, under Georges Bidault, Pierre-Henri Teitgen, François de Menthon and Francisque Gay.

Further to the left, the Socialists, though less hard hit than the Radicals, were demoralised and divided. Their pacifism inclined them to support the Munich settlement, but clashed with their awareness that democracy, which was in peril, needed to be defended. Most of the deputies who had voted against Pétain on 10 July 1940 were Socialists; but some supported him and some of these went so far as to work for a permanent understanding between France and Germany with a view to avoiding further wars. This sentiment was to be considered admirable at the time of the European Common Market but was premature in 1940, and the great majority of French Socialists rejected it. Many of these joined the Resistance, but they were disinclined to form a purely Socialist resistance movement as they did not wish to hinder recruiting into non-partisan groups. In this, they were following the directives that reached them from the party leader, Léon Blum, in his prison at Riom. They did, however, form a Comité d'Action socialiste (CAS), with H. Ribière as secretary-general. Daniel Mayer, formerly a sub-editor on the Socialist paper Le Populaire, later took over from Ribière. Two committees were formed, one for each of the zones of France. Ribière was the leading figure in the northern one; Mayer served on the southern one, along with other politicians, such as Félix Gouin (who came to London) and Gaston Defferre.

As for de Gaulle, the Socialists were frankly suspicious of him. What they knew of the adventurous or right-wing character of some of his early followers displeased them, and the French proverb qui se ressemble s'assemble ("Birds of a feather . . .") seemed to them apt. Besides, de Gaulle was a general, and therefore, by definition, a militarist and a reactionary. They suspected him of dictatorial ambitions and were naturally receptive to the anti-Gaullist tittle-tattle that reached them from the Socialists in the anti-Gaullist "Jean-Jaurès group" in London.

This attitude of reserve or hostility changed completely, however, when the Socialist Resistance decided to find out for themselves what kind of a man de Gaulle really was, when it was seen that he was there to stay, and when he himself decided to put some political views on paper.

For de Gaulle, too, had been acquiring a political identity. Being de Gaulle's, it was of course a singular one, not easy to define. He, too, was apolitical when he came to London, apart from a negative rejection of the "regime of parties" that had provoked the fall of the Republic. He himself was born and raised in a *milieu* that was in most respects typical of the conservative upper *bourgeoisie* or minor aristocracy; though money was not naturally respected and de Gaulle *père* had been a Dreyfusard. Part of the trauma Charles de Gaulle underwent with the defeat, the armistice and the emergence of a collaborationist regime in his beloved France was caused, however, by the realisation of painful facts: the army, to which de Gaulle belonged, had acquiesced in the defeat; and the class to which he belonged, along with the world of money, had supported Pétain. His alienation from his class background was, therefore, complete.

But not only had de Gaulle's "own" people flocked to the enemy and the traitors, but manifestly it was the left that was joining the Resistance in the greatest numbers.

All these factors combined to precondition de Gaulle towards political radicalism. Christian Pineau's trip to London in the spring of 1942, and his conversion to Gaullism, were important developments. Pineau had feared he might find a narrow-minded professional soldier, and was delighted to find a potential national leader with "advanced" social and economic views. On Pineau's advice, de Gaulle incorporated some of these views (and perhaps some of Pineau's) in a message to the Resistance, which was published in the clandestine press on 23 June 1942. This arresting document has not been accorded the attention it deserves. Certainly, it marked a fundamental stage in de Gaulle's evolution. In it, he denounced both the former regime and the existing one, called for *revolution*, and defined his war aims: the complete restoration of territorial integrity; the return of democratic liberties and the free election of a sovereign National Assembly; the punishment of the enemy leaders and of traitors; social security; and a "powerful renewal of the resources of the nation and the Empire by means of a state intervention".[5] Ambiguous though this message was on the future polity of the French State – and it could not be otherwise since de Gaulle was calling for a sovereign assembly – its principles were ones that any French Socialist could live with.

De Gaulle and Blum exchanged letters about this time, and the Socialist party declared itself in favour of Free France. The logical next

[5] For text, De Gaulle, *Discours*, Vol. I, pp. 205–7. For background, Passy, Vol. II, pp. 71–5.

step was the arrival in London of the prominent Socialist resister, André Philip, and his appointment in July 1942 as de Gaulle's commissioner for the Interior. But the Socialist party was also powerfully represented in Passy's BCRA: by Pierre Bloch, Louis Vallon and Pierre Brossolette.

The following year the Socialist party (which essentially had consisted of Blum and those who listened to him) formally reconstituted itself. In part, this was a natural preparation for post-liberation politics; but the real spur was the re-emergence of the Communist party and its claim – which the Socialists, with good reason, contested – to be the only party in the Resistance. Until the Socialists had formally reconstituted themselves, the Communist claim was literally correct; and damaging. The new Socialist party, as befitted the circumstances, purged itself ruthlessly by excluding all former party members who had voted for Pétain and all those who had joined the Légion des Combattants.

The re-emergence of the totalitarian left was, however, undoubtedly the most important phenomenon of Resistance politics. During the time when the Resistance groups were organising themselves, the Communist party was weak and inactive; by the end of the war it was by far the strongest political group in France, and universally accepted as a patriotic and even a democratic organisation. How did the Communists accomplish this feat?

The answer lies in a combination of circumstances favourable to them but not of their own making; and in their own qualities of clandestine organisation, courage and duplicity. The Communist party's fidelity to Moscow's line seems, in retrospect, astonishing and at times almost suicidal. From 1935 to 1939, it was in the vanguard of the struggle against Fascism and appeasement: but the Nazi-Soviet Pact of August 1939 turned the Communists into neutralists overnight. When war was declared in September, the Daladier government banned the party and interned its top leaders. (Maurice Thorez deserted from the army, into which he had been conscripted, and spent the war years in Moscow.)

When the Nazi authorities moved into Paris, the party requested authority to resume (open) publication of L'Humanité on the ground that it would preach Franco-Soviet friendship as a complement to the German-Soviet Pact.[6]

The Nazis spurned this advance, but for months, through its illegal publications, the party went on preaching solidarity between the French

[6] Michel, Courants, p. 557, quoting Daladier, Réponse aux Chefs Communistes. Part V of Courants is an extended discussion of the wartime policy, or rather policies, of the French Communist party, on which the present chapter draws freely; as it does, also, from the same author's shorter Résistance, ch. IV.

workers and German soldiers and denouncing saboteurs. For its pains, the Nazis allowed the Vichy police to persecute party members and handed over the Communists interned by Daladier on the Isle of Yeu to the Vichy authorities, who transferred them to North Africa.

The Yeu incident, which took place in mid-September, marked a change of line. Henceforth, the party press denounced the Vichy government (whose legality, however, it did not contest) and the conditions of the occupation. Also denounced were the evils of Nazism; but the party went on denouncing de Gaulle as a lackey of the English and in the pay of the City of London, while the Cross of Lorraine was bracketed with the Swastika.

The German invasion of Russia on 22 June 1941, however, changed the party's line as radically as had the Nazi-Soviet Pact, but in the opposite direction. Instantly, the war ceased to be a clash between rival imperialisms and became a great patriotic struggle to save the home of the revolution and the fatherland of the workers. The Front National had already been formed, and was initially anti-Nazi, but in words not deeds; now it was activated. It excluded bosses and capitalists initially, though they were eventually admitted; meanwhile, everyone else was welcome, specifically including ex-Fascists who had seen the error of their ways. No Communist-controlled National Front anywhere was ever more universal or more successful, while party control through the well-trained officials of the Front remained absolute. Those who joined the National Front usually belonged already to some Resistance organisation and were ignorant of party control over the Front. Indeed, Marxist-Leninist doctrine was swept out of sight, apparently forgotten. Instead, the party extolled the virtues, deeds and names of the French Revolution of 1789.

Communist assassinations of German officers and French "traitors", strikes and acts of sabotage multiplied. Itself inactive for so long, the Communist party now turned on the Free French and the Resistance groups, accusing them of *attentisme*. Party members suffered at least their share of deportations and executions. Once again, the stupidity of the enemy played into the hands of the Communists. For Vichy, to alarm public opinion, systematically attributed all acts of resistance to them. Their prestige as the most active and effective resisters was thereby inflated.

The Communists had a dual political aim: to gain control over the trade union movement, and over the Resistance as a whole. Neither objective was entirely achieved, but progress in both directions was rapid. In May 1943, the main trade union body – the CGT, from which the Communists had been expelled – was reconstituted, with three Communists in the central committee of nine.

To control the Resistance as a whole was a tougher undertaking. The tactic was to join the larger movements as individuals and press for adherence to the Front National. The measure of the party's success is that it came to be accepted as a patriotic party like any other, the past forgiven if not forgotten. But full control eluded the Communists. Their presence prevented the creation of a great national party of the Resistance, which the majority of non-Communist resisters hoped to set up.

Just as the forced entry of the Soviet Union into the war had turned the French Communists into resisters, so Stalin's policy of recognition and aid for de Gaulle's National Committee brought them into a *de facto* alliance with the Free French. It was, however, an alliance, not an act of allegiance, and the distinction is important. At the beginning of 1943, the party sent a representative, Fernand Grenier, to London, where he worked under Soustelle, purveying, says de Gaulle, a "rigorous" Gaullism.[7] Thereafter, the Communist resisters in France adopted the Cross of Lorraine and the V of Victory, but displayed them next to their own Hammer and Sickle.

Yet when Giraud entered the scene, the Communists, once again following the Moscow line, gave their support impartially to both generals. When Grenier arrived in Algiers at the end of 1943, he defended this duality by referring to the need for national unity. And, alone among the resisters, the Communists also sent a representative (named Pourtalet) to General Giraud's headquarters. The pay-off came when Giraud armed the Communist *maquis* in Corsica.[8]

For his part, de Gaulle carefully refrained from reminding the Communists of their recent indifference to the war and hostility towards himself. And although his telegram to Free French headquarters from Jerusalem on 24 June 1941 mentioned the "vices and even the crimes of the Soviet regime", he was too aware of the usefulness of Russian support, both in the war as a whole and in his own quarrels with the "Anglo-Saxons" to repeat such charges in public. But he was alive to the double game of the French Communists, and in his memoirs describes their attempts to draw non-Communists into their Resistance organisations, while themselves infiltrating into non-Communist groups. But:

I myself wanted them to serve. To defeat the enemy, there were no forces that should be left out and I thought that theirs would weigh

[7] De Gaulle, *L'Unité*, p. 90.   [8] Michel, *Courants*, pp. 613–14.

heavily in the kind of war which the occupation imposed. But they would have to do it as part of a whole, and not to beat about the bush, in subservience to me [*sous ma coupe*]. . . . In the world's ceaseless movement all doctrines, all schools, all revolts have their moment. Communism will pass away. But France shall not pass away.[9]

These rival political ambitions and formations explain the deep concern de Gaulle felt – in addition to his personal distress – when the news of Jean Moulin's death reached him in Algiers. That death, he learned, was the consequence of another casualty: a few days earlier, General Delestraint, whom de Gaulle had appointed commander of the Secret Army of the Resistance, was arrested by the Gestapo on 9 June 1943, as he was changing trains on the Paris *métro*. The appointment had been made in March, and it was Jean Moulin who had brought him to London to meet de Gaulle. Both men had returned to France, and to their deaths, on the 24th of that month; for General Delestraint was never heard of again. In the few weeks before his arrest, he had not been able to accomplish much, and it was to review the situation that Moulin had called the meeting at Lyon that had led to his own arrest.

It was not easy to find a successor for Delestraint; Jean Moulin, strictly speaking, was irreplaceable, but a man had to be found to be General de Gaulle's delegate-general with the Resistance. Colonel Marchal was appointed to head the Secret Army, but was arrested almost immediately after arriving in Paris,[10] and the post remained unfilled until the spring of 1944.

De Gaulle did not want a politician as delegate-general but a public servant of stature acceptable to all tendencies and capable, when liberation came, of assuring public order.[11] Months elapsed before he could find his man. He then picked Emile Bollaert, who had outstanding service as a prefect and who had resigned in 1940 rather than take the oath to Marshal Pétain. He was still in France at the time of his appointment in September 1943, and had never met de Gaulle. It was therefore arranged that he should come to Algiers for a meeting and briefing. The appalling luck of the Free French continued, however, for he was arrested by the Germans as he was about to embark from a lonely spot on the Breton coast. He was deported to Buchenwald, but survived the war. The search for a similar candidate took several more months, and it was not until March 1944 that de Gaulle was able to appoint

---

[9] De Gaulle, *L'Appel*, p. 232.
[11] De Gaulle, *L'Unité*, p. 164.

[10] Gorce, p. 311.

Alexandre Parodi, a former member of the *conseil d'Etat* and director-general (permanent under-secretary) of the ministry of Labour, to be his delegate-general with the Resistance.

The resisters, meanwhile, had done some reorganising of their own. The Conseil National de la Résistance (CNR) had chosen a new chairman, Georges Bidault, who was acceptable to de Gaulle but was not appointed by him and who, unlike Moulin, did not have the double attribution of delegate-general and chairman of the CNR. It was not, however, Bidault's appointment that worried de Gaulle so much as the fact that three of the five members of the permanent office of the CNR were Communists or sympathisers,[12] while the new military action committee (COMAC) was controlled by the Communists. The vacuum in the command of the Secret Army made this situation still more dangerous: for Colonel de Jussieu, appointed to succeed Marchal, was arrested in his turn. In the end, a Communist, Malleret-Joinville, was appointed commander, from within the Resistance and without reference to Algiers.

In this situation, de Gaulle was beginning to discover the disadvantages of being in North Africa instead of in London.[13] The North African wavelengths were less familiar to French listeners than the London ones, and reception was not as clear. Moreover, clandestine communications by air were more difficult and hazardous.

One comfort for the general was that he now had his family with him. His wife had come first, with their sick daughter, Anne. Then Elizabeth joined them from Oxford, and was employed in the office dealing with the foreign press. Philippe was still at sea in the Channel and Atlantic. The family lived simply in the Villa des Oliviers. There, in the evenings, de Gaulle worked alone on his speeches, the only one of his duties he appears to have found a burden. From time to time they entertained, but the menus, because of rationing, were short. Every now and then they managed to spend Sunday in a cottage in Kabylia.

News came of their relatives. Not all of it was good. The general's brother Xavier was in hiding at Nyons and able to send useful information to Algiers. Xavier's daughter, Geneviève, had been captured by the Germans and sent to Ravensbrück, while his eldest son was fighting in Italy. Charles de Gaulle's sister, Mme Alfred Cailliau, had fallen into the Gestapo's hands and was gaoled first at Fresnes, then in Germany, while her husband, aged sixty-seven, was sent to Buchenwald. One of

---

[12] The party member was Pierre Villon, the sympathisers were Pascal Copeau and Louis Saillant (who later became the secretary-general of the Communist-controlled World Federation of Trade Unions). The other members were Bidault himself and Maxime Blocq-Mascart of the "right-wing" Organisation civile et militaire (OCM).
[13] De Gaulle, *L'Unité*, pp. 166–7; *see also* pp. 173–4.

their sons had been killed in action during the battle of France and three others had joined the Free French forces, as had three sons of Charles de Gaulle's paralysed brother, Jacques, who himself had found refuge in Switzerland. His brother Pierre was arrested by the Germans in 1943 and sent to Eisenberg concentration camp. His wife and five children had made their way to Morocco after crossing the Pyrenees on foot.

But at least de Gaulle now had Algiers well under control. On 17 September 1943, a decree of the National Liberation Committee called for the creation of a Consultative Assembly of the Resistance, a kind of provisional parliament and pendant to the provisional government. On 3 October, the National Committee, taking note of the *de facto* situation, formally appointed de Gaulle as its sole president, leaving Giraud to his command.

It remained for de Gaulle to call the first session of the Consultative Assembly and reorganise the National Committee – with the same objectives in each case: to see that the new political and social trends that had emerged in France within the Resistance should be as faithfully represented as possible in Algiers, and to demonstrate the harmony which now, he thought, prevailed between external and internal wings of the Resistance.

Both events took place in November. On the 3rd, the Assembly met. Its composition, as decreed on 17 September, and its selection by nomination of interested groups, were of course artificial, but not excessively so in the circumstances. Fifty members had been nominated by the Resistance organisations and twenty by the political parties, the latter consisting as far as possible of former deputies who had denied their vote of confidence to Pétain. A dozen Communists – those who had been arrested in 1939 and deported to North Africa – were also members: they had been freed by General Giraud. Then there were twenty representatives of the Resistance from the Empire; and ten counsellors-general from Algeria.

The new provisional government was announced on the 9th. There were seven professional politicians among the new commissioners. Two were Radicals, and both were to become premiers under the Fourth Republic: Henri Queuille (commissioner of State), and Pierre Mendès France (Finance). Three were Socialists: André Philip (relations with the Consultative Assembly); André Le Trocquer (War and Air); and Adrien Tixier (Labour and Social Security). The solitary representative of the moderate right was Louis Jacquinot (Navy), and there was one Christian Democrat, François de Menthon (Justice). The Resistance had five commissioners: René Pleven (Colonies); Emmanuel d'Astier (Interior);

Professor René Capitant (Education); André Diethelm (Supply and Production); and Henri Frénay (Prisoners, Deportees and Refugees). Then there were the notables and technicians: General Catroux (Moslem affairs); Henri Bonnet (Information); René Massigli (Foreign affairs); René Mayer (Communications and Merchant Navy); and Jean Monnet (head of the Raw Materials and Arms mission with the rank of commissioner but based in the United States).

General Giraud was out, of course, and so were General Georges (who opted for retirement; "with dignity" says de Gaulle), Dr Abadie (who wanted to get back to his scientific work), General Legentilhomme (who had asked to be posted to London, and was), and Couve de Murville.

The new team was impressive, but not very new-looking. And there were two omissions from the list, one of them glaring. De Gaulle had hoped to include a representative of the Church in Mgr Hincky, but failed to obtain explicit hierarchical approval and was therefore unable to proceed. His memoirs provide no explanation for this failure, which may have been due to Catholic suspicions of Communist strength in the Resistance. But the Communist party, in the event, was unrepresented in the new government, and this was the more glaring omission. It was de Gaulle's first direct experience of negotiations with Communists. Negotiations had, in fact, dragged on since the end of August, the party haggling over names, de Gaulle's programme, and assignments. In the end, de Gaulle tired of the bargaining and went ahead with his appointments.[14]

The party seems to have been divided on the issue of whether to join the National Liberation Committee. The intransigent wing, led by André Marty, wanted no truck with parliamentary government, even in its attenuated Algerian form, and advocated intensive preparations for revolution. The more moderate wing, advised by Maurice Thorez (still in Moscow but pleading to be allowed to return unpunished for his desertion), favoured infiltration of the State from within. In March 1944, the Thorez faction at last won the day and the party authorised Fernand Grenier and François Billoux to join the committee. They moved in on 4 April, Grenier as commissioner for Air, and Billoux as commissioner of State without portfolio. This meant finding new jobs for André Le Trocquer, who was made commissioner for Liberated Territories, and André Diethelm, who replaced Le Trocquer as commissioner for War; Paul Giacobbi took over the economic responsibilities of Diethelm.

After the November reshuffle the Giraud problem remained – but residually. On the 13th, the National Committee confirmed his

[14] ibid. p. 150.

appointment as commander-in-chief of the French Armed Forces. Stubborn as ever, the general was less than satisfied with his lot. Having lost the political battle, into which he should never have ventured, he was now determined to hang on to the massive Intelligence Service of the Army General Staff, which had served Vichy until November 1942, before being transferred to Algiers on Giraud's own orders.

The loyalty of this service was not in question. Its chiefs, Colonels Ronin and Rivet, had done their best whenever possible to frustrate the Germans. Its continuance as a separate service, responsible only to the C.-in-C., was, however, unrealistic now that Giraud had ceased to be joint-president of the National Committee. On 27 November 1943, the committee decreed that the General Staff Intelligence Service should be merged forthwith with de Gaulle's own secret services. Jacques Soustelle, who was only thirty-one, was appointed director-general of the combined secret services, directly responsible to General de Gaulle. It was not proposed to declare redundancies, but to absorb the General Staff team in the new and enlarged service, which was to be known as the Direction Générale des Services spéciaux (DGSS).[15] But Giraud would not hear of giving up his intelligence service, and months went by while it and the DGSS existed and worked separately. Since Giraud's service sent its own agents into France, in ignorance of Soustelle's arrangements, the situation soon became untenable.

It was not, however, till April 1944 that de Gaulle, after some unfortunate incident, gave Giraud an ultimatum. But Giraud, pig-headed and self-righteous to the end, continued to prevaricate. Thereupon, the National Committee withdrew by decree his appointment as commander-in-chief and instead appointed him inspector-general. To soften the blow, de Gaulle wrote him two letters: an official one praising the services he had rendered, and a personal one appealing to him to give an example of abnegation in the painful circumstances of the nation, and accept his new assignment.

Giraud decided, however, to retire. Declining the Military Medal that was offered to him, he declared, "I want to be commander-in-chief or nothing."[16]

Nobody seemed sorry to see him go, or indeed to take much notice of the fact that he had gone.

For de Gaulle, a much greater battle loomed ahead: the battle for France herself.

[15] Soustelle, Vol. II, p. 292. Passy became Soustelle's *Directeur technique* (Foot, p. 23); the DGSS had twin services in Algiers and London.
[16] De Gaulle, *L'Unité*, p. 168.

Chapter 13 ✤ The Agony of France

For France, in her long agony, the end was in sight. With his visceral concern for the motherland, General de Gaulle felt every fresh instance of Nazi barbarism, each new humiliation, and – as far as he could learn the facts – each further sign of Laval's villainy or Pétain's stately weakness. It is impossible to grasp the magnitude of the problems that loomed ahead for the Gaullist movement and their leader without considering events in France herself.

The Vichy regime had become both more impotent and more repressive as the war years wore on. The French people, with few exceptions, had turned to Pétain in defeat, as the father-figure who would guide and protect them from German frightfulness in the difficult days ahead. Their trust in him was total and their love uncritical. These sentiments did not extend to Laval, the most powerful political personality to have survived the collapse of the Third Republic, nor to the rest of Pétain's *entourage*.

From the first, Laval was the advocate of "loyal" collaboration (though not without reservations); whereas Pétain hoped for neutrality and autonomy under the "protection" of the armistice. Laval's great error lay in assuming that the British would shortly be defeated as the French had been. He saw ahead a Europe of totalitarian states dominated by Nazi Germany, in which France's only chance lay in total collaboration, to the extent of declaring war on her former Allies, the British. The alternative, he thought, was the "polonisation" of France – that is, the destruction of any vestiges of a French State and the imposition of direct Nazi rule through a Gauleiter.

It was relatively easy to sustain this logic during the first period of Laval's ascendancy – during the second half of 1940. By the time he returned to power, in April 1942, it was evident that the assumption of a swift British defeat had not been realised. But Laval's self-confidence remained unshaken. He thought it possible to collaborate with Germany to defeat Bolshevism, while keeping on good terms with the United States. The Germans, he reasoned, would defeat the Russians in the

East; and in the West, he, Laval, would be the go-between in a compromise peace between Germany and the United States, with the British powerless to affect the course of events.[1]

Neither the armistice,[2] with its formal limitations on German encroachments, nor the imitative flattery of Pétain's National Revolution, stopped the Nazis from systematically pillaging the country they occupied. An occupation mark was issued and made legal tender at an artificial rate of 20 francs (compared with the legal rate of 16 before the war). During the first three months of the occupation, more than 500 French machine-tools were seized and transported to Germany; 85 per cent of the French steel industry was placed under Nazi control, or simply annexed by the Germans; under a decree of 20 June, all exports of raw materials or produce from occupied France were controlled by the Nazis.

Despite these exactions, the behaviour of the well-disciplined occupying troops, especially in the early months, was ostentatiously "correct". But as the power of the Gestapo and related services spread, and the Resistance had its first successes, the impression of a well-behaved invader rapidly wore thin. Hunger and cold soon damped any initial euphoria among the French civilian population. In September 1940 the daily food ration was fixed at 1,800 calories (compared with the 3,000 to 3,500 reckoned necessary to adults in sedentary occupations). Those with means supplemented their rations on the black market. But the majority were less fortunate.

In 1941, with the first stirrings of the Resistance, the Nazis began the practice, which they continued on an ever-increasing scale throughout the occupation, of shooting hostages in retaliation for anti-German attacks. The most notorious case is known as the "Châteaubriant episode". At 8 a.m. on 20 October 1941, the Feld-Kommandant of Nantes, Lieutenant-Colonel Holz, was killed by persons unknown near the cathedral. General von Stulpnagel announced that fifty hostages would be executed as a reprisal. On the 21st, sixteen were shot at Nantes. Next day twenty-seven political detainees in the concentration camp of Châteaubriant were executed in their turn, and in Paris five more were shot, bringing the total to forty-eight. Thereupon, von Stulpnagel announced that fifty more hostages would be executed if the murderers of Colonel Holz were not unmasked within forty-eight hours.

So moved was Pétain by this barbarism that he conceived the plan of offering himself to the Germans as a hostage, to shame them into dropping their policy of arbitrary arrests and executions. But he was

---

[1] Rob. Aron, Vichy, pp. 508 et seq.   [2] See above, Part II, chapter 2.

talked out of it, and in the end did not even protest. This reticence probably marked the beginning of the end of his personal popularity.

Inevitably, the brutalities of the Nazis adversely affected the character of the Vichy regime. Three policies were open to the men of Vichy: to collaborate with the invaders; to resist all encroachments on the rights of unoccupied France, as defined by the armistice; or to sit on the fence. Laval was the arch-advocate of the first course. Flandin, who briefly succeeded him (13 December 1940 to 9 February 1941), urged resistance, and the brevity of his tenure of office reflected Pétain's view that the best policy was no policy; to avoid being drawn into a military commitment against France's former allies, to try to gain time when faced with Nazi demands, and to give in when it became unavoidable.

Pétain's choice as the executant of his non-policy was Admiral Darlan, but this narrowly ambitious man lacked both the skill of the politician and the vision of the statesman. Although anti-German as well as anti-British, he always, in the end, gave in to the Nazis. It was under his authority that the minister of the Interior, Pierre Pucheu, recruited among the Légion française des Combattants candidates for a ruthless instrument of repression, akin in some respects to the Nazi SS: the Service d'Ordre Légionnaire (SOL) whose oath read, "I swear to struggle against democracy, against the Gaullist dissidence and against the Jewish plague."[3]

Darlan had lasted fourteen months, from 9 February 1941 to 18 April 1942. Persistent German pressure, coupled with Laval's powerful advocacy of his own policy, then brought the latter back to office as Prime Minister, though only for a relatively brief period (18 April to 27 November 1942). Until Laval's return, the distinction between occupied and unoccupied France had remained, despite increasing oppression in the free zone. Refugees crossing the dividing line felt the relief of relative freedom. Now, the dividing line was increasingly blurred. Before it was possible to read the Swiss newspapers or see British films; now, both were banned. On 22 June 1942, the anniversary of the German invasion of Russia, Laval expressed the hope of a German victory over Bolshevism, and called on French workers to sign on for work in Germany, so that French prisoners-of-war might be repatriated. Later, such exhortations yielded to threats of forced labour if insufficient numbers volunteered.

Soon Nazi police moved into "unoccupied" France in pursuit of Resistance fighters. And the SOL, under its sadistic leader, Joseph Darnand, became a state within the State, much as Himmler's SS was wherever it operated. In emulation of the Nazis, the SOL rounded up

[2] Rob. Aron, *Vichy*, pp. 421; *see also* pp. 502 *et seq.*

261

thousands of Jews, of both sexes and all ages, piled them into trains without sanitary facilities and delivered them to the Germans.

Although Laval was the arch-advocate of collaboration, it should not be thought that he always or automatically gave in to German demands. His technique was to negotiate, in the hope of achieving a concession that fell short of the conqueror's requirements. As human lives were often at stake, the outcome, in many cases, was that fewer people suffered or died than might have otherwise. The fact remains that he sent many of his countrymen to suffering or death. In the end he and the Germans, between them, virtually "Polonised" France.

Two days after his return, the Germans began shooting hostages again: between 20 April and 24 May 1942, they executed 201. On 6 May the dreaded Reinhard Heydrich, Hitler's henchman and the scourge of Czechoslovakia, arrived in Paris. Refusing to see Laval, he announced the direct subordination of the French police and administration to the German authorities, and the devolution of Vichy's authority, for what it was worth, to the collaborationist parties of the French totalitarians, Jacques Doriot and Marcel Déat, both of whom were heavily subsidised by the Germans and lost no opportunity to satirise the Vichy regime. On the 27th, Heydrich was assassinated in Czechoslovakia. The Gauleiter of Thuringia, Sauckel, a typically brutal Nazi of the worst type, now arrived in Paris, where he immediately ordered the Vichy government to deliver 350,000 workers for the German factories. As usual, Laval sought to negotiate and was elated when Sauckel agreed in principle to a "relief" programme, under which three French workers would be exchanged for one repatriated prisoner-of-war.

The next German demand was for the immediate rounding up of all Jews in both zones of France. Again, Laval negotiated. On 23 July, it was agreed that the Germans would only deport foreign Jews from occupied France, and that only foreign Jews would be delivered to them from the free zone. During the next two months, the Vichy authorities delivered 10,410 Jews, mostly refugees from Germany, into Nazi hands.

Meanwhile, Sauckel let it be known that the response to Laval's appeal for volunteers for work in Germany was not good enough. There had been 12,000 in June, 23,000 in July and 18,000 in August – well short of the 350,000 required. Faced with a German ultimatum on 29 August, Laval on 4 September promulgated a law providing for the mobilisation of all males aged eighteen to fifty and single women between twenty-one and thirty-five. Once again, Laval sought to avoid Polonisation by the Nazis by doing the job of Gauleiter for them.

With the Allied landings in North Africa, the scuttling of the French fleet on 27 November 1942, and the occupation of the free zone of France by the German armed forces a fortnight earlier, the Vichy regime entered its final phase of ultimate degradation. Laval remained premier; Pétain stayed increasingly in the background or was simply ignored by his ministers.

On 14 January 1943 Sauckel demanded 250,000 more workers by mid-March: either Laval would provide them, or the Germans would help themselves. A month of negotiations followed, culminating on 17 February in the notorious Service obligatoire du Travail (SOT) which made all French citizens born in 1920, 1921 and 1922 liable to forced labour. In return, Laval secured some concessions, such as the free travel and correspondence between the nothern and southern zones.

It was the SOT, above all, that caused the spontaneous creation of the famous *maquis* groups of the French Resistance. Until then, the Resistance had consisted of small groups operating in the towns. Now young men in ever-increasing numbers took to the hills to escape forced labour. They grouped themselves in the higher and wilder regions of France, in Auvergne, in Savoie, in Corrèze, in Vercors. Armed by British parachute drops and financed from London and Algiers, they were to form the nucleus of the Forces françaises de l'Intérieur (FFI), which played an important part in the liberation of France.

A new horror visited France at that time, with the creation on 30 January 1943 of a militia, under Darnand, which absorbed the SOL and supplemented its personnel from among the criminal population.

There seemed no end to Nazi frightfulness. On 3 January 1943, following an explosion in a Marseilles brothel frequented by Wehrmacht soldiers, the German command ordered the destruction of the Old Port. The deed was done on the 23rd and 20,000 local inhabitants were sent to concentration camps. Then there was the wholesale destruction of villages, the most horrific being that of Oradour-sur-Glane on 10 June 1944, where the SS division Das Reich burned alive more than 600 women and children in the local church.

This, then, was the plight to which France had been reduced on the eve of the liberation. By then, the last vestiges of Vichy's independence had gone. Pétain, now eighty-eight, was powerless to resist Laval's machinations. On Hitler's orders, transmitted through Abetz to Laval, three arch-collaborationists – Marcel Déat, Philippe Henriot and Joseph Darnand – were brought into the cabinet. The old man, who had impotently resisted these appointments, burned his private hoard of papers – to the loss of history.

Against this sordid background, the story of the end of Pierre Pucheu, the first of the Vichy ministers to be executed, is tragically intelligible. Pucheu had been Darlan's minister of the Interior. In 1942, having made his way to Spain, he requested General Giraud's permission to serve in the army in Morocco. Permission was granted early in 1943 on condition that he kept out of politics.[4] Instead, he made no secret of his identity. Embarrassed by this indiscretion, the "civil and military commander-in-chief" placed him under house arrest. The question now arose – in the late summer – should Pucheu be brought to trial?

De Gaulle and his National Liberation Committee unanimously decided that he should. Since the French High Court could not be summoned, he was called to account before the Army Tribunal. The trial began on 4 March 1944 on charges that included treason and illegal arrests. An embarrassed Giraud, who explained that he did not know what had been going on in France when Pucheu was in office since he himself was in German hands, pleaded for mercy, on the ground that this was a time for reconciliation so that all Frenchmen with the will should fight the common enemy. Much of the evidence was of a personal, passionate and denunciatory character; documentary proof of the allegations was, of course, missing. Pucheu was condemned to death, despite his powerful self-defence.

A further question now arose: should the sentence be carried out? Giraud interceded with de Gaulle, both in person and in writing, in favour of a reprieve.[5] De Gaulle, however, left Giraud's letter unanswered and decided that for reasons of State (raison d'Etat), the execution must be carried out. He gave the necessary orders without bothering to notify Giraud that his plea had not been granted.

Pucheu faced death bravely at dawn on 22 March 1944. He told his lawyer: "I have been ready for a long time. My death will be more useful to France than my reprieve. You will tell everybody how I died. You will tell your political friends, our friends that this really is a political assassination. And above all, don't let General de Gaulle invoke reasons of State. . . . Reasons of State? That's in the purest tradition of national-socialism."[6]

---

[4] Paillat, L'Echiquier, Vol. II, p. 371.
[5] In his memoirs (L'Unité, p. 179), de Gaulle mentions a personal visit from Giraud, but not a letter; see Paillat, L'Echiquier, Vol. II, pp. 381–3.
[6] Paillat, L'Echiquier, Vol. II, pp. 384–5. De Gaulle in his memoirs pays tribute to Pucheu's bravery, and quotes him as shouting before the firing squad, in reference to the general: "That man, who today carries the supreme hopes of France, if my life can serve him in the mission he is accomplishing, let him take it! I give it to him." These remarks are noble, but the suggestion that Pucheu ever uttered them strains the imagination.

He insisted on shaking hands with every member of the firing squad, and, in a little speech, denounced Giraud for having "dishonoured" himself by failing in his word. He then gave the command to fire, and died without flinching.

What, then, were de Gaulle's "reasons of State"? In his memoirs he argues, pertinently, that, at the time, the Resistance was about to become an essential element in the forthcoming battle of liberation. Meanwhile, Laval and Darnand, in collusion with the Germans, were trying to smash it. It was essential, therefore, to show "our fighters" that culprits would be brought to justice.

Paillat adduces less exalted reasons, which cannot be ignored: indeed, they do not discredit the reasons given by de Gaulle, but complement them. One of them was the attitude of the National Council of the Resistance, and especially of its Communist members. The council had "sentenced" Pucheu to death and conveyed its decision to de Gaulle. Fernand Grenier, one of the Communist delegates in Algiers, was among the most virulent of the witnesses for the prosecution during the trial. And de Gaulle, at the time of the trial, was negotiating with Grenier and his fellow-Communist, François Billoux, for their entry into the National Liberation Committee. They accepted the posts he was offering them only a few days after Pucheu's execution, on 4 April 1944.

The other reason was Giraud. The question of a reprieve for Pucheu came up at the time when de Gaulle was planning to relieve Giraud of his command.[7] To ignore Giraud's plea for Pucheu contributed to discredit the former. De Gaulle was not of course to know that Pucheu would denounce Giraud before the firing squad. This was a bonus, which the whispering Gaullist *mafia* swiftly carried through Algiers. On 8 April, de Gaulle summoned his former chief and informed him that his command was at an end. Pucheu's execution therefore did serve de Gaulle's reasons of State, and in more senses than one.[8]

Pucheu's trial and execution was the first juridical settlement of

[7] *See above,* p. 58.
[8] The question of Pucheu's actual guilt is, of course, another story. De Gaulle declares (*L'Unité*, p. 179) that when the Germans presented Pucheu with a list of hostages for execution, he countered with a list of his own preferences for shooting; and that the Germans "gave him that odious satisfaction". This is an over-simplification. Pucheu appears to have objected to many names on a German list on the grounds that they were veterans of the First World War. The Germans presented him with an alternative list of names, mostly of Communists; Pucheu raised no objections, and the executions were carried out. (Rob. Aron, *Vichy*, pp. 387–9.) In his defence, Pucheu pleaded that he had successfully battled with the Germans to cut down the number of hostages. But he seemed insensitive to the fact that by indulging in such haggling, he had made himself a party to sending Frenchmen to their deaths. At his trial, it should be added, the question of hostages was dropped.

accounts by Vichy's opponents during the Second World War. There were to be many others before the war ended and after; and numerous private killings and kangaroo court executions. For in all but name, a civil war was going on in France. And as in Spain, the problem before the victors was how to control and divert the thirst for revenge into juridical channels. It was de Gaulle's problem, as it had been Franco's. And although French justice proved less ruthless than Spain's, the number of *unofficial* executions in France greatly exceeed those of similar cases in Spain at the end of the Civil War.

To a large extent, this was undoubtedly due to the fact that whereas Franco's official justice, however summary, travelled with his advancing army, the Free French were minority partners in the liberation of their own country and operating from outside France. They were, however, acutely aware of the problem of private reprisals in the wake of the departing Germans, and the National Committee tried, in the summer of 1944, to guard against them. "No private citizen," wrote de Gaulle, "has the right to punish the guilty. That is the business of the State."[9] On 26 June and on 26 August 1944, two ordinances defined the conditions under which the crimes and misdemeanours of collaboration might be dealt with. The basis for legal action already existed in the statute book in the offence of "intelligence with the enemy". But the circumstances of wartime France were unprecedented, and fresh arrangements were needed. The ordinary law courts were not competent to try cases of collaboration, and the ordinary magistrates, having taken the oath to Vichy, had disqualified themselves. New courts of Justice were therefore created, to consist of appointed magistrates and four assessors, two of whom would be representatives of the Resistance. The execution of orders from the Vichy government would, in certain cases, be accepted as extenuating circumstances. The leading dignitaries of the regime, however, were to be tried before the High Court. For the new offence of collaboration, a new penalty was devised: "national indignity", comprising the loss of political rights, ineligibility for State employment and, in the worst instances, exile.

The ordinances dealing with collaboration were a small part only of the work of the Consultative Assembly, which aimed at sweeping away all vestiges of Vichy's legislation and restoring "Republican legality". The ordinance of 9 August 1944 in effect declared all Vichy's laws and regulations null and void, under the principle that "the Republic has never ceased to exist". But this was too easy and too sweeping. In practice, individual Vichy measures had to be considered on their

9 De Gaulle, *L'Unité*, p. 177.

merits; not all of them had been bad, while with some it was not enough merely to declare them lapsed: the repeal of anti-Jewish laws did not, for instance, restore confiscated Jewish property to its rightful owners.[10]

Much patient scrutiny was therefore needed, before the delegates of the Resistance could go on – as they did – to draw up precise provisions for the restoration of democratic institutions in France. Since these provisions proved largely unrealistic in the face of the conditions prevailing at the time of the liberation, they need not detain us here. Throughout the months of the Assembly's deliberations, de Gaulle's relations with it were stormy, although he often did as the Assembly had requested after a show of going his own way.[11] His clashes with the delegates were a foretaste of his later difficulties with elected deputies. Broadly speaking the internal Resistance wanted one kind of polity – much the same as the Third Republic – while he envisaged another and stronger one.

In the spring of 1944, on the eve of the Normandy landings, General de Gaulle indeed not only knew the kind of justice he would administer to those of his compatriots who had been his enemies; he also knew, in broad outline, the kind of State he planned to establish in liberated France, and had projects for a European organisation and a liberalised colonial empire with autonomy for its component parts overseas. All these subjects were covered in a remarkable and prophetic speech he delivered before the Provisional Consultative Assembly in Algiers on 18 March 1944. Since much of his future policy, in his first and second periods in power in metropolitan France, is contained in this discourse, it is worth recalling the main points of it.[12]

ON THE AUTHORITY OF THE NATIONAL LIBERATION COMMITTEE

Any attempt to maintain Vichy organisations, however partially or however concealed, would be intolerable. So would be any attempt at the "artificial formation of powers external to the government".[13] All citizens were under the strictest obligation to follow the instructions of the authorities nominated by the Committee of Liberation.

[10] Dorothy Pickles, *France between the Republics*, pp. 115–16.
[11] For a detailed account of the Consultative Assembly's work, and of de Gaulle's clashes with it, and with some of his own Ministers, see Yves Maxime Danan, *La Vie politique à Alger de 1940 à 1944*, especially pp. 263 *et seq.*, and 300 *et seq.*
[12] For full text, De Gaulle, *Discours*, Vol. I, pp. 380–90.
[13] This cryptic phrase referred to Allied plans for circumventing the authority of the Gaullists, or pre-empting their forthcoming bid for power, for instance by sending President Lebrun (who had never formally resigned) to Algiers (see De Gaulle, *L'Unité*, pp. 160–2).

ON THE FOURTH REPUBLIC

Democracy in France would be a social democracy, giving everybody the right and freedom of work, guaranteeing security for all in an economic system designed to exploit national resources for the benefit of the nation as a whole and not of private interests. The direction and control of the State were to be exercised with the regular "concourse" of those who work and those who take the risks.[14] While the profit motive was recognised, black-market fortunes would be confiscated. No coalitions of private interests, private monopolies, or trusts would be tolerated. Freedom of the individual, of the press, of the trade unions and of information would be restored. There would be a national poll with a view to forming a National Constituent Assembly whose task would be to build the Fourth Republic. Suffrage would be universal, for women as well as men.[15]

THE FUTURE OF EUROPE AND THE WORLD

De Gaulle expounded a favourite theme: linking the two world wars as a single Thirty Years War, he declared that France had saved the world on the Marne, at Verdun and in 1918 through the indomitable energy of men like Poincaré, Clemenceau and Foch. Great Britain in turn had saved it when Churchill stood alone. Soviet Russia was now saving it through the tremendous effort of its armies and people under Marshal Stalin's leadership. And in the end, the United States would have saved it through its decisive intervention under Roosevelt's driving force. It was clear that the power and unity of these four great States were essential to the future of humanity. They were friends and would remain friends.

Europe, said de Gaulle, had been reduced and humiliated by Hitlerism, and the nations of Europe had no voice in the camp of freedom. But Europe still existed. First, the cause of its decline – "the frenetic power of Prussianised Germanism" – must be removed. After that, France's rightful place must be restored. Then France could play her European role to the advantage of all. In the old continent, thus reborn, groups of states should be formed, without any loss of sovereignty. As far as France was concerned, a sort of Western European group could be formed, on an economic basis, and with as wide a membership as possible.[16] Such a group could be prolonged into Africa and have close rela-

---

[14] Evidently an early Gaullist definition of what is now generally known as "participation".

[15] French women were, in fact, given the vote for the first time under the ordinance of 21 April 1944.

[16] A. W. DePorte, in his interesting study, De Gaulle's Foreign Policy (1944–1946) (hence-

tions with the Arab States of the Near East; the Channel, the Rhine and the Mediterranean would be its arteries.

THE FRENCH EMPIRE

On this point, de Gaulle was less than explicit, merely remarking that the Fourth Republic would "certainly be completed by arrangements within the French community for the destiny of peoples linked with our own destiny".

De Gaulle had already, indeed, said as much as he could say about the future of the French Empire, in his speech of 30 January 1944, at the opening of a conference in Brazzaville of representatives of the French territories of Africa. The "Brazzaville speech", as it is usually known, has an honoured place in the Gaullist annals. There have been many references to its generosity and far-sightedness, and both qualities are present in the typically Gaullian text, with its oratorical rotundities and erudite ambiguities. But too much has sometimes been read into it. De Gaulle was not promising independence or anything like it. He was, however, deeply conscious of the vital role the African possessions had played in the Free French movement. Without them, he would have lacked a base, except on foreign soil. He was grateful to them and wished to show it. And he did so with a distant vision of local autonomy, and in these convoluted words:

> We believe that, as regards the life of the world of tomorrow, autarchy would be neither desirable, nor even possible, for anyone. We believe, in particular, that from the point of view of the development of its resources and its greater communications, the African continent should constitute, to a large extent, a whole. But, in French Africa, as in all the other territories where men live under our flag there would be no progress that could be called progress, if men, on their native soil, did not benefit from it morally and materially, if they could not raise themselves little by little to the level where they will be able to participate at home in the management of their own affairs. It is the duty of France to make it possible for this to happen.
>
> Such is the goal towards which we have to proceed. We do not conceal from ourselves the length of the stages on the way....

forth, DePorte), pp. 47–8, makes the point that by implication, and studied omission, Britain had no part in de Gaulle's concept of Europe. Certainly his policy of a *Europe des états*, during his second period in power, and his veto on the admission of Great Britain into the European Economic Community, are directly consistent with his speech in March 1944. What de Gaulle envisaged was nothing less than the hegemony of France in a revitalised Western Europe.

When de Gaulle reached power in metropolitan France, therefore, he was not burdened with a promise of independence for the colonies, nor even with that of a rapid timetable towards the very limited self-rule he then envisaged. Indeed, one of his first concerns was to restore France's full authority in those overseas possessions where it was seriously challenged – in the colony and protectorates of Indo-China.[17]

As for his ideas for the Fourth Republic and the future of Europe, many frustrations lay ahead. And nearly fifteen years were to elapse before he could even make a start on his more grandiose designs.

[17] Cochinchina (South Vietnam) was a colony. Annam and Tonking (Central and North Vietnam), Laos and Cambodia were protectorates.

Part IV ⚜ The Liberation and After 1944–1946

Chapter 1 ❖ Jostling for Position

As the end drew closer, the jostling for position intensified. De Gaulle did not doubt that he would emerge as the unquestioned master of France, even if others bore the brunt of the battle for her liberation. His difficulty lay in the reluctance of other interested parties – especially outside France, but even within – to acknowledge in advance the inevitability of his control. More than ever, Roosevelt was determined to ignore his political claims, and in this determination, he enjoyed Churchill's full backing. Yet once again, in the face of systematic snubs and humiliations from his major allies, de Gaulle's will was to prevail. By the same token, Roosevelt's dream of a post-war world in which America and Russia would make the rules and impose their solutions, with Britain and China as junior partners and France excluded as of no account, was never fully to materialise.

In the crucial period between September 1943 and June 1944, however, de Gaulle was kept out of most Allied decisions, or informed of them after they had been taken. Thus on 27 September 1943 his foreign minister, Massigli, was given the text of the armistice with Italy, by the British and American representatives. The document had taken account of French views but had not been submitted to the French for their comments at the drafting stage.[1] The text was presented to Marshal Badoglio, the Italian acting chief of State, for signature later that day, although the signing did not take place until the next day, at Malta.

It was the same with the meeting of foreign ministers that took place immediately after in Moscow: the Russians were hosts, and the British and American ministers were presented, but the French were not invited. When Cordell Hull, the American secretary of State, called on de Gaulle in Algiers on his way to Moscow, he told the general that the meeting would probably set up an inter-Allied commission on Italian affairs. "Perhaps," he said, "you will be asked to join."

"We shall see," replied de Gaulle, who went on to explain that French help and French bases would be necessary to expel the Germans from

[1] De Gaulle, L'Unité, pp. 190–1; for further matter, see also pp. 203, 207, 210–11.

Italy. France was ready to help, but would have to have an equal voice in the future of Italy.

The message went home. On 16 November, the Allied envoys – Macmillan, Murphy and Bogomolov – called on Massigli and invited the French Liberation Committee to join the inter-Allied commission. Massigli accepted.

This relatively minor victory could not compensate de Gaulle for his "government's" exclusion from the two Big Three conferences – at Cairo in late November, and at Tehran from 2 to 7 December.[2] The general noted sourly that neither Churchill, at sea off North Africa on his way to Cairo, nor Roosevelt, flying to the same destination, had bothered to get in touch with him. But his pain at such neglect was as nothing beside his frustration at not being consulted on the future of Europe and the plans for her liberation. If, as he learned, the debate at Tehran had touched on the respective merits of Churchill's plans for a vast operation to liberate the Balkans and strike at the Danube, as against landing in his beloved France, was this not a subject upon which his views should have been sought?

Deprived of access to the inner circle of the great powers, he consoled himself with contacts with lesser figures, such as General Mihailovich, the leader of the Chetnik irregulars of Yugoslavia, Dr Beneš of Czechoslovakia and General Sosnkowski of Poland. In February 1944, he conferred a *Croix de Guerre* on Mihailovich, as a sign of support at a time when the Chetnik leader was losing ground and when Allied help was being switched to Tito's partisans. Beneš visited him in Algiers on 2 January 1944, on his return from Moscow, where he had signed with Stalin a treaty of friendship and mutual assistance (which in no way inhibited the Soviet dictator from adding Czechoslovakia to his satellite empire only four years later). Beneš invited de Gaulle to look at the map, which showed beyond doubt that his country could be liberated only by the Red Army. Despite Stalin's deviousness and ambitions, he was comforted in the knowledge that the Soviet dictator had agreed that the Russian command would not interfere in Czechoslovak politics. More realistically, he added that after the war Britain's only interest would lie in safeguarding the Alps and the Rhine, and in the Mediterranean; while Roosevelt's sole concern would be to "bring the boys home".

That this was a true reading of Allied intentions, de Gaulle had no doubt, especially as Stalin's intentions in respect of Poland began to take shape. It seemed clear that in the final analysis, Roosevelt would give

---

[2] At Cairo, the Big Three were Churchill, Roosevelt and Chiang Kai-shek; at Tehran, Stalin, Churchill and Roosevelt.

Stalin a free hand to install a puppet government in Warsaw and that Churchill, for all his misgivings, would not actively oppose the virtual annexation of Poland. It was particularly galling to him, in the light of the sentimental attachment between Poland and France, and of his own service in Poland in the 1920s, that he should be powerless to intervene.

It was indeed beyond the power of anyone in the West to do anything to help the tragic secret army of General Bor-Komorowski when it rose against the Germans in Warsaw at the end of July 1944 and was crushed; while the Russians, who had incited them to rise, waited for them to die so that they could place their own Polish "Committee of National Liberation" in power in their own good time and without competition from the Polish Resistance. But de Gaulle, while accepting the principle of Soviet seizures of Polish territory against territorial compensation at Germany's expense, was firmly convinced that the Western allies, given the will, could have prevented Stalin from handing over the country to his puppets. It would have sufficed, he thought, for Britain, France and America, acting in concert, to denounce such plans, reserving the right for their warships to use the Baltic seaports, if necessary, against the grant of similar access for Soviet shipping to the North Sea. Whether joint action would have stopped Stalin may be doubted; that it might have halted him for a time is at least possible. But nothing was done.

One small thing, however, lay in de Gaulle's power, and he did it. In September 1939 the Polish government had deposited a large stock of gold in the Bank of France; and in June 1940 this had been transferred to Bamako, in what was then the French Sudan (now Mali). When the Polish premier-in-exile, Mikolajczyk, requested the French National Committee to return the gold, de Gaulle concurred. Having got wind of this request, the Soviet representative, Bogomolov, put pressure on the French to deny it. Getting nowhere, he called on de Gaulle and declared: "The Soviet government strongly protests against the transfer of Polish gold to the refugee government in London. For this will not be the future government of Poland."

Glad perhaps of a chance to be haughty towards the Russians, as he he had so often been towards the British and Americans, de Gaulle replied that the government in London was still the legal government, recognised as such by all the Allies, including the Russians, that Polish forces were fighting side by side with the French in Italy, and finally that he could not see by what right the Soviet Union was intervening in an affair that concerned France and Poland exclusively. Bogomolov left in unconcealed ill humour.

275

Throughout this period, de Gaulle maintained close and friendly relations with the Polish leaders: General Sosnkowski, who had succeeded Sikorski when he had lost his life in a plane crash at Gibraltar; General Anders, whom de Gaulle met with the Polish forces in March 1944 before Monte Cassino in Italy; Rackiewicz, the president of the Polish Republic; and Romer, the foreign minister.

A small mercy for de Gaulle in this more than usually trying period was the change in America's diplomatic representation with the French committee. Robert Murphy, whom de Gaulle had never liked and always distrusted, was to be transferred to Italy. His successor, Edwin Wilson, carried the encouraging title of "United States representative" with the committee, unlike Murphy who was more imprecisely termed President Roosevelt's "personal representative". De Gaulle took an instant liking to him and felt he had the man's embarrassed sympathy in the permanent misunderstanding that separated the general from the American president.

At the same time, Harold Macmillan, still British minister of State, also left for Italy, and was succeeded by Duff Cooper. Despite early difficulties and clashes, de Gaulle and Macmillan had developed mutual understanding and esteem. De Gaulle, indeed, praises his "lofty spirit, his clear intelligence". But for Duff Cooper, his praise was boundless. His appointment as ambassador in Algiers, de Gaulle wrote, was "one of the shrewdest and most amiable gestures towards France ever made by the government of His Majesty in the United Kingdom".

Bogomolov continued to represent the Soviet Union, but he was superseded, for a time, by Andrei Vishinsky, the dreaded prosecutor in Moscow's notorious purge trials, who had been given temporary charge of Italian affairs. To his surprise, de Gaulle found him not only astute, but engaging. But he could not always conceal the implacable nature of the orders under which he worked. One day, within earshot of others, de Gaulle remarked to Vishinsky, "It was a mistake on our part not to have put into practice with you, before 1939, an open alliance against Hitler. But how wrong you were to reach an understanding with him and allow us to be crushed!" Vishinsky stiffened, his face livid. He seemed, says de Gaulle, to ward off some mysterious threat. "No! No!" he murmured. "This must never, never be be said!"

Perhaps the worst of de Gaulle's frustrations and humiliations lay ahead. It was for him a point of honour that his forces should play their part in the liberation of his country, that he should be consulted about Allied plans, that the authority of his provisional government should be recognised unreservedly and that he himself should, at the first possible opportunity, be seen on French soil. As early as September 1943, the Liberation Committee had sent Washington and London a memorandum outlining a programme of collaboration and coordination between the French administration and the Allied forces. The local authorities would meet Allied requests for communications and public services; in the rear, the French government would respond to the requests of General Eisenhower as Allied supreme commander. A French administrative liaison corps had been recruited, trained and sent to London in September, under Hettier de Boislambert. In March 1944, de Gaulle had appointed Generals Koenig and Cochet as assistants to the Allied commanders-in-chief of the Northern and Mediterranean theatres respectively; while André le Trocquer had been appointed national delegate-commissioner for the liberated territories.

The Allied chiefs of staff seemed pleased enough with these arrangements. But nothing could be done to put them into effect, because Roosevelt allowed the months to pass without replying to de Gaulle's memorandum, in the face of *démarches* from Monnet and Hoppenot, the Liberation Committee's representative in Washington, and of urgent requests from Eisenhower. At last, in April, the president instructed Eisenhower that he himself, as Allied commander-in-chief, was to assume full powers in France. When Eisenhower pleaded to be relieved of this political burden, the president modified the form but not the substance of his instructions.

In de Gaulle's eyes, Roosevelt's plans were about as realistic as the dreams of Alice in Wonderland. He had nursed similar plans, in far more favourable circumstances, in North Africa, and had been undone. The Darlan-Clark agreement, denounced by de Gaulle, was a dead letter, and the authority of de Gaulle's government was unchallenged in the French-speaking territories. If Roosevelt tried to play the same game in France, he would be up against the fact that the only ministers and officials the Allies met would be those appointed by de Gaulle, and the only French troops those under his authority.

Eisenhower did not share his political leader's views. He had dropped in to see de Gaulle on 30 December, before leaving to take up his new command, and with characteristic generosity, had said, "I had been warned against you. Now I recognise that this judgment was mistaken. . . . I need your help and have come to ask for it."

"At last!" replied de Gaulle. "You are a real man, for you know how to say 'I was wrong.' "[3]

³ Eisenhower does not mention this exchange in *Crusade*.

A new *bête noire* now plagued de Gaulle: AMGOT. Unwilling to the last to concede recognition, even provisionally, to de Gaulle's government, Roosevelt planned to hand over the administration of liberated France to this "Allied Military Government, Occupied Territories". A proliferation of technicians, businessmen, theoreticians, propagandists and "Frenchmen of yesterday freshly naturalised Yankee", AMGOT aroused in de Gaulle the same distaste he was later to feel for NATO and the U.N.

Since Churchill's attitude towards de Gaulle was meticulously aligned on Roosevelt's, his relations with the general continued to be acrimonious. The acrimony was deepened by yet another Levantine crisis in November 1943, and a sordid quarrel over a Frenchman who may or may not have been a British agent, and may or may not have been planted on the Gaullist secret service.[4] Relations were not improved, despite the superficial cordiality of the occasion, by de Gaulle's meeting with the Prime Minister at Marrakesh in January 1944. Churchill, taken ill at Tunis on his way home from Tehran, had gone to southern Morocco to recover. Duff Cooper asked de Gaulle if, in the circumstances, he would go to Marrakesh. Since Churchill was Churchill, and not in good health, de Gaulle waived his entitlement to receive the Prime Minister in Algiers, Churchill being "in French territory". But he declined an invitation at short notice to bring Mme de Gaulle with him and spend the night at the villa Churchill and his wife were occupying.[5]

Instead, he arrived alone nine days later, on 12 January 1944, and accepted an invitation to lunch. Duff Cooper and Lady Diana were present, and so was Lord Beaverbrook. De Gaulle, says Churchill, was in the best of humour. He spoke English throughout the meal, and Churchill, "to make things equal", spoke French.

After lunch, he sought to disarm de Gaulle by murmuring in an audible aside, "I'm doing rather well, aren't I? Now that the general speaks English so well, he understands my French perfectly." His reward was a guffaw from de Gaulle.

Churchill then listed his current grievances. Why, he enquired, had the Free French authorities arrested Peyrouton, Boisson and Flandin? And why had he driven General Giraud and General Georges off the committee? He reminded de Gaulle that President Roosevelt had picked Peyrouton as governor of Algeria and that Boisson's position had been

---

[4] For a study in mutual incomprehension, *see* de Gaulle's account of the Lebanese crisis (*L'Unité*, pp. 194–9), and Churchill's (Vol. V, pp. 164–5). For contrasting accounts of the "agent" – the "Dufour affair" – *see* de Gaulle, *L'Unité*, pp. 217 *et seq.*; and E. H. Cookridge, *Inside SOE*, pp. 206–7.

[5] Churchill, Vol. V, p. 401.

guaranteed by Roosevelt as well. The Prime Minister had studied Flandin's dossier and found that nothing very serious was held against him. As for Giraud and Georges, Roosevelt had chosen the first, and Churchill had brought the second over.

Still in the best of humour (this time by de Gaulle's account), the general replied that the interest Roosevelt and Churchill were taking in French internal affairs was a proof of France's recovery. He did not wish to disappoint them by obstructing the course of justice, which would cause revolutionary convulsions in France later on. He wished no harm to Flandin and Peyrouton. He recognised the worth and good intentions of the first, and the service the second had rendered by handing over his post when he, de Gaulle, had arrived. But he thought it consistent with the national interest that both men should be required to explain their actions as ministers of Vichy before a High Court. As for Governor-General Boisson, what happened to him was up to his superiors. And the presence or absence of Generals Giraud and Georges was a matter for him alone to decide.

To preserve appearances and restore their surface cordiality, de Gaulle proposed that they should jointly review the garrison the following day; which they did, to local acclaim.

The next Anglo-French clash took place in April, when Duff Cooper twice visited de Gaulle, on the 14th and 17th, with messages from Churchill. If only, Churchill said through his ambassador, de Gaulle could meet the president man to man! In particular, the question of recognition of the Committee of National Liberation would probably be solved. The Prime Minister declared his readiness to arrange for de Gaulle to be invited to Washington.

Churchill, by now, should have known de Gaulle better than to suppose he would accept so indirect a proposal. De Gaulle told Duff Cooper that he was little attracted by this non-invitation, coming as it did after other non-invitations. If the president of the United States wished to receive the president of the French government, he needed only to ask him to come. In that event, he would go. But why should he solicit an invitation through Churchill, at a time when Roosevelt openly professed that any authority in France would be responsible to him? For his part, he had nothing to ask of the president. The formality of recognition was no longer of interest to the French government. The important thing was to be recognised by the French nation, and that could now be taken for granted. At one time, the Allies could have helped the French committee to gain stature. But they had not done so. Now it no longer mattered.

He warned the ambassador that there would be chaos in France if the Allied command tried to usurp his government's authority.

As in the darkest days of the war, retribution was swift: the French were notified that henceforth their coded communications would no longer be transmitted between London and Algiers. The French retaliated by forbidding their ambassador in London, Viénot, and their military delegate, General Koenig, to transact any business with the Allies.

The stalemate was ended on 23 May, when Duff Cooper brought an invitation from Churchill for de Gaulle to go to London to settle the questions of recognition and of administrative collaboration in France. He added an important rider: the British government wished him to be present in Great Britain at the time of the Allied landings.

De Gaulle thanked Duff Cooper, but declared that the committee, which was about to proclaim itself the government of France, was no longer interested in recognition. Nor did he see the point in entering into negotiations with the British on administrative matters, since the Americans would not be present. He was, however, ready to go to London, but only on condition that restrictions on the transmission of coded messages were immediately lifted.

Three days later the committee duly declared itself to be the provisional government of the French Republic, and decided that de Gaulle would not be accompanied by a minister on his journey to London, since there were to be no negotiations.[6] Duff Cooper brought a written guarantee that coded communications were restored; and de Gaulle got ready to leave.

Now came a devious approach from the American president. On 27 May, Admiral Fenard, who headed de Gaulle's naval mission in Washington, arrived in Algiers with a breathless air and a personal message from the White House. The president, he declared, had formally asked him to convey an invitation to de Gaulle to come to Washington. But because of the attitude the president had adopted hitherto, there could be no announcement. If de Gaulle accepted this semi-official approach, the embassies could make the arrangements without any need to disclose which side the initiative came from.

This was not a time to take offence. But neither was it a time for effusive acceptance. The potential advantages of going to Washington were still great, but de Gaulle would go in his own good time. So he instructed Admiral Fenard to return to Washington and say General de

[6] Churchill, Vol. V, p. 553, in a letter to Roosevelt on 4 June, said de Gaulle's committee had decided by a large majority that he should accept the Prime Minister's invitation but that Massigli and several others had to threaten to resign before he would give his consent. De Gaulle does not record any such discussion.

Gaulle had taken note of the president's wishes. It was, however, out of the question for him to go to Washington in the immediate future, since he was about to leave for London. The contact could be renewed later.

The real message Fenard had brought was unstated but implicitly clear. It was that de Gaulle, once again, was going to be the winner in a long contest of wills. There might be further crises ahead, but the outcome was no longer in doubt: de Gaulle's concept of France's independence was going to prevail.[7]

On 2 June an urgent message came from Churchill: Would de Gaulle come to London forthwith? The Prime Minister had graciously sent his personal plane to Algiers, and in it the general travelled, together with five assistants, including Palewski, General Billotte and Geoffroy de Courcel. They reached London, after stops at Casablanca and Gibraltar, on the morning of 4 June 1944.

Churchill had had a train fitted out as his personal headquarters. It took him, with his personal staff and a privileged trio – Field-Marshal Smuts, Ernest Bevin and General Ismay – to a siding next to General Eisenhower's headquarters near Portsmouth. From there, he could watch the preparations for the invasion of occupied France. And it was there, on 4 June, that he received General de Gaulle, who was escorted by Anthony Eden.

De Gaulle found Smuts rather embarrassed. Not long before, he had made some widely reported remarks to the effect that France was no longer a great power and might as well join the Commonwealth. Over lunch, Churchill explained that he had hoped de Gaulle would arrive just before D-day, but the weather was discouraging and the vast operation had had to be postponed. Many of the 150,000 troops embarked for the first wave of the assault were packed uncomfortably into small craft. 11,000 planes and 4,000 ships had been assembled. The Prime Minister deeply regretted the loss of life that had been unavoidably caused by the preliminary bombing of French railways.[8]

De Gaulle had listened fascinated to Churchill's description of the plans for the great battle ahead. He expressed warm admiration for the great role that was about to be played by the Royal Navy. But when it came to business, says Churchill, de Gaulle was "bristling". There was a minor clash between the two men over coded messages, and a major one over relations with Roosevelt. De Gaulle had to give Churchill further reassurances that he would make no mention at all of the invasion

[7] De Gaulle, L'Unité, p. 222.
[8] Churchill, Vol. V, pp. 554–5. In fact, Churchill had originally proposed that de Gaulle should be invited to London *after* D-day, but had been overruled by the war cabinet.

preparations through the cipher facilities. Testily, the general explained that he must have the facilities, but only to liaise with Algiers over the course of the Italian campaign.

The clash over Roosevelt was predictably acrimonious. Churchill's reminder that by dropping Giraud he had offended Roosevelt did nothing to improve de Gaulle's temper. When the Prime Minister urged him to reach an understanding with the British over cooperation in France, then go to Washington to submit it to the president, de Gaulle replied with acerbity, "What makes you think I should submit to Roosevelt my candidature for power in France? The French government exists. In that domain I have nothing to ask of the United States of America, or for that matter of Great Britain."

De Gaulle now brought out the most unwelcome bit of information that had come his way since his arrival. It concerned AMGOT. "I have just learned," he said, "that despite our warnings, the troops and auxiliary services that are about to disembark are being provided with so-called French money, manufactured abroad, which the government of the Republic absolutely refuses to recognise and which, by orders of the inter-Allied command, will be enforced as legal tender in French territory."

"Besides," interposed General Billotte, who was sitting opposite Bevin, "the notes were printed with a spelling mistake."[9]

De Gaulle carried on: "Now I understand that tomorrow General Eisenhower, on instructions from the president of the United States and with your assent, is to proclaim that he is taking France under his authority. How do you expect us to make a deal on this basis?"

Now it was Churchill's turn to explode. With a show of passion which de Gaulle took to be aimed at impressing the British half of his audience, he exclaimed: "And you! How do you expect us British to take up a different position from that of the United States? We are going to liberate Europe, but we couldn't do it without the Americans. Let's be quite clear about this. Each time we have to choose between Europe and the open seas, we shall always choose the open seas. Each time I have to choose between you and Roosevelt, I shall always choose Roosevelt!"[10]

[9] Galante, p. 145.
[10] De Gaulle, L'Unité, p. 224. Churchill's account (Vol. V, p. 556) is rather different. Whether de Gaulle went to Washington or not was his own affair, but in the event of a split between the Committee of National Liberation and the United States the British would almost certainly side with the Americans. "About the administration of liberated French soil," he wrote, "if General de Gaulle wanted us to ask the President to give him the title-deeds of France the answer was 'No'. If he wanted us to ask the President to agree that the committee was the principal body with whom he should deal in France the answer was 'Yes'. De Gaulle replied that he quite understood that if the USA and France disagreed Britain would side with the USA. With this ungracious remark the interview ended."

De Gaulle adds that Bevin came to him when the lunch had ended and said in a tone audible to others: "The Prime Minister has told you that in all cases he would take the side of the president of the United States. I want you to know that he spoke for himself and not in the name of the British cabinet."

Churchill then took de Gaulle to Eisenhower's headquarters, where the commander-in-chief and General Bedell Smith received him with great courtesy. Having given de Gaulle a clear and impressive exposition of Allied plans, Eisenhower asked him what he would do at this stage, having regard to the fact that the weather was very bad, but that if the landings were not launched on or before the 7th, the moon and the tide would make a further attempt impossible for another month.

De Gaulle replied that the decision was entirely up to Eisenhower and he would support the generalissimo without reserve. But if he were in Eisenhower's place, he would not delay any further.

When de Gaulle was about to take his leave, Eisenhower, with evident embarrassment, handed him a typewritten document. It was the text of a proclamation from him to the peoples of Western Europe, including France. De Gaulle ran his eyes over it and immediately declared that it was unsatisfactory.

"It is only a draft," said Eisenhower. "I am ready to modify it according to your observations."

It was agreed that de Gaulle would propose precise changes the following day.

According to Churchill's account, the Prime Minister expected de Gaulle to dine with him, then return to London in his train, but the general "drew himself up and stated that he preferred to motor with his French officers separately". De Gaulle makes no mention of this, but it is clear that he had much to discuss with his *entourage*. He was in fact in a sombre mood, for the text of the Eisenhower proclamation was indeed quite unacceptable. His address to the Norwegian, Dutch, Belgian and Luxembourg peoples was unexceptionable, being strictly concerned with military matters. But the tone changed when he turned to the French, who were invited to carry out his orders. There was no mention at all of de Gaulle or of the National Committee, still less of its new title of "provisional government". Indeed, the French people were to be told that once they were liberated, they themselves could "choose their representatives and their government".

Without much hope, de Gaulle and his assistants redrafted the text and had it delivered to Eisenhower's headquarters the following morning, 5 June. A message came back, saying it was too late, since the proclamation was already printed; de Gaulle learned indeed that it had been printed a week before. The landings were to take place that night and by then the proclamation, in thousands of leaflets, would have been dropped over France and other countries.[11]

On his arrival in London, de Gaulle checked in at the Connaught Hotel, as in the old days, and used his old office in Carlton Gardens. And as before, Charles Peake of the Foreign Office presented his compliments and his accreditation as liaison man. Seeing him again gave de Gaulle pleasure, for he regarded Peake as a friend; but he felt sorry for him, since dealing with the Gaullists had never been an easy passage. Indeed, the first thing Peake did was to convey yet another snub.

Next day, with the battle for the liberation joined at last, the exiled European leaders – the king of Norway, the queen of the Netherlands, the grand-duchess of Luxembourg and the premier of Belgium – were to speak to their peoples over the radio. Then Eisenhower would read his proclamation. Only after that would General de Gaulle go before the microphone.

If this was the scenario, said de Gaulle, it was not on as far as he was concerned. If he were to speak immediately after the commander-in-chief, he would appear to be supporting a form of words of which he disapproved. Moreover, he objected to being placed last in the queue of distinguished speakers. If he spoke at all, it could only be in an entirely separate programme.

At 2 a.m., Pierre Viénot knocked on de Gaulle's door. Announcing he had come straight from 10 Downing Street, he said the Prime Minister had summoned him to let him know, in no uncertain terms, how angry he was with de Gaulle. Presently Peake also arrived. Calmly, de Gaulle said the other speakers could go ahead as arranged, but without him. He himself hoped he would be allowed to use the BBC in the evening.

As usual, he got his way. It was 6 p.m. and he was, for programme purposes, alone. It was an emotional moment, long awaited. "For the sons of France," said the familiar voice, "wherever they are, whoever they may be, the simple and sacred duty is to fight the enemy by all means at their disposal. . . . The orders given by the French government and by the French leaders it has appointed must be applied exactly. . . .

[11] Eisenhower does not record the incident, but mentions that his staff thought the argument about recognition was "in a sense" academic, since in the early stages of the operation at least, de Gaulle would be the only valid authority anyway. Roosevelt's strict instructions were to avoid prejudging the verdict of the French people; Eisenhower felt that *de facto* recognition of his administration would not have violated the spirit of the president's directives. (Eisenhower, *Crusade*, pp. 272–3.)

Behind the heavy cloud of our blood and our tears, the sun of our great ness is now reappearing!'"[12]

The problem of cooperation between the French and the Allies re-mained, of course, unresolved. Eden, having taken over from Churchill the attempt to negotiate an agreement with de Gaulle, came to dinner at the Connaught on the 8th, accompanied by Duff Cooper. Viénot was present on the French side. Why not, asked Eden, bring Massigli over to London to sign a Franco-British agreement? Once agreement had been reached, the Americans could scarcely veto it. He offered to go to Wash-ington at the same time as de Gaulle, to make sure Roosevelt underwrote a Franco-British accord.

But de Gaulle was not so easily deflected from his chosen path. He had not come to London to negotiate, he explained. Eden nevertheless con-signed the substance of his proposals to paper, and the government in Algiers was asked its opinion. It stood firm. Massigli stayed in Algiers. And Viénot replied to Eden, saying that if the British government wished to discuss the French proposals of 1943, it could do so through ambassadorial channels.

Having counter-snubbed the British, de Gaulle sought publicity for his views. On 10 June, he gave an interview to a news agency, in which he denounced the AMGOT currency as valueless and underlined the ab-surdity of a situation in which the Allied forces would lack any liaison machinery with local authorities in France. Indeed he had decided that the French administrative liaison officials trained by Boislambert would not now accompany the British and American service staffs, as this would be condoning the usurpation of French authority. A few observers only would go along.

A storm of attacks against him broke out in the American press; and a counter-storm of defence from Walter Lippmann and other champions of de Gaulle. In Britain, most of the press supported him and criticised Roosevelt for obstinacy.

That day, Eisenhower, who was in Normandy in one of the bridge-heads, sent his chief of staff, General Bedell Smith, to Carlton Gardens to plead with de Gaulle to visit President Roosevelt without further delay. General Marshall, the chairman of the Joint Chief of Staff who had just arrived in London, supported Bedell Smith's mission. Admiral Fenard also turned up again with a further message from Roosevelt naming possible dates for their meeting. And in Algiers, Seldon Chapin.

[12] For full text, *see* de Gaulle, *Discours*, Vol. I, pp. 409–10.

deputising for Ambassador Wilson, was similarly pressing. To all, at that time, de Gaulle still declined to commit himself.

He wanted, first, to build up public support for his position. The agency interview had helped. And to this end he multiplied his contacts and exchanges of visits with the exiled leaders in London, including the Czechs and Poles. All supported his stand. And between 8 and 20 June, in the face of urgent pleas from the British and Americans to await developments, the Czechoslovaks, Poles, Belgians, Luxembourgers, Yugoslavs, and Norwegians all officially recognised the provisional government of the French Republic. The Dutch alone declined to act – probably, as de Gaulle surmised, because they thought that by deferring to Washington they would gain more understanding than hitherto for their position in the Dutch East Indies.

De Gaulle had been hoping for some days to visit the Normandy bridgehead, but the Allies were in no hurry to provide him with the necessary facilities. As late as the 12th, a letter from Churchill, delivered to Eden during a dinner for de Gaulle, raised further objections to his plan. But Eden, having consulted his colleagues around the table, including Clement Attlee, said the way was now clear. Next day, de Gaulle boarded the French destroyer *La Combattante* at Portsmouth. With him were ten of his top assistants. Seven of them were to return to England with de Gaulle. Three, however, were to stay in France and constitute the kernel of the Gaullist administration in the liberated areas. Needless to say, de Gaulle had not told the British or Americans that this was what he was planning to do. The chosen trio were Pierre Laroque, who had been until then the secretary-general of the Gaullist office in London; François Coulet, who for three months after the departure of the Germans and Italians from Corsica had been doing a similar job there; and Colonel de Chevigné. On 12 June, de Gaulle had summoned Coulet and told him that he was to be left behind as regional commissioner of the Republic, with Laroque as his juridical assistant and de Chevigné as military delegate.[13]

Having anchored off the coast, *La Combattante* discharged its human cargo; and its material one, which consisted of quantities of Free French money destined to make the hated AMGOT currency irrelevant. The French party went ashore near the village of Courseulles with a Canadian regiment that was then disembarking. General Montgomery, who was to brief the visitors, had despatched cars for them. But first, de Gaulle sent Coulet off to Bayeux, where he was to prepare the ground for de Gaulle's arrival.

[13] Robert Aron, *Histoire de la Libération de la France* (henceforth Rob. Aron, *Libération*), pp. 25 and 77.

Montgomery, who was in excellent humour, gave his lecture in his motorised office, under the portrayed eyes of Rommel, the man he had defeated in North Africa but had not ceased to admire. "Monty" and de Gaulle were later to become firm friends. But de Gaulle, interested though he was in the progress of the fighting, had pressing matters on his mind and was anxious to get to Bayeux. There, Coulet awaited him with the mayor and the municipal council. At the last minute, somebody had remembered to remove the portrait of Pétain that adorned a wall in the salon. It had proved recalcitrant and yielded only to stern treatment just before de Gaulle arrived.[14]

Surprised at the sight of the general, the locals cheered, smiled or wept. As he walked the streets, men, women and children crowded around him, following him and swelling to constitute a procession. It was de Gaulle's first *bain de foule* on metropolitan soil, and he savoured every moment of its patriotic emotion. Similar scenes followed in other places, and on the 15th, back in Portsmouth, then in London, he had the joy of reading the headlines his visit to France had occasioned in the British press.

That afternoon, Eden called on de Gaulle at Carlton Gardens. Now, he said, Roosevelt only awaited his visit to revise his position. For form's sake, the foreign secretary repeated his regret that the French government had not adopted the procedure suggested by the British. He now proposed, however, that Viénot and he should work out a draft which he would communicate to Washington and which could be signed simultaneously by the British, Americans and French. This time, de Gaulle raised no objections.

The general was planning to return to Algiers on the evening of 16 June. Before doing so, he wanted to restore amicable relations with Churchill, and sent him a letter to thank him for all he had done, reaffirming France's "indissoluble attachment" to Great Britain and praising the immortal honour the Prime Minister had earned through his unrelenting leadership of the British war effort.

Evidently still vexed, Churchill replied with thanks for de Gaulle's compliments, but an expression of chagrin for the failure of the British and French to reach agreement during de Gaulle's visit, which he, Churchill, had personally arranged. He hoped this would not prove to have been the last chance, and he advised de Gaulle to visit Roosevelt and try to re-establish good relations with the United States, which were a precious part of the French heritage.

On his way back to Algiers, de Gaulle called in at Naples, where

[14] ibid. p. 82.

Couve de Murville introduced him to the permanent head of the Italian Foreign ministry, Signor Prunas. After a visit to the front and talks with Juin, Alexander, Wilson and Clark, he went on to Rome, where he had a long talk with Pope Pius XII.[15]

De Gaulle had carefully considered the timing of events. He had been in no hurry to visit Roosevelt because he knew that it would take some time for the Allied forces to consolidate the Normandy bridgeheads and because he wanted to demonstrate before the world that he would be greeted in France as her natural and unquestioned leader. Now, however, time was running out. The great Allied offensive was to start in August. The time had come to go to Washington.

But the ground needed to be carefully prepared. The matter was exhaustively debated within the French provisional government, and it was agreed that de Gaulle should go, but in a manner showing that he was not coming cap in hand, or indeed with negotiations of any kind in mind. Thus no minister was to accompany him, and he would be President Roosevelt's personal guest throughout his stay. De Gaulle hoped that two inferences would be drawn from these circumstances: that he was paying personal homage, in France's name, to the war effort of the mightiest western country and to the friendship of the French and American peoples; and that any talks would constitute an equal exchange of views between two heads of government. If the Americans wished to discuss civil and military relations between the Allied armies and the French administration, they would be invited to do so through normal diplomatic channels after the general's departure.

Though so often delayed, and held finally in circumstances that were less than satisfactory, de Gaulle's visit to Roosevelt was a great personal success for him. The president had set the keynote by sending his own plane for de Gaulle and an *entourage* of half a dozen advisers, including the inevitable Palewski. On arrival in Washington on 6 July 1944, de Gaulle was escorted to the White House. With his broad smile and famous charm, the president was in the doorway to greet him, with Cordell Hull at his side. After tea, the president and the general had a first long talk without their advisers; and two further talks followed, on the 7th and 8th.

After their first talk, General de Gaulle was taken to Blair House, "the ancient and curious dwelling which the American government is accustomed to reserve for the accommodation of its guests". A year earlier, General Giraud, Roosevelt's choice as leader of the Free French, had been

[15] For an account of de Gaulle's talk with the pope, *see* de Gaulle, *L'Unité*, pp. 233 *et seq.*

accorded similar honours. Now Giraud, defeated and discredited, had returned to obscurity, and it was the turn of the grudgingly accepted junior general to be the president's guest.

This was, then, de Gaulle's first exposure to the great power centre of official America, and he was impressed by the overwhelming self-confidence of the *élite*; wryly aware, too, of the fact that optimism becomes those whose means are more than adequate. Three banquets had been arranged, the first at the White House, the others at the departments of State and of War; and the French, on their side, were hosts to the Americans in a reception at their provisional Embassy – since the Vichy authorities still occupied the normal official quarters.

Either at the banquets, or at Blair House, de Gaulle met and conversed with some of the most powerful of the great administrators whose empires had spread as America's wartime power had grown. Robert P. Patterson, the secretary for War, and James V. Forrestal, the secretary for the Navy, were those whose departments had expanded most spectacularly in step with the needs of war. General George C. Marshall, chairman of the Joint Chiefs of Staff, also met de Gaulle, who found him reserved in conversation, in contrast with the boldness and world scale of his strategy. Then there was the "ardent and imaginative" Admiral Ernest J. King, commander-in-chief of the U.S. fleet; General H. H. Arnold, commander of the Army Air Forces; and the chairmen of the Senate and House of Representatives foreign affairs committees, Senator Tom Connally and Congressman Sol Bloom, respectively.

But among the wry satisfactions de Gaulle derived from his visit, perhaps the choicest was his encounter with the former ambassador to Vichy, Admiral William D. Leahy. The admiral, says de Gaulle, surprised by a turn of events that defied his conformism, seemed astonished to see the general there but ready to make the best of it. Leahy, in his own account of the meeting, writes that he "found him more agreeable in manner and appearance than I had expected". He adds that de Gaulle "made a very good impression" and he himself "had a better opinion of him after talking with him". But not good enough, apparently, to modify the fixed *a priori* political judgment he shared with President Roosevelt, for: "I remained unconvinced that he and his Committee of Liberation necessarily represented the form of government that the people of France wished to have after their nation's liberation from the Nazis."[16]

[16] Leahy, pp. 287–8. Two comments might perhaps be made on this judgment. One is that the "people of France" were deeply divided during the war, and that Pétain and de Gaulle symbolised this division, which continued into the liberation with a brutal settlement of accounts at the expense of the Vichyists. The other is that when the

Echoing the admiral, Cordell Hull was to record that de Gaulle "went out of his way to make himself agreeable to the president, to me, and to other members of the government, and to assure us emphatically and repeatedly that he had no intention of forcing himself or his committee upon France as her future government".[17] De Gaulle's references to Hull are more patronising. He found the aged secretary of State a man of conscience and high spirituality, but hampered by his rudimentary knowledge of things not American, and by the president's intervention in his domain.

Between dutiful visits to the tomb of the unknown soldier in Arlington Park, to the dying First World War General Pershing in hospital and to the George Washington monument, de Gaulle held court at Blair House, where his callers included the liberal and idealistic vice-president, Henry Wallace, with his dream of a victory for the "common man".

But the real object was, if possible, to achieve a meeting of minds with Roosevelt, and by this criterion his visit was a failure; for Roosevelt, who was at the summit of his power, had no concern other than that of making de Gaulle understand that France would count for nothing in the post-war world as the president saw it. De Gaulle, from his position of weakness and contested legitimacy, was trying to get the president to understand that, with him at the helm, a regenerated France would carry a far from negligible weight. Their conversations were thus, as the French say, "dialogues of the deaf".

The two men met in Roosevelt's study near his table which de Gaulle found encumbered with "surprising objects" such as souvenirs, insignia and good luck fetishes. On the morning of 7 July,[18] Roosevelt launched into a vast but impressionistic description of his plans for a world liberated from the fear of Nazi Germany. It was a grandiose vision, presented not didactically as a professor would put it, or eloquently as a politician might, but with the deft touches of the artist and charmer; and therefore all the more difficult to answer with reasoned argument. The whole, moreover, though expressive of a will to power, was presented, "as is human", in idealistic terms.

Isolationism, the president declared, was a great error, but it belonged

French voters came to decide on their form of government, as de Gaulle had promised them they would but which did not happen until late in 1946, they ignored his constitutional views. A year earlier, however, the elected representatives of the French people had decided that they wanted him as Prime Minister. It was he who walked out.
[17] Hull, Vol. 2, p. 1,433.
[18] De Gaulle's account (*L'Unité*, pp. 237 et seq.) does not distinguish between his separate conversations with Roosevelt, synthesising them as one. My account draws on other sources, including Funk (pp. 277–83), Hull, Leahy and Rosenman (1944–45 vol.)

to the past. For the future, he envisaged a directorate of the Big Four, of whom the United States, the Soviet Union and Great Britain were the first three, and the fourth not France but China. The United Nations would constitute a kind of parliament that would give a democratic aspect to the power of the Big Four and help to contain Soviet ambitions. But on the western side, only one power would really count – America. For as Roosevelt made clear, Chiang Kai-shek's China would need American aid, and the British, with the future of their empire uncertain, would be subservient to America's will. Since self-determination was to be a guiding principle of America's post-war policy, new sovereignties would arise in Africa, Asia and Australasia. Against this great prospect, the problems of old Europe, east and west, seemed to Roosevelt secondary.

In any case, either because they would need American aid, or because America, in her new world role, would need widely scattered military bases, many states both new and old would become clients of the U.S.A. Indeed, France by inference would be among them since she would need American aid and since Roosevelt stated that his country would need bases on French territory, specifically mentioning Dakar as an example.

De Gaulle wanted Roosevelt to understand that he had no intention of surrendering any part of the French empire. He was ready, however, to lend a sympathetic ear to American proposals on international security. As regards self-determination for dependent peoples, he was the first to believe that the colonial powers would have to give up any direct administration of dependent territories. Instead, forms of association would have to be worked out. But emancipation could not take place against the metropolitan powers, on pain of unleashing a xenophobic anarchy that would be a danger to the world as a whole. France, he said, would move towards a French union, in which Indo-China, for instance, would be represented within a federal system.

Quite apart from the question of France's colonies, however, de Gaulle had found Roosevelt's vision of American hegemony deeply disquieting, for Europe and for France. Nor was he going to leave it unchallenged. The president's plan, he said, might well put the West in peril. If Western Europe was to be regarded as secondary, would not Roosevelt be weakening the cause of civilisation, which he professed to wish to defend? If he wanted to win the assent of the Soviet Union to his new order, would he not find it necessary to make concessions to the Russians, at the expense of Polish, Baltic, Danubian and Balkan interests, and to the detriment of the general balance? How could he be sure.

moreover, that China, after the trials that were forging her nationalism, would be the same as she used to be?

"It is the West that must be rehabilitated," de Gaulle went on. "If the West finds itself again, the rest of the world, whether it likes it or not, will take it for its model. If it declines, barbarism will in the end sweep everything away. And Western Europe, despite its divisions [*déchirements*], is essential to the West. Nothing could take the place of its valour, its power, the far-flung influence of its ancient peoples. This is true above all of France which, among the great nations of Europe is the only one that was, is and always will be your ally.

"I know that you are getting ready to help her materially, and this will be of great value to her. But it is in the political sphere that she must regain her vigour, her self-confidence and therefore her role. How can she do this if she is kept out of the great world decisions, if she loses her African and Asian extensions, in short if the settlement of the war gives her, in the end, the psychology of the vanquished?"

Roosevelt's horizons were broad enough to comprehend de Gaulle's arguments. In any case, his feelings for France – or at any rate for France as he had once conceived her – were strong. But he did not hide his disappointment in, and irritation over, the French defeat and the unworthy reactions of so many Frenchmen, many of them known to him personally. With some bitterness, the president described his own feelings at the spectacle of France's political impotence in pre-war years. "I myself, the president of the United States," he exclaimed, "have sometimes found myself unable to remember the name of the current head of the French government. For the time being, you are there and you see with what attentions my country is greeting you. But will you still be there when the tragedy is over?"

Easy though it might have been to refute some of Roosevelt's views, de Gaulle refrained from expressing the arguments that were running through his head; from reminding the president how much America's isolation had contributed to France's discouragement after the First World War and her reverses in the second; or how his attitude towards the general and Fighting France had helped to maintain the "wait and see" mood of so much of the French *élite*, thus favouring a return to the political inconstancy which the president himself rightly condemned. Instead, he observed that the president's remarks had finally proved to him that in relations between states, neither logic nor sentiment counted for much in comparison with the realities of power; that the important thing was what one could take and hold on to; and that France could rely only on herself to recover her place in the world.

Roosevelt smiled and said: "We'll do what we can. But it is true that to serve France nobody can take the place of the French people."

Before lunch (says Funk) de Gaulle raised the question of Germany's future and staked a claim for some kind of French control over the Rhineland. But Roosevelt, who was hoping to incorporate northern Germany in the American occupation zone and had not, at that stage, reached agreement with his two major allies, confined himself to general remarks.

At lunch, the two men were joined by thirty-eight others. The president, says Leahy, "gave a very pleasing, friendly talk in which he skilfully avoided any political implications". "There are no great problems," he declared, "between the French and the Americans, or between General de Gaulle and myself. They are going to work out all right, if they will just leave a few of us alone to sit around the table."[19]

This was one way of disguising a fundamental divergence of views. It is true, however, that at the humdrum level of immediate arrangements, agreement was at hand. De Gaulle had expressly ruled out any discussion of an administrative accord as an objective of his trip. But it happened anyway, for that day the draft agreement, originally drawn up by the British and French and later submitted to the American Treasury and War departments, was brought to Leahy for presentation to the president. But Roosevelt did not deal with it until after de Gaulle's departure on the 10th,[20] before announcing it at his press conference on the 11th. De Gaulle himself did not see the final text until after his return to Algiers on the 13th, when it struck him as not only satisfactory but remarkably similar to the proposals he had made a year earlier. For the provisional government of the French Republic was named and recognised as the sole authority administering France; as alone qualified to liaise with the Allied forces and provide them with the necessary services; and as the sole source of currency, to be exchanged for the dollars and pounds of the liberating Allies.

But that was as far as agreement went. When General Béthouart called on Leahy on the last day of de Gaulle's visit, to request American assistance to recover Indo-China from the Japanese, the answer was that Indo-China could not at that time be included within the sphere of interest of the American chiefs of staff. Persevering, Béthouart went to the Pentagon to enquire whether the United States would be prepared to arm five more French divisions, in addition to the eight covered by the Anfa agreement; and to transport a French expeditionary force to Indo-China. There were negative answers to both questions. General Eisenhower and other field commanders had let it be known that France did

[19] Rosenman (1944–45 vol.), p. 195.   [20] Not, as Funk says, on the 8th.

not, in their opinion, need more forces than already agreed. The joint chiefs concluded that any further rearmament must be relegated to the post-war period and was therefore a political, not an operational, problem and beyond their competence.

Despite the paucity of results, the warmth of the American hospitality had created a certain euphoria in allied quarters. In London, however, Churchill remained cautious. He wrote to Eden on 10 July – the day of de Gaulle's departure but before the announcement of the administrative agreement – to say that it would be most unwise to ask the Americans and Russians to join the British in recognising the French provisional government "until the result of the president's honeymoon with de Gaulle is made known". There was no point in a premature debate in parliament "which might have spoiled all this happy kissing".[21]

De Gaulle now took his leave of the president. He was to learn later that in a letter to an American businessman, Roosevelt had asked him to make sure de Gaulle did not learn of a deal being negotiated with a French company, for if de Gaulle heard about it, he would be certain to have the director of the company removed. In the same letter, which de Gaulle quotes in full but only in translation in his memoirs, the president commented that de Gaulle was "amenable" (*traitable*) when future problems were under discussion, so long as France was treated on a world basis. He was very touchy about France's honour. But Roosevelt thought him essentially egotistical. "I was never to know," writes de Gaulle, "whether Roosevelt thought that . . . Charles de Gaulle was egotistical for France or for himself."[22]

After a brief stop in New York, de Gaulle went on to Canada, where the Prime Minister, Mackenzie King – "dignified and strong in his simplicity" – gave him a warm welcome. He was the guest of the earl and countess of Athlone, the earl being at that time governor-general of the dominion. In the round of speeches and ceremonies, only one event was noteworthy: de Gaulle's visit to Montreal on 12 July. A vast crowd assembled to see and hear the general, whom the mayor introduced with heady words: "Show General de Gaulle that Montreal is the second French city in the world!" A thunder of cheers followed.

It was there, twenty-three years later, that de Gaulle was to startle the world, shock his cabinet and deeply offend the Canadian government by shouting: "*Vive le Québec libre!*"

That evening, he flew back to Algiers, where news of his belated victory over the administration of France awaited him.

21 Churchill, Vol. VI, pp. 213–14.   22 De Gaulle, *L'Unité*, pp. 240–1 and 662.

Chapter 2 ✤ De Gaulle's Parisian Triumph

Within a fortnight of General de Gaulle's return to Algiers, the Allied offensive was breaking out of Normandy and driving towards Paris. On the eastern front, the Russian armies were pouring into Poland towards the Danube and into the Balkans. In Italy, General Alexander's multinational forces, having liberated Rome on 4 June, were striking northwards towards the river Po. The landings in the French Riviera – operation Anvil – were impending.

Although the French provisional government had been recognised as the *de facto* administration of liberated France, it had not been recognised as France's provisional government, for even at this late stage, neither Roosevelt nor Churchill (who deferred to the president) was yet ready to acknowledge the possibility of previous error. De Gaulle's humiliations and frustrations therefore continued, though on a diminishing scale. He had been kept out of the decision-making in Overlord, but his unyielding tactics had brought him victory elsewhere in the hard-fought matter of consultation.

The occasion for the showdown de Gaulle had been seeking came at the end of 1943. The major allies had agreed on Overlord but were not unanimous about Anvil. Roosevelt and his commanders favoured Anvil; but Churchill had long been wedded to his theory that the action should go where German resistance was likely to be weakest – the "soft underbelly" of the Axis: from Italy to Greece and Yugoslavia and through to the Danube basin. For his part, de Gaulle was convinced Churchill was wrong, and that the "soft underbelly" was a misnomer for the rebarbative Balkan mountain chains where men and machines trained or designed for fast advances over the plains would be slowed to a standstill. His strategic conviction was, of course, strengthened by patriotic sentiment: he wanted France to be liberated, and an operation in the Balkans was not the quickest way to do it.[1]

[1] De Gaulle, *L'Unité*, p. 258; for further matter, *see also* pp. 260–3.

The trouble, as usual, was that his opinion was not being sought. Nor was that of General Giraud who, at that stage, was still the Free French commander-in-chief. "Never," was he later to lament, "did the Anglo-Saxons consent to treat us as veritable allies. Never did they consult us, from government to government, on any of their arrangements. By policy or by expediency, they sought to use the French forces for the goals they themselves had fixed, as though those forces belonged to them, and on the ground that they were helping to arm them."

Three French divisions were already fighting in Italy, and in December Eisenhower requested a fourth. The French National Defence Committee agreed and chose the 1st Free French Division. Eisenhower, however, let it be known that he preferred the 9th Colonial. This was the opening de Gaulle had been waiting for. He immediately notified the Allied High Command that the 9th Colonial was not at Eisenhower's disposal and would be staying in North Africa. Predictable indignation ensued. Eisenhower invoked arrangements he had made directly with Giraud, though without de Gaulle's knowledge; and the Anfa agreement between Giraud and Roosevelt, which laid down that French troops armed by the Americans would be fully at the disposal of the American command.[2]

For de Gaulle, these references to arrangements to which he had not been a party could only strengthen his resolve. He confirmed his decision, but notified the Allied envoys, Edwin Wilson and Harold Macmillan, that his government was ready to discuss with their governments the conditions under which the French forces could be used "on the same footing as the American and British forces". Angrily, the Allied general staff protested that such behaviour would compromise current operations. The envoys declared that the matter was of no concern of their government and should be settled between General Eisenhower and the Liberation Committee. But de Gaulle knew that he had the whip hand, for the French forces were needed in Italy but would not leave North Africa until he gave the command.

On 27 December, the Allies gave in and agreed to attend a meeting under de Gaulle's chairmanship. Wilson and Macmillan were there; Eisenhower was travelling but General Bedell Smith took his place. Massigli and Giraud were in de Gaulle's "corner". At his loftiest, de Gaulle explained that the 1st Division – but none other – having been put at the disposal of the Allied commander-in-chief, would be sent to Italy as soon as a formal request for it was made. It must be understood, of course, that no French forces could be used in any operational theatre

[2] Eisenhower does not mention this incident in *Crusade*.

except on orders from the French government. He was, on the other hand, "naturally disposed" to cooperate with the Allies. But it could only be in full knowledge of the facts. The French, however, were not associated with Allied plans. In case it should be useful, the French had prepared a draft agreement to ensure cooperation between the three governments and commands in the conduct of the war.

"If this agreement is concluded," he went on inexorably, "all is well. If it is not, the French government will place its forces under the Allied command only under conditions it will itself determine and under the reserve that it may take them back, in part or in whole, when the national interest may seem to call for it."

In case his meaning remained obscure, he went on to specify that the French would not reinforce their forces in Italy, or even leave them there much longer, unless they had a guarantee that Anvil would take place. And he demanded further guarantees: that all French forces in Italy and North Africa would take part in Anvil; that a French division would be transported to England in good time to take part in Overlord and liberate Paris. If these guarantees, once given, were called in question, the French government would *ipso facto* resume control over its forces.

These were plain words. Next day, Massigli confirmed their gist in letters to Wilson and Macmillan. Their reply was that their governments were studying de Gaulle's proposals; meanwhile, they were at liberty to give him the guarantees he sought, as regards the French operations. Thereupon, the transport of French troops to Italy was resumed. And an era of Franco-Allied cooperation began, during which de Gaulle established cordial and confident relations with the Allied military commanders. It was another victory for de Gaulle, in a skirmish that might easily have been avoided with tact and foresight on the Allied side.

Although de Gaulle had never doubted the usefulness, to the Allies themselves, of such relations, he gave the British and American leaders full credit for overcoming their understandable reluctance to deal with a man who was the exception to so many rules. What were men like Bedell Smith and Air Marshal Tedder, or like General Maitland Wilson and Admiral Cunningham, to think of "this chief of State without a constitution, without voters, without a capital, who spoke in the name of France; this officer wearing so few stars, whose ministers, generals, admirals, governors and ambassadors of his country obeyed his orders without question; this Frenchman who had been condemned by the 'legal' government, vilified by many notables, fought against by a part of the armed forces"? (Not long after, in Paris, Churchill "was struck by the awe, and even apprehension, with which half a dozen high generals treated de Gaulle, in spite of the fact that he had only one star on his uniform and they had lots".[3])

On the eve of the great operations in Normandy and southern France, the French forces, though still modest in comparison with the gigantic Allied and German armies, had ceased to be negligible. Manpower was short, and while gaps at the unskilled level could be filled by recruitment from the autochthonous populations of North Africa and the African colonies, the commissioned ranks and the skilled attributions could go only to the French themselves, of whom there were few. In Algeria, Tunisia and Morocco, put together, there were no more than 1,200,000 European French men and women. By calling up all classes back to 1918, 116,000 were enlisted. Then there were the 15,000 youths of Free France, 13,000 from Corsica and 18,000 young volunteers of both sexes who had escaped to North Africa through Spain. From all these sources, by the spring of 1944, a fighting army of 230,000 men had been raised, together with 150,000 home troops; a fleet of 320,000 tons manned by 50,000 seamen, a merchant navy of 1,200,000 tons, two-thirds of which had French crews; and an air force of 500 first-line aircraft with 30,000 personnel.[4] True, this impressive force, so much of which had been organised and trained by General Giraud, was partly colonial and dependent on American supplies. But de Gaulle was surely justified in thinking that its political and moral value to the Allied cause, quite apart from its fighting quality, transcended its relative insignificance and continued dependence.

Nor was the French side short, at that stage, of gifted commanders. General Juin – who had been a classmate of de Gaulle's at Saint-Cyr – was the first to command the only army de Gaulle's government was able to put into the field, appropriately termed the 1st. His qualities of solidity and general straightforwardness, seasoned with occasional cunning, contrasted with the mobility and panache of his successor, General de Lattre de Tassigny, who was later to acquire legendary stature in Indo-China. On the eve of Anvil (which was launched on 15 August 1944), de Gaulle appointed Juin to the highest rank in his gift: chief of the general staff of National Defence.

Among the lesser commanders, two – Generals Leclerc and Koenig – deserve special mention. General Leclerc (de Hautecloque), had won fame with his long drive from black to northern Africa. It had been agreed between the French and their allies that the honour of liberating

---

[3] Churchill, Vol. VI, p. 219. De Gaulle, of course, actually had two stars, not one.
[4] De Gaulle, L'Unité, pp. 246-9.

Paris should fall to a French force and that it should be Leclerc's famous 2nd Armoured Division. Although short of vehicles on its arrival in England,[5] its deficiencies were soon made good; and by common consent, it was not to take part in the earlier Normandy operations, so that the troops, under their dynamic and imaginative commander, should be fresh when launched against the capital.

Koenig – the victor of Bir-Hakim – had been given an important complementary command: that of the French forces of the Interior (Forces françaises de l'Intérieur, or FFI). The FFI had been formally created by de Gaulle on 1 February 1944,[6] to put some order into the confused picture of separate and sometimes rival armed groups of the French Resistance.[7] At the end of March, de Gaulle appointed Koenig superior commander of the French Forces in Great Britain, and military delegate for the Northern Theatre of Operations; it was in the latter capacity that he was commander of the Resistance forces, but there was no mention of the FFI in de Gaulle's order. The air force general, Cochet, who was to work in Algiers, was appointed military delegate for the southern zone, in anticipation of landings in southern France.

[5] Churchill, Vol. V, pp. 545–6.
[6] Michel, *Résistance*, p. 106. De Gaulle (*L'Unité*, p. 256) dates the creation of the FFI in March 1944, but was evidently writing from memory. He also states that Koenig was given his London appointment in April; but the relevant document, on pp. 684–5 of *L'Unité*, is dated 28 March.
[7] Apart from the proliferating regional groups, each with its own name, the following armed organisations existed in France at the beginning of 1944:
Armée secrète (AS): created by de Gaulle, on Jean Moulin's suggestion, at the beginning of 1943, as the military arm of the unified Resistance. Its first commander was divisional General Delestraint. The German police chief, Kaltenbrunner, estimated its membership at 80,000 in June 1943.
Francs-Tireurs et partisans français (FTPF or FTP): the military arm of the Communist-controlled Front National. First mentioned in September 1941.
Milices patriotiques: a para-military body recruited by the Communists within existing Resistance movements. The Patriotic Militias were given auxiliary police duties: their primary function was to assist the projected national insurrection, and help turn it into a Communist revolution.
Organisation de Résistance de l'armée (ORA): Mainly composed of regular army officers disillusioned with Pétain. Mostly Giraudist, the ORA was initially commanded by General Frère. On his arrest in June 1943, he was succeeded by General Verneau, who was arrested in turn in September, the command then going to General Revers, who was to be the central figure in the crisis arising out of a leakage of intelligence to the enemy in Indo-China in 1950. The ORA organised the escape routes of thousands of soldiers from France to Algeria, through Spain.
From September 1943, there was some attempt to coordinate the activities of all these groups, through a "National Military delegate" appointed by the Gaullist authorities in London and Algiers. The first incumbent was Colonel Marchal who, in time, was arrested and committed suicide. He was succeeded by Mangin, then Bourgès-Maunoury and finally by Jacques Chaban-Delmas. The last two made political names for themselves under the Fourth Republic, and Chaban-Delmas became President Pompidou's premier after the departure of General de Gaulle in 1969.
See Michel, *Résistance*, chs. XI and XII; and Rob. Aron, *Libération*, Part II, ch. 1.

Although the French were not to be taken into the Allied secrets of Overlord, Koenig was given the information he needed to liaise with the FFI, and some, though not enough, material assistance. He was not, however, given full control over the network of French agents set up by the British SOE until after the Normandy landings. But from the moment of his arrival in London, he was fully consulted on the use to which the FFI could be put as auxiliaries to the Allied forces. There were to be three zones. In the battle zone, reliable intelligence was all that was asked of them. The requirements for the "rear zone" – which covered the areas immediately beyond the battle zone – were more strenuous. The FFI were required to carry out systematic acts of sabotage. As the Allies advanced, the rear zone was of course gradually absorbed into the growing battle zone. A third zone, styled "non-operational", covered difficult or inaccessible areas and those unlikely to become part of the battle zone. There, the unleashed *maquisards* were to paralyse the rail system, cut the roads, flood the canals, sabotage the power stations and attack fuel and arms depots.

As Michel points out, to carry out such tasks satisfactorily on such a scale would have required a massive programme of air-dropped armaments and paratroops. In fact, the British and Americans merely air-dropped teams of three or four men, known as "Yedburghs", to organise sabotage groups of about forty men each. Arms were insufficient. It was estimated that the FFI needed sixty tons of arms a day, but deliveries did not exceed about twenty tons. On D-day only half the FFI were armed, and that half only with light weapons.[8]

Despite these inadequacies, many of the FFI groups were already in action before D-day. But after 6 June, the insurrection of the Resistance spread rapidly. Many Frenchmen who had hesitated to embark on a life of clandestinity now reported for duty. For the Communists, the insurrection was to be the prelude to the revolution whereby they hoped to face General de Gaulle with an accomplished fact at the time of his return. But in the minds of most resisters one thought predominated: the time had come to turn the tables on the Germans and liberate their country.

The plans carefully worked out in London were not necessarily strictly executed. In Normandy, however, circumstances dictated a fairly close adherence to the battle zone routine. In Calvados department, for example, more than half the population had been evacuated, and with seventeen divisions the Germans roughly equalled the remaining local inhabitants in numbers. Sabotage and sudden harassment were there-

---

[8] Michel, *Résistance*, p. 108; *see also* pp. 110–11.

fore the most the FFI could attempt. In Brittany, however, the FFI were enormously effective from the start. By the end of June, they had paralysed all trains in the region. In July, having grown from 5,000 to 20,000, they carried out 200 acts of sabotage on the rail system, cut the telephone lines at 300 places, carried out fifty ambushes and made thirty attacks on enemy positions.

When the American 3rd Army broke through at Avranches, at the end of July, the FFI were able to guide the Allies, guard prisoners and harass the retreating Germans. By mid-August, they had grown to 80,000 men. When the Americans turned eastwards, the FFI cleaned up enemy resistance in the Breton departments, capturing nearly 20,000 prisoners in two months.

Further south, in the Dordogne Valley, the FFI constantly harassed the German army, which was moving towards the northern battle zone. The notorious Das Reich division, responsible for the Oradour massacre, was among those that suffered most from FFI attacks. (The infamous General von Brodowski, who had ordered the massacre, was captured by the French 1st Army, and shot by an FFI guard "while attempting to escape"; the description of the mode of death, so often used by the Nazis to justify indiscriminate killings, appears to have fitted the facts of his own case.[9]) In twenty-eight departments of the centre and south-west, the FFI could be given sole credit for the liberation. Limoges was one of their prizes.

One of the most tragic episodes of the insurrection took place in the sub-Alpine hills of Vercors, in east-central France. About 3,500 resisters had taken refuge there in June. Armed with the contents of 1,500 parachute containers, they were given special attention from London and Algiers. A mission of British, French and American officers was sent from England and instructors came from Algiers. A landing strip was prepared. Vercors was to be an important centre for the harassment of the Germans.

The German army, however, decided to reduce the Vercors redoubt. The attack began on 14 July, with air bombardments and the machine-gunning of the defenders. The FFI held out for ten days against 20,000 Germans, losing 750 killed. German losses were probably heavier. In their fury, the Germans killed off many wounded and indulged in an orgy of massacres in the villages of the region. The Vercors tragedy was the subject of bitter recriminations among the Gaullists. It was thought in Algiers that all the defenders of Vercors had been killed. One of the Vercors leaders had sent a telegram accusing the French and their

[9] Rob. Aron, *Libération*, p. 547.

allies of doing nothing to help and calling them "criminals and cowards". On 27 July 1944, Fernand Grenier, commissioner for Air and one of the two Communist ministers in de Gaulle's government, gave a press conference in which he quoted this telegram and dissociated himself from the "criminal policy" of withholding aid from "our brothers in France". The next day the government met at the Palais d'Eté. De Gaulle arrived in a cold fury. Disdaining to shake hands with any of the commissioners, as he usually did, he launched into a rebuke of Grenier which, according to one account, ended with the words: "You know how to exploit dead men." He called on Grenier to disclaim what he had said in writing, or resign.

Grenier asked for permission to consult his fellow-Communist in the government, François Billoux, commissioner for Liberated Territories. Left alone, the two men telephoned Marty at Communist Headquarters. Grenier then drafted a disclaimer, and handed it to de Gaulle when the commissioners reassembled. De Gaulle read it and declared that it did not go far enough. Grenier rewrote his text, which the general accepted. He was allowed to remain in the government, but de Gaulle dismissed him on 9 September 1944.[10]

On 15 August, Anvil was at last launched, when the first elements of the French 1st Army and the 6th American Corps landed in Provence. General Patch commanded the Americans, and General de Lattre the French. The Americans were to drive northwards towards Grenoble, and the French mission was to capture Toulon and Marseilles before moving up the Rhône Valley.

Here, too, the FFI played an important part in the Allied successes. They had been given the jobs of securing the Allied right flank on the Italian side and disorganising enemy communication lines. By the 15th, these jobs had largely been accomplished. Three of the reserve divisions of the German 19th Army were immobilised by the *maquisards*. On the 17th, the German command decided to withdraw the 19th Army. Next day, de Lattre took Toulon and started driving towards Marseilles.

But the most dramatic developments were taking place on the northern front. Leclerc's 2nd Division had landed in Normandy, as agreed, on 1 August. It was attached to General Patton's 3rd Army command and the agreement that it would be the first to enter Paris was to be honoured. General Eisenhower, however, was determined to avoid a frontal assault on the capital, for fear of a repetition of the

---

[10] In his account of the Vercors incident (*L'Unité*, pp. 282–3), de Gaulle makes no mention of the Grenier incident, which is summarily described by Soustelle, *Envers* (Vol. II, pp. 410–12), and in greater detail by Rob. Aron (*Libération*, pp. 282–5).

horrors of Stalingrad, or of another desperate and tragic insurrection, as in Warsaw.[11] Koenig, on the other hand, wanted an uprising in Paris, for patriotic as well as military reasons. If the people of Paris themselves liberated their capital, they might be spared an Allied administration; they would be able to affirm French sovereignty and demonstrate that the Resistance was no myth. But it was all a question of timing. Koenig did not want the insurrection to start until the Allied armies were at the gates of Paris, in case the Germans smashed it before it had a chance to take over.

The Communists, who dominated the Resistance in Paris, saw the situation in quite different terms. For them, the essential thing was to get their authority established, in the interests of the revolution, before de Gaulle arrived. They therefore favoured an early uprising. In this, they were helped by the mood of the Parisian workers, whose patience was at snapping point early in August. In fact, the first act of the insurrection was a general strike of railway workers in the Parisian region, which began on the 12th. Two days later, on Bastille Day, militant Communists organised a mass demonstration. On the 15th, by order of the Resistance, the police went on strike. Three days later, the Communist party called on the people of Paris to rise. On the 19th, Communist resisters started taking over Les Halles – the Covent Garden of Paris – which fell to them a day later. Distribution of foodstuffs to the Resistance in requisitioned German lorries began immediately.

On the day of the attack on the market, de Gaulle left Casablanca by air for France, via Gibraltar. He landed at Maupertuis, near Cherbourg, in Normandy on the evening of Sunday, 20 August. Two men who enjoyed his special confidence were in Paris: Chaban-Delmas, the government's military delegate, who had returned there on the 16th after consultations in London; and Alexandre Parodi, whom he had appointed on the 14th as minister-delegate for non-liberated territories with authority to speak in de Gaulle's name.[12] At Maupertuis, the general was met by Koenig, Coulet – the man he had left at Bayeux as commissioner in Normandy – and an officer from General Eisenhower's headquarters. While the American accompanied the French party to headquarters, Koenig told him the news, as he had heard it from Parodi and Chaban-Delmas. The police had taken the prefecture and were firing on the Germans; and the Resistance was seizing public buildings.

But Koenig also brought the latest news about the last-minute attempts by Laval to turn the situation to his advantage. De Gaulle had heard the start of the story in Algiers at the beginning of the month.

[11] Churchill, Vol. VI, p. 31.   [12] De Gaulle, L'Unité, p. 293.

Laval's idea, which he pursued with his usual skill and with desperate courage, was to change the character of his government in ways that would make it acceptable to the Allies, and face de Gaulle with the accomplished fact of an administration in power in the French capital while de Gaulle's own government was still denied *de jure* recognition. To this end, he planned to get rid of the pro-German extremists in his government – Déat, Darnand, Bonnard and Brinon – to free Edouard Herriot, the last president of the Chamber of Deputies and persuade him to convene the parliamentarians; and to take measures to suppress the hated militia. First he secured German approval for his plan and assured himself, through one Enfière – an American agent responsible, wrote de Gaulle, to Allen Dulles's secret organisation in Berne, which used him to keep in touch with Herriot, with whom he was on friendly terms – that the Americans would not oppose his plan. Indeed, as de Gaulle thought, any proposal to restore the sovereignty of the French parliament would have much to commend itself to Roosevelt. Next, on the 12th, Laval in person freed Herriot from his place of detention in a lunatic asylum at Maréville, near Nancy. Herriot and his wife, delighted to be freed, accompanied Laval to Paris by car on the 13th. Back in the capital, Herriot visited his tailor and ordered himself a suit to his generous measurements, and accepted an invitation to dine with Laval and Abetz. But he declined to commit himself to accepting Laval's plan.

The whole project collapsed on 18 August when the Gestapo, alerted by Brinon and Déat, ordered Laval to go forthwith to Belfort in eastern France; there he was later joined by Marshal Pétain, who had refused to come to Paris and lend his fading authority to Laval's plans. As for Herriot, to his relief, he was returned to Maréville.[13] Laval's last throw had misfired: it was the end of Vichy.

With uncharacteristic generosity, de Gaulle commented in his memoirs:

> Laval had played. He had lost. He had the courage to admit that he was responsible for the consequences. Doubtless in his government, deploying in support of the untenable all the resources of his cunning, he sought to serve his country. May that much be left to him! It is a fact that in the depths of misfortune, those of the French who, in small numbers, chose to crawl through the mud of dishonour, did not disown their motherland.

---

[13] The fullest account of Laval's plan is in Rob. Aron, *Vichy*, pp. 685 *et seq. See also* de Gaulle, *L'Unité*, pp. 289–90, and 298–99.

At all events, the collapse of Laval's plans meant that henceforth only two obstacles barred de Gaulle's way: the Communist leaders of the Parisian Resistance, and – possibly – a last show of American ill-will. His conversation with Eisenhower on the 20th fed his suspicions. The supreme commander briefed him on the military situation. It was, of course, brilliant. But one point struck de Gaulle forcibly: Patton's 3rd Army had split, so that one column was striking north of the Seine towards Lorraine, while the other was moving south towards Melun. But there was no sign of an assault on Paris. Why not, de Gaulle asked?

Eisenhower seemed embarrassed. A battle for Paris, he explained, might lead to dreadful destruction and heavy loss of civilian lives. De Gaulle admitted this, but argued that any further delay was unjustified now that the Resistance had risen.

To this, Eisenhower replied that the Resistance had acted too soon.

"Why too soon?" asked de Gaulle, "since your forces are already at this hour on the Seine?"

The supreme commander thereupon assured de Gaulle that the order to march on Paris would soon be given and would be reserved for Leclerc and his division.

De Gaulle parted from him with a warning that the liberation of Paris was of such national importance that if marching orders were unduly delayed, he himself would order the 2nd Armoured Division to attack.

From this unsatisfactory encounter, de Gaulle deduced that Roosevelt had ordered the delay in the hope that Laval's plot to reconvene the Chamber of Deputies under Herriot would succeed. And his suspicions were strengthened when he learned that the Leclerc division, until then attached to Patton's army, had for the past three days been transferred to the 1st Army under General Hodges, where it was being kept under close watch. Moreover, the agreement on cooperation between the Allied armies and the French administration, announced by Roosevelt on 11 July, had still not been signed by Koenig and Eisenhower because the supreme commander had not yet received the necessary authority from Washington.[14]

Well-informed though General de Gaulle was about events in Paris, there were some developments that had not yet come to his knowledge. One concerned German policy towards the capital. At the beginning of August, Hitler had appointed a new commander for Greater Paris, to replace General von Stulpnagel, allegedly implicated in the bomb plot to assassinate Hitler on 20 July. The new man, General von Choltitz, who had been commanding the 84th Army Corps in Normandy, came

[14] De Gaulle, L'Unité, pp. 295–7; see also pp. 300–6.

with a frightful but quite undeserved reputation. He was credited with the destruction of Warsaw with 277,000 dead, although at the time, he was on the Siegfried Line. Moreover, he came armed with personal orders from the Fuehrer to destroy Paris extensively and exact "the most widespread and bloody reprisals" if attacked from within the city. Monuments were to become heaps of ruins and the water supplies were to be cut off, so that typhus and cholera should spread.

Von Choltitz, however, had a secret. He had met Hitler shortly after the bomb plot, and decided, on seeing the pitiful human wreck that he had become, foaming at the mouth, with wandering eyes, requiring frequent jabs of stimulants, that the Fuehrer was now irretrievably insane. He had therefore decided to ignore Hitler's orders, which, when the insurrection began, became ever more pressing and demented.[15] The fact was that this small, plump, monocled man, though a firm disciplinarian, was humane and not without a sense of humour. Above all, he abhorred the cruelties and massacres of the SS which to his mind dishonoured the German uniform. Not, had Hitler but known, the man for the job of destroying Paris.

Nor did de Gaulle learn until later that there had been a clash between his two principal men in Paris, Parodi and Chaban-Delmas, about the desirability of launching the insurrection. It was, of course, a time of agonising choices, for all concerned. The Resistance was divided on the issue. The Parisian Liberation Committee (CPL), with Tollet, a Communist and militant trade unionist, at its head, was determined that the city should be liberated by insurrectional means. The Gaullist delegation was simply ready to do what Koenig, from London, told them to do: if the order was for an insurrection, they would go ahead; if to wait, they would wait. And the orders were clear on one point: if there was to be an insurrection, it would have to be timed to coincide with the impending entry of Leclerc's troops into Paris.

But when was Leclerc coming? On 19 August, when the National Council of the Resistance (CNR) met in the Rue de Grenelle to decide whether the insurrection should go ahead, information from London was that Leclerc's entry might be delayed for weeks. Tollet of the CPL wanted an immediate rising. A majority of the CNR sided with him. Parodi, who was the sole representative of the Gaullist delegation, was isolated. His orders were to wait. If he voted in favour of the insurrection, against London's orders, and it proved premature, leading to defeat, destruction and reprisals, his responsibility would be heavy. But if voted against, and the insurrection went ahead anyway and was suc-

[15] Rob. Aron, *Libération*, pp. 365–6; *see also* pp. 376, 400.

cessful, the Communists would take the credit for liberating Paris; and carry off the administrative prizes that went with victory. All these considerations passed through Parodi's mind that morning. And the thought that was uppermost was that it was essential to preserve the unity of the Resistance, so that de Gaulle, on his arrival, should meet a united movement and not a Communist-led majority, with a Gaullist minority of dissidents. So he voted in favour of the insurrection.

That afternoon, at a meeting of the Gaullists, Chaban-Delmas vehemently reproached Parodi with having forgotten the order to wait. Parodi explained his reasons; above all, he dwelt on the fact that with the strikes already declared, events had gone too far for minority opposition. That afternoon, a mysterious personage, claiming to represent the British Intelligence Service, called on Parodi and requested permission to telegraph London immediately to urge a speedier Allied advance on Paris. Parodi naturally agreed. The stranger never reappeared, but evidently did his work.

An unexpected initiative now further complicated the situation. The Swedish consul-general in Paris, Raoul Nordling, called on von Choltitz to request an amnesty for French prisoners and a truce between the German authorities and the insurgents. Von Choltitz agreed to both. Nordling was thus able to secure the release of 4,000 Frenchmen, some of whom were certainly spared deportation or massacre. As for the truce, which was subsequently negotiated in Nordling's presence, it was short-lived, but was used by the humane von Choltitz as an excuse to release Parodi and two other Gaullists who had fallen into German hands on the 20th while carrying incriminating documents.

While these events were occurring, de Gaulle was making a triumphal tour of liberated towns in Normandy, Brittany and on the road to Paris. From Rennes, de Gaulle wrote a personal letter to Eisenhower, relaying the news he had been getting from Paris and urging an immediate advance on the capital. The letter was to be delivered on 22 August by Koenig who, after adding explanatory comments, returned to London, from where communications with the Resistance in Paris were better organised than in the liberated towns.

Meanwhile, de Gaulle pushed on. At Laval, he was greeted by his commissioner, Michel Debré (later premier of France), and was handed a letter from Leclerc. The impatient French commander had sent a vanguard, under Major de Guillebon, to Paris to make preliminary contacts with the Resistance. For this, he had been roundly reprimanded by the American General Gerow, commanding the 5th Army Corps. De Gaulle wrote back approving Leclerc's initiative.

A few hours after reading de Gaulle's letter, Eisenhower at last ordered the French 2nd Armoured Division to advance on Paris. At Le Mans, more messages from Paris awaited de Gaulle. From these he learned of the truce, which annoyed him all the more for being out of tune with the belated decision to give Leclerc his marching orders. Next morning, the 23rd, however, as he was on the point of leaving Le Mans, a further message informed him that the truce was breaking down, although it had permitted the release of Parodi and of the other Gaullists arrested with him.

The triumphal progress continued. Wherever de Gaulle went, he found flags unfurled and heard cries of *"Vive de Gaulle!"* He felt himself "carried on by a kind of river of joy". That afternoon, de Gaulle's motorcade overtook Leclerc's division.

The two men met at Rambouillet, and Leclerc explained his battle plan to de Gaulle, who instructed him to set up his headquarters in Montparnasse station. "You are lucky," de Gaulle said to the younger man, thinking of the joys of military action in favourable circumstances, which were no longer his now that he was concerned with affairs of State.

The BBC, a trifle prematurely, was already announcing the liberation of Paris by the FFI. King George VI, said the announcer, would be sending de Gaulle a telegram of congratulations. Why this anticipation of events? De Gaulle thought he could deduce the answer from the contrast between the warm and jubilant tone of the BBC and the sour reserve of the voice of America. London, he thought, was forcing the issue of support for de Gaulle on the reluctant Americans.

For de Gaulle, the hour he had awaited so long was at hand. It was an emotional moment for the patriot that he was. But for the statesman, it was a time for clear thinking. If he had obeyed sentiment, he would have gone straight to the Town Hall to meet the leaders of the Resistance, including the Parisian Liberation Committee, who had their headquarters there. But reasons of State dictated a different course. On the evening of the 23rd, he sent a message to the newly appointed Gaullist police chief, Luizet, to explain that he would be setting up his own headquarters in the vacant War Ministry, before meeting the Resistance leaders. By this gesture, he would be demonstrating that his first concern was to re-establish the authority of the State.

It was part of de Gaulle's reasoning that no concessions at all should be made to the recent past: no recognition of the sovereignty of a parliament that had betrayed the country, and no acknowledgment of

Marshal Pétain's "French State". That evening, a strange delegation visited him. It consisted of four ill-assorted men. There were two Frenchmen, Alexandre de Saint-Phalle, a businessman associated with the Gaullist delegation in Paris; and Jean Laurent, director of the Banque d'Indochine; a Swede, Rolf Nordling, brother of the consul-general; and an Austrian, Baron Poch-Pastor, aide-de-camp to von Choltitz and an agent of the Allies. The baron and the Swede had passes issued by von Choltitz; the Frenchmen's passes had been delivered by Parodi. The four men had left Paris on the night of the 22nd to try to persuade the American command to send regular troops to Paris as soon as possible, while the truce was on. They had seen Eisenhower, who told them Leclerc was on the way. They had then decided to call on de Gaulle. De Saint-Phalle had a proposal to make. As soon as de Gaulle got to Paris, he said, he should convoke the "national" Assembly, so that a parliamentary vote should confer legality on his government. De Gaulle declined.

On the evening of the 24th, Leclerc's Division reached Paris after fierce fighting on the outskirts. Striding back and forth on the terrace of his quarters in Rambouillet, de Gaulle was working out his plans for the following days, while reading messages from the scene of battle. One thing was certain: there would be no power vacuum at the centre of the kind that had caused the disaster of 1940.

On the 25th, de Gaulle's car reached the Porte d'Orléans, and entered the Avenue d'Orléans, which was black with cheering crowds. Instead of driving towards the Hôtel de Ville, as the crowd had evidently supposed he would, he took the route for Montparnasse. There, Leclerc told him that von Choltitz had just signed an instrument of surrender, and was now giving orders to his garrison to lay down their arms. De Gaulle caught sight of his son, an ensign with the 1st Regiment of Marines, who was off to the Palais-Bourbon, accompanied by a German major, to receive the surrender of its occupants.

With Leclerc was Colonel Rol-Tanguy, the Communist chief of the FFI in Paris. De Gaulle congratulated both men. Later, Leclerc handed him a copy of the surrender document, which he read with evident disapproval. Why, he asked, had Leclerc agreed to Rol-Tanguy's suggestion that the text should record the German general's surrender to both men on equal terms? It was his, Leclerc's, responsibility, as the superior officer, to accept von Choltitz's surrender. Moreover, did he not understand that Rol-Tanguy's insistence was part of an unacceptable plan? To help Leclerc understand, he gave him the text of a proclamation made that morning by the CNR which referred to itself as "the French nation" and made no mention of General de Gaulle or his government. Leclerc got the point; and de Gaulle warmly embraced him.

Arriving at the War Ministry, de Gaulle found it eerily unchanged. Not a chair was out of place; the same attendants were on duty. Taking possession of the ministerial office, which Reynaud and he had vacated together on the night of 10 June 1940, de Gaulle reflected that only one thing was missing: the State. And he was there to restore it.

Luizet and Parodi, both radiant but exhausted after a sleepless week, reported to him. Two problems worried them, they said: public order and food supplies. And there was another cause for concern: the CNR and the Liberation Committee were irritated with him for not having gone straight to the Hôtel de Ville to greet them. De Gaulle explained his reasons, and said it was up to the CNR to visit him where he now was. He was talked out of his refusal by Parodi and Luizet, yielding to the argument that he must not disappoint the great crowd that awaited him before the Hôtel de Ville.[16]

Plans were then made for the great parade which de Gaulle intended to lead the following day. Before de Gaulle left for the Town Hall, a message came from Koenig. It was an apology for his failure to greet de Gaulle. His excuse was a good one. Eisenhower had requested his presence to sign the famous agreement on cooperation between the Allied forces and the French administration. Better late than never, was de Gaulle's thought.

On his way to the Hôtel de Ville, de Gaulle called at the Prefecture of Police to review the police, on whom he would have to depend for the maintenance of public order in the dangerously exalted atmosphere that prevailed in the capital. Then, accompanied by Parodi, Le Trocquer, Juin and Luizet, he made his way through the dense and enthusiastic crowd to the Hôtel de Ville.

There to greet him, at the foot of the steps, were three leaders of the Resistance: Georges Bidault (another future premier); Marcel Flouret, the Gaullist prefect of the Seine department, whose recent nomination had been fiercely resisted by the Communists, who had tried in vain to smear him as a Pétainist and a German spy; and the Communist André Tollet. With cheers in his ears and tears in the eyes of Resistance fighters, de Gaulle was led to the salon, where the members of the CNR and of the Liberation Committee were assembled. It was a dramatic and complex encounter. The drama was self-evident: the leaders of the internal Resistance were face to face, many of them for the first time, with the man who had inspired and led the Resistance from outside

16 Rob. Aron, *Libération*, p. 440; see also pp. 377–9.

France. The complexity was inherent in the conflicting motives and ambitions of those present.

Marrane, a Communist deputising for Tollet, made a warm speech, and Bidault, the historian, a learned one. De Gaulle then responded with an improvised oration, of which several versions exist. In his memoirs, de Gaulle emphasises the sentimental side of the gathering and glosses over the tensions. He does, however, mention that his speech included a call for unity, and the full text reproduced in the appendices quotes the pregnant sentence: "The nation would not admit that, in the situation in which she finds herself, this unity should be broken."

This sentence, and the whole of the passage that follows it, is deleted from the officially approved *Discours et Messages* published in 1970. The fact is worth mentioning, for the version quoted by Robert Aron in his painstaking reconstruction of events not only includes the passage mentioned, but several more sentences that do not appear in either the memoirs or the *Discours et Messages*. If this version is accepted, then it is clear that on that day of liberation, de Gaulle, instead of thanking the Resistance and praising it, as its leaders had expected, rebuked them and warned them. For de Gaulle's further words were:

> . . . the French people has decided, by instinct and by reason, to satisfy two conditions without which nothing great can be done, which are order and ardour. A Republican order, under *the only valid authority, that of the State*; the concentrated ardour that will allow the legal and fraternal building of the edifice of renewal. That is the meaning of the manly acclamations of our towns and villages, purged at last of the enemy. That is what the great voice of liberated Paris is saying.[17]

Aron argues that de Gaulle's words passed over the heads of his audience, who were carried away with the emotions of the occasion, but this seems unlikely. Bidault next appealed to the general to appear on the balcony and proclaim the Republic before the people of Paris. The general had no objection to receiving the acclamations of the people of Paris. But he refused utterly to proclaim the Republic, for to do so would be to recognise the Vichy interlude by inference; and also, the authority of the CNR, whereas the only authority was his own. In his most cutting tone, he snapped at Bidault, "No. The Republic has never ceased to exist."

He then stepped over the iron barrier of one of the windows, to the

17 My italics. cf. de Gaulle, *L'Unité*, pp. 709–10; Rob. Aron, *Libération*, p. 442; de Gaulle, *Discours*, Vol. I, pp. 439–40.

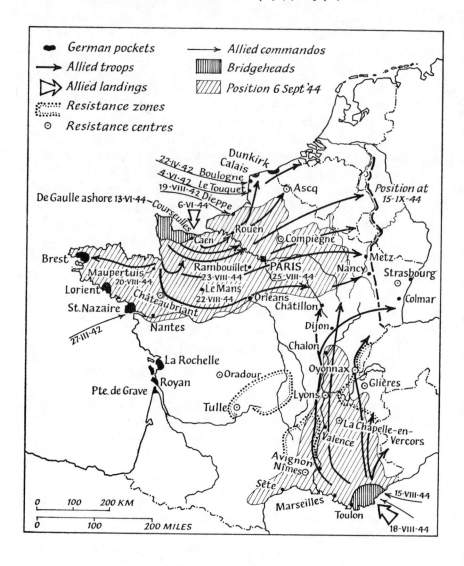

The Liberation of France 1944

apprehension of those who watched him and feared he might slip, and opened his arms in the famous and characteristic greeting of General de Gaulle, to the wild clamour of the people below.

Having climbed back into the offices, the general left without waiting for the members of the CNR to be introduced to him.

De Gaulle had carefully planned his apotheosis on Saturday, 26 August. Regardless of security, protocol and custom, he was going to walk most of the distance from the Arc de Triomphe to Notre Dame Cathedral in the Ile de la Cité. He was aware of the personal risks, which he matched against his need for popular acclaim. He had instructed Leclerc, however, to detach certain units from the 2nd Armoured Division and post them at strategic points along the route. On learning of this order, General Gerow protested in a letter to Leclerc telling him to ignore de Gaulle's instructions and return his troops to their fighting duties. A copy of the letter was brought to de Gaulle himself by an American messenger. This unamiable intervention was, of course, ignored by de Gaulle and Leclerc.

The general had not bothered to inform the CNR of his plans,[18] which did not prevent Bidault from taking what he felt to be his place next to him at the appointed hour. At three o'clock, de Gaulle arrived at the Arc de Triomphe, where he saw the Resistance leaders, including the Communists; the two ministers, Parodi and Le Trocquer; the high officers, Juin, Koenig, Leclerc and d'Argenlieu; the new prefects, Flouret and Luizet; the military delegate, Chaban-Delmas; and many lesser figures. A sea of people enveloped the Place de l'Etoile and the Champs-Elysées, and blackened the balconies and roof-tops.

Slowly and calmly, raising his long arms from time to time to acknowledge the cheers and tears of the Parisians, de Gaulle made his way to the great Gothic cathedral of medieval France, which in his eyes symbolised the history of France.

At the Rue de Rivoli, de Gaulle boarded a car for the last stage of the journey. After a brief halt at the Hôtel de Ville, de Gaulle reached the cathedral square. As soon as he alighted from his car, rifle shots rang out. The crowd panicked, many lying down on the pavements, and others jostling de Gaulle. As though nothing were happening, calm and majestic as ever, the general walked slowly into the cathedral. There, more firing occurred. Outside, it had seemed to come from the roof-tops, and the FFI on the ground, together with Leclerc's regulars, had fired

[18] Rob. Aron, *Libération*, p. 443; *see also* pp. 448–9.

in the direction, as they thought, of the original shots. In the cathedral, the shots were coming from the eaves.

Who was firing against whom? In a letter written the following day, de Gaulle blamed the incidents on the general nervous tension of the combatants. In his memoirs, written some twelve years later, he opted for another explanation: the Communists in the Resistance had aimed at provoking incidents that would justify revolutionary measures and a state of emergency from which they would hope to benefit. In fact, firing had broken out simultaneously in various parts of the city, suggesting a plot rather than mass hysteria. Attempts were made to blame the Germans and last-ditch members of the militia; but neither Germans nor militiamen were found.

The cardinal-archbishop of Paris, Mgr Suhard, was not in his cathedral to greet de Gaulle. This had been his wish, but he had incurred the anger of the Resistance by solemnly receiving Pétain as chief of State and officiating at the funeral of the Vichy Propaganda minister, Philippe Henriot, and the Resistance requested him to stay away. De Gaulle, who would have liked him to be there both as a symbol of national unity and because he respected the Church's traditional recognition of existing power, consented to his absence to avoid unpleasant incidents. But he sent his personal regrets to the cardinal and undertook to see him before long.

Although the absence of electric current had silenced the great organ, a superb *Magnificat* was sung. As the firing continued, however, de Gaulle cut the service short.

That night, the Germans raided Paris, hitting the Halle aux Vins, destroying 500 houses and causing 1,000 casualties. All Sunday, 27 August, the 2nd Armoured Division was locked in fierce fighting on the outskirts of Paris. The 28th brought excellent news. The last Germans were being driven out of the capital. The 1st Army, having taken Toulon and Marseilles, were driving towards Lyon. General Patch's forces had reached Grenoble. Bourgès-Maunoury, military delegate in the south-east, sent word that the *maquisards* were now in full control in the Alps, and in the Ain, Drôme, Ardèche, Cantal and Puy-de-Dôme departments.

From de Gaulle's point of view, the iron was hot and he proposed to strike. There could be no central authority but his, and the Resistance must be made aware of it. That morning of the 28th, he decided to have a showdown. First, the twenty principal leaders of the Parisian partisans were summoned to de Gaulle's office. After congratulating them, he announced that their forces were to be incorporated into the regular army. Next came the secretaries-general who, being appointees

ot the provisional government, merely wished to be given his instructions. Lastly, the Central Council of the Resistance were brought before
the general.

This was the moment. Not all the members of the council were
rebellious. But some, de Gaulle knew, were planning to transform the
CNR into a permanent authority, in effect, a parallel government, while
"patriotic" militias, carefully selected from among the fighters of the
Resistance, would impose a revolutionary order of their own. The CNR
had drawn up its own legislative programme, intended to guide the
government. All this was intolerable.

After the expected congratulations, de Gaulle informed the council
of its fate. Now that Paris was liberated, he said, the CNR belonged
to history and had lost its *raison d'être*: it was to be dissolved and
absorbed into the Provisional Assembly, which would be brought over
from Algiers and would thereby be enlarged. Any governing would be
done by the government. The FFI would be absorbed in the national
army; henceforth, they would be responsible to the War Ministry; and
the Action Committee – COMAC – would disappear. Public order would
be maintained by the police and *gendarmerie,* with help if necessary
from the regular forces. There was no need for any militias, which would
be dissolved forthwith. General Koenig, now appointed military governor
of Paris, would supervise the incorporation of the irregulars into the army.

Some members of the council heard of these harsh dispositions with
resignation, while others protested vehemently. De Gaulle had not,
however, summoned the Resistance Council to start an argument, and
cut the protesters short by declaring the audience closed.

De Gaulle had hoped by this show of decisiveness and authority to
nip the incipient revolution in the bud. But he was more apprehensive
than his demeanour had disclosed, or even than he was later to admit
in his memoirs.

There was indeed much to be apprehensive about. It was not only
Paris that was threatened by revolutionary ferment: a number of provincial cities were more or less cut off from the capital and its authority.
Such were Bordeaux, Toulouse, Limoges and Montpellier. The Gaullist
authorities had not yet worked themselves in; the local commissioners
of the Republic found their authority flouted by the local leader of the
Communist-controlled FTP; summary tribunals were being set up and
collaborators or "class enemies" were being tortured and executed.[19]

When Eisenhower called on de Gaulle later that day, de Gaulle informed him that for reasons of public order he proposed to keep the

[19] ibid. pp. 575–6.

Leclerc division at his disposal for a few days longer. This is as far as his account goes, in the memoirs. But Eisenhower, with less reason for reticence, was to disclose that de Gaulle had urgently requested the temporary loan of two American divisions, with which to make a show of force.[20] The supreme commander, though he understood de Gaulle's problem, could not spare two divisions, however. As a compromise, it was agreed that the following day two of the American divisions on their way to the front would take part in a march-past on the Champs-Elysées, in the presence of General Bradley and de Gaulle. This, it was hoped, would have the effect of a show of force, while not weakening the Allied war effort.

Three months later, de Gaulle was to confide in Colonel Passy: "The Communists had grabbed all the sources of production. I couldn't smash them, for to do that I should have had to bring back from the front several of our five divisions. But it was indispensable to keep them at the front so that France could take her place with honour among the victors."[21]

On leaving him, Eisenhower, in whose ears de Gaulle's words of confidence and esteem were still ringing, issued an announcement to the effect that the Allied military command, in accordance with the agreements previously concluded, had transferred to the French administration the powers it had exercised in France. How, de Gaulle asked, could the Allies transfer what they had never had or exercised? He answered his own question by reference to the self-respect of the president, especially as the election campaign had begun in the United States.[22]

And now came a triumph of another kind. A message from Pétain reached de Gaulle. Strictly speaking, the message was from a former Vichy minister, Admiral Auphan, and was conveyed by General Juin. Before being taken into custody by the Germans, Pétain had sent a secret document, dated 11 August 1944, to the admiral, authorising him to make contact on his behalf with General de Gaulle, to reconcile "all Frenchmen of good faith". But he added a rider: "So long as the principle of legitimacy which I incarnate is safeguarded."

What a reversal of roles this was! The marshal of France, once de Gaulle's chief, now wished to reach an understanding with the man whose condemnation to death he had approved. Once again, de Gaulle faced a choice between sentiment and reasons of State. Once again, he did not hesitate. There would be no reply.

[20] Eisenhower, *Crusade*, p. 326. "... there seemed," wrote Eisenhower, "a touch of the sardonic in the picture of France's symbol of liberation having to ask for Allied forces to establish a similar position in the heart of the freed capital."
[21] Rob. Aron, *Libération*, p. 575.   [22] De Gaulle, *L'Unité*, p. 319.

It was not, he felt, the old man who had allowed foreign invaders to usurp the government of France, who could claim legitimacy. One man only incarnated legitimacy: the man who had refused to acknowledge defeat and had led the nation back to self-respect. That man was General de Gaulle.

Chapter 3 ❧ Trial of Strength

De Gaulle had imposed his authority on liberated Paris, overcoming the pre-emptive bids of the Communist Resistance; but only just. It remained for him to carry his rule to the furthest parts of France, and this was to prove even more arduous.

France was starving and shabby, cruel and anarchic. The destruction was vast, and nowhere more than in communications. This not only hampered economic recovery: it made government from the centre almost impossible, encouraged disorder and facilitated local bids for autonomy. Of the French Railways' pre-war stable of 12,000 locomotives, only 2,800 were left. Three thousand bridges had been blown up. It was impossible to travel by rail from Paris to Lyon, Marseilles, Toulouse, Bordeaux, Nantes, Lille or Nancy. Nine-tenths of the country's three million motor vehicles had been destroyed, and an acute shortage of petrol made travel in those that remained hazardous. The shops were empty and the factories idle.[1]

Economically, the country was moribund. Psychologically, it was dazed yet euphoric, eager for rebirth. Within weeks of the landings, virtually the whole of France had been liberated. The shock of freedom from German oppression after four years of occupation was heady. Many equated liberation with peace, but the war went on, and French soldiers were fighting still, though further every day from the capital of France.

For most French men and women, liberation meant the right to speak their minds and meet as they pleased without having to account for their actions to the occupying power or its French collaborators, and without fear of the physical consequences. For a smaller number, it

[1] Charles de Gaulle, *Mémoires de Guerre: Le Salut, 1944–6* (henceforth, de Gaulle, *Salut*), pp. 1 and 2.

meant the right, or at any rate the chance, to pay off old scores with informers and torturers, or even with personal enemies not involved in the politics of the occupation. During the last months of the German presence, and especially in the weeks and months following the Normandy and Midi landings, the pent-up hostility between collaborators and resisters turned into a civil war; although it has never been formally given that name.

In June 1944 the illegal tribunals of the *maquisards* began their work, which continued even after the establishment on 13 September of special tribunals which substituted the official purge for the summary "justice" of the Resistance.[2] Throughout France, and especially in the south, kangaroo courts had been condemning thousands to death without benefit of trial, sentence being carried out immediately. Many private murders, more or less disguised as political reprisals, completed the horrific picture.

How many people were put to death in this time of violence, which stretched on in attenuated form until early in 1945? As with Spain during and after the Civil War, the evidence is not easy to come by. Robert Aron, the meticulous historian of this most sordid period of recent French history, puts the figure of executions or private killings at 40,000, while ten times that number[3] – he states – were arrested without proper trial.[4] Many of the executions took place in public before excited and sometimes inebriated audiences; a large number were preceded by tortures. Women who had been, or were thought to have been, the mistresses of Germans or of militiamen, were treated with special brutality: they were shaved, on the head and pubis, beaten, burned with cigarette lighters, or had their nipples cut off before being raped.

[2] ibid. pp. 37–8.
[3] Robert Aron, *Histoire de l'Epuration*, Vol. I, pp. 474 *et seq.* (henceforth, Rob. Aron, *Epuration*).
[4] ibid. p. 433. Elsewhere (in the earlier *Libération*, p. 655) the same author gives the total of executions as between 30,000 and 40,000; but more credence must be given to the higher figure, to which he inclined after more detailed researches. It is worth noting that he rejects the total of 9,675 summary executions given by the premier and minister of the Interior, Henri Queuille, on 19 July 1951, in reply to a written parliamentary question by Maître Isorni. Gorce (p. 341) uncritically accepts this official figure, although he gives Robert Aron as one of his sources, and does not even raise the possibility that it may have been higher. Robert Aron, incidentally, also rejects a much larger figure – 105,000 – which he attributes to Adrien Tixier, minister of the Interior, in a conversation in February 1945 with Colonel Passy. De Gaulle himself (*Salut*, p. 38) gives another set of figures: 10,842 executions without trial, including 6,675 before the liberation; and 779 after due process of law. He then wraps the problem up in a sentimental passage about mother France nursing and mourning her dead children. On p. 108, however, he gives another figure – 768 – for officially sanctioned executions. But the evidence painstakingly collected and presented in Aron's *Epuration*, Vol. I, seems unlikely to be controverted.

Attempts have been made to put the blame for the atrocities of the liberation exclusively on the Communists. True, from his Moscow refuge, Maurice Thorez had called on "the people of France" on 10 August to show "no quarter for the vile auxiliaries of the Hitlerite executioners, for all those criminals who have on their hands the blood of patriots."[5] But the record shows that many French Communists did not await this dispensation from above to start killing; nor were the summary executions committed only by Communists. Thorez sanctioned, and indeed called for, civil war. But the settlement of accounts had already started, and would have taken place without his encouragement.

This was the reality of liberated France that confronted de Gaulle at the end of August 1944. Nor can he himself be entirely exempted from blame for the unofficial civil war. In his eyes, those who had sided with Vichy had, in effect, ceased to be Frenchmen. This Manichaean approach was widely applauded by the Frenchmen who had been persecuted by Vichy. By sanctioning the execution of Pucheu, for "reasons of State" and while France was still occupied, the general had set an example which thousands of maquisards, lacking his concern for legitimacy, were to imitate on private account. But this, to him, was intolerable. There could only be one authority: that of the State, which he represented. Only the State could issue currency, make laws and carry them out. And the State's monopoly of the death penalty must be restored and preserved.

In mid-September he set out on a tour of inspection of the provinces. Events had been moving swiftly. On 31 August the provisional government had been transferred from Algiers to Paris, but not all its ministers arrived that day: some had lingered in the south, inspecting the French 1st Army, and one – Massigli – had gone to London to facilitate the foreign contacts of liberated France.[6] De Gaulle wanted to keep as many of his Algiers ministers as possible, but knew the time had come to include members of the internal Resistance. Within a fortnight, all the men of Algiers had arrived in Paris, and de Gaulle had been able to consult them and sound out the new men. On 9 September he announced his government.

It was a reasonably satisfactory blend of the tendencies that supported General de Gaulle, whether through blind fidelity, as in the case of the original followers, or because they really had no choice, as with the Communists. There were now to be two ministers of State. Jules Jean-

[5] Thorez's call was printed thirteen days later, in L'Humanité (Rob. Aron, Epuration, Vol. I, p. 481).
[6] De Gaulle, Salut, p. 4.

neney, who had been president of the Senate under the Third Republic, was one. He was given the difficult job of supervising the transition from the emergency and provisional to the normal and permanent administration of the Republic. General Catroux, the other, was to continue in charge of Muslim affairs and the government-general of Algeria. Those remaining in their former posts were Diethelm (War), Jacquinot (Navy), Pleven (Colonies), Mayer (Transport and Public Works), Capitant (Education), Giacobbi (Food) and Frénay (Prisoners, Deportees and Refugees).

The newcomers fell into two categories: those who had been in Algiers or London but in different jobs, and the men of the Interior who had not yet held ministerial office. The most interesting of the former group was Pierre Mendès France, who had been handling finance at Algiers and who was now made minister of the National Economy – a job from which his uncompromising advocacy of austerity soon led to his withdrawal. Two others in that group were Adrien Tixier (Interior) and the Communist François Billoux (Public Health). The men of the internal Resistance were headed, at least symbolically, by Georges Bidault, who had been president of the CNR, and who now became foreign minister – a post in which de Gaulle was unlikely to allow him much initiative. The other "resisters" were: Aimé Lepercq (Finance), Robert Lacoste (Production), François Tanguy-Prigent (Agriculture), Alexandre Parodi (Labour), Augustin Laurent (Postal Services), Pierre-Henri Teitgen (Information) and Charles Tillon. The last-named, who was the other Communist in de Gaulle's new government, took over as Air minister from his fellow party member, Fernand Grenier – the man who had clashed with de Gaulle over the party line on the Vercors defenders.

Seven others among the National commissioners in Algiers also left the government. Two wanted to go into politics: Henri Queuille, who would later become premier; and Emmanuel d'Astier, whom de Gaulle had wanted to send to Washington as ambassador[7] but who, to de Gaulle's distaste, had expressed his preference for the parliamentary game. In his stead, de Gaulle appointed Henri Bonnet to the Washington embassy, the status of which had been given de facto, though not yet de jure recognition by the American administration. Massigli was sent to London as ambassador, in succession to Pierre Viénot, who had died in July. André Le Trocquer became president of the Paris Municipal Council; and Jean Monnet resumed his post as head of the economic mission in the United States, a function that was incompatible with the holding of a ministerial portfolio.

[7] Gorce, p. 349.

Having announced his new government, de Gaulle wanted to explain his policies before starting off on his tour of the provinces, which he knew would be a crucial and difficult stage in his fight to re-establish the central authority of the State. On 12 September, then, before an invited audience of 8,000 at the Palais de Chaillot, de Gaulle rose to speak. Those present amounted, between them, to a representative assembly selected on corporative principles. The Council of the Resistance was represented, and so were the directing committees of the movements and networks, the Municipal Council, the Civil Service, the University of Paris, industry and commerce, the trade unions, the press, the bar and other professional groups. Unlike the docile mass audiences he had addressed in London, and even the Provisional Assembly in Algiers, this cross-section of the groups that would be running France was not a crowd whose support de Gaulle could take for granted. And he sensed as much – despite the thunderous applause that greeted him initially – in the glances exchanged, in the "tonality" of the enthusiasm and in the volume of the clapping, which was not uncritically uniform but varied according to what he was saying.

Although he had sprinkled his speech with patriotic phrases and appeals, and with praises for France's allies, this was no empty oration. For de Gaulle had a precise message to put over:

Despite the defeat of 1940, France claimed, by virtue of the fact that she had never ceased to be in the war (the fundamental Gaullist claim) and was playing an increasingly important part in it, the right to an equal say in the future of Germany and in any peace settlement.

It was not enough for France to regain her rank: she must now keep it. And this could be done only if national unity was maintained under its government.

As soon as the entire national territory was liberated, and all prisoners and deportees had returned, the nation would be called upon to elect, by universal suffrage including women, its future sovereign National Assembly.

Until then, the government would carry on, with the help of an enlarged Consultative Assembly, of which the Resistance would naturally form the core.

The laws of the Republic would continue in force until the election of the new Assembly (in other words, the laws of Vichy were null and void).

The war was not over yet. To fight it, large units were needed, and the manpower for them would come from the forces of the Interior. A new division was being formed in Brittany, and another would be formed in the Paris region.

Reconstruction was on the way, but losses in materials and production had been heavy, and recovery was bound to be slow. While freedom and enterprise would be preserved, private interests would have to yield to the general interest. The great sources of wealth would be exploited for the common good and not for the advantage of vested interests. There should be security and dignity for all. Those who had enriched themselves by working for the enemy would be compelled to make restitution.

Essentially, this was the message de Gaulle had agreed with Pineau, the Socialist representative of the Resistance, in June 1942, plus the adaptations which the new situation called for. Its Socialist content was unmistakable. By foreshadowing, in effect, a welfare State, de Gaulle was being true to himself in the sense that, as always except in 1940, he was identifying himself with the national mood. But as it happened, and as he was aware, no other policy was politically possible at the time, since the Vichy regime was identified with "big business" and the Resistance with the parties of the left. Paradoxically, however, the representatives of big business in the Palais de Chaillot that day were not averse from the notion that the State should take on the major burdens of reconstruction, since their own depleted resources would scarcely have sufficed. Moreover, his promise of freedom for enterprise was reassuring. Indeed, the most hostile among the listeners were probably the Communists and left-wing Socialists. For de Gaulle was serving notice on them that he would not tolerate a class war; that the "patriotic militias", which the Communist-led Resistance regarded as the spearhead of the revolution, were to be absorbed into the armed forces; and that the existing government would resist any challenge to its authority until the sovereign people had chosen its representatives by free elections. If there was to be a revolution, it would be made from above, under his leadership, not from below through insurrection.

Beyond his audience, too, de Gaulle was publicly staking France's claim to a seat in the councils of the mighty; but the great Powers were no more disposed to listen to him now that he was the visible head of the French government than they had been when he was merely the exiled leader of a patriotic rump.

Two days later, while the battle of the Rhine was starting, de Gaulle repeated his message, in condensed form, in a national broadcast. Now he was ready to face the provincial dissidents.

Having failed to gain control of Paris, the Communists were making a more effective bid for power elsewhere. The government had decreed that a single Liberation Committee, representing all the elements of the Resistance, should be formed in each department, to assist the prefect appointed from Paris. Instead, the party had set up numerous unofficial committees of its own which put pressure on local mayors, and conducted its own witch-hunts with selected murders, to make people understand who was likely to be boss.[8]

In seeking out the enemy – for this was what his journey amounted to – de Gaulle knew that he had one asset which nobody else could match: overwhelming personal popularity and prestige. He had neither a political organisation nor an underground network he could call his own. In Algiers, when he had arrived to challenge Giraud and the "Anglo-Saxons", the Gaullist "*mafia*" had paved the way. Now, the men he had appointed stood alone with events out of their control. He needed to stiffen their backbone and bolster their authority, transferring to these lesser men something of the power he hoped to derive from the acclamations of the crowd.

Broadly speaking, this simple plan worked. Between 14 September and 6 November, General de Gaulle made no fewer than six extended provincial trips, returning to Paris between times. By the end of November, he knew his authority was respected through most of France, even though the illegal executions were to continue a few weeks longer.

The first of de Gaulle's absences from Paris was the toughest: it took him to Lyon, Marseilles, Toulon, Toulouse, Bordeaux, Saintes (near La Rochelle) and Orleans. As a northerner, with his outer coldness and his austerity, de Gaulle was always out of his element in southern cities, with their noisy exuberance and natural disorder. It was true of Algiers, and equally of Marseilles, Toulon and Toulouse. But incompatibility of temperament was only one of the things that made him irritable. Others were the pretensions of the freshly promoted Resistance officers, the parallel administrations set up by the Communists (especially in Toulouse) and the presence of British agents who behaved as though SOE were in control of France. Compassion for the local inhabitants in their material sufferings hardly mitigated his ill-temper, for, as he knew, it was only by hard work, in conditions of order, that recovery could begin. Revolutionary plots, general unruliness and sloppiness, and southern volubility were so many obstacles to be overcome.

Until he reached the Loire, therefore, de Gaulle was in an execrable

[8] De Gaulle, *Salut*, pp. 9 *et seq.* For a full account of the Communist conspiracy at this time, *see* Rob. Aron, *Libération*, Part V, ch. 4.

mood, with cutting remarks ready at the slighest provocation. At Toulouse, for instance, a young *maquis* leader introduced himself as "Colonel Ravanel".

"No," snapped de Gaulle, who had done his homework on Resistance *noms de guerre*, "Lieutenant Asher."

On another occasion, after inspecting a row of colonels whose insignia had obviously only just been sewn on their tunics, he sighted a young subaltern and asked in a loud voice, "You, over there, don't you know how to sew?"[9]

Devastation and misery reigned almost everywhere. In Lyon, all but two of the bridges across the Rhône were destroyed, the stations were out of action, and factories reduced to ruins. In Marseilles, where the Germans had razed the Old Port, Allied bombardments and the battle for the city had laid whole quarters to waste. There, de Gaulle found "an anonymous dictatorship" set up by the Communists. He gave orders to send such Resistance units as wished to fight to the Alsace front, and the others, whose revolutionary desires were apparent, to be dissolved.

But Toulouse, which de Gaulle reached on the 16th, was the most threatened by insurrectionary turbulence. Ravanel, the young man whom he had rebuked, had set up what amounted to a Soviet, partly controlling both the city and the surrounding countryside. Nor was the Resistance the only irritant to de Gaulle. A Spanish Republican division was being formed, with the aim of marching on Barcelona. And a senior British army officer originally sent to join the *maquis* of the Gers region was giving himself airs. To complete the show, there was a battalion of Russians who had deserted General Vlassov's army, having decided that they did not wish to fight with the Nazis.

In the general effervescence, de Gaulle's commissioner, Pierre Bertaux, exercised a minimal authority. Greeting the general on his arrival at Toulouse airport, Bertaux found him in his blackest mood, which his account of the local situation did nothing to improve. When Bertaux mentioned the British officer, de Gaulle exploded: "Didn't you have him arrested?"

"No," murmured Bertaux. "He had 700 armed men with him."

"I hope at least you haven't invited him to lunch with me."

"Yes, of course. He fought with the *maquis* for nearly two years, invoking your name."

"Well, you will tell him that I don't want to take a meal with him."

[9] This story, though in character with mood and occasion, is possibly apocryphal. Lacouture, who tells it (p. 130), says the incident took place in Montpellier, which was not on the general's itinerary, although the Communist threat was worse there than anywhere else except Toulouse and Limoges.

A stormy interview ensued. As the British officer, red with anger, left the general's temporary office, de Gaulle snapped at Bertaux: "You will give him twenty-four hours to get out of French territory. If he stays on, have him arrested." He left.[10]

As for the armed men, de Gaulle inspected them *en masse* – the Resistance units, the Russians and the Spaniards. He thanked them, one and all, but told the Spaniards that he could not allow them to cross the Pyrenees. Then he took practical measures to ensure Gaullist order. The gendarmes, having been laid off, were sent back to their duties; General Collet, who had been brought over from Morocco, was placed in command of the military region, and a detachment of the 1st Army was sent to Tarbes and Perpignan to make sure the Spaniards did not try to transgress the frontier.

After a formal lunch at the Prefecture, Bertaux asked de Gaulle what were his plans for the future. Gravely, almost in the form of a soliloquy, the general replied, "I shall be retiring. I have a mission and it's drawing to a close. I must go. Some day, France may yet need a pure image. . . . If Joan of Arc were married, she wouldn't be Joan of Arc. I must go."

At Bordeaux, next day, de Gaulle found an apprehensive population, for the Germans were not far away and it was feared they might return any moment. A number of armed Resistance groups were refusing to obey the orders of the local authorities. After inspecting them, de Gaulle summoned their chiefs and gave them a straight choice between obeying the orders of the local military commander or going to gaol. They chose obedience.

In the more orderly cities further north, de Gaulle found himself in a better temper. Back in Paris on the 18th, he left again on the 25th, for Lorraine (where the natural hostility towards the Germans had avoided any political problems). In his native town of Lille, on the 30th, de Gaulle, moved by the sight of the pallid and emaciated faces of the crowd, found himself more than ever convinced that the liberation of the country must be "accompanied by a profound social transformation".[11] Visits to Normandy, Champagne and the Alps followed. Over the past few weeks, he had been seen, on his own estimate, by ten million Frenchmen, and drawn strength from the fervour of their welcome.

By the end of November, it was clear that de Gaulle had won his trial of strength with the Communists. But it would be too simple to suppose that the force of his charisma alone – great though it was –

[10] Rob. Aron, *Libération*, pp. 605–6.   [11] De Gaulle, *Salut*, p. 18.

had brought him victory. The fact is that the Communists, though organised for insurrection and bubbling over with the urge to launch it, failed to act. The explanation must be sought both in the internal politics of the French Communist party and in the higher policies of Stalin; and the story needs to be followed through to the time of de Gaulle's visit to Moscow at the end of 1944.

The party leadership – through COMAC[12] – had placed its men in key positions in the FFI, with insurrectionary intent. It had tolerated, or positively approved, local excesses and atrocities. But it never gave the order to seize power.[13] Two factions were at variance within the party's Politburo. The militants, led by Lecoeur and Tillon, knowing they could count on their troops at the time of the liberation, wanted to take advantage of the temporary breakdown of law and order to seize power. The Moscow faction, led by Duclos and Frachon, would not give the orders unless the word came from Moscow. But the word never came. The Communist leaders in the Resistance – Lecoeur and Tillon – had probably decided to seize power in Paris, but were circumvented by de Gaulle's arrival. Almost certainly, they had decided, without waiting for Moscow's orders, to proclaim a Soviet republic in southern France: orders to that effect were discovered by non-Communist Resistance leaders in the Dordogne area. But the FTP forces, though dominated by the Communists, escaped their total control. Many members of the FTP were not Communists and would not have obeyed orders to seize power. Even within the FTP, therefore, revolutionary unity could not be assumed.

The key, however, was in Moscow. Stalin's ambitions, as his armies rolled westwards, were vast but finite. He wanted the whole of eastern Europe, and felt confident that he could gain his ends in agreement with Roosevelt, with Churchill's reluctant assent. But he had no wish to spoil his grand design by allowing a revolution (which might fail) to be launched in France.

Although his motives in visiting Stalin were several, one of them was undoubtedly to persuade the Soviet dictator to "lay off" France. He took a calculated risk, on the eve of his departure for Moscow on 24 November 1944, by granting Thorez a free pardon for his desertion five years earlier. This enabled the Communist leader, who had personally petitioned him several times, to return to France.[14] De Gaulle's aims were doubtless to gain favour with Stalin as well as to mollify the Communists. Events proved the risk to have been justified.

[12] See above, p. 255.   [13] Rob. Aron, Libération, pp. 633 et seq.
[14] De Gaulle, Salut, p. 100.

At this time, the Communists were intensifying their recruiting campaign for the "patriotic militias", in defiance of government directives. This was to be the instrument of revolution. Even the Moscow faction was not against this recruitment, for even if the order to act did not come, the "Muscovites" thought the militias would be a useful bargaining counter in the coming struggle for political power. On 27 October, Duclos himself had publicly declared himself in favour of the militias. Next day, de Gaulle formally barred them, to a chorus of protests from the Resistance and bomb outrages that claimed many victims.[15] On 27 November – three days after de Gaulle's departure – Thorez was back in Paris. On the 30th, addressing a mass meeting at the Vélodrome d'Hiver, he gave orders that were simultaneously patriotic and subversive: "Make War" (on whom – the Germans or the French?); "Create a powerful French army" (to fight whom?); "Rapidly reconstruct industry" (in whose service?); "Unite" (with whom?). The ambiguity was intentional: de Gaulle was about to arrive in Moscow; Stalin had not made his intentions known; Thorez did not know how far he could go.

On 21 January, however – five weeks after de Gaulle's return to Paris, that is, after a reasonable delay for decisions to be taken in Moscow and transmitted to the French Politburo – the central committee of the French party met at Ivry and heard Thorez declare his opposition to the maintenance of the patriotic militias.[16] "These armed groups," he declared, "had their *raison d'être* before and during the insurrection against the Hitlerite occupier and his Vichyist accomplices. But now the situation is different. Public security must be ensured by the regular police forces constituted to that end. The civic guards, and, in a general way, *all* irregular armed groups must no longer be kept in being."[17]

What had happened between de Gaulle and Stalin to explain this about-turn? Beyond confirming that the subject of Thorez did come up in his Moscow discussions, de Gaulle has nothing to say about it in his memoirs. According to de Gaulle, it was Stalin who brought up the French Communist's name. De Gaulle stayed silent, with an air of disapproval on his face, and Stalin exclaimed, "Don't be angry over my indiscretion! Just allow me to say that I know Thorez and that, in my opinion, he is a good Frenchman. If I were in your place, I wouldn't put him in prison." And he added, with a smile, "At least, not straightaway!"

[15] ibid. pp. 39–40.   [16] Rob. Aron, *Libération*, p. 637.
[17] My italics.

De Gaulle's disdainful answer was: "The French government treats Frenchmen according to the services which it expects from them."[18]

It seems unlikely that de Gaulle actually made a "deal" with Stalin over Thorez. This would have been out of character. But he knew Stalin wanted Thorez to go back to Paris; and it has since become clear that Stalin did not want a revolution in France. Hence his interest in having Thorez – who had not fought in the Resistance – resume control over the French Communist party, which, during the war, had developed tendencies that were (from Moscow's viewpoint) dangerously anarchic. Besides, de Gaulle's reply, though disdainful, contained a hint that if Thorez behaved himself there was a job waiting for him; as there was.

A last factor in the explanation of the Communist failure to launch an insurrection is in Thorez's own psychology. Not having fought in the Resistance, having in fact spent a rather inglorious war in Moscow, he had every incentive to destroy the power which the Communist leaders of the Resistance had acquired during his long absence. Stalin's policy therefore happened to coincide with his own self-interest. These factors played at least as great a part as de Gaulle's courage and prestige in sparing France a Communist revolution.

Henceforth, while the Communists' invective continued, de Gaulle was relieved of the fear of a revolution; indeed, there was not even a strike for the remainder of his period of power. And although the Communists made life difficult for him in parliamentary terms, they refrained from personal abuse and cheered him with the rest when he appeared in public.[19]

---

[18] De Gaulle, Salut, p. 63. De Gaulle may have expurgated his own account. According to another version, what Stalin said was: "Be nice, wait a little before having him shot." (Rob. Aron, Libération, p. 635.) Robert Aron describes this account as probably apocryphal, but it is more in line with Stalin's character than de Gaulle's reporting.
[19] De Gaulle, Salut, p. 100.

Chapter 4 ⚜ Foreign Disappointments

De Gaulle's international humiliations did not end with his achievement of power and popular acclaim in Paris. Recognition of his government by America and Britain did not come until towards the end of October 1944 – two months after his Parisian triumph. The French were kept out of the Allied discussions on the future of Europe and the creation of the United Nations; they were unrepresented at the summit conferences at Yalta and Potsdam. The general's one apparent success in foreign affairs – the signing of a treaty with Stalin – was shown up in its hollowness when Stalin resisted Churchill's plea that France should be awarded an occupation zone in Germany. The Prime Minister's stand prevailed; but relations between France and Britain continued sourly, especially in the Levant, and it was irritating to de Gaulle that France's "rights" in Germany should have been secured by the much envied ally of the first hour and not by the new ally in the east he had so assiduously wooed.

Not all the snubs administered by France's allies could be imputed to de Gaulle's presence at the head of affairs. Indeed, in all that concerned the future of Germany and Europe as a whole, it was de Gaulle's misfortune as well as his peculiar glory that he happened to be the Prime Minister of a nation lately defeated, whose contribution to the common cause had been marginal and remained minor as the Allied forces closed on Hitler's Reich. Under any other head of government, France might have been completely ignored during this period, instead of merely relegated to a position of inferiority and grudgingly given the things de Gaulle felt were his by right.

If this thought occurred to de Gaulle, he kept it to himself. With his usual sense of realism, he was aware that in the long run no European settlement that left France's views out of account could be valid. Geography would see to that: soon the French armies would be on the Rhine and the Danube, and at the war's end "America would find herself in her hemisphere and England on her island".[1] It was therefore only

[1] De Gaulle, *Salut*, p. 48; for further matter, *see* pp. 45–57.

a matter of holding firm; a habit for which de Gaulle had given himself much training.

As far as recognition was concerned, similar considerations applied, but only to a degree. Had there been no French provisional government at the time of liberation, then the question of recognition would not even have arisen: General Eisenhower would have exercised in fact the powers "conferred" upon him by Roosevelt, which had turned out to be irrelevant because of the speed with which de Gaulle's administration had asserted its authority. But personalities undoubtedly played a part in the delay. A provisional government headed by a less dominant, abrasive character than de Gaulle would probably have received America's recognition upon entering Paris, for all the president's democratic reservations. But the antipathy de Gaulle aroused in Roosevelt was profound, and did not diminish – quite the contrary – as the time approached when the president would be called upon to admit, by implication, his error of judgment.

On this issue, as on so many others, Churchill deferred to Roosevelt, but seems to have been only marginally more eager to advance the date of recognition. On the eve of the French entry into Paris, he was telling Eden that he strongly deprecated further commitments to the French National Committee, "whose interest in seizing the title-deeds of France is obvious", until it had been enlarged.[2]

By the end of September it was clear that the *maquis* was rallying to de Gaulle, and on the 28th, Churchill told the House of Commons that it would now seem possible to transform the Consultative Assembly into an elected body, to which the National Liberation Committee (as he still called it) would be responsible. "Such a step, once taken . . ." he said, "would render possible that recognition of the provisional government of France . . . which we all desire to bring about at the earliest moment."

A fortnight later, from Moscow, Churchill cabled Roosevelt to say that the French had found it impracticable to proceed with the original Algiers plan of elections in liberated areas. Nevertheless, progress had been made in enlarging the Assembly. There was no doubt that the provisional government had the support of the majority of the French people, and he therefore suggested that "we can now safely recognise General de Gaulle's administration as the provisional government of France".

But the president, replying six days later, could see no reason for

[2] Prime Minister to foreign secretary, 18 August 1944. Churchill, Vol. VI, p. 214; *see also* pp. 218–20.

haste. Nothing should be done, he told Churchill, until the French had set up a real " zone of interior" (as distinct from the "forward zone" under Eisenhower's authority) and until the enlargement of the Assembly had been effectively completed. Sourly, he added, "I would not be satisfied with de Gaulle merely saying that he was going to do it."

Despite this late delaying action, recognition came – rather suddenly, and to the surprise of Churchill, who was still in Moscow – only three days later, on 23 October 1944. The form it took could scarcely have been better calculated to irritate de Gaulle, for at the White House and in Downing Street it was explained ("to save face," says de Gaulle) that Eisenhower now considered it possible to "transfer his authority on French territory to the de Gaulle government". Since de Gaulle, from the start, had seen to it that Eisenhower never exercised more than a theoretical authority, except over the forces under his command, de Gaulle had little reason to be pleased. When asked, at a press conference two days later, for his impressions of the attitude of the Allies, he replied with characteristic aloofness: "The French government is satisfied that they should now be willing to call it by its name."

In practical terms, recognition meant an immediate bustle of diplomatic activity, but mostly of a purely formal kind, such as the opening or reopening of embassies and the presentation of letters of accreditation. But what de Gaulle had never ceased to hope for – an equal voice in Allied councils – was no more forthcoming after than before. Many problems of foreign policy were of concern to General de Gaulle, but none was more pressing, more vitally important, than the future of Germany. Three times in seventy years German armies had invaded France. To de Gaulle, the lessons of history were clear: when the German states were united, and therefore strong, imperialism and the will to domination had resulted. Dismemberment, then, was the logical solution. The German states, as they had been before the German empire emerged in 1871 in the wake of the Franco-Prussian war, should be given back their sovereignty under a loose federal structure. The Ruhr should have a special statute under international control; and the Saar, while retaining its German character, should be economically tied to France, so that its coal production could constitute war reparations.

While France's moral right to a voice in her powerful and aggressive neighbour's future could scarcely be contested, the facts of power excluded France from Allied deliberations. For more than a year, a European Advisory Commission, consisting of British, Soviet and American delegates but on which France was not represented, had been meeting

331

in London to consider Germany and other European problems. In September 1944, the American president and the British Prime Minister had met in Quebec to concert their policies, and nobody had thought it necessary to let de Gaulle know what had been decided. In October, Churchill and Eden had gone to Moscow to sound out Stalin; but had not kept him informed.

Recognition, however, did mean that de Gaulle could begin to act as host in his own home, and he took advantage of the new situation, on 30 October, to invite Churchill and Eden to visit Paris. "For form's sake, and without illusions" (as de Gaulle put it), Roosevelt and Cordell Hull received a similar invitation; which they declined.

As with previous Anglo-French wartime encounters, the Churchill visit to Paris was an emotional success, but yielded little of immediately practical benefit to the French side. The Prime Minister and Eden landed at Orly on 10 November. Churchill had brought his wife and their daughter Mary with him and evidently much enjoyed not only the Republican pomp of the arrangements but the fact that he was to sleep in the same bed and use the same bathroom that Field-Marshal Goering had had in the Quai d'Orsay. At a formal luncheon in the War Ministry, de Gaulle paid a moving tribute to Churchill's leadership, and Churchill told de Gaulle how impressed he had been by the obvious unanimity of the French people.

When it came to business, the British were, says de Gaulle, less forthcoming. They were prepared to provide only minimal aid to arm the French forces; nor were they disposed to persuade the Americans to do more. While recognising that France ought to have an occupation zone in Germany, they were not prepared to define it. From Churchill's lips, de Gaulle heard the British had just agreed in Moscow to Stalin's proposals for the acquisition of territory at Poland's expense, and for the division of the Balkans into two spheres of influence. The premier, he heard, had summoned three Polish ministers – Mikolajczyk, Romer and Grabski – and constrained them to make the necessary arrangements with the Moscow-protected Lublin Committee. As for the Balkans, Churchill explained the proposed spheres of influence in precise percentages: in Rumania, 90 per cent to the Russians and 10 per cent to the British; in Bulgaria, 75 per cent and 25 per cent; in Greece, 90 per cent to the British and 10 per cent to the Russians; and in Yugoslavia and Hungary, equal shares.

Describing the visit in a letter to Roosevelt a few days later, Churchill said he had pointed out that de Gaulle's request for equipment, which was intended for eight more divisions, could only be met by

America, but could not be shipped before Germany's defeat, all shipping space being earmarked for the supply of the forces now fighting. He was at pains to deny a Reuter message, "emanating no doubt unofficially from Paris", reporting agreement that France should be assigned certain areas, including the Ruhr and Rhineland, as an occupation zone. Nothing, he said, had been decided.

On the 13th, Churchill inspected the French forces, under General de Lattre, at that time preparing for battle near Besançon. De Gaulle was with him, and took the occasion to press his arguments from the eloquence of despair. Churchill had proposed a formal treaty of alliance between their two countries. What was the use of signing an ambiguous document, asked de Gaulle, unless the two powers could agree on a common policy? Britain was stronger than France but had suffered heavy losses and her position was relatively weaker than it had been, in comparison with Russia and America. But the two great powers, embarrassed by their rivalry, would be able to accomplish little. Let France and Britain together build the peace.

Churchill's reply, though conciliatory in tone, disappointed de Gaulle. Britain would not separate herself from France, he declared. But through his personal relations with Roosevelt, he could persuade him to do the right things. As for Stalin, his appetite was huge and nothing could be done at present to prevent him from assuaging it. But the time for digestion would come, and that was when the Russians would start getting into difficulties.

"As for France," Churchill added, "thanks to you, she is coming back. Don't get impatient! Already the doors are opening. Later on, they will be wide open. We shall be seeing you, quite naturally, take a seat at the boardroom table. Nothing will stop us then from operating together. Until then, leave it to me!"

To de Gaulle, these words made it quite plain that the British would be playing their own game in the world; as Roosevelt had made it plain that he would be playing his; and as the Russians would shortly be showing that they were playing theirs.

Only one concrete advantage for France had come out of Churchill's visit. He had brought de Gaulle a joint invitation from the British, the Americans and the Russians to the French to take part, on equal terms, in the work of the European Advisory Commission in London. It was an appreciable step forward. But it was not, from de Gaulle's standpoint, enough.

On 14 November, de Gaulle went back to Paris, and Churchill visited Eisenhower's headquarters at Rheims before returning to London. An exchange of written courtesies between de Gaulle and Churchill sealed their inconclusive meetings.

Immediately after Churchill's return to England, the Russians invited de Gaulle to visit Stalin in Moscow. Once again, as in the darkest days of the war, de Gaulle saw a chance to seek in Moscow what he could not find in London. He accepted, and thought it useful, before his departure, to make a public statement of France's claims in any future settlement.

It was 22 November 1944, and his forum was the Consultative Assembly, but his real audience was in the ministries and chancelleries of the world. He served notice that France would again be a diplomatic power of the first rank, claiming a seat, as of right, on the directing council of the United Nations.

To say this was to touch a raw spot, for in September and October, representatives of Britain, the United States, Russia and China – but not of France – had met at Dumbarton Oaks, California, to draw up plans for the future U.N. It had been agreed that there was to be a Security Council consisting of the countries represented at Dumbarton Oaks, and Senator Connally had made a comment de Gaulle was un- likely to forget: "That's as it should be," said the chairman of the Senate Foreign Relations Committee, "for the United States, England, Russia and China are the four nations that have shed their blood for the rest of the world, whereas France's part in the war has only been that of a small country."

Above all, that day, de Gaulle wanted the Big Three leaders of the grand alliance to understand that no settlement of the German problem would be valid, or respected, unless France was a party to it. He made an intentionally plural reference to "the German peoples"; and went on to declare France's readiness to take part in the construction of a united Europe. There followed a reference to the wrongs Italy had done to France: when these had been righted, France offered a frank reconcilia- tion and friendship to the Italians.

Never had de Gaulle felt more acutely the gap that separated him from his immediate audience – the politicians now listening to him. Their minds were on higher and more nebulous matters, such as "the coming triumph of justice and liberty through the crushing of Fascism", "the solidarity of the democracies", or "France's revolutionary mission". But they had no objection to his going to Moscow and even to his signing a pact there.

De Gaulle and his *entourage* – which included Bidault, Generals Juin and Palewski, with the Russian ambassador, Bogomolov, as guide – took off on 24 November, but did not reach Moscow until Saturday, 2

December, having stopped at Cairo, Tehran, Baku and Stalingrad on the long journey. The general's first meeting with Stalin took place on the evening of his arrival. His description of the Russian dictator is one of the literary gems of the war memoirs:

> Stalin was possessed of the will of power. Trained by a lifetime of plotting to mask his features and his soul, to dispense with illusions, with pity, with sincerity, to see in each man an obstacle or a danger, everything in him was manoeuvre, mistrust and obstinacy. The revolution, the party, the State, the war, had offered him the chances and the means of dominating. He had succeeded, using in full the twists and turns of Marxist exegesis and totalitarian rigours, bringing into play a superhuman boldness and astuteness, subjugating or liquidating others.
>
> Thereupon, alone face to face with Russia, Stalin saw her as mysterious, stronger and more durable than all theories and all regimes. He loved her in his way. She herself accepted him as a tsar for the duration of a terrible period and supported Bolshevism in order to use it as an instrument.

A long corridor lined with police led de Gaulle to Stalin's office in the Kremlin. The foreign minister, Molotov, was there to do the introductions, and "Marshal" Stalin appeared. During the fifteen scattered hours of conversation that followed, de Gaulle, seeing through his ruses and genial exterior to the overweening ambition beyond, appreciated his "sort of shadowy charm".

Whether talking or listening, Stalin doodled incessantly. Once again, to the fact of another country's power de Gaulle could oppose only the strength of his own will and personality. Stalin made it clear that any French claims, for instance in the Rhineland, the Ruhr and the Saar, could be settled only in negotiations with Russia, Britain and America. In contrast, the advancement of Russia's western boundaries at Poland's expense was already agreed, with compensation for Poland to Germany's detriment. The Oder and the Neisse would therefore constitute Germany's eastern frontier line.

"Let us together study a Franco-Russian pact," said Stalin, "so that our two countries may together guard against any new German aggression."

De Gaulle could not resist an allusion which he knew would sting Stalin and Molotov – not to the Soviet-Nazi Pact (that would have been too rudely provocative), but to the Franco-Russian alliance negotiated by Laval in 1935. The indignant Russians exclaimed that because of

335

Laval, the 1935 pact had never been applied either in the spirit or in the letter.

"I am not Pierre Laval," countered de Gaulle, who explained that he had mentioned the 1935 treaty, as he already had mentioned the 1892 alliance, to show that in the face of the German danger it was natural for France and Russia to act together.

When it came to the detailed negotiations, de Gaulle and his team soon found – with something of the shock of discovery – that the Russians play their cards close to their chests, have an infinite capacity to spin out a game, and conceal their intentions to the fifty-ninth minute of the eleventh hour. There were, of course, distractions – the ballet, a reception at the Spiridonovka Palace, lavish banquets, a meeting with the officially approved "Francophile" writers, among them Ilya Ehrenburg. But at the negotiating table, the French were being given a foretaste of the methods that were to infuriate western diplomats during the years of the cold war.

First, the procedural and formalistic objections. France, said Molotov, had a provisional government, so who would ratify the treaty and how could the Russians be sure it would be ratified? The French negotiators, Dejean and Bidault, made little headway. Then de Gaulle intervened and silenced the Russians by pointing out that they had signed a pact with Beneš, whose government also was provisional and who, moreover, lived in London.

Then came the partial disclosure of motives, the haggling, the veiled menace. For, as de Gaulle now discovered, this was to be a haggle, not the empty conferment of a scrap of paper. What, then, did the French have to offer the mighty Russians? The answer, it turned out, was Poland. What Stalin was after was French endorsement of his Polish plans, and more French support in putting pressure on the Poles to accept their fate.

It was now 6 December. Whatever influence the French might have on the Poles – "all the Poles", said de Gaulle significantly – would be exercised in the direction of an independent Poland friendly both to Russia and to France. He had little difficulty in accepting the Oder–Neisse line as the western, and the Curzon line – which Stalin had mentioned – as the eastern boundaries of Poland. But, mindful no doubt of his own commitment to elections, he declared that the future government of Poland could not be imposed in advance, but could be decided only by the Polish people in a free vote.

Now Stalin raised his voice. Russia's policy towards Poland, he declared, had taken a great turning. Always, Poland had provided a corridor for the Germans to invade Russia. The Oder–Neisse line could end all that. But the government in Warsaw would have to be "democratic".

And the dictator launched into a virulent diatribe against the Polish leaders in their London exile. They were reactionaries and responsible for the premature Warsaw rising, which they ordered irresponsibly without consulting the Russians who were not yet in a position to intervene. "Why don't you use your influence to recommend to them the necessary solution?" he exclaimed. "Why do you take up the same sterile position as America and England have adopted until now? What we expect of you, I must tell you, is that you should act with realism and in the same direction as ourselves." And he added, softly: "Especially as London and Washington have not said their last word."

Despite this outburst, de Gaulle again expressed the view that the Poles should decide on their future government through universal suffrage. He had expected a sharp rejoinder, but Stalin merely smiled and murmured: "Ah well! We'll reach an understanding anyway."

When the general asked about the Balkans, Stalin castigated the Yugoslav Chetnik leader, Mihailovich, and accused the British of harbouring him in Cairo. Bulgaria and Rumania would be punished, he said, and would have to become "democratic". The same applied to Hungary, which had made a first step by arresting the regent, Admiral Horthy.

Suddenly, then, the Russians threw an entirely unexpected card on the table. A telegram had come from Churchill. Since de Gaulle was in Moscow negotiating a treaty, said the Prime Minister, why not make it a tripartite one, between Russia, Britain and France? Stalin thought this a good idea, but it held no appeal for de Gaulle. His first objection was the habitual one: why had Churchill, in a matter that concerned France equally with Russia and Britain, consulted Stalin alone? Then again, it seemed to him that France and Russia had special reasons, which Britain did not share, for fearing German invasion. It was therefore natural that they should make bilateral arrangements. Besides, he wished at some time to formalise the *de facto* alliance between France and Britain, and did not want to do this until he had settled certain fundamental questions with London, such as the future of Germany, the Rhine and the Levant.

The talks were resumed on 8 December, in what was to be the final working session of the visit. De Gaulle repeated his views and claims on Germany, and Stalin repeated his silence. The general then once more went over his objections to the tripartite pact proposed by Churchill. And in case Stalin should think that the French would stay in Moscow until a pact was signed, he confirmed that they would be leaving Moscow as originally planned, on the morning of the 10th.

Suddenly, Stalin changed direction. "After all, you're right!" he exclaimed. "I don't see why the two of us should not draw up a pact." But Poland was a fundamental question for Russia. No understanding could be reached with the anti-Russian Poles of London. "If you share our way of thinking, recognise the Lublin Committee publicly and make an official arrangement with it. Then we'll be able to conclude a pact with you."

And Stalin went on with an argument that was curiously similar to the one de Gaulle himself had used repeatedly in his dealings with the western Allies earlier that year. He pointed out that the Russians had recognised the Polish National Liberation Committee, which was taking over the administration of Poland as the Russian armies advanced. If the French needed anything, for instance to enquire about the fate of French prisoners-of-war and deportees in Poland, they would have to turn to Lublin anyway.

"As for Churchill," he concluded, "I shall telegraph him that his plan is not acceptable. He will certainly be offended. That won't be the first time. He himself has offended me pretty often."[3]

Now de Gaulle thought everything was clear. Stalin must have put all his cards on the table. Unyielding as usual, he declared that France was ready to conclude a security pact with Russia, but while she had nothing against the Lublin Committee, she had no intention of recognising it as the government of Poland. If any questions needed attention, they could be dealt with by the appointment of a simple delegate, without diplomatic status, who could be sent to Lublin.

Had de Gaulle won? Stalin made no further comment. Instead, with apparent good grace, he declared himself delighted at the prospect of meeting the French again at dinner the following evening.

De Gaulle was wrong. Stalin had several more cards up his sleeve. The first was produced by Molotov the next day, when, in an atmosphere of resentful gloom, he showed the French two drafts: one of an agreement under which the French recognised the Lublin Committee, and the other of a communiqué announcing the fact to the world. De Gaulle inferred from this manoeuvre that the Russians must suppose that a treaty was essential to him for reasons of domestic politics; and instructed his negotiators to reject the texts out of hand.

The next card consisted of the principal members of the Lublin Com-

---

[3] Stalin was mistaken, for Churchill took the Franco-Soviet Pact in his stride. See Churchill, Vol. VI, pp. 226–7.

mittee, who had been brought from Galicia several days earlier. Bierut, the chairman; Osubka-Morawski (Foreign Affairs); and General Rola Zymierski (Defence). De Gaulle saw no very good reason not to meet them, but was not impressed when he did. To his eloquent words about the sufferings of Poland, they responded with details of their social and economic plans, so that he gained the impression they were reciting verses written for them in advance.

De Gaulle proposed the appointment of a French officer, Major Christian Fouchet, to discuss the question of French prisoners and deportees with the Poles, and raised no objection to their appointing a man of their own as their delegate in Paris. But, he reiterated, he had no intention of withdrawing recognition from Mikolajczyk's government in London. With some dignity, Osubka-Morawski then declared that under those conditions, the appointment of the French officer had better be deferred; and took his leave.

Stalin's last card was quite different and far more spectacular. He played it at the banquet where the French, together with the American ambassador, Averell Harriman, and the British *chargé d'affaires*, John Balfour, were the guests in the company of forty high Russian personalities headed by Stalin and Molotov. The luxury of the table and the lavishness of the courses had a stupefying effect on de Gaulle. But the conversation was of secondary interest until the time came for the toasts. This, for Stalin, was the occasion for a display of his absolute power, the crushing weight of all the Russias.

Every Frenchman present was toasted, and there were toasts for the British and Americans. Then came the turn of the Russians. Thirty times, Stalin lifted his glass, pointing each time with his spare index finger at the man he had singled out for attention. Each of them heard a message which contained at the same time praise for his work, a personal threat, sometimes veiled, sometimes explicit, of his fate if he failed, and a curtain line extolling the might of Russia.

To the inspector of artillery: "Voronov! To your health! To you falls the mission of deploying on the battlefield our gun system. It's thanks to this system that the enemy is crushed in breadth and depth. Go to it! More power to your cannon!"

To the Naval chief of staff: "Admiral Kuznetsov! People don't know enough about what our navy is doing. Have patience! One day we shall dominate the seas!"

To the aeronautical engineer Yacovlev, designer of the fighter Yack: "I salute you! Your planes are sweeping the sky. But we must have many more of them and better ones. It's up to you to make them!"

THE LIBERATION AND AFTER (1944-1946)

To Novikov, the Air chief of staff: "You're the one who's using our planes. If you don't make the best use of them, you know what will happen to you."

Then, pointing to another man: "There he is! He's the director of rear operations. It's up to him to bring the material and the men up to the front. He'd better do it the right way! Otherwise, he will be hanged, as we do it in this country."

Each of the designated men, having heard Stalin's little speech, ran forward to clink his glass against the dictator's. After dinner, de Gaulle, whose manner had been growing visibly colder as Stalin's theatricals went on, saw with some distaste that the French diplomats had gathered around Molotov and the others and were listening to yet another harangue about recognition of the Lublin Committee. Seeing his expression, Stalin shouted: "Ah, those diplomats! What chatterboxes! There's only one way to shut them up: mow them down with a machine-gun. Bulganin, go and get one!"

Leaving the momentarily silenced diplomats alone, he led de Gaulle into a projection room where a Soviet propaganda film of 1938 was shown. De Gaulle found it conformist and naïve. The Germans were invading Russia and being repulsed by the gallant Russian people. Now it was Germany's turn to be invaded. Soon revolution broke out in Germany, and peace reigned over the ruins of Fascism.

Stalin was laughing and clapping. "I fear the end of the story doesn't please Mr de Gaulle." Annoyed, the general replied: "Your victory pleases me all right. Especially as at the start of the real war things did not happen as they did in the film between you and the Germans."

By now, de Gaulle's mind was made up. Bidault had confirmed his view that there was no sign of yielding on the Russian side on the question of the Lublin Committee. There was no point, therefore, in staying on. At midnight, when the light came on, he rose from his seat, presented his thanks for the hospitality received, declared his satisfaction at the frank exchange of views that had taken place, and said: "I shall now take my leave. . . . Good-bye, *monsieur le Maréchal!*" Not seeming to understand, Stalin said, "Stay on. They're going to show another film."

De Gaulle's answer was to extend his hand. Stalin took it and let him go. On reaching the door, de Gaulle turned to salute the audience, which looked at him as though dumbstruck.

Pale with apprehension, Molotov ran after him, his face reflecting his evident fear of the consequences of failure. As always in such situations, de Gaulle was calm. On reaching the Embassy, he found Bidault had stayed behind and sent a messenger to fetch him. Dejean and Garreau were instructed to talk on, but without authority to make commitments.

As de Gaulle had half expected, Maurice Dejean knocked on his door at 2 a.m. He had had a long talk with Stalin and Molotov, he said, and the Russians had agreed that the treaty could go ahead so long as it was accompanied by a statement recording the exchange of delegates between Paris and Lublin.

It was going to be a late night. De Gaulle told his assistant the only text he would agree to was one that simply announced the arrival of Major Fouchet in Lublin.

Back went Dejean to Molotov, who in turn went to Stalin, who had never ceased to supervise the negotiations, while returning from time to time to consume more vodka with his guests. Agreed, said the Russians, but with one last condition: the arrival of Fouchet in Lublin should be announced at the same time as the treaty. But that was just what de Gaulle did not want. The treaty, he said firmly, was to be dated 10 December: Fouchet's arrival in Galicia should not be made known until the 28th at the earliest.

This time, the Russians gave in. Bidault brought de Gaulle the text of the treaty, which recorded the determination of both countries to pursue the war until final victory, not to conclude a separate peace; and thereafter to take measures in common against any new German menace. De Gaulle gave his approval, and at 4 a.m. went to Molotov's office to sign the treaty. "We must celebrate this," said Stalin, and ordered supper to be served.

Softly, he said to de Gaulle: "You held firm. My compliments! I like to deal with someone who knows what he wants, even if he doesn't share my views."

After effusive farewells, Stalin caught sight of his interpreter, Podzerov. His face darkened and his voice took on a cutting edge: "You, you know too much! I have a good mind to send you to Siberia."

As he left the room with his party, de Gaulle glanced back and saw Stalin, seated alone at the table. He had started eating again.

Why had de Gaulle gone to Russia, and why had Stalin given him the treaty he wanted without securing his signature to an agreement with the Poles of Lublin? De Gaulle's motives are, of course, clearer than Stalin's. The British and Americans were still denying France the status of a great power, which was the deepest purpose of all that he had attempted and accomplished since 1940. He had hoped Stalin would confer that status on him by the fact of signing a treaty with him, and in this, Stalin proved obliging. On his return to Paris, the treaty was indeed hailed as France's re-entry as a great power.[4]

Why, however, was Stalin ready to give de Gaulle what he wanted? The answer must surely be found in French internal politics. In terms of actual power, de Gaulle had nothing to offer Stalin except, possibly, goodwill should the Russians fall out with their major wartime allies. But the French Communist party, whose leader, Thorez, had spent the war years in Moscow, was of the utmost importance to him. Stalin's evident mistake, during the early phase of the Franco-Soviet negotiations, lay in supposing that de Gaulle would go to considerable lengths to ensure a friendly Communist party at home by pleasing Moscow – that he would go so far as to drop the London Poles and support the Lublin group. But this was a miscalculation. De Gaulle already had the support of the Communist party, and although he might have lost it if he had failed to gain Stalin's goodwill, he felt sure that his calculated risk in allowing Thorez to return to Paris on the eve of his own departure for Moscow would pay off. It was a further risk to have walked out on Stalin after the film show. But that, too, paid off. By then, Stalin knew he would have to write off the attempt to gain respectability for the Lublin Poles. But he knew, also, that if he allowed de Gaulle to return empty-handed, the general's prestige would be weakened. And it suited him to have de Gaulle in power, with Communists in his government. In opposition, the Communists might have started plotting revolution again, and this was just what Stalin did not want. By luck, firmness and good judgment, de Gaulle had got what he wanted in Moscow.

From de Gaulle's point of view, however, the Moscow success, though real, was limited. He was about to be disappointed in a matter of far greater importance to him; one, indeed, in which success would have represented the culmination of all his efforts since June 1940. For the Big Three were about to meet at Yalta to debate the future of Europe and the world, and he was not going to be there. Of all the bitter pills the unknown French colonel and temporary junior general had had to swallow, this was quite the bitterest. He was never to forget it, or to forgive the man he held responsible for his exclusion – Roosevelt – or indeed the country of which Roosevelt was the president; nor, indeed, was he ever to forgive the man who had the impudence to stand up for France's interests – Churchill – much less feel the slightest gratitude towards him.

De Gaulle had returned to Paris via Tehran and Tunis. Though ready

[4] For an intelligent discussion of the Franco-Soviet Pact, see DePorte, pp. 74–83.

to bask in the euphoria created by the Franco-Soviet treaty, while it lasted, he soon had the disagreeable news that Churchill, Stalin and Roosevelt were to meet to discuss the fate of Germany after "unconditional surrender", the future of the Balkans and central Europe, and the convening of an assembly to organise the United Nations. And he learned these facts in what, to him, was the most disagreeable way possible: through the British and American press, and not through a diplomatic communication from the governments concerned, let alone private messages from the Big Three.

He has left his own account in the war memoirs, but it needs to be supplemented from other sources, especially Churchill and the Harry Hopkins papers. As de Gaulle himself put it, writing long after the painful event, the news was unwelcome but in no way surprising: "Whatever may have been the progress accomplished on the road that would lead France to her place, I was too well aware of where we had started to believe we were already there."[5]

With the benefit of hindsight and of access to other people's memoirs, he surmised that although neither Churchill nor Stalin could have been eager to invite him, the man who was determined to keep him out was Roosevelt. Indeed, on 6 December, while de Gaulle was in Moscow, Roosevelt wrote to Churchill to say: "I still adhere to my position that any attempts to include de Gaulle in the meeting of the three of us would merely introduce a complicating and undesirable factor."[6]

Having decided that de Gaulle should not be invited to Yalta, Roosevelt did think of sweetening the pill. Indeed, he and his advisers thought of three devices, each calculated to make the decision more palatable, to demonstrate goodwill and to show de Gaulle that France was not being entirely forgotten. Predictably, all three failed, and the only surprising thing about the attempts is that the Americans should have been surprised – as they evidently were – at their failure.

The first device was a complimentary passage about France in Roosevelt's State of the Union message on 6 January 1945, upon his re-election to the presidency. The passage was inserted on the wise advise of Harry Hopkins, who had to plead very strongly for its inclusion, which Roosevelt had evidently not thought necessary.[7] Roosevelt's listeners heard him praise the Resistance and the Frenchman who had refused to surrender after the disaster of 1940. France's vital interest in a lasting solution to the German problem was recognised, and so was the contribution she could make, resuming "her proper position of strength and

[5] De Gaulle, *Salut*, p. 80.   [6] Churchill, Vol. VI, p. 226.
[7] Sherwood, *Hopkins*, Vol. II, p. 838.

leadership". The president's advisers were confident that these words marked the end of the Vichy policy and would be so recognised by the French. But in this, Harry Hopkins was soon to be disillusioned.

The president's second initiative was to send Hopkins to Paris in an attempt to improve Franco-American relations. He had a cordial talk with Bidault, who expressed his devotion to de Gaulle but admitted that the general was a difficult man to handle because he made no effort to please. Hopkins nevertheless thought that a frank admission of past errors and an expressed willingness to start afresh would melt the general's reserve. This was, of course, to misunderstand a man with de Gaulle's clear-eyed awareness of the difference between shadow and substance. When they met on 27 January 1945, the general was "neither responsive nor conciliatory".[8] "If," said de Gaulle, "you really mean that you believe that relations between the United States and France are not all that they should be, why don't you do something about it? One way would have been to invite France to Yalta." The interview, which had begun coldly, ended frostily.

Hopkins, echoing Roosevelt's sentiments, had explained the reasons for America's deep disappointment in France; and de Gaulle had retaliated by recalling France's sufferings in three wars, and listing the ways in which, he felt, the Americans had let her down: by their inactivity while Hitler was swallowing Europe, by their neutrality when France was being overrun, by the rejection of Reynaud's appeal to Roosevelt, when a promise of help would have kept France in the war; and not least, by their continued support of the French leaders who had capitulated to Germany.

Germany's difference with France, the general went on, could not be decided by the Americans, the British or the Russians. "The French," he declared bitterly, "have the impression that you no longer consider the greatness of France as necessary to the world or yourselves." It was up to the Americans to do what needed to be done to put Franco-American relations on a new and better footing.

Before leaving Paris, Hopkins and Jefferson Caffery had lunch with Bidault and, not wishing to leave entirely empty-handed, suggested that arrangements might be made for de Gaulle to attend the final stages of the Yalta conference, when European questions were to be discussed. He also expressed the president's "cordial desire" to meet de Gaulle somewhere on French territory in the Mediterranean on his way home from the conference. This was Roosevelt's third attempt to placate de Gaulle

[8] In the words of the U.S. ambassador in Paris, Jefferson Caffery, quoted in Sherwood, *Hopkins*, Vol. II, p. 839.

without giving him the things he really wanted. It was the most disastrous of the three and, as we shall see, actually set relations back still further.

Without de Gaulle, then, the Big Three assembled in the splendid imperial villas and palaces of Yalta on 3 February 1945. That afternoon, Roosevelt asked Stalin how he had got on with de Gaulle during the general's recent visit. Surprisingly, Stalin replied that he had found de Gaulle "an uncomplicated individual"; less surprisingly, he added that he had found the general unrealistic in his assessment of France's contribution to the winning of the war.[9] In the discussions that followed, the dictator was to show what he meant by the second comment by resisting suggestions that France should be given an occupation zone in Germany and a seat on the proposed Allied Control Commission for Germany. Any hopes de Gaulle might have entertained that Stalin would support French claims as a result of the Franco-Soviet treaty were thus dashed within weeks of its signature.

The conference opened formally on the 5th. When the question of the occupation of Germany by the Allied armies came up, Roosevelt at first sided with Stalin in opposing any concessions to the French. It was Churchill who stood up for the French. This was not entirely for altruistic reasons. There was a formidably practical motive as well. At the first formal meeting the president had declared that the United States did not propose to keep an army of occupation in Germany for longer than two years. This immediately faced Churchill with the problem of how the Western occupation zones were to be manned. To do it alone would be far beyond Britain's strength. It followed that France's participation was an absolute necessity. Accordingly, Churchill pressed France's claims with determined vigour.[10] At the second formal meeting, Stalin agreed that France should have an occupation zone, but only if it were carved out of the British and American zones; but he strongly opposed the inclusion of France in the control machinery.[11] Roosevelt sided with Stalin. Eden pointed out that the French were unlikely to accept a zone unless they had a say in the decision-making. In the end, Hopkins persuaded the president to go along with Churchill on the grounds that it would be easier to deal with the French if they were on the Control Commission than if they were kept out of it. Stalin – who had nothing to lose since the Soviet occupation zone was to be left intact – then followed the president's lead.

The Big Three went on to consider arrangements for the creation of

[9] ibid. p. 843. [10] Churchill, Vol. VI, pp. 308 et seq.
[11] Sherwood, Hopkins, Vol. II, pp. 849 et seq.

the United Nations Organisation, with its Security Council and right of veto for its permanent members, there again, deciding that France could not be kept out. On separating, on 12 February, they published a long communiqué enshrining all these decisions and others concerning Poland, Yugoslavia and other East European countries, euphemistically described as "liberated" and now under Soviet occupation. The frontiers of Poland were established as between the Curzon line to the east and the Oder–Neisse line to the west. There was no mention of free elections, nor, specifically, of the London government, although it was vaguely stipulated that the provisional government (that is, the Lublin Committee) should be enlarged by the inclusion of "democratic leaders residing in Poland or abroad". Although the provisions for Yugoslavia included reference to ratification by a National Assembly, the effect was that Tito's dictatorship was recognised *de facto*, as was the primacy of the Lublin Committee. In other words, in all that concerned eastern Europe (except Greece), Stalin had got his way. He had also indeed got his way, against Roosevelt's initial objections, by gaining acceptance of the inclusion of the Ukraine and Byelorussia as separate member-states of the U.N., despite their total control from Moscow.

In Paris, during the week of the Crimean talks, de Gaulle was nursing his stately discontents. On 5 February, the official start of the conference, he broadcast a warning that France would not in any way be bound by decisions negotiated in her absence. When the communiqué was published on the 12th, however, its contents mollified him to some extent. More gratifying still was a visit from the American ambassador, Jefferson Caffery, who was the bearer of three communications. The first was a formal invitation to France to join the Big Three in the Control Commission for Germany. The second expressed the hope that France, although "circumstances" had prevented her from taking part in the Yalta discussions, would nevertheless subscribe to the common "Declaration relating to Liberated Europe" and take on any obligations that might arise from it. The German arrangements were, in fact, what de Gaulle had hoped for and demanded as of right. The declaration on liberated Europe was unacceptable to him, since it conflicted with the moral obligations inherent in his friendly relations with the exiled Poles and Yugoslavs; there is no doubt that had he been present at Yalta, he would have fiercely contested the virtual handover of eastern Europe to Stalin. And the awareness that he would have done this was doubtless one of the reasons why Stalin, in common with Roosevelt, was determined to keep him out.

The third communication was a memorandum from the American

president inviting France, in the name of the Big Three, to become one of the convening powers of the forthcoming conference of the United Nations, and to take part in the consultations which the Americans, Russians, British and Chinese were to hold to give precise form to the arrangements agreed at Dumbarton Oaks.

Had matters rested there, de Gaulle, while nursing his resentment at his exclusion from Yalta, would simply have given his conditional assent to the decisions of the conference, and past humiliations might have been, if not forgotten, then at least attenuated. But Harry Hopkins, from the best of intentions, did not leave well alone. Before leaving Paris, he had mentioned Roosevelt's readiness to meet de Gaulle after the Yalta conference, and the French Foreign minister had tried to discourage him.[12] Now, however, Caffery asked for a second audience on the same day. This time, he brought a personal message from Roosevelt, expressing his desire to meet him and naming Algiers as the meeting place. If, said the president, de Gaulle agreed, he would name a date.

De Gaulle was in no mood to meet the American president. To see him on the morrow of a conference from which Roosevelt had excluded him seemed an ill-chosen moment. Nor did he see any practical advantage in a meeting, since the decisions of Yalta had already been taken; indeed, if he met Roosevelt, the world would gain the impression that he accepted decisions taken in his absence, whereas he disapproved of the fate arbitrarily meted out not only to the enemy countries – Hungary, Rumania and Bulgaria – but especially to the Allied Poles and Yugoslavs. He even suspected that the Big Three must have made arrangements concerning French interests in Syria, the Lebanon and Indo-China behind the backs of the French. If no such matters had been discussed at Yalta, why had France been kept out?

But there was worse, for Roosevelt had committed the insulting solecism, in the general's eyes, of inviting him to a meeting in "France", that is, in Algiers. True, the president did not recognise Algiers as France; all the more reason to remind him of the fact. Moreover, on his way to Algeria, the president was host aboard his cruiser, the *Quincy*, to the presidents of Syria and the Lebanon, both under French mandate. And now, he expected de Gaulle to follow them to the same place and the same presence. All this was intolerable to de Gaulle's national pride.

Having consulted his ministers, he therefore requested Caffery on 13 February to let the president know that it was impossible for him to go to Algiers at such short notice; that in November the French government had invited the president to come to Paris and regretted his inability

[12] De Gaulle, *Salut*, p. 87.

to accept, but that it would be happy to see him there at any time; but that if he nevertheless desired to stop at Algiers, would he kindly let the French authorities know so that the governor-general of Algeria could be instructed to meet the president's wishes?

A storm of disapproval now broke about de Gaulle's head, especially in the American press. Roosevelt himself, in a speech before Congress on 3 March, made a mocking reference to *prima donna* behaviour. But in France, too, the reactions were severe. The Communists took de Gaulle to task for his evident disapproval of the concessions the president had made to Stalin; the politicians, for his insult to the great democratic leader. De Gaulle, however, though disappointed once again by his countrymen's indifference to national dignity as he conceived it, remained unshaken.

A few weeks later, Franklin Delano Roosevelt died. It was 12 April and the last great Soviet offensive that was to take the Russians into Berlin began that day. De Gaulle, whose sense of history was unaffected by recent personal rebuffs, cabled Roosevelt's successor, President Harry Truman, to praise the late president's "imperishable example". Roosevelt's death had, incidentally, robbed him of the prospect, which he was certain would not have been long delayed, of reaching a belated understanding with the American leader. In this expectation he would doubtless have been proved right, for the logic of France's position in Europe was unassailable and had just been recognised by the allocation of an occupation zone in Germany and the invitation to become one of the conveners of the San Francisco conference.

In deed if not in word, de Gaulle had thus restored France's position as one of the great powers.

Chapter 5 ✦ International Discords

Although the Allies, in their disputes and diplomacy, were anticipating victory, the war went on, no less bitter now that the great armies were closing in on Germany. To all who could read a map, Hitler's defeat loomed ahead. But the discipline of the German people and their forces held to the last: indeed the dreadful logic of "unconditional surrender" could only mean a fight to the bitter end.

On 16 December 1944, the German supreme commander in the West, General von Rundstedt, under direct orders from Hitler, launched a sudden and powerful offensive in the Ardennes mountains of Belgium, hoping to drive all the way to Antwerp. The site was well chosen, for the Allied forces were thin in this sector and were rapidly driven back to the Meuse. Although General de Lattre's 1st French Army was fighting in Alsace, far to the south, they were immediately affected by the German offensive. In their sector, too, the Germans were attacking in the Colmar pocket, and Eisenhower feared that the Ardennes offensive would outflank the American and French forces to the south. To counter it, the Allies would have to straighten their line by falling back on the Vosges mountains. From Allied Supreme Headquarters came the order to de Lattre to evacuate Strasbourg, which the French had captured after fierce fighting on 23 November.

To de Gaulle, this order, whatever the strategic necessity behind it, was intolerable. The moral and national symbolism of the Alsatian capital had escaped Eisenhower. The province of Alsace had changed hands between France and Germany in each of the three wars within a man's memory. To quit now without a fight would be to bring back the Gestapo, to disappoint the hopes of the people, to cast discredit on de Gaulle himself. Here, yet again, was one of those situations which de Gaulle had sought to avoid since June 1940. His claims to sovereignty over his own forces and his own soil were at stake. In September 1944 the fight for autonomy had been won in that from that time de Lattre's forces had ceased to be integrated in General Patch's 7th Army and fought separately on an equal footing.[1] But overall orders still came from Eisenhower's headquarters and the war on the western front was still being run as an "Anglo-Saxon" operation, the French being informed of decisions only after they had been taken.[2]

On 30 December de Gaulle sent General du Vigier, whom he had named governor of Strasbourg, with urgent messages for de Lattre and the American General Devers on the same front to the effect that Strasbourg must be defended. Lightly armed ex-Resistance forces, totalling 50,000 men, were immediately sent to the Metz area, north-west of Strasbourg, to cover any sudden American retreat that might endanger the Alsatian capital.

The danger was great, for Eisenhower understandably was diverting as many forces as he thought could be spared to the Ardennes front. Rundstedt, moreover, had achieved maximum surprise, and administered a further psychological shock by producing the first jet fighters ever used in war, turning to profit a British invention which the Germans had been quicker to exploit than the Allies.[3]

On New Year's Day 1945, de Gaulle ordered de Lattre to hold Strasbourg even if the Allies were forced back to the Vosges. At the same time, he wrote to General Eisenhower, explaining the reasons for his decision, and telegraphed Roosevelt and Churchill to inform them that he could not consent to orders that threatened France with the gravest consequences. By that time, it is true, the German advance had been blunted in what had become popularly known as the "battle of the Bulge". But as Eisenhower put it later, "the Strasbourg question was . . . to plague me throughout the duration of the Ardennes battle."[4]

De Lattre, though agonisingly conscious of the value of Strasbourg, was at first unreceptive to de Gaulle's order. Replying to his leader on 3 January, he made it clear that he thought the execution of the order would have to await the assent of the Allied Supreme Command. He ought to have known that this was not the way de Gaulle would see the problem. Immediately came de Gaulle's telegraphed reply. "Your last communication," said de Gaulle, "was little to my liking. . . . The 1st Army and you yourself are part of the Allied machinery for the sole reason that the French government has so arranged it, and only until

---

[1] Rob. Aron, *Libération*, pp. 680–1.

[2] In his war memoirs, de Gaulle justifies his indignation by claiming that in the final reckoning, nearly a quarter of the troops under Eisenhower's command were French (*Salut*, p. 132), but this was certainly an exaggerated claim. Robert Aron is nearer the mark when he points out that the French forces totalled scarcely more than one-tenth of the Allied forces in the western front (*Libération*, p. 680).

[3] De Gaulle, *Salut*, p. 145; for further matter, *see also* pp. 149, 155, 171.

[4] Eisenhower, *Crusade*, p. 385.

such time as it decides otherwise." De Lattre wired back that the new defensive arrangements were being carried out.

That afternoon, de Gaulle, accompanied by General Juin, went to Versailles. "Mr Churchill," he wrote later, with his usual ingratitude for the Prime Minister's support, "had thought it necessary to come too, alerted by my message and ready, apparently, to use his good offices."

The visitors found Eisenhower full of his military worries. "For France," de Gaulle explained, any retreat in Alsace would be a "national disaster". German reprisals were to be feared. He had given the order to hold Strasbourg and it would be a pity if Allied unity were to break on this issue. He requested Eisenhower to reconsider his decision and order General Devers to hold firm in Alsace.

But de Gaulle's reasons, Eisenhower objected, were political. "Armies," lectured de Gaulle, "are made to serve the policies of states." Besides, the fate of Strasbourg was of extreme moral importance.

Churchill concurred. "All my life," he declared, "I have seen the place Alsace holds in the sentiments of the French." He shared de Gaulle's view that this had to be taken into account.

Shaken but unconvinced, Eisenhower resorted to veiled threats. If the French 1st Army started operating independently, he said, the Americans might withhold petrol and ammunition supplies. De Gaulle invited him, in his turn, to consider the consequences. If the enemy were allowed to crush the isolated French, the people, in their fury, might withhold the use of the railways and communications facilities.

The supreme commander, "with the frankness that was one of the better sides of his likable character", gave in and ordered Devers to suspend the withdrawal. The two men parted good friends on the steps of the Trianon.

The Strasbourg affair was not the last of de Gaulle's war-time clashes with his allies. Nor was the time of diplomatic humiliations yet over. His stubborn will and prodigious efforts had given him mastery over France, but his constant claim to "be" France was a two-edged weapon. His image of France was of a proud nation restored by his own example and leadership to a premier place in the world. But the shadow of the other France – the France of defeat and collaboration – was too deep, the memory of Western disillusionment too strong for his own concept to be readily accepted by the rest of the world. The British and Americans, and the Russians even more, were conscious that France's sovereignty could not have been restored by the unaided efforts of de

Gaulle's followers. They could not accept de Gaulle's France at his valuation. The France they remembered was to play no part in the reshaping of the post-war world. De Gaulle, in other words, had not yet worked his passage home.

Though de Gaulle was haughtily unwilling to concede an inch of his claims, he must have been bitterly aware of the true position. His immediate objective, then, was to build an unassailable position on the ground in Germany. In pushing ahead as fast as his limited means would allow, de Gaulle was not solely motivated by the lust for personal glory in competition with others. His overriding aim was to establish *de facto* French positions from which it would be impossible to evict his men. De Lattre, for instance, would have to race Patch to Stuttgart, and in a telegram on 29 March 1945 he ordered the commander of the French 1st Army to cross the Rhine, "even if the Americans do not agree and if you should have to cross it in rowing boats". By 4 April, 130,000 Frenchmen, with 20,000 vehicles, had reached the right bank, and that day Karlsruhe was taken. Three days later, de Gaulle himself crossed the Rhine and paid a visit to the devastated town.

On all fronts now, the Allied drives were fusing into one vast operation. In the northern sector of the western front, Montgomery was pushing towards Hamburg, Kiel and Lübeck. In the centre, Bradley was driving towards the Elbe. In the south, Patch and his uneasy French allies were competing for mastery of Württemberg. Meanwhile, on the eastern front, powerful Russian attacks were being launched from the Danube Valley, Poland and East Prussia.

Aware though he was of the vast strategic picture, de Gaulle was focusing his eyes and his will on the Patch–de Lattre sector. In his haste, de Lattre had left a powerful German force in the Black Forest region and turned to reduce it. On 15 April, however, de Gaulle reminded him that he was expected to capture Stuttgart. Next day, however, General Devers ordered his own forces to take the city and warned de Lattre "against a premature advance of the French 1st Army". The French, he declared, were to confine themselves to mopping up in the Black Forest.

But de Lattre knew who his master was and immediately ordered his forces to resume the drive on Stuttgart. On the 20th they entered the ruined city, and on the 21st de Lattre reported the "complete success of the operations in progress during the past fortnight in Württemberg, the Black Forest and Baden".

The inevitable American reaction was not long delayed. On the 24th General Devers ordered de Lattre to evacuate Stuttgart. De Gaulle, to whom the matter was referred, replied that orders remained unchanged. "I order you," he wrote, "to maintain a French garrison at Stuttgart and forthwith to institute a military government. . . . In the event of American comments, you will reply that the orders of your government are to hold and administer the territories conquered by your troops until such time as the French occupation zone has been fixed in agreement between the interested governments." Meanwhile the passage of American forces through the city was in no way to be hindered.

Since it was clear that this was a case of higher political strategy and not of local insubordination, Devers referred the whole question to Eisenhower. At this point, rival accounts diverge. Let us take de Gaulle's first. According to his account, Eisenhower sent him a resigned letter on 28 April to say that while the French action contravened the agreements on the rearmament of the French forces, he proposed to accept the situation, since he could not entertain the idea of suspending supplies and wanted to avoid anything that would impair the "exemplary spirit of cooperation between the French and American forces in the battle". Delighted, de Gaulle explained in reply that the situation was in no way Eisenhower's responsibility but resulted from the lack of any agreement between the Americans and the British on the one hand and the French on the other concerning the occupation of German territories. On 2 May Eisenhower wrote again to say he quite understood de Gaulle's position and was happy that de Gaulle understood his. To a sour communication from President Truman, de Gaulle replied complaining that the Allies had failed to consult France on questions that concerned her intimately, such as the occupation of adjacent German territory. The French stayed on in Stuttgart.

Eisenhower, in his account, explains that Stuttgart had been placed in the zone of Patch's 7th Army because the supply routes would run through the city. He goes on:

> The city was captured by the French, who afterwards refused to evacuate or permit its use by Patch. So unyielding were the French in their assertion that national prestige was involved that the argument was referred to me. I instructed Devers to stand firm and to require compliance with his plan. The French still proved obstinate and referred the matter to Paris. Not content with this, General de Gaulle continued to maintain an unyielding attitude on the governmental level in his reply to a sharply worded message from the president of the United States on the subject. In the meantime, I had warned the French commander that under the circumstances it was necessary

353

for me to inform the Combined Chiefs of Staff that I could no longer count with certainty on the operational use of any French forces they might be contemplating equipping in the future. This threat of a possible curtailment of equipment for the French forces proved effective, and the French finally complied.[5]

Both protagonists, then, claimed victory.

In the midst of his German preoccupations, dramatic news from the Far East had reached General de Gaulle. The Japanese, who had imposed their will on the Vichy authorities in French Indo-China under the Tokyo Treaty of May 1941, suddenly turned on the garrisons in Tonking, Annam and Cochinchina (together constituting what is now known as Vietnam). The date of the Japanese *coup de force* was 9 March 1945. Although de Gaulle had never been to the Far East, the fate of French Indo-China had long been on his mind. It was from there that the first major "notable" – General Catroux – had responded to his call of 18 June 1940. Admiral Decoux, who had succeeded him as Vichy's governor-general, went much further in the direction of Fascism than his collaborationist loyalty need have taken him. After Vichy's eviction, he secretly made obeisance to de Gaulle,[6] but his recent past of vilification of the Free French disqualified him as a defender of France's imperial interests. If France had a fight on her hands in the Far East, a Gaullist force would have to take it on, and for reasons that transcended symbolism: for if the French were not able to defend their own interests, the probable outcome would be the loss of France's Far Eastern possessions and a division of spoils among the allies.

Not only had de Gaulle expected a Japanese coup, he had even hoped for it, since it might be expected to provide him with a chance to assert France's dominion. To this end, as early as 1943, he had named General Mordant, ostensibly Vichy's commander of the Indo-China forces, as commander of the Gaullist forces there, against the day when the Japanese should attack. Instructions had later been air-dropped to him and to Admiral Decoux, once he had decided to change sides. When the time came, however, the swiftness of the Japanese action caught the French off balance. When Decoux and his representative in Hanoi, General Aymé, turned down a Japanese ultimatum, both were arrested.

[5] Eisenhower, *Crusade*, p. 450. Note 16 (p. 545) quotes *6th Army Group History*, Chapter IX, April 1945, pp. 273, 281, 282. Messages FWD-20127 (SCAF 319), 28 April 1945; and FWD-20425 (SCAF 328), General Eisenhower to CCS, AGO. Also, *Diary, Office C-in-C*, Book XV, under date 3 May 1945, for Truman–de Gaulle exchanges.
[6] De Gaulle, *Salut*, p. 164.

General Mordant himself was soon found and also captured. Those garrisons that were not immediately overwhelmed resisted bravely, and isolated groups fought on for weeks in Tonking, but by the end of April all resistance was over, and remnants of the French forces took refuge in China.

In these latest French misfortunes, the British showed understanding and sympathy, but the Americans did not. For months past, a French intelligence and security mission, headed by General Blaizot, had worked in Calcutta, not only organising a network of agents in Indo-China but providing the intelligence that guided British air action from Burma and American from China. But the Americans had consistently declined to arm a French expeditionary force, to which the British would have given hospitality in Burma. And now, when the French remnants were fighting their way to the China border, American air cover was withheld. General Sabattier, whom de Gaulle had appointed delegate-general after Mordant's capture, made contact with the American Command at Lai Chao, in China, but his appeal for help was rejected.[7]

At all events, some 6,000 troops, most of them Europeans, had found their way to China, of the original forces of 12,000 Europeans and 38,000 indigenous recruits. Though defeated, they had fought bravely – and had killed 4,000 Japanese, including 200 officers. For the time being, de Gaulle's government could do no more, but a claim had been staked, and authenticated in blood.

And now, in Europe, the end was near. On 28 April a group of Italian partisans executed Mussolini and his mistress and hung them upside down in Como. On the 30th Hitler took his own life in the Berlin bunker that had become his headquarters in the last desperate days of the *Götterdämmerung* that brought to its close the Reich that was to last a thousand years. That day, Marshal Pétain gave himself up into the hands of the French authorities on the Swiss frontier, and French troops began an Alpine offensive that was to take them into Italy and precipitate another "demarcation" dispute with the Americans. On 2 May, the last German defenders of Berlin capitulated to the Russians, and on the 4th, Leclerc's 2nd Armoured Division, in a fitting climax to the spectacular military journey that had begun at Lake Tchad, captured Hitler's mountain retreat at Berchtesgaden.

In *extremis*, Himmler had addressed a memorandum to de Gaulle, as part of a "peace" plan with which he sought to convince the western

[7] For contrasting accounts, see de Gaulle, *Salut*, pp. 181–3 on the one hand; and, on the other, Churchill, Vol. VI, pp. 493–4; and Eisenhower, *Crusade*, pp. 450–1.

Allies that they should conclude a separate and unconditional peace with him, leaving the Germans to continue the fight against the invading Russians to the east.[8] The message to de Gaulle might be described as an auxiliary document, not a circular but specially drafted for its recipient.

> You have won! [it declared] When one knows whence you started, one must, General de Gaulle, doff one's hat and bow very low. . . . But now, what are you going to do? Hand over to the Anglo-Saxons? They will treat you like a satellite and will make you lose your honour. Associate yourself with the Soviets? They will impose their law on France and will liquidate you personally. . . . In reality, the only path that might lead your people to greatness and independence is that of an understanding with defeated Germany. Proclaim it straight-away! Make contact, without delay, with those men who, in the Reich, still enjoy a *de facto* power and want to lead their country in a new direction. . . . They are ready for it. They ask you for it. . . . If you overcome the spirit of revenge, if you seize the occasion which history offers you today, you will be the greatest man of all time.[9]

Though recognising the cunningly chosen areas of truth in the sur-rounding shell of flattery, de Gaulle treated this missive with the con-temptuous silence it deserved.[10]

It was all over. On 7 May, General Jodl, named by Hitler's appointed successor, Grand Admiral Doenitz, went to Rheims, bearing for the supreme Allied commander the final act of capitulation. Two days later, on special instructions from de Gaulle and in the face of the opposition of the Russians and the surprised indignation of the German Field-Marshal Keitel, General de Lattre de Tassigny signed the ratifica-tion of Germany's surrender in Berlin. Technically, he signed as a wit-ness only, not a full participant. But de Gaulle felt honour had been saved; and the tricolour was among the flags that formed a panoply above the heads of the assembled military leaders, victors and vanquished.

Victory in Europe day – 8 May 1945 – brought de Gaulle news of outbreaks of violence in two Arab areas under the French flag: the Levant and Algeria. In his war memoirs, de Gaulle is expansive on the first, which he felt able to blame on the British, and curiously reticent about the second, in which he could have found little or nothing to

---

[8] *See* Chester Wilmot, *The Struggle for Europe*, pp. 702–4.
[9] De Gaulle, *Salut*, pp. 175–6.
[10] Franco, in receipt of a similar "peace" feeler from Himmler in December 1943, had treated it seriously. It is true that Himmler was stronger then than in Hitler's last days. *See* Crozier, *Franco*, pp. 374–5.

France's credit. All he found to say about the Algerian troubles fitted into one sentence: "In Algeria, a beginning of insurrection, occurring in the Constantinois and synchronised with the Syrian riots in the month of May, was snuffed out by the Governor-General Chataigneau."[11] The use of the word "synchronised" was evidently designed to suggest a collusive conspiracy between Levantine and Algerian Moslems, or even that the perfidious British (roundly blamed for the events of Syria and Lebanon) must have had a hand in the Algerian disturbances as well. But no known evidence justifies either interpretation. No reader could guess from the sentence just quoted that the Algerian disturbances were on a major scale, with great loss of blood, or that they must have provoked agonising debate within the French cabinet. The only real similarity between the troubles in the Levant and Algeria is that both began with victory celebrations on VE day.

The Algerian celebrations, in Sétif, rapidly turned into systematic mass-acres of Europeans there and in other towns. The repression was extremely severe, involving naval, air and ground operations, and resulted in thousands of casualties.[12] The whole affair was successfully hushed up at the time, although some accounts appeared in the American press. Writing thirteen or fourteen years after the events, de Gaulle preserved official secrecy in the misleading sentence I have quoted. The full truth will not be known until – and if – French cabinet documents of the period are released. But the scale of the operations makes it clear that they must have been ordered from Paris; and that the Communist ministers in de Gaulle's government shared the responsibility for the decisions taken. During this crucial period, all parties in de Gaulle's coalition accepted his ruling that France's authority must be restored over all her overseas possessions, whatever might happen later.[13] Certainly there was no disposition to sympathise with the nationalist aspirations of dependent peoples who wished to turn the Allied victory to their advantage. By associating themselves with this view, the French Communists alienated the Algerian nationalists – a fact that was later to embarrass them and which they tried to live down, without ever quite succeeding, during and after the Algerian war of 1954–62.

De Gaulle was far more prodigal with details of the simultaneous

[11] De Gaulle, Salut, p. 223.

[12] For further details, see Brian Crozier, The Rebels (henceforth, Crozier, Rebels), pp. 197–9.

[13] At this stage, de Gaulle was experiencing only minor difficulties with Algeria's neighbours, Tunisia and Morocco. The sultan of Morocco and the bey of Tunis visited him in Paris in turn in June and July; neither asked for full independence, and de Gaulle accepted their proposals for contractual associations with France.

events in Syria and Lebanon, but his account is so sharply at variance with Winston Churchill's, not only in interpretation but also on the facts, that it is difficult with any confidence to reconstruct what happened.[14] Churchill, for instance, says the disorders followed the arrival of French troops, sent against British advice, at Beirut on 17 May. De Gaulle says the first riots occurred on the 8th, when Arab soldiers of a British division which had just arrived from Palestine insulted France while on a victory parade. Again, de Gaulle states that the French had ordered a cease-fire on 30 May, after bloody incidents, especially in Syria; whereas Churchill says the cease-fire order was not given till the 31st. The dates are important, for Churchill says the French cease-fire order was given in response to a British request presented on the 31st on instructions from London; whereas de Gaulle states that the order was given independently from Paris the previous day.

When it comes to interpreting the events, the divergence is even sharper. De Gaulle saw in the anti-French incidents yet another proof of nefarious British plans to drive the French out of Syria and the Lebanon to their own advantage. He supports his argument with allegations that British agents advised the Syrian and Lebanese politicians to sponsor violence against the French, using British arms.

In Churchill's account, the British role is conciliatory. In his statement on 27 February 1945 in the House of Commons, he had declared Britain's respect for the independence of the two states, as proclaimed in 1941, and also for France's special position there. On his way home from Yalta, he had met the president of Syria in Cairo and urged him to make a peaceful settlement with France; negotiations had followed. On 4 May he had sent a friendly message to de Gaulle (who acknowledges the tone of the message but questions its sincerity), "explaining that we had no ambitions of any kind in the Levant states and would withdraw all our troops from Syria and the Lebanon as soon as the new treaty was concluded and in operation". He had also, however, mentioned that the British had to keep their war communications throughout the Middle East free from disturbance and interruption. In these circumstances, the arrival of French reinforcements "was bound to be looked upon as a means of pressure, and might have serious consequences".

At all events, the Syrian and Lebanese governments broke off negotiations after the French reinforcements had arrived, and the disorders reached a climax on 29 May, when fighting broke out in Damascus between French troops and Syrians. The French bombarded the city,

[14] De Gaulle, Salut, pp. 184–99; and Churchill, Vol. VI, pp. 489–93.

from the air and with heavy guns, causing some 500 Syrian deaths. Churchill's message to de Gaulle on the 31st expressed profound regret at the order, now given, to the British commander-in-chief, Middle East, to intervene. "In order to avoid collision between British and French forces," the message went on, "we request you immediately to order the French troops to cease fire and to withdraw to their barracks."

To General de Gaulle's acute annoyance, Churchill's message was read to the House by the foreign secretary before it had reached him. The general interpreted this circumstance as evidence of the Prime Minister's determination to inflict a public humiliation on France, and even to provoke the downfall of his government. Churchill, however, merely states that "by an error in transmission, and with no intentional discourtesy", the message had been read to the House about three-quarters of an hour before it reached the general.

Since, in any case, the message had been made public, de Gaulle did not feel the need to reply to it, and merely had a public statement on it issued on 1 June, presenting his version of the cease-fire. He followed this up next day with a press conference in which he disposed of Churchill's version of the situation with characteristically mordant sarcasm.

The worst of the crisis, however, was over, although some acrimony in Anglo-French relations persisted.[15] It is not easy to apportion praise and blame. The whole affair was a typical clash between French logic and British common sense, aggravated by de Gaulle's normal intransigence. On paper, there is no doubt that he was within his rights in sending reinforcements to the Levant, since under the Lyttelton-de Gaulle agreement of 23 July 1941 responsibility for the maintenance of order in Syria and the Lebanon fell to France, the mandatory power. True again, British forces in the area numbered hundreds of thousands at the time, and there is some force in de Gaulle's argument that the despatch of a mere 2,500 French troops, some of whom were to relieve Senegalese forces due to be repatriated, should not make much difference to the local situation. On the other hand, by his own admission, there were many signs of agitation towards the end of April (indeed that was why reinforcements were to be sent), and the Syrian government of Shukri al-Kuwatli had adopted a shrill anti-French tone and continually stepped up its demands. In these circumstances, and while negotiations were going on, the Syrians were bound to consider the arrival of French troops, even in small numbers, as a

---

[15] On 27 May 1945, at the height of the crisis, however, de Gaulle solemnly decorated Field-Marshal Montgomery at a ceremony in Paris.

provocation, and the British advice not to send them was probably sound. Moreover, if, as de Gaulle alleges, the British had really wanted to wrest control over Syria and the Lebanon, the arrival of a derisory French force would not have stopped them. But it is clear from subsequent events that they had no such intentions. The British had been the mandatory in Iraq, whose independence they had recognised in 1931; and they retained mandates in Palestine and Transjordan. Both were to be shed in the violent aftermath of the war. As for Syria and the Lebanon, their sovereignty was recognised by their being invited to the United Nations conference at San Francisco. In February 1946, they appealed to the Security Council for the immediate withdrawal of French and British troops. The evacuation was completed by 15 April.

De Gaulle had expected, or at least hoped for, public support in France for his firm stand in the Near East, but in this he was disappointed. The press was critical, and so were most of the politicians when the Consultative Assembly debated the affair on 17 June. De Gaulle's own speech was applauded, because he was de Gaulle; but the Assembly proceeded to pass a submissive resolution, from which de Gaulle publicly dissociated himself.

In a sense, however, de Gaulle had the last word. Churchill, in his message of 31 May, had proposed tripartite talks – between Britain, the United States and France – in London, to resolve the Levant problem. De Gaulle countered that it should be considered by the five powers that were to be permanent members of the Security Council; which would have added Russia and China to the British tripartite formula. This proposal was rejected by the British and Americans, as was a further proposal that the whole question should be referred to the United Nations. In the absence of talks, then, as de Gaulle had calculated, the U.N. eventually took over the League of Nations mandates and France was therefore able to surrender her mandates to the new world body without intervention by other powers.

While de Gaulle was thus ready, at this early stage, to use the U.N. for national aims, his attitude towards the new organisation was one of realistic reserve. On reflection, he had decided to reject the invitation to France to one of the sponsoring powers, on the grounds that it did not suit her to invite fifty-one nations to subscribe to a constitution that had been negotiated in the absence of the French, first at Dumbarton Oaks, and later at Yalta. The French were nevertheless present throughout the inaugural conference held at San Francisco from 25 April to 26 June. Indeed, France took her place as of right, as one of the permanent members of the Security Council, and obtained agreement that French should be, with English and Russian, one of the official U.N. languages.[16] But de Gaulle, who years later was to describe the U.N. as "that thingummybob" (*ce machin*), did not share the late President Roosevelt's simple faith in it as an instrument of peace; nor was he willing, like Churchill, to allow it to be thought that he did, or, like Stalin, to pretend that he did.

The painful reality was that France was still not accepted in the concert of great powers, as was shown when the British, Americans and Russians met at Potsdam on 17 July without French participation. Writing years after the event, de Gaulle recorded his irritation at this fresh exclusion, but consoled himself with the thought that by the time the Potsdam conference took place, the fate of Europe had already been decided and his presence would not have made much difference. Had he been invited to the Tehran and Yalta conferences, he argued, he would have been in position to protest against the unnatural division of Europe that was being perpetrated to appease the Russians. Indeed the American forces, in accordance with the Yalta provisions, had withdrawn from their furthest positions so that the Russians could take over the territories which they coveted and which had been allocated to them. Nor did de Gaulle see any point in bringing the Russians into the war in the Far East when atomic bombs were about to be dropped on Japan. He seems also (unless wise after the event) to have foreseen the advantage which the belated Russian offensive would bring to the Chinese Communists in their civil war against Chiang Kai-shek: a consideration that seems to have escaped other statesmen of the period, except Stalin.

On 25 July, before the Potsdam conference had ended, news came of Churchill's unexpected and overwhelming defeat in the British general election. De Gaulle's tribute to the old warrior in his war memoirs is one of their most justly famous passages. For all their clashes, he recognised that without Churchill's help, his own enterprise would have come to naught. Churchill, he knew, had France's interests at heart, even if his own ambitions had at times led him astray. He had greatly admired him; but he had also envied him the resources of the State that were at the service of his outstanding powers of leadership. Now that Churchill was gone, he foresaw the time when he, too, would have to abandon power.

Though kept out of Potsdam, the French were invited to take part in the projected conference of the Big Four foreign ministers, to be held in London with the object of discussing the possible bases of peace treaties

[16] De Gaulle, *Salut*, pp. 199–201.

between their respective countries and Germany. In July, the European Commission in London, of which France was a member, had given the French almost complete satisfaction in the demarcation of France's occupation zone in Germany. Apart from Cologne, which de Gaulle would have liked but the British insisted on including in their own zone, he was given everything he had asked for, including an equal share in the administration of Berlin and Vienna.

Before the foreign ministers met, de Gaulle went to Washington to meet President Truman. The new president had been pressing him to come for three months, apparently wishing to efface the unpleasantness caused by de Gaulle's refusal of Roosevelt's request for a meeting in Algiers. De Gaulle had accepted Truman's invitation, relayed through Georges Bidault who had led the French delegation in San Francisco, but on condition that the meeting should not take place immediately before, or immediately after, the Potsdam conference from which France was to be excluded. Taking the hint, Truman took care not to land in Paris on his way to and from Potsdam.

De Gaulle flew to Washington on 21 August, arriving the following day. With him were Bidault, General Juin and, as usual, Palewski. They were met by the secretary of State, James Byrnes, General Marshall, and the American ambassador in Paris, Jefferson Caffery. In the ceremonies that followed, de Gaulle had the subtle pleasure of conferring the Legion of Honour on the contrite Admiral Leahy, his opponent of Vichy days, as well as on Generals Marshall, Arnold and Somerwell, and Admiral King.

The general's talks with Truman lasted about seven hours and were spread over 22, 23 and 25 August. He was greatly struck by the contrast between the expansive and idealistic Roosevelt and the matter-of-fact, down to earth Truman. Not for Truman the dreams of universal peace nourished by his predecessor. Instead, he saw a world dominated by the rivalry between the Soviet Union and the rest – a world in which quarrels between states and revolutionary violence were alike to be avoided. But he, too, in his simplicity, had his recipe to solve all problems: independence for all and American-style democracy, with universal acceptance of American leadership. It is true that President Truman's education in world affairs was only beginning.

De Gaulle nevertheless had some success in making Truman understand France's point of view. The European balance, he said, had been disturbed by the transformation, with the consent of America and Britain, of the countries of eastern Europe into satellites of the Soviet Union. The imposition of a federal system on Germany, by removing the German menace, would provoke dissension in eastern Europe, and therefore offered the only chance of restoring the natural European order.

The president did not comment on these ideas. But he agreed to support the establishment of a Franco-Anglo-American commission in the Ruhr, without prejudice to its future; to allocate a fair share of Ruhr coal to France; and not to oppose the measures France proposed to take in the Saar. A long-term loan of $650 million, which Jean Monnet had been negotiating for some months, was finally agreed.

As regards Africa and Asia, de Gaulle pledged himself to conferring independence upon her dependencies, while reserving the choice of timing and conditions for France alone. There followed an outburst against the British for their recent behaviour in the Levant, which elicited an admission that perhaps the Americans had given too much credit to the British side of the dispute.

On Indo-China, de Gaulle expressed French misgivings without ambiguity. The president had declared that his government would not oppose the return of French power there. De Gaulle paid tribute to America's overwhelming share in the victory that would make France's return possible, and declared that he intended that the peoples of Indo-China should have regimes of their own choice. In the meantime, however, France utterly rejected the arrangements – originally made at the Cairo conference in 1943, then confirmed by Potsdam – whereby British troops were to take over from the Japanese in the south of Indo-China, and Chinese Nationalists in the north. Nor was he unaware that American agents, assembled under General Wedemeyer in China, were about to cross into Tonking to make contact with the revolutionary regime of Ho Chi Minh.

Truman could only repeat that the United States would not impede France's return to Indo-China. The two men parted on this note, and thereafter, says de Gaulle, never an acid word was exchanged between them.

Another curious omission from de Gaulle's account of this period must now be mentioned. On 18 August, the emperor of Annam,[17] Bao Dai, addressed an appeal to General de Gaulle, couched in noble French not dissimilar to de Gaulle's own. One passage of it read:

You have suffered too much during four deadly years not to understand that the Vietnamese people, who have a history of twenty

[17] Strictly speaking, Annam is the central province of Vietnam, but before the war, the term was currently applied to the whole of Vietnam, and the people now known as Vietnamese were called Annamites.

centuries and an often glorious past, no longer wish, can no longer support, any foreign domination.[18]

De Gaulle, however, ignored this appeal and, as far as is known, did not even acknowledge Bao Dai's letter. In view of his well-deserved reputation for epistolary courtesy, it is worth asking why. The most likely reason is that he considered the letter importunate at a time when he was planning to restore the French presence in Indo-China. Another possible reason is that he may have been misinformed, or have drawn the wrong inferences from the information available to him, about Bao Dai's importance in the Vietnamese equation, and the circumstances in which he came to write to de Gaulle.

It is relevant to point out that at the time of writing, Bao Dai was not a free agent. When the Japanese struck at the Vichy administration on 9 March 1945, they arrested Bao Dai in his palace at Hué, in central Vietnam, and forced him to proclaim the independence of Vietnam and form a puppet government. Nobody recognised either his proclamation or his government. In China and North Vietnam, meanwhile, the Communist leader, Ho Chi Minh, was setting up a clandestine administration with the aim of taking over from the Japanese after their expected defeat but before the French had a chance to return.

In August, events moved swiftly. On the 6th, the Americans dropped their first atom bomb, on Hiroshima. Next day, Ho Chi Minh set up a Vietnamese People's Liberation Committee under his own chairmanship. On the 10th, the Japanese cabinet decided to make an offer of surrender; and four days later, Tokyo accepted the Allied terms. Immediately after that, Ho Chi Minh's agents "persuaded" Bao Dai, at gun point, to abdicate, hand over the imperial seals (representing the "mandate of Heaven") and join their provisional government.[19] It was after this that Bao Dai wrote his appeal to de Gaulle. To the extent that de Gaulle was informed of these events, he would have been entitled to suppose that Bao Dai was merely doing what he was told and could be ignored. Subsequent events were to show, however, that although Bao Dai may have written his appeal under duress, he meant every word of it.

[18] For full text, see Philippe Devillers, Histoire du Viêt-Nam de 1940 à 1952 (1952), p. 138.

[19] Aidan Crawley wrongly states on p. 319 of his De Gaulle (henceforth, Crawley), that the Japanese "installed Bao Dai as their puppet emperor". In fact, he inherited his throne, which he ascended in 1925, aged twelve. Nor is it true to say, as Mr Crawley does, that "the people of Vietnam, led by Communists in the north and Nationalists in the south, rose against Bao Dai and forced him to abdicate". The "people" had nothing to do with his abdication; nor was it possible, in 1945, to draw a clear distinction between Vietnamese Nationalists and Communists: the Communists, in fact, were in control of the Nationalist movement.

The fact is that de Gaulle had his own plans for Indo-China. On 22 August, while he was in America, a young Resistance leader, Jean Sainteny, whom he had sent to Kunming in charge of a French intelligence network called M5, flew to Hanoi in an American Dakota. With him were four companions, and the five men took formal possession of the French governor-general's palace. The Communist General Vo Nguyen Giap led a delegation to see him on 27 August, and next day Ho Chi Minh announced a second provisional government with the key posts in Communist hands and Bao Dai as his "supreme counsellor".

It was a confusing time, for not only were the French trying to get back and the Vietnamese to claim independence; not only was the country being occupied by the Chinese to the north and the British to the south; but the Americans were also playing a game of their own. In the Dakota with Sainteny and his companions was the local representative of the Office of Strategic Services (OSS, the precursor of the CIA), Major Patti. And Patti's orders were to encourage the Vietnamese Nationalists. Nor was he much concerned with distinguishing between Nationalists and Communists: for this was still the short-lived era of hopes for Russo-American collaboration, initiated so lately by President Roosevelt and Marshal Stalin. Indeed, the preamble to the constitution of the "Democratic Republic of Vietnam", which was proclaimed by Ho Chi Minh on 2 September, borrowed heavily from the American Declaration of Independence, and Patti was present at the ceremony.

At this stage, "independence" went far beyond anything de Gaulle contemplated in respect of France's Indo-Chinese dependencies. On 24 March 1945, his provisional government had offered the Indo-Chinese peoples "freedom" and "economic autonomy" within the French Union. But these concepts fell well short of sovereignty. On 15 June, de Gaulle had appointed General Leclerc commander of a proposed expeditionary force destined to reconquer Indo-China – at a time when it looked as though the Americans would have to invade Japan and fight every inch of the way. But the events of August changed everything. Leclerc was still to go to Indo-China, but to restore order and French sovereignty, not to fight the Japanese. Meantime, on 14 August de Gaulle had sent him to Tokyo Bay, to sign, on behalf of France, Emperor Hirohito's act of surrender, aboard the American battleship *Missouri*. Next day, de Gaulle appointed Admiral d'Argenlieu high commissioner in Indo-China. Sainteny himself was to be commissioner of the Republic for Tonking.

These plans were, however, seriously impeded by the Potsdam arrangements. A mixed British–Indian force under Major-General Douglas

Gracey landed in Saigon from the first week of September. Unlike the Americans, the British had no desire to keep the French out, and Leclerc's force arrived in Saigon on 5 October.[20] Gracey, who on arrival had found a riotous situation, had been freeing and arming French prisoners-of-war; the Communists, on their side, had been murdering French civilians. Leclerc, however, gradually restored order, and the British left at the end of October.

In the north, the Chinese were far less cooperative. Commanded by the Nationalist General Lu Han, they descended on the land like locusts, pillaging and looting. There was no telling how long they would stay. Since the Chinese Prime Minister, T. V. Soong, happened to be in Washington during de Gaulle's stay, the general complained to him about the Chinese occupation and was given formal assurances that it was purely temporary. On 19 September, Soong called on de Gaulle in Paris and listened to de Gaulle's complaints about the behaviour of Lu Han's troops. "My government," Soong declared, "is going to see that this state of affairs ceases and withdraw its forces from Indo-China." But Lu Han did not budge. He did not leave, in fact, until protracted Franco-Chinese negotiations had produced a formal agreement securing free port rights at Haiphong for China. By that time, de Gaulle was out of power.

In the late summer of 1945, however, the Chinese presence was yet another obstacle in the way of General de Gaulle's plans for the restoration of France's authority; along with the proclamation of the Democratic Republic and with Bao Dai's decision to work with Ho Chi Minh. Since it looked as though Bao Dai was "lost", de Gaulle cast around for an alternative candidate to the throne of Annam, now vacant. He secretly toyed with the idea of offering it to Prince Vinh Sanh, who had himself – under the name of Duy Tan – been emperor until dethroned by the French in 1916. The prince, though the French had deposed him, had insisted on serving in the Free French forces and was now an air force major. On 14 December 1945, de Gaulle had a private talk with him and explored the possibility of restoring him to his throne. De Gaulle's view was that Prince Vinh Sanh was a strong personality; and indeed he was highly respected. Nothing, however, came of this project. In time, the French Fourth Republic was to turn to Bao Dai, who had many assets, including intelligence, but signally lacked the character which the immense difficulties of the Vietnamese situation required.

After a triumphant reception in New York, a more subdued one in

[20] De Gaulle, *Salut*, p. 231.

Chicago, and a satisfactory visit to Canada, de Gaulle returned to Paris in time to keep an eye on the London conference of foreign ministers, which was convened on 11 September 1945. For twenty-three days the ministers – Bidault, Byrnes, Bevin and Molotov – discussed the problems of Europe and of the Italian colonies, reaching deadlock on all subjects. In preparation for the conference, de Gaulle had granted an interview on 10 September to the Paris correspondent of *The Times*, Gerald Norman, in which he commented on the absurdity, as he saw it, of Britain's negotiating arrangements on the future of Germany without French participation. How, he asked, could this be reconciled with Britain's present desire for a Franco-British treaty? He went on to plead for the internationalisation of the Rhineland and the Ruhr, for the security and economic well-being of western Europe, and as an essential precondition to any German settlement. Now, at the conference, Bidault elaborated de Gaulle's plan, including proposals for the creation of a Franco-Saarian economic union, of autonomous states in the Palatinate, Hesse and Rhineland and for their integration into a western economic and strategic system.

These proposals were not ill received. But the conference as a whole was an acute disappointment to the French, who at Molotov's insistence were excluded (along with the Chinese) from all discussions on the Balkans. The debate on Germany came to an abrupt halt when Molotov claimed that in the event of adoption of the French plan, Soviet troops would have to participate in the occupation of the western areas. Earlier, the debate on the future of the Italian colonies had been similarly jerked to a halt when Molotov had asserted Russia's right to a mandate over Tripolitania.

The conference, in fact, merely faced the Western ministers with the consequences of the decisions already taken at Tehran, Yalta and Potsdam. What Russia held, in eastern Europe, was not for discussion; but if any changes were contemplated in areas under Western control, the Russians claimed the right to participate in them. The division of Europe was an accomplished fact; and de Gaulle's lamentations were not misplaced, however ineffectual.

Although aware that, except in marginal aspects, his plan for the future of Germany was unlikely to materialise, de Gaulle had wider visions of a Western group, with the Rhine, the Channel and the Mediterranean as its "arteries". In the further future, he saw such a group as part of a still more grandiose association of all the peoples of Europe. After a visit to the French zone of Germany, the general outlined these visions to enthusiastic audiences in Brussels on 11 October. Next day, at a press conference in Paris, he elaborated his ideas, but not with any precision.[21]

It is useless to speculate how far he would have gone in the direction of such European ideas had he remained in power after 1946. But it is clear that he continued to regard them, however unrealistic they seemed to others, as a guiding programme even after his return to power in 1958. Indeed, the concept of "Europe from the Atlantic to the Urals", which gained wide currency during his second period of power, was merely a revival of his 1945 ideas under a different name.

[21] De Gaulle, *Salut*, p. 222. For texts of one of his Brussels speeches, and of his press conference of 12 October, *see* De Gaulle, *Discours*, Vol. I, pp. 625–6, and 627–41, respectively. It should be noted that when writing his war memoirs, he refined his concept in a passage in *Salut*, pp. 179–80, which makes it clear that his "association" would have excluded Britain, and indeed have constituted a third force between the Atlantic world and the Soviet bloc: "To cause the States that border the Rhine, the Alps, the Pyrenees, to group together. To make of this organisation one of the three global powers and, if it is necessary one day the arbiter between the two camps, the Soviet and the Anglo-Saxon." But this was not the way he put it in 1945.

Chapter 6 ⚜ Vichy on Trial

During his period of power at the head of the provisional government, de Gaulle was beset by nagging worries about the legitimacy of his claim to rule over the French people. It was fundamental to the Gaullist myth that the men of Vichy had forfeited any claims of their own by surrendering the sovereignty of France, for the first time in French history. He, conversely, had won the title to rule, at least provisionally, by defending that sovereignty, even though at first he had done so virtually single-handed. Since everything he had done, and was to do, for the nation and the State presupposed acceptance of the myth, it is understandable that the claim to legitimacy should have become a great and permanent obsession of his.

The obsession underlay his decision to bring the major figures of the Vichy regime to trial, either in person or *in absentia*; for it was essential to his claim for legitimacy that their own claim should be publicly denounced. But there was of course more to the great purge than that. The unofficial settlements of accounts that had claimed so many victims in the months that followed the Normandy landings could not be allowed to go on. Anarchy was intolerable to de Gaulle. A formal purge had to be substituted for private vengeance, and collaborators and traitors brought to trial. In his war memoirs, de Gaulle claimed that justice was done, but this simple claim needs critical scrutiny. Something, of course, did need to be done. As in Spain after the Civil War, passions were running high, and the chilling statistics he quotes show why. The collaborators of the Germans had sent some 60,000 of their compatriots to their deaths and 200,000 into deportation, of whom no more than 50,000 had survived. Vichy's own tribunals had, in addition, sentenced 35,000 men and women to various penalties, interned 35,000 officials and reduced 15,000 servicemen to the ranks on charges of alleged participation in the Resistance.

In the face of such massive evidence of inhumanity, the exercise of Gaullist justice does not seem to have been unduly severe. Of 2,071 death sentences passed, only 768 were carried out.[1] These were the ones where de Gaulle, to whom all death sentences were submitted, could find no extenuating circumstances that might justify a reprieve. In all cases, those executed had of their own volition sent their countrymen to their deaths or directly helped the enemy. Some 39,900 were sentenced to various terms of detention; 18,000 were acquitted. About 14,000 Vichy officials were penalised in various ways, 5,000 of them losing their jobs. In some places riots marred the proceedings and about twenty prisoners were lynched by mobs in scattered localities.

It is hard to dispute de Gaulle's view that in the emotionally charged atmosphere of that time, "normal" courts of justice could not have been entrusted with the task of judging and punishing collaborators. The situation was exceptional, and exceptional procedures were necessary. To this end, de Gaulle created the High Court (*Haute-Cour*) by decree on 18 November 1944. Its specific purpose was to pass judgment upon acts of intelligence with the enemy and prejudicial to the external security of the State, committed at the highest level.

While de Gaulle frankly recognised that a judicial machine created in such circumstances could not be anything but political, he glossed over the extent to which it fell short of normal standards of impartiality. The High Court consisted of five professional magistrates, all of the top rank, and twenty-four jurors. These jurors were drawn at random from two lists: one comprising fifty senators or deputies of the old parliament who had declined to vote in favour of the delegation of powers to Marshal Pétain in the famous vote of 10 July 1940. The second consisted of

[1] De Gaulle's figure on p. 108 of *Salut*. On p. 38, however, he gives a figure of 779.

nominees of the Resistance organisations. Neither list could be considered impartial, let alone favourably prejudiced towards the accused.[2]

Two of the magistrates have been scathingly criticised for their performance at the trials. One, the public prosecutor Mornet, had won a certain notoriety by demanding and obtaining the death sentence against the spy Mata Hari in 1917, although he later confessed that what she had done hardly merited the supreme penalty. More relevantly, he was to call for the death sentence against Pétain, then whisper to one of the jurors, "You know, I have called for death, but you must not vote for it."[3] More surprisingly, Mornet himself had served Vichy for four years.

The historian Robert Aron makes the grave charge that neither Mornet nor the president of the High Court, Mongibeaux, bothered to study the documentary evidence available in Pétain's case.[4] Despite the composition of the court and the attitude of the magistrates, who seemed less concerned with establishing the facts than with confirming a man's assumed guilt, it is fair to say that seven of the nineteen high personages it tried were acquitted. Exactly the same number – seven – were sentenced to death, two of them in their absence. One of these was Marcel Déat, who took refuge in Italy and died undetected ten years later.[5] The other, Abel Bonnard, had gone to Spain. Back in France, he appeared before the High Court in 1960, and was pardoned.

The first two trials by the High Court were those of Admiral Estéva and General Dentz, in March and April 1945, respectively. Estéva, as resident-general in Tunisia, had allowed the German forces to disembark and prevented the local French forces from joining the Free French. He was sentenced to life detention, military and civil degradation and confiscation of property; he was released after six years and died some months later. Dentz, as high commissioner in the Levant, had given the Germans all the facilities they asked for and resisted the British and Free French forces. He was condemned to death, but instantly reprieved by de Gaulle, and served a life sentence.

But Estéva and Dentz were, relatively, small fry. The full spotlight of the world's publicity fell upon the trials of Pétain and Laval, which followed in August and October.

This much is clear from de Gaulle's war memoirs. But he is reticent about motives and miserly with relevant facts, and one needs to turn elsewhere to fill in the gaps. Apart from personal embarrassment, de

---

[2] See Rob. Aron, *Epuration*, Vol. II, pp. 409 *et seq.*
[3] ibid. p. 410, quoting Pétrus Faure, *Un Témoin Raconte*, p. 213.
[4] ibid. pp. 412, 413, 426, 427.
[5] Alexander Werth, *France 1940-55* (henceforth, Werth, *France*), pp. 121-2.

Gaulle had hoped for a trial *in absentia*, which could have been turned into an undefended denunciation of Pétain's work, but with the emphasis less on the Vichy regime as such than on the marshal's acceptance of the General Staff's decision to come to terms with the Germans. Everything, he believed, flowed from that: the deepening corruption of the regime and the increasing brutality of its behaviour under German pressure, the provision of labour and cannon-fodder for the Nazis, the denunciations, tortures and executions of Frenchmen. In effect, de Gaulle wanted the trial of Pétain to provide a judicial endorsement of his version of recent French history. This would have been easier to achieve had Pétain been absent. The last thing he wanted was a trial in the flesh of a national figure, now eighty-nine, whose appearance was bound to arouse pity and perhaps sympathy. When General de Lattre asked him what he should do if his forces came across Pétain and his followers while advancing into Germany, in the Sigmaringen district, where they had taken refuge, de Gaulle replied that any former Vichy ministers should be arrested, but not Pétain, as he wished to avoid a meeting.[6] He hoped, in fact, that something would turn up that would keep Pétain out of France.

Pétain himself, however, was to frustrate de Gaulle's evasive tactics. He persuaded the Germans to take him to Switzerland, where he arrived on 23 April. The Swiss ambassador in Paris, Karl Burckhardt, immediately brought the news to de Gaulle, who remarked that the French government was in no hurry to extradite Pétain. A few hours later, however, Burckhardt returned to say that Pétain himself had now asked to be taken back to France. The die was cast, and de Gaulle sent General Koenig to the frontier to escort Pétain to his place of detention in the Fort of Montrouge.

So much is in de Gaulle's memoirs. But there was more to it than that. According to Jacques Isorni another Swiss diplomat, Stucki, formerly minister to Vichy, had been involved in the arrangements for Pétain's return to France and had received an extraordinary request from de Gaulle. He was to ask the Swiss authorities to keep Pétain on their soil. A petition for extradition was about to reach them, the message ran, but they were requested to turn it down – but without disclosing that their refusal was at France's request.[7]

Can one believe the story of this tortuous manoeuvre? The source, admittedly, is suspect, for Isorni was Pétain's lawyer who, as a young man, brilliantly defended him at his trial. His account, however, has not

[6] De Gaulle, *Salut*, pp. 111–12.
[7] J. Isorni, *Pétain a sauvé la France* (Paris, 1965), p. 14.

been contested. Moreover, it is consistent with de Gaulle's known reluctance to bring Pétain back, and with de Gaulle's occasionally Machiavellian methods.[8]

The High Court were now faced with the unexpected task of finding evidence against him. They did not try very hard. Neither Pétain's personal papers, nor Vichy's State archives, both of which were available, were studied at all seriously until after Pétain had been brought to trial.[9]

In the end, the trial disappointed de Gaulle, while it could scarcely have satisfied Pétain. For Pétain, too, had his reasons for coming back: he saw in his inevitable trial a way of reasserting, before the public opinion of France and the world, the legitimacy of his government, and of vindicating its actions, including the appointment of Laval as premier which he was to present as part of a double game to deceive the Germans. Both de Gaulle and the senior barrister charged with defending Pétain – Fernand Payen – would have been happy for him to plead diminished responsibility on account of his age, which would possibly have secured him an acquittal. But this would have been incompatible with Pétain's own reasons for allowing himself to be tried, and with his conception of his own dignity, and he turned down Payen's suggestion. Isorni, the junior counsel, then helped him draft an initial statement, which became a sort of political testament and self-exculpatory pleading.

The marshal and his wife had been held in conditions that fell short of ordinary decency, and he was brought to court in the vehicle known colloquially as a *panier à salade* and reserved for common criminals.[10] For lack of premises in a suitable state of repair, the trial was held in a small court room in the Palais de Justice. There, in the midst of the crowded and uncomfortable benches, an armchair had been provided for the defendant, who was wearing the battledress of a marshal of France with only one decoration, the Military Medal. The trial began on 23 July. Security precautions were stringent and police not only surrounded the Palais de Justice but took up positions on the rooftops of adjacent buildings.

At the outset, Pétain read his statement, upon which he rested his own defence. Thereafter, he declined to answer any questions, confining himself to a further and shorter statement when all the evidence had

[8] Rob. Aron, *Epuration*, Vol. II, p. 452.
[9] ibid. pp. 416–19. *See also* Louis Noguères, *Le Veritable Procès du Maréchal* (1955), in which the author, who succeeded Mongibeaux as president of the High Court, assembled the documents on which the evidence for and against Pétain should have rested.
[10] Rob. Aron, *Epuration*, Vol. II, p. 471.

been heard. The trial partook of the nature of a theatre rather than a court of justice. Famous or notorious figures of the Third Republic – Daladier, Reynaud and Weygand among them – came as witnesses, each more concerned to defend his own role in the tragic events of recent memory than to throw light on Pétain's behaviour. The most sensational appearance was that of Pierre Laval. A German plane had flown him to Spain where he had sought asylum; but Franco had sent him back to Germany. The American forces had handed him over to the Gaullist authorities, and he himself was about to face trial. Bowed and much aged, unkempt as ever, his hair almost white, his complexion darker than ever in contrast, he had lost none of his persuasive skill. His evidence was designed to make the accusers of Vichy grasp the dreadful reality of trying to govern France under the heel of the German conqueror.

On 15 August, the court declared Pétain guilty and sentenced him to death, but with a recommendation for mercy. De Gaulle had already decided that the old man should not be put to death. He therefore signed the act of clemency, commuting the death penalty to detention for life. The marshal was then flown, first to the Fort of Portalet, in the Pyrenees, and later to the Isle of Yeu off the Atlantic coast. There he remained until just before his death on 23 July 1951, aged ninety-five.

During his long captivity, Pétain often spoke of de Gaulle, expressing admiration for his qualities – especially his astonishing memory, which Pétain envied –but misgivings on account of his excessive ambition. On one occasion, he told the chaplain, Canon Ponthoreau: "I condemned him to death, he condemned me to death: we're quits. I had written in the margin of the sentence that it should not be carried out. He must have done the same, since I am here."[11]

For all that, the trial of Pétain deeply disappointed de Gaulle. For instead of providing the clear denunciation of the armistice he had hoped for, and which would have vindicated his own claim to "legitimacy", it had merely thrown light on the sordid aspects of the Vichy regime which were only of incidental concern to him.

Next on the list of eminent accused was Joseph Darnand, perhaps the most infamous of the Vichy regime's henchmen. A man of great physical courage, which he had displayed during the battle of France and to which de Gaulle pays tribute in his war memoirs, he had ordered or sanctioned tortures and massacres of Resistance men and women. His trial, which was brief, was comparatively well conducted. It ended with a death sentence on 3 October, which was carried out without delay.

[11] Tournoux, *Pétain*, p. 487.

Laval's trial, which followed immediately, was a sordid Roman circus, in which the rancorous hatreds of the liberation found their lowest level. Scorning the advice of his counsel, who wished to demonstrate that he had been misled and committed errors of judgment, he decided to take full responsibility for his actions and argue that in all cases he had chosen consciously the lesser of two evils. The prosecution had scarcely bothered to master its brief and its preliminary cross-examination had been, as Laval had no difficulty in demonstrating, cursory beyond the point of negligence. Eloquent as ever, the accused provoked the magistrates and the jury, who rose to his bait with shouted insults. Thereupon, he refused to take any further part in the proceedings, evidently hoping to force a declaration that there had been a mis-trial. With his customary skill, he had brought out the fact that his judges had administered the laws of Vichy; and – more damaging still – that his trial was being rushed so that the parliamentary jurors could take part in the general elections, which had been fixed for 21 October. Indeed, whereas the hearings in Pétain's trial had been spread over twenty days, in Laval's they were compressed into five.

None of this saved Laval from the death sentence, which was pronounced on 9 October 1945. Three days later, Laval's lawyers called on de Gaulle to request a re-trial. The general listened to them coldly and made no comment. But he immediately wrote to his minister of Justice, Pierre-Henri Teitgen, to ask his advice. Teitgen, who was in Brittany, replied the following day, in effect referring the decision back to de Gaulle. The latter decided not to order a re-trial.

When the officials came to fetch Laval, he had just swallowed a dose of cyanide, which he had hidden in his overcoat. It is thought that the deadliness of the poison had been reduced through contact with impurities, the phial having split, though not widely enough for the cyanide to escape. Rushed to hospital and subjected to a stomach-pump, he recovered sufficiently to be led to the firing squad. A cigarette in his mouth, he died shouting: "Vive la France!" Laval's death rounded off de Gaulle's work of retribution against the Vichy regime, although trials went on up to 1949, and were revived in 1954 to deal with people previously tried in absentia who gave themselves up. In all 108 trials of Vichy ministers and officials were held.

Chapter 7 ✤ The Patient Stirs

The home base on which de Gaulle was trying to build a foreign policy was in desperately poor shape. During the winter of 1944–5, the official food ration provided only 1,200 calories a day – when it was obtainable. Forty per cent more children died in Paris that winter than in 1943 during the occupation. By the spring of 1945 the food shortage had further worsened and on 19 March, when ration cards were not honoured, 5,000 housewives gathered to demonstrate before the Hôtel de Ville.[1] In several provincial cities there were food and coal riots; for there was no coal for private use and through the long winter, one of the harshest in memory, most French people shivered in their semi-starvation. In such conditions, the black market flourished. Those who owned bicycles used them to pick up supplies in the countryside. They were the fortunate ones. Some 20,000 in devastated Caen were without accommodation, let alone transport. Trains were infrequent; hospitals were starved of supplies; and the newspapers, for part of the time, were down to half a sheet. This was not what the French had expected from their liberation.

The immediate miseries were indeed only the visible evidence of deeper wounds. Liberated France was a ruin. Half a million buildings had been destroyed, whether in the fighting of 1940, the Allied air raids, or the bombardments of the liberation, and a further million and a half badly damaged. More factories, proportionately, had been hit than private dwellings, but six million Frenchmen were homeless. The demographic losses were high – much higher than might have been inferred from France's relatively minor part in the war. About 250,000 Frenchmen had been killed in combat, but 160,000 more had lost their lives in air raids or bombardments or had been massacred by the Germans; in addition, 150,000 had died in Nazi concentration camps and 75,000 had failed to survive prisoner-of-war camps or forced labour. The grand total of war dead, then, came to 635,000; and to these, if economic loss was to be assessed, must be added some 585,000 men incapacitated for

[1] Werth, *France*, pp. 236–7.

reasons connected with the war.[2] Overwhelmingly, those affected had been young in a country whose static birth-rate had reduced it from the most populated in Europe to the fifth most populated in less than 150 years.

Nor were lives and dwellings the only losses suffered. Bombs, mines and trench-digging had put nearly two and a half million acres of land out of commission, and over thirty-seven million acres more had lost their productivity through neglect. Tools, grain and fertilisers were lacking. Moreover, the Germans had systematically bled France white under the terms of the armistice, since it was up to them to interpret the blanket clause providing that "the costs of the occupation forces are chargeable to the French government". The occupiers had helped themselves to the capital goods they needed and made the French pay for the coal and other raw materials imported into France to serve German needs. The occupation had cost France 2,000 milliards of francs at 1938 prices. But there was no monetary tag for the under-nourishment, the loss of life and the moral depression the invaders had inflicted on a nation which, a generation earlier, they had already grievously damaged.

De Gaulle was deeply conscious of the long-term implications of all this spoliation, which directly affected his constant aim of restoring French greatness. Though preoccupied with foreign affairs, he did not, as has sometimes been alleged, neglect home problems. Indeed the two were intimately connected, since economic health was indispensable to a foreign policy as he conceived it.

The coal which French industry desperately needed was to come from the economic union with the Saar, and from the Ruhr, which was to provide fifty million tons a year. In addition, during this first period of power, the coalfields of the Nord and Pas-de-Calais departments, and later of the Loire, were nationalised. Gas and electricity were taken over by the State, and a State petroleum research organisation began to prospect for oil. Uranium was abundant in the French sub-soil, and an Atomic Energy Commission was set up to exploit it. A High Commissariat for the Plan undertook the gigantic job of assessing France's needs for capital equipment and providing it. The financial side of reconstruction, too, was taken over by the State, when the Banque de France and various credit institutions were nationalised. A great State-controlled airline, Air France, was created by the merger of a number of private but subsidised companies. The Renault works, whose owner was alleged to have collaborated with the Germans, were taken over by the government. And in August 1945, the Ecole Nationale d'Administration was created, as a training centre for high officials.

[2] De Gaulle, *Salut*, pp. 233–6.

With nationalisation went a social policy which, to the surprise of many who thought of de Gaulle in stereotyped terms as a member of the military caste and of the *grande bourgeoisie*,[3] was radical; though not quite revolutionary enough for the furthest left among his Resistance followers. Ever since Pineau had, to his surprise, found de Gaulle receptive to the socialist ideas of the Resistance, the general had encouraged his assistants, both in London and in Algiers, to form study groups and lay plans for social change. In 1944 and 1945, these plans were largely turned into realities. Automatic insurance was provided for all wage-earners and generous family allowances were instituted. On the land, tenant farmers were guaranteed against eviction, and given "first refusal" in the event of a sale.[4]

The motivation for this social policy was complex. De Gaulle's championship of the poor was neither an affectation nor a politically calculated attitude. The military caste, to which he belonged, had betrayed France by accepting defeat, and disowned him, first by refusing to take his advice, then by condemning him to death. The *grande bourgeoisie*, with honourable exceptions, had been blind to the German danger, then had collaborated with Vichy. In manners and speech, de Gaulle was what birth and upbringing had made him; but he felt alienated from his social *milieu*. Although it would be wrong to attribute his social policy to this alienation, it did not displease him to take note of the discomfiture of the class into which he was born, which he called *les privilégiés*. Nor was he indifferent to the sufferings of the people after the liberation; but compassion alone was not his motive. Nor, it is certain, did he encourage nationalisation and welfare merely to please the Resistance; although it gave him a certain pleasure to take the wind out of the sails of the Communists, who, as he noted, complained of "reactionary links" that prevented him from going far enough, but took care not to oppose him. Although each of these things played a part in his home policy, all were subordinated, in his eyes, to the drive to restore France's greatness. To nationalise the sources of energy and credit was to strengthen the State and enable it to control the economy; to reduce the misery of the workers and their families and to give the peasants security of tenure was to mitigate their discontents and involve them in the work of national reconstruction. Years later, in the 1960s, de Gaulle and his ministers were to join in the fashionable espousal of workers' "participation" in industry; but to de Gaulle at least, the idea was not new. The word

[3] *See* Werth, *France*, Part II, chapters 1 and 2, "De Gaulle, the noble anachronism", and "Was de Gaulle a *grand bourgeois* at heart?"
[4] De Gaulle, *Salut*, pp. 95–8.

"participation" itself appears on page 97 of *Le Salut* in a description of the *Comités d'entreprise* that were set up in February 1945, with the object of involving management and workers in each other's problems. His ultimate aim was "the association of capital, labour and technology [*technique*], in which I see the human structure of the economy of tomorrow".

While the reforms went on, de Gaulle sourly watched the revival of the political groups and parties. It suited the Communists, for reasons we have examined, to work with de Gaulle; but he never doubted that their ultimate aim was to gain a monopoly of power. In February 1945 the Socialists had set up a "committee of understanding" with the Communists; but the Socialist leader, Léon Blum, was determinedly anti-Communist, and this embryo of a new "popular front" was still-born. New parties sprang up: Georges Bidault's Christian Democratic Mouvement Républicain Populaire (MRP), and François Mitterrand's Union Démocratique et Socialiste de la Résistance (UDSR). Soon the MRP, UDSR, "moderates", and Socialists together easily outnumbered the Communists on the Conseil National de la Résistance. This led the Communists and fellow-travellers to set up a rival Conseil Central de la Renaissance Française, but this artificial body soon collapsed for lack of support.[5]

There was much talk of "revolution", but the word meant different things to different people and groups. Most advocates of "revolution" were vague about its implications; the Communists knew very well what they understood by it, but kept their further plans silent; Bidault talked of "revolution within the law", but this was more a slogan than a programme. In the end, de Gaulle decided that by "revolution", most of the politicians understood not a plan of action, but a term to express their permanent dissatisfaction with whatever the government was doing, even if they had originally advocated it.[6]

De Gaulle's relations with the Consultative Assembly were ambiguous. Whenever he appeared, he was greeted with formal respect, and if he spoke, with prolonged applause. On the other hand, his programme was constantly criticised. And while he himself escaped criticism, the same was not true of his ministers: the minister of State, Jules Jeanneney, the Finance minister, François de Menthon, the minister of Information, Pierre-Henri Teitgen, and the minister for Prisoners, Henri Frénay, were each in turn subjected to tumultuous, and even scurrilous, attacks in the Assembly. As de Gaulle surmised, this agitation was the parliamentarians' way of signifying their discontent with a purely con-

[5] Werth, *France*, pp. 265–6. [6] De Gaulle, *Salut*, p. 102; *see also* pp. 105–6.

sultative role. On 19 March 1945, a delegation representing all political groups called on the general to demand that in future no decisions should be taken against the Assembly's stated views.

"The people," replied de Gaulle in his lofty way, "has sole sovereignty. Until it is in a position to express its will, I have taken it upon myself to lead it."

When the delegates exclaimed that they represented the Resistance and therefore were entitled to express the will of the people in the absence of legal powers, de Gaulle went on calmly: "You are mandated by the movements and parties of the Resistance. This certainly gives you the right to make yourselves heard. That is why, in fact, I have instituted a Consultative Assembly and nominated you as members of it. . . . You are associated with the government's action through the questions you put to it, the explanations that are given to you and the advice you formulate. But I shall not go beyond this. Besides, I invite you to consider that the French Resistance was greater than the movements and that France is greater than the Resistance. Well, it is in the name of France as a whole, not a fraction, however valuable it may be, that I am carrying out my mission. Until the forthcoming general elections, I am answerable to the country itself for its destiny, and to it only."

In ill-humour, the delegates withdrew; but thereafter, says de Gaulle, the Assembly calmed down and settled to its work, at least for a time.

One of the most pressing of the tasks before it, in the spring of 1945, was the Budget. It was thought impossible to raise more than 175,000 million francs in taxation, which barely equalled military expenditure alone. But some 215,000 million francs were needed for other public expenditures. Two rival financial theses, each with its champion, confronted each other. One, defended by Pierre Mendès France, the Economics minister, advocated austerity. The other, whose champion was the Finance minister, René Pleven, called for expansion. Inflation was at the heart of the debate. Mendès France wanted to call in all banknotes and exchange them for fresh notes worth only a quarter of the face value of the old; the remaining three-quarters would be credited to owners but the accounts thus increased would be frozen, except for modest current needs. This would drastically reduce purchasing power and beat the black market. Simultaneously, the prices of all necessities would be frozen at a low enough level to allow the poorer consumers to live. Only luxuries could find their own price level. Clearly, such measures would gravely affect tax revenues; but a massive tax on capital would put that right.

Against this, Pleven argued that inflation was the symptom, not the cause, of France's economic plight. The occupying power, by requisitioning raw materials, starving France of imports and conscripting French labour, had virtually halted industry. Now, the immediate needs of reconstruction prevented recovery. The most urgent need was to revive production. But brutal measures of austerity, by removing all incentives, would make revival impossible. Confidence in the State and credence in its currency would be ruined. The road to recovery lay in stimulation of the economy, in expansion. If too much liquidity resulted, the surplus could be mopped up by floating bonds which would encourage savings and give every taxpayer the feeling that he owned what he earned. For the same reasons, there should be no tax on capital. The profits of black marketeers and racketeers should be confiscated, but legitimate enterprise should not be penalised.

It is a measure of de Gaulle's prestige that the exponents of each thesis looked to him as the guarantor of success. Mendès France argued that the general's authority would ensure acceptance of the harsh measures he had proposed; Pleven, that with de Gaulle at the helm public confidence would ensure recovery and expansion.

The debate took a long time to mature, then to reach crisis point. In Algiers, de Gaulle had entrusted Mendès France with the fundamental thinking about France's economic future. When liberation came, the general gave him what he wanted most: a ministry of the National Economy which could coordinate all the country's economic activities. But the Finance ministry went to a conservative banker, Lepercq. Economics and finance therefore started moving in opposite directions.[7]

In the desperate circumstances of the liberation, inflation was, in any case, inevitable. In September 1944 the government decreed a 50 per cent rise in wages. Prices duly rose and were blocked in November. But the price control mechanism broke down and a further increase in wages came in April 1945. In the meantime, in November, Mendès France had first proposed his austerity programme. He was immediately opposed by Lepercq, who counter-proposed a large State loan. It was the classic clash between State socialism and private enterprise. Three days later, however – on 9 November 1944 – Lepercq was killed in a car crash.

Mendès France undoubtedly hoped he would succeed Lepercq, but was aware of the unpopularity of his proposals. He therefore did not offer himself for the job, but proposed instead a friend and fellow-Radical, Giacobbi, who had made a success of the ministry of Food. De Gaulle, however, picked Pleven, who was minister of the Colonies. On taking

[7] Jacques Fauvet, *La IVème République* (henceforth, Fauvet, *IVème*), pp. 36–40.

office, Pleven adopted his predecessor's policy, and thereby clashed with Mendès France who, on 18 January 1945, wrote a letter of resignation, addressed to de Gaulle. It was an exceptional communication, for a letter of resignation: running to eighteen pages, it listed the arguments in favour of austerity, and castigated his opponents as miracle-makers whose remedies would condemn France to the indefinite devaluation of the franc.[8]

De Gaulle declined to accept the letter. Instead, he invited both Mendès France and Pleven to his official residence in the Bois de Boulogne. It was a Sunday, and (writes Jacques Fauvet) it was the first time the general had devoted a whole day to economic and financial questions. Himself an austere man, his instinct was to support Mendès France. But this was not a time to provoke public protests by adopting harsh financial measures. His reason, therefore, inclined him towards Pleven. At one time, bewildered by the contradictory views reaching him from both sides, he turned to Mendès France and protested: "But aren't all the experts against you?" Mendès France's reply was devastating: "I know a certain Colonel de Gaulle who before the war had 'all the experts' against him."[9] By evening, however, he had persuaded Mendès France not to resign and Pleven to make some concessions to the other man.

The truth is that, for all de Gaulle's esteem for Mendès France, which bordered on admiration, the intellectual processes of the two men were incompatible. De Gaulle liked concise summaries of difficult questions, preferably on one sheet of paper. Mendès France, who had a horror of over-simplification, found this difficult if not impossible. He would bring reports of thirty pages to the general who called them the "prophecies of Jeremiah". "You will summarise this," he would say with an air that was both mocking and displeased; and sigh under his breath: "*De profundis, clamavi ad te Domine.*"[10]

In the Assembly, Mendès France had been supported by two Socialists, Jules Moch and André Philip. With inflation galloping on, the Economics minister renewed his proposals in March. Pleven again raised objections, exclaiming, "I'm not going to add rationing of money to all the other forms of rationing."[11]

Mendès France found himself isolated. Apart from Moch and Philip, there was nobody to support him. Two of the Socialist ministers, Robert

[8] This letter is quoted in full in the appendices of *Salut*, pp. 426–36. Also quoted are Pleven's report of 24 February 1945 on the money supply (pp. 440–8), and Mendès France's final and briefer letter of resignation, dated 2 April 1945 (p. 460).
[9] Ronald Matthews, *The Death of the Fourth Republic* (1954), p. 189.
[10] Galante, p. 198.   [11] Fauvet, IVème, p. 39.

Lacoste (Production), and François Tanguy-Prigent (Agriculture) favoured expansion. So did the "moderates", and at the other end of the political scale, the Communists, who scrawled slogans on the walls accusing Mendès France of wanting to cut the value of the people's money. There was virtually no opposition to Pleven.

On 2 April Mendès France renewed his resignation – in a shorter letter. This time, de Gaulle accepted it. It had long been clear that no further compromise was possible. He could not have both Mendès France's austerity and Pleven's expansionism. His decision in favour of Pleven rewarded him with the ministry of the National Economy as well as that of Finance. The decision was not, however, made on technical grounds, for as de Gaulle put it, there was no absolute truth in economics, any more than in politics or strategy. In the sick and wounded country that was France, the important thing was to avoid "perilous convulsions".

While accepting Mendès France's resignation, de Gaulle took care to remain on good terms with him and reassure him of continued esteem. Indeed, he reserved the right, at some future date, and should circumstances change, to reinstate him and apply his surgical remedies. But this time was never to come.

Who, in restrospect, was right? Since Mendès France's plan was not put into effect, its validity cannot be disproved. But on social and political grounds, there seems little doubt that it would have been disastrous and that de Gaulle was right to reject it. On economic and financial grounds, the history of the provisional government and of the Fourth Republic that succeeded it, tended to confirm de Gaulle's view that there is no absolute truth in economics. For inflation did continue, and with it the need, at intervals, to devalue the currency. On the other hand, production did recover. By the end of 1945, economic activity had doubled, in comparison with conditions at the liberation; and money supply had been reduced. Pleven, on balance, was more right than Mendès France, in the circumstances of 1945. In later years, a dose or two of Mendèsiste austerity would have done the country no harm.

Before long, the talents of René Pleven and the resolve of the government were put to a severe test, with the return from Germany of France's prisoners-of-war. The collapse of the Reich suddenly freed two and a half million French servicemen and civilian deportees in their hands. By 1 June 1945, only three weeks after VE day, a million had returned; most of the rest came home within a further month. Two years earlier, de Gaulle's French Committee in Algiers had set up a ministry of Prisoners, Deportees and Refugees, and the minister, Henri

Frenay, the former Resistance leader, had prepared detailed plans for the reception. The suddenness of the crisis and the weight of numbers involved were bound, however, to strain the best-laid arrangements.

There was no special difficulty about repatriating prisoners freed in the French zone, and relatively little about those in the British and American zones. But it was a different story for those stranded in Russia, where Soviet suspicions and bureaucratic procrastination, added to the problems of distance, created additional delays. The most difficult cases of all were those of the Alsatians and Lorrainers who had been forcibly incorporated into the *Wehrmacht*. Many of these unfortunates had fought on the eastern front and had fallen into Russian hands. Scattered now in Soviet prisoner-of-war camps, they were hard put to it to establish their claims to French citizenship and their right to be repatriated. General Catroux, now ambassador in Moscow, directed enquiries, not always successful and inevitably slow.

To feed, clothe and rehabilitate two and a half million men, to prevent a collapse of their morale on meeting the realities of France's poverty after their dreams of the country they had known – all this was necessary, but agonisingly difficult. Reception centres had been set up and doles were distributed along with elementary necessities. But there was little to go round and the difficulties were unscrupulously exploited by political groups for their own ends.

Foremost in this sordid game were the Communists, who had gained control of the "National Movement of the Prisoners" and used it to organise protest marches and launch a scurrilous campaign against the minister for Prisoners. "Frénay to the gallows!" clamoured the placards brandished by the "Movement", parading in front of hospitals and reception centres.

De Gaulle put a stop to all this agitation in strictly military style. Summoning the leaders of the "Movement" to his office, he gave them an ultimatum. "What is going on is intolerable," he said. "I insist that it should be brought to an end and I shall hold you responsible."

The predictable reply was: "It is an explosion of justified anger on the part of the prisoners. We are powerless to stop it."

De Gaulle was not the kind of man to swallow a specious excuse. "Public order," he declared, "must be maintained. Either you have no power over your own people; in that event, you must immediately say so to me in writing and announce your resignation. Or else you really are the leaders; if so, you will give me a formal commitment that all agitation shall cease today. Unless you give me before leaving, either the letter or the promise, you will be placed under arrest in the ante-

383

chamber. I can only spare you three minutes to make up your minds."

After a brief conference near the window, the men came back and said: "We understand. Agreed. We can guarantee that the demonstrations will cease." And so they did, that very day.[12]

While the prisoners were returning, de Gaulle authorised Pleven to launch his recovery (*assainissement*) plan, which was drastic enough, though not nearly so traumatic as the measures envisaged by Mendès France. The operation was spread out between 4 and 15 June. All bank-notes and short-term bonds were to be handed in and exchanged on a one-for-one basis against new pieces of paper. The object of the exercise was dual: it was to complete the national inventory of the country's wealth, completing what was already known about land and property, stocks, shares and debentures; and it was to flush out illicit fortunes. Those who handed in their money rendered themselves liable to taxation, but any money they failed to hand in, perhaps for fear of prosecution, became worthless. This applied to sums removed by the Germans in French money. Accounts, however, were not frozen. Within two months, the money in circulation dropped from 580 milliard to 444 milliard francs.

Two ordinances on 30 June constituted the next stage. The first gave the State authority to limit prices; the second gave details of penalties for evasion of the new regulations. Armed now with all the information he needed, Pleven, under authority of a further ordinance dated 15 August, raised a special "solidarity tax" – a sweeping system of levies on inheritances, on wartime profits and on company funds. The purposes of the solidarity tax, as announced, were to cover the exceptional expenditures occasioned by the return of the prisoners, the demobilisation and re-patriation of servicemen, the despatch of the expeditionary corps to Indo-China, and the public reconstruction programme.

As de Gaulle wryly noted, the Pleven plan was attacked in the Assembly, both by the left for not hitting business hard enough, and on the right for hampering business activity; but was in the end approved by a large majority. It was the last time his government was to carry the day in the provisional parliament.

[12] De Gaulle, *Salut*, pp. 243–5. For a description of the state of mind of returned prisoners, Werth, *France*, pp. 250–2.

Chapter 8 ✤ De Gaulle Steps Down

Although an autocrat by nature, de Gaulle was not, and was never to be, a dictator in the fullest sense of the term. Not wishing to prejudge the people's will, or to give an example of conspicuous luxury in the midst of the national poverty, he had declined to take up residence in the Elysée Palace. For the same reason, he made no use of the president's country residence at Rambouillet. Instead, he had rented, at his own expense, a mansion on the edge of the Bois de Boulogne. There he lived, with his wife and their two daughters, their son being absent and at war. In the evenings, from time to time, they entertained. But after the guests had left, de Gaulle returned to his study, to pore over files, write his speeches or – during the purge – consider the appeals of those under death sentences. On Sundays he walked for hours in the woods. It was, at that time, his only relaxation.[1]

His working days were spent in the old Hôtel Brienne, in the rue Saint-Dominique, on the Left Bank. There he gave his audiences and receptions, occasionally presiding over the Council of Ministers. Normally, however, the cabinet met in the Hôtel Matignon, as it still does. The key people, more important in their way than the ministers, were Louis Joxe who, as secretary-general of the cabinet, organised the flow of work; René Cassin, vice-chairman of the Council of State, which dealt with constitutional problems; and Gaston Palewski, whose task was to bring de Gaulle the foreign telegrams, reports, messages and analyses of the French and foreign press and radio.

At cabinet meetings de Gaulle listened to what everyone had to say. When, as in most cases, a consensus emerged, de Gaulle usually went along with it. When opinions were divided, he expressed his own view, which became that of the cabinet.

An incessant flow of speeches, whether in the Assembly, on the radio, at public meetings, and press conferences, punctuated his busy statesman's life. On rare occasions, he allowed the mood or emotion of the moment to carry him forward with an improvised speech. But as a

[1] De Gaulle, *Salut*, pp. 125–8; see also pp. 237 *et seq.*

rule, he worked and reworked on the texts, never failing to memorise them so that. as delivered, they gave the impression of spontaneity or facility. Despite the vast number of his speeches and his not inconsiderable literary production, however, writing never came easily to him.

The general's work routine was frequently interrupted by absences. On eleven occasions, he left Paris on tours of inspection of the armed forces. There were many visits to the provinces and, of course, his trip to Russia, taking in the Levant on the outward and North Africa on the return journey. In one period of eight months, he was away for a total of seventy days.

As 1945 wore on, de Gaulle became ever more deeply convinced that a return to the "regime of parties" would be disastrous for France. During the year, he carefully considered, only to reject, the idea of prolonging indefinitely the kind of monarchy by consent which he had established. He thought it likely that he could have hung on to power, but he knew that he could not have done so without disturbances that would probably turn to violence. He was accepted not only for what he was and had done, but because he had never ceased to promise that as soon as possible he would submit his record to the people's will, freely expressed at elections. Because he was, and intended to remain, above parties and sectional interests, he had no organised machine behind him. The Resistance had united behind him but was now split into its component parts, each pursuing particular interests. The army would have supported his continued rule, but the outcome – a military dictatorship – could not have been justified in a country now at peace, no longer threatened from abroad and in no mood for national adventures of the kind that had been initiated by the two Napoleons.

Having rejected his own despotism, as he put it, de Gaulle was nevertheless convinced that the country needed a strong regime: one that should no longer be at the mercy of shifting parliamentary majorities. At one time the parties had reflected the idealism of their founders. Now the idealism had gone. There was no room left for disinterest; personal ambitions, the jostling for position, the tactical necessities of professional politicians – these were the realities. Since no party on its own was strong enough to rule, sordid bargains in the division of electoral spoils were inevitable. In this panorama, the Communists stood apart, knowing what they wanted, which could only – if they had their way – place France in servitude to the Soviet Union.

There was only one way out, as de Gaulle saw it: a presidential system, with a leader above parties and chosen directly by the people, and an executive chosen by the leader, outside parliament and therefore freed from obligations to sectarian interests, serving the nation and community as a whole.

It was clear that the parties themselves would fight as hard as they knew to preserve their own sovereignty and the political games that were their life-blood. In the end, the people themselves would have to decide, in a suitable referendum. If they approved his ideas, the parties would have to make the best of it and work with him. If they disapproved, there would be nothing left for him but to go. The general was aware of the fragility of this dependence on popular favour. For the people of France never ceased to disappoint him by their failure to live up to his idea of their country. Changeable, facile, individualist, quarrelsome, capable of great things when well led in great crises, but swift to return to mediocrity, and now tired and anxious to play games, without the ambition for national grandeur which was de Gaulle's offering to them: knowing or sensing all this, de Gaulle felt a kind of anguish.

For a few days, it is true, he had allowed himself to think that he could pull it off. These were the days that followed the German surrender. On 15 May the Consultative Assembly had greeted his speech with unanimous waves of applause and a superb impromptu rendering of the *Marseillaise*. Then again, the former leaders of the Third Republic, as they returned one by one from Nazi detention, called on him to assure him of their loyalty, devotion and support. Paul Reynaud, Edouard Daladier and Albert Sarraut were the first to call. Léon Blum, on his release, publicly declared: "France is being resuscitated, thanks to General de Gaulle. We were lucky to have had a General de Gaulle. From the depths of my prison, I always hoped that my party would support him. All France has confidence in him. For our country his presence is an irreplaceable guarantee of internal concord." Edouard Herriot, whom the Russians had liberated, broadcast from Moscow: "My conviction is that the country has grouped itself around Charles de Gaulle, at whose disposal I place myself without reservations." But such utterances, however sincerely meant at the time, were not necessarily followed up in practice. Everybody wanted de Gaulle, but only on condition that he did not try to impose his views on them.

By VE day, indeed, behind the rejoicing and the show of unanimity, the political leaders were absorbed by the municipal elections – the first of any kind since the liberation, which were seen as a dress rehearsal for the general elections to be held in the autumn. There were two ballots, on 29 April and 13 May. Resistance candidates predominated and a divided opinion about the future constitution emerged: the Radicals and moderates wanted simply to return to the constitution of 1875

– that of the Third Republic – while the Marxists and Leftists called for a single and sovereign chamber. What was common to both groups were that they wanted parliament, whether it consisted of one house or two, to have all the power.

On 2 June 1945, de Gaulle gave the first public indication of the way his mind was working on France's constitutional future, but only in the form of the options open and of the one that most clearly met with his disapproval. In response to a question at the end of the press conference he had called to present his version of the Syrian crisis, he declared:

> Three solutions are conceivable. Either to *return to the errors of yesterday*, to have a Chamber and a Senate elected separately, then to bring them together at Versailles as a national Assembly that either would, or would not, modify the constitution of 1875. Or to consider that constitution as dead and proceed to elections for a constituent Assembly that would do as it pleased. *Or else, finally, to consult the country on the terms that would serve as a basis for [further] consultation and to which its representatives would have to conform.*[2]

Although de Gaulle did not reveal his own thinking with any precision, he had said enough to set the cat among the pigeons. He had expressed disapproval of a return to the Third Republic and evoked the possibility of a referendum. It was soon clear that he had embarked on a collision course with the parties and their leaders. One after the other, they passed resolutions or made speeches condemning the idea of a referendum. The Communists, Socialists and Christian Democrats (MRP) called for a sovereign single chamber; and the Radicals for the system under which they had flourished – that of the Third Republic.

Nor was de Gaulle to find any support from the liberated statesmen of the Third Republic. In prison, Blum had written in favour of a presidential system; at liberty, he had soon returned to his old habits, turning down de Gaulle's offer of a portfolio and publicly declaring, in a speech on 20 May – only six days after his return to France – "No man has the right to power. But we ourselves have the right to be ungrateful."

---

[2] ibid. pp. 255–6. Once again, de Gaulle's version of his own words in his memoirs differs in a number of details from that given in the official *Discours* (Vol. I [1970], pp. 571–2), which omits the words I have italicised above. We must, I think, assume the version given in the war memoirs is the correct one, if only because of the arguments de Gaulle develops, which are based on the passages omitted from the later text. Incidentally, de Gaulle gives the date of the press conference as 3 June, whereas it took place on the 2nd, as correctly stated on p. 194 of *Salut*. The questioner, according to *Discours*, was the famous novelist François Mauriac.

Herriot was an even bigger disappointment. Swallowing his reticence towards this most typical representative of the Third Republic, de Gaulle had sent his personal aircraft to Beirut to bring him back to Paris after his liberation by the Russians. But Herriot, too, had turned down the job de Gaulle offered him. All he dreamed of was a return to his old haunts and habits; and in particular, of the revival of his ailing Radical–Socialist party. It was the same with the right-wing politician, Louis Marin, a Lorrainer who had supported de Gaulle without reserve while the Germans were being expelled from French territory, but now took his distance from the general. He, too, turned down the offer of a ministry and found nothing attractive in the idea of limiting the powers of the deputies.

To accommodate some of the distinguished figures that were now returning from captivity and were willing to serve in the provisional government, de Gaulle now reshuffled his team. Christian Pineau, who had just emerged from Buchenwald concentration camp, replaced his fellow Socialist Paul Ramadier as minister of Supply. Eugène Thomas, back from deportation, became minister of Posts, in place of Augustin Laurent who was retiring for health reasons. François de Menthon was sent to Nuremberg to represent France at the War Crimes Tribunal, and his portfolio of Justice was given to Pierre-Henri Teitgen.

After long consultations with Jeanneney, de Gaulle drew up a formal electoral proposal, which combined elections with a referendum. On 9 July, he presented it to the Council of Ministers. Since most of his ministers belonged to political parties, all of which had declared their disapproval of his ideas, he announced at the outset that he accepted in advance any resignations that might be tendered. However, not one of the ministers resigned, and the proposal was accepted unanimously.

It was an ingenious plan. The country would vote for an Assembly in October. Simultaneously, the electors would answer two questions with a straight Yes or No:

1. Do you want the Assembly elected today to be constituent?
2. If the electoral body has answered Yes to the first question, do you approve that the public powers should be – until the entry into force of the new constitution – organised in conformity with the provisions of the bill whose text appears on the reverse of this bulletin?[3]

If a majority of the electors voted No to the first question then the second would become irrelevant: for a No would simply mean that the

[3] Fauvet, IVème, p. 51; see also p. 52.

Third Republic was reinstated as it had been, and elections for a Senate would follow. A Yes to the first question, followed by a Yes to the second, meant that the powers of the Assembly would be limited in various ways and would last only seven months. During that time, it would draw up a constitution which would be put to the people in a further referendum. If, however, a Yes to the first question were followed by a No to the second, then the Assembly would be sovereign and would last as long as it wished.

The election-referendum was to take place on 21 October 1945. At its meeting on 9 July, the cabinet also decided that Departmental Council (Conseil-Général) elections should take place on 23 and 30 September.

Having decided on the form of the questions to be put to the sovereign people, de Gaulle made known his personal preference in a broadcast on 12 July. He called for a double Yes, meaning "no return to the Third Republic" and a Constituent Assembly of limited powers and duration. An acrimonious debate followed in the Consultative Assembly, on 27 and 28 July. With passion, de Gaulle defended himself against a charge of Bonapartism which several members had hurled at him. Far from wishing to strangle the Republic, he remarked, he had pulled it out of the tomb. Did this, he asked, bear any resemblance to Napoleon I's 18 Brumaire, or Napoleon III's 2 December? There must be an end to the haggling and intrigues of the old regime. Between 1875 and 1940, France had had 102 governments. During the same period, Great Britain had had twenty and the United States fourteen.

The Assembly listened to him with respect; then by 210 votes to 19 rejected the government's proposals in their entirety. They failed utterly, however, to agree on an alternative. Thereupon, under an ordinance dated 17 August, de Gaulle proclaimed the electoral law, which was substantially the same as the original draft.

Again, a bitter wrangle followed, this time concerning the method of voting, each party clamouring for the arrangements most likely to give it a majority in the new Assembly. De Gaulle opted for the system least likely to allow the Communists to dominate it: voting for party lists instead of individual candidates, with proportional representation not, as the left wanted, on the national scale, but at the departmental level. When the trade union boss, Léon Jouhaux, as leader of the hastily constituted movement opposing his voting procedure, asked to see him on 1 September, de Gaulle refused point-blank on the ground that a trade unionist should keep out of politics. The Communists attacked the referendum as a barely disguised plebiscite for de Gaulle and launched a vicious campaign to deprive de Gaulle of the support of the one party that seemed likely to stand by him – the MRP – by eliminating it from the race. Bidault, its leader and president of the National Council of the Resistance, heard his party described as a "machine to pick up Pétainists".

In the end, 96 per cent of the voters voted Yes to the first question; that is, No to the Third Republic. The Communists and Radicals who, for different reasons, had called for No to the second, failed to carry the day: 66 per cent said Yes to a limited constituent Assembly. De Gaulle, then, had got his way, but in an atmosphere that boded ill for further success.

In the Assembly of 586 members, the Communists had 160 seats, the Socialists 142 and the Popular Republicans 152; the Radicals were eclipsed, with only 29 members. For the first and last time in French political history, the Communists and Socialists, with 302 seats between them, had an absolute majority. A Popular Front government looked possible, and logical – but for one thing: de Gaulle's presence. To secure a Popular Front government, the Communists would have had to make sure de Gaulle did not become the Prime Minister; and this turned out to be beyond their power.

The new Constituent Assembly met for the first time on 6 November. Although de Gaulle had not yet decided to retire, he was already certain that his retirement could not long be deferred. And when it came, he wanted to be able to leave untarnished by intrigues or manoeuvres. As he wrote later: "They would take me as I was, or they wouldn't take me at all."[4]

The first act of the new parliamentarians was to elect a president, that is, a speaker. Their choice was the Socialist Félix Gouin. Their next obligation was to choose a Prime Minister. Was it going to be de Gaulle? The initial speeches were peppered with slyly critical references to his policy, which were applauded, and conventional praise of his person, which evoked little response. He himself, true to character, did not put his name forward as a candidate.

After a week of embarrassing discussions, the Assembly unanimously voted him president of the Council of the provisional government, on 13 November. The general was touched when Churchill, who had lunched with him in Paris that day, wrote to congratulate him on his election. Remembering the circumstances of his own removal from power earlier that year, Churchill recalled Plutarch's dictum that "Ingratitude towards great men is the mark of strong peoples", and

[4] De Gaulle, *Salut*, p. 273; *see also* pp. 275–87.

added: "Plutarch told a lie!" But de Gaulle had no illusions. The deputies had voted for him out of respect for his record, but they had no intention of supporting his programme.

And indeed, a political crisis immediately followed de Gaulle's election. When he tried to form a government, the Communist leader, Thorez, claimed at least one of the principal ministerial posts – which he defined as Defence, the Interior and Foreign Affairs – for his party. Here was an issue on which no compromise was possible. Had de Gaulle given in, he would have handed the Communists a master card to play in a crisis. But if he refused, it might turn out to be impossible to form a government. And in that event, the Communists would have demonstrated that they held the whip hand.

With his usual decisiveness, de Gaulle met the challenge head-on. He told Thorez that his party could not have any of the ministries it claimed: only the economic portfolios were on offer. "Furious diatribes" followed (writes de Gaulle), in which the Communists accused him of insulting the memory of the 75,000 party members shot by the Germans – an arbitrary claim, according to de Gaulle, since the true figure was no more than a fifth of that number. From the Socialists as well as the Communists, however, he was under pressure to give in for the sake of national unity. Since he was determined not to yield, he wrote on the 17th to the president of the Assembly – not to resign, which would have been fatal, but to return his mandate, an ambiguous formula which left it open to assume it again. Next day, in a radio speech, he appealed to the people to understand why he could not give the Communists the power to dominate France's policy, by giving them "the diplomacy which expresses it, the army which supports it or the police which protects it". He was ready to form a government with whomsoever was prepared to follow him. Failing this, he would quit immediately and without bitterness.

His ultimatum carried the day. After a heated debate, which he did not attend, the Assembly re-elected him President of the Council, the Communists abstaining. Without delay, they came to see him, offering their services in any capacity and without conditions. Their reward was to be given four of the "economic" ministries in the government de Gaulle announced on 21 November: National Economy, Labour, Production and Armaments. Four Socialists and four Popular Republicans also entered the government, together with two members of the Democratic Union of the Resistance (Pleven and Soustelle), a Radical and two independents (one of them André Malraux, the writer).

Very soon de Gaulle's victory was shown to be Pyrrhic. True, he was able to get some of the major bills of the preceding government on to the statute book. The Bank of France was duly nationalised and a National Credit Council, responsible to the Finance minister, was set up. Again, the production of electricity and gas was transferred to the State, and the National School of Administration – brain-child of Michel Debré – was created. But two more major crises came in quick succession. The first was on 15 December, when all employees in the public service threatened to strike if their wages were not immediately raised. Ironically, the Communists, who were set on staying in the government, rescued the government by supporting minor pay rises and other financial concessions.

The second crisis concerned the Budget, and burst on 1 January 1946, when the Socialists, without prior warning, called for a 20 per cent cut in the Defence allocations. Once again, the Communists, who had the Armaments ministry, came to the rescue, by opposing any reductions. But their attitude, this time, was ambiguous, for they let it be known that if the Socialists insisted on pressing the point, the Communists would have no choice but to support them.

By then, de Gaulle's mind was made up. The Assembly's Constitutional Commission had been in session since 4 December 1945 and, by the end of the year, it had reached agreement on proposals that would remove all authority from the future president of the Republic and subordinate the government to the National Assembly. This he knew although the *rapporteur* of the commission, François de Menthou, had declined to tell him what had been decided, on the grounds that he was not a member. These proposals were the exact opposite of de Gaulle's, and he did not propose to live with them. On that New Year's day, therefore, he rose to castigate the parliamentarians in terms that were to prove prophetic.

"The issue that separates us," he said, with due solemnity, "is a general conception of government and of its relations with the national representation. We have begun to rebuild the Republic. After me, you will continue to do so. I must tell you in conscience – and doubtless this is the last time I shall speak in this enclosure – that if you do so in misunderstanding of our political history of the past fifty years, if you take no account of the absolute necessities of authority, of dignity, of the responsibility of the government, you will head towards a situation such that, one day or another, I predict, you will bitterly regret you have taken the path you now follow."

The deputies listened absent-mindedly, but when it came to it, voted almost unanimously in favour of the Budget. Twelve years were to elapse before the awful truth of de Gaulle's prophecy was to become apparent.

The only question now left for de Gaulle to decide was the exact date of his retirement. An interlude for meditation seemed indicated. He chose to spend it at Antibes, on the Mediterranean coast. It was the first holiday he had allowed himself in more than seven years, and it lasted a week. He knew now that he would go quietly, without attacking anybody and without accepting any post, whether public or private.

Returning on 14 January, he spent the week signing the decrees and laws that had accumulated during his absence. He called a number of his ministers to his office to let them know that his departure was now imminent.

On the 16th, Herriot, who had not forgiven the French public, especially in his headquarters at Lyon, for failing to greet him as he used to be greeted, and whose soul was full of envy, sought to embarrass de Gaulle by calling on him to cancel the medals and citations awarded three years earlier by General Giraud to French servicemen who had lost their lives or suffered severe wounds when fighting against the Americans. These awards had just been confirmed, with de Gaulle's approval, in the *Journal Officiel*. Disgusted with Herriot's choice of an issue on which to challenge him, de Gaulle turned on the Radical leader, declaring that he was the best judge of the validity of the awards, since "I myself never had anything to do with Vichy or with the enemy, except by cannon fire". This allusion to Herriot's lunch, on the eve of the liberation of Paris, with Laval and Abetz, silenced Herriot but confirmed de Gaulle in his contempt for professional politicians.

On Sunday, 20 January, all de Gaulle's ministers gathered at his invitation in his office in the rue Saint-Dominique. Three only were absent: Auriol and Bidault who were in London, and Soustelle who was in Gabon. This was the last scene, and it was very brief. De Gaulle entered, shook hands with everybody and without inviting them to be seated, delivered his carefully prepared statement:

The exclusive regime of the parties has come back. I disapprove of it. But, short of establishing by force a dictatorship which I don't want and which would probably turn out badly, I lack the means to prevent this experiment. I must therefore retire. This day, I shall address to the president of the National Assembly a letter informing him of the government's resignation. I thank each of you very sincerely for the help you have given me and I ask you to stay at your posts to ensure the despatch of business until your successors are appointed.

Sad rather than surprised, the ministers stayed silent, and de Gaulle took his leave.

After he had left, Thorez remarked: "There's a certain grandeur about this departure."

In his formal letter to the president of the Assembly, de Gaulle avoided all polemics. He had only stayed in power after 13 November 1945, he declared, to ensure a smooth transition. He outlined some of his government's achievements, and wished success to the next government.

For all that, the politicians were worried. Vincent Auriol returned precipitately from London and, fearing that de Gaulle would go on the air to arouse the people's anger against the parties, wrote to him on the 20th to say that if this were his intention, he would be dividing the country "to the advantage and satisfaction of the enemies of democracy".

But Auriol need not have worried. De Gaulle had no wish to pour fuel on the flames. He was content with silence, for he was confident that soon enough the Fourth Republic would collapse and the people of France clamour for his return. He was right in all respects except the vital one of time. By the time the call came, in 1958, he was a much older man.

Part V ⚜ The Fourth Republic 1946–1958

Chapter 1 ⚜ Birth and Challenge

De Gaulle had hoped his departure from power would be marked by popular demonstrations. To his disappointment, there was none. His property at Colombey – La Boisserie – had been damaged by enemy action and while it was being made habitable, he rented for himself and his family the Royal Hunting Lodge at Marly, near Paris. It is probable that even if La Boisserie had been in good repair, he would have preferred, at least for the time being, to live near Paris. For by so doing he was showing that he considered his absence from power to be temporary. He was, indeed, convinced that an early crisis would bring him back to power on his own terms, on a wave of popular acclaim.

The coolness of the populace was the more disappointing. When neither crowds nor delegations called at Marly, he sent a messenger to find out whether the police had put up cordons. No impediment was discovered. Flatteringly, the minister of the Interior, Adrien Tixier, shared de Gaulle's expectation of a popular clamour. De Gaulle's hope was Tixier's apprehension. He summoned the commissioners of the Republic to Paris for a crisis briefing, told them the situation was "grave", then sent them back with alacrity to their provincial posts.[1] But he need not have worried: having been liberated, the French people – and their press – were ready to lose interest in General de Gaulle. Within a week, his name no longer rated front-page treatment.[2]

Insults would have been more tolerable than indifference. In his disappointment, de Gaulle began hurling insults to those of his faithful followers who visited him. "The French," he exclaimed "are cattle."

His remarks to visitors were startling alternations between the ripest barrack-room language and philosophical speculations. One moment he would be denouncing the "*politichiens*" – his contemptuous neologism for the politicians – the "vinegar-pissers", the "sterilisers", the "eunuchs of the Fourth Republic", the "paralytics of politics", or using other even less readily translatable epithets. The next, he would solemnly

---

[1] J.-R. Tournoux, *La Tragédie du Général*, p. 26 (henceforth, Tournoux, *Tragédie*).
[2] Crawley, p. 292.

proclaim the approach of the Third World War, with the Russians in Paris and a second 18 June on the way. Indeed, his faith in the imminence of his return to power was directly linked with his belief in the imminence of war. For the indifference of the people had made it clear that only a great national crisis would bring him back, and in that context, no crisis could equal another war.

The fascinating game of parliamentary musical chairs was back in favour. De Gaulle had spoilt the sport; now the politicians could show, to their own satisfaction, how closely the Fourth Republic was to resemble the Third. As the MRP leader, Georges Bidault, put it: "There is an impossible great man and several possible average men."[3] The average men became the players, and essentially, in this first post-Gaullist phase, the game consisted of ringing the permutations made possible by the parliamentary dominance of three parties – the Communists, the Christian Democrats (MRP), and the Socialists. The rules of the game were drawn up in a protocol signed by representatives of the three parties on 24 January 1946, only four days after de Gaulle's resignation. The politicians promised not to indulge in offensive or insulting polemics. "In the government, in the Assembly, the press and the country," they pledged themselves to develop "a spirit of loyal solidarity for decisions taken in common". As time went on, these admirable sentiments were less and less respected.

A reassuring figure, Félix Gouin, the Socialist president (that is, speaker) of the Assembly, was voted Prime Minister, by 497 of the 555 votes cast; three Assemblymen had voted forlornly for the departed general. The spectre of another Popular Front began to haunt the chamber, for when it came to the issue of the constitution, the Socialists sided with the Communists in pressing for a text which the Christian Democrats could not accept, if only because the preamble omitted any guarantee to the Catholic schools.[4] They had other reasons for objecting to the draft, and so had the opposition parties, including Mendès France's Radicals, for it envisaged a virtually unfettered single chamber, with a weak president of the Republic: the perfect recipe for a gradual and constitutional take-over by the Communist party.

To the general surprise of the politicians, however, the voters of France turned down the constitution proposals in a referendum on 5 May, by some ten and a half million to nine and a half million. It was the first time in the country's history that a negative verdict had been

[3] Fauvet, IVème, p. 70.
[4] See Philip Williams, Politics in Post-War France (henceforth, Williams), p. 17.

returned in a direct appeal to the people. As Jacques Fauvet shrewdly notes, this was the first time that a referendum had been presented by an amorphous assembly and not by some outstanding personality – a Louis-Napoleon, for instance.[5] Unlike previous "consultations", this one was not, in its effect, a plebiscite. The voters were asked for a straight answer to a straight question; and gave it. During the campaign for and against the constitution, de Gaulle, sunk in his frustrated resentment, said nothing in public. And he abstained from voting.[6]

The general's period of self-restraint was, however, coming to an end. By now, La Boisserie had been made habitable and he had moved there with his wife and their sick daughter, Anne. The other daughter, Elisabeth, had been married, on 3 January 1946, to Squadron-Leader Alain de Boissieu; their son Philippe shortly afterwards became engaged to Henriette de Montalembert.[7] In the poverty-stricken village of Colombey, on its high plateau, a genteel poverty now visited the squire of the manor in his turn. For all his claims to permanent "legitimacy", de Gaulle was conscious of the provisional nature of the power he had exercised, and had declined the honours that would have been his for the asking. His sole income at that time was his pension as a brigadier-general. In April 1946 Félix Gouin had instructed the minister of War to draft a decree under which de Gaulle's army rank would have been raised to the highest the land could offer. But it would have been out of character for de Gaulle to accept from lesser men a promotion which neither circumstances nor his military prowess had brought him. So, when informed of the president's wishes, he replied:

> In answer to your letter ... since 18 June 1940, the date on which I ceased to conform to a pattern and embarked on a fairly exceptional course, events have been such and on such a scale that it would be impossible to regularise a situation that is entirely without precedent. Moreover, no one apparently thought it necessary to change anything during the five years, seven months and three days of an epic struggle. An administrative solution which might be applied today would be strange and even ridiculous. The proper course is to leave things as they are. Death will take care of the difficulty in time, if there is a difficulty to take care of.[8]

In the same spirit, he handed over to the air force the DC4 he had received from President Truman as a personal gift, and sold his large American car – to an artist named Florelle. Yvonne de Gaulle took

[5] Fauvet, IVème, p. 73.
[7] Gorce, p. 448.
[6] L'Année Politique, 1946, p. 161.
[8] Edward Ashcroft, De Gaulle, p. 199.

driving lessons, passed her test and was soon driving a more modest French car in the village and to neighbouring towns for provisions.[9] Money was short, and the diet was often austere. Wine was reserved for guests, and some – including Ambassador Dejean on one occasion – had to make do with water. De Gaulle's appetite matched his size, but his tastes were rustic enough to fit a limited purse: plenty of cabbage, tripe *à la mode de Caen*, pig's trotters, all delighted him, with the occasional luxury of *boeuf bourguignon*.

The three acres of parkland that surrounded La Boisserie were de Gaulle's solace, and he never tired of walking through the formal gardens, which Yvonne de Gaulle kept in trim with the help of a part-time gardener. The large flower bed in the centre had been planted in the form of a Cross of Lorraine. From the tower which de Gaulle had added to the eighteenth-century building, he had a choice of three views. There he whiled away the lengthening hours, re-editing his earlier literary works; and there, some years later, he was to write his war memoirs.

As the long continental winter of Haute-Marne turned slowly into spring, the weight of his boredom became intolerable. There was a limit to the relief that could be obtained from his daily torrent of imprecations, or from the frequent expression of his gnawing envy of President Truman. To be forgotten was intolerable; to be silent, a suffering no longer to be endured. It had to end. And the referendum of 5 May provided the general with a good excuse to break his silence.

On 16 June 1946 de Gaulle launched his premeditated attack on the government and the constitution that had just been defeated at the polls.[10] He spoke at Bayeux, the first liberated French town, during the festivities commemorating his visit there at the time of the Normandy landings. The *discours de Bayeux* is of great importance; for although it had no immediate consequences, it precisely foreshadowed the constitution of the Fifth Republic, promulgated about twelve years later.

"During a period of time which does not exceed twice a man's lifetime," said de Gaulle, "France was invaded seven times and lived under thirteen regimes."[11] The rivalry of parties was ill suited to the dangerous times that lay ahead. Because of the inadequacy of the regime of parties, the threat of a dictatorship always hung over the democracies. How and

[9] Tournoux, *Tragédie*, p. 29 n.
[10] Strictly speaking, this was not de Gaulle's first public speech since his resignation, for he had spoken a few patriotic, but not specially significant, words at the tomb of Clemenceau in Vendée on 12 May on the double occasion of the anniversary of victory in Europe and of the Joan of Arc national day.
[11] For full text, *see* De Gaulle, *Discours*, Vol. II, p. 7.

why, he asked, had the First, Second and Third Republics ended? How and why had Italy's democracy, the Weimar Republic and the Spanish Republic yielded to the dictatorships that followed? And yet, dictatorship was not the answer. After the anarchy of a failed democracy, it gave a first impression of dynamic purpose. But it was essentially an adventure. As time went on, the dictator was impelled to launch ever more grandiose schemes, both at home and abroad, until in the end all collapsed in suffering and blood.

After the preamble, the prescription. The elected Assembly had, of course, the right to vote laws and budgets. But its wisdom was limited. It was essential that there should be a second Assembly, elected upon different principles and representing local interests, professional and family interests, and the territories of France overseas. This second house should have powers of amendment; and, together with the elected local councils of the overseas territories, it should constitute the grand council of the French Union. It was obvious, de Gaulle went on, that the executive power should not proceed from parliament, on pain of reducing the government to an "assemblage of delegations". True, this had happened with the provisional government, but the procedure was justified by abnormal circumstances and the vacuum of power. The chief of State should be above party, and should be elected by a college comprising not only parliament but a much wider membership. He should be the president of the French Union as well as of the Republic. And, above all, he should have the responsibility of choosing the premier and lesser ministers. To him would fall the task of presiding over cabinet meetings and of arbitrating in contentious issues, referring the most intractable to the French voters. If ever the country should be in danger, the chief of State would be the guarantor of national independence and of the treaties concluded by France.

In the circumstances of that time, de Gaulle knew he was addressing his words not only to the government as a whole and the people in general, but to one man in particular: Georges Bidault, leader of the Mouvement Républicain Populaire. But for strong reasons, Bidault had little incentive to listen. Born of the Resistance, the MRP was widely regarded as de Gaulle's creature. But Bidault, who had felt oppressed in de Gaulle's presence, had been relieved to see him go: the attractions of power at a less exalted level than the general's were potent. Moreover, the MRP's opposition to the constitution had paid rapid political dividends. Appalled by the adverse vote in the referendum, which had shown that many Socialists had voted against party policy, the Socialist leaders abruptly turned against the Communists in the election campaign that immediately followed. Daniel Mayer announced that they would not support a government led by Maurice Thorez; And André le Troecquer went further by denouncing Thorez as a deserter and exclaiming, "With Thorez in power, we would be serving the cause of Russia."[12]

Little did this about-turn serve them: in the general election of 2 June 1946 the Communists gained votes and the Socialists lost 500,000. It was the beginning of the long Socialist slide to political insignificance. The big gainers were the MRP, who attracted more than five and a half million votes to displace the Communists as the leading party in France. On 19 June Bidault became premier of another tripartite coalition.

Though now in power and with the strength of popular support, Bidault was too conscious of the lateness of his success and its precariousness to ignore the general entirely. That he feared him still is clear. But political expediency ruled out a slavish response to the Bayeux speech. A purely Gaullist constitution might itself be rejected, and if it were, more weary months of provisional government would follow. Moreover, the MRP did not enjoy working with the Communists: its moral discomfort was patent. Better then, Bidault's followers reasoned, to draw up another compromise constitution, improving on the first and with a high chance of electoral acceptance. Only thus could the "tripartism" be broken and the provisional era ended.[13]

The Christian Democrats therefore sat down with the Socialists to draft a fresh text. The Communists, however, also sat on the drafting commission. Although they and the Socialists had lost their absolute majority in the Assembly, they were able to deprive the MRP of the clause it wanted guaranteeing freedom for the Catholic schools. But they could not prevent the adoption of MRP proposals for the election of a chief of State by secret ballot of both houses, instead of the public vote of a single Assembly.

As a precaution, Bidault sent two of his MRP colleagues, Maurice Schumann and Pierre-Henri Teitgen, to Colombey to plead the cause of the new constitutional draft. They were coldly received. "Your constitution," General de Gaulle declared, "resembles that of 5 May like a sister."

The second constitutional referendum had been arranged for 13 October. Weeks earlier, de Gaulle had launched his campaign against the revised draft. On 27 August, when the second Constituent Assembly was about to debate it, he made a detailed rebuttal of it in a statement to the press. In a further statement, this time in question-and-answer

---

[12] Fauvet, IVème, p. 76; for further matter, see also pp. 79 and 81.
[13] Williams, p. 18.

form, when the Assembly was preparing to vote on the final draft on 19 September, he solemnly warned the parliamentarians against approving it. Finally, on 29 September, at Épinal, he delivered an eloquent anathema upon the whole concept of the Constitution.[14] In the early hours of the 29th – a Sunday – the Assembly had, however, adopted the draft by 540 votes to 106. The general had miscalculated the political consequences of his interventions. Himself disdainful of parliamentary arithmetic, he had neglected to do his sums. The Communists did not like the MRP-Socialist text; but de Gaulle's denunciations scared them into supporting it, for fear of something closer to the Bayeux model.

De Gaulle, however, was also addressing the French people, over the heads of their elected representatives. And on that plane, his words were not without effect, although he failed to sway the decision. On 13 October, more than nine million voters said Yes to the feeble text he had denounced, and fewer than eight million said No. Significantly, about as many as had opposed the text abstained altogether. The constitution of the Fourth Republic was thus approved by a minority of elegible French men and women. But this did not invalidate it. Despite the evidence of apathy, many ordinary people, and most parliamentarians, were relieved that France, at last and at least, had a constitution, for now the work of national reconstruction, so long delayed, could begin. Now, too, the politicians could settle down to their games and intrigues, without worrying too much about their immediate survival. It would not be long before de Gaulle's strictures were proved well founded. But the Fourth Republic had twelve years of life before it.

Indignant Gaullists made the pilgrimage to Colombey and, undoubtedly with the general's approval, launched a virulent campaign against the "faithless" MRP. René Capitant, the left-wing Gaullist, set up a Gaullist Union to defend the ideas in the Bayeux speech. Not waiting for the referendum, he had begun to hit at the Christian Democrats in August. In October the general's brother-in-law, J. Vendroux, who had just resigned from the MRP, published the text of a letter from de Gaulle congratulating him on voting against the constitution. The letter went on to castigate MRP leaders, though not by name. In November Jacques Chaban-Delmas told an audience of 2,000 that on a recent visit to Colombey de Gaulle had said of the MRP that initially he had thought this new party, whose members were honest and patriotic men, would "purify" French political life, but had been

[14] For texts, see De Gaulle, *Discours*, Vol. II, pp. 18–34. Fauvet, *IVème*, p. 79, and other authorities wrongly date the Epinal speech on the 22nd and the Assembly vote on the 30th. In his speech, however, de Gaulle referred to the adoption of the draft "last night".

disappointed in its performance: he still thought its leaders were men of principle, but "because they are incapable, they are dangerous". One of the listeners was Bidault himself, who sprang to his feet to reply, "I note that we are being judged honest and principled, but incapable. If you know others more honest and more capable, send them along to take our places."[15] Colonel Passy, de Gaulle's wartime secret service chief, made a speech attacking Maurice Schumann.

Wearily, the voters went to the polls on 10 November 1946, for the fifth time in a year: at least, many of them did. Abstainers reached 21.9 per cent, the highest figure since 1919. Having failed to abort the constitution, de Gaulle had made only one intervention in the electoral campaign – a press statement, once again denouncing the party system but without singling out any one party for abuse. The Christian Democrats lost the 500,000 votes they had gained in the previous election, but might have lost more if they had had to face attacks by de Gaulle himself instead of by his followers. The decline of the Socialists continued, and the Communists, with a slight increase in their vote, emerged once again as the strongest party. In the final tally for Metropolitan France, the Communists had 166 seats, the MRP 158 and the Socialists 90; outside the tripartite parties, the Radicals (with their allies, the Rassemblement des Gauches Républicaines or RGR) held 55 seats and the Conservatives 70.

The election almost, but not quite, killed tripartism. The MRP had campaigned on the slogan "Bidault without Thorez", and could scarcely now consent to taking part in a coalition that included the Communists. The Socialists, on the other hand, conscious of their weakness, declined to govern without the Communists. As if to prove that de Gaulle's contempt for parliamentary manoeuvres was not misplaced, the new National Assembly started off with a crisis. As the strongest party, the Communists put up Thorez for the premiership; lacking the MRP's votes, he failed to get a majority. Next day, the Communists turned the tables on the Christian Democrats, whose candidate, Bidault, obtained even fewer votes than Thorez had. In the end – but not until 16 December – Léon Blum headed a government of Socialists only, with the temporary confidence of 575 deputies and only 15 against. It was too good to last: a month later, Blum was out of office.

Blum's brief passage at the helm coincided with the start of the Indo-China war, which was to sap the feeble strength of the Fourth Republic over the ensuing seven and a half years. On 19 December 1946 the troops of the Vietnamese Communist and nationalist leader, Ho Chi

[15] Fauvet, IVème, p. 81; Tournoux, Tragédie, p. 31.

The First Indo-China War

Minh, massacred forty Frenchmen in Hanoi. It was the beginning of a
long premeditated uprising organised by Ho Chi Minh, his military
commander Vo Nguyen Giap, and their political organisation, the
League for the Independence of Vietnam, better known as the Vietminh.
Less than a month earlier – on 23 November – the French fleet had

bombarded the Vietnamese quarter of Haiphong, killing or wounding many thousands.[16]

It is idle to speculate how General de Gaulle would have handled this situation, and the Indo-China war as a whole, had he been in power when it began. All one can do is to recall the part he played when he *was* in power, and the opinions he expressed later. It is clear that in 1945 and 1946 he had no thoughts at all of recognising the independence of any part of France's possessions in Indo-China, nor of any other component of the Empire.[17] Indeed, he believed France's status as a great power depended upon the retention of the overseas territories, whatever arrangements might have to be made to meet local demands for self-rule.

He had asked the western Allies for ships to send an expeditionary force to Indo-China, but had been frustrated, at least temporarily, by President Roosevelt's anti-colonial attitude. In the end, 80,000 troops had gone in September 1945 under the command of General Leclerc. With them went Admiral Thierry d'Argenlieu as high commissioner. Nine years later, at a press conference on 30 June 1954, de Gaulle defined the instructions he had given to Leclerc and d'Argenlieu in 1945 in terms that are worth recalling if only because they show how hindsight can distort the facts. The two men (said de Gaulle) were instructed to regain a solid foothold in Cochinchina and southern Annam, as well as in Cambodia and Laos, but not to force France's will on northern Annam and Tonking until he gave orders to that effect. They were, however, to make as many political contacts as possible with the northerners. De Gaulle was not at that stage in a hurry. He intended to frustrate American pretensions to interfere in Indo-China. In time, there would be elections to local assemblies on the five parts of Indo-China. Having thus found people to talk to, "France" – that is, de Gaulle – could decide what her policy should be.[18]

This reconstruction of the past, however, was uttered after the fall of Dien Bien Phu and at the close of the Indo-China war. His attitude at the time was quite different. Leclerc's papers, extensively quoted by Claude Paillat, make it clear beyond doubt that as soon as circumstances should make it possible, the French expeditionary force were to take

[16] The dead alone numbered 6,000, wrote Jean Sainteny (*Histoire d'une paix Manquée*, p. 216, henceforth, Sainteny).
[17] That these were indeed de Gaulle's views was confirmed to me, in a conversation in Paris in November 1968, by Pierre Mendès France, a frequent caller at Colombey during the general's "exile".
[18] Unless otherwise indicated, this account of the Indo-China situation is based upon Claude Paillat, *Vingt Ans qui Dechirèrent la France*, Vol. I, *Le Guêpier* (henceforth, *Guêpier*), pp. 151 *et seq.*

over Tonking as well. Indeed, in a number of press conferences between 1947 and 1951, the general spoke of Indo-China in intransigent terms. On 29 March 1949, for instance, he described the Ho Chi Minh solution as "capitulation".

While d'Argenlieu and Leclerc were restoring France's authority in Cochinchina, Jean Sainteny, as commissioner of the Republic, was attempting to reassert France's political presence in Tonking. It was uphill work, for he faced the *de facto* government established, with American encouragement, under Ho Chi Minh and ex-Emperor Bao Dai (whose appeal for independence de Gaulle had ignored). Leclerc and Sainteny on the one hand, and d'Argenlieu on the other, were unfortunately in disagreement on the proper interpretation of de Gaulle's policy and indeed over the respective merits of military and political action after de Gaulle had resigned. Leclerc, quick-tempered but utterly honest, worshipped by his subordinates, was totally out of sympathy with d'Argenlieu – the former Carmelite monk turned sailor – who was both authoritarian and indecisive.

Though a military man, Leclerc was convinced that the French would have to come to terms with the Vietnamese nationalists. In a telegraphed report to General Juin and Admiral d'Argenlieu on 14 February 1946, he declared that the Vietnamese interpretation of "independence" (a word the French were determined not to use) was exactly what the French understood by "autonomy"; he therefore proposed that the forbidden word should be used, and that the French government should declare its readiness to concede independence within the French Union *in advance* of the arrival of military forces in Tonking. By then, of course, de Gaulle was out of office; but these views were anathema to him, and to d'Argenlieu, who justly claimed, throughout this troubled period, that he was acting in complete agreement with de Gaulle.[19]

When Leclerc telegraphed his report, he had already restored order in Cochinchina and southern Annam, but he was reluctant to use force in the north, if only because he realised the tenacity of the hold the Vietminh now had over the population and knew that the forces at France's disposal were hopelessly inadequate to restore French authority. After weeks of negotiations, Sainteny and Ho Chi Minh – between whom a curious bond of sympathy had been forged – signed the provisional agreements of 6 March 1946. The French government

[19] In conversation with me in Paris in January 1969, Jean Sainteny said: "D'Argenlieu had an influence on the general. It was not a good one." Mendès France, during the conversation previously mentioned, also told me, with evident truth, that d'Argenlieu had de Gaulle's confidence.

recognised "the Republic of Vietnam as a free State, having its own government, its parliament, its army and its treasury". But the word "independence" was not used, and it was stipulated that the Republic formed part of the Indo-Chinese Federation (along with Laos and Cambodia). As for the unity of the three *ky* or provinces of Vietnam (Tonking, Annam and Cochinchina) – which Ho Chi Minh claimed, as Bao Dai did later – it was laid down that the matter would be decided by referendum.

Ultimate authority on the spot, however, was vested in Admiral d'Argenlieu, who disapproved of the agreements and denounced them privately as "another Munich". He consented to meet Ho Chi Minh on 24 March. Predictably, there was an immediate antipathy between the two men, both in their way fanatics, but in utterly different causes. Ho Chi Minh went away complaining of French duplicity; on his side, the admiral resolved to torpedo the arrangements made. His first step to this end was to allow the formation on 26 March of a "provisional government of the Republic of Cochinchina". On 10 June, the "Autonomous Republic of Cochinchina" was proclaimed, in clear violation of the agreements of 6 March, and the admiral, who had certainly encouraged the Cochinchinese to go ahead, immediately recognised it. He had already "shown the flag" in the north by sending General Valluy to Haiphong on 6 March – the day of Sainteny's agreement with Ho Chi Minh – and Leclerc to Hanoi on the 18th.

Ho Chi Minh learned of the proclamation of the Republic of Conchinchina on the plane that was taking him to France for further talks with the French government, and Sainteny had great difficulty in restraining him from returning to Hanoi.[20] The conference between the Vietminh delegates and the French nevertheless opened as planned at Fontainebleau on 6 July – to furious diatribes from the Vietminh, who complained, not without cause, that the French were planning to break the agreements of 6 March. On the 17th, Leclerc's resignation – which he had been pressing on Juin for weeks – was at last accepted. At the end of April, he had written to Juin to complain of Admiral d'Argenlieu's indecisiveness and "lack of intellectual probity". As if to show the truth of these charges, the high commissioner called a conference on 1 August at Dalat in the Vietnamese highlands, to discuss the constitution of an

[20] *See* Sainteny for his account of these events. When the book was published in 1954, de Gaulle sent for him and said, "In the end, it looks as though you will turn out to have been right." But in the spring of 1946, over coffee after lunch, de Gaulle had reproached him with making a deal with Ho Chi Minh before Leclerc's army had reached Tonking. Sainteny did not see de Gaulle again for seven years. (Conversation between author and Sainteny.)

Indo-Chinese federation. Since this was one of the points at issue between the French and the Vietminh and was scheduled for discussion at Fontainebleau, it was now plain that the talks were unlikely to be productive. They ended on 14 September with a lame *modus vivendi* agreement whose only purpose was to save Ho Chi Minh's face. Four days earlier, d'Argenlieu had unilaterally opened a French customs post at Haiphong, ostensibly to control the traffic in arms and petrol which the Vietminh was fostering. Soon, however, the French were imposing a complete naval blockade on the approaches to the harbour. Terroristic attempts and clashes between the Vietminh and French forces were multiplying.

What followed was a tragedy of personal feuds and absenteeism in high places. D'Argenlieu (the high commissioner) and Sainteny (the commissioner for Tonking) were both in France; their deputies in Saigon and Hanoi respectively were General Valluy, the commander-in-chief for Indo-China, and General Morlière, the general officer commanding in the north. But the principal actor was a less prominent man, Colonel Dèbes, who commanded the garrison at Haiphong, and whose immediate superior was therefore General Morlière. Dèbes, who had served under Morlière elsewhere, had quarrelled with him and tried, whenever possible, to circumvent him. Morlière, a Freemason, believed in accommodation with the Vietminh and dreaded having to take any action that would expose him to the criticism of left-wing politicians in Paris, whom he frequented on occasion. Dèbes believed in teaching the Vietminh a lesson; and so, in a less impulsive way, did Valluy.

On 21 November, Dèbes sent an ultimatum to the local Vietminh committee: they were to clear certain quarters of Haiphong and disarm the Vietnamese by 9 a.m. on 23 November. Failing that, the colonel would take any measures necessary. The key point is that Dèbes issued his ultimatum in the name of "the General High Commissioner of the French Republic in Indo-China", that is, General Valluy, but without consulting Valluy. Having issued the ultimatum, he informed Valluy but not Morlière who, as his immediate superior, should have been the first to be told. Valluy, however, though he reprimanded the colonel for not having "cleared" the ultimatum with him before issuing it, ordered Morlière to give Dèbes all support. When the Vietminh failed to respond by the appointed time, Dèbes requested the fleet to open fire; which it did with devastating effect. Over the next week, ground forces and paratroops "cleaned up" the town.

On the day of the bombardment, Sainteny – returning in all haste to his post – touched down at Saigon, where he conferred with

Valluy; who, however, thought it unnecessary to inform him of the French ultimatum.[21] Less than a month later, the Vietminh attack on the French garrison in Hanoi marked the start of the Indo-China war.

Ghastly though the bombardment of Haiphong had been, it was no more than a late contributory cause of the war; for in Ho Chi Minh's absence, the most extreme Vietminh group, led by Giap, had made thorough preparations for an insurrection. Ho Chi Minh was less extreme only in the sense that he had hoped to achieve independence through negotiations and without fighting for it; but when the time came, he led the fight for control over Indo-China, first against the French then against the Americans, until his death in 1969.

Shortly after the outbreak of the war, General Leclerc was summoned by Léon Blum (during his brief period in power[22]), who proposed to send him to Indo-China, at first as commander-in-chief, then as high commissioner in succession to Admiral d'Argenlieu, whom the Socialist leader wished to replace. Leclerc said he would have to consult de Gaulle, whom he still considered his chief, before replying. He therefore wrote to the general who, on 13 January 1947, replied in a letter defending the admiral and putting the blame for the Indo-China situation entirely on the men who had been governing France for a year – Gouin, Bidault and Blum. Instead of going to Indo-China, said de Gaulle, Leclerc should support d'Argenlieu. It is fair to speculate (as Claude Paillat does) that de Gaulle, who was on the eve of returning to politics, wished above all to prevent the appointment to so exposed a post as commander-in-chief in Indo-China, of one of the most "glorious" of the original Gaullists, who might soon be made a scapegoat for the failures of the Fourth Republic. Leclerc therefore turned down Blum's offer, on the grounds that Valluy ("who deserves an extra star") was able to stay on and that he – Leclerc – had no qualifications for the post of high commissioner. Moreover, he argued, to recall d'Argenlieu would be to admit a French failure in the eyes of the enemy and of the world.

On the 16th Blum fell, and his successor, Paul Ramadier (also a Socialist), immediately renewed the offer to Leclerc. Once again, Leclerc said he would have to consult General de Gaulle; but before doing so, he was persuaded to talk to the president of the Republic, Vincent Auriol (yet another Socialist). The interview took place on 8 February, and the president strongly pressed Leclerc to accept.

This time, Leclerc sought a meeting with de Gaulle, which took place

21 Fauvet, IVème, p. 95.
22 Political developments are dealt with more fully later in this chapter.

412

at the Gaullist headquarters in the Rue de Solférino. De Gaulle, in a furious temper, accused Leclerc of paying too much attention to the blandishments of the regime. Leclerc, who had a temper of his own, retorted that all de Gaulle knew about Indo-China was what d'Argenlieu told him. He went on to accuse his leader of having started the rot by losing Syria and the Lebanon. "It wasn't me, it was Catroux," exclaimed de Gaulle.

In the end, however, de Gaulle calmed down and told Leclerc that France should insist on an Indo-Chinese federation and refuse all concessions to the Vietminh on Cochinchina (which, unlike the other divisions of Indo-China, was a colony, not a protectorate). He declined, however, to resolve Leclerc's dilemma whether or not to accept the government's offer.[23]

On 10 February, still without committing himself, Leclerc wrote to Ramadier to say he would draft a report on the Indo-China situation. This he did forthwith. Three days later, however, he wrote again to the premier to decline, definitively, to take up any appointment in Indo-China. The government thereupon decided to send a former Resistance leader, Emile Bollaert, to Indo-China on a six-month's mission of enquiry, and with the aim of appointing him as high commissioner at the end of it. Getting wind of this scheme, d'Argenlieu threatened to resign; and, to his surprise, was taken at his word. On 5 March, then, Bollaert was appointed high commissioner.

Would de Gaulle's unyielding attitude have changed under the pressure of events? It is hard to say, if only because his conduct of affairs would undoubtedly have been more skilful than that of the politicians of the Fourth Republic, and might have yielded successes that were beyond their grasp. Ho Chi Minh seems to have thought that with de Gaulle in power, his own problems would have been simplified, for in a letter to a French politician in September 1955 he declared: "If de Gaulle had stayed on, things would have worked out differently. The independence of Vietnam would doubtless have been achieved without Dien Bien Phu, and the prospects for unification would be clearer than now seems likely."[24] But such speculations do not rest on any solid foundations. As Tournoux observes, de Gaulle's views might have changed; and then again, they might not have. In Algeria, some years later, the general was intransigent at first, then conciliatory. But that was six or seven years after Dien Bien Phu, the fall of which had

---

[23] The most complete account of the Leclerc incident is in Paillat, *Guêpier*, pp. 233–7; see also Tournoux, *Tragédie*, p. 49 n.
[24] Tournoux, *Tragédie*, p. 176 n.

provoked de Gaulle to coin yet another epithet to describe the politicians: *les capitulards.*[25]

When the Indo-China war began, at the end of 1946, however, all General de Gaulle could do was to look on and curse the regime for its handling of the situation. True, the politicians had other things on their minds besides Indo-China. Their first preoccupation was to preside over the birth of the Fourth Republic, after the long labour of the Constituent Assembly. The election of the first National Assembly on 10 November 1946 did not complete the process. Next came the election on the 24th of the "grand electors" who in turn, on 8 December, chose the members of the Upper House, which was termed the Council of the Republic and replaced the old Senate. Now the parliament was fully formed and could elect a chief of State. (On 28 December, de Gaulle had publicly denied the disquieting rumour that he would present himself as a candidate: he was not, he said, going to "preside, in impotence, over the impotence of the State".[26])

On a bright cold day – 16 January 1947 – both houses met in the dirty, ill-heated Palace of Versailles, and their choice fell upon a Socialist, Vincent Auriol. When all the wrangling and all the voting had finished, the other "presidents" were: Edouard Herriot (Radical), for the Assembly; Champetier de Ribes (MRP), for the Council of the Republic; and for the more important presidency of the Council, or premiership, the Socialist Paul Ramadier, a Greek scholar and childhood friend of President Auriol. The most striking thing about the Fourth Republic, at the time of its birth, was thus its close resemblance to the Third: for each of the four "presidents" had been a prominent figure in the defunct Republic. Who (asks Fauvet) would have believed it at the time of the liberation of Paris?[27]

Characteristically, the new regime began with a row and an unnecessary vote of confidence. The row was over Ramadier's appointment of a Communist, François Billoux, as Defence minister, against determined but abortive MRP protests. (The MRP itself got Foreign Affairs, with Bidault back in his old job.) The unnecessary vote of confidence

---

[25] General Ely, on being appointed commander-in-chief and high commissioner in Indo-China in June 1954, called on de Gaulle at Colombey to seek the general's approval for his plan to send a further three divisions of conscripts to the war. De Gaulle immediately approved; and indeed thought four divisions would be more appropriate. His prescription was to establish a position of force, and only then negotiate with Ho Chi Minh. Evoking the decisions of 1945, he said – already with a slight distortion through hindsight: "I brought France back to Indo-China, but it was not I who laid hands on Hanoi. We should have left Ho Chi Minh and Bao Dai facing each other after consolidating in Cochinchina. And then, just waited...."
[26] De Gaulle, *Discours*, Vol. II, p. 37.   [27] Fauvet, *IVème*, p. 103.

came because, out of force of Third Republic habit, Ramadier solicited the support of the Assembly for his constituted team. And again from force of habit nobody contested this procedure, which had no basis in the new constitution. For his pains, Ramadier saw his majority – initially the unanimous votes of the 549 deputies present – reduced by 28 votes. By now, it was 28 January.

Over the next few months, political, economic and social tensions grew dangerously in France.[28] The Ramadier coalition had begun with the Socialists and Communists in idyllic harmony, but this euphoria did not last. Indeed, there was no single question on which all the ministers could agree. Indo-China was perhaps the most divisive issue of all. When the National Assembly first met, the dean of parliamentarians, the Communist Marcel Cachin, presided, as tradition demanded. But tradition also demanded that he should refrain from partisanship: yet he immediately made highly partisan comments on the outbreak of hostilities. On 19 March the Communist party's Central Committee denounced the allocation of funds for "the war against Vietnam". The day before, the Communist Defence minister, Billoux, had remained seated when his colleagues rose in response to a tribute from the premier to the French Expeditionary Force; and the parliamentary party had abstained from the vote of confidence called by Ramadier. On 29 March, another overseas crisis further divided the government, when an insurrection broke out in Madagascar. A ferocious repression restored order, however, and unlike the Indo-China crisis, this one was short-lived. But on 16 April, the Communist ministers walked out of the cabinet meeting in protest against the proposed lifting of the parliamentary immunity of four Malagasy parliamentarians. Imperturbably, Ramadier declared that ministerial solidarity remained unimpaired.[29]

Domestic issues were equally contentious, and in the end they were to bring the Ramadier government down and with it the tripartite formula. The Finance minister, Robert Schuman, perhaps the most conservative of the MRP ministers, threatened to resign when the Socialists proposed to nationalise the steel and chemical industries and the merchant marine. But the principle of nationalisation was only one aspect of the bigger problem of how the economy was to be managed. During his month in office Léon Blum had cut all retail prices by 5 per cent in a desperate attempt to stem the flood of inflation which, during the last six months of 1946, had sent the cost of living up by 50 per cent. The "Blum experiment", as it was called, worked – but only for a few

[28] See Dorothy Pickles, French Politics (henceforth, Pickles, French Politics), pp. 73 et seq.
[29] Fauvet, IVème, p. 108; see also p. 112.

weeks. Then hoarding and black marketing caused shortages and the spiral of price increases and wage claims started off again.

During this dismal period General de Gaulle, tiring rapidly of his brooding at Colombey, decided to return to politics. The first alarm signal was a stay of several days in Paris in mid-February, which occasioned a special cabinet meeting on the 14th. His political contacts seemed to be multiplying, and so were the anti-regime speeches of the Gaullists. What was he up to? Nobody seemed to know.

Every day a couple of hundred letters reached him from all over the country. From time to time, one of them contained a Communist party membership card, torn in half to show the ex-member's disillusionment. Did all this mean that the French voters were turning away from the left? That they looked to him to save them from the regime, to "save France" as he had done once before? He had little difficulty in believing that this was the message. Besides, he had a strong sense of impending doom. Some catastrophe, he felt sure, was on the way: probably another world war. France would need him soon, so he had better anticipate the call. The first 18 June had been his call to France, and it had come *in extremis*. He was determined that the second one should be made before it was too late, so that nobody could reproach him, should a catastrophe happen, with having done nothing to avert it. Something had to be done, and because he was de Gaulle it could only be something spectacular, likely to fire the imagination of the French people, and of the world.

On 30 March, in a speech on the cliffs at Bruneval, in Normandy, General de Gaulle gave a hint of his intentions, but in characteristically Delphic form. At that place, on 27 February 1942, British and Canadian forces, aided by a French Resistance group, had destroyed a German radar station, and a modest monument now commemorated the fact. The Resistance, he proclaimed – with more attention to rhetoric than historical truth – had been "one and indivisible", as was France. But now "the voices of division, that is to say, of decadence", were being heard again. And he ended with these ambiguous words: "The day will come when, rejecting the sterile games and reforming the ill-constructed framework in which the nation was losing its way and the State disqualifying itself, the immense mass of French people will rally round France."[30]

What did this mean? Bearing in mind the ease with which de Gaulle identified himself with France, was this not a warning of an impending *coup d'état*? That month the general had, it seemed, deliberately in-

[30] for full text, *see* De Gaulle, *Discours*, Vol. II, pp. 41-6.

sulted the President of the Republic by turning down an invitation to lunch on the occasion of a visit to Paris by the prince-regent of Belgium. At Bruneval, thousands of enthusiastic followers had yelled themselves hoarse with cries of *"De Gaulle au pouvoir!"* To many observers, to many politicians, only the worst interpretation fitted the general's sibylline words. That day, at Avignon, having heard what de Gaulle had said, Ramadier exclaimed, "There is no supreme saviour, no Caesar!" On 3 April the premier startled the president of the Republic by revealing to him that between midnight and 2 a.m. on 2 April, he had been at La Boisserie, in a *tête-à-tête* with the general. Later on 2 April, the Council of Ministers had heard an account of the visit from the premier himself. Thorez, the Communist minister of State and vice-premier, objected on the grounds that there could be "neither equality nor a dialogue between a citizen acting politically against his government, and the president of the Council". His MRP co-equal, Teitgen – also minister of State and vice-premier – with the support of Robert Schuman, thereupon reminded their colleagues that de Gaulle had saved Strasbourg by insisting on keeping the French forces there at a time when Eisenhower had wanted to withdraw them.

"There had to be an end to equivocation," Ramadier told President Auriol. "I dispensed with all protocol. I left the Hôtel Matignon by an unobtrusive door. The director of my military secretariat, General Bonnafé, an airman of Free France, had taken the chauffeur's place." He had told the general, in a courteous and even cordial interview, that nobody forgot the gratitude which the country owed him. But it was no longer possible to overlook the distinction between de Gaulle the liberator and de Gaulle the politician. He appealed to the general to help the Fourth Republic.[31]

But de Gaulle replied:

> The present constitution will not ensure the greatness of France, the sole object of my preoccupations and supreme goal of my life. The regime of parties is harmful [*malfaisant*]. It prevents the execution of a great external policy, just as it compromises internal peace and stability.
>
> You reproach me with having become a political leader. Yes, it's true, I *am* a political leader. The Resistance was not only a national phenomenon, *Monsieur le Président*, it was also political. I am maintaining my role, that is all.

[31] My account of Ramadier's report to the president is drawn from *Tragédie* (pp. 36–8), by that indefatigable collector of confidences, J.-R. Tournoux.

I shall remain the nation's guide. You mustn't be surprised therefore if I make other speeches, and if I take up a position on the problems that effect the future of the Motherland. Don't expect me to give up.

It was I who restored the Republic. Do you think I now want to overthrow it?

Such an accusation is grotesque. . . . I serve France only. I shall always serve France alone.

Politely, de Gaulle escorted the premier to his car. His parting words were: "You may reassure the warriors. I'm not going to be a Boulanger."

"Well," exclaimed President Auriol on hearing Ramadier's account, "let him take note that I'm not going to be a Hindenburg!"

A week later, on 7 April, de Gaulle attended a huge meeting at Strasbourg, organised by the "Alsatian Committee for Gratitude to America". For the occasion, he declared that if any new tyranny should arise "we can be sure in advance that the United States and France would agree to oppose it". But that was not what the crowd had come to hear. With his usual sense of drama, General de Gaulle led up to his theme of overwhelming problems and the inadequacy of the political parties to deal with them. He explained his own dilemma as he saw it. He had ruled out any "plebiscitary adventure" which would have led to disastrous upheavals. There were therefore only two possible solutions:

Either to enter into the game of the parties, which would, I believe, have wasted without any advantage that sort of national capital which events have made me stand for. Or else to let the parties carry out their experiment, but not without having previously reserved for the people themselves the opportunity of deciding by way of a referendum the kind of regime to be adopted. I chose the second solution. . . . We know how things turned out.

He refrained from blaming anybody, for some of the men concerned were very worthy and capable of directing public affairs, but they were paralysed or led astray by the system. At last came the "punch line":

The time has come to form and organise the rally of the French people which, within the framework of the law, will promote and lead to triumph, above differences of opinion, the great effort of common salvation and the profound reform of the State. And so, tomorrow, in line with the common actions and will, the French Republic shall build the new France!

So that was it: a rally of the French people. It was now clear that what de Gaulle had in mind was a vast popular movement, rather than a party, which should transcend the political parties and draw its strength from them. A small group of privileged Gaullists had known for some weeks that this was what he was planning. One of them was Jacques Soustelle, who had directed the Gaullist secret services during the last phase of the war, and who was one of the guests at a small meeting in the house of de Gaulle's brother-in-law, Jacques Vendroux, where the general himself had chosen the name "Rassemblement du Peuple Français".[32] On de Gaulle's instructions, Soustelle had spread the word to a limited number of friends and acquaintances, all former members of the internal or external Resistance.

The die, then, was cast: General de Gaulle was challenging the Republic.

[32] Jacques Soustelle, *Vingt-Huit Ans de Gaullisme* (henceforth, Soustelle, *Gaullisme*), p. 40.

Chapter 2 ❧ Triumph and Collapse

Of all the phases of de Gaulle's life, the phase of the Rally of the French People was the most controversial, and the one that does him least biographical honour. It would be wrong, however, to dismiss it as simply an experiment in Nuremberg-style Fascism;[1] and unfair to see it as merely a paroxysm of envy and frustrated personal ambition – although these sentiments played their part in his behaviour at that time. The truth is that, as always, de Gaulle identified himself with the nation, and his fortunes with its needs. On the one hand he was bored by retirement, envious of the men who directed France's destinies, and contemptuous of their abilities. On the other, he foresaw (and hoped for, rather than feared) calamitous international events, which he believed the men of the Fourth Republic to be quite incapable of dealing with. His desperate longing to return to power therefore merged with a

[1] As does the left-wing writer Alexander Werth in *De Gaulle* (Political Leaders of the Twentieth Century. Penguin, 1965–7), (henceforth Werth, *De Gaulle*); see c. 6, 2, the title of which – *De Gaulle turns Fascist Demagogue* – is characteristic of this writer's tendency to reduce complex issues to convenient labels.

burning desire to save the motherland a second time. The Rally was his instrument to achieve this double aim. At first, its flame glowed brightly, turning to incandescence; but as quickly as it had gained life, it declined and died, leaving de Gaulle more bitter than ever.

The critics who describe the de Gaulle of the Rally as "a Fascist demagogue" rest their case on the theatrical staging of his public appearances and on his passionate denunciations of the Communists. That the rallies of the Rassemblement had many of the trappings of Hitler's can be verified from pictures and newsreels. The giant standards of the Cross of Lorraine, the lofty orator's stand, the impassioned, even hysterical speeches, the cult of the heroic leader, the calls to unity above party, the appeals to nationalism, the shrill exposures of a Bolshevik danger: in all this, it was understandable to see the rise of a French Fuehrer. Nor is it extenuating to plead that all this political theatre was the work of the famous writer André Malraux, himself a veteran of the fight against Fascism in the Spanish Civil War; for a word from de Gaulle would have changed the style and presentation. That he did not utter the word is proof enough that this was the way he wanted things to be – that Malraux's way, indeed, was his. But the critics make insufficient allowance for de Gaulle's demonstrated aversion from the vulgar temptations of a Nazi-style dictatorship; or for the cold war that was beginning to rend Europe at this time and for which de Gaulle was in no way responsible although he exploited it to his political advantage.

As early as May 1945, in a letter to President Truman, Winston Churchill had expressed his apprehensions about Russia's behaviour in Europe, coining a phrase that was to become famous: "An iron curtain is drawn down upon their front." Ten months later, he startled the world with his speech at Fulton, Missouri, denouncing the Soviet Union's imperialism. And indeed, Stalin showed no sign of surrendering his control over the territories "liberated" from the Nazis by the Red Army. True, in 1946 the Soviet forces were withdrawn from the Iranian province of Azerbaidjan, where the Russians had set up a Communist regime; but this withdrawal, under strong American pressure, was the exception that proved the tenacious rule. In the Far East, the Russians had occupied Manchuria and North Korea, setting up a Communist regime in the latter. In eastern Europe, their grip was tightening. In Greece, Stalin's Communist emissaries had attempted to seize power. All western proposals – including de Gaulle's own – for the future of Germany and the reconstruction of Europe had met with Stalin's veto. Total failure awaited the conference of foreign ministers in Moscow in

March 1947. And on the 12th of that month the president of the United States, reflecting the realities of the post-war world, publicly protested against Communist intimidation in Poland, Rumania and Bulgaria, and announced a policy of aid to Greece and Turkey which became known as the "Truman doctrine" and marked the beginning of the abdication of British power and its replacement by American.

It was in this international climate that de Gaulle had launched his rally of the French people. And the domestic circumstances closely mirrored the international setting. The outbreak of war in Indo-China, and of rebellion in Madagascar, alienated the Communist ministers within the coalition government. Despite the worsening international climate, it probably suited Stalin that the western Communist parties should continue to be represented in government. But it no longer suited President Truman, whose message of 12 March made it clear that the presence of ministers dedicated essentially to Moscow's interests was now incompatible with western interests. In Belgium and Italy, the Communist ministers were accordingly forced out. And in France, domestic developments shortly made a similar outcome inevitable.

Since January 1946, a general commissariat under Jean Monnet had been drawing up an ambitious plan to modernise and re-equip the economy. In the spring of 1947, the plan was about to be launched, but it would be years before its beneficial effects could be felt. Prices were rising and the CGT, now Communist-dominated, called for a minimum wage. April brought a wheat shortage and towards the end of the month a strike broke out at the Renault works. Party discipline being what it was, the Communist secretary of the Paris Trades Council denounced the strike leaders as "Hitlero-Trotskyists in the pay of de Gaulle".[2] But the party leaders suddenly understood that they were in danger of losing control of the CGT to non-Communists more militant than they. The Communist ministers thereupon dissociated themselves from the Ramadier government's plans to stabilise wages; and the CGT officially espoused the cause of the Renault workers when the party voted solidly against him. Since the Communist ministers nevertheless refused to resign. Ramadier had no option but to dismiss them; which he did on 5 May, the day after the vote. In their stead, he appointed Socialist and MRP ministers.

It was the end of *tripartisme*. Released from their residual ministerial restraints, the Communists threw their highly disciplined machine into the fostering of industrial unrest, with the public services and the nationalised industries as their special target. Exasperated, Ramadier exclaimed

[2] Pickles, *French Politics*, p. 77; see also p. 78.

on 3 June 1947 that there was now "a strike movement, spreading from industry to industry and centre to centre; an orchestration produced by a hidden conductor. . . . It looks as if the aim were to undermine either Republican authority or nationalisation, and every time the blow falls it is the national economy and the national currency that suffer."

Under attack from one side by General de Gaulle's rally and from below by the Communists, Ramadier's coalition struggled on. In time, the Radicals, MRP and Socialists who mainly comprised it came to be known as the Third Force – that is, an alternative to the extremes of Left and Right represented by the Communists and Gaullists.[3]

Ramadier had lost no time in denying to de Gaulle any help which the honours of past office might have brought him. He had used, or abused, these privileges – outriders, a guard of honour, police protection – when making his political come-back with the speech at Bruneval on 30 March. Two days later, when Ramadier made his much criticised pilgrimage to Colombey, he told the general that henceforth such honours would be withheld whenever de Gaulle made an *unofficial* public appearance; nor would his speeches on such occasions be broadcast on the State radio system.[4]

But it would have taken more than such administrative pinpricks to slow down, let alone halt de Gaulle's triumphal progress. Within twenty-four hours of his speech of 14 April explicitly launching the RPF, 12,700 Parisians had joined. By 1 May, 800,000 French men and women had sought membership. Moving from temporary headquarters at 6 Square Rapp, the RPF opened shop at 5 rue de Solférino.[5] On 29 May, de Gaulle and five others – André Malraux, Rémy, Léon Mazeaud, Pasteur Valéry-Radot, and Jacques Soustelle – signed the articles of association of the RPF. Of these, only Rémy (the Resistance leader) and Soustelle had been part of the Free French movement. De Gaulle, as chairman, inevitably dominated the movement, whose precocious successes owed almost everything to the magic of his name. Malraux's stage-management, however, was an important contributory factor; and so, to a lesser degree, were Soustelle's organising and oratorical abilities.

There was a romantic surge in those early days of the Rassemblement. Malraux, especially, contributed to it with his obscure but exalted

---

[3] Strictly speaking, de Gaulle was never, either then or later, in the fullest sense a man of the right. But it is a fact that his Rally attracted many followers whom the right-wing label suited better than him; while the Communists and fellow-travellers took care to label him a "Fascist".

[4] Gorce, p. 478.

[5] Where the Association Nationale pour le Soutien à l'Oeuvre du Général de Gaulle – the guardians, as it were, of Gaullist purity – established its permanent headquarters.

speeches, full of allusions to the glories of French history that passed well over the heads of his listeners. Hard though it might be to know just what he was trying to say, his enthusiasm was contagious. De Gaulle himself dwelt usually on themes that were well beyond the interests or comprehension of his audiences: on the greatness of France, so sadly betrayed by the politicians, on great questions of international policy, the mention of which expressed the deep-seated frustrations of his exclusion from power. But the tens of thousands of ordinary men and women who listened to him were preoccupied with more mundane matters, such as food shortages, rising prices and inadequate wages – in which the great man had only a minimal interest. "I haven't liberated France," he used to exclaim, "to worry about the macaroni ration!"[6] Despite the intellectual and emotional gap between his lofty preoccupations and the daily anxieties of his new followers, they were, for a time, ready to flock to his banner and help him with their votes. And the secret of this initial success lay not only in his incomparable prestige but in his capacity to descend from the heights of his world vision to the earthly invectives of his fulminations against the little men who governed them. They wanted scapegoats and he gave them what they wanted: the politicians (and the regime, a more abstract concept, but still comprehensible) and especially the Communists – the "separatists", as he soon started calling them, whose lies in the service of a foreign power he condemned repeatedly.

De Gaulle switched with great facility from noble historical perspectives to the demagoguery of fear. His message, tirelessly reiterated, was this, in substance: France is in danger, from an external foe – Russia – even more powerful than was Hitler's Germany; the weak regime and the little men at its head were incapable of saving the mother-country; he, de Gaulle, had saved France once and was ready to save her again; whereas the Communists were traitors, ready only to betray her. As time went on, another "enemy" entered de Gaulle's oratorical demonology, an embarrassing one by reason of its friendliness and generosity: the Americans. On 5 June 1947, the American Secretary of State, General George C. Marshall, chose the unsensational forum of Harvard University's "commencement exercises" to launch the European Recovery Programme, known as the "Marshall Plan". If, he declared, the European countries devastated by the war, were to agree among themselves about their needs on a cooperative basis, the United States would support them "so far as it may be practical for us to do so".

This generous offer, which was to transform Europe's economic

6 Soustelle, *Gaullisme*, p. 41.

423

prospects, was immediately welcomed by the British and French governments. De Gaulle could hardly dissociate himself from an initiative on
which so many hopes rested; yet on the first occasion that presented
itself for a public comment – in a speech at Lille on 29 June – he laid
down, typically, that any aid received from the United States should be
subject to negotiations on equal terms.[7] Addressing British and American
correspondents on 9 July, however, he warmly welcomed the Marshall
Plan, although describing it, in effect, as a noble recognition on America's
part that her interests and Europe's coincided – in other words, as a case
of enlightened self-interest.[8] But a year later, when it was plain that
Marshall Aid was not only saving France as a country, but prolonging
the life of the Fourth Republic, de Gaulle began to attack the conditions
under which it was made available. It was true that American assistance
carried "strings" – such as fiscal reforms, monetary stabilisation and
even the ending, as soon as possible, of the Indo-China war – an interference which many Frenchmen (not least de Gaulle himself) found
humiliating. The American ambassador in Paris, Jefferson Caffery,
thought it well to assure the Gaullists that Marshall Aid was not intended to bolster the Third Force, as such, but to help France's recovery;
should de Gaulle return to power, his government, too, would qualify
for assistance.[9]

Between 29 June and 9 July 1947, the dates of de Gaulle's first two
comments on the Marshall Plan, momentous developments had fatally
deepened the rift in Europe. With characteristic generosity, General
Marshall had offered aid to his eastern as well as his western allies. The
British and French Foreign ministers, Ernest Bevin and Georges Bidault,
invited their Soviet colleague, Vyacheslav Molotov, to Paris to talk it
over. But Molotov came at the end of June armed with Stalin's intransigent orders, refusing all cooperation on the ground that the Marshall
Plan would violate the sovereignty of any country accepting it. For one
brief, mad moment the Czech government accepted the Anglo-French
invitation of 4 July to join the other European governments in conferring
on how to set up what became the Organisation for European Economic
Cooperation – the precondition of Marshall Aid; but a threatening telephone call from Moscow caused the Czechs hastily to change their minds.

---

[7] De Gaulle, *Discours*, Vol. II, p. 84. [8] ibid. p. 92.
[9] *See*, in particular, de Gaulle's press conference of 17 November 1948 (ibid. Vol. II, pp.
236–8), and his speech at Bordeaux on 25 September 1949 delivered within a few days of
the consecutive devaluations of the pound and the franc (ibid. p. 306). Tournoux,
Tragédie (pp. 74–7), has interesting passages on RPF attitudes towards Marshall Aid, and
quotes ironical sentences from the November 1948 press conference which do not appear
in the approved version of *Discours*.

Only Russia and Spain had not been invited. And besides Czechoslovakia, all East European countries "liberated" by the Red Army declined the Anglo-French invitation. The division of Europe was now an accomplished fact: Churchill's "iron curtain" had descended.

In France this fact was reflected, though not immediately, in the actions of the Communist party. Was there, at that time, a failure of communication between Stalin and Thorez? We cannot be certain, but as Jacques Fauvet points out, the French party was still – in June – merely calling for its rightful place in the government, while the wave of strikes gathered speed; and it was not until September that it denounced "the eviction of the Communist ministers [which had taken place in May] under pressure from the United States".[10] And when, in October 1947, Stalin's right-hand man, Andrei Zhdanov, set up the Cominform – successor to the Comintern – the Central Committee of the French Communist party at last admitted that it had "been tardy in appreciating with the necessary precision the profound changes that have occurred in the international situation . . . and the total subordination of French policy to the demands of the United States". This was the party's declaration of war on the Fourth Republic – on Stalin's behalf. From then on, its iron organisation and disciplined energies were mobilised to subvert and undermine the State, by its propaganda and an ever more menacing series of strikes.

It was against this background that the Rally of the French People waxed. Who, then, were the hundreds of thousands who flocked to join it, and the millions who were soon voting for its candidates? It was a varied, almost a motley, clientele. For Rémy, Soustelle and other ex-Free French or ex-Resisters, the RPF was simply a second "18 June" – a renewal of the Gaullist mission, temporarily interrupted.[11] But for the mass of ordinary members, such mystical motivation was incomprehensible. Most of them, for one reason or another, were discontented with their lot and sceptical of the ability of the existing parties and leaders to improve it. They included, at first, members of other parties – since the rally declared itself not to be a party; but many, too, who belonged to no party, and these included small shopkeepers (the kind who later joined Poujade's populist movement of the 1950s), bank clerks and indeed the anonymous mass whom Malraux described, in a dismissive phase, as the "rush-hour Métro crowd". Conservatives and traditionalists, attracted though they were by de Gaulle's unyielding attitude on colonial matters and by the authoritarian aspects of his constitutional proposals, found it hard to support the RPF. Many had supported Pétain and Vichy, and

[10] Fauvet, IVème, p. 127.   [11] See Soustelle, Gaullisme, p. 41.

they abhorred the general's radical social ideas and his readiness to nationalise industries. But minor Vichyites in their thousands crowded the recruitment offices. During the war, they had opted for the marshal's paternal protection; now they turned to the man who had defeated him, and who also promised fatherly authority and leadership.[12] But the movement also attracted many men of "technocratic" qualifications – engineers, doctors, architects, lawyers, civil servants, generals – who saw hope in the "order" which de Gaulle promised to substitute for France's perennial Republican anarchy.

At the top were many personalities who had already achieved, or would soon achieve, fame: academics like Raymond Aron, writers like Paul Claudel, left-wing politicians like Louis Vallon, Radical-Socialists like Michel Debré and Paul Giacobbi. Some, but not all, remained faithful to the general. Others found it impossible to accept the absolute subservience to his views which fidelity implied. In 1952 de Gaulle summoned a dissident Gaullist deputy, Vigier, gave him five minutes to confess his "sins", and expelled him when he declined.

On 27 July 1947, gratified by the initial response to his appeal, de Gaulle first used the term "separatists" to describe his former comrades-in-arms of the Resistance, the Communists. Speaking at Rennes, he reminded his audience that at the time of the liberation he had given them every opportunity ιo play their part in the national community. But they had preferred to play Russia's game. Now Soviet Russia had extended its hold over 400 million people, forming a bloc that confined Sweden, Turkey, Greece and Italy. "Its frontier," he exclaimed, "is separated from ours by only 500 kilometres, that is hardly the length of two stages of the cycling Tour de France!"[13] This telling image was much quoted thereafter.

General de Gaulle was thus taking on the whole of the political establishment of France: the anti-democratic Communists as well as the conventional parties. Not surprisingly, both sides hit back. The Communists dug into their own rich vocabulary of invective, denouncing the "Fascist" general and comparing him with Hitler. Their strong-arm boys tried to wreck Gaullist meetings, where they met the strong-arm boys of the RPF in fisticuffs or mutual bombardments of minor missiles. The other parties chose subtler methods. At the outset – as early as April 1947 – the MRP forbade its members to join the rally of the French people.[14] Other parties followed suit and banned the *double appartenance,* or dual membership. Thereby, despite the general's wishes, the

12 *See* Williams, pp. 132 *et seq.; see also* p. 129.
13 De Gaulle, *Discours,* Vol. II, p. 102.　　　　14 Pickles, *French Politics,* p. 97.

RPF was gradually transformed into a political party like any other; as subsequent parliamentary history was to show.

The first big test of the new Gaullist resurgence came in October 1947 with the municipal elections. It was passed triumphantly: in the 334 towns with more than 9,000 inhabitants, the RPF polled nearly 40 per cent of the votes. In Paris the Gaullist share of the vote exceeded 40 per cent in all *arrondissements* and 70 per cent in two.[15] The results seemed to show that the rally would have topped the poll in a general election held at that time. Jubilation in Gaullist quarters was correspondingly great. But rejoicing was tempered by sober analysis. For one thing, municipal elections can never precisely reflect the state of political opinion on a national basis. For another, the RPF contested very few rural seats, and the 334 towns represented no more than one quarter of the total electorate. The results, however, were deeply alarming to the established parties. The MRP, especially, felt damaged, having lost some 750,000 votes, mostly to the rally. The published lists, moreover, showed that many Radicals and Moderates had fought on the RPF ticket. Between them, the Socialists, Radicals and MRP (the first and third being essentially the Third Force) had attracted only 35 per cent of the voters – 5 per cent less than the RPF alone; and the Communist share, at 19 per cent, placed the "separatists" well below the Gaullists. "Every day," exclaimed de Gaulle in a statement on 27 October 1947, ". . . will show more clearly that the separatists have none of the characteristics of a French party but are merely the delegates of a foreign dictatorship for which the misery of men is but the springboard of its ruthless domination." He invited the Third Force parties, in effect, to commit suicide by calling for an immediate dissolution.

But the politicians were not yet ready to die. Had they listened to de Gaulle, the Republic they had created would have been swept away. But there were disinterested, as well as personal, reasons for them not to listen. They settled down, then, to weather the storms. And what storms there were! Not only was de Gaulle trying to bring their house tumbling down, but the Communist-led trade unions started a new and more vicious round of revolutionary strikes which, on 12 November 1947, forced Ramadier to resign as premier. By the end of the month one and a half million workers were out (the Communists said three million). Workers who wanted to return were intimidated, and in some cases beaten up; there was sabotage on the railways and charges of ballot-faking were heard.

On the 19th, Léon Blum – now seventy-five – made a bid for the

[15] ibid. p. 97; and Gorce, p. 486.

premiership which failed but was memorable, for his speech that day launched the concept of a "Third Force".[16] "The danger," he declared "is a double one. On one side, international communism had openly declared war on French democracy. On the other, a party has been formed whose objective – perhaps its only objective – is to deprive national sovereignty of its fundamental rights . . . . The vote which you are about to take will indicate whether there is or is not such a thing as what I have called the third force, or at least whether it is capable of becoming aware of itself, of acting and of governing."

The Third Force was, in fact, hardly a force at all. The totalitarian left and de Gaulle's authoritarian Rally were, at that time, genuine forces. The parties in the middle, which broadly speaking preferred their imperfect democracy to the alternatives on offer, did not become one merely by assuming the name of Third Force, which they did on 10 January 1948, when a provisional committee of Radicals, Socialists and MRP was set up. But their force of inertia was not to be despised. While never inspiring, they rang the changes in parliamentary arithmetic for more than ten further years.

But at the end of 1947 nothing looked more fragile than the power of the French parliament. When the deputies assembled on 29 November to debate bills to strengthen security measures against sabotage, the Communists resorted to verbal, and sometimes to physical, violence in the chamber. When Robert Schuman, Lorrainer and good European, who had spent part of his boyhood in Germany, became president of the Council, the parliamentary leader of the Communist party, Jacques Duclos, shouted: "Voilà le boche!" Though Jules Moch, the new minister of the Interior, was Jewish and a veteran of two world wars, he was greeted with cries of "Heil Hitler!"[17]

The tide, however, was turning, although those who lived through the crisis had no means of knowing it. On payment of an inflationary wage increase the workers went back to work during the first two weeks of December. Exasperated by Communist methods, the non-Communist trade unionists, who were in the minority, broke away to form their own trade union body, the Confédération Générale du Travail-Force Ouvrière. Nearly three million tons of coal had been lost and rising prices swiftly swallowed up wage rises that were uncovered by rising production.

Seizing his opportunity, General de Gaulle launched a bid for the

---

[16] As Mrs Pickles points out (French Politics, p. 85), a small movement of that name did exist in the 1930s: its aim was a middle way between capitalism and communism.
[17] Fauvet, IVème, p. 136.

support of workers and bosses alike. In a speech at Saint-Etienne on 4 January 1948, he called for an association between capital and labour. In every enterprise, he proposed, workers, foremen and bosses should form committees that would determine wages and salaries according to the value of the output. Only that, he reasoned, could give everybody pride of work and satisfactory remuneration. Moreover, the worker-management committees should send representatives to a Council of the Republic, where they would sit alongside the delegates of local assemblies.[18]

With its echoes of Mussolini's corporate State, these proposals provided further ammunition for de Gaulle's enemies on the left, who wished to brand him a "Fascist". The system he proposed in 1948 had indeed marked similarities to that which was later introduced into Yugoslavia under Marshal Tito; and it was the forerunner of the system of "participation" formally proposed many years later (in 1965) by the left-wing Gaullist, Louis Vallon.

The immediate effect of de Gaulle's words, however, was a significant increase in the working-class membership of the RPF. A paper for Gaullist workers – whose title, *The Worker's Spark (Etincelle Ouvrière)*, was curiously reminiscent of Lenin's *Spark (Iskra)* – was launched. When the rally held its first congress, at Marseilles in April 1948, it was claimed that 145,000 factory groups had been set up. By then, a total membership of one and a half million was said to have been achieved. But neither then nor later did the Gaullists seriously challenge Communist power among the organised workers.

The Third Force was both well-and ill-served by international events. The best stroke of international luck was Marshall Aid: on 2 January 1948 Georges Bidault, the Foreign minister, signed the agreement under which France was to receive $280 million in goods and money. The country's economic and financial difficulties were not, of course, immediately solved, either by Marshall Aid or by the Monnet Plan. But the awareness that without them conditions would probably be far worse created some resistance to de Gaulle's blandishments and prophecies of doom. To that extent, his attacks on the government for becoming a dependency of the United States aroused relatively little interest.

Every new twist in the cold war, on the other hand, strengthened his appeal as the "man of storms", a saviour once and again now a saviour-presumptive. The most dramatic of these events in 1948 was the Communist take-over in Prague on 25 February (which caused de Gaulle, on 7 March, to make a fresh call for a general election). But the governments

[18] De Gaulle, *Discours*, Vol. II, pp. 167–8.

of the threatened western countries had already begun to steal his thunder by organising their defences. In January 1948 France and Britain proposed to the Benelux States (Belgium, Netherlands and Luxembourg) an extension of the Franco-British treaty of Dunkirk. At this time, the British and French (but especially the latter) were still obsessed by the danger, as they saw it, of a revival of German militarism. But the coup of Prague made them understand, tardily, that the real threat to European security came from further east. And the treaty of Brussels, signed on 17 March – three weeks after the Communist take-over in Czechoslovakia – said nothing about the German threat: instead, it referred in general terms to the possibility of an "armed aggression in Europe". The next move was to associate the Americans with European defence efforts, which alone were too feeble to deter the Soviet giant. Early in June, the American secretary of State, General Marshall, con-ferred in London with the signatories of the Brussels treaty to consider the future of the British, French and American occupation zones of Germany. The outcome was a proposal for the unification of the three zones and the inauguration of a democratic Constitution.[19] On learning of these recommendations, which Bidault had accepted, though with ill-grace, de Gaulle was deeply angered. Since the liberation, and even earlier, the general had thought that the solution of the German problem lay in permanent dismemberment, or rather in the revival of the German princely states in a loose federation. He wanted a guaranteed share of the Ruhr's coal for France and the incorporation of the Saar into the French economy. And now, in London, Bidault had thrown all these ideas and claims to the winds. On 9 June the general issued a long statement, describing the London proposals as "creating a Reich in Frankfurt". Now, he said (prophetically), there was nothing to stop the Russians creating a rival Reich in Berlin or Leipzig, and he saw great dangers for France in the rivalry between the two. "We are on the edge of a precipice," he declared. And he went on to re-state France's claims upon the Ruhr and the Saar and to call for the rejection of "the strange 'communiqué' of London".

Though not without effect, the general's intervention did not carry the day, for on 17 June the Assembly approved the London proposals by the narrow majority of 297 votes to 289. The negotiations, however, cost Bidault his job, and on 26 July, Robert Schuman, himself yielding the premiership to the Radical André Marie, took over as Foreign minister; to the relief of, among others, President Auriol, who had long

[19] See G. de Carmoy, Les Politiques Etrangères de la France 1944–66 (henceforth, De Carmoy), pp. 22–3.

tired of Bidault's supple evasiveness in the exposition of his foreign policy. Even if Bidault had no other claim to fame, however, he would have to be credited with the germ of the idea that was to become the Atlantic treaty, for it was he who, in a message to General Marshall on 4 March, had first proposed urgent consultations between the United States and Europe on common defence measures.[20]

Before talks could take place, the American government had to free itself from constitutional obstacles to external alliances in peace-time. It was not, therefore, till December 1948 that the negotiations could begin. For six months, the British and American air forces had been engaged in a desperate attempt to supply the two and a quarter million people of West Berlin with the necessities of life, in the face of a Soviet blockade of the sectors controlled by the western powers. Under this stimulus, the West found unity, and on 4 April 1949 the Atlantic treaty was signed. Within a month, the Russians called off the Berlin blockade.

During this prolonged tension, de Gaulle had continued to make capital out of the supposed impotence of the regime and his own readiness to guide the nation to safety and prosperity. The Marie government had lasted only a month, and Schuman's attempt to return to power collapsed two months later. On 11 September, however, the Radical Henri Queuille formed a government which, against all odds, was to survive thirteen months, though mainly by doing very little – a course that has led to the association of *immobilisme* with Queuille's name.

Only a week after Queuille's investiture, de Gaulle was involved in an incident which did much harm to the reputation of his movement. He had gone to Grenoble to preside over an RPF meeting. Communists tried to disrupt it, and clashed with armed Gaullists. One Communist was killed, and fourteen people on both sides were seriously injured. In a statement on the 21st, the minister of the Interior disclosed that only de Gaulle's supporters had carried arms. He went on to complain that the cost of State security measures to protect de Gaulle on his provincial tours since the beginning of the year had exceeded ten million francs. Questioned about the riot at a press conference on 1 October, on the occasion of the meeting of the National Council of the RPF, the general found it strange that the "separatists" had been allowed on the scene of his "patriotic demonstration", and that arms had been found on Gaullists who had been searched by the police. There followed an astonishing piece of political arithmetic. On the suggestion of André Malraux, supporters of de Gaulle had been invited to buy special Gaullist stamps and send them to him as a token of support and a

[20] Fauvet, *IVème*, p. 142.

contribution to RPF funds. A million such letters, each carrying ordinary ten-franc stamps, had reached him, de Gaulle declared; so he owed nothing to anybody. Unmoved, the government deprived de Gaulle of the guard of honour to which he had hitherto been entitled as a former commander-in-chief in wartime, and of which he had already been deprived on unofficial appearances.

About this time, a new round of price rises made further industrial strife inevitable. Once again the Communists were ready to exploit the situation for revolutionary ends. On 1 October, the gas and electricity workers declared a twenty-four hour strike, and three days later a national coal strike began. On the 11th, Jules Moch told his Socialist party that the Cominform was financing the miners and dockers (who had joined in the stoppages) and that Zhdanov – Stalin's right-hand man – had ordered the French Communist party to sabotage the Marshall Plan.[21] When the CGT, refusing a ballot, ordered a strike of maintenance men, there were serious clashes between strikers and the police, in which 479 members of the security forces were badly injured. Nearly 1,000 arrests followed. After a further wave of violence, the men began drifting back to work, and on 27 November the strikes were called off. A year of industrial peace followed.

The Third Force had begun, in fact, to steal the general's thunder in home as well as foreign affairs. He could fulminate against the "separa-atists"; but Jules Moch, the toughest minister of the Interior of the Fourth Republic, could actually arrest them. He could raise the spectre of Stalin's hordes threatening the homeland, but Bidault and Schuman – lesser men though they might be – could play their part in common schemes for western defence. As a saviour, de Gaulle was beginning to look unnecessary; soon, he would come to seem at the least a nuisance, at worst an agitator. Never was his lust for power greater than during those frustrating years. His only solace was in the *bains de foule* ("crowd baths") which fed his sense of identification with the nation. Life, at all events, was less dull than during the solitary year spent at Colombey. But power was what he longed for, and it pained him that it should be held, if not exercised, by others. In private, his imprecations and philo-sophical soliloquies continued, often as though his visitors were simply not there.[22] Indeed, when at times the politicians did use their power de Gaulle's frustration and even humiliation were all the greater. The Grenoble riot and its sequel was a case in point. But there was worse to come. In June 1949 two RPF municipal councillors were among the sixteen arrested on suspicion of plotting a *coup d'état*. Once again,

21 Pickles, *French Politics*, pp. 103–4. 22 Tournoux, *Tragédie*, p. 69.

there was ammunition for those who accused de Gaulle of wanting to establish a Fascist dictatorship, although it was clear enough that this never was among his ambitions. His repeated denials deserved more credit than they received, and those who made or believed the charges deeply misunderstood the personage. De Gaulle was never a Bonaparte, still less a Boulanger: he was a sovereign by disposition. His aim was never to seize power but to have it conferred on him by the people's will and reign over them with their consent. The manner of his two departures, in 1946 and 1969, proved the point.[23] The "plot" of 1949 and the Grenoble disorders did, however, show that the RPF had been penetrated by men of the extreme right who did not share de Gaulle's almost mystical attachment to the sanction of the popular will.

Although the decline of the RPF had already begun by the end of 1948, it still had a good deal of life in it, as three elections were to show. The first were to have been Cantonal (departmental council) elections, in which General de Gaulle hoped to repeat his triumph of the municipal poll a year earlier. But Dr Queuille, sensing that the country was alarmed at the risks of civil war implied by the Grenoble incident and the new wave of strikes, decided, with parliament's support, to postpone the cantonales for six months, until March 1949. This earned him some public invective from de Gaulle, who described the reasons for postponement as "ignoble".[24] The next test of Gaullist strength was therefore the election of councillors of the Republic – that is, members of the Upper House (who, on being elected, promptly called themselves "senators", thus expressing the general parliamentary nostalgia for the Third Repubic). At first sight, the elections showed that the Gaullists had repeated their municipal triumph, since no fewer than 130 of the "senators" had sought RPF support, whatever their individual party affiliations. Once elected, however, most of them declined Gaullist discipline, and only fifty-eight accepted it, of whom fifty-six were members of the rally.[25] Communist representation had fallen from 84 to 21; the right-wing parties had 68 seats and, with 128 seats between them, those

[23] Asked about his political intentions in the early days of the RPF, de Gaulle referred to charges that he wanted a plebiscite, and said: "What is a plebiscite? . . . It is the case of a man who, having taken power by violence, turns to the people and says: 'Tell me I was right!' There has never been any question of a plebiscite in any of the proposals I have made on the subject of constitutional changes. There has never been any question of anything except powers proceeding from the people and freely conferring a mandate on a man of its choice. When President Lincoln or President Roosevelt were elected by the citizens of the United States to run the government of the United States, these were not plebiscites!" De Gaulle, Discours, Vol. II p. 69.
[24] Fauvet, IVème, p. 152.
[25] Pickles, French Politics, p. 106; Williams, p. 36; for corrected figures, see L'Année Politique, 1949; see also Pickles, ibid. pp. 107–8.

of the Third Force had no difficulty in playing the legitimate role assigned to the Upper House, which was one of second thoughts and revision. The Gaullists, on the other hand, were frustrated in their clear intention of using the Council of the Republic to block government bills and provoke a general election.

The Cantonal elections were held in March 1949 in a tranquillising atmosphere of falling prices, more abundant food and the external re-assurance of America's readiness to help the West defend itself against the Soviet menace. Marshall Aid was beginning to yield results and there was a feeling of returning normality. Only half the Cantons were involved, and those of the Paris region were not among them. Apathy was in the air, and no more than half the electors voted. These were never conditions under which de Gaulle's magnetism showed itself to best advantage. The Gaullists, then, polled only 25.3 per cent of the votes – only slightly more than the Communists, with 23.5 per cent. This left the Third Force parties with only a small majority; but the fate of their government was not at stake, and on the whole the results reflected the increasing prestige of the Queuille administration. Although de Gaulle immediately called a press conference, it was clear that the results had deeply disappointed him. He was indeed reduced to producing his own account of RPF candidates elected on the first round of the double ballot in an effort to prove that Gaullist support was stronger than the final results purported to show.[26] But this kind of arithmetical sophistry fell short of the more exalted themes that best became him, and this was an unusually subdued performance.[27]

During the press conference of 29 March, de Gaulle expressed some views on the Atlantic treaty, which was about to be signed. The ceremony took place on 4 April, and he immediately issued a short statement cautiously welcoming it, but calling on France to reserve final judgment until she knew under what conditions she would be getting the arms she would need to play her part in the common defence effort, under what

[26] Press Conference of 29 March, De Gaulle, *Discours*, Vol. II, pp. 267 *et seq.*

[27] It is not true, however, to say, as the usually accurate Jacques Fauvet does (*IVème*, p. 153), that after this press conference, the general, for the first time for three years, kept silent for several months. In fact, he made a statement (on the Atlantic pact) on 4 April 1949, issued a communiqué on 7 August, delivered speeches on 1 May, 22 May, 18 June, 25 September, 2 October and 23 October, and held a press conference on 14 November – on the whole, a normally productive year. At the press conference of 29 March, incidentally, he was sounded about popular demands, then being heard, for a general amnesty for Vichy's collaborators. While defending the sentence of death passed on Marshal Pétain, he then declared himself in favour of the old man's release from the fortress on the Isle of Yeu. In April 1950, however, when Colonel Rémy, the Resistance leader, wrote an article advocating the marshal's rehabilitation, he was forced to resign from the Gaullist executive (Williams, p. 133). Pétain, however, was neither released nor rehabilitated, and died at Yeu in 1951.

conditions she could count on being rescued in the event of an aggression against her, and what her commitments would be, should she have to send help to others.[28]

Already, however, the general's remarks on world affairs were of diminishing interest. His political strategy was essentially a short-term one in that it rested on the supposition that he could force a general election. The politicians, who had nothing to lose by passive resistance, sheltered under the protection of the constitution de Gaulle had reviled, which gave the National Assembly a life of five years, that is, until November 1951. Having weathered the storms of 1947 and 1948, the Assembly was not again in peril from de Gaulle until the world crisis of 25 June 1950, when the Communist forces of Soviet-protected North Korea invaded the non-Communist Republic in the south.

In Europe the creation of NATO, and America's then monopoly of the atomic bomb, had helped to reduce the impact of de Gaulle's cries of alarm. Now that a shooting war had broken out across one of the dividing lines of the cold war, was the world again to be engulfed in a major conflict? Once again de Gaulle suffered the agonies of a mere spectator at great events. He watched while President Truman, taking advantage of the extraordinary miscalculation whereby the Russians were boycotting the United Nations Security Council and therefore could not use their veto, arranged for a military counter-intervention by American and other U.N. forces. As a participant in public life, all he could do was to raise the alarm yet again and declare his readiness to guide the nation through the perilous times ahead. In tones of mounting vehemence he gave an interview to the correspondent of the United Press on 10 July, issued a statement on 17 August and, on 21 October, addressed a mass meeting of the RPF at the Vélodrome d'Hiver. On 3 October the Vietnamese Communist forces, ably led by General Vo Nguyen Giap, had compelled the French garrison to evacuate the fortress of Caobang, on the Tonking–China border. This gave de Gaulle the chance to point out that the French had been fighting for five years in Indo-China and to draw a parallel between that and the American involvement in Korea.

At a time when France is involved in a series of grave events I address myself – there is still time! – to the present tenants of the Republic, to tell them loudly but without passion: your regime is bad! Already in 1940, it took us to the brink and the storm swept it away. It was without the regime, and for good reasons, that France extricated

[28] De Gaulle, *Discours*, Vol. II, p. 282.

435

herself. But after the victory, you rebuilt it, still worse than it had been earlier. No matter what I have shouted to you, you have not wanted to understand that ... France can do without a just and strong State only at her peril. ...

As for me ... the nation knows that I am ready at any moment to take charge of power, while leaning on all those ready to help me support the burden.[29]

It seems more than likely that if parliament had been dissolved at that time, the Gaullists would have been swept into power with an absolute majority, which they could have used to introduce a new constitution.[30] But, kept out of power and deprived of a role to fit his stature, de Gaulle consoled himself with praise for the only American soldier whom he recognised as cast in the same heroic mould as himself – General Douglas MacArthur. To visitors, he contrasted MacArthur and other American generals: Marshall ("the messenger boy of the State Department") and Ridgway ("a chameleon who does an about-turn in twenty-four hours"). On 15 April, four days after MacArthur's dramatic dismissal by President Truman for wanting to drop atomic bombs on China's Manchurian bases, de Gaulle paid homage to him in a speech at Rheims. There was no doubt a parallel to be drawn between his own case and that of MacArthur, a soldier "whose boldness was feared after full advantage had been taken of it".[31]

Shortly after de Gaulle had praised MacArthur, his Rally and the politicians started preparing for the first general election since 1946. After a series of crises, the National Assembly had voted to abridge its own life – not by as much as de Gaulle would have wished, but by about five months. The poll had been fixed for 17 June 1951, and under a new electoral law which was calculated to reduce as much as possible the representation of the two anti-parliamentary groupings: the Communist party and the rally of the French people. It was a complicated procedure, but its essentials were these: each party was required to present a list for each constituency contested, each list to contain as many candidates as there were seats to be filled. A party whose list obtained an absolute majority took all the seats. But it was realised that this was going to be a rare occurrence (only one list did obtain an absolute majority), so parties were given the right to form associations amongst themselves,

[29] ibid. p. 389. [30] Lacouture, De Gaulle, p. 150.
[31] "... dont on redoutait l'audace, après en avoir profité" (Tournoux, Tragédie, p. 104). These words, however, do not appear in the approved version of de Gaulle's speeches (De Gaulle, Discours, Vol. II, p. 416), which quoted him as rendering "deserved homage to the legendary services of this great allied soldier", and "in the name of France".

known as *apparentements*. If a group of associated parties won an absolute majority, the seats were divided between them on a proportional basis.[32]

Since the democratic parties refused to work with the Communists, the latter were handicapped under the new law. The Gaullists need not have been similarly handicapped, but de Gaulle himself decided against associations, with only three approved exceptions. Despite these circumstances, the Communists emerged as the largest single party, although they had lost 400,000 votes: nearly five million electors, or 25.6 per cent of the total, voted Communist. The Gaullists came next with more than four million and 21.56 per cent. The new law, however, hit the Communists harder than the Gaullists. As a result, there were 121 Gaullists in the new Assembly and only 106 Communists. The democratic parties (especially the MRP and Socialists) had taken a beating, but thanks to the new law they held, between them, a small majority in a house of 626 deputies. If voting had taken place under the previous electoral system there would have been 181 Communist and 155 Gaullist deputies. In that event – which de Gaulle had hoped for – the Assembly would have proved unworkable and a way would have been opened for his return to power.

The results were thus paradoxically a relative success for the Gaullists and an absolute failure for the general. At a press conference on 22 June de Gaulle complained that 36,000 votes had been needed for each Gaullist seat, whereas 26,000 had sufficed for the Socialists, 23,000 for the Christian Democrats (MRP), and only 20,000 for Radicals and Moderates (conservatives). The Gaullists were ready, however, to form a government.[33] He went on to outline a seven-point programme:

Constitutional reform, including a provision for a referendum or a dissolution in the event of deadlock in parliament.

Electoral reform.

Association of labour and capital, especially in the nationalised industries.

The reorganisation of national defence.

Family allowances to enable families to choose schools for their children (a reference to the quarrel between the supporters of lay and of religious schools).

[32] For a fuller description of the system of *apparentements*, see Pickles, *French Politics*, pp. 137–8.
[33] De Gaulle, *Discours*, Vol. II, pp. 438 *et seq.*

Direct negotiations between France and Germany with the object of creating an effective European federation.

The negotiation of precise agreements with other western countries, "in particular, the United States", for cooperation on common defence within the Atlantic alliance.

On 1 July, de Gaulle presided over a meeting of the National Council of the RPF at Levallois-Perret.[34] He raised the possibility of sharing power with those aiming at the same national objectives. Neither he nor Jacques Soustelle, the RPF's secretary-general, was, however, under any illusions about the readiness of other groups to work with them.

Their apprehensions were well founded. Jeers and insults greeted the arrival of the RPF deputies, and against their heated protests they were relegated to the extreme right of the hemicycle of the Assembly. (De Gaulle regarded the Rally as a movement of the left.)

It did not occur to President Auriol to call on Soustelle, who had himself been elected as leader of the Gaullists' parliamentary group, to form a government. Instead, after the habitual crisis, he turned to an ex-Gaullist, René Pleven, of the small but important Union Démocratique et Socialiste de la Résistance (UDSR). Since the UDSR had launched Soustelle himself and other leading Gaullists (such as Malraux and Capitant) on their political careers, Soustelle referred to it ironically in the Assembly as a kind of "parthenogenesis". This provoked a turmoil of protests on the part of deputies who did not know the meaning of the word but suspected it to be insulting. They quietened down when Edouard Herriot, who was in the chair, assured them that it was not.

Soustelle himself was later to incur, quite unwittingly, the wrath of the general for the crime of apparent readiness to come to terms with the "system". The occasion arose on the fall of the Edgar Faure government on 29 February 1952, after five hectic weeks in power, during which the premier lost nearly ten pounds in weight. This time, Soustelle was one of those invited in turn to form a government. Loyally, Soustelle journeyed to Colombey to ask the general how he should answer.

"It is out of the question that you should become president of the Council. Either the parties would oppose it, or else it would mean that you would enter into an inadmissible combination."

"I quite agree," said Soustelle, then went on unwisely: "But the advantage of an affirmative reply is that, while the round of talks was going on, we would have access to the radio and the press, to publish

[34] Soustelle, *Gaullisme*, pp. 72 et seq., including p. 74 n.

our statements, our communiqués. Let us take advantage of the chance given us to affirm our ideas, to denounce the electoral alliances and to call for a national re-grouping.

"Then again, I could, in the course of my soundings, open all the State files and find out the exact situation in the country. I haven't a chance of being appointed, and there is no question, of course, of carrying the matter to a vote. In any case, tomorrow in Paris, after giving my reply to the president of the Republic, we shall re-examine the situation in your presence, in the course of the weekly meeting of the Executive Council."

Without saying No, de Gaulle concluded the interview by saying: "If my name comes into the conversation, you can say to M. Auriol that, should he be worried by national and international events, and should he, in his conscience, feel that it might be useful to make contact with General de Gaulle, well, I shan't turn him down. The meeting could take place at Marly, in a house where I once lived, where M. Vincent Auriol once saw me anyway, after I had left the government and when he himself was president of the National Assembly.

"My proposal goes beyond the person of M. Vincent Auriol. It goes beyond mine. It is a question that could one day be of public interest."[35]

Back in Paris, Soustelle duly called on President Auriol. Emerging from the Elysée, he made a statement to the press on the way the RPF proposed to handle the crisis. Unknown to him, however, General de Gaulle, surrounded by Companions of the Liberation, was working himself up into a sardonic rage. "So, he had to go and say his piece before the microphones, go the rounds of the wooden horses, drop in at the circus." Then, in sarcastic tones: "What job do you think M. *le Président du Conseil* is going to offer me? Under-secretary of State for the Fine Arts? Or perhaps Physical Education?"

In a whisper, André Malraux is said to have asked: "Would he be jealous, by any chance?"

This scene, which the bold and patient Jean-Raymond Tournoux has reconstructed, appears to be authentic, and throws an interesting light on de Gaulle's intolerance at the slightest sign of competition. Soustelle had made himself guilty in his eyes, and those of the Companions, of a form of *lèse-majesté*. He had, to all appearances, played the parliamentary game; worse still, in his statement to the press, the general's name was not mentioned.

Of all this, however, the unfortunate Soustelle was ignorant. In his version of the incident he declares that he had to wait fifteen years, until

[35] Tournoux, *Tragédie*, pp. 127–8.

the publication of Tournoux's *La Tragédie du Général* in 1967, to learn that the general had made these disparaging remarks. Not once, he says, did de Gaulle criticise what he had done, or attempt to stop him.[36]

From that time forward, General de Gaulle gradually lost interest in the movement he himself had created. It had failed in its main purpose of bringing down the Fourth Republic, and its parliamentary group had allowed itself to be corrupted, as he saw it, by the attractions of the game he most despised. In March 1952, immediately after Soustelle's failure to form a government, twenty-seven RPF deputies "compromised" with the system by voting in favour of the election of the conservative Antoine Pinay as Prime Minister. During the rest of the year, the rally rapidly lost leaders and rank-and-file. When new disciplinary rules were imposed in July, a quarter of the Gaullist deputies resigned and formed a new conservative group. Further right-wing defections were followed, in January 1953, by a decision of the parliamentary RPF to support the election of another Prime Minister, the Radical René Mayer. This decision, taken in defiance of de Gaulle, brought the Gaullists automatically into the government's majority. At the end of April, the decline of the movement was marked by heavy losses in the municipal elections.

As if to signal his indifference, General de Gaulle had spent the month of March in Africa. On 6 May, after returning to Paris and three days after the results of the municipal elections had been published, he formally dissociated himself from the Rally. Henceforth, he declared, any RPF deputies could act as they pleased, but not in the name of the movement. He did not, however, dissolve it, but called on members to regroup themselves throughout the country. Typically, he had not bothered to consult the RPF leaders before publishing this statement which put an end to their common endeavours. For lack of leadership, he lamented, the country was back to its old divisions. The end of illlusions was coming.

[36] Soustelle, *Gaullisme*, pp. 90–1.

Chapter 3 ✦ In the Wilderness

Although de Gaulle had "dropped" the Rally, he had not yet retired, in the fullest sense of the word. From time to time, he would make a speech, or issue a statement. But from mid-1952 on, the bulk of his time was devoted not to politics – his bid for power having failed – but to writing. For he had begun his war memoirs.

Never did an author write more consciously with posterity in mind. Although de Gaulle had predicted the downfall of the Fourth Republic on resigning as premier in 1946, and had done his utmost – from 1947 on – to make his prophecy come true, he had ceased to believe in the imminence of his return to power. He had not, of course, abandoned his belief in the essential impermanence of the system which he had repeatedly denounced. But its resilience after each crisis that ought to have been its last had surprised and disappointed him. It might hang on for years, only to crash when he was too old to return, or even after his death. There being no guarantee that he would ever be given a second chance to play a part on the national and world stage, the time had come for him to present his own evaluation of his place in history. This is indeed a normal purpose of statesmen's memoirs. But in his case, the grandeur of his aspirations – frustrated though they had been – as well as his absorption in history and his love of literature, implied that nothing short of a masterpiece would be suitable. Accordingly, the *Mémoires de Guerre* are more than a compilation of reminiscences in three volumes: they are a monument to de Gaulle, by de Gaulle.

Although de Gaulle had already written so much, if the texts of his many speeches are added to the slender volumes of his earlier output, he wrote painfully, without natural fluency. He neither dictated – as Churchill did – nor typed, as professional authors do, but wrote in longhand, using a fountain pen with black ink. Alone in his tower at La Boisserie, he covered the pages in his almost illegible scrawl; then made them still more difficult to decipher by innumerable deletions and changes. Only two people helped him: René Thibault, of the Quai d'Orsay, who helped in selecting and obtaining the text of the documents that supported his narative; and his daughter Elisabeth, highly practised in reading her father's difficult writing, who did the typing.

Between bouts of writing, de Gaulle read voraciously. He went through Bergson again, and his beloved Chateaubriand. He re-read Saint-Simon, Péguy, Epictetus, Barrès and La Rochefoucauld. Bismarck fascinated him, as did all German writers on the arts of war and politics. He neglected neither Sartre, nor those distinguished followers of de Gaulle, Malraux and Mauriac. He read Ernest Hemingway's *The Old Man and the Sea* at one sitting, casting himself, naturally, as the old man. Ever thirsty for knowledge, he even read gardening manuals, and textbooks on aerodynamics, cybernetics and saddle-making.[1] An unexpected taste developed for Françoise Sagan's slender novels, less, it seems, for their content than for their polished syntax.

But his eyesight deteriorated fast during his "exile". Formerly an inveterate smoker, he dropped tobacco. It made no difference, but he did not resume it. Later, he was to undergo an operation for the removal of a cataract, although out of concern for his "image" he was hardly ever seen wearing spectacles in public.

From the start, Charles and Yvonne de Gaulle had agreed that the bulk of the royalties earned by the memoirs should go to the charitable trust they had set up for handicapped children, and to other selected charities. The trust was named the Fondation Anne de Gaulle, after their mentally retarded daughter. During all her years, de Gaulle had loved and played with her, protecting her from the curious, including photographers in quest of sensation.[2] The de Gaulles were haunted, however, by the fear that they would die before Anne, leaving her defenceless. When they returned to La Boisserie after de Gaulle's resignation in 1946 they set about establishing the trust. Premises were found: a castle on fifteen hectares of wooded land near the village of Milon-la-Chapelle, not far from Rambouillet, in the Valley of Chevreuse. A staff was found: the nuns of Saint-Jacut were ready to take it on. Money was more difficult to find, and initially the de Gaulles funded the project from their own modest resources. At all events, the home was opened in 1946, and they now felt that should Anne survive them, she would be properly looked after.

---

[1] Tournoux, *Tragédie*, pp. 231–2.

[2] Galante records that de Gaulle refused to allow any of his children to appear in publicity photographs of the couple at home in wartime England, reasoning that the presence or absence of Anne would be equally likely to occasion comment. Churchill, says Galante, had entrusted £500 to General Spears to give de Gaulle an international "image", and Spears had hired a public relations man to get pictures and stories about the general into the press (Galante, pp. 71–2; *see also* pp. 79–81).

Two years later, however, shortly before her twentieth birthday, Anne died of pneumonia. At her graveside, after a time of tears and silence, de Gaulle took Yvonne's hand and said: "Come. Now she is like the others. . . ."[3]

The founding of the home had landed de Gaulle in financial difficulties, from which he was extricated by Georges Pompidou, later to be the general's choice as premier, and later still to become president of the Republic. A master at the Lycée Henri IV, and the compiler of an anthology of French verse, Pompidou was a product of the famous Ecole Normale Supérieure and the holder of the onerously acquired certificate known as the *Agrégation*. Though in no way connected with the Resistance (or, for that matter, Vichy), he had joined de Gaulle's secretariat in 1944, during the provisional government period, when he played a self-effacing role. Later, during the general's period in the political wilderness known to the faithful as *la traversée du désert*, he became de Gaulle's right-hand man, heading his personal secretariat and acting as his intermediary in monetary matters.[4] In 1951 the Fondation Anne de Gaulle was running into serious financial straits. It looked as though de Gaulle would have to raise a mortgage on La Boisserie. By this time, however, Pompidou was general manager of the Banque Rothschild, and he arranged for a loan.

Several publishers competed for the honour of bringing out the memoirs and de Gaulle's choice fell on the Librairie Plon, which had published the works of Foch, Joffre, Poincaré, Clemenceau, Lloyd George and Churchill – a distinguished company de Gaulle was keen to share.

Pompidou opened negotiations in the autumn of 1953. By this time, the first volume was nearing completion, and Yvonne de Gaulle had persuaded her husband that he should publish the whole work during his lifetime and not, as he had initially envisaged, after his death. On 1 April the managing director of Plon, Maurice Bourdelle, and the literary director, Charles Orengo, called on Pompidou at his home, 25 rue de Charlemagne. Pompidou showed them the completed typescript, which they studied. On the 8th de Gaulle met Bourdelle and Orengo in Paris at the Hotel Lapérouse, where he kept rooms and which he used as his *pied-à-terre* every Wednesday. On 22 April, the de Gaulles entertained the two men, and their wives, at a lunch to mark the signing of the contract.[5]

[3] Lacouture, *De Gaulle*, p. 145.
[4] Philippe Alexandre, *Le Duel De Gaulle–Pompidou* (1970), p. 24 (henceforth, Alexandre).
[5] Gorce, pp. 513–14; *see also* pp. 515 and 520.

Meticulous as ever, de Gaulle personally corrected the proofs and attended to every question of fact brought to his attention, either by the publishers or, after the first edition had appeared, by readers. The first volume, *L'Appel*, was delivered from the presses on 5 October 1954; the second, *L'Unité*, on 29 May 1956; and the third, *Le Salut*, not until 25 September 1959, by which time he was back in power. Paul-Marie de la Gorce records a curious change of author's preferences between the appearances of the first and second volumes. For the first, de Gaulle had drawn up a list of fifty-five recipients for complimentary copies printed on special paper. When the publishing date for the second volume was drawing near, the publishers sent the list back to him for approval. The general replied to say he had not intended, this time, to include Jacques Soustelle on the list, but since arrangements had been made for him to get a copy, he would not make an issue of it – a measure of the coolness that had developed between de Gaulle and one of his most faithful followers, whose misdemeanours were to have played the parliamentary game, won personal acclaim as governor-general of Algeria, and (later) stuck to principles once defended by de Gaulle after the general had abandoned them.

The war memoirs were an immediate best-seller. By December 1963, without counting foreign language editions, 30,000 copies of each volume had been printed in the illustrated edition; 228,000 of the ordinary edition of the first volume and 273,000 of the paperback; 169,000 and 225,000 respectively of the second volume; and 186,000 and 225,000 of the third. These vast sales brought in huge royalties, into which de Gaulle dipped generously not only for the Fondation Anne de Gaulle, but for the French Red Cross, various other charities and the commune and parish of Colombey-les-deux-Eglises.

For de Gaulle, despite his literary consolations, his sojourn in the wilderness was an increasingly melancholy period. Every government crisis confirmed the essential truth of his critique of the system; yet the resilience of it never ceased to surprise and disappoint him: though moribund, it was reluctant to die, and indeed at times seemed full of life. Great events, some of them tragic, were happening in the world, and to his chagrin and frustration he had no say in them. Lacking all power, and with a diminishing audience, all he could do was to make an occasional speech or pronouncement, at rare and lengthening intervals; and in the end confine himself to private comments that were in turn embittered or resigned. The table of contents of the collected speeches (*Discours et Messages*, Volume II) is negatively eloquent on this score. Even in 1953, the year of disillusionment in the RPF, he made two public speeches, issued five statements and gave two lengthy press conferences. In 1954, there were two short statements of his "wishes" to his followers, two more general pronouncements, one press conference and one speech. The following year, he neither made speeches nor issued statements but gave one press conference – on 30 June – in which he announced that he would no longer intervene in public affairs; in 1956, there were two short speeches only; and in 1957, only a brief communiqué.

During these five years he kept up the habit of going to Paris in mid-week, but as time went on fewer and fewer men of note wanted to see him. Olivier Guichard, who headed the Gaullist secretariat, always made sure there was somebody in Suite 11 at the Hotel Lapérouse, so that the great man's journey should not have been in vain. But towards the end, the guest was likely to be just a faithful Companion of the Liberation, or even, if all else failed, a man from Plon's to discuss some technical detail of the war memoirs.

By the end of 1957, then, Charles de Gaulle was virtually a forgotten man, remembered as a legend, admired as a writer, but no longer taken seriously, except by a very few, as a potential saviour of France. Yet he was within a few months of his sensational return to power, in roughly the kind of circumstances he had foreseen, except that destiny had taken twelve years to realise what was expected of it.

For de Gaulle, the five years to 1957 were a time of bitterness and impotence; for France they were eventful, if unedifying; for the world, dramatic. If any one man ruined the political chances of de Gaulle and of his Rally of the French People, it was Antoine Pinay – everyone's idea of the average Frenchman and therefore the antithesis of the general. During his nine and a half months as premier (6 March to 23 December 1952), this level-headed businessman made Gaullism seem irrelevant by quietly halting inflation and starting the Fourth Republic on the course of economic recovery and expansion. During this period, however, what Jacques Fauvet has called "the infernal circle of terrorism and repression" began in Tunisia and Morocco; the Algerian war was still two years off.[6]

In the Far East, the Korean war had ground to a halt in the latter half of 1951, although a formal truce was not signed until 27 July 1953. France's own war in Indo-China, however, went on. The death of the successful commander-in-chief, General de Lattre de Tassigny, early in 1952 was followed by French strategic withdrawals. The war was sapping the Republic through the continuing drain on money, resources

[6] Fauvet, IVème, p. 219.

445

and manpower; and above all, perhaps, through demoralising scandals and evidences of corruption.[7]

In 1953, France had two governments: that of the Radical René Mayer, which began on 7 January and lasted only four and a half months; and that of the Republican Independent (that is, conservative) Joseph Laniel, which was one of the longest (26 June 1953 to 12 June 1954). The thirty-seven days between Mayer's fall and Laniel's advent stood as the longest ministerial crisis of the Fourth Republic. Continuity in foreign policy was provided by the presence of Georges Bidault (MRP) at the Quai d'Orsay throughout this period. From his predecessor, Robert Schuman, Bidault had inherited the unpopular project for a European army, enshrined in a treaty (signed at Bonn on 26 May 1952) to create a "European Defence Community" (EDC). Bidault, however, was in no hurry to have it ratified.

During the Mayer government, General Henri Navarre was sent to Indo-China as the new commander-in-chief. It proved a disastrous appointment. Navarre chose to draw the Vietminh (Communist) forces into battle at Dien Bien Phu, near the Laos border. It was a catastrophic choice, for Dien Bien Phu was in a hollow, surrounded by hills that gave cover to Vietminh artillery, and could be supplied only by air. The Laniel government – if possible, even more *immobiliste* than the Queuille administration of 1950 – declined to allocate the credits Navarre needed, but without ordering him to modify his plans.[8]

In December 1953, the Fourth Republic further discredited itself when the parliamentarians, in conclave at Versailles Palace, voted no fewer than thirteen times to choose a new chief of State. The winner was a worthy Norman businessman, René Coty.

Three other events punctuated the Laniel period: the French premier joined Churchill and President Eisenhower in a summit conference in Bermuda (4–8 December 1953); the sultan of Morocco, Mohammed ben Youssef, was deposed (thus shelving, not solving, the Moroccan problem); and a conference on Indo-China opened at Geneva on 15 April 1954. On 6 May Dien Bien Phu fell after a long siege, and France's will to continue the war was broken.

Laniel's fall on 12 June brought to power a lonely and uncompromising figure: Pierre Mendès France. On the 16th, he made the unprecedented wager that he would bring peace to Indo-China by 20 July or resign. He won his bet (but only just, the clocks at the Palais des Nations having

[7] ibid. pp. 159 *et seq.*
[8] Both Navarre and Laniel later wrote books, each blaming the other for what ensued: H. Navarre, *Agonie de l'Indochine* (1956) and J. Laniel, *Le Drame Indochinois* (1957).

been stopped for a few hours to enable him to "win" and stay in office). The war had lasted seven and a half years and cost the French Union 92,000 killed and 114,000 wounded.

In his remaining months in office, Mendès France ended terrorism in Tunisia by recognising the country's internal autonomy; allowed the EDC project to be defeated in parliament; but cleared the way for West Germany to rearm and enter NATO through the treaty of Paris (23 October 1954). On 1 November the Algerian war began: it was to last approximately as long as the Indo-China war.

Mendès France fell on 3 February 1955, to be succeeded by his Finance minister, Edgar Faure. Though readier to compromise than his predecessor, Faure lasted only until 2 January 1956, when general elections were held. It had fallen to Faure to represent France at the summit conference of July 1955, at Geneva, along with President Eisenhower, Sir Anthony Eden and Marshal Bulganin of the Soviet Union; to commit France to the creation of a European Common Market; and to consent to the return of the Nationalist leader Habib Bourguiba to Tunis, and of the sultan to Morocco.

The elections brought the Socialist leader, Guy Mollet, to power. His year – 1956 – was that of the Hungarian uprising and the Suez expedition. The most startling thing that happened under Mollet's authority, however, was the diversion to French soil of a plane carrying Algerian revolutionary leaders, who were promptly interned. His reign lasted long enough for France to sign the treaty of Rome on 25 March 1957, but not long enough for him to raise taxes to finance the Algerian war. His request to that end brought about his downfall in May.

The Fourth Republic now entered its terminal malady. The Radical Bourgès-Maunoury, who succeeded Mollet on 12 June 1957, was in office for only ten weeks, during a month and a half of which parliament was in recess. But this was time enough for the Prime Minister to get approval for slightly heavier taxes than those whose refusal had brought down Mollet, and to introduce a bill for a general administrative law (loi-cadre) which he saw as the basis for a gradualist solution to the Algerian problem. Both the youngish premier (he was forty-three) and his loi-cadre were, however, more than the settler lobby could tolerate; and Jacques Soustelle, back in parliament after his stint as governor-general of Algeria, led the attack which forced Bourgès-Maunoury out of office on 30 September.

One of the longest ministerial crises followed. After thirty-five days of it, Félix Gaillard (MRP), who had been the outgoing premier's Finance minister, found himself in power. The Treasury by now was empty, and

Gaillard's first action was to borrow 200 milliard francs from the Banque de France. Shortly after, he sought a massive dollar loan to balance France's external account.

In Algeria, the war was going rather well for the French in military terms. In Algiers, the grip of the Moslem terrorists had been broken by ruthless measures that included torture. In the country, the revolutionary army was suffering heavy losses and was gradually being driven outside Algeria, to set up camp on Tunisian and Moroccan soil. But this was a revolutionary war, in which military successes do not necessarily bring victory. In the more important areas of morale, public opinion at home and abroad, and the financing of hostilities, France was losing. The "rebels" were having successes of their own in organising sympathy for their cause, both in France and in the United Nations. The failure of the French government, including the minister-resident in Algiers, to denounce torture and other excesses of the repression, was bringing it into widespread discredit.

And then came Sakhiet, one of the more traumatic experiences of the Republic. On 8 February 1958, in daylight, French bombers with fighter escort heavily bombarded the village of Sakhiet-Sidi-Youssef, on the Algerian–Tunisian border, killing sixty-nine Tunisian civilians, including twenty-one children. This, it seemed, was the ultimate defiance of Paris by Algiers. Not far from there, on 11 January, sixteen French soldiers had been killed in an ambush by Algerian revolutionaries coming from Tunisia. Without bothering to consult the government, the army had simply decided to administer a "lesson" to the Tunisians.

When told of the incident, however, Gaillard declined to condemn it. Righteously indignant, President Bourguiba put the matter in the hands of the United Nations Security Council; and on 17 February, both the French and the Tunisian governments accepted the "good offices" for mediation purposes of Britain and the United States. For fifty days Sir Harold Beeley of the Foreign Office, and Robert Murphy (de Gaulle's wartime *bête noire* in North Africa) of the State Department travelled back and forth between Paris and Tunis, not without success. But this foreign interference in France's sovereign affairs had brought the indignation of the Algiers lobby to boiling point. On 15 April Gaillard was forced out. Only one more premier now remained before de Gaulle's return to power.

General de Gaulle had, of course, been powerless to control this dismal sequence of events. Occasionally, however, he tried to influence it, especially during the time of his active association with the RPF. Later on, he merely philosophised, more often in private than in public.

Between 1955 and 1957, he seems to have despaired of ever returning to power, and his private soliloquies were increasingly gloomy and disillusioned. It was during the long period that preceded and ended his stay "in the wilderness", however (that is from 1952 to 1958), that de Gaulle's thoughts on France and the world finally crystallised. If his words at that time had been read or heeded (to the extent that they were publicly available) the shocked surprise that greeted his later actions would have been unnecessary. This applies, in particular, to his views on the need, as he saw it, for a confederal Europe without American links.

Here, then, is a brief selection of de Gaulle's opinions, including some that illustrate his character rather than his policy.

THE EUROPEAN DEFENCE COMMUNITY

"It is my duty to warn the nation that these treaties [that is, the EDC treaty and the Bonn Conventions of 1952 defining relations between the western occupying powers and the German Federal Republic] are, for our country, protocols of abandonment ... it is pretended to establish a 'defence community' and create an army described as 'European' under American command. Higgledy-piggledy with defeated Germany and Italy, France is to pour out her men, her arms, her money, in a stateless [apatride] mixture." 6 June 1952.

De Gaulle returned to this theme time and again, until the defeat of the EDC project in the National Assembly.

EUROPE

In his wartime statements on the future of Europe, de Gaulle made no provision for Britain: he thought in terms of a loose confederation that would serve to contain a Germany broken up into princely states, and led, naturally, by France.[9] Then, on 12 November 1953, the general said:

"The West must complete its means of defence. That implies the creation of a truly European alliance, organised in a confederation of which England would be a part and which Germany could enter with the necessary commitments and limits. That implies, on the other hand, *a revision of the conditions of the American alliance*, to adapt the latter, first to our own independence, and also to our situation as a power, not only European, but African, Asian, Oceanic, which we are and want to remain." (Emphasis added.)

[9] A useful anthology of de Gaulle's views on Europe is contained in R. Massip, *De Gaulle et l'Europe* (Flammarion, 1963), see also Lord Gladwyn, *De Gaulle's Europe*, pp. 31–55.

"I see Europe as she is. I see her stretching from Gibraltar to the Urals, from Spitzberg to Sicily." 7 April 1954.

NATO

"What is the Atlantic Pact? It is a declaration of intent . . . [to which] I subscribe entirely. . . . In any case, the Atlantic alliance needs an effective policy and an organisation. . . . It is an error . . . to want to cut up the world in slices of security. . . . We must have the courage to consider the danger on its existing scale, that is on a world scale, and to build at the same time, in the Atlantic, the Pacific, in Asia, in Europe, in Africa, the common security of the free peoples. . . ." 10 March 1952.

WESTERN EUROPEAN UNION

Welcoming the rejection of EDC by the French Assembly, de Gaulle said:

". . . the agreements reached after that, in London and Paris, are in themselves far preferable. For these agreements . . . leave France, in principle, the possibility of having an army, a face, an external action." 4 December 1954.

THE AMERICANS

In a passage on Nato and the EDC project, de Gaulle said:

"The way things are happening, it even seems – I am obliged to say this – as if America were playing today, under cover of the Atlantic Pact and the European army, on a special *de facto* alliance between herself and Germany." 10 March 1952.

In reply to a question on "foreign pressures" on France to ratify the European army treaty, de Gaulle declared:

"Nothing . . . is as curious as the public or hidden interventions of the United States to constrain our country to ratify a treaty that condemns her to decline. Yes, curious! For after all, the United States is not a party to this treaty . . . if it thinks the system of fusion is such a good idea for the French and such a good idea for the Germans, why doesn't it merge with Canada, Mexico, Brazil or Argentina?" 12 November 1953.

Referring to the threat by the American secretary of State, John Foster Dulles, of an "agonising reappraisal" of policy if France did not ratify the EDC treaty, de Gaulle said:

"Whatever harassed ministers may say on occasion, I don't believe in sudden and dramatic revisions in the attitude of great states, for instance that of America. . . . Preparing for world war, she deploys great efforts to arm all countries liable to combat man to man with the Communist armies, and she takes care to take over the command of their forces, but she herself has chosen a peripheral strategy which would commit the smallest possible number of her own children." 7 April 1954.

THE UNITED NATIONS

"The United Nations organisation sets itself up as a tribunal to pass judgment on France's work in Africa." 8 October 1952.

This was a reference to a move by thirteen African and Asian states to place Morocco on the agenda of the forthcoming session of the General Assembly.

NORTH AFRICA

Referring to the concept of association within the French Union, de Gaulle said:

"The association could take . . . either the form of a link of a federal nature between states, for example between Morocco or Tunisia and France, or else that of the integration of a territory with its own character, for example Algeria, in a community larger than France. . . ." 30 June 1955.

THE LATINS

"There are some 250 million Latins in the world, not only in Europe, but in Latin America and in Africa. That is as many as the Anglo-Saxons, as many as the Slavs, three times as many as the Germanic peoples. Their cultural power is the foremost in the world. Their economic potential is very great. . . . If they could organise themselves in a practical manner, starting with the economic and cultural domains, they would constitute a great asset of equilibrium, for the lack of which the world is in danger of dying." 7 April 1954.

DICTATORSHIP

"I had the material means to establish a dictatorship. . . . I must confess, without requesting absolution, that events forced me to exercise a dictatorship during nearly six years. But France was gagged at the time; she was in mortal peril. . . . Should I have maintained that dictatorship? My answer to my own question was 'No!' . . . Dictatorship always ends badly in France if it is maintained when circumstances have returned to normal." 6 July 1952.

"Of course I could have called in Leclerc and expelled the Assembly." (In an interview with J.-R. Tournoux.)[10]

10 Tournoux, *Tragédie*, p. 152.

THE SUEZ EXPEDITION

"If I, de Gaulle, had been the master, because I represent legitimacy, as soon as the man named Nasser had announced this summer the nationalisation of the Suez Canal, I should have seized the microphone and I should have announced on the spot, for the world to hear: 'Listen carefully, Mr Nasser, I don't know if you really are going to nationalise the canal, but I, de Gaulle, am sending two divisions to Egypt. In two hours my paratroops will have taken Cairo. And no force in the whole world is going to stop them!'" (In private conversation.)[11]

After the failure of the expedition, de Gaulle commented: "We left it to the British to do the organising, and they organised very badly. Why did we let them command everything? They commanded at sea, they commanded on the ground, they commanded in the air.... One has to be called Guy Mollet or Pineau, one must be a Socialist to believe in the military virtues of the English.

"Yes, yes, Waterloo! But at Waterloo the English were dealing with an exhausted Napoleon who had been running around Europe for fifteen years....

"We should have warned the Americans and told them: 'This is what we plan to do. If you don't accept, that's the end of the Atlantic Pact.' And they would have accepted.

"Today, they're threatening to cut off our supplies of petrol. Well, I would say to them: 'From tonight at zero hundred hours, American troops will lose the right to move on French roads, and there will be no more American bases in France until further notice.'" (In an interview with Tournoux.)[12]

It is fascinating, but fruitless, in the light of such remarks, whether made in public or in private, to reflect how different the history of the post-war years might have been had de Gaulle remained in power, instead of returning to it after years of inactivity in 1958.

[11] ibid. p. 209.   [12] ibid. pp. 214–15.

Chapter 4 ✤ De Gaulle Returns

Between 1956 and 1958 the French army became politicised. This fact is central to an understanding of the circumstances that brought General de Gaulle back to power. The general public in France was, however, quite unaware of what was happening; and so, indeed, were the embassies and foreign correspondents in Paris, and most academic observers of the French scene.[1] This unawareness helps to explain the impact and success of the general's political intervention, when it came.

The state of mind of the French army early in 1958 is easily understandable. Despite prodigious efforts and expenditure, much heroism and occasional successes, the war in Indo-China had been lost. The disaster of Dien Bien Phu was a national and military humiliation, which was difficult to blame on the politicians. Nevertheless, many army officers felt the politicians had let them down, and the Geneva settlement of 1954 was regarded by many of them as a sell-out. Within a few months of the end of the Indo-China war, the war in Algeria had begun. The army was determined that this time there would be no Dien Bien Phu, and, above all, no political and diplomatic sell-out. Yet it was plain to the men who were doing the fighting that the Fourth Republic was coming apart, and that the soldiers could place less and less reliance on the will of the politicians to fight on until final victory. The appointment of the Anglo-American "good offices" team in the wake of the bombing of the Tunisian village of Sakhiet[2] confirmed them in their suspicions. Another sell-out, they felt, was on the way. Their patience, sorely tried over the past twelve years of almost continuous fighting, was now exhausted.

Understandable though this psychology was, it was not, however, the whole story. There had been much intellectual as well as emotional soul-searching within the army. Unreliable though the politicians had proved to be, their unreliability and spinelessness alone did not fully

[1] *See* Brian Crozier, *The Masters of Power* (henceforth, Crozier, *Power*), p. 20 n. A re-reading of the British and even the French press of the early months of 1958 is instructive for its evidences of unreality.
[2] *See above* p. 448.

account for the failure of the army to dominate the military situation in Indo-China. While the war was on, the military hierarchy never came properly to grips with the problem. But many of the younger officers, especially during the final phase, had undergone the horrors of political indoctrination in Vietminh hands, where they had made forced acquaintance with the works of Mao Tse-tung and his Vietnamese disciples, Vo Nguyen Giap and Truong Chinh (at that time the secretary-general of the Vietnamese Workers' – that is, Communist – party). When the war was over, and especially when the Algerian war began, there was much cogitation in military quarters about the theoretical and practical lessons of the French defeat. The secret, which the army had discovered too late to bring victory in Indo-China, was the Sino-Vietnamese doctrine of "revolutionary war". From the doctrine, the soldiers retained above all Mao's dictum that the army should move among the people as the fish in water: the army, in other words, must help, and be helped by, the people – with food and intelligence, for instance. From their personal observations in Indo-China, they could see that the Vietminh had set up a parallel administration in areas under its control, which raised taxes, conscripted the young and built roads.

During the Indo-China war, the army had dismissed Mao's experience as irrelevant to its problems. Now, translations of his works were made and the more intellectual of the French officers set about elaborating a counter-theory of revolutionary war, by means of which the French would use Mao's and Giap's principles to turn the tables on the revolutionaries of the Algerian Front de Libération Nationale (FLN) themselves deeply influenced by the same theories. As a consequence of the Second World War experience, the army had added a "Fifth Bureau", charged with psychological war, to the traditional four bureaux dealing respectively with personnel, intelligence, operations and supplies.

Those who ran the Fifth Bureau saw it as their duty not only to influence the Algerian Moslem population, but also to indoctrinate the conscripts in their charge in the counter-theory of revolutionary war and in the principles of *activisme*: that is, of the army's right and duty to intervene in social and political affairs.[3] One of the liveliest of the proponents of activism was Colonel Jean Lacheroy, whose views were reported to the War ministry. Finding them alarming, the ministry had him transferred from Algiers to Paris. Shortsightedly, however, Lacheroy was given teaching responsibilities that enabled him to continue the indoctrination process nearer the centre of power. His articles in the ministry's house magazine, the *Revue Militaire d'Information*, especially

[3] *See* Brian Crozier, "The General's Generals", *Encounter* (April 1960).

in 1957, provided the intellectual basis of military activism. Not surprisingly, Lacheroy was one of the plotters whose efforts brought down the Fourth Republic. (Later, disillusioned by de Gaulle's Algerian policy, he joined the Organisation of the Secret Army – OAS – and became a fugitive from justice.)

Whole books have been written on the plots that brought de Gaulle back to power.[4] Not all those who wanted to tear down the Fourth Republic wanted to bring back de Gaulle; nor was the fate of Algeria necessarily their dominant motive, although Algeria was the catalyst that temporarily united them. The plotters, agitators and other opponents of the regime fell broadly into four groups: the Gaullists, the extreme right-wingers, the generals and the Algerian whites, known as "pieds-noirs". The motives of this opposition being mixed and sometimes contradictory, there was much overlapping between the groups. The cleverest among them were the Gaullists, whose extraordinary success was to persuade or manoeuvre the other groups into accepting the proposition that their interests would best be served by the return of the general. Many who clamoured for his return lived to regret it, and even to fight his authority. As for de Gaulle himself, he was soon to show that his twelve years in the wilderness had not been wasted. It was not only an older man who emerged from the shadows, but a more subtle and cunning politician.

The leaders of the Gaullist group were Michel Debré, Jacques Soustelle and Chaban-Delmas. Unlike the second and third of these, Senator Debré, a former commissioner of the Republic in de Gaulle's provisional government, had never compromised with the Fourth Republic. An able constitutional lawyer of Jewish origin, he had greeted each of its ministerial crises with an appeal for the general's return. Of the dwindling band of the truly faithful, none was stauncher than he. He was, as the saying went, pur et dur. A bitterly effective pamphleteer, he wrote a devastating attack on the politicians – Ces Princes qui nous Gouvernent – and launched an angry periodical, Le Courrier de la Colère ("The Angry Mail") with the aim of popularising the view that de Gaulle's return alone would keep Algeria French. He was later rewarded for his zeal by being made the general's first Prime Minister under the Fifth Republic.

[4] For instance, the rather breathless account of the Bromberger brothers, Les 13 Complots du 13 Mai; J. R. Tournoux, Secrets d'Etat (henceforth, Tournoux, Secrets); and the more slender 13 Mai: histoire secrète d'une révolution, by Dominique Pado (henceforth, Pado). The best summary I know is in Pierre Viansson-Ponté, Histoire de la République Gaullienne (henceforth, Viansson-Ponté, République), Vol. I, pp. 23 et seq., from which I draw in this chapter.

Soustelle, unlike Debré, had compromised with the system, although in its final phase he had acquired a fresh reputation as the most effective demolisher of its governments in the National Assembly. As governor-general of Algeria, however, he had taken his distance from the political parties, including the Gaullist group of Républicains Sociaux. Although a passionate defender of French Algeria, he was committed, not to the defence of the white settlers' privileges, but to the idealistic solution of *intégration*, that is, of the complete equality of the communities, including proportionate representation in the French parliament. On 15 April it was Soustelle who in a coldly impassioned speech brought down the government of Félix Gaillard, thus provoking what was to be the penultimate ministerial crisis of the Fourth Republic.

Chaban-Delmas, who was Gaillard's Defence minister, had his own man of confidence in Algiers, Léon Delbecque. Having fought in the Resistance, Delbecque had joined the rally of the French people. His official job in Algiers was "Technical Counsellor" to the Defence ministry's liaison bureau, known as the "Antenna". The commander-in-chief, General Salan, had regarded his arrival with deep suspicion. Delbecque, son of a northern industrialist and a born organiser, quickly established a network of informants and launched what amounted to a propaganda service to prepare for de Gaulle's return. Soon, Salan was among those influenced by it.[5] Between December 1957 and May 1958 Delbecque travelled back and forth between Paris and Algiers twenty-seven times.[6] He took advantage of one of his Parisian visits to call on General de Gaulle, to whom he reported that public sentiment, in Algeria as well as in metropolitan France, among the Moslems as well as among the settlers and within the army, now favoured the general's return to power. De Gaulle was sceptical but gave Delbecque to understand that if the call came, he would respond to it. Delbecque had hoped for an unambiguous declaration of intent, but rightly judged that the movement he was organising could count on de Gaulle when the crisis had ripened.

The extreme right-wingers were less important than the Gaullists, though they contributed to the psychosis of fear that increasingly paralysed the politicians in Paris. Their leaders were two civilians, a former Cagoulard and Pétainist, Dr Martin, in his sixties, and a much younger man, Robert Martel, who was a *colon* from the Mitidja region; and two soldiers, General Cherrière, lately retired as commander of the Land Forces in Algeria, and Air Force General Lionel-Max Chassin,

---

[5] Tournoux, *Secrets*, pp. 229–30; *see also* pp. 230–1 and 187.
[6] Fauvet, *IVème*, p. 344.

formerly the air force commander in Indo-China, who had a reputation as an intellectual. Romantic and conspiratorial, the right-wing group advocated a Christian and corporative State inspired by Portugal and Vichy (whilst disclaiming racism or fascism). For these men, de Gaulle's return would have been a catastrophe for France. Wishfully, they had convinced themselves that he was not, in any case, ready to come back, even if asked to do so, and thought it safe to conspire to overthrow the Fourth Republic to their own ends. General Cherrière himself was convinced that before long he would be chief of State.

The military group was more divided and confused than either the Gaullists or the extreme right-wingers. All they knew for certain was that the politicians were leading them towards a defeat (indeed, Robert Lacoste, the minister-resident, had publicly conjured up the spectre of a "diplomatic Dien Bien Phu"), and that they would not allow Paris to betray them. One of the most prominent, General Jouhaud, was himself a *pied-noir*. There were, however, Gaullists and activists among the generals. Their unity, then, was doubtful. Their asset was the possession of military power; their handicap lay in the self-doubts inherent in the conflict between hostility towards the regime and the habits of obedience and discipline.

When the point of no return was reached, on 13 May 1958, the most important soldier turned out to be General Massu, the tough commander of the *élite* paratroop division, whose political knowledge was nil but who opted for de Gaulle at a crucial time and swung the army behind him. It was Massu who, between March and October 1957, had cleaned up Algiers of the FLN terrorists, by ruthless methods that included a liberal use of torture.[6a] In the short term, his success in Algiers was undeniable; in the longer term, his methods undoubtedly drove yet another nail into the coffin of the Fourth Republic and brought further international support for the Algerian revolutionaries. He was, however, a hero to the army, and especially to the dreaded *paras*. His decision to support de Gaulle was therefore decisive on the day.

Then there were the *pieds-noirs*. They, too, were divided and confused, except on the proposition that Algeria must remain French. They had more to lose than any other faction, and sought support wherever they could find it; even, if need be, from de Gaulle, whom most of them, as ex-Pétainists, detested. Their spokesmen in parliament were commonly at that time known as the "four musketeers" – Soustelle, Bidault, André

[6a] In his book, *La Vraie Bataille d'Alger* (1971), Jacques Massu gives explicit details of tortures used and defends them as justified by the urgent need for information (*see esp.*, pp. 163 *et seq.*).

Morice, who had given his name to the system of fortifications (the *ligne Morice*) that was supposed to keep the Algerian revolutionary army in its Tunisian bases, and Roger Duchet, one of the leaders of the conservative Indépendants. Only one of the four, Soustelle, was a Gaullist. Morice and Duchet had their own political affiliations; and Bidault, the MRP leader, detested the general.

In later years, the Gaullists spread the myth that the general had no knowledge of the plots and counter-plots that were to bring him back to power. He himself, in his *Mémoires d'Espoir*,[7] was to contribute to this impression. But while it is clear that he held himself aloof from the conspiracies, it is certainly untrue that he knew nothing about them. Delbecque's visit was a case in point. In addition, however, de Gaulle, emerging from his period of oblivion, had many visitors in the early months of 1958, including two of his most faithful followers, Olivier Guichard and Jacques Foccart, who (says Soustelle) were told everything that went on, and passed it on to the general.[8] But until quite late in the day, de Gaulle continued to greet the news that reached him with scepticism and even pessimism. He did not doubt that the Fourth Republic was doomed; but, disappointed in his earlier expectations of its imminent collapse, he was reluctant now to supose that his chance to return to power was approaching. Indeed, as late as 27 March 1958 he told war veterans at the Gaullist headquarters in the Rue Solférino that "this situation could go on for thirty or forty years, which is nothing in the history of a nation". It was this remark, relayed to General Cherrière, that convinced the neo-Fascists that they need not fear any competition from de Gaulle. When one of the most faithful Gaullists, Roger Frey, wrote to him about that time to say he was sure the hour of the appeal to de Gaulle was approaching, de Gaulle dismissed the thought with these words: "Nothing will happen. . . . Why shouldn't France be happy with M. Gaillard, since M. Gaillard is so pleased with himself?"

It is tempting to credit de Gaulle with more prescience than such remarks indicate. But it seems more likely that his scepticism, inactivity and public silence at this time was due to the inertia of his lengthening retirement than to a desire for dissimulation. Between 1947 and 1953 he had repeatedly tried to rock the foundations of the Fourth Republic, and had failed. Now, he was going to wait until power was offered to him. If it were not, then his historical pessimism would cover his disappointment. A powerful motive in his refusal to commit himself was un-

[7] Soustelle, *Gaullisme*, p. 145; Tournoux, *Secrets*, p. 233; *see also* pp. 226–7 and 252–3.
[8] De Gaulle, *Mémoires d'Espoir: Le Renouveau 1958–1962* (henceforth, De Gaulle, *Renouveau*).

doubtedly, however, a desire to keep all options open. Certainly, he was not going to commit his name in advance to one group of plotters rather than another. Nor, on the other hand, was he going to disown any of them. Nobody would be able to say that he had come to power through a military *putsch*, or at any rate a *putsch* led by himself. If anything illegal was to happen, he would not be a party to it; but it was not for him to condemn the illegal acts others might commit if, in consequence, he were to return to power. For, in his eyes, he represented the *legitimacy* of the nation, a permanent state which could not be equated with the transient phenomena of *legality*. Indeed, he himself had achieved legitimacy by an act of disobedience (illegal in the eyes of most Frenchmen) in 1940. In January 1958 de Gaulle told Tournoux that he no longer considered the French government as legitimate, since it no longer ensured the defence or security of its territories.[9]

As the weeks went by, de Gaulle's prolonged public silence itself became an ominous factor in the evolving crisis. A year or two earlier, politicians and people were indifferent at his self-effacement. Now they longed for him to say something: some of them would have been relieved to hear him disclaim any further political aspirations; others hoped he would declare himself ready to take over, and thereby give the Fourth Republic its *coup de grâce*.

The question-marks inherent in the general's public silence were, if anything, made more enigmatic by the ambiguous confidences he had been making to visitors, each of whom he contrived to leave with the impression that de Gaulle was on his side. Thus Louis Terrenoire, former resister and MRP deputy, and the journalist Roger Stéphane called on the man of Colombey in search of a "liberal" and a "leftist"; and were not disappointed. Edmond Michelet and Maurice Schumann left his company with the clear impression that he so desired peace in Algeria that he would be prepared, if necessary, to concede complete independence to the revolutionaries. But General Petit, assistant to the chief of the General Staff, and Robert Lacoste, while still minister-resident, were delighted to hear (as they thought) de Gaulle encourage them in their policy of repressing the "rebellion".[10] Yet was independence really what de Gaulle had in mind? One visitor whose confidences reached me in March 1958 was astonished to hear the general outline a vision of the future of North Africa in terms of a commonwealth embracing France

---

[9] Tournoux, *Secrets*, p. 228. Some months earlier, Michel Debré, the "high priest" of Gaullism, had written in *Ces Princes qui nous Gouvernent*: "Legitimacy is the key word of difficult periods. A legal government may be illegitimate, an illegal authority may be legitimate."

[10] Viansson-Ponté, *République*, Vol. I, pp. 48–50.

and the French possessions in "black" Africa, as well as the countries of the Maghreb. In this commonwealth, Algeria was to be no less equal than the others even if she had to wait some years for equality.[11]

On 15 March Debré, Soustelle and Frey met one of the arch-exponents of Algérie Française, Alain de Sérigny, an ex-Pétainist, editor of the *Echo d'Alger*, who expressed doubts about de Gaulle's intentions. Debré exclaimed indignantly, "How can you have even a second's doubt about General de Gaulle's will to keep Algeria French?" Soustelle supported him: "He is categorically opposed to secession!"

Some weeks earlier de Gaulle, in one of his darker moods, had said to Maurice Schumann: "I shall never come back to power. Never. It's finished now." Gloomily, Schumann passed on these remarks to Michel Debré, who retorted with conviction: "If he's told you that he will never come back to power, it means he's hoping to hear you say the opposite. That's all he thinks about."

Events were to prove Debré right. They gathered an ominous momentum after the fall of Félix Gaillard on 15 April. President Coty, who lacked the supreme power de Gaulle thought a president ought to have, was nevertheless the greatest living expert in parliamentary arithmetic (this was, after all, part of his job); and he had already come to the conclusion that the Fourth Republic had virtually ceased to be governable. He had only two politicians in reserve: René Pleven, a former Gaullist and adept at parliamentary consultations; and Pierre Pflimlin, a patriotic Alsatian and one of the leaders of the MRP. After that – and this was Coty's secret – he would have no option but to turn to General de Gaulle.[12] Logically, of course, he ought to have invited one of the "four musketeers" to form a government. But it was clear that while the Algerian lobby in Paris was capable of bringing down governments, it was not capable of commanding a majority of its own. Nevertheless, the president went through the motions of doing the logical thing, by inviting Georges Bidault to have a try. Bidault, however, was disowned by his own party, and had to give up the attempt three days later, on the 23rd.

On the 26th, Pleven was given his chance. That day in Algiers silent demonstrators paraded the streets bearing placards calling for a "government of Public Safety".[13] Nobody in Paris took much notice, or was aware that its organiser was Léon Delbecque, or would have known who

[11] *The Economist Foreign Report*, 13 March 1958.
[12] Tournoux, *Secrets*, pp. 243–4.
[13] I use this mis-translation of "*salut public*" (public salvation) because it has been in general use in English history books ever since the "Committee of Public Safety" of the great French revolution.

Delbecque was had they been told his name. On 8 May, at 3 a.m., Pleven formed a government; and at 1 p.m., he withdrew when the Radicals withdrew their support. For form's sake, the president then called in three Radical leaders, before turning, as he had originally intended, to Pflimlin. In the ornate office at the Elysée Palace, Coty looked Pflimlin in the eye, and said: "You are my last card. If you too fail, there will only be one way out: to call on General de Gaulle."

What the president did not say was that three days earlier he had sent the head of his military household, General Ganeval, in secret, to Jacques Foccart's flat in the Avenue de l'Opéra, to take soundings on de Gaulle's intentions. Foccart – later to be given special responsibility for African affairs, with general control over the secret services – was the general's man of confidence. A former head of the Free French transport arrangements, he was neither an intellectual nor a politician: his qualities were absolute loyalty, unquestioning obedience and, not least, total discretion.

With Foccart and Ganeval that day were de Gaulle's aide-de-camp, Colonel Gaston de Bonneval, and the head of his personal secretariat, Olivier Guichard. Later, President Coty learned with astonished dismay that de Gaulle refused to appear before the Assembly to plead for his investiture. Instead, he wanted a vote of confidence in his absence, and conveyed to him in writing. In any case, he thought it was too soon to make his detailed conditions known.[14] The situation, then, was unsatisfactory. But it was impossible for Coty to sound de Gaulle out further unless through a personal meeting, which Coty rejected on the grounds that it was contrary to the dignity of his office, would need to be secret, but would not remain so long, and when known, would have grave consequences. Besides, he told a friend: "What am I supposed to do? Wear a false beard?"

One thing was clear: if it was too early for de Gaulle, it would have to be too early for Coty. So the president went ahead with his invitation to Pflimlin.

But it was later than either man thought. Confident in the righteousness of his position, which indeed was sanctioned by the constitution, Pierre Pflimlin sat down in the Hôtel Matignon to compose his speech of investiture. It was 9 May. In Algiers that evening the top representatives of the armed forces – Generals Salan, Jouhaud, Allard and Massu, and Admiral Auboyneau – sat down to draft an anguished telegram to the president of the Republic, which, however, they addressed, as military hierarchy obliged them, to the chief of the General Staff of National Defence, General Ely.

14 Viansson-Ponté, *République*, pp. 28–9.

Although Pflimlin was unaware of it, the soldiers had decided that they would have no part of him. His sins were two: he had voted against Bidault as premier, and on 23 April, in an article in *Le Nouvel Alsacien*, he had raised the possibility of negotiations with the FLN. That was enough to brand him as a liberal and a scuttler. The cable from Algiers did not, however, mention Pflimlin by name. Instead, three times in two sentences, it expressed the fear of the army and of the population of Algeria of being *abandoned* by the metropolis:

> The army in Algeria is worried ... about the French population of the Interior which feels itself abandoned, and about the French Moslems who, in ever growing numbers, have given back their confidence to France, trusting our reiterated promises never to abandon them.
> The French army would unanimously feel a sense of outrage at any abandonment of this national patrimony.

The telegram ended by asking General Ely to "draw the attention of the president of the Republic to our anguish, which only a government firmly determined to maintain our flag in Algeria can efface". [15]

Then came 13 May. The date has become a symbol, standing for salvation or a Spanish-style *pronunciamento*, depending on the viewpoint. In Paris, Pflimlin summoned the National Assembly to meet at 3 p.m. to vote its confidence in him. In Algiers, three hours later, and with the Assembly still in session, a huge crowd massed on the Forum – the great open space before the building of the government-general. On the surface, what then occurred was a spontaneous happening, a case for students of mob psychology. In reality, the mob was driven as well as led. The neo-Fascists had about a thousand members of their secret army among the crowd; Poujadists were there, and so were trained teams brought from the *bled* by a tall, bearded student leader, Pierre Lagaillarde, who was to win brief fame that day.[16] It was he who, after haranguing the crowd, gave the order for an assault on the government-general building. Under the hot Algiers sunshine, the excited crowd poured into the huge building, sacking desks and filing cabinets and throwing the contents out of the windows. Nonplussed, the army and security forces stood by and looked on.

In Paris, Félix Gaillard, still acting Prime Minister, since Pflimlin had not yet got his vote of confidence, was in constant touch by telephone with Salan in the government-general building. With Gaillard were General Ely and Robert Lacoste, who had been recalled from Algiers

---

[15] Fauvet, *IVème*, p. 346.   [16] Tournoux, *Secrets*, pp. 278–9; *see also* pp. 294–5.

– for good – three days earlier. Learning that the building was being occupied by the mob, Gaillard delegated full civil as well as military powers to Salan. The crowd in the Forum greeted the news with boos. At a loss now, Gaillard ordered Salan to "sub-delegate" his powers to the popular Massu. This time there were cheers from the Forum.

Amidst noise and confusion, the generals were drafting the proclamation of a "Committee of Public Safety". Salan was acutely unhappy, but concealed the fact under an expressionless face which, together with his long service in Indo-China and his love for things oriental (including, it was said, opium), had earned him the nickname of *le Chinois*. Unwilling to commit himself to an act that might later be termed insubordination, Salan kept quiet. Massu took over, declaring himself ready to be the chairman of the committee. He started writing down names. There were colonels among them and neo-Fascists, Gaullists and *pieds-noirs*.

Ramrod-straight and with his beak of a nose held high, Massu went on to the great balcony. Cheers, then silence, greeted him. As he read out the names, renewed cheers broke out. Back inside, Massu drafted a telegram to the president of the Republic, which he read to the excited crowd:

> We announce the creation of a civil and military Committee of Public Safety, chaired by myself, General Massu.

As suddenly as they had gathered, the crowd withdrew, but not to disperse. A rumour that Jacques Soustelle was about to land at Maison Blanche airport had drawn them in that direction. It was a false report, but it cleared the Forum and reduced the fever.

Léon Delbecque, who had walked over much of the government-general building, rejoined Salan and helped him to draft yet another telegram to General Ely for President Coty. It was now nearly 11 p.m. The Gaullists present tried to persuade Salan to include a specific reference to General de Gaulle, but Salan was swayed by more cautious counsels, and the relevant portions of the final text read as follows:

> . . . in the face of grave disorders that threaten national unity and which cannot be stopped without risk of bloodshed, the responsible military authorities consider it an imperative necessity to appeal to a national arbiter to constitute a government of Public Safety able to reassure Algerian public opinion. An appeal for calm by this high authority, affirming the categorical will to keep Algeria French, is alone capable of restoring the situation.

At 3.30 a.m. in Paris, Pflimlin found himself, for what it was worth, president of the Council, with 274 votes in favour and 120 against, with 137 abstentions (the latter mainly Communists). Half an hour later, in Algiers, General Massu reappeared on the balcony and (inaccurately) told those still there to hear that the new premier had been confirmed in office with the complicity of the Communists. He announced, on doubtful authority, that Soustelle would shortly be in Algiers, and, more rashly, implored de Gaulle to break his silence by calling for a government of Public Safety which alone could save Algeria from the diplomatic Dien Bien Phu evoked by Lacoste. It was clear, but clumsy; but then, Massu was no orator.

When 14 May dawned, however, the facts were these: in Paris, a properly constituted government had been formed; and in Algiers, an illegal committee existed, not headed, but sanctioned, on the other hand, by a general to whom Paris had delegated plenary powers. This was not quite the situation the Gaullists, or de Gaulle himself, had envisaged. Was this the time to go into action? Some sixth sense told the general that it was not. During the hectic fortnight that followed, his followers were sometimes to feel that he had lost, or fluffed, his chance, and never more than during the night of 13 to 14 May. But they were soon to find out that he was the best judge of timing.

In a sense, then, 14 May was an anticlimax, albeit an eventful one. The new premier began the day (which was the end of his long night) with a broadcast solemnly declaring that France and Algeria would never be severed and asserting that the new government would ensure respect for the laws of the Republic. Nobody paid much attention. President Coty, invoking Article 33 of the constitution, which made him chief of the armed forces, ordered all servicemen to return to their duties under the authority of the government. As far as the men in uniform in Algeria were concerned, he might as well not have spoken.

In Paris, right-wing demonstrators marched down the Champs-Elysées, shouting: "*Massu au pouvoir!*" and left-wing demonstrators gathered in the Place de la République shouting: "*Massu au poteau!*" – "Massu to the gallows!" Impotent in Algeria, the government struck where it could, arresting about fifty members of right-wing organisations, together with six army officers. All demonstrations were banned.

De Gaulle, arriving at his office in the Rue de Solférino, found an unexpected letter of support from one of the men who detested him most: Georges Bidault. But this alone was not enough to make him break his silence. He also learned that Massu had sent him a telegram the previous day, which had not been delivered. "Now the system is even stopping my mail," he grumbled.[17]

In Algiers, Delbecque and his companions wondered whether Salan was now going to have them arrested, and in turn debated whether to seize the commander-in-chief, in the end deciding it was too risky. Salan himself went around in a daze, wondering, as he said more than once, whether he was in danger of assassination. On the telephone, he told Pflimlin, with every mark of respect, that he would carry out the government's orders. He had, in fact, entered a twilight world where he was at once the government's delegate and the highest-ranking rebel against its authority.

The decisive day was the 15th. Salan, not entirely of his own volition, took further steps towards his personal Rubicon, but stopped himself at the edge. And General de Gaulle at last broke his silence.

In Algiers, on the morning of another glorious Mediterranean day, General Salan stepped on to the balcony of the government-general building and greeted the huge and mobile crowd below. Briefly, he savoured the first shouts he had yet heard saying "Vive Salan!" Somebody placed a microphone within speaking distance, and he found words which the crowd wanted to hear. "Vive la France!" "Vive l'Algérie française!" With these words, the general started turning away from the microphone. Delbecque, however, was at his elbow, and prompted him: "Vive de Gaulle!" Almost mechanically, Salan turned back to the microphone and, in his turn, shouted: "Vive de Gaulle!"

Later that day Salan, who had never been a Gaullist and whose wife was fiercely anti-de Gaulle, wondered aloud whether he had really, as people said, shouted the fatal words, and if so, why.

De Gaulle was back at Colombey, after his weekly visit to Paris. He had spent much of the night listening to the radio and answering telephone calls, most of which were pleas for him to act, or at any rate to say something. At 10 a.m. on 15 May, the general at last decided to make a statement. It was short, carefully ambiguous and stylistically noble. He handed it to his aide-de-camp, Colonel de Bonneval, and instructed him to embargo it for release at 17.00 hours. The colonel drove off to Paris and de Gaulle left the house on foot for his daily walk in the woods around La Boisserie.

That evening three hundred journalists jostled each other in the inadequate space of the Gaullist headquarters. At 5 p.m. they began flashing the message to the world. Seventeen minutes later the teleprinters at the Palais-Bourbon conveyed the general's words to the Prime Minister:

[17] Pado, p. 49.

The degradation of the State inevitably brings in its train the alienation of the associated peoples, agitation within the army in combat, national dislocation, the loss of independence. For twelve years, France, grappling with problems too arduous for the regime of parties, has been engaged in this disastrous process.

Once before, the country, in the depths of its being, gave me its trust to lead it, in its entirety, to salvation.

Today, before the trials that once again press upon it, it should know that I hold myself ready to take over the powers of the Republic.

In Paris, in Algiers and abroad, the question everybody was asking was: what did it mean? Two things only were clear: de Gaulle was ready to come back; and if he did, the system of the Fourth Republic would be destroyed. That, indeed, was his price for returning. Everything else had to be inferred or guessed. There was no mention of Algeria, for instance. De Gaulle's reference to "the alienation of the associated peoples" could be interpreted as a call for a commonwealth of independent states, or as an appeal for integration: whether the solution proposed (whatever it was) included or excluded Algeria was left to the imagination. Like Franco, who in his time had written so many ambiguous, though less stylish, declarations, this one made its author all things to all men.

In Algiers especially, but in Paris too, General de Gaulle's statement gave the impression of being a direct response to Salan's involuntary "*Vive de Gaulle!*" Nor did he say which powers he was ready to take over: those of a chief of State, or those of a Prime Minister? Or both? De Gaulle must have known that his statement would provoke such questions.[18] At all events, the politicians, the generals and ordinary people were now convinced that de Gaulle was coming back. The impatience of all but the politicians to act accordingly and get rid of the Fourth Republic grew correspondingly.

The general's declaration brought immediate statements of protest from the Communist and Socialist parties. The Communists he could ignore: they walked alone. But the Socialists had to be taken into

[18] If Dominique Pado's and J.-R. Tournoux's accounts are compared, the one supplementing the other, the inference must be that de Gaulle decided to issue his statement quite independently of Salan's "Long live de Gaulle!" Tournoux, *Secrets*, p. 298, gives the time of Salan's speech as 10.15 a.m. on 15 May. Pado, in *13 Mai*, says General de Gaulle made his decision at 10 a.m. that morning. De Gaulle's own account throws no light on the sequence of events, for in *Renouveau*, p. 24, he wrongly dates Salan's speech on the 14th. P.-M. de la Gorce, however, says that although de Gaulle had indeed drafted his statement before learning of Salan's exclamation, it was the news that Salan had invoked his name which made him decide that his statement should be published.

466

account, for he needed their support in parliament if his plan to return by legal means only was to succeed. Embarrassingly, the Socialist statement drew attention to the fact that de Gaulle had failed to rebuke the military leaders for their "grave acts of indiscipline" against the president of the Republic. In Algiers, however, the Committee of Public Safety expressed its "deep pleasure" at the general's declaration.

In his solitude at Colombey, the general could measure the gap that still separated him from complete success. Although the situation had begun to move in the right direction, from his standpoint, it was still precarious. Too many elements escaped his control. The Assembly, though impotent, was unwilling to commit suicide. Pflimlin's minister for Algeria, André Mutter, and his Defence minister, Pierre de Chevigné, were proclaiming their determination to restore the government's authority over the military. Vain though this threat was, it stood between de Gaulle and an understanding with Parliament. He could have led the rebellious generals, but at the cost of his claim to represent the nation and to hold the law in respect. Besides, the hidden leaders of the mob that had seized the government-general building were "ultras", Poujadists, neo-Fascists, willing to risk civil war to smash the regime, whereas the Gaullists in Algiers wished merely to frighten the politicians and show up their impotence. The ultras did not want de Gaulle; they would acccept him only if no other way existed of bringing down the Republic and keeping Algeria French.

Since he could not directly control events – yet – all de Gaulle could do was to watch and wait, turning to his advantage any development that lent itself to exploitation. This he did with masterly skill. It was up to the Gaullists to create such openings; and this they too did skilfully. Thus on the 16th Chaban-Delmas – the man who had placed Léon Delbecque in Algiers – astutely suggested to the Socialist leader, Guy Mollet, now vice-premier, that he should challenge de Gaulle to pledge himself to respect Republican legality.[19] That afternoon Mollet told the Assembly of his "great esteem and great admiration" for de Gaulle and called on him to clarify three points: recognition of the Pflimlin government as the only legitimate one; disavowal of the Committee of Public Safety and respect for constitutional processes, should he be invited to form a new government.

The Socialist party's statement had, if only mildly, hindered de Gaulle's plans. But Mollet's speech helped him, first by its friendly tone, which gave de Gaulle to suppose that here, at least, was a potential ally in parliament; then by the opportunity it gave de Gaulle for manoeuvre.

[19] Gorce, p. 550.

A man less versed in the arts of power might have yielded to the temptation to reply immediately. Not so de Gaulle. Instead, he announced that he would give a press conference on the afternoon of the 19th.

This was a trump card. For it automatically prolonged the crisis by three more days. In the unlikely event that the government should regain its authority, de Gaulle would have been able to blame the entire crisis on the feebleness of the regime, and, without fear of contradiction, forecast further disorders. More likely, the stalemate would continue, the Algiers rebels would be strengthened, and de Gaulle would begin to be more widely accepted as the only possible arbiter, the one man who could save France from civil strife.

In Algiers that day, an unprecedented scene took place. Thousands of Moslems of both sexes walked from the labyrinthine Casbah and from the bled to the Forum, flying tricolour flags. On arriving, to the cheers of the Europeans already there, members of both communities embraced each other, proclaiming themselves brothers. Moslem women tore off their veils and joined in the fun.[20] Those most discomfited by this unexpected turn of events were the FLN revolutionaries.

Salan, meanwhile, was showing signs – alarming to the insurgents – of wishing to work his passage home to legality. Delbecque, having taken care to tap the official telephones, learned that he and his companions were shortly to be arrested. Accompanied by another fervent Gaullist, Lieutenant Léon Neuwirth, he called on Salan and extracted a promise of cooperation from the commander-in-chief. But Salan was playing a curious game, telling some visitors he was a Republican and others that he was not. When two ultras – the Corsican lawyer Jean-Baptiste Biaggi, and a close friend and fellow-conspirator, Alain Griotteray – landed at Algiers airport, Salan had them arrested.

Massu, tired of these complications in his soldierly life, was threatening to arrest everybody. One of the candidates for arrest was the picturesque Colonel Thomazo, known as "leather-nose" from the device (actually made of plastic fibre) that filled the hole where his nose had been before he had lost it in battle. Thomazo, too, was a plotter, on the neo-Fascist side, and the territorial units under his command were considered in Paris to be thoroughly seditious. To mark the point, Paris ordered their dissolution on the 16th. Fortunately for the Gaullists, a puzzled officer brought the order to Delbecque to ask his advice.

[20] Some newspaper reports at the time derided the whole thing on the ground that it was organised by the psychological warfare department of the army, to the extent of providing lorries to bring Moslems in from the countryside. That some stimulus was given seems probable; but I incline to the view that the demonstration was largely spontaneous.

Delbecque advised him to keep his men under arms; and tore up the official order.[21]

The plot – or plots – looked indeed as though they might be collapsing, when a dramatic diversion changed the whole outlook. The central character in this new phase of the drama was Jacques Soustelle, the former governor-general of Algeria. Ever since 13 May he had been, as it were, straining at the security leash placed around his neck by Jules Moch's security police. During the Assembly debate that gave Pflimlin his majority he had tried, but failed, to find a seat aboard Salan's plane, bound for Algiers from Villacoublay military airport. Back in Paris, at 2 a.m. on the Esplanade des Invalides he had bumped into Chaban-Delmas. Though Chaban-Delmas was the man who had placed Léon Delbecque in Algiers, he was now in a mood of deep pessimism and wanted to abandon all action in favour of de Gaulle's return. "Don't compromise your political career," he advised Soustelle; but (says Soustelle), he was doubtless thinking mainly of his own.[22]

Debré, however, pressed Soustelle urgently to go to Algiers: he himself was immobilised at home with acute sciatica. From the morning of the 14th, however, Soustelle was practically under house arrest, with a close police surveillance on his flat. In the end, he escaped next day in a car driven by his landlord's daughter, crouching unseen in the space normally taken up by the back seats, which had been removed (and not, as was widely reported at the time, in the boot, which would not have accommodated his two-hundred-pound bulk). He was driven to Geneva, whence he flew to Algiers, landing at 1.30 p.m. on the 17th.

Salan, through Massu, had tried to send a message to Soustelle on no account to come to Algeria. Since Soustelle had vanished, the message was never delivered. The airport police were alerted and when the former governor-general's familiar face, with his thick black-rimmed glasses, was seen, he and his party were immediately escorted to the VIP room. Salan, told of Soustelle's arrival, immediately had himself driven to the airport, where he tried to persuade the politician to go back to Paris. One of Soustelle's companions, however, telephoned Delbecque and gave him the news. "Tell Salan," said Delbecque, "that he won't get back to Algiers alive if he sends the boss home. I'm going to gather the people." Thus, instead of being arrested or sent back to Paris, Soustelle enjoyed a triumphant reception by a deliriously happy crowd in the Forum. That night, he slept at the Villa des Oliviers in the room where de Gaulle had slept in 1943.

Reporting to Paris on Soustelle's arrival, Salan expressed alarm at the

[21] Tournoux, *Secrets*, p. 311; *see also* pp. 312–15. [22] Soustelle, *Gaullisme*, p. 142.

possibility that he himself might be arrested. The Council of Ministers was plunged into deep gloom at the thought that a professional was now available to lead the Algiers plotters.

That day – 17 May – Jules Moch's ministry of the Interior announced a state of emergency for three months, with courts-martial to try such offences as sedition, subversion and treason. Several extremist movements of the right were dissolved and their leaders arrested. That day, too, General Ely resigned as chief of the General Staff, apparently because some of his leading men, including General Challe, had been arrested. General Lorillot, Salan's predecessor as C.-in-C., was appointed to succeed Ely.

But Jules Moch's characteristically energetic measures cloaked a profound impotence on the part of the police, the gendarmerie and the Compagnies Républicaines de Sécurité, or riot squads. One and all, as he was later to reveal, had become unreliable almost overnight, their sympathies manifestly with the rebels of Algeria.

Came the 19th. Panic-stricken, the ministers feared civil war if they banned de Gaulle's conference, or if, through some tragic failure of security, he were assassinated on the occasion. All approaches to the Hôtel Palais d'Orsay were cordoned off and only authorised persons, with a permit shown, were allowed through the police barriers. About 1,200 journalists packed the hotel to the doors when the general made his appearance at 3 p.m. Some thirty cameramen and a hundred photographers dazzled him and his audience with their flashes.

It was his first public appearance for three years. He had put on weight during his retirement; and aged. Both facts occasioned much comment. So did the relative thinness of his voice, compared with the raucous tones of his oratorical maturity. In addition, he was visibly more nervous than he used to be. His almost infallible memory, however, did not let him down, and he did not once consult the text of his lengthy opening statement. He thought, he said modestly, that he might be useful, since the regime of parties had failed and because he was a man alone, who belonged to nobody and yet to everybody.

On later occasions, de Gaulle's press conferences were to consist largely of questions carefully planted by selected journalists. On this occasion they seemed spontaneous, and de Gaulle was in no way spared the awkward ones.

What did he mean, someone asked, by "the powers of the Republic"? In his Delphic way, he replied that such powers could only be those that were delegated by the Republic. And he went on to recall that he had saved the Republic, and to enumerate the reforms he had introduced.

The army, he said in reply to another question, had done well to forestall disorders. And what, asked a correspondent, about Guy Mollet's questions in the lobbies of the Assembly?

Acutely conscious of his need for Socialist support, de Gaulle said: "I shall begin by telling you that I have a lot of esteem for Guy Mollet." As for the question: "I answer that if de Gaulle should find himself delegated with exceptional powers for an exceptional task at an exceptional time, that could obviously not be done according to the usual procedure and with the customary rites of which everybody now has had more than enough."

Then came a question that was uppermost in the minds of many people: "Do you not think that at the precise moment when you launched your appeal, the rebellion in Algeria was crumbling away? You have given fresh courage to the sedition-mongers. Your press conference will strengthen them."

De Gaulle was studiously non-committal: "Responsibilities will be studied later. Today there is a fact. Some people call 'sedition-mongers' those leaders who have not been the object of any sanction on the part of the public authorities – to whom the public authorities have even delegated full powers. And I, who am not at present the public authority, why would you have me call them sedition-mongers?"

Was he going to attack public liberties, if he came back to power?

"Have I ever done so?" asked the old man. "On the contrary, I restored them when they had disappeared. Is it credible that I am going to begin a career as a dictator at the age of sixty-seven?"

He ended with the words: "Now I shall return to my village and I shall remain there at the disposal of the country."

Extremist members of the Action Committee of war veterans had planned a mass demonstration, culminating in the occupation of public buildings, for 19 May. They were dissuaded from it by Olivier Guichard and Jacques Foccart, who explained to them that de Gaulle was determined not to return to power by means of a *coup de force*. The attempt did not take place, and the fact that it did not lent credibility to the claim that only the Gaullists could now prevent the violent overthrow of the legal government.

Another week of agonising tension followed, nevertheless. Wild rumours were circulating. Shortly after de Gaulle's press conference, Roger Frey, the former Nouméa planter who had become secretary-general to the Gaullist parliamentary group, reached Algiers. There he elaborated, with the help of Lucien Neuwirth, a further twist to the war of nerves on the politicians, by sending off "personal" radio messages to imaginary people in France, on the model of the wartime BBC, so that uninformed monitors would gain the impression that a vast conspiracy was under way. Jules Moch and his police were among those thus deceived.[23] Militant Gaullist women collected the private telephone numbers of the ministers and took turns to telephone them with warning messages. Other Gaullist women organised the printing and distribution in various parts of the country of tens of thousands of postcards inviting the politicians to get out and hand over to de Gaulle. Soon they were reaching the Elysée and the Hôtel Matignon by the van load.

Ministers began sleeping at friends' places instead of their own homes. Pflimlin, whose holiday home had been damaged by plastic explosives, stayed in his office for days on end, held upright by a massive intake of Dexedrine tablets.

On 21 May, Lagaillarde arrived in Paris with a plan to rally the students and the veterans of Indo-China and capture the Communist party's training school for *cadres*. Once in Paris, however, he changed his mind and decided to try to forestall de Gaulle's return by seizing the National Assembly the way he had seized the official headquarters in Algiers. Threats from the Gaullists made him drop his plans and return to Algeria.

Perhaps the most extraordinary aspect of the crisis was the general indifference of ordinary French people, unaware perhaps how close the country was to civil war. When the weekend came, Parisians in their tens of thousands drove off into the country for their habitual relaxation.

On 24 May local paratroopers in Corsica, led by a handful of notables who had arrived from Algiers with an official *ordre de mission* signed by General Salan, seized power on behalf of the Committee of Public Safety; then set up one of their own. The leader of the *coup*, Pascal Arrighi, was a Radical deputy from the island, badly wounded when fighting in the Resistance, whose plan had been greeted with enthusiasm by Delbecque and Soustelle who thought the best way of meeting the intense competition from the neo-Fascists was to act in Corsica rather than in metropolitan France. Valiantly, Jules Moch sent 160 security police from Nice to restore the legitimate authority; but on arriving at Ajaccio, they immediately joined the insurgents. The impotence of the regime was now total.

De Gaulle, still at Colombey, took note of it with a mixture of pleasure and despondency. Conflicting assessments of legality and legitimacy still stood between him and power. Unwilling to be bullied, the politicians still clung to office. He could see, if they could not, that if they clung on

[23] ibid. pp. 146–7 n.

much longer, their chance of averting bloodshed by turning his way would vanish forever. De Gaulle therefore decided to force their hand.

Several of them, in any case, had shown their desire to call him back. Bidault had done so publicly on the 21st. On the 22nd, the conservative ex-premier, Antoine Pinay, had called on him at La Boisserie where he found a smiling, liberal de Gaulle declaring his readiness to meet the politicians, not least the Prime Minister. On the 23rd, varying his tactics, he requested General Lorillot, then still chief of staff of the army, to ask Salan on his behalf for a personal report on developments in Algiers – in the knowledge that this message would be reported to the premier's office.

On the morning of the 26th the Colombey postman delivered a letter from Guy Mollet, in which the Socialist leader renewed his appeal to the general to condemn the "sedition" of the Algiers generals. This, of course, de Gaulle could not do, for if he did and failed, he would be discredited, while if he succeeded, he would no longer be needed. However, Mollet also said that he understood the state of mind of the officer corps and the anguish of the European community. What he feared was that the Communists – he called them the "Bolsheviks" – might take advantage of the confrontation between the State and the army.[24] General de Gaulle concluded that the letter was Mollet's way of declaring at least his conditional allegiance.

That morning, he sent a personal message to Pierre Pflimlin proposing a meeting that night at the former imperial residence at Saint-Cloud, whose conservator, Félix Bruneau, was a friend of the general's. De Gaulle found the premier "calm and dignified".[25] The general explained why he could not condemn the rebels; and the premier explained why he could not abandon his post. They argued back and forth for two and a half hours before separating at 2 a.m. without having reached any kind of agreement, except on the need to keep the meeting secret; and, in the event that it should become known, to say that further contacts were envisaged.[26]

The minister of the Interior had reported to the cabinet that the Corsican operation was supposed to be repeated in metropolitan France, first in the provinces, then in Paris, on the night of 27 to 28 May. The news was brought to de Gaulle, who now decided on the most cunning deceit of his career, and perhaps the most decisive. With his usual masterly ambiguity, he drafted the following statement, which was published at 12.30 on the afternoon of the 27th:

[24] Gorce, p. 564.
[25] De Gaulle, *Renouveau*, p. 28.
[26] Tournoux, *Secrets*, pp. 344–6.

I began yesterday the regular process needed to establish a Republican government capable of ensuring the unity and independence of the country.

I believe this process will be continued and that the country will show, by its calm and its dignity, that it wishes it to succeed.

Under these conditions, any action endangering public order, from whatever side it originates, could have grave consequences. Even though I understand the circumstances, I could not give my approval.

I expect the land, sea and air forces in Algeria to maintain exemplary behaviour under the orders of their commanders, General Salan, Admiral Auboyneau, and General Jouhaud. To these leaders, I express my confidence and my intention to make contact with them shortly.

On reading the text, Pflimlin, who could scarcely believe his eyes, was outraged and wanted to expose the general's deception. He was dissuaded from so rash an action by President Coty. Later, Jules Moch was to write that de Gaulle's statement had averted civil war and was made solely with that intention; he dismissed any suggestion of ulterior motives,[27] such as trying to force the pace of events. When the general himself told the story, more than a decade later, however, he wrote: "That morning, I hastened the march forward." Of the statement itself, he wrote: "Thus, leaving the augurs of the corridors of the Palais-Bourbon and the sub-editors' rooms to work out for themselves what the 'regular process' might be that was to lead to my advent, I told the military leaders to stop any further intervention. And in fact, they did."[28]

A "process" (*processus*) is not, of course, a "procedure". While everybody was working out the difference, the government finally crumbled. On 28 May, exhausted and in despair, Pflimlin handed in his resignation to President Coty, but remained at his post until a successor could be found.

That day, Salan's emissary, General Dulac, accompanied by three other officers, called on de Gaulle at La Boisserie. From Dulac's lips, de Gaulle heard the alarming details of "Operation Resurrection" for the seizure of Paris by paratroops. Since his policy was to refrain from any criticism of the army, he did not ask his visitors to drop the plan. Indeed, he expressed the view that the military means envisaged were insufficient. If, he said, the parties continue to oppose my return, "then do the necessary!"[29]

De Gaulle was almost back; but, irritatingly for him, not quite. It

[27] ibid. p. 349, quoting article by J. Moch in *Le Midi Libre* in June 1958.
[28] De Gaulle, *Mémoires d'Espoir, L'Effort: 1962* (henceforth, De Gaulle, *L'Effort*), p. 29.
[29] Soustelle, *Gaullisme*, p. 147; cf. Gorce, pp. 569–70, who does not dispute the facts but argues, rightly in my view, that at a time when the government had fallen and the

still remained for him to win over the parliamentarians, and above all the Socialists who, on the afternoon of the 27th, had voted by 112 votes to 3 in favour of a resolution stating that they would "in no circumstances rally to the candidature of General de Gaulle". Fortunately, de Gaulle had already had a letter from Guy Mollet and, on the 26th, had received a further letter from an equally eminent Socialist leader, Vincent Auriol, formerly president of the Republic. Auriol, too, had asked him to denounce the Algiers sedition, adding that if he did, the "responsible men of the Republic" would regain confidence in him and loyally cooperate with him in a limited programme giving him plenary powers. In his reply, which did not reach Auriol until the 29th, de Gaulle lamented the sectarianism that seemed to be preventing him from again saving the Republic, while there was still time. If this happened, those who were doing the preventing would bear a heavy responsibility, "As for me, all that will be left for me, until I die, will be to stay with my sorrow."

At President Coty's request, de Gaulle met the chairmen of the National Assembly and of the Council of the Republic, André le Trocquer and Gaston Monnerville, at Saint-Cloud, on the evening of the 28th. Le Trocquer, one of the Socialist leaders, was brutally hostile and resolutely opposed de Gaulle's candidature. Monnerville, however, was in favour, and tried to explain to de Gaulle the minimum conditions under which he could return to power legally. As usual, the general had started off from a position of maximum intransigence: he wanted plenary powers, including constituent ones, for two years, during which time parliament would be in recess. Moreover, he wanted to dispense with the traditional visits to the chairmen of the two chambers (the men whom, in fact, he was at that moment addressing), and with the usual consultations with party leaders; and even to stay away from the debate on his own investiture.[30]

Le Trocquer exploded: "All this is unconstitutional. I have known you pretty well since Algiers. You have the soul of a dictator. You're too fond of personal power!"

With cold scorn, de Gaulle gave his standard reply: "It was I who restored the Republic, Monsieur Le Trocquer."

---

general's chances of being invited to succeed Pflimlin stood high, nothing could have been worse, from de Gaulle's standpoint, than a military operation in France. On the other hand, the talk with Dulac informed him about the views of individual commanders in Algiers. It is hard to dispute Gorce's contention that it was important, at this delicate stage, for de Gaulle not to dissociate himself from the Committee of Public Safety. Had he done so, the ultras would have ordered the paratroops to strike.
[30] Tournoux, *Secrets*, pp. 382–5.

Monnerville, a coloured man from French Guiana, broke into the explosive exchanges that followed with soothing arguments about the constitutional niceties. De Gaulle, professing an improbable unawareness of these points in a constitution which he must often have dissected the better to attack it, heard the President of the Council of the Republic say that if legal forms were to be respected, then the maximum duration of special powers would be six months.

According to Tournoux's detailed account of this meeting, de Gaulle had tears in his eyes as he took his leave. Anger, however, predominates over sorrow in de Gaulle's own far briefer story. "Very well, then," he said, addressing Le Trocquer, "if parliament listens to you, all that will be left for me to do is to leave you to sort things out with the paratroops and to go back to my retreat and nurse my sorrow." And on leaving the lodge, he remarked to the secretary-general of the Elysée, Charles Merveilleux du Vignaux, that he was sorry that he had come all that way for nothing. He did not get back to Colombey until 5 a.m.[31]

President Coty, who was in his pyjamas, greeted Monnerville and Le Trocquer at the Elysée in the early hours, and heard their conflicting accounts of the stormy meeting with de Gaulle. He went to sleep exhausted, but at 8 a.m. decided that the time had come – neither too late nor too early – to make a public appeal to de Gaulle. He could not have done it any sooner, but any further delay would have been fatal, for already the deputies were talking of forming another government in the usual way; had they done so, there is no doubt the paratroops would have landed in Paris. That morning, Coty drafted a message to both chambers, which was read to them at 3 p.m. In it, he evoked the dangers of civil war and called on "the most illustrious of Frenchmen, who, during the darkest years of our history, was our leader for the conquest of liberty and who, having achieved national unanimity around his person, spurned dictatorship, to establish the Republic". The message was heard in total silence.

On hearing the text over the telephone, de Gaulle agreed immediately to meet the president of the Republic. Hoping to avoid the photographers, he entered the Elysée at about 7.30 p.m. by the side entrance in the Avenue de Marigny. The photographers, however, were there all the same. It was an emotional meeting, at which the two men quickly reached agreement. A communiqué drafted by de Gaulle was immediately published. Characteristically, it was as striking for its omissions as for what it actually said. De Gaulle called for plenary powers "for a determinate period" and for a mandate, to be submitted

[31] De Gaulle, L'Effort, p. 30.

476

to the country by referendum, for constitutional changes, "in particular concerning the separation and balance of powers as well as the relations between the French Republic and the peoples associated with it". He did not say precisely how long he would need special powers, nor mention the sovereignty of parliament.

It was evident that de Gaulle was on the point of achieving his ambition to return to power. Yet his mood, at this decisive moment, was one of gloom. It was painfully apparent to him that Coty had appealed to him because there was no other way, not because there was an irresistible wave of enthusiasm for his return. Even among the Algiers plotters, only a small but skilful minority really wanted him. As for the parliamentarians, they considered him, not without reason, as their enemy. He now felt certain they would give him majority approval; but among those who would probably vote against were a handful of men, especially Pierre Mendès France, whom he held in high esteem. Despite the imminence of danger, the country's mood was still predominantly apathetic. The Communist-controlled CGT had called for a general strike on 26 May, but the response was feeble. This, however, did not amount to a popular clamour for General de Gaulle. On the 28th, 200,000 demonstrators, headed by Daladier, Pineau, Mendès France, Ramadier and the Communist Duclos, had marched in orderly silence across Paris to show their attachment to the dying Republic.

On the day of de Gaulle's meeting with Coty, however, the general's exchange of letters with Vincent Auriol was made public, and the effect within the Socialist party was dramatic. On the 30th, Auriol first, then two other Socialists – Guy Mollet and Maurice Deixonne – called on de Gaulle at Colombey. At his most eloquent, the general passionately rejected charges that he wished to set up a dictatorship. The three men went back to Paris convinced and converted. Next day, the Socialist parliamentary group voted, by a majority, in favour of his return.

That day, the 31st, was a Wednesday, and de Gaulle, as usual, went to the Hôtel Lapérouse. The security services had insisted that he should not use his usual suite, No. 11, and he was placed in No. 28 – which, ironically, was normally used by Jean Jardin, formerly Laval's *directeur de cabinet*.[32] There, on Georges Pompidou's advice, he was host to twenty-six parliamentarians, representing all the groups except the Communists.

Now de Gaulle was ready to face the Assembly. But he had stuck to his refusal to take part in the debate on his investiture. Instead, on 1

[32] Gorce, p. 573.

477

June, he mounted the rostrum and read the customary declaration of candidates for the premiership. In a few short phrases, he depicted the decadence and crisis of the State. He appealed for the confidence of parliament and for approval of his proposals for constitutional reform, which would be submitted to the people at a referendum. Once the Assemblies had voted, he declared, they would go into recess until "the date fixed for the opening of their next ordinary session" – that is, until Tuesday, 7 October. This relatively modest request showed that, in the end, he had taken Gaston Monnerville's advice.

Having spoken, de Gaulle left the chamber. In the debate that followed, Mendès France and Mitterrand expressed their personal esteem for the general but declared themselves unable to support his return under threat of force. Both men were among the 224 who voted against the investiture; there were 32 abstentions. There was, however, an absolute majority, the Ayes totalling 329.

Next day, however, the deputies were astonished and gratified when the general returned. In striking contrast to his forbidding mien of the previous day, he was full of charm and courtesy. He expressed "all the honour and pleasure I feel to be in your midst". The deputies heard him with delight. Many crowded round him to shake his hand, as though he had always been one of them. Without much further argument, they voted in favour of three bills, renewing the government's special powers in Algeria (a routine measure); conferring special powers on the new government for six months; and empowering the government to make constitutional reforms and submit them to a national referendum.

De Gaulle had won. At 9.15 on 3 June, he called unannounced on Gaston Monnerville, and thanked him for his advice. "I shall never forget," he told the chairman of the Upper House.

Part VI ✣ The Fifth Republic

Chapter 1 ⚜ De Gaulle breaks the Opposition (1958–1962)

In June 1958, de Gaulle was back in power,[1] but the circumstances of his return were of contested legality, and his authority was accordingly precarious. During the next three or four years, his dominant concern was to consolidate his power, by breaking the opposition and resolving, as far as he was able, the dreadful colonial problems which the Fourth Republic had been unable to cope with and which, in the end, had caused its downfall.

Foremost among these was Algeria, which aroused intense passions in metropolitan France as well as in North Africa, and indeed in the world at large. But the future of France's possessions overseas, especially in Africa, also clamoured for attention. And so, too – frustratingly for de Gaulle – did France's relations with foreign countries. The frustration lay in the fact that until de Gaulle had solved the problems that had brought down preceding governments, he could do no more than feel his way in foreign affairs, lacking the means to conduct the policy of "grandeur" to which he aspired. Indeed he was never to acquire means commensurate with his ambitions. But this was not a truth he willingly faced.

In all the issues that confronted him – his own power, the future of France's relations with former dependencies and with foreign countries, the containment of the opposition – the instrument that was to enable the general to act was the constitution of the new Republic. Ever since 16

[1] Strictly speaking, the government General de Gaulle formed in June 1958 was the last of the Fourth Republic, not the first of the Fifth. But his return to power so evidently represented a break in political continuity that I have thought it logical to begin Part VI at this point. I have also deemed it useful from the reader's standpoint to deal with developments under appropriate chapter headings, maintaining chronology in each subject, instead of giving detailed treatment to each event as it occurred, irrespective of its character. To some extent, this was the method used by de Gaulle himself in his fragmentary *Mémoires d'Espoir*; but my chapter headings are not identical with his. During the first period, de Gaulle's consolidation of his personal power was intimately interwoven with his treatment of Algerian and other overseas problems, and I consider them all, in varying degrees, in this first chapter.

June 1946 he had thought and dreamt about it, fashioning its clauses and provisions in his mind by word and on paper. Now reality was catching up with the dream. As he had forecast, the constitution of the Fourth Republic had contained the seeds of its own destruction. A strong man, with a strong policy, he sought a strong basic law. But this alone, though essential, was not enough: the struggle that followed the general's return to power was less a matter of texts and votes than of a clash of wills and guile; both of which de Gaulle had in greater measure than the luke-warm, the doubters and his enemies.

De Gaulle's sardonic sense of humour, normally exercised at the expense of others, did not readily adapt itself to the irony of his own situation. He had originally achieved power as a rebel; and now he was returning to power as a result of a rebellion within the army of which he had once been an active member. That was why he could not disown the Algiers dissidents, as the frightened politicians in Paris had asked. Yet it was clear to him that as soon as he was back in power the army would constitute a potential challenge to his own authority. For the soldiers, and the settlers of Algeria behind them, had brought him back for a specific purpose – to keep Algeria French. And they would continue to support him only as long as he stuck unwaveringly to the course they thought they had charted for him. Whatever de Gaulle may have said to selected people or proclaimed to the world, however, he was not wedded unconditionally to French Algeria. His approach was inevitably more pragmatic than that. For the army and the settlers, Algérie française was all; for him, it was only one element in the complex picture of his deferred ambitions, along with his burning desire to restore France's "greatness", to play a major role in contemporary history, to lead Europe and to break the hegemony of the United States in western international relations.

Within four years of his return to power, General de Gaulle had conceded the FLN's claim to the independence of Algeria. In the process, he had alienated or dismissed a number of his closest companions, broken the careers of various army officers, sustained and mastered two major challenges to his authority, and weathered two attempts on his life. Inevitably, such traumatic events aroused fiercely partisan passions, on one side or another. On the right, de Gaulle's supporters either abandoned their principles, in their unconditional loyalty, or stuck to their principles and suffered in consequence. Among the first group were men like Michel Debré and Roger Frey; among the second, the most prominent was Jacques Soustelle. Some of those who had originally supported the general's return, such as Jean-Jacques Susini, the pied-noir leader, turned to violence and terrorism through the Organisation de l'Armée Secrète (OAS). On the left (such labels being convenient though unsatisfactory), the general's followers felt their faith in him to be vindicated by the advent of Algeria to sovereignty, along with the general emancipation of French Africa. Of such were Louis Vallon and René Capitant.

The truth, however, was both simpler and more complex than any group of de Gaulle's 1958 supporters were capable of supposing. Like all politically ambitious men, but more than lesser men, de Gaulle's overriding priority was the retention of power. He was not, however, in the true sense, a dictator, and he was proud enough not to wish to stay in power against the wishes of the majority of the people, as he showed more than once in his extraordinary career. It is quite mistaken to accuse him, as some of his detractors have done, of deliberately misleading the public by appearing to defend French Algeria when his real intention, from the start, was to abandon it. But it is equally misleading to praise him, as his left-wing supporters do, for a supposedly masterful policy of decolonising Algeria by stages. There can be no doubt that, ideally, de Gaulle would have liked to give the army a complete victory in Algeria, to have persuaded or forced the FLN to lay down their arms, and to have carried the great majority of the population of Algeria – Christian and Moslem – with him in a policy of permanent association between Algeria and France. But he was unable to do these things; and to be fair to him, his chances of doing them, which might have been high had he returned to power, say, in 1955, were very low from 1958 on.

"Victory" in Algeria, in the sense of military and diplomatic success, would have enabled de Gaulle to turn to world affairs (his main preoccupation) with a greatly strengthened hand. When it became apparent that he would never achieve success in these terms, he switched from a policy of victory to one of avoiding defeat. Either way, he was determined to get France out of the Algerian *impasse*, which, as he could see, blocked her economic and diplomatic recovery and her military-technological modernisation. He settled, then, for military success and diplomatic failure. That he was able to part with Algeria without a civil war in France was a great though negative achievement which, in all probability, would have been beyond the capacity of any other leader France possessed. But his enemies, including many erstwhile supporters, would never forgive him for it.[2]

[2] In his unfinished *Mémoires d'Espoir (Renouveau*, pp. 48 *et seq.*) de Gaulle analyses his attitude to Algeria without, I think, excessive wisdom from hindsight. He quotes from his press conference of 30 June 1955 (*Discours*, Vol. II, pp. 637–9) to show that even then he was publicly advocating "association" instead of "domination" as the right policy for

In June 1958, however, the outcome still lay in the indeterminate future. De Gaulle knew, broadly speaking, where he was going, but had no precise idea how he would get there. What he did know was that the situation was still dangerously explosive, and that any premature disclosure of ultimate intentions might remove him from the power he had so lately achieved. He was bound, therefore, to dissemble.

In a sense, his first cabinet was an act of dissimulation. It was essential that it should be broadly based, providing reassurance to the Gaullists and to the proponents of French Algeria, while not appearing to threaten the democratic principles. As Prime Minister (with President Coty still in office), de Gaulle chose four ministers of State: Louis Jacquinot (conservative), Houphouët-Boigny of the Ivory Coast, Pierre Pflimlin (MRP), and Guy Mollet (Socialist). The conservative ex-premier, Antoine Pinay, was the Finance minister. The faithful Debré was the minister of Justice (*garde des sceaux*) and de Gaulle immediately put him to work on drafting a constitution inspired by the Bayeux speech of 1946. For he rightly sensed that the Algiers rebels had consented to his return to power only as a way of bringing down the Fourth Republic, and would try to remove him if he disappointed their Algerian hopes. By setting up new Republican institutions de Gaulle hoped to forestall them. Sourly, Debré commented on some of his new colleagues: "Houphouët, that black man; Pflimlin, that knave; Mollet, that primitive; and Pinay, that ass."[3]

Couve de Murville, *inspecteur des Finances* and an accomplished civil servant, became Foreign minister, a post he was to hold for ten years. The Interior went to the little-known Pelletier, and the armed forces and France Overseas to Guillaumat and Cornut-Gentille. A Socialist, Max Lejeune, was charged with Saharan affairs. But the most famous name in the cabinet, next to de Gaulle's own, was that of André Malraux, the writer and master-producer of the great rallies of the RPF, whose mandate was to ensure that the Gaullist second coming should achieve dis-

---

France in North Africa. He might have added that on the same occasion he advocated "integration" for Algeria, but only "in a community larger than France". In his memoirs, he goes on to say that he ruled out as Utopian "any idea of the assimilation of the Moslems to the French people", which, he argued, might have been conceivable a hundred years earlier, but only if it had been possible to implant millions of metropolitan French in Algeria and millions of Algerians in France. As things stood, he aimed from the first at self-determination for Algeria, and a privileged position for France in that country, in conditions that would enable the French population, under the protection of the army, to decide for themselves whether they wished to stay there or settle in the metropolis. The terms on which Algeria eventually achieved independence fell short of these aims, of course; and in their implementation, even more than in the letter of the terms.

[3] Viansson-Ponté, *République*, Vol. I, p. 58, see also p. 59.

tinction in the Fine Arts. A late-comer to the cabinet was Jacques Soustelle, whose presence in Algiers at a critical time had powerfully contributed to the general's return but whose sin was an excessive popularity with the French of Algiers. He had confidently promised General Salan that he would be in charge of Algerian affairs. Instead, de Gaulle kept this key portfolio to himself, choosing as his secretary-general in Algeria René Brouillet, a man whose chief qualification for the job (as Soustelle bitterly remarks[4]) was undoubtedly that he knew nothing about the subject. Weeks later, on 7 July, when Soustelle had given up hope and was packing to resume his ethnological studies in Mexico, de Gaulle offered him the relatively minor post of Information minister; which he accepted. To have excluded Soustelle altogether would doubtless have been dangerous. When Soustelle made his first appearance in the Council of Ministers, de Gaulle is reported to have exclaimed: "All we need now is Pierre Poujade, Maurice Thorez and Ferhat Abbas, and everything will be complete." The minister of Labour, Bacon (MRP), who was physically small and slight, was the object of a more dismissive greeting: "At least that one won't get in the way!"

On 4 June 1958, the day after securing the powers he sought from the National Assembly, General de Gaulle flew to Algiers. With him went three of his ministers, Jacquinot, Guillaumat and Lejeune; and General Ely, whom de Gaulle had just reinstated as chief of the General Staff. Beflagged and loud with enthusiasm, Algiers greeted de Gaulle. Appearing on the balcony of the government building overlooking the massed white and Moslem faces below, he raised his arms in the familiar V sign of French Rally days and declaimed four words which produced a storm of applause. Carefully chosen, but substantially void, the words were: "*Je vous ai compris*" – "I have understood you." This guileful response to the perennial complaint of the *pieds-noirs* that the metropolitans did not understand them struck the responsive chord he needed to establish a *rapport* with his audience.

He went on to say that from that day, all the inhabitants of Algeria were French in the full sense, with equal rights and duties; all would vote in the forthcoming French general election, and – unlike previous general elections in Algeria – there would be no separate electoral colleges for French and Moslem voters. This sounded like "integration", although de Gaulle was careful not to use the word.

The respect accorded to the general did not, he learned immediately afterwards, extend to his ministers, two of whom – Jacquinot and

4 Soustelle, *Gaullisme*, p. 169.

Lejeune – were seized before they could join de Gaulle and Generals Salan and Ely on the balcony, and locked up in an office.

As his tour of inspection went on, de Gaulle found more and more causes for irritation. On 6 June at Oran he refused at first to see the local Committee of Public Safety, then yielded, but only to ask them caustically: "Surely you're not still playing at revolution?" Later that day, on the parade ground, he lost his temper when the cries of "Vive de Gaulle" were overwhelmed by shouts of "The army in power! Vive Soustelle!" Pounding on the table with his fist, de Gaulle retaliated: "Will you please be quiet! Be quiet!" Further shouts for Soustelle, in Algiers, made him turn to a neighbour and say, in cruder terms than this translation: "Those bastards make me sick!"[5] When the committee called on him to proclaim "integration", on threat of further disorders, de Gaulle told them that should these materialise, they would all go to gaol.

In all his speeches – at Algiers, Bône, Constantine, Oran and Mostaganem – de Gaulle praised the army, and stuck to his main theme of equality between the communities of Algeria. He is widely reported to have promised his audience at Oran that Algeria would remain French forever, but there is no doubt that de Gaulle was merely referring to the will of the inhabitants to remain French, without committing himself for the future. In the following convoluted passage his listeners heard, or thought they heard, a pledge:

> It is, in particular, in the immense opportunity that is going to be offered in three months to the totality of French citizens, a matter of Algeria in her entirety, with her ten million inhabitants, participating with all her heart like the others with the same right, with the will to demonstrate thereby that she is organically a French land today and for ever.[6]

There is no doubt, indeed, that de Gaulle had gone to Algeria determined not to use either the word "integration" or the slogan of "French Algeria" which was being pressed on him from all sides. At Mostaganem, on 7 June, however, he did shout: "Vive l'Algérie française!" But he

[5] De Gaulle, Renouveau, pp. 53–4; Tournoux, Tragédie, p. 289; Viansson-Ponté, République, Vol. I, p. 91.

[6] My literal translation, made at the time. Maurice Allais in L'Algérie d'Evian (henceforth, Allais), p. 120, was among those who thought de Gaulle had made a pledge that day; so was Viansson-Ponté (République, Vol. I, p. 91). Prudently, the official collection of his speeches (Discours, Vol. III) omits the text of the Oran speech; and indeed of those de Gaulle made at Bône, Constantine and Mostaganem: only the Algiers one appears. My own belief that no pledge was intended is based on my contemporary study of the newspaper reports.

later expressed surprise that he had done so and said the phrase had "escaped" from him, adding: "After all, one says in current speech, 'French Canada, Swiss Canada'. . . . It was superficial."

On the day of his Mostaganem speech, 7 June 1958, de Gaulle returned to Paris. Within the next few days, agreements which de Gaulle had proposed to the chiefs of State of Morocco and Tunisia on his return to power came into force. They provided for the withdrawal of French troops from both national territories, with the exception of Bizerta in Tunisia, and Meknès, Port-Lyautey, Marrakesh and Agadir in Morocco. On the 10th, heedless of the general's warnings, the Algeria–Sahara Committee of Public Safety passed a resolution calling for the abolition of political parties and the formation of a "true government of Public Safety" under de Gaulle; for the abrogation of the loi-cadre (framework law) for Algeria passed by the Gaillard government and for the total integration of Algeria and the Sahara with France.

His irritation rising once again, de Gaulle cabled back to Salan, rejecting the resolution as "unfortunate and untimely". After some days for reflection, the committee, on 21 June, passed another resolution, this time declaring that it was "indissolubly united behind General de Gaulle", and that it would continue its mission "in a totally unpolitical spirit". Already some of those who had reluctantly joined the Gaullists to save French Algeria were beginning to realise that it was not going to be easy to control the old man.

Deliberately, however, the general blew hot and cold, for on 9 June, immediately after his return from Algeria, he had confirmed General Salan as commander-in-chief and named him "delegate-general" in Algeria; while a few days later he had appointed Generals Allard and Massu as super-prefect and prefect, respectively, of Algiers. These appointments, while recognising existing realities, offered the additional advantage of lulling potential adversaries with a false sense of security. For de Gaulle was to show later that he was as quick to remove these men as he had once been to give them jobs.

The Committees of Public Safety, which had so powerfully contributed to bring him back to power, were in his eyes one of the more deplorable realities of the situation. He was to lose no opportunity to cut them down to size. Back in Algeria, from 1 to 4 July, de Gaulle took Guy Mollet with him, refused to see the Algiers Committee and left the city, having caused the news of his arrival to be withheld from the population.[7] After an extensive tour of military installations, however, he returned to Algiers where he made a speech on 3 July foreshadowing

[7] Viansson-Ponté, République, Vol. I, p. 94.

new economic measures and disclosing that Moslem women, for the first time, would exercise voting rights in the forthcoming elections.

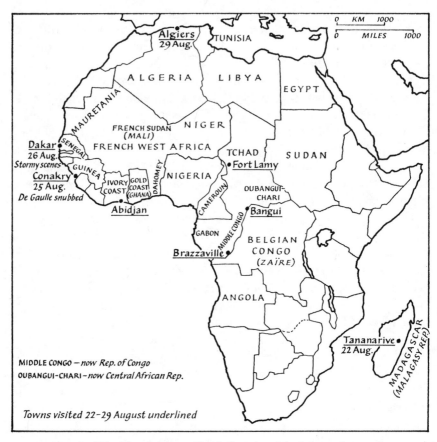

De Gaulle's African Trip – The Referendum of 28 September 1958

From now on, de Gaulle systematically let fall, at irregular intervals, hints on the future status of Algeria which, he soon made plain, was bound to fall well short of integration or permanent French domination. On the 13th, for instance, in a speech in Paris, he outlined his plan for new federal links between France and her possessions overseas, in which, he said, Algeria would have "a place of choice". Whatever this obscure formula meant, it could not mean integration.

Now de Gaulle was ready to meet the leaders and peoples of French-speaking Africa. Debré's constitutional committee was making rapid progress, and de Gaulle knew exactly what he sought from the Africans. Wherever possible, he wanted an overwhelming vote of confidence (in effect, a plebiscite, although he deprecated the term, which he considered discredited by Napoleonic usage[8]). But his trip was to be, in modern parlance, a "hard sell". The choice he would place before the African heads of State would be, in effect, between all and nothing. Or, alternatively, take it or leave it. If they saw to it that their peoples voted in favour of de Gaulle's constitution in the forthcoming referendum, they would gain all the advantages of sovereignty, plus France's friendship, in all its generosity. If, however, they voted no, then *all links would be severed*, and they would be on their own, without France's aid or blessing. There could be no half-way house in de Gaulle's vision of a Franco-African community.

The journey lasted only nine days – from 20 to 29 August – but in that time, de Gaulle and his *entourage* visited Madagascar, Tchad, Middle Congo (Brazzaville), Oubangui-Chari (now the Central African Republic), Ivory Coast, Guinea and Senegal. In all places except the last two, de Gaulle received a rapturous welcome that left him in no doubt of the way the voting would go. Nor was there any serious doubt about the outcome in Upper Volta, Dahomey, Gabon, Niger or Mauretania. The doubts were concentrated on Guinea and Senegal; even Sudan – later to federate, then break with Senegal under the name of Mali, which it retained for itself alone – seemed safe.

All the drama in de Gaulla's African tour was concentrated in his stays in Conakry (Guinea) and Dakar (Senegal), especially the former. Sékou Touré, a militant former trade union leader and a powerful personality, had gained absolute power over Guinea, establishing single-party rule over what de Gaulle termed "a totalitarian republic". All the way from the airport to the capital, on 25 August 1958, well-drilled crowds shouted "Independence!" and displayed banners with that single word upon them.

Sékou Touré was not prepared to accept the stark choice offered by de Gaulle. He wanted unconditional independence, but saw no reason why this should rule out friendly relations between his country and France. The speech he had prepared, couched in the peremptory language he normally used, was shown to French officials, who could not find in it anything he had not been saying for months, but persuaded him to write in a favourable reference to de Gaulle's Brazzaville speech of 1944. The amended text, with key passages heavily underlined in red ink, was handed to General de Gaulle who, however, rolled it up without reading it.[9] When Sékou Touré started speaking, therefore, the matter of

---

[8] De Gaulle, L'*Effort*, p. 19; see also Tournoux, *Tragédie*, p. 484.
[9] Jean Lacouture, *Cinq Hommes et la France* (henceforth, Lacouture, *Cinq Hommes*), p. 351. His account of the visit to Conakry, which he witnessed (ibid. pp. 347 *et seq.*) is the most informative I have seen.

his words – and even more, the defiant manner of their delivery – came as a shock. One sentence, in particular, impressed de Gaulle: "We prefer poverty in freedom to riches in slavery." He paid less attention to another passage: "Our heart, our reason, as well as our most evident interests, make us choose, without hesitation, interdependence and freedom in this union [with France] rather than to define our position without France and against France." Frenetic shouts and cheers greeted each of the leader's sentences.

Sadly, rather than angrily, de Gaulle replied: "There has been talk of independence. I say here, louder still than elsewhere, that independence is at the disposal of Guinea. She may take it by saying 'No' to the proposals before her, and in that event, I guarantee that the metropolis will not raise any obstacle."[10]

De Gaulle's account suggests, however, that anger predominated over sadness; or at the least, that anger soon gained the upper hand. According to the general's version, he replied that France had done a lot for Guinea, one proof being that the president had just delivered his speech in very good French. Those freely joining the proposed Community would be entitled to French aid, and Guinea was entirely free to say "Yes" or "No"; but if she said "No", that would mean separation, and France would draw its own conclusions.[11]

That evening, at the French reception in the Government Palace, de Gaulle saw Sékou Touré alone[12] and made the position plainer still, in these words: "Don't get things wrong! The French Republic you are now dealing with is no longer the one you have known and which used cunning instead of decision. As far as France today is concerned, colonialism is finished. That amounts to saying that she is indifferent to your retrospective reproaches. From now on, she accepts to lend her help to the State which you are going to create. But she is quite prepared to cut her losses. She has lived a very long time without Guinea. She will go on living a very long time if the two are separated. In that event, it goes without saying that we shall immediately withdraw

---

[10] De Gaulle's speech, which was at least partly improvised, is not recorded in the semi-official Discours, although this passage appears in Année Politique, 1958, p. 549 and in Cinq Hommes, together with the quotation from Sékou Touré's speech I have translated. [11] De Gaulle, Renouveau, p. 60.
[12] According to Lacouture, de Gaulle chose not to meet Sékou Touré at the reception; but de Gaulle's account must, I think, be preferred. Lacouture, however, records that General de Gaulle declined Sékou Touré's offer to accompany him by plane to Dakar; and that the minister for France Overseas, Bernard Cornut-Gentille (who, with Jacques Foccart, charged with African affairs in de Gaulle's secretariat, accompanied him on the African tour) cancelled an invitation to spend the night as guest of Sékou Touré, preferring his hotel room. I have no reason to doubt these details, which are in character with de Gaulle's normal behaviour towards those out of favour.

our administrative, technical and educational assistance and that we shall cease all subsidies to your budget. I add that, having regard to the links which have united our two countries, you must not doubt that a 'No' solemnly addressed by yourselves to the solidarity which France proposes, will mean that our relations will lose the character of friendship and preference among the states of the world."

Next morning, the road to the airport was deserted. "Adieu, Guinea!" said de Gaulle to Sékou Touré, who had come to say goodbye.

At Dakar, too, the atmosphere was tense. The premier, Mamadou Dia, was not there to greet the general, and clamorous demonstrations in favour of independence rose to his ears as he faced the crowd. "First," shouted de Gaulle, "a word to those carrying banners. If they want independence the way they understand it, let them take it on 28 September [the day of the referendum]. But if they don't take it then, let them make what France proposes to them: the Franco-African Community." As they listened, the shouters fell silent, and as he went on, they applauded.

On his way back to Paris, the general stopped briefly at Algiers, where he met various Algerians of both communities and made a radio speech on 29 August, explaining Algeria's part in the referendum. More significantly, on this third visit, he gave General Massu a dressing down for his excessively visible role in the Public Safety Committee; and overruling objections from the "ultras", he insisted on seeing both Moslems and liberal Europeans in private.

By the time General de Gaulle got back to Paris, the text of the new constitution was ready. On this issue above all, the fulfilment of an ancient dream, the general had forced the pace. Michel Debré, with his team of eighteen jurists, had worked at top speed to add flesh to the bare bones of the Bayeux speech. But simultaneously, a second team, under the chairmanship of de Gaulle himself (when he was not travelling), met at the Hôtel Matignon. It consisted of the four ministers of State; Pompidou, as the general's *directeur de cabinet*; Raymond Janot, another member of de Gaulle's secretariat; and René Cassin, vice-chairman of the Council of State and one of the original London Gaullists. Debré, however, also attended these meetings, which essentially provided the raw material of the proposals which his own committee was charged with drafting in legal form. As the text advanced, it was submitted to the Council of Ministers, but in a manner that discouraged contributions from those whose misfortune it was to belong to the dying system.[13]

---

[13] Viansson-Ponté, *République*, Vol. I, pp. 62–7, citing Pierre Avril, *Le Régime politique de la Vème République*.

In mid-July, conscious that time was not on his side in the race to forestall a possible challenge from those who might wish to remove him, he intervened to speed up the procedure. Instead of long discussions of each clause, he prescribed that the restricted cabinet committee over which he himself presided should simply choose between alternative drafts submitted. He then rapidly constituted, as the measures voted by parliament obliged him to do, a Consultative Constitutional Committee, consisting of thirty-nine members, one third of whom were chosen by the general, and the rest by the Assembly and Senate. Even among the thirteen members chosen by de Gaulle, the Gaullists were in a minority. The other group ranged wide over the political spectrum, but excluded the Communists; among the parliamentarians were two Senegalese, Léopold Senghor and Lamine Gueye.

The Consultative Committee met for the first time on 29 July, and completed its work on 14 August, when the approved draft constitution emerged. The committee had made improvements in drafting, but had left the text substantially unchanged. The general had, of course, been given the constitution he wanted, but it was not in all particulars his own brain-child. Not unexpectedly, de Gaulle had paid closest attention to the articles defining presidential powers. The president of the Fifth Republic – initially, he presumed, Charles de Gaulle – was to be elected for a term of seven years by the indirect suffrage of an electoral college of parliamentarians, departmental councillors and other notables. He was to have the right to choose his own Prime Minister, to dissolve parliament, to call a referendum on specified issues if proposed either by the government (if parliament was sitting) or jointly by the two Assemblies; and above all, at times of grave crisis, to assume plenary powers under Article 16, which was inevitably to become the most controversial provision in the constitution. The restricted cabinet committee is credited especially with the drafting of the provisions concerning parliamentary procedure; and Michel Debré with articles guaranteeing the primacy of the government over parliament. In sum, then, the new constitution was of a quasi-presidential type, owing more to the American model than previous French constitutions did.

A peculiarly French problem, however, was that of relations between France and the overseas dependencies within the framework of the new "Community". Was the relationship to be "federal" or "confederal"? In other words, was the Community to consist of sovereign states loosely grouped together for certain defined purposes, or of partially self-governing states in a federal system, leaving the normal attributes of sovereignty – such as foreign affairs, defence and the currency – under central (that is, French) control? The strongest advocate of confederation was the Senegalese poet-politician, Senghor; the federalists were led by Debré and Houphouët-Boigny.[14] In the end, the federalists won, and their views on sovereign attributes were enshrined in Articles 78 and 80–2.[15]

Now de Gaulle had his instrument of power; but before he could use it, he had to submit it to the popular will through the proposed referendum. No issue could have been simpler or starker. The voters were merely to be asked whether they wanted the Gaullist constitution, or did not. There was never any strong likelihood that they would not, for to vote against would imply renewed drift and, this time, the strong probability of a *coup d'état* and a straight military dictatorship. Even in the eyes of most of his opponents the general had at least the merit of being "the devil they knew". In "France Overseas", it is true, there was a further element of choice. The general himself decreed that each territory could decide whether to retain its existing status, to join the community as a partially self-governing state, be incorporated into France itself as an overseas *département*, or secede from the French Community altogether. For with brutal logic, de Gaulle gave France's dependencies a form of self-determination: what they called "independence" he called "secession". If they wanted French aid and protection, then the best they could hope for was local self-rule; if they wanted to run their foreign policies as well, then all links, including sentiment, would be severed. It was to explain this choice that de Gaulle had travelled Africa.

At home, too, the dismal nature of the alternative was plain enough, but the Gaullists were determined nevertheless to leave nothing to chance. Under the direction of Soustelle, whose assistance the general had almost spurned, an irresistible propaganda machine was mobilised. The master-component was French Radio-Television, in which Soustelle in the space of one month dismissed ten top executives, replacing them with members of the minute Gaullist parliamentary party, the Social Republicans. Time allotted to opponents of the new constitution was severely rationed. Sky-writing exhorted the people to vote (for abstentions were feared), and propaganda films exalted the general's image

---

[14] Viansson-Ponté, *République*, Vol. I, p. 66.
[15] For an analysis of the Gaullist constitution and its practical applications, *see* Dorothy Pickles, *The Fifth French Republic* (1960–2) (henceforth, Pickles, *Fifth Republic*). which includes a translation of the text by William Pickles that originally appeared in his *French Constitution of October 4 1958* (1960). The same text also appears in Alfred Fabre-Luce, *The Trial of Charles de Gaulle* (henceforth, Fabre-Luce, *Trial*), the English version of that author's *Haute-Cour* which was banned in France.

while vilifying the Fourth Republic. Posters by the million plastered walls all over France, Algeria and the territories; while an electoral journal, *France-Référendum* was distributed free in tens of millions. Against this massive barrage the opposition, with the exception of the Communist party, was muted. And this, too, was part of the picture: for it was to the advantage of the Gaullists that the alternatives to de Gaulle should seem to be either the generals or the Communists.[16]

On 3 September the government gave its final seal of approval to the constitutional draft, and on the 4th, in a speech in the Place de la République, de Gaulle presented it and appealed for its approval. When referendum-day came, on 28 September, the results overwhelmed even the most optimistic of the Gaullists: with fewer abstentions than at any time since 1936, nearly 80 per cent of metropolitan voters said Yes. Overseas the percentage reached 95.[17] Only Guinea, as expected, voted No, and the consequences outlined by de Gaulle immediately followed. All archives were removed from official buildings, and even the telephones were ripped out. All aid ceased, and a grain ship, bound for Conakry, was diverted from its course. Sékou Touré had to be taught a lesson: that it did not pay to say No to de Gaulle. The leaders of the rest of French-speaking Africa, who had said Yes, duly took note; although within a year most of them would be claiming the independence they had earlier prudently declined.

The constitution of the Fifth Republic was duly promulgated on 5 October. Having won what, in effect, was a personal plebiscite, de Gaulle faced the further constitutional hurdles (relatively minor ones, in the circumstances) of the parliamentary elections and his own

[16] Viansson-Ponté, *République*, I, pp. 67–73. *See also* Philip Williams and Martin Harrison, in D. H. E. Butler (ed.), *Elections Abroad*, ch. I, "France 1958".

[17] Between 14 October and 18 December 1958, the following territories opted for the status of "States of the Community": Madagascar, French Soudan, Senegal, Gabon, Mauretania, Middle Congo, Tchad, Oubangui-Chari, Ivory Coast, Dahomey, Upper Volta and Niger. The following decided, however, to remain "Overseas Territories of the French Republic": French Somali Coast, Comoro Archipelago, French Polynesia, New Caledonia, and the Islands of Saint-Pierre and Miquelon. Between 22 January and 20 April 1959 the new states of the Community adopted their constitutions. All termed themselves Republics, using their former names, except the following: Central African Republic (Oubangui-Chari), Republic of the Congo (Middle Congo), Islamic Republic of Mauretania, and Malagasy Republic (*République malgache*, formerly Madagascar). Soudan and Senegal federated in January 1959 as the Federation of Mali, but broke up on 22 September 1960; thereupon, Senegal kept its name, and the former Soudan became the Republic of Mali. The U.N. Trust territory of Togo became independent as the *République Togolaise* on 27 April 1960; the part of Cameroons under French trusteeship became an independent Republic on 1 January 1960 and joined the former British trusteeship territory to form the Federal Republic of Cameroun on 1 October 1961. In June and July 1960, the various states of Community opted for full independence. The Community thus became "ex-Community", but cooperation agreements between the new Republics and France preserved a special relationship.

election to the presidency, before the final but important formality of taking possession of the Elysée Palace. The Algerian problem, however, remained unsolved, and could at any moment jeopardise all his carefully laid plans. There was no alternative, he knew, to the policy of gradualism he had adopted; only thus could the time bomb be de-fused. On 2 and 3 October he was back in Algeria, this time with a vast plan of economic expansion which he announced in a speech on the 3rd, at Constantine (and which was immediately dubbed "the Constantine plan"). Although circumstances were to prevent its fulfilment, it was an imaginative concept which, if allowed to continue to its natural term of five years, would have brought the Moslem population of Algeria far closer to French levels, in education, income and opportunity. Had this stage been reached, the "integration" for which the "ultras" clamoured, would at least have been a more practical possibility than it then was. But once again, de Gaulle carefully forebore to use the word; instead, he said Algeria would have "its own personality" while "linked in close solidarity with metropolitan France".

These were not words the "ultras" heard with pleasure, and to reduce their power, de Gaulle issued a directive to General Salan, forbidding military officers to stand as candidates in the general elections in Algeria and ordering them to withdraw forthwith from the Committees of Public Safety. On the 14th General Massu and other military members of the Algeria-Sahara Committee of Public Safety duly resigned; and next day, the committee, under its civilian chairman, the Moslem Dr Sid Cara, called for a general strike in Algiers in protest against "the political parties who wish to liquidate Algeria" and to demand the return of the military members. Salan, however, persuaded the committee to call off the strike.

At this time, General de Gaulle nursed a lingering hope that the reforms and economic measures he was taking would make continued hostilities seem irrelevant in the eyes of the Moslem rebels of the FLN. To this end, at a press conference on 23 October 1958, he called for a "peace of the brave" which, he said, could be achieved either through local cease-fires, or through negotiations between the French government and the "external organisation" of the FLN. He now used the flexible word "association" to describe future relations between France and Algeria.

The Moslem leaders, however, had only lately – on 19 September 1958 – announced the transformation of the Front de Libération Nationale into a provisional government of the Algerian Republic (GPRA, from its French initials). Operating in Tunis, intransigent as are, by definition, all politically-motivated groups who turn to terrorism, they ignored de

Gaulle's offer of negotiations. From the general's point of view, however, his offer was a psychological step forward, for he had launched, for the first time, the notion of negotiated settlement, which was exactly what the settlers, with their standing demand for unconditional surrender, found intolerable.

The next preoccupation was the elections – though less for the general, who affected a lordly aloofness from such vulgarities, than for the Gaullists. In the elections of 1956, they had polled less than 4.5 per cent of the votes. Now they were on the crest of the wave, with the man who symbolised their faith and hopes back in power. They lacked, nevertheless, a broadly based political party that would carry them to power and provide the parliamentary machinery that would execute, instead of hindering, the general's programme. Ironically, in the light of their subsequent relations, it was Jacques Soustelle who provided it, just as it was he who had organised the massive propaganda effort that had all but obliterated dissentient voices during the referendum campaign.

Immediately after the referendum Soustelle invited the leaders of three Gaullist groups to his office in the Avenue de Friedland. These were the parliamentary groups – Républicains Sociaux – Soustelle's own Union for the French Renewal, and the Convention Républicaine, led by the energetic conspirator who had done most to give the Algiers rebellion a Gaullist twist, Léon Delbecque. From the federation, and later the merger, of these three bodies came the Union pour la nouvelle République (UNR), which through successive name changes was to be the ruling party of the Fifth Republic. The central committee of the UNR consisted of Chaban-Delmas, Roger Frey, Debré, Michelet, Pierre Picard, Delbecque, Marie-Madeleine Fourcade, Marcenet, Veyssière, Ali Mallem and, of course, Soustelle, who became its secretary-general. For troops, the leaders turned to the old groups of the defunct Rally of the French People and to the hangers-on of the Committees of Public Safety. Inevitably, this composition gave the UNR, at least initially, a "right-wing" and extremist look, which could not have been to de Gaulle's taste.

Very rapidly, under pressure of events, the UNR organised itself in the constituencies. There was much heated discussion within the government on the provisions of the new electoral law, since it was obvious that the voting system chosen would profoundly affect the composition of the National Assembly. In the end, General de Gaulle personally intervened,[18] against the advice of most of the Gaullists in favour of the "one-member, two-ballot" system (*serutin uninominal à deux tours*),

[18] Viansson-Ponté, *République*, Vol. I, p. 74.

under which each party could nominate a single candidate for each constituency, who could be elected on the first ballot, but only if he obtained at least half of the votes cast plus one, and if the votes in favour totalled at least a quarter of the electorate. If he failed by these tests, there would be a second ballot. This system, as de Gaulle rightly supposed, encouraged non-Gaullist candidates to drop out after an initial stalemate, and the voters in general to vote for the Gaullist candidate on the second, a week later. Although the general had dissociated himself from the UNR and forbidden its candidates to use his name, "even as an adjective", this injunction was widely and ingeniously ignored. ("If de Gaulle were here," a candidate would say, "he would vote for. . . .")

When the first ballot was held, on 23 November, the startling result was that only thirty-nine of the 465 candidates were elected. As the general had hoped, the second ballot brought a massive switch to the Gaullists, with the left-wing vote largely split between Socialist and Communist candidates. The outcome (writes Dorothy Pickles) was "probably the most unrepresentative Assembly in French history". True, the UNR, with 28.1 per cent of the votes cast, led the poll, ahead of the Communists (20.5), the conservatives (18.5), the Socialists (13.8), the Christian Democrats or MRP (9.11) and the Radicals (5.7). But the composition of the chamber did not reflect these percentages. The seven million electors who voted for Socialist and Communist candidates returned only 50 deputies, while only half the number (three and a half million) of voters sent 200 UNR candidates to the National Assembly.[19]

Representatives or not, the new Assembly was startlingly new: of the 537 outgoing deputies, only 131 had been re-elected. Among those eliminated – temporarily – from political life were six ex-premiers: Mendès France, Laniel, Daladier, Bourgès-Maunoury, Edgar Faure and Ramadier. (Most would soon return, by being elected to the upper house.) Who was to lead, and if necessary discipline, this fresh, inexperienced and untried gathering? Unexpectedly, Jacques Chaban-Delmas announced his candidacy. Young (forty-three), athletic and good-looking, a former Rugby international player, a general in the Resistance, and mayor of Bordeaux for the past eleven years, he was a politician born, who had not hesitated to take office under the Fourth Republic. Yet it was he who had sent Delbecque to Algiers, thereby paving the way for de Gaulle's return. Everybody had credited him with further ministerial ambitions; but he now wanted to be the president of the Assembly (or speaker, in English parlance).

[19] Pickles, *Fifth Republic*, p. 59. See also Soustelle, *Gaullisme*, pp. 178–9.

On hearing the news, de Gaulle did not hide his displeasure. He had already promised the aged ex-premier, Paul Reynaud – the one politician of the Third Republic who had wholeheartedly espoused de Gaulle's theories of mechanised war – that he could count on the general's support if he stood for this high but powerless office. De Gaulle summoned Soustelle to his office to explain this unfortunate circumstance and instruct him to break the news to Chaban-Delmas and request him to withdraw. Debré was asked to support Soustelle in this delicate mission.

To their surprise, Chaban-Delmas heard them out with cool self-possession, then declared that much as he would like to please the general, it was too late, since so many deputies had promised him their support. On the first ballot he was so far ahead of Reynaud that the old man withdrew. Would he, then, incur the general's anger? Not in the least. Recognising in the dashing new speaker something of the audacity that was his own hallmark, de Gaulle wrote him in longhand a letter of warm felicitation, which the delighted recipient showed off to all whom he met in the corridors of the Palais-Bourbon.[20]

For de Gaulle there remained one last institutional hurdle, but an important and in some respects less than straightforward one: to be elected president of the Republic. It was less than straightforward because he had never until now presented himself as a candidate for any office; the formality had not been required of him when the National Assembly twice elected him president of the provisional government in 1945, after having led France, in his own words, "by virtue of events alone".[21] According to ex-President Coty's account,[22] de Gaulle went through a period of agonising doubt before deciding to present himself for election. As late as the end of November 1958 he called on Coty and, with some embarrassment, asked whether he should be a candidate. The embarrassment, which may not have been feigned, was due to the fact that Coty had been elected president at the end of 1953 for a term of seven years. He therefore had two years still to go, and it was known that he would have liked to complete his term had the death of the Fourth Republic not interrupted it. Not unexpectedly, Coty pointed out that difficulties might arise if de Gaulle were to continue as premier under the new constitution. It was only then, says Coty, that de Gaulle agreed to stand.

Since the new constitution had so obviously been conceived with de Gaulle in the presidential role, the general had made up his mind

[20] Jacques Soustelle, l'Espérance Trahie (henceforth, Soustelle, Espérance), pp. 72–3. De Gaulle does not mention this incident in Mémoires d'Espoir.
[21] De Gaulle, Renouveau, p. 39.   [22] Tournoux, Tragédie, pp. 300 et seq.

from the start that he would have himself elected, and that his "consultation" of President Coty was no more than a courtesy to a man whom he held in relative esteem (relative, that is, to his general contempt for the men of the Fourth Republic), and who had had the great merit of not standing in his way in May and June 1958. The gesture, then, deserves praise, although it was followed not long after by an act of discourtesy that was to leave Coty hurt and bewildered.

By consenting to the drafters' provision for the indirect electing of the president, de Gaulle had played safe, not being at that stage sure enough of popular support to entrust himself to universal suffrage. (He was later to amend the constitution to allow for direct presidential elections.) On 21 December, the "notables" duly gave de Gaulle 78 per cent of their 80,000 votes, with the Communist candidate, Georges Marrane, as runner-up (10,000) and a small vote (7,000) for Albert Chatelet, standing as candidate of a leftist "Union of Democratic Forces".

On 8 January 1959 the new president formally called on the outgoing one, who greeted him with the words: "The first among Frenchmen is now the first man in France."[23] To loud cheers of "Merci, Coty" and "Vive de Gaulle", the two men rode side by side in the presidential car to the Arc de Triomphe for the traditional homage to the Unknown Soldier. It had been agreed that once the ceremony was over, de Gaulle would accompany Coty to his own car, and only then return to the Elysée – henceforth his home – in the presidential car. But at the last moment, surrounded by enthusiastic supporters, de Gaulle forgot, or omitted, to do what had been agreed, and Coty was left to his own devices. De Gaulle, however, later "forgot" something else that had been tacitly understood between him and Coty: that the latter should be appointed president of the Constitutional Council, of which he was a member, ex officio. It seems probable therefore (as Viansson-Ponté argues) that a snub was intended. Certainly de Gaulle's treatment of Coty was consistent with de Gaulle's known view of himself as a man without a predecessor and who did not need a "transfer of powers" from a powerless president.

With de Gaulle at the Arc de Triomphe were the president of the Senate, Gaston Monnerville (who had authority under the constitution to take the president's place in case of necessity), the president of the Assembly, Chaban-Delmas, and the man everybody knew de Gaulle had chosen as his first premier, Michel Debré. Which of the three would the new president choose for the honour of accompanying him on the

[23] De Gaulle's version (*Renouveau*, p. 39). Tournoux, *Tragédie*, p. 301, and Viansson-Ponté, *République*, Vol. I, p. 83 give slightly different versions.

journey back to the Elysée, and therefore as a sign of possible future favour? To the general surprise, and the particular disappointment of the three concerned, de Gaulle signalled to his able and self-effacing *directeur de cabinet*, Georges Pompidou. This was surely the most unconscious of the general's prophecies, for he certainly had no notion at that time that he was singling out the man who, in fact, would succeed him as president of the Republic.

The worst was yet to come in General de Gaulle's confrontation with the army and the settlers. Between the general and presidential elections – from 3 to 7 December 1958 – he had made his fifth and last trip of the year to Algeria, in which he concentrated on technical problems implicit in the Constantine Plan and the continued war. He made, for instance, a tour of the Saharan oilfields, inspected the electrified barrier on the Tunisian border and looked at agricultural centres.

On his return, his government issued decrees, dated 12 December, marking the restoration of civil government in Algeria, except in defence, internal security and the maintenance of order. Paul Delouvrier, at that time head of the Finance Division of the European Coal and Steel Community, was appointed delegate-general of the French government in Algeria, under the direct authority of the Prime Minister. The time had now come to remove the potentially dangerous General Salan from his post. This was achieved by an administrative invention, the new post of inspector-general of Defence, in which capacity he was supposed to advise the government on "important questions relating to the defence of the Republic and the Community". This non-post, however, was soon to be abolished, once its main purpose – the removal of Salan from Algiers – had been accomplished.

To succeed Salan as commander-in-chief in Algeria, de Gaulle promoted Salan's deputy, General Maurice Challe, one of the generals arrested under the Pflimlin government. General Jacques Allard, until then "super-prefect" for the Algiers region, became Challe's deputy. De Gaulle had turned to Challe, an air force general, because he had a high confidence in the man's ability to carry the attack on the FLN and gradually reduce the pockets under their control; for the thing de Gaulle most feared during this delicate phase when he was trying to lay the bases for negotiations was some spectacular military reverse for the French forces, which would have played into the hands of the ultras and caused many passive Moslems to declare themselves for the rebels.[24] In military terms, Challe did what was expected of him. On the political

[24] De Gaulle, *Renouveau*, p. 67.

side, however, he too some two years later would go into dissidence against de Gaulle.

And these were only the most spectacular changes. By March 1959 it was estimated that some 1,500 officers had been either retired or transferred from Algeria to other places. De Gaulle was determined to remove as many as possible of the army officers who had been exposed to the ideological poisons of Algeria.

For his part, he still hoped late in 1958, and early in 1959, for a peace of reconciliation, leaving an independent Algeria still linked with France in ways to be determined. In the ceremony at the Elysée on 8 January, when he took over from President Coty, he made a short speech foreshadowing a "place of choice" within the community for "a pacified and transformed Algeria, developing her own personality in her own way and closely linked with France". Hoping to soften Moslem intransigence, he presided five days later over a cabinet meeting which announced sweeping measures of clemency. Some seven thousand suspects would be released from internment camps in Algeria, and 180 persons under death sentences were reprieved. More significantly, Messali Hadj, the aged leader of the Mouvement National Algérien (MNA), rival to the FLN, was released from internment on Belle-Ile and shortly afterwards moved into a flat outside Paris. Still more significantly, the FLN leader Ben Bella, who had been seized when an airliner on which he was travelling from Rabat in Morocco to Tunis was diverted, was transferred with four of his companions from the grim Santé prison in Paris to more agreeable conditions in the fortress of the Ile d'Aix. This was widely, and rightly, interpreted as the first step in the transformation of Ben Bella and his companions from the status of outlaws to that of *interlocuteurs valables* – the kind of people one could, at a suitable time, negotiate with.

These acts of clemency infuriated Jacques Soustelle, whose thinking on Algeria was dominated by two elements: one of them emotional – his passionate identification with the "anguish" of the settlers and of those Moslems who had opted for the French connection; the other intellectual – the knowledge that the war that was being fought in Algeria was not an ordinary war but something new, as in Indo-China, a "revolutionary" or subversive war.[25] It was true enough that de Gaulle dismissed the Algerian war as just another Kabyle insurrection, like the one in 1857, which Marshal Randon crushed with 100,000 men.[26] There is some substance in Soustelle's reproach that just as the Second World War generals were thinking in terms of the First World

---

[25] Soustelle, *Espérance*, pp. 88 *et seq.*   [26] Tournoux, *Tragédie*, p. 346.

War, so de Gaulle, faced with the age of revolutionary wars, thought in terms of conventional war, even though he was aware of such technological developments as thermo-nuclear weapons.

But of course Soustelle and de Gaulle were pursuing different objectives. Soustelle believed (despite the evidence of its unreality) in the idea of "integration" of a France–Algeria of equal citizens. De Gaulle knew this objective to be unrealistic. He sought to give the army absolute mastery on the ground, but knew that even if the rebellion appeared to be crushed, there was nothing to stop it reviving in five or ten years. He wanted to bring the FLN to the negotiating table, but preferably as merely one of a group of negotiators, who should include the Moslems favourable to France, and the MNA, who would have settled for autonomy instead of independence. Logically, he should also have wished to consult the *pieds-noirs*, but he was never able to give any kind of emotional commitment to their cause. More and more, as the war dragged on, he saw it as the great obstacle that stood between him and his dreams of grandeur for France. And because as the war dragged on he felt himself getting older and feared to lose his remaining chances of playing a world role, he became increasingly willing, or resigned, to negotiate with the FLN alone.

Throughout 1959, however, the general's strategy was to move towards self-determination for all Algerians, in conditions which, he hoped, would take the wind out of the sails of the Algerian Moslem rebels. His reference to "a place of choice" for Algeria in his Elysée speech of 8 January was a first stage in the process. The second came on 25 March, in the course of his first Elysée press conference, with a typically cryptic reference to "the transformation in which Algeria will find her new personality". He followed this up on 29 April with a brutal but effective interview with Pierre Laffont, editor of *L'Echo d'Oran*, which appeared in that paper the following day. "What the activists want, and those who follow them," he said, "is to preserve 'Daddy's Algeria'. But 'Daddy's Algeria' is dead. Those who do not understand that will die as well." This sneer (for that is what it was) caused much appreciative laughter in Paris and elsewhere, but was interpreted among the Europeans of Algeria as an alarming sign that General de Gaulle was ready to "abandon" them. Less notice was taken of a passage in the same interview in which he said of the FLN: "It represents an important force, but it does not represent Algeria, not even the Moslems of Algeria."[27]

[27] In his indignation, Soustelle quotes both passages in *Espérance* (pp. 103–4); de Gaulle, however, quotes only the reference to *l'Algérie de papa* (*Renouveau*, p. 75), evidently loth to recall his dismissal of the FLN as sole negotiating partners in 1959, but not averse from quoting his own *bon mot*.

In May, the municipal elections in Algeria, held for the first time under the single college, brought Moslem majorities to many local councils, including Algiers. On 1 May too came the first sign of interest in negotiations on the part of the FLN, when Ferhat Abbas, the former moderate who had become "Prime Minister" of the Algerian provisional government, said in Beirut: "We are ready to meet General de Gaulle on neutral ground, without prior conditions. . . . We would be prepared for discussions with the French government. . . . It is not ruled out that the National Liberation Front should send a delegation to Paris."[28]

Towards the end of August de Gaulle, accompanied by his minister for the Armed Forces, Pierre Guillaumat, and by his top soldier, General Ely, made a tour of inspection of military zones. His official purpose was to see for himself what the army had accomplished in recent offensives against the army of National Liberation. On the visible evidence, these attacks had been highly successful. But de Gaulle learned things that finally convinced him the fight was hopeless. As he was leaving a Kabyle village that had greeted him with cheers and the Marseillaise, the mayor approached him and murmured: "*Mon général,* don't be taken in. Everybody here wants independence."

At Saida, where he was introduced to ex-*fellaghas* (guerrilla fighters) who had joined the French in a special commando, a young Moslem medical officer working with them said, his eyes filled with tears: "What we want, what we need, is to be responsible for ourselves and not others on our behalf."

These insights were supplemented by arithmetical evidence. More than 400,000 troops were tied down in defensive or administrative jobs in the towns and villages and along the frontiers. The actual fighting was done by only some forty thousand combat troops – about the same number as were fighting on the FLN side. The supposition that the French were bringing overwhelming force to bear on the Moslems was therefore an illusion. The French army saw the war as a crusade. De Gaulle now saw it as a "chimerical struggle" that would divide the army and the nation, and which offered dangerous temptations towards adventurism for the higher officers. He therefore took advantage of his brief tour to give General Challe and some of his closest subordinates an insight into his thinking. To win battles was not enough, he explained; the era of direct European rule was over and nothing could be done without the consent of the Algerian population. Then came a solemn warning: "As for all of you, listen to me well. You are not the

28 De Gaulle, *Renouveau,* p. 76; see also pp. 78–80.

army for the sake of the army. You are the army of France. You exist only for her and for her service. Well, I myself, at my level and my responsibilities, must be obeyed by the army so that France should survive. I am sure you will do this, and thank you on France's behalf." General Challe, according to de Gaulle, declared that the president could count on him.

In many speeches in the provinces de Gaulle had continued to drop hints about his Algerian policy. Now on 16 September 1959, in an important speech that reached an audience of millions through radio and television, he at last publicly grasped the nettle. He offered the Algerians self-determination within four years of the restoration of peace, and defined it as a free choice between secession – his favourite word for independence – complete integration with France (*Francisation*), and internal self-government in close association with France. He declared that the FLN would have the same right as other tendencies – "no more and no less" – to express their views; and he made it clear that the conditions must include the withdrawal of the French forces from Algeria before the Algerians could determine their own future. Messali Hadj welcomed de Gaulle's offer unreservedly, but nobody paid much attention.

At his press conference on 10 November, de Gaulle repeated his offer of self-determination, with specific guarantees of safety for any FLN delegates who wished to come to France for talks. The FLN reacted by naming Ben Bella and other leaders in French hands as their delegates; and de Gaulle had to make it clear that he was referring to "those who are still fighting, not those who are *hors de combat*".

Thoroughly alarmed by now, five of the more extreme European movements in Algeria demonstrated against the president's policy. The polarisation of Algerian politics was now proceeding fast. Judging the time ripe for a renewal of urban terrorism, the FLN started a fresh wave of incidents which between 1 December and 10 January 1960 caused twenty-two deaths of Europeans. In the week before Christmas 1959 Georges Bidault had visited Algeria, making inflammatory speeches that brought him enthusiastic shouts of "*Bidault au pouvoir!*" On 7 January yet another movement, "SOS Algeria", issued a manifesto proclaiming resistance to General de Gaulle's policy of "scuttle".

The spark that was to detonate this explosive situation came with the so-called "Massu affair". In an interview with the Munich newspaper *Süddeutsche Zeitung*, the popular paratroop commander, General Jacques Massu, rashly declared: "We no longer understand the policy of de Gaulle," and added that the army would never leave Algeria. When a telephone call from Michel Debré made him realise how seriously his words were being taken, he naively explained that his talk with Herr Kempski, the chief correspondent of the *Süddeutsche Zeitung*, was a private one, not intended for publication. Summoned to Paris, he was dismissed on 22 January from all his military and civil posts and replaced as commander of the Algiers Army Corps by General Jean Crépin.

In so acting, General de Gaulle went against the advice of General Challe, who was in Paris, and of several ministers who feared that the dismissal of Massu would provoke an explosion in Algiers. They were right; although foreknowledge that they were would not have stopped de Gaulle. On the 23rd, Pierre Lagaillarde – who was now a deputy in the National Assembly – donned his parachutist's uniform to lead a troop of demonstrators and occupy the university buildings. Other demonstrators were led by Joseph Ortiz, an Algiers café proprietor who had founded an armed and semi-clandestine organisation called the French National Front (FNF), and Jean-Jacques Susini, a militant student leader. The demonstrators, shouting "Hang de Gaulle" (*De Gaulle au poteau*), announced that they would stay put until Massu had returned to Algiers. In line with French revolutionary tradition, paving stones were ripped out to make barricades.

At first General Challe reacted energetically, denouncing the agitators and bringing in troop reinforcements to confront them. Soon, however, he was engaged in parleys with the "revolutionaries", and on 28 January both he and the delegate-general, Paul Delouvrier, left Algiers to set up temporary headquarters in the air force base at Reghaia sixteen miles to the east. There, Delouvrier delivered an emotional appeal to the demonstrators, and the strikers who had joined them, to rally round de Gaulle. By that time, however, the soldiers, sensing Challe's and Delouvrier's indecision, were fraternising with the activists, in what de Gaulle termed a "scandalous fun-fair" (*kermesse*).

This was, of course, the kind of situation that de Gaulle – *l'homme des tempêtes* – particularly relished. All round him were doubters and disapprovers. Although his fidelity to the general was infinite, Michel Debré was tortured by intellectual doubts and moral scruples. Guillaumat was pessimistic; Cornut-Gentille (Posts and Telegraphs) thought the insurgents should be brought to heel by a blockade, not by force, and criticised de Gaulle's policy, at least by implication; Soustelle criticised it frankly, and passionately defended the French of Algiers.[29] Only Edmond Michelet, the minister of Justice, favoured firmness.

[29] An apparently authentic account of a cabinet meeting and of talks at the Elysée during the crisis appears in Tournoux, *Tragédie*, pp. 349 *et seq.*

At the Elysée Marshal Juin, who was de Gaulle's senior at Saint-Cyr and now, as the only living marshal of France, his hierarchical superior, had a stormy scene with the president and declared: "If you give the order to fire, I shall publicly take position against you."

Throughout de Gaulle remained calm and convinced that in the end the "insurrection of the barricades" would collapse in the face of his authority. But the continued defiance of the activists astonished him. On the 25th in a radio speech he had described the events of the previous day as "an evil blow struck against France"; but the demonstrators took no notice. Now, four days later, he put on his uniform of a brigadier-general and faced the television cameras.

"Frenchmen of Algeria," he said, "how can you doubt that if, one day, the Moslems decided freely and formally that the Algeria of tomorrow must be closely united with France, nothing would give greater joy to the fatherland and to de Gaulle than to see them choose, between this solution and that, the one that would be most French?"

For the past twenty years, he declared, he had incarnated the "national legitimacy", and: "In the last resort, public order will have to be restored."

These powerful words had a delayed effect on the vacillating military and civilian leaders. If Tournoux's precise account is accepted, both Crépin and Delouvrier telephoned from Algiers to try to dissuade de Gaulle from giving orders to fire on the rebels. De Gaulle, however, declared himself ready to use the Foreign Legion, and when Delouvrier protested that blood would flow, de Gaulle exclaimed: "That is just what I want." He added, however: "But you will see, blood will *not* flow. They shout a lot, but they're cowards. . . . Not one of them will move. They're all bawlers."

In the end, no shots were fired. There were fisticuffs between soldiers and demonstrators on 31 January, and after a night of talks the rebels evacuated all their camps. Most of the insurgents were incorporated into the army. Lagaillarde, Susini and other leaders were arrested and flown to Paris for trial. They included the influential editor of the *Echo d'Alger*, Alain de Sérigny. Ortiz slipped through the security cordons and escaped to Spain.

Next day – 2 February 1960 – the National Assembly approved a bill granting the government special powers for one year. On the 5th, de Gaulle reshuffled his cabinet. The two ministers who had opposed his policy – Cornut-Gentille and Soustelle – were out; the first with the president's thanks, the second without a word, although de Gaulle owed him so much. Roger Frey and Pierre Guillaumat both became ministers attached to the Prime Minister's office, with a variety of responsibilities which, in Guillaumat's case, included France's atomic and space programmes. Louis Terrenoire, who before the war had been regional secretary of the Catholic trade unions, became minister of Information, and Pierre Messmer, who had served with the Free French forces, took over the portfolio of the Armed Forces from Guillaumat.

Sweeping changes were now made in Algeria, involving the re-organisation of the police, the disbandment of the territorial units (a kind of home guard), which had sided with the rebels behind the barricades, and especially the dissolution of the Cinquième Bureau for psychological war, which, as de Gaulle knew, had become a centre for subversive activities. Most of the extremist organisations were also declared illegal.

Having, in effect, broken the settlers, de Gaulle now had to break the powerful section of the army that opposed him, either because it sided with the settlers or because it identified the army's Algerian mission with the general struggle against "communism". He did not, however, seek a confrontation which, in the end, was forced on him. Indeed, he hoped to convert the army to his views on the need for change in Algeria, and to this end, between 3 and 5 March 1960, he toured army messes there. In consequence, this journey was immediately dubbed *la tournée des popotes*. De Gaulle used it to talk informally to army officers and to make speeches that were never to be published in full. From de la Gorce's partial quotations, and from other reports then available, it seems that the general gave soldiers to understand that there would be no exclusive negotiations with the Moslem provisional government. The war, he told them, would go on for many long months and it was up to the army to smash the power of the insurgents. In the end, however, the Algerians themselves would have to decide their fate; and their choice would doubtless be an "Algerian Algeria linked with France". As for the French army, it would not continue indefinitely to be in effect a garrison army in colonial territory. Higher things were in store for it, one day.[30]

De Gaulle's words alarmed the army's extremists, since they seemed to confirm that the end result of their endeavours, even if military victory was theirs, would be outside their control. His message, however, was beginning to get through to the FLN, and in March 1960 the leaders

[30] Gorce, pp. 646–7. *See also* Brian Crozier and Gerard Mansell, "France and Algeria", *International Affairs* (London), Vol. 36, No. 3, July 1960. De Gaulle himself (*Renouveau*, p. 92) substantially confirms de la Gorce's fuller account.

of the rebel Willaya IV (fourth military zone in and around Algiers) made contact with the French authorities and declared their interest in negotiations. In total secrecy, General de Gaulle himself advised them that he was prepared to meet their representatives. The meeting took place at the Elysée on the evening of 10 June. With de Gaulle, who was in uniform, were two of his aides, Bernard Tricot (later to become secretary-general at the Elysée) and Colonel Mathon, of the Prime Minister's military secretariat. The Moslems were Si Salah, commander of Willaya IV, and Captain Si Lakhdar. Behind a curtain was an ADC with a sub-machine gun trained on the Algerians.[31] Far though de Gaulle had already travelled towards a meeting of minds with the Moslem nationalists, he was not yet ready to talk politics. He merely told them that the Algerians, including the insurgents, would indeed be free to determine their future, but he ruled out any meeting between French representatives and the captured FLN leader, Ben Bella. He told them, however, that he was about to renew his offer of a cease-fire.[32]

On 14 June in a major speech de Gaulle pledged that "all points of view" (*tendances*) would take part in supervising the proposed referendum on the future of Algeria. He also referred to the "Algerian people". Both phrases alarmed the settlers and army activists, who translated all "*tendances*" as an open invitation to the bomb-throwers of the FLN; and "Algerian people" as recognition in advance of a separate Algerian nation.

In his speech, de Gaulle had invited the FLN to send emissaries to France to find an "honourable end" to the fighting. This time the provisional government responded, and on the 25th two representatives, Ali Boumendjel and Mohammed Ben Yahia, arrived at Melun under safe conduct and with massive security precautions. But if de Gaulle had hoped that the Algerians would agree to lay down their arms and take their chance in a free vote, he was soon disabused. The emissaries demanded direct negotiations between Ferhat Abbas, their provisional Prime Minister, and President de Gaulle; the release of Ben Bella; and freedom to set up an office in France during the proposed negotiations. The French – Roger Moris, secretary-general for Algerian Affairs, and General de Gastines, deputy commander of the Paris military region – retorted that it was out of the question to negotiate with them or to release Ben Bella while murders and ambushes continued. They were ready to talk about arrangements for a cease-fire and self-determination,

[31] Viansson-Ponté, *République*, Vol. I, p. 275.
[32] Gorce, pp. 648–9; De Gaulle, *Renouveau*, pp. 104–5.

and nothing more. After four days of deadlock, the talks were broken off, though courteously.[33]

The Melun meeting coincided with reprisals against the Moslem leaders who had met de Gaulle. Si Lakhdar was seized and murdered by men of Willaya III (Kabylia), and Si Salah was interned by his own men of Willaya IV. He too lost his life when the men guarding him fell into a French ambush on 20 July 1961 – a year later.

If the Melun talks had served a useful purpose, it was that of re-assuring the settlers that de Gaulle was not prepared to discuss Algeria's future with the terrorists. He now pressed on with his gradualist plans. On 18 July 1960 he set up commissions of elected Algerian councillors to lay the ground for the projected reforms under the Constantine Plan. An oratorical silence followed, while the war went on. Then, at a press conference on 5 September, de Gaulle repeated his offer to let "all points of view" take part in the act of self-determination, and his hope that the outcome would be an "Algerian Algeria" linked with France. But he also declared that there could be no negotiations with the insurgents so long as murders went on.

That day the trial opened in Paris of sixteen alleged members of the so-called "Jeanson network" – named after Francis Jeanson, a Sorbonne lecturer – which was said to have collected funds for the FLN and organised escape facilities for deserters from the French army. On the 14th, General Salan, who had been living in Algiers since his retirement, issued a statement on the trial which by implication criticised de Gaulle's policy of self-determination. Summoned to Paris, he was forbidden to return to Algeria. At the end of October he took up residence in Barcelona.

A few days later, on 3 November, another emotive trial began in Paris – that of nineteen men accused of complicity in the barricades affair. The tribunal, though a military one, dealt with them leniently. Colonel Jean Gardes, the former head of the psychological warfare bureau, and the only military man on trial, was acquitted. The civilians were released on probation, and the most active of them, including Lagaillarde and Susini, joined Salan in Spain. From there, Susini in particular organised the terrorist Organisation de l'Armée Secrète (OAS), making clandestine trips to Algeria when the need arose.

In this tense atmosphere, de Gaulle took another calculated step forward. On 4 November, in a speech to the nation, he used for the first time the term "Algerian Republic". Typically, it was used in a context

---

[33] De Gaulle, *Renouveau*, pp. 94–5. De Gaulle wrongly states that the talks started on 20 June and that they lasted nine days.

that denied its existence. He could not, he said, accept the rebel leaders' claim to be "the government of the Algerian Republic, a republic which will one day exist but has never yet existed".[34] But this was a "denial" that implicitly forecast what was being denied, and it was as a forecast that his listeners understood it. To the Moslem insurgents he held out an offer "to take part, without restriction, in the parleys relating to the future consultation, then in the campaign which will take place freely on this subject, and finally on the verification of the ballot, asking simply that there should be agreement to stop killing each other".

It is hard in retrospect to see what else General de Gaulle could have said, given the continued intransigence of the FLN and his determination to rid France of its Algerian burden. But predictably his speech completed the polarisation of the forces involved in the Algerian drama. Activists in Algeria and France set up new fronts for French Algeria which instantly enlisted a mass membership. In Paris Marshal Juin publicly dissociated himself from the policy of "abandoning our Algerian brothers" and solemnly broke "a friendship of fifty years" (with de Gaulle). In Algiers, on Armistice day, OAS groups set off a series of plastic explosions.

On the 16th, however, it was announced in Paris that General de Gaulle had decided to ask the people – in Algeria as well as in France – to decide whether or not self-determination should be offered to Algeria. The Communist party denounced this proposal; and so from Tunis did the Algerian provisional government, which attacked it for denying the Algerian people their right to independence.

The referendum on self-determination was to be held on 8 January 1961. A month earlier de Gaulle made his final visit to Algeria, which lasted from 9 to 13 December. It was a sombre return. Wisely, he had decided to avoid Algiers and Oran, but on the 11th blood was shed in communal clashes in both towns. In other places mainly European audiences heard him in sullen silence; but wherever the Moslems were predominant, he was cheered. In military terms, he noted, the war was virtually over. But the chances of harmony between the two communities seemed slight. More than ever, he was resolved to extricate France from the the trap.

Although more than 40 per cent of the 4,760,000 registered voters

---

[34] According to Viansson-Ponté (*République*, Vol. I, p. 314), the term "Algerian Republic" did not occur in the original text distributed to ministers and recorded by de Gaulle on the morning of 4 November. He decided to insert it, and re-recorded his speech with the change. The revised video-tape was sent to Algiers by air for simultaneous transmission with Paris. Michel Debré, who was in the plane, was told of the change only after take-off, when it was too late to revert to the earlier version.

abstained from the ballot on 8 January, the outcome clearly vindicated de Gaulle's policy. Overall, twenty-one million of the twenty-seven million voters went to the polls, and 76 per cent of them said yes. In Algeria, the percentage was 70.

Negotiations with the FLN now seemed inevitable but they were not going to be easy, and before they could get properly under way de Gaulle was faced with the most serious challenge yet to his authority – this time from four rebellious generals: Challe, Salan, Jouhaud and Zeller. The occasion was unprecedented. Salan's feelings were well known, for he had openly proclaimed them. Edmond Jouhaud, alone among the four, was a *pied-noir*. Heavily built and hot-tempered, he had nevertheless played on the whole a moderating role in the Algiers Committee of Public Safety in 1958. But he was known to favour "integration", and de Gaulle had removed him, much as he had removed Salan, by appointing him to the honorific post of "inspector-general of the Army of the Air".

Another malcontent, with less cause, was André Zeller. He had played no part in the events of 13 May 1958; but, as chief of the general staff of the land army from 1 July that year, he had allowed his office to be used as a meeting place for ultras, some of whom he "placed" in key posts. On his retirement in 1959 he immediately took part in activist politics.[35]

The most surprising participant in the plot was Maurice Challe, but he too had cause for discontent. In December 1958 de Gaulle had appointed him as commander-in-chief in Algeria, to succeed Salan. An airman (like Jouhaud), he had planned the brilliantly executed French airborne landings during the Anglo-French expedition of 1956. He did well in Algeria, and his offensives drastically reduced FLN activities. He had expected to be rewarded by succeeding General Ely as chief of the general staff of National Defence – the highest military post in France. Instead, he was appointed Allied commander-in-chief in Central Europe. This was cause for resentment; so, too, was de Gaulle's anti-NATO policy, of which he disapproved, but which, in his new job, he had to live with. When the plotters asked him to lead the proposed *putsch* in April 1961, he accepted.

The real plotters, in fact, were not the generals, but five colonels, all of them deeply involved since the Indo-China defeat in the "crusade" of the army extremists: Argoud, Broizat, Godard, Gardes and Lacheroy,

---

[35] Jacques Fauvet and Jean Planchais, *La Fronde des Généraux*, pp. 59–62. This remains the best account of "the affair of the generals". Robert Buchard's more "journalistic" book, *Organisation de l'Armée Secrète* (2 vols, henceforth, Buchard), contributes some picturesque details of the preliminary arrangements, however.

all seeing themselves as crusaders in a titanic struggle to save the West from Communism. Generals Challe and Zeller reached Algiers secretly on the evening of 20 April in an aircraft provided by the air force commanders. Jouhaud was already there, and Salan got there three days later in a Spanish plane, having slipped out of his Madrid hotel unseen by his police guard.

Within hours of his arrival Challe had secured the obedience of several regiments of paratroopers. The delegate-general of the government, Jean Morin, had been arrested; and so had the commander-in-chief, General Gambiez, the prefect of Police, René Jannin, and one of de Gaulle's ministers, Robert Buron. The main public buildings had been seized. It was a classic *coup de force*, and the *pronunciamiento* duly followed, on the morning of 22 April. The form of it was an order in seven articles, signed by Challe, Jouhaud, Zeller and the absent Salan. Article 5 was possibly the one that General de Gaulle read with the liveliest interest. It read, in part:

> Those individuals who have taken a direct part in the attempt to abandon Algeria and the Sahara will be placed under arrest and brought before a military tribunal, which will be set up to judge crimes committed against the security of the State. . . .

Radio Algiers announced that the army had taken over control of Algeria, that the *gendarmerie* and Republican riot squads (CRS) had joined in, and that the three generals (Salan was not named) headed the movement.

This, then, was the most daunting challenge so far to de Gaulle's authority. He met it, in keeping with his character, by an inflexible display of personal authority. He despatched his newly appointed minister of State for Algerian Affairs, Louis Joxe, and his new chief of the general staff of National Defence, General Olié, to Algiers, at their great personal risk, within hours of the rebel proclamation, to make dissident middle-rankers repent. He suspended all air and sea transport to Algeria. He proclaimed a state of emergency, and with the support of the required authorities, assumed exceptional powers under Article 16 of the constitution.

As at the time of the affair of the barricades, some of de Gaulle's ministers panicked. To one of them, he barked: "Stop whining!" With heavy irony, he asked his team: "Do you think I should leave now, or only when the paratroopers arrive?"[36] What astonished de Gaulle was that Challe, whose military prowess he admired, should have done this

[36] Tournoux, *Tragédie*, p. 376.

thing, and that the four generals should have dared to defy him. His ministers might panic, but he stayed calm, secure in the belief that Challe would lose his nerve, and in the knowledge that his usual weapon – radio and television – would turn the tables in his favour. And so it turned out. It was announced that the general would go on the air at 8 p.m. on 23 April, and the announcement alone was a blow in the war of nerves, for on one side of the Mediterranean anticipation strengthened the faint of heart, while on the other it weakened resolve. As in January 1960, de Gaulle appeared on the screen in his uniform of a two-star general, outranked by the men who defied him but a visible reminder of the traditions of military authority and obedience.

An insurrectional power [he said] has established itself in Algeria by a military *pronunciamiento*. Those guilty of the usurpation have exploited the passions of the *cadres* of certain specialised units, the inflamed adherence of a part of the population of European extraction, led astray by fears and myths, and the powerlessness of the authorities submerged by the military conspiracy.

In appearance, this power consists of a quadroon[37] of retired generals. In reality it is in the hands of a group of partisan, ambitious and fanatical officers. . . . But they see and understand the nation and the world as distorted by their frenzy. Their undertaking is leading straight to a national disaster. . . .

Referring to this "odious and stupid adventure", he went on:

Thus the State is flouted, the nation defied, our power shaken, our international prestige reduced, our place and our role in Africa compromised. And by whom? Alas! alas! by men whose duty, honour and *raison d'être* are to serve and to obey.

In the name of France, I order that all means, I repeat all means, be used to bar the way everywhere to these men, until they are brought down.

He forbade all Frenchmen to carry out orders given by the rebels. He threatened the "usurpers" with the full rigour of the law. He invoked the "French and republican legitimacy which the nation has conferred on me, which I shall maintain, whatever happens, until the term of my mandate or until I lose my strength or my life". And he ended, as so often, with the incantatory appeal: "Frenchwomen, Frenchmen! Help me!"

[37] The word de Gaulle used, improperly but with pejorative intent, was "*quarteron*", which has precisely the same meaning as "quarteroon" or "quadroon" in English, and is just as meaningless in de Gaulle's usage.

Later that evening, an agitated Debré also broadcast over the national network, but in quite another vein. Information had reached the French government that the rebels were planning to land some 1,500 paratroopers on one of the airfields near Paris. The Prime Minister now appealed to the people of the capital to go to the airfield and talk the paratroopers out of their folly. Since it was unlikely that fanatical paratroopers would listen to the voice of popular reason, some sought another meaning to this jittery injunction and thought they had found it in the fact that hundreds of thousands of Parisians, on foot, on bicycles or in their cars, would have so jammed the approaches to the capital that even if the paratroopers had landed, they would have got bogged down in the human mass.

But they never did land. De Gaulle's magic had worked again, as he knew it would. The rebellion began to lose impetus on the 24th. On the 25th many serving officers who had sided with Challe decided that they had been mistaken. That afternoon Challe himself made up his mind to stop the revolt. Next morning he gave himself up. Zeller, who had fled in civilian clothes, followed suit a few days later. Salan and Jouhaud, however, together with Godard and other OAS colonels, went underground to continue the struggle.

Fearing a repetition of the lenient treatment that had been given to the insurgents of January 1960, de Gaulle set up a new Higher Military Tribunal under Article 16 of the constitution, to try the rebel leaders and those who had followed them. On 29 April Joxe and Olié, who had returned to Algiers to complete the suppression, announced that nearly 200 officers had been arrested, 140 civilian officials suspended and – in the Algiers region alone – 160 civilians arrested or interned. All Algiers newspapers were suspended. In metropolitan France, too, there were numerous arrests and searches.

Brought to trial at the end of May, Challe and Zeller were both sentenced to fifteen years' imprisonment and stripped of rank and honours. Salan and Jouhaud were condemned to death *in absentia*; and so were the plotting colonels – Argoud, Broizat, Gardes, Godard and Lacheroy.

Shortly after the generals had been brought to trial, de Gaulle faced a challenge of another kind in Tunisia, and reacted to it with ruthless despatch. It was more than a challenge, indeed: a rash act of defiance on the part of the Tunisian president, Habib Bourguiba. Rashness was not normally associated with Bourguiba, who had won his country's independence of French rule – on 1 June 1956 – by gradualist tactics. Since the Algerian provisional government was quartered in Tunis he was, however, in a delicate position. In 1958 he had negotiated a phased withdrawal of French troops from Tunisia, which was completed on 11 October. But the great air-naval base at Bizerta remained in French hands. The memory of the French bombing of Sakhiet in February 1958 inhibited Bourguiba from taking provocative action. Moreover, he admired de Gaulle, was aware of the general's difficulties with his army, and wanted to avoid doing anything that might prejudice an Algerian settlement.

Bourguiba had never met de Gaulle until, on 27 February 1961, he was the French president's guest at Rambouillet. The Algerian war was discussed, and so was Bizerta. Bourguiba emerged elated in the belief that de Gaulle had made a promise to evacuate Bizerta; but de Gaulle almost certainly had merely made one of his sibylline utterances.

Towards the end of June, the French began extending the runway of the main Bizerta airstrip, for use by the new Mystère jet fighters. Tunisia's ruling party, the Néo-Destour, found this provocative, and on 4 July declared that priority would be given to "the evacuation and liquidation of the Bizerta military base". On the 6th, Bourguiba wrote to de Gaulle, re-stating an earlier claim to a strip of Algerian territory, and calling for the evacuation of Bizerta. That day, mass demonstrations against the French presence there began throughout Tunisia. After angry diplomatic exchanges, Bourguiba told the National Assembly that a blockade of Bizerta would begin on the 19th. On the 18th, a French note was delivered: there could be no negotiations under threat, it said, and Bourguiba was warned of the consequences of the action he was proposing to take. At 2.15 p.m. on the 19th, Tunisian National Guards armed with rifles fired on a French helicopter. Next day French troops opened fire on Tunisian demonstrators, then attacked the Tunisian barricades, with support from rocket air raids and naval shelling. At the end of that day the French had lost five men, but the Tunisians could count 110 dead and 500 wounded.

On the 21st, after the Tunisians had rejected a French ultimatum, French bombers struck at military targets. At 2 p.m. the dreaded *paras* launched an attack on the Tunisian barracks, advancing against desperate resistance. At 11.30 p.m. the French announced that Bizerta had fallen; the streets were littered with the bodies of men, women and children machine-gunned by the invaders. Next day, the French mortared the medieval Arab Casbah where the defenders had retreated. In all, 1,300 Tunisians had been killed and 639 taken prisoner. The French had lost only 21 dead and 101 wounded.

The Tunisians, strictly speaking, had been the aggressors. For this, General de Gaulle had taught them the kind of lesson it was impossible for him to teach the Algerians or his own French rebels. In this context, at any rate, Gaullian France remained a great power.

De Gaulle's victory in his confrontation with a major section of the army was not, as many supposed at the time, the last battle in the new war the OAS had declared against his State, but the first. There was never again, however, to be so direct a clash, or one at that level of eminence. Instead, a campaign of attrition began in which, for a while, the Secret Army scored its atrocious points at will, causing pain and shedding blood with ruthless abandon. To understand why in the end it failed, one may first ask what these desperate men were trying to achieve, or rather to prevent. Their strategic aims were plain: to oust de Gaulle by paralysing the State; to keep Algeria French and thus deny its territory to Soviet Communism. ("Do you want Mers-el-Kébir and Algiers to become Soviet bases tomorrow?" Challe had asked in his broadcast on 22 April.) For these were the theoreticians of counter-revolution, those who knew, or thought they knew, the secrets and cure of revolutionary war. In their apprehension of Soviet strategic interest in Mediterranean bases they were displaying, as time showed, a certain prescience, even if their equation of Algerian nationalism with international Communism was simplistic.

To the ends described, they devised tactics of great ferocity: the murder of "traitors", or of mere servants of the regime: destruction of property; outrages against the Moslems designed to provoke a mass uprising that would force army reprisals and wreck any negotiations with the FLN; and the assassination of General de Gaulle himself.

There were at least four plots against the general's life: in September 1961, and in May, June and August 1962. The first and last reached the stage of execution, but failed, the first through a technical hitch, the last by a kind of miracle; the other plots were uncovered before the arrangements were complete. In the first, the conspirators had hidden 90 lb of explosive plastic in a gas cylinder which also contained butane gas, and a petrol can containing petrol, oil and soap flakes under a heap of sand beside the road from Paris to Colombey. On the night of 8 September 1961, as the president's car passed the spot, a sheet of flame suddenly enveloped it. But the plastic failed to explode. On 22 August 1962, a group of men opened fire on the presidential car from a yellow shooting-brake on the side of the road, as he was being driven to the military airfield at Villacoublay. The chauffeur accelerated, but a hundred yards further on another group fired from a blue car in a side street. About a hundred and fifty shots were fired in all, of which fourteen hit de Gaulle's massive, custom-built Citroën; one, which broke the rear window, passed within inches of de Gaulle's head, and two others hit, but without puncturing, the bullet-proof tyres. "And yet," wrote de Gaulle, "– incredible luck! – none of us was hit. May de Gaulle then continue to follow his path and his vocation!"[38]

The plot which had so narrowly failed was organised by Lieutenant-Colonel Jean-Marie Bastien-Thiry, aged thirty-five, one of France's leading experts on guided missiles. Happily married and the father of three daughters, he disdained plentiful chances of escape and stayed at home awaiting his arrest, which came on 15 September. He then made a full and remarkable confession. A practising Catholic, he invoked St Thomas Aquinas in sanction for his attempted "tyrannicide", and cited von Stauffenberg's attempt to assassinate Hitler as a precedent. In his eyes, de Gaulle was Satan and anti-Christ, and it was his duty to remove the tyrant. He described the attempted assassination with cool detachment, referring to it simply as "the problem".

Was he insane? Three years earlier he had spent a short period in a mental clinic, with nervous depression. But at his insistence the defence did not plead insanity; and indeed he appeared to be fully aware of what he had done and why. Far from wanting to be reprieved, he hoped with all his being for a death sentence. By a majority of three to two, the judges met his wish.

It was generally assumed that de Gaulle would exercise his prerogative of mercy, and at first this seems to have been his intention. However, on reading the transcript of the trial, in which the accused went out of his way to claim conscious responsibility for his acts, the general changed his mind. Thereupon, say witnesses, a great serenity came over Bastien-Thiry, who passed his remaining time in prayer; and died with his rosary in hand. It was 11 March 1963.

Why did de Gaulle, who had pardoned so many others in their time, deny a reprieve to Bastien-Thiry? Not, it is certain, because he himself was to have been murdered. Tournoux is probably right when he avers that de Gaulle had understood the younger man: to have condemned him to live out his life would have been the worse punishment, for it would have deprived him of the aura of martyrdom which he sought.

"The French need martyrs," confided de Gaulle to a friend. "They should choose them well. I could have given them one of those idiot

38 De Gaulle, *Renouveau*, p. 138.

generals. I gave them Bastien-Thiry. They can make a martyr of him, if they want to, when I'm gone. He deserves it."[39]

Long before de Gaulle's death, however, Bastien-Thiry's name had been elevated to sainthood and martyrdom by those who hated the general.

By the time of Bastien-Thiry's execution, the OAS – to which he did not belong, although it had helped him recruit his assassination squad – had spent itself. But from the late spring of 1961 until the end of June 1962 it committed many sanguinary excesses, often in competition with the FLN, whose military weakness in the countryside coincided with a revival of urban terrorism. According to de Gaulle, the rat-hunts (*ratonnades*) of the OAS in the Moslem quarters of Algerian towns resulted in 12,000 deaths of men, women and children. In addition, several hundred police, *gendarmes* and CRS, and about thirty officials, were killed or wounded. In metropolitan France there were about a thousand plastic explosions.[40]

Against this background, de Gaulle's representatives negotiated Algeria's future with the FLN. A first round of talks began on 20 May 1961 at Evian, whose mayor, Camille Blanc, had been murdered by an OAS explosion on 31 March. A second round began on 7 March 1962, also at Evian, and resulted on the 18th in a cease-fire and agreements on Franco-Algerian cooperation, after self-determination through a referendum.

In Algeria, after a "scorched earth" policy that seemed devised to leave the country as the French had found it in 1830, the OAS suddenly changed course and sought to negotiate a separate deal with the FLN. On 17 June agreement was reached between the deputy-premier of the Algerian provisional government, Belkacem Krim (the chief negotiator at Evian), and Jean-Jacques Susini for the OAS. There was to be an amnesty on both sides; Europeans were to be allowed to join the local security forces, and the OAS would call off its terrorism and encourage the Europeans to stay in Algeria.

The FLN having also banned all demonstrations, there was complete order when the referendum was held. Of the electorate of six and a half million, 91.8 per cent went to the polls; and of those who did, 99.7 voted yes to Algerian independence.

---

[39] Tournoux, *Tragédie*, p. 454. The account of the Bastien-Thiry case is one of the most striking things in Tournoux's book, which also reproduces his confession in full, together with reports of the physicians and psychiatrists who examined him. De Gaulle does not mention the case; Gorce (p. 678) says de Gaulle wanted to make an example of Bastien-Thiry.
[40] De Gaulle, *Renouveau*, p. 129; see also p. 135.

The Krim-Susini agreement, however, was a dead letter. Within a few weeks of independence, more than 800,000 of Algeria's 900,000 Europeans had sought refuge in France. And within three months, some 10,000 of the Moslems who had served in the French army had been massacred by the new masters of Algeria.[41]

In France, meanwhile, de Gaulle had completed his punishment of the "quadroon" of generals who had defied him in April 1961. On 25 March Jouhaud was arrested in Oran and flown to Paris for trial. Salan, in turn, was seized in Algiers on 20 April. By a quirk of the Higher Military Tribunal, however, Jouhaud was condemned to death, but Salan only to life imprisonment. It is clear from de Gaulle's memoirs that he thought both men deserved to be executed. It was, however, unthinkable to allow the relatively junior Jouhaud to be executed if Salan, his superior, was to escape. Rather unwillingly, de Gaulle accepted the argument to that effect presented by Georges Pompidou, who by that time had succeeded Debré as Prime Minister, and of the minister of Justice, Jean Foyer. Both generals therefore kept their lives.

In the end, then, de Gaulle had managed, though at frightful cost, to decolonise Algeria, against his initial desires and in the face of passionate resistance from many of his countrymen. He had broken the internal resistance within the army and freed it to be the instrument, as he planned, of the policy of grandeur which had always been his dream.

[41] For a full and fair account of the Franco-Algerian negotiations, see D. Pickles, *Algeria and France: from Colonialism to Cooperation* (1963). For the story of the secret pre-negotiations, see Brian Crozier, *The Masters of Power* (1969), pp. 38–43 (henceforth, Crozier, *Power*). The Krim-Susini negotiations are described in the same author's *The Morning After* (1963), pp. 108–13; and the massacre of the pro-French Moslems is dealt with in Allais.

Chapter 2 ⚜ The Atlantic Directorate Affair

When de Gaulle returned to power, he was sixty-seven and felt his age. He confided his fears to his personal physician, Dr Lipchwitz, and others. "I've come back ten years too late. . . ." To René Pleven and other Companions of the Liberation, he remarked: "I'm the man of 1940. In reality, I'm twenty years too old to face up to destiny." Their reassurances failed to console him, although they pointed out that some foreign statesmen were even older.[1] One man, however, did reassure him: Dr Adenauer, the West German chancellor. When the two men first met at Colombey in September 1958, Adenauer pointed out that he was fourteen years older than de Gaulle, and told him that in his view, there was an "age barrier" a man could cross, much as a pilot crashes through the sound barrier. Once this had happened, said the chancellor, one could go on indefinitely. For the next few weeks, de Gaulle, delighted, told everybody he met: "I've crossed the age barrier. I can go on indefinitely."

In fact, although he could not know it for certain, he had twelve years of life left and eleven of political power. Enough, by his own reckoning, to do some of the things he had hoped to do. In a historical, as distinct from a personal, sense, however, he had achieved supreme power too late to play in France's name the dominant role to which he had always aspired; too late, perhaps, by fifty years or so. Not only did the current facts of international power out-date his grandiose schemes and concepts, but he had in addition to face the dreadful problem of Algeria, which, while it lasted, blocked the roads he aspired to follow.

Despite his age and the continuing Algerian crisis, however, de Gaulle lost no time in staking France's claim to a share in world leadership. His principal foreign policy aim was to break the American hegemony in the western alliance. This objective, amounting almost to an obsession, underlay the famous but abortive memorandum he addressed to President

[1] Tournoux, *Tragédie*, p. 295.

Eisenhower and the British Prime Minister, Mr Macmillan, on 17 September 1958, proposing the creation of a three-power directorate of the alliance. The memorandum, in effect, was a statement of de Gaulle's optimum hopes. Had it been accepted, he would have achieved his principal aim at one stroke. It is unlikely that the general ever expected so simple an outcome, and indeed, as if to anticipate a refusal, his memorandum contained a veiled, but unmistakable threat of non-cooperation with NATO in that event.

To have accepted General de Gaulle's request would have amounted in American eyes to conferring super-power status on a country that lacked the essential qualification: the possession of nuclear weapons. De Gaulle, who well understood this, therefore let it be known that France was a willing buyer of such weapons, but only on the condition that once acquired they would be under France's sole and sovereign control. Failing that, and in any event, France was going to become an atomic power in her own right and by her own efforts, whether or not aid and advice were forthcoming.

Anticipating non-cooperation on the part of France's major allies, de Gaulle was resolved if not to break the American hegemony, then at least to restore France's independence as he conceived it; and with it, if this proved possible, to establish France's leadership of western Europe, and consolidate her influence in the Third World. In practice, this meant a gradual withdrawal of France from NATO; a determined attempt to take advantage of France's membership of the European Economic Community and of her veto under the treaty of Rome, to wean West Germany away from dependence on the United States, in favour of French leadership and support; and a deliberate closing of the European door on Britain until such time as the British should learn the error of their ways and sever their "special relationship" with the Americans.[2]

In the event, only those parts of the plan that lay strictly within France's power – withdrawal from NATO, keeping Britain out of "Europe", and retaining, at great financial cost, the support of the former dependencies in Africa – were realised. De Gaulle did establish a measure of ascendancy over Dr Adenauer, but not over his successors, and he

---

[2] In his incomplete *Mémoires d'Espoir*, de Gaulle did not spell out his intentions with such candour. He explains, not untruthfully, that he based his European policy on reconciliation between France and Germany, expresses doubts about the genuineness of Macmillan's "Europeanness" and affirms France's determination to resist supranational integration, whether in Europe or in NATO. He defines his Russian policy as the quest for "*détente*, then *entente* and cooperation", with similar intentions in regard to China; all this under cover of "a nuclear power such that none should be able to attack us without risking frightful wounds" (*Renouveau*, p. 214, and the chapters entitled "Europe" and "The World", taken as a whole).

failed to persuade the Germans to drop the Americans in France's favour. Similarly, he kept the British out of the European common market, but did not dent the "special relationship". His foreign policy achievements, in short, were mainly negative; against this, he did succeed in making France the third possessor of nuclear weapons, but not in persuading the Americans to take France's nuclear credentials seriously enough to accept his proposed triumvirate of western power.

It is perhaps not sufficiently understood, even today, that although de Gaulle followed his ideas on NATO through to their logical conclusion, he was not the first to express French misgivings on France's place in the western alliance. There had been frequent expressions of French dissatisfaction over the years, mainly on the grounds that France could not rely on support from her allies in overseas questions, such as Algeria and other colonial problems, or the Suez expedition.[3] De Gaulle himself had frequently, while out of power, called for greater French responsibilities within the alliance, and hinted in private that France might leave NATO if he returned.

When de Gaulle returned to power, memories of his wartime intransigence were still lively, and his speeches and even his private comments had gained wide currency. Not unnaturally, France's allies soon sought to find out how they now stood with him. The first was Macmillan, who had talks with de Gaulle at the Hôtel Matignon on 29 and 30 June 1958. France, the general said in substance, wanted a western atomic standing group in which control would be shared by the principal western powers. She would share in any decisions to use nuclear weapons. What was needed, he argued, was a world organisation directed by America, Britain and France. NATO itself should be given wider geographical limits and have changes in its command structure – a reference to the complaint, frequently made by past French governments, that key jobs in NATO were virtually controlled by the Americans and British. In any event, de Gaulle told the Prime Minister, France was determined

[3] For instance, Félix Gaillard, who fell in consequence of the bombing of the Tunisian village of Sakhiet, declared in the presence of the American ambassador and before the Franco-American Association on 4 December 1957: "If the Atlantic Alliance had only a local character ... and if outside a specified frontier Allied interests were in conflict or were ignored, it would be particularly grave, especially for France and Britain." Several years earlier – in February 1953 – Bidault, then Foreign minister, told his British colleague, Sir Anthony Eden, in private conversation that one of the principal arguments against French participation in the European Defence Community was that France would "lose the basis of her present satisfactory relationship with the United Kingdom and the United States". By this he meant that within the EDC France's status would be no greater than, for instance, Germany's. He proposed to meet this objection by placing the alliance under the control and direction of "a tripartite political group". (Private information.) In effect, then, Pidault's thinking anticipated de Gaulle's 1958 memorandum by five years.

to have atomic weapons even if they were produced by other countries. Macmillan's reply is not recorded in his own account of the meeting.[4] It would be consistent with what is now known of his general readiness to help de Gaulle, however, if he had pointed out to the general that he would stand no chance of qualifying for American assistance under the Atomic Energy Act unless he first went ahead and tested a French bomb.

Almost immediately after Macmillan had gone, the American secretary of State, John Foster Dulles, turned up in Paris. Franco-American exchanges at the Quai d'Orsay had suggested that his willingness or otherwise to cooperate with France in the atomic field would determine the success of his visit, which took place on 5 July. By this token, it was a failure. Dulles, speaking with some emotion, evoked America's friendship with France and appealed for French participation in the European security system. Within that system, the U.S. was, he declared, ready to provide atomic arms for France and thus save the French the enormous expense of producing their own. The important thing was to break Soviet imperialism and with it Communism's ambition to dominate the world.

De Gaulle, agreeing that preparations against a possible Soviet aggression must be made, thought it highly unlikely. Should it take place, of course, France would without doubt be at the side of the United States. But the "Russian fact" was at least as important as the "Communist fact", and Russia was interested in détente and peace. France, too, would work towards détente while preparing for the worst. But a France without world responsibilities was without value:

> That is why she does not approve of NATO, which does not give her her proper share in decision-making and which limits itself to Europe. That is also why she is to provide herself with an atomic armament. That way, our defence and our policy can be independent, which is what we want above all else. If you agree to sell us bombs, we shall willingly buy them, so long as they belong to us entirely and without restrictions.

Dulles, says de Gaulle, left it at that and took his leave.[5]

Although de Gaulle does not record the fact, the situation in the Lebanon was also discussed during Dulles's visit.[6] The point at issue was

[4] Harold Macmillan, Riding the Storm, 1956–9, pp. 446 et seq. (henceforth, Macmillan, Storm).
[5] De Gaulle, Renouveau, pp. 220–1.
[6] See David Schoenbrun, The Three lives of Charles de Gaulle, pp. 278 et seq. (henceforth, Schoenbrun, Lives).

whether France should participate in any western intervention in that country, in which a virtual civil war had developed since May. President Chamoun of the Lebanon thought the French should take part; so did the Pflimlin government when the crisis first broke; and so in turn did General de Gaulle. The British and Americans, however, strongly opposed French participation, on the ground that it would provoke excessive hostility among Arab countries, especially Jordan and Iraq – both at that time friendly to Britain and the U.S. (although the Iraqi monarchy was shortly to be overthrown by Abdel Qarim Qassim, who took his country out of the Baghdad Pact) – because of France's war against the Algerian revolutionaries. In the event, French participation was confined to sending French warships to patrol off Beirut – a gesture which de Gaulle, in his memoirs, presents as a deliberate decision to act separately from the Anglo-Saxons, without hinting that he would have preferred to act with them.[7] Later, the French were to complain that they had not been consulted about or even informed of the American landing. But it is clear from George Ball's account of the 5 July conversation that the subject was discussed between Dulles and de Gaulle.[8]

De Gaulle, then, had left the British and Americans in no doubt over his attitude to NATO, of his proposed "solution" to the problem of consultation, or of his intention to "go it alone" should he fail to get his way. The memorandum dated 17 September 1958 and addressed a week later to President Eisenhower and Macmillan cannot, therefore, have come as a surprise. There is a difference, however, between a statesman's expression of his views in private conversation, and their embodiment in a formal communication, since at that point they become public policy and cannot be ignored by recipients.

In his memorandum, then, de Gaulle asserted that "the present organisation of the western alliance no longer answers the essential security requirements of the free world as a whole". Risks were shared, but decision-making was not. The area of operations of the Atlantic Alliance no longer corresponded to political and strategic realities. For instance, events in the Middle East and Africa were of direct interest to Europe. French responsibilities extended to Africa, the Indian Ocean and the Pacific, as did those of Great Britain and the United States. The increasing range of ships, aircraft and missiles made the military assumptions of NATO obsolete. Equally, the assumption that the United States would keep its initial monopoly of atomic weapons had ceased to be valid, and the delegation to Washington of decisions on

[7] De Gaulle, *Renouveau*, p. 217.
[8] George W. Ball, *The Discipline of Power*, p. 129 (henceforth, Ball).

defence could no longer be justified. The French government therefore proposed that

> political and strategic questions of world importance should be en-trusted to a new body, consisting of the United States of America, Great Britain and France. This body should have the responsibility of taking joint decisions on all political matters affecting world security, and of drawing up, and if necessary putting into action, strategic plans, especially those involving the use of nuclear weapons. It should also be responsible for the organisation of the defence, where appropriate, of individual operational regions, such as the Arctic, the Atlantic, the Pacific and the Indian Ocean. These regions could in turn be subdivided if necessary.

There followed the veiled but unmistakable threat: "The French government regards such an organisation for security as indispensable. Henceforth the whole development of its present participation in NATO is predicated on this." Finally, de Gaulle proposed the "earliest possible consultations" between the three governments concerned, initially through the embassies and the standing group of Big-Three ambassadors in Washington.

Though forewarned of General de Gaulle's ideas, Eisenhower and Macmillan were embarrassed by his memorandum. Playing for time, and hoping to delay as long as possible any formal discussions on the substance of the general's proposals, British and American diplomats repeatedly pressed the French for clarifications over the next few weeks. In fact, their purport was plain enough, and in both London and Washington it was quickly agreed that they had to be rejected. Nor were the reasons exclusively confined, as de Gaulle may have thought, to the natural jealousy of the "Anglo-Saxons" at the idea of a French intrusion into their closed and privileged world. Both the British and the Americans, but especially the latter, feared repercussions within the alliance, particularly among the Germans. The Anglo-American special relationship was tacitly accepted because it had grown naturally out of history, language and the common possession of nuclear weapons. Even the Germans accepted it, since they themselves were forbidden to manu-facture or possess atomic weapons under the allied dispositions that restored, in other respects, their sovereignty. But it would be quite a different matter if, at French initiative, a new and privileged group were to be created, to which the alliance as a whole was to be subordinated; for in that event, those outside the group, including West Germany, would have no more than second-class status. As always, divided

Germany was central to allied preoccupations in Europe. If tripartism, Gaullist style, were set up, wouldn't Adenauer and his people draw the conclusion that his policies of cooperation with the West had failed, and seek an accommodation with Russia?

Then again, Dulles was worried about reactions from the Third World once it was known that NATO's sphere of interest was to be extended to non-European countries. Selwyn Lloyd, for Britain, saw this problem mainly in terms of the Commonwealth. He and Macmillan were worried, too, as were their officials, lest tripartism should so dilute the special relationship that it would cease to mean anything. Then there was the technical obstacle of the modified Atomic Energy Act; how "substantial" would France's progress in her autonomous atomic weaponry programme have to be to qualify for Congressional approval for U.S. aid in this field, let alone for the authority to allow a foreign power to share in the decision to use nuclear weapons? A final argument concerned French intentions and the durability of de Gaulle's regime. Although the general's memorandum indirectly threatened France's withdrawal from NATO, it was felt in London and Washington that de Gaulle could not, in the existing climate of cold war, go far in the direction of a truly neutralist foreign policy. Nor could there be any certainty, in the tense early months of his return, that he would remain in power long enough to matter. The temptation to discount his threat and call his bluff was therefore strong.

All told, these arguments ruled out any acceptance of the general's proposals. But it was realised, at least in London, that they had to be taken seriously and that some attempt must be made to meet his wishes, without jeopardising essential interests.[9] The irony of the situation was not lost on senior officials: for years everybody had lamented the lack of leadership in France, and it was felt that it would be invidious to be too openly resentful of the leadership now so plainly manifesting itself.

Evasiveness, therefore, was the course chosen. Early in October 1958 Macmillan and Eisenhower both sent acknowledgements to General de Gaulle, saying that it was not possible to answer his proposals immediately, since they raised such important issues. The British and Americans, however, disagreed on the best way to handle de Gaulle. Dulles called the British ambassador, Sir Harold Caccia, to the State Department on 17 October, to say he had decided to reject the general's suggestion of tripartite talks on the grounds that they would falsely give NATO the impression that the three powers wanted to settle world affairs on their own. Instead, he would invite the French to exploratory bilateral talks.[10]

[9] Private information.   [10] Private information.

This was not the way the British wanted to go about it, for Britain was at that time engaged in delicate discussions with the French, and other Europeans, on the British proposal for a European Free Trade Area. It was therefore important not to drive de Gaulle away from the British into a position in which he would place all his faith upon a community of the Six. Since the substance of de Gaulle's proposals was going to be rejected anyway, it was all the more important to concede the form of his request for tripartite talks.

In the event, the British view prevailed. On the 21st, unenthusiastic replies from the American president and the British premier were sent to de Gaulle. They were not identical, and the president's was the more discouraging. While ready to explore ways of improving the alliance, he saw "very serious problems" in any effort to extend the coverage of the North Atlantic Treaty; moreover, he thought consultation on areas beyond Europe had, in any case, been greatly extended in recent times. Macmillan thanked de Gaulle for drawing attention to problems within the alliance, but sought clarification on two points. Was the proposed new tripartite body to operate on the principle of unanimity – that is, with a veto for each member? And would it replace some of NATO's functions or would NATO "continue in a subordinate role alongside other regional organisations"? Since the answers to both questions were plain enough and had already emerged from diplomatic soundings, Macmillan's reply was part of the exercise of gaining time.

De Gaulle, meanwhile, had had two meetings with Konrad Adenauer, whose approval of his policies, either overt or more likely tacit, was necessary to him. The first meeting took place on 14 and 15 September 1958, at Colombey-les-deux-Eglises, which de Gaulle chose in preference to more formal places in Paris as a sign of his desire to offer personal friendship and courtesy to the German leader.[11] Essentially, the conversations between the two men, which de Gaulle reports at length, amounted to a declaration of intent on both sides to make a fresh start in Franco-German relations, on a basis of reconciliation and complementary needs and talents. De Gaulle told Adenauer of his intention to take France out of NATO, some day or other, as she would soon have nuclear weapons and there could be no question of military integration once this happened. But he said nothing about his then impending decision to propose an Atlantic directorate from which Germany would be excluded.

Adenauer therefore had cause for grave offence on learning of de Gaulle's initiative – as he did when the memorandum was delivered to

[11] De Gaulle, *Renouveau*, p. 184.

Macmillan and Eisenhower, the Quai d'Orsay having given the West German ambassador a summary of it on 24 September. The chancellor is said to have reacted "most splenetically, with the cold rage and frustration of the deceived".[12] When Macmillan visited Bonn on 8 October, he heard Adenauer angrily denounce de Gaulle, and calmed him down with recollections of the general as he had known him in wartime. He declined, very properly, to give Adenauer a copy of the memorandum.[13]

Despite this anger, the general had, in a deeper way, conquered the chancellor, who at their first meeting did not trouble to hide his admiration. Moreover, Adenauer had sincerely decided that reconciliation with France must become a firm principle of West German foreign policy. In conjunction, these private and official sentiments sufficed to overcome his resentment, and a return meeting took place at Bad Kreuznach on 26 November. With de Gaulle were his premier, Michel Debré, and his Foreign minister, Couve de Murville. On the German side, the deputy chancellor and Economics minister, Ludwig Erhard, was present, and so was the Foreign minister, Heinrich von Brentano. For this was a working meeting, designed to give practical expression to the new Franco-German friendship. De Gaulle, who had been reticent at Colombey about the British proposals for a free trade area,[14] now frankly expressed his unalterable opposition to them, on the ground that they would dilute the exclusive club of the Six by opening it first to England and then the rest of the West. It was agreed that on the EEC side the negotiations should now be broken off. In return, de Gaulle gave Adenauer a reassurance that France would oppose any change in the status of West Berlin, as being advocated at the time by Nikita Khrushchev.[15] De Gaulle's tripartite proposals, by then known to the Germans, were apparently not discussed.

On leaving Bad Kreuznach, then, de Gaulle probably felt that, within reason, Adenauer could be persuaded to accept virtually any European or world initiative he might take. Certainly his relations with the German chancellor were closer than with any other foreign statesman, and the general provides quantitative evidence of the fact in his second set of memoirs, recording that between 1958 and mid-1962 the two men met fifteen times, conversed for one hundred hours and exchanged forty letters. There is some independent evidence that these exchanges, especially the tête-à-tête ones, tended at times to be dialogues of the deaf.

---

[12] John Newhouse, De Gaulle and the Anglo-Saxons, pp. 73–4 (henceforth, Newhouse).
[13] Macmillan, Storm, p. 454.   [14] Private information.
[15] De Gaulle, Renouveau, pp. 190–1.

To what extent this reflected the age of the interlocutors, each absorbed in his own thoughts, or the ability of Adenauer to close his mind to things he did not wish to hear, is hard to say.

At all events, by the time of the Bad Kreuznach meeting, de Gaulle knew that neither President Eisenhower nor Harold Macmillan was likely to give him a facile victory. In fact, the tripartite consultations at ambassadorial level, which was the "Anglo-Saxon" device for fobbing him off with less than the substance of what he wanted, were about to begin. They began in Washington on 4 December, and a further meeting took place there on the 10th. The French delegation was led by the ambassador, Hervé Alphand, and the British likewise by Sir Harold Caccia. On the American side, perhaps with needless lack of tact, the head of the team was de Gaulle's wartime *bête noire*, Robert Murphy, who soon confided to Sir Harold his view that it was not going to be easy to spin the talks out for very much longer.[16]

When the American secretary of State next called on de Gaulle, on 15 December 1958, he was greeted with discourteous hostility. Dulles was in Paris for the NATO ministerial meeting; when he called on the president at the Hôtel Matignon, de Gaulle did not, as he had done in July, go to the door to welcome him. When shown into de Gaulle's Louis XVI office, he was faced with a relentless catalogue of French grievances. The United States, he complained, had abstained in a vote in the UN General Assembly on an Afro-Asian resolution demanding independence for Algeria, which had been defeated by only one vote; America had supported Guinea's application for membership of the United Nations, a course which de Gaulle found "inadmissible"; Dulles had opposed the Atlantic directorate idea in a recent meeting with the Italian premier, Amintore Fanfani; four American officials had attended a reception in New York for the Algerian National Liberation Front; moreover, members of the FLN had been granted U.S. visas.[17]

For good measure, de Gaulle is said to have observed that it was unrealistic to be allies in one place and not in another. This was a clear reference to the crisis that began on 27 November 1958 when the Soviet leader, Nikita Khrushchev, gave the western allies six months to get out of West Berlin.[18]

At the 15 December meeting Dulles also told de Gaulle that however

[16] Private information.
[17] Newhouse, p. 81, quoting the Paris Gaullist paper, *Paris-Presse L'Intransigeant*, 17 December 1958. De Gaulle makes no mention of this meeting in his *Mémoires d'Espoir*.
[18] For a full account of the crisis, including de Gaulle's role, *see* Crozier, *Power*, pp. 149 *et seq.*

useful tripartite consultations on individual problems might be, a formal tripartite organisation was impossible. De Gaulle emphatically retorted that an organisation was necessary. He did not, however, reject informal consultations, which continued from time to time.

It was already clear to him, beyond doubt, that his proposals did not stand even a remote chance of acceptance and that he could now, therefore, consider himself free to act as he pleased in respect of NATO. It is possible, and even likely (as Guy de Carmoy suggests), that he put his proposals forward with the object of provoking a refusal, thereby justifying the gradual resumption of France's freedom of action.[19] At all events, he decided, early in 1959, to make the first in a series of spectacular moves marking France's independence of NATO restrictions.

On 6 March, the French government announced that it had decided to withdraw its Mediterranean fleet from NATO control, on the ground that in the event of war, the first concern of the French forces would be to defend the coasts of France and North Africa. But the military rationalisation was less important than the true political motivation, which emerged on the 25th at a press conference in which de Gaulle explained that the restrictions under NATO, from which France had now extricated herself, would have made it impossible for the French to defend their interests in, say, the Middle East, North Africa, Black Africa and the Red Sea. Strictly speaking, this was untrue in that the integration of the French fleet would have applied only in wartime. Indeed, de Gaulle had said the French government would be prepared to cooperate with allied naval forces in wartime. Nor was it true, as he claimed on that occasion, that the zone of NATO action did not extend south of the Mediterranean, since Article 6 of the treaty, inserted at French request at the time of the original negotiations, extended the geographical coverage of the alliance. De Gaulle's announcement on the Mediterranean fleet, which did nothing to improve allied unity, must be seen against this background. On 21 February 1959 Macmillan and Selwyn Lloyd had gone to Moscow in an effort to reduce the international temperature. The news, however, was received without enthusiasm in Bonn and Paris. Later suggestions that President Eisenhower and Khrushchev should meet à deux were also sourly received by de Gaulle, who was credited with telling his entourage that this kind of thing would relieve America's allies of any obligations of solidarity in their dealings with the Soviet Union.

That month – February 1959 – de Gaulle had a third and final visit from Dulles, who was to die three months later. De Gaulle records the

19 De Carmoy, p. 332.

visit in his *Mémoires d'Espoir*,[20] but nothing of what was said. Yet John Newhouse's account of it, based on a conversation with one of Dulles's aides, makes it clear that the secretary of State offered de Gaulle a major concession: in effect, a French veto on American nuclear weapons deployed in continental Europe.[21] The word "veto" does not appear to have been used, but whatever phrase was actually used – "advance authorisation" or some equivalent – meant the same. It seems clear that this was the price Dulles was prepared to pay in return for French cooperation in NATO and probably on the storage of American nuclear weapons on French soil.

True, Dulles's offer fell short of the French veto on America's use of nuclear weapons anywhere that was implicit in de Gaulle's memorandum. But it was so substantial a step in that direction that de Gaulle might have been expected to accept it, or at least to have shown willingness to discuss it, if his original proposals had been sincerely intended. The general, however, did not respond, and Dulles (according to Newhouse) later told his aide that he had not seemed to grasp the significance of what he was offering. If so, it is just possible that an interesting opportunity was missed for linguistic reasons, since the conversation was conducted in French and in a *tête-à-tête*. (Dulles, who had studied at the Sorbonne, did speak French, but not of high quality.) It seems more likely that de Gaulle was taken aback and unwilling to take Dulles's offer seriously. At all events, he made no effort to enquire whether it could be treated as a basis for negotiations with President Eisenhower.

As the history of the next few years shows, indeed, de Gaulle's interest in concessions from his American and British allies was either limited or non-existent: he wanted the whole cake of tripartism, not an occasional slice, however tasty.

In general, the controlled Radio-Diffusion-Télévision Française (RTF) was anti-American in tone; but a friendly note was sounded when Eisenhower was about to visit Paris on 2 and 3 September 1959. Towards the American president himself, as distinct from his country, French radio and television coverage was especially warm, and this fact reflected de Gaulle's own esteem for General Eisenhower as "the most glorious symbol" (as he puts it in *Mémoires d'Espoir*[22]) of Franco-American brotherhood in arms.

De Gaulle himself estimated that a million Parisians turned out to greet "Ike", who was touched by the size as well as the warmth of the

---

[20] De Gaulle, *Renouveau*, p. 221.   [21] Newhouse, pp. 82–3.
[22] De Gaulle, *Renouveau*, p. 222; *see also* pp. 223 *et seq.*

welcome. But propitious though the atmosphere was, there was no yielding on either side when the two men got down to business. De Gaulle's published record of the conversation differs markedly from the account Eisenhower in person sent to Macmillan for his information.[23] The differences are worth mentioning. In de Gaulle's view, the American president was well pleased with the subservience of America's NATO allies. The only things that mattered were the two super-powers and the relations between them; where America led, it was up to other western countries to follow. He was in favour, however, of reaching some sort of agreement with Russia, especially to limit expenditure on armaments. He had sent Vice-President Nixon to Moscow, and Khrushchev would soon be visiting the United States, where Eisenhower hoped he would see something of the American way of life and be able to reflect on the achievements of their respective regimes.

De Gaulle warned Eisenhower against treating East-West relations solely on an ideological basis. Of course Communism weighed heavily on international relations, but would Peter the Great have behaved differently from Stalin in a similar situation after a great war? A technical understanding about armaments was all very well, but the world would still remain divided into two hostile blocs. The only way out of this situation was a gradual improvement in relations between European states and Russia, on a state-to-state basis, so that heavy defence expenditure would come to seem unnecessary. France intended to play her part in this process, and to this end Khrushchev would shortly be invited to visit Paris. He thought Germany could be reunified only in the context of an *entente* of Europe as a whole.

Eisenhower evoked the proposals then current for a summit conference between Russia, America, Britain and France. To this, said de Gaulle, he would raise no objections, but first he wanted to see Khrushchev.

Next Eisenhower turned to NATO and France's role in it. He was worried about the French decision to make atomic weapons, and took up Dulles's earlier offer to provide France with such arms, on condition that the Americans controlled their use through the need for approval by the commander-in-chief of the alliance.

That, said de Gaulle, was precisely why France was going to make her own atomic weapons. Was this not, asked Eisenhower, a sign of distrust of the United States? This rejoinder provoked a lengthy speech from de Gaulle. If Russia attacked France, he said, France and America

---

[23] *See* Dwight D. Eisenhower, *Waging Peace, 1956–1961*, pp. 424–30. My own account complements Eisenhower's here and there.

would be allies. But whereas Russia and America had the means of mutual deterrence, this was not true of France and Russia. How could the French be certain that the U.S. would risk total destruction if France was attacked but not America? Because of this uncertainty, France had to have her own deterrent.

"Why do you doubt that the United States would identify its fate with Europe's?" asked Eisenhower.

And de Gaulle reminded him that during the First World War, American help came only after three years of almost mortal trials; and in the second, only after France had been crushed. Nor was this at all strange. That was why France, although faithful to the alliance, was against integration in NATO. As for harmonising – "if one dares to apply this celestial word to that infernal subject" – the use of French and American bombs, this could be done in the framework of direct cooperation between the three atomic powers which he had proposed.

But surely, the American president objected, given the prohibitive cost of such armaments, France would not be able, by a long way, to reach the Soviet level? In reply de Gaulle gave him the doctrine of the French deterrent in its simplest and purest form: "You know very well that on the scale of megatons, a few rounds of bombs would destroy any country. For our deterrent to be effective, all we need is enough to kill the enemy once, even if he has the means to kill us ten times over."

Thereafter, writes de Gaulle, despite the reproaches and invectives heaped upon him from American quarters, there was never a rupture, or even a quarrel between the two governments. This was one way of describing a gradual deterioration of relations that did, it is true, stop short of an outright break, but only just.

In his letter to Macmillan, Eisenhower put quite a different complexion on his Paris talks. De Gaulle, he wrote, had seemed "satisfied with our discussion regarding the decision to use nuclear weapons. I made the point . . . that unless the situation were one of surprise attack, with bombers overhead, we would of course never unleash the use of nuclear weapons without consulting our principal allies." De Gaulle had said he understood that American legislation would make it difficult to give France assistance with the development of nuclear weapons and he did not want any help in this respect.

Algeria, wrote Eisenhower, received most attention during the talks, but there had been a "relatively brief" consideration of integration, ending in a clear agreement on the idea of "conferring informally among ourselves regarding matters that lie beyond NATO". Eisenhower had mentioned the idea of setting up *ad hoc* staff committees, and de Gaulle had agreed that it would be unwise to establish formal or permanent institutions.[24] Since de Gaulle's memorandum had envisaged a formal tripartite "directorate", it seems improbable that he would have agreed with Eisenhower on the unwisdom of establishing permanent institutions; but in saying that he did, Eisenhower may have wished simply to reassure Macmillan that no such arrangements were contemplated.

The idea of informal consultations was, in fact, to be pressed on de Gaulle, and in his reply to Eisenhower, dated 16 September, Macmillan declared himself in favour of such consultations on both political and military matters. Early in October American sources in Paris were saying that de Gaulle had replied to a later letter from Eisenhower on outstanding NATO issues in "the most amiable terms" but without making the slightest concessions of substance.

Having said what he wanted to say in private, de Gaulle now made two public pronouncements. The first, at the Ecole Militaire on 3 November 1959, was one of the most important speeches he ever made, though a relatively short one. He defended France's right to provide for her autonomous defence as she always had done in history. He denounced integration of the allied forces as having outlived the usefulness it may have had in the crisis that gave birth to NATO, and told the young soldiers in his audience that the great task for the years ahead was to build France's deterrent – the *force de frappe*.

De Gaulle was, of course, addressing the world at large as well as his countrymen; but in a very special sense, that day, he was giving notice to the army that the thankless job it was engaged on in Algeria would not go on forever, and that a higher destiny awaited it.

A week later, at the second of his twice-yearly press conferences, the general stressed the importance of his forthcoming meeting with Khrushchev, as a preliminary to the proposed four-power summit, and declared that France would not join in any proposed ban on nuclear bomb tests. He referred ironically to an attempt in the Political Committee of the United Nations to censure France for its forthcoming test in the Sahara, and asked why the U.N. had not similarly criticised the world's first three nuclear powers for the 200 tests they had conducted hitherto.

The intransigence of de Gaulle's mood was thus in no doubt when the British Prime Minister and the American president conferred with

[24] Private information. Macmillan does not mention this letter, or his reply to it, in *Storm*.

him at Rambouillet on 20 December. The "Anglo-Saxons", agreeing that it was out of the question to offer de Gaulle the full substance of his directorate, now proposed, however, a limited form of tripartism. With Macmillan's prior assent, Eisenhower suggested that a limited form of tripartite machinery be established on a discreet basis. Although this clearly fell short of de Gaulle's own proposals, he did not say no; the precise form of the machinery, however, remained undefined.[25]

In the phase of "limited tripartism" that now opened, Macmillan was generally cast as counsel for de Gaulle's defence, for motives that included sentiment as well as self-interest, since he clearly hoped that de Gaulle would recognise the role he was playing by easing Britain's entry into the EEC. In this, of course, he was disappointed; gratitude was not one of the general's characteristics. Time and again, however, the Americans thought of new reasons for not doing as the Prime Minister suggested. Thus on 30 December 1959 Christian Herter, who had succeeded the late John Foster Dulles as secretary of State, wrote to Selwyn Lloyd and Couve de Murville, the British and French Foreign ministers, proposing that instead of formal machinery, it would be better if representatives of the three countries met from time to time, for instance in private working dinners.

Six weeks later, France was "in business" as an atomic power: her first atomic device was successfully tested at Reggane in the deep desert, on 13 February 1960. On 13 March de Gaulle told the British Prime Minister, when they met at Rambouillet, that he attached the greatest importance to the tripartite arrangements proposed by President Eisenhower, but the Herter suggestions had disappointed him. For groups of officials to meet at dinner was not good enough, although if the ambassadors were present it would be better. But better still would be continuing meetings of the three heads of government. He went on to make his standard attack on the "absurdity" of NATO.

At Rambouillet, de Gaulle, elated by the success of France's first atomic test, sounded the Prime Minister's reactions to the idea of a Franco-British nuclear cooperation. Macmillan answered that he would be in favour, in principle, but that existing arrangements with the United States would create difficulties. De Gaulle took this as a final refusal and deduced that France would have to continue to "go it alone".[26]

---

[25] Private information. Most of the remaining material in this chapter comes from various international private sources; exceptions are indicated.
[26] Maurice Couve de Murville, *Une Politique Etrangère 1958–69*, pp. 64–5 (henceforth, Couve de Murville). The author implies that this was the only time Macmillan and de Gaulle discussed a possible nuclear cooperation between their two countries. But there were further discussions on the subject.

The general's visits to Britain and the United States in April[27] left tripartism where it had been. In this context, indeed, nothing further of consequence happened until 18 May 1960 – the day after the dramatic collapse of the four-power summit meeting in Paris. President Eisenhower, fresh from the discomfiture of the Soviet success in shooting down an American U.2 "spy plane" over Russia, and of Khrushchev's use of the incident to discredit him, observed that the events of the past few days had shown that the three western governments ought to seek ways of communicating with each other that should be both more rapid and more intimate than the existing ones. De Gaulle reminded the president and Prime Minister of his 1958 memorandum, to which, he complained, "little attention has been given". He added that he would be sending them a further communication on the same lines but more precisely phrased.

In a speech on the 31st, de Gaulle analysed the lessons of the collapsed summit meeting, as he saw them. "Our recent trial," he declared, "has demonstrated the profound solidarity of the westerners. Doubtless President Eisenhower, Prime Minister Macmillan and myself each have our problems and our temperaments. But in the face of the events, the three friends that we are had no trouble in reaching agreement in wisdom and firmness." The alliance had emerged as a living reality. But it would be stronger still when France had her own deterrent. And he went on to affirm the need to "build" western Europe.

A few days earlier – on the 25th – the Prime Minister had made proposals of his own for improving co-operation between de Gaulle, Eisenhower and himself. He pointed out that the Foreign ministers of the three powers already met four times a year – at the twice-yearly NATO ministerial councils, at the SEATO council and at the UN General Assembly. But they could do better still, by meeting every two or three months, with an agenda prepared in advance and with the approval of the heads of government. In addition, the heads of government could meet informally from time to time.

On 1 June the three western ambassadors met in Washington in Herter's house: it was the beginning of the kind of limited tripartism which was as far as the Americans wanted to go but which failed to satisfy General de Gaulle. It was to continue, nevertheless, for about eighteen months; but did nothing to reduce the acrimony that was inherent in de Gaulle's deep-seated antagonism towards the western alliance as constituted.

On 10 June de Gaulle, as he had foreshadowed, sent further pro-

[27] These are described in the next chapter.

posals to the Prime Minister and president.[28] He accepted the Macmillan formula of regular meetings of the foreign ministers and less frequent ones of the heads of State or government. All this would strengthen political cooperation, but, he complained, it would do nothing to further the very necessary strategic cooperation, and in default of it, political cooperation lost much of its value. He proposed that strategic questions could be dealt with by the standing group acting outside NATO. In some cases, the three Defence ministers or commanders-in-chief could meet; finally, strategic questions could also be dealt with in the tripartite meetings of heads of State or government.

Predictably, de Gaulle's new communication provoked considerable dissension in London and Washington. In both places, the chief executive was initially inclined to be conciliatory, but was talked into taking a harder line by his officials. In Macmillan's case, the toughest opposition came from the ministry of Defence, but the Foreign Office also had representations to make. Initially, the Prime Minister's inclination was to accept de Gaulle's proposals, on condition that consultation should remain "unobtrusive". In the end, however, he decided, as so often in the history of Anglo-American relations since the Churchill-Roosevelt era, merely to seek the president's views.

Eisenhower, on his side, was at the outset equally conciliatory. The first White House draft reply to de Gaulle, though cautiously worded, was open to the interpretation that the Americans were now prepared to grant most of the general's requests on military tripartism, political tripartism being regarded as almost an accomplished fact. In it Eisenhower had expressed his belief that there were "means of arranging military discussions here which meet the concerns you mention". He was prepared to have military representatives take part in "wide-ranging talks on all subjects of interest to you". An acceptable French representative was General André Beaufre, who had just been appointed France's representative to the NATO standing group. The draft went on to drop hints about some of the things the Americans would like to see resolved, such as the status of fleet commands in the Mediterranean, the integration of defence in western Europe and the stationing of medium-range ballistic missiles.

Even the toned-down American proposals, conveyed to Macmillan in a letter from Eisenhower dated 1 July 1960, went a long way to meeting de Gaulle. The president now proposed military talks in

---

[28] This communication, and subsequent exchanges, are mentioned briefly in *Hearings before the U.S. Senate, 89th Congress, Second Session* (Summer 1966), pp. 501–8, the relevant passages of which are quoted in Newhouse, p. 117. My own account fills out the blanks. *See also* Schoenbrun, *Lives*, pp. 295–7.

Washington by "appropriate military representatives". While this still fell short of global strategic planning in the sense de Gaulle understood it, it was a considerable advance on previous offers. The British were deeply sceptical. Did the Americans really want global strategic discussions? For this was the long-term implication of the new draft. Were they now prepared to accept France as a nuclear power and help her in that capacity? If not, it was reasoned, such open-ended commitments could do more harm than good. On 21 July, Selwyn Lloyd told the Prime Minister he was really worried about allowing the Americans to put forward a proposition which could not be implemented. The British proposed changes in the draft.

In the end, Eisenhower's reply to de Gaulle was delayed until 2 August. It took a harder line in that it asked for concessions on NATO in return for consultations. The United States, said the president, was "prepared to have our military representatives engage in talks on subjects of interest to you in various parts of the world previously outside the NATO area". For this purpose, the French representative in the standing group was acceptable. But if "a close European military cooperation" was to develop between them, a viable NATO would have to be perfected. Macmillan's endorsement, which reached de Gaulle at the same time, stressed that the Washington meetings should take place "unobtrusively".

De Gaulle, however, had no time for furtive tripartism, as he soon made plain. Did he, in fact, really want tripartism at all? If he had, would he not have accepted Eisenhower's offer, using it as a basis for further progress on Gaullist lines? At all events, de Gaulle's reaction was to propose a sudden jump into tripartism at the top. In letters to Eisenhower and Macmillan on 9 August 1960, he called for a Big Three summit meeting at Bermuda in mid-September. He went on to list four main areas for discussion:

1. The need for closer tripartite cooperation.
2. An extension of NATO's geographical coverage.
3. The need, as he saw it, to do away with military integration within the alliance.
4. The possibilities for agreement in the situation as it then was.

"Basically," wrote de Gaulle, "our views and intentions are doubtless fairly close together, if we three together can really grapple with this problem, it seems to me we can work out a common formula." Then came a negative note: the formula for enhanced military cooperation put forward in President Eisenhower's letter of 2 August was "too restrictive". It would not, thought de Gaulle, "result in common action" or

538

a more effective alliance. The Congo crisis – a reference to the break-down of law and order under the first independent government of the former Belgian colony – highlighted their disagreement. This could have been an opportunity for exercising their responsibilities; instead these had been drowned in the "composite mixture" of the United Nations. Throughout the world, unfolding events showed France that her allies were behaving as though they were not allies.

Such candour was bound to embarrass the policy-makers in London and Washington, and did. By now, Eisenhower was entering the final phase of his second term as president, and his authority was diminishing as the presidential elections drew near. The State Department used this as an argument against the utility of a summit. But the French had a counter-argument ready: the proposed Bermuda meeting would establish a precedent for the incoming administration. In other words, top-level tripartism would be a going concern.

In both capitals the usual objections were raised: it would be difficult to justify a summit with the French in the eyes of other allies; and what, it was asked, would Khrushchev be driven to do if Berlin dominated the agenda? Once again, Macmillan tried to find a way of satisfying de Gaulle without offending Adenauer, Fanfani and the rest. His suggestion was a farewell visit to Europe by President Eisenhower, which could provide a pretext for a tripartite summit.

At the beginning of September, Eisenhower sent a lengthy reply to de Gaulle. Borrowing a favourite device of the French, he accepted the idea of a summit meeting "in principle", and thought it could take place in December (that is, well after the meeting of Foreign ministers which was due in September). The president's letter then systematically took up de Gaulle's challenge on specific issues. He gave warning against the possibility of an American withdrawal from Europe. "Real political and military tripartite cooperation", he said, could not be organised if it implied the subordination of American relations with other allies, who were no longer willing to let others speak for them, or if it implied the reorganisation and consequent withdrawal of American forces from Europe. A return to the pre-war system of alliances would be much less effective than the present alliance, particularly in the field of automatic collective reaction to attack.

As for the Congo, Eisenhower went on, what had struck him had been the "frequency and fullness" of the consultations between the Americans and French – a list of which, between 1 June and 22 August, was attached to the letter. If the two governments' positions still remained "somewhat apart" after all these contacts, it was doubtful whether more formal or elaborate tripartite arrangements at whatever level could have made any difference.

The letter ended on a harder note. The president said he could not understand "the basic philosophy of France today". The French rejected a close union within NATO; yet they proposed a close tripartite union, which implied a veto and the imposition of decisions on other members of the alliance. Did France envisage speaking for the continent in the proposed tripartite forum, and if so was it wise to diminish the close relationship between the United States and Germany which drew the Federal Republic closely to the West?

On the "Anglo-Saxon" side, the special relationship was still working, and Macmillan, in a short letter dated 1 September 1960, also raised the possibility of a summit in December. He supported de Gaulle, however, in that he endorsed the French argument that it was important to create a pattern to be followed by the incoming American administration.

That day, the British ambassador in Paris, Sir Gladwyn Jebb (later Lord Gladwyn), reported that de Gaulle derived no satisfaction from Eisenhower's reply. The general had told him he thought there was only a "faint chance" of getting the Americans to change their views. He regretted the American refusal to face the facts on the Congo. It was no good citing the number of occasions on which officials had met; what was needed was some tripartite decisions at the highest level.

Once again, de Gaulle thought, the time had come to switch from secret to public diplomacy. He summoned the press to a conference at the Elysée. Carefully inspired questions enabled him to say what he thought of current events in the Congo, and about the need to reform NATO. Of the former, he said that if the western powers had concerted their policies, they could have prevented the "bloody anarchy that exists in this new State". This would have been better than effacing themselves behind "the inadequate and very costly action of the so-called United Nations" ("des nations dites Unies"). On the latter, he reaffirmed his fidelity to the alliance, but repeated his familiar call for an extension of its geographical coverage, against integration, and for French control over atomic weapons on home soil.

Not unreasonably, these statements were considered in Washington as a public reply and rebuff to President Eisenhower. De Gaulle, however, had already decided that no useful purpose would be served in accepting Eisenhower's tentative proposal for a summit in December, for in a short formal note to the president, dated 6 September, he made no reference to it. This closed the de Gaulle–Eisenhower correspondence on tripartism.

When the Foreign ministers flew to New York for the autumn session of the U.N. General Assembly, they met in tripartite conclave, much as Macmillan had proposed in May. Military matters were not discussed, but the talks covered most outstanding world problems, on all of which, except two, there was agreement. The two exceptions were NATO and Algeria.

There was a further round of ambassadorial tripartism in Paris on 14 and 15 December, when NATO's ministerial council met. Surprisingly, there was agreement on western objectives in the Congo; and also one set of parallel instructions to the Big Three ambassadors in Vientiane. East-West relations, Berlin and contingency planning were also discussed. The atmosphere, for much of the time, was far from harmonious, with Herter and Couve de Murville often in confrontation on support for the UN in the Congo, and on American policy in Laos.

Throughout this period and for some time ahead, de Gaulle's foreign, as distinct from Algerian, policy was dominated by the search for his concept of a "Europe of States". In June 1960 British Officials drew attention to the possibility that France, through tripartism, might claim the right to speak for the six members of the EEC as a whole within de Gaulle's proposed directorate. That de Gaulle was indeed thinking on these lines was confirmed when the president of the French National Assembly, Jacques Chaban-Delmas, on a visit to Washington in March 1961, claimed that France represented western Europe, just as Britain represented the Commonwealth, and therefore had as much right as Britain had to be admitted to American counsels.

De Gaulle's claims faced Macmillan with a cruel dilemma. Earlier in his premiership he had invested much time and prestige in the British project for a European Free Trade Area, which would have converted the common market (EEC) into a wider but looser organisation. Not unnaturally, the EEC took the view that this amounted to seeking membership of their club without paying the dues. De Gaulle emphatically shared this view.[29] Predictably, the Free Trade Area talks collapsed at the end of 1958, and later Macmillan sought British membership of the Common Market. Once this decision had been taken, the need to seek French support was vital. De Gaulle's proposal for an Atlantic directorate seemed to offer a way. But the Prime Minister's field of manoeuvre was severely restricted. He had to consider the special relationship with the U.S.; he was deeply conscious of the need to keep

[29] De Gaulle, *Renouveau*, p. 199.

West Germany in the alliance; and he could not forget the Commonwealth. Moreover, he was under constant pressure from the permanent officials.

In January 1961, for instance, the Foreign Office view was that whatever the price paid for French support of Britain's Common Market application, it should not weaken NATO, stimulate Franco-German rivalry, or encourage the Germans to turn eastward. It was hoped, therefore, that de Gaulle might be placated through discreet tripartism as proposed by the Prime Minister in May 1960. The status of the standing group should be raised, giving it authority over the Supreme Allied Commander, Europe; and the British and French nuclear forces should be placed under a multilateral NATO system.

Nuclear "multilateralism" was, indeed, beginning to be fashionable, remote though the possibility was that it would meet with de Gaulle's favour, and therefore that it would ever come to anything. During January 1961 Foreign Office and Defence ministry views were expressed on the subject. Macmillan listened, then made up his own mind. At his next meeting with de Gaulle, which took place at Rambouillet on 28 January 1961, he supported the case for arrangements between Britain and the EEC with arguments in favour of nuclear cooperation between Britain, France and the United States. To Macmillan's disappointment, however, de Gaulle listened with evident indifference, due at least in part, one supposes, to the general's realistic awareness that Macmillan was "offering" something – tripartite nuclear cooperation – that was not in his gift.

Despite this setback, however, the Prime Minister continued to support tripartism, Gaullist-style. On 28 April 1961, for instance, he sent President Kennedy, lately come to office and about to meet de Gaulle, a memorandum defending tripartite leadership for the non-Communist world. Indeed, he went further than ever before, arguing in favour of tripartite consultations before using nuclear weapons; joint arrangements for their use; Anglo-American willingness to consider helping France to develop her nuclear potential; and a review of the command structure within NATO to maintain "maximum national identity of the troops" and redistribute the senior posts. De Gaulle himself could scarcely have put his case better.

In an interim reply, the new president made it clear that his motivation for meeting de Gaulle's wishes was considerably weaker than Macmillan's. There was to be no American help for France in her nuclear programme; the most he could offer was closer political consultation and rather more sharing of nuclear information.

John F. Kennedy had already exchanged more than one letter with General de Gaulle. In February, he had asked for de Gaulle's support in American moves to turn over to the United Nations the military, political and administrative direction of Congo-Leopoldville.[30] And in March he had asked de Gaulle to endorse his project for placing Laos under the protection of the South-East Asia Treaty Organisation (to which both the United States and France – the latter no more than nominally – belonged). In his lordly way, de Gaulle had turned down both requests.

In *Mémoires d'Espoir*, General de Gaulle devotes one of his magisterial descriptive passages to Kennedy who, to face his daunting problems, had "the credit open to his youth, but also the doubts that surround a novice". Despite all the obstacles, the new president

> is resolved to make his career in the service of liberty, of justice and of progress. It is true that, persuaded of the duty of the United States and himself to redress grievances, he would be led at first to interventions which calculation did not justify. But the experience of the statesman would doubtless have contained, little by little, the impulses of the idealist. John Kennedy had the means and, without the crime that killed him, he might have had the time to impress his mark on the age.[31]

Despite the inauspicious beginnings of their correspondence, two more letters came from President Kennedy. In the first, in April, he accepted with all pleasure de Gaulle's invitation to visit France; the second, in May, was to inform de Gaulle that he intended, after Paris to go on to Vienna to meet Khrushchev. Between the two communications, he had suffered the painful reverse of the Bay of Pigs operation – the CIA-supported attempted invasion of Cuba by exiles from Florida.

Before Kennedy's departure from Washington the French ambassador, Hervé Alphand, is said to have put as much pressure as he could muster on the State Department to have the president briefed to revive the question of the Atlantic directorate. The president, however, was advised by his officials to keep off the subject. Once in de Gaulle's presence in Paris, where he arrived to a warm welcome on 31 May, he decided to raise it of his own accord.[32] He offered no more, however, than a renewal of Eisenhower's pledge that France would be consulted on the use of nuclear weapons "anywhere in the world", unless the threat of attack

[30] Now Zaïre, and previously Congo-Kinshasa, so termed to distinguish it from the former French colony, Congo-Brazzaville, across the Congo river.
[31] De Gaulle, *Renouveau*, pp. 266–7.
[32] Other aspects of Kennedy's visit to Paris are dealt with in the next chapter.

was so imminent as to threaten the survival of the United States. This was not the kind of statement that impressed General de Gaulle.

Tripartite discussions continued, mostly in Washington, during the rest of the year. But they were conducted in an increasingly acrimonious atmosphere, and the meeting of the Big Three foreign ministers during the NATO ministerial council gathering in Paris in December 1961 may be regarded as the end of tripartism on the pattern originally proposed by Macmillan, although later meetings were held from time to time on an *ad hoc* basis.

In the spring of 1962 the Prime Minister took the initiative in seeking another meeting with de Gaulle. It took place at the Château de Champs on 2 and 3 June, and was mainly concerned with an attempt on Macmillan's part to seek clarification of France's attitude towards Britain's application to enter the EEC. But Macmillan also sought to win de Gaulle's elusive goodwill by offering to "Europeanise" Britain's nuclear deterrent. The formula, as it stood, was vague, but surely (Macmillan thought) imaginative enough to arouse de Gaulle's curiosity. De Gaulle, however, made absolutely no response to Macmillan's overtures, although (as Newhouse reports) the Prime Minister brought up the subject on several occasions during the talks.[33]

For all his persistence, Macmillan had not done the one thing that might have gained him de Gaulle's support: he had not offered to sever Britain's special nuclear relationship with America. For this there were good and well-known reasons; but without a severance of this kind, de Gaulle was simply not interested in Macmillan's nuclear proposals. The failure of the Château de Champs talks was disguised in an anodyne communiqué: on the face of it, Franco-British relations were still friendly.

The same could not be said of Franco-American relations, which continued to deteriorate during 1962 and 1963.[34] Nor was the blame entirely de Gaulle's, although it is clear enough that his foreign policy

[33] Newhouse, pp. 173–80. According to Newhouse, Macmillan, who faced a foreign policy debate in the House of Commons in the following week, wanted to avoid criticism for having offered de Gaulle a nuclear deal. To this end, official leaks from Downing Street inspired press stories in advance of the Château de Champs meeting to the effect that no kind of nuclear bargaining was envisaged. Either there, or at the Rambouillet meeting in December 1962, Macmillan probably went even further than Newhouse says in proposing a Franco-British nuclear deal. Lord Gladwyn, at that time Britain's ambassador in Paris, made an elliptical reference to "the proposal for setting up a Franco-British strategic and nuclear force" in an interview in *Le Figaro* of 9 November 1971 to mark the first anniversary of de Gaulle's death. According to Gladwyn, this proposal could not succeed because of the existing links between London and Washington; "but obviously," he added, "Mr Macmillan could also not have accepted the creation of an Anglo-American nuclear force!"

[34] For an interesting and authentic account of this process, *see* Newhouse, chapters 6–8.

was incompatible with good relations with Washington. The Americans, too, had some responsibility for the downward slide; for knowing de Gaulle's determined opposition to multinational arrangements, President Kennedy nevertheless allowed his Defence secretary, Robert McNamara, to press with increasing insistence for military integration within NATO and for the extinction of independent nuclear forces.

The logical conclusion of de Gaulle's policy came in March 1966, with the withdrawal of France from all military aspects of the western alliance. But to see this dramatic event in perspective it is necessary to return a little in time and look at de Gaulle's foreign policy against a wider background than his demand for an Atlantic directorate, which in the end had yielded no more than the pallid and limited tripartism with which Harold Macmillan had tried to content him.

Chapter 3 ✤ Europe and the World

Yalta was the intolerable lump that stuck in de Gaulle's throat. France – that is, General de Gaulle – had been kept out of the conference that was to determine the shape of the post-war world. The memory of this exclusion never ceased to rankle. The other slights heaped upon the Free French leader by President Roosevelt were bad enough – especially the attempt to substitute Giraud for de Gaulle in North Africa. But most of them, including the Giraud business, provided the general with victories for his stubbornness. Yalta was different: France's interests were involved and the man who, all his life, had had "a certain idea of France" was not there.

General de Gaulle's foreign policy – its systematic anti-Americanism, to the point of eccentricity and beyond; its anti-British bias to the extent that Britain followed America's lead; its taste for a deal with Russia – can largely be traced back to the giant grievance of Yalta and the accumulated pinpricks that punctuated his dealings with Roosevelt and with Churchill. The rest – *l'Europe des Etats* or the discounting of ideologies, for instance – had deeper roots, in de Gaulle's nationalism and his reading of history.

In his public role as in his private yearnings, the driving force in de Gaulle's life was his ambition to restore France's *grandeur*. In common with some other great men, Charles de Gaulle was both a visionary and a realist, and the two competed within him. As time went on during his second period in power the realist tended to win less frequently. He had relinquished power in 1946 because the constitution that had been drafted and approved against his wishes had not given him the kind of State he needed even to attempt a policy of "greatness". He had returned, much later than he had hoped, because the desperate crisis of 1958 seemed likely to give him *carte blanche* to create the plebiscitary monarchy he wanted. But it was his cruel destiny to be frustrated by circumstances. Paradoxically, the Algerian war, which had given him his second chance, blocked the future, while it lasted. In the end, he had grown impatient with it; so impatient that in his urgent haste to be rid of the burden while a few years of active life remained, he had virtually given the country away.

In the meantime – between 1958 and 1962 – he had looked at the game, studied the cards in his hand and tentatively played a few. It was a poor hand, and he was bitterly aware of it. But nobody was going to keep him out of the game; if the cards were poor, bluff might take him far; and there was always the hope that a trump would turn up, or more likely, that his opponents' mistakes would yield a few easy tricks. Often enough, this latter hope was realised; for as men and leaders, the other players were not in his class, however overwhelming the strength of their own hands.

In playing his game, he was not going to allow himself to be circumscribed by the limitations of his own constitution. In fact, he had made it clear to his supporters, at the outset, that he would brook no interference in what he termed the *domaine réservé* – foreign policy, defence in all its aspects (including strategy and intelligence), Community affairs and Algeria. The reserved sector was first publicly spelt out by the president of the National Assembly, Jacques Chaban-Delmas, at the Gaullist party's inaugural conference at Bordeaux in November 1959. He later made it clear that in the subjects covered by the "reserved sector", not only did General de Gaulle intend to lay down policy, but he expected the Gaullists to refrain from offering advice or criticism, whereas they were free to do so in other aspects of the government's work.[1] Soustelle was not the only Gaullist who did not take docilely to presidential restrictiveness.

As France's allies were to learn through hard experience, the Gaullian

[1] Philip Williams and Martin Harrison, *Politics and Society in de Gaulle's Republic* (henceforth, Williams and Harrison), pp. 193–4.

concept of foreign relations was governed by thoughts occasionally expressed in private, of which the most telling and typical was: "War is against our enemies, peace against our friends."[2]

What, then, was the role de Gaulle envisaged, for France and for himself? He spelt it out repeatedly, in various passages of the third volume of his war memoirs (Le Salut),[3] and in speeches and at press conferences. But he did not put it in the same words twice, nor is there either consistency in the content, nor clarity in the presentation.[4] Two main strands do, however, emerge. One is the idea of a "Third Force" (or neutralist Europe), the most coherent description of which occurs on pages 179 and 180 of Le Salut, which consists of reflections after the capitulation of Germany on 7 May 1945:

> ... it seems to me that the new period will allow me, perhaps, to make a start on the execution of the vast plan I have formed for my country.
>
> To ensure her security in western Europe, by preventing a new Reich from threatening her again. To collaborate with West and East, if necessary to contract on one side, or else on the other, the necessary alliances, without ever accepting any kind of dependence. To prevent the risks, still diffused, of dislocation, to obtain the progressive transformation of the French Union into a free association. To cause a grouping, from the political, economic, strategic viewpoints, of the states that border on the Rhine, the Alps, the Pyrenees. To make of this organisation one of three world powers and, if need be one day, the arbiter between the two camps, the Soviet and the Anglo-Saxon.

[2] J.-R. Tournoux, Le Mois de Mai du Général (henceforth, Tournoux, Mai), p. 427.

[3] It should be remembered that Le Salut, although completed some time before, did not appear until October 1959. It has been suggested that de Gaulle held up publication until convinced that nothing was going to come of his Atlantic directorate idea (see above, ch. 2). Certainly, he had opportunities to revise the text in the light of American and British response to his plan, first launched in September 1958.

[4] René Courtin, in his interesting and (as it turned out) prophetic little work, L'Europe de l'Atlantique à l'Oural (1963; henceforth, Courtin), collects the most significant passages in his annexes. As M. Courtin pointed out (p. 24 n.), de Gaulle claims (on p. 22 of Le Salut) to have launched a "grandiose project" and a "vast design" in a speech at Brussels on 11 October 1945, and to have repeated it at a press conference in Paris the following day; but neither text is reproduced in de Gaulle's extensive documentary appendix. M. Courtin failed to find the text of the Brussels speech, and the relevant passage in the press conference is a disappointingly vague call for "a European organisation", apparently to consist of the French, Belgians, Dutch and Rhinelanders (Rhénans). The "missing" speech is, in fact, reproduced in Discours, Vol. I (1940–6), pp. 625–6. It is almost equally vague, and the relevant passage merely calls for the "re-establishment of our Occident", defined as "the countries [contrées] bounded by the Mediterranean, the Atlantic, the North Sea and the Rhine". Certainly neither the speech nor the press conference matches the inflated description of "vast design" or "grandiose project".

This passage, at any rate, bears the signs of retouching with hindsight, if it is compared with the much vaguer public reflections which the general made in October of the same year.

The other strand is the famous formula, "Europe from the Atlantic to the Urals". Now the first point to note about this phrase (in all its variants) is that it is incompatible with "Third Force Europe" if either is meant to be the "vast design" or "grandiose project" to which de Gaulle often referred. An uncommitted western Europe is not, however, incompatible with "Europe from the Atlantic to the Urals" if it is considered a first stage in the wider grouping. And, just as in mathematics the part cannot be greater than the whole, so the grander Gaullist formula comprises and supersedes the lesser.[5] De Gaulle's true vision and aim, however unrealistic, his truly "vast" and "grandiose" design, encompassed European Russia as well as western Europe.

He said so in many speeches and in answer to many questions. But he was no more consistent on this score than on the more restricted one of western Europe. Contradictory quotations could be made. A fairly consistent thread, however, runs through numerous declarations: France and Germany must unite in friendship as the heart of a West European organisation that would balance, or counter-balance, the United States; overtures should be made to Moscow, and in time, *détente* should lead to *entente*. At times, de Gaulle stated that America would have to give its approval to this design (for example, in his press conference of 29 March 1949). At other times, there was no mention of America. Nor did the phrase "Atlantic to the Urals" imply ignorance on de Gaulle's part that the Urals do not constitute the Soviet Union's eastern boundary. His concept referred to Europe and the Europeans as heirs to a common civilisation: he dismissed Siberia and Soviet Asia in general as a conglomerate of non-European tribal groups, and on one occasion contrasted "Russia, a white nation of Europe" with "the yellow multitude that is China".[6]

Important as de Gaulle's words were, they were less important than his deeds. His vision was one thing: his attempts to execute it were another. Always, aspiration clashed with reality. During the Second World War, and especially towards the end of it, de Gaulle had frequently advocated the dismemberment of Germany and its reversion to

[5] Not all commentators would agree with this interpretation. Massip, for instance, dismisses the "Atlantic to the Urals" notion as harmless day-dreaming. Among those who take it seriously, as I do, are Courtin, de Carmoy (pp. 501–2), and Newhouse. It is, in any case, impossible to dismiss the view that de Gaulle did not exclude a reversal of alliances, in the light of events between 1963 and 1969.
[6] This racialist touch occurs in the press conference of 10 November 1959.

the congeries of principalities that preceded Bismarck. But the major allies did not heed him. Although France was represented (against Russian objections) at the formal capitulation of Germany, de Gaulle was excluded from the Potsdam conference as he had been from Yalta. A few months later, he deprived himself of his own power, such as it was, in France. From 1946 to 1958 – the post-war years – he had no say in public affairs. By the time of his return the German Federal Republic had existed (in sovereignty) for three years, and the Soviet-protected German Democratic Republic for nine; two super-powers dominated the world, and France was not one of them; western Europe was protected by the North Atlantic Treaty Organisation, in which the United States wielded authority as well as power; a Communist government was in power in China; the emancipation of Europe's dependencies was well advanced, and France, having lost Indo-China as the result of a lengthy war, was in the throes of another, in Algeria; Britain had nuclear weapons, and France had not; not least, the treaty of Rome had been signed, and the European Economic Community (the Six) was being built.

It was in the face of these realities that General de Gaulle launched his Atlantic directorate proposals. In the unlikely event of their acceptance by President Eisenhower, NATO would probably have been shattered at one blow. But it seems unlikely, given de Gaulle's reluctance to accept the crumbs of "tripartism" proffered by his allies, that he was ever really interested in tripartism as such; his aim was to break the chain of consequences that flowed from Yalta. To this end, he proposed to exclude America from European affairs, including Europe's defence; to make France a nuclear power; to detach West Germany from dependence on America; to keep Britain (seen as America's extension) out of "Europe"; and to substitute France for America as Russia's "interlocutor" in the settlement of world problems.

It is hard to say whether even de Gaulle thought this monumental programme had the slightest chance of success. Certainly he behaved as though he did. But as its unreality became increasingly manifest, his actions, more and more, became those of a frustrated and embittered old man. Blocked or thwarted in the positive aspects of his programme, he turned more and more to negative or destructive actions, the effect of which was to alienate France's friends without enhancing France's influence, except among those countries of the Third World among whom he had acquired prestige for his rapid decolonisation and his defiance or humiliation of America and, to a lesser extent, Britain.

De Gaulle's wooing of Germany, especially while Adenauer was alive, was persistent and intermittently successful, though at times curiously callous. Having gone out of his way to charm the chancellor at their first meeting in September 1958, he outraged the old man's feelings by concealing his intention to launch the Atlantic directorate idea a fortnight later.[7] Six months after that, he caused alarm in Bonn by casually "giving away" Germany's claim to territories east of the Oder–Neisse line. The occasion was his press conference of 25 March 1959, and the words he used were these:

> ... The reunification of the two fractions into a single Germany, which would be entirely free, seems to us the natural destiny of the German people, so long as the latter does not call in question its present frontiers, to the west, to the east, to the north and to the south, and that it should aim at integrating itself one day in a contractual organisation of the whole of Europe for cooperation, freedom and peace.[8]

At that time, the official attitude in Bonn was that Germany's frontiers should be as they were in 1938; that is, that they should include the lands which the Russians had handed to Poland in compensation for Polish territory annexed by Russia. These "Polish" lands were called "eastern Germany", and the territory administered by the German Democratic Republic, which the rest of the world called "East Germany", was known in the Federal Republic as "central Germany". Nevertheless, in private conversation, the West German authorities would readily concede that there could be no return to the pre-war boundaries; but they were unwilling to make the concession formally, preferring to hold it in reserve as a bargaining point in any future negotiations with Moscow on German reunification. And now, without prior consultation or warning, de Gaulle had given away his friend Adenauer's bargaining position.

Why did de Gaulle do it? Some weeks earlier, Harold Macmillan had returned from a trip to Moscow in which he had tried to explore Khrushchev's intentions. Khrushchev's Berlin ultimatum, which was due to expire on 27 May 1959, still hung over the alliance, for it was not yet clear beyond doubt that the Soviet leader was bluffing. This was a time for allied unity, especially in public utterances. Yet de Gaulle chose this moment to make a public concession at the expense of the government with which he hoped to establish special links and whose fate was more closely affected by the outcome of the crisis than any other. The timing of his statement was, however, deliberate, and stemmed almost

[7] See above, pp. 527–8.   [8] De Gaulle, Discours, Vol. II, p. 85.

certainly from pique at Macmillan's solo trip, on which he had made sour and even hostile comments in private. In a sense, Macmillan had stolen some of his thunder, for if any European was to seek a *rapprochement* with the Kremlin, it could only be de Gaulle. As the context shows, the statement was designed less to humiliate Adenauer than to resume his intermittent hints at a Franco-Soviet dialogue, in the framework of Europe from the Atlantic to the Urals. The discomfiture of Adenauer was incidental, but consistent with de Gaulle's view of Germany as France's junior political partner, fit for snubbing from time to time.

Dr Adenauer responded with a private letter to de Gaulle pleading with him not to raise the frontier issue again.[9] De Gaulle agreed, and with one exception kept off the subject for the remainder of Adenauer's lifetime. The exception was the press conference of 10 November 1959, in which he took cognisance of a journalist's question about the Oder–Neisse line, but merely to point out that he had already said what he had to say and had not changed his mind.[10]

Despite occasional snubs, de Gaulle went to extraordinary lengths to persuade the Germans to exchange America's nuclear protection for France's, dropping the Atlantic policy in favour of an independent Franco-German policy of pan-European reconciliation. The climax of these endeavours came in the autumn of 1962, when the general, without going so far as to breach the ban on Germany's possession of nuclear weapons, tried to involve them with the *force de frappe*. What the French proposed, in a secret diplomatic initiative, was a joint Franco-German strategic air command under a French commander-in-chief. There was to be a joint training scheme for the manning of France's Mirage bombers, with French as the working language – a Gaullian touch that would have effectively ruled out any German air cooperation with the Americans.[11]

The Germans, unwilling to exchange the real security of the American nuclear umbrella for the doubtful protection of France's fledgling bomb,

---

[9] Newhouse, p. 97.   [10] De Gaulle, *Discours*, Vol. III, p. 142.

[11] Private sources. What with Macmillan's proposals to de Gaulle (*see above*, p. 544), and de Gaulle's to Adenaur, nuclear inducements had became fashionable, In de Gaulle's case, moreover, there was an interesting precedent. On 31 March 1958 the French and West German Defence ministers – at that time, Jacques Chaban-Delmas and Franz-Josef Strauss – signed a convention for a joint defence research programme. Shortly afterwards the two men, on a trip to French installations at Colomb-Béchar in the Sahara, signed a secret protocol under which West Germany was to be given French nuclear weapons, under joint control, in return for financial contributions to their development. But the Fourth Republic fell shortly afterwards and nothing came of the "Protocol of Colomb-Béchar". (For partial confirmation, *see* Alfred Grosser, *La IVe République et sa Politique extérieure* (1961), p. 343, and Newhouse, pp. 16–17.)

declined. As a result, the Franco-German "special relationship" died without having ever fully come to life. But this did not stop de Gaulle, only three months later, from signing the Franco-German treaty with Adenauer. This was the Gaullian way: he had written the script, and he was going to act his part, even if the stage had collapsed under him.

Adenauer was willing, however, to go a long way to meet de Gaulle, although not as far as the general would have liked. In the often stormy ministerial meetings of the Six, for instance, Germany frequently supported France, at least while Adenauer was alive. And when de Gaulle vetoed Britain's application to join the EEC, Adenauer offered no support for the British. It was characteristic of his dilemma, however, that at about the same time, he accepted President Kennedy's invitation to participate in the proposed multilateral nuclear force, which de Gaulle had refused.[12]

Again, at about that time came the culminating point of Franco-German relations – the signing of the treaty of cooperation between the two countries on 22 January 1963. It was Adenauer's idea but he and de Gaulle had different reasons for welcoming it. In Adenauer's eyes, it signalled the achievement of reconciliation between two major European countries that had so often been at war with each other. He was particularly pleased with the provisions for exchanges in the fields of education and youth, the effects of which were that German would be given preference over English in French schools, and that more young people would get to know each other's countries. De Gaulle, however, saw the treaty primarily as an instrument to enable him to establish his influence, extending perhaps in time to a right of veto, over German foreign policy. The most controversial clause provided that: "The two governments shall consult each other before any decision, on all important questions of foreign policy, and in the first place on questions of common interest, with a view to reaching, as far as possible, analogous decisions." To this end, there were provisions for twice-yearly meetings of heads of State or government, quarterly meetings of foreign ministers and frequent meetings of authorities in the fields of defence, education and youth.

The controversial clause quoted above implied consultations in such matters as NATO, the proposed multilateral nuclear force, relations with Moscow and the development of the common market – on all of which de Gaulle held decided views that did not coincide with those of the German government. The possibilities of friction were therefore evident. Adenauer chose not to see them; his Foreign minister, Gerhard

12 De Carmoy, p. 444.

Schroeder, was more clear-sighted and was appropriately unenthusiastic about the treaty. So was the Bundestag, when the question of ratification came before it. In the end, the German deputies agreed to ratify it but only on condition that it should be preceded by a preamble stating that it "does not affect the rights and obligations of the multilateral treaties" concluded by Germany, and that it should further "a particularly close cooperation between Europe and the United States . . . common defence in the framework of the North Atlantic alliance and the integration of the forces of the countries belonging to that alliance" and "the unification of Europe following the path begun by the creation of the European communities and by including Great Britain".

The preamble thus carefully enunciated the policy goals which de Gaulle opposed and was determined to destroy. It was soon clear, indeed, that the Franco-German treaty was not going to make Germany the docile instrument of de Gaulle's policy. Later that year, on the eve of the first twice-yearly summit meeting under the treaty, on 4 and 5 July 1963, de Gaulle told French parliamentarians: "You know, treaties are like girls and roses: they last as long as they last." And he quoted a famous line from Victor Hugo's *Les Orientales*: "*Hélas, que j'en ai vu mourir, de jeunes filles.*"[13]

As with Germany, so with Europe. De Gaulle had had no say in the treaty of Rome, and he abhorred the supranational Europe which the architects of the European movement – Jean Monnet and Robert Schuman – saw as the end result of their labours. The European Economic Community, however, was not, as it stood, a truly supranational organisation, since it stipulated unanimity in ministerial council meetings: in other words, each member country had a veto over policy decisions. De Gaulle therefore resolved to use his veto to further French interests, especially in agriculture, and to block any moves of which he disapproved for more recondite reasons, such as the admission of Britain into the club of the Six. The end result he envisaged was the opposite of that dreamt of by the "Europeans": they wanted integration; he wanted an *Europe des Etats*.[14] Paradoxically, this aspiration was almost identical with Macmillan's concept of Europe. The difference was that Macmillan wanted Britain to be one of the "states" of Europe, and de Gaulle did not. This led to the well-known description of de Gaulle's Europe as *l'Europe à l'anglaise sans les Anglais*.

[13] Newhouse, p. 243.
[14] The phrase sometimes attributed to de Gaulle's is "*l'Europe des Patries*" (Europe of the Fatherlands). De Gaulle, however, disowned "Europe of the Fatherlands" in his press conference of 15 May 1962.

Since this was his concept, he had no time for the European Commission in Brussels, or for the supranational pretensions of its president, Walter Hallstein, whom he charged with furthering German ambitions under the cloak of supranationality.[15] Deeming the treaty of Rome to have neglected French agricultural interests, de Gaulle insisted on the inclusion of agriculture in the second phase of the creation of the common market. When he met with German resistance in the second half of 1961, he instructed the French ministerial team, led by the Foreign minister, Couve de Murville, to make it clear that France would quit the EEC if she did not get her way. On the eve of the fateful debate in Brussels he wrote, then telegraphed, to Adenauer to confirm the ultimatum. On 14 January 1962 he duly got his way, with the adoption of a common agricultural policy. Nor was he in any way abusing French rights under the treaty of Rome in so acting: other leaders might, however, have done what he did with less drama.

It was the same with the search for a European political organisation. At a meeting of heads of State and government, at Bad Godesberg, on 18 and 19 July 1961, there had been general agreement on a common European policy, and even de Gaulle had raised no objections to the final declaration, which mentioned the alliance of Europe with the United States and other free peoples and affirmed that the political union of Europe would strengthen the Atlantic Alliance. De Gaulle, however, soon had second thoughts. A commission had been set up in Paris, under the chairmanship of a faithful Gaullist, Christian Fouchet, then ambassador to Denmark. It set to work to draft a treaty establishing a "Union of States".

As presented to the EEC governments on 2 November, this first draft of the "Fouchet Plan" followed the Bad Godesberg decisions fairly closely, but made no mention of the Atlantic Alliance, referring instead to the need to strengthen the security of member-states in cooperation with other free nations. It ran into strong opposition from the Dutch and Belgians who wanted to bring the British into the negotiations.[16] A second Fouchet draft was presented on 18 January 1962. This time there was no mention of cooperation with other free nations in defence matters, and the role of the European Assembly was reduced. The second draft caused consternation. The acrimonious discussions that ensued broke down completely in April, when the Dutch and Belgians refused to continue negotiating unless the French withdrew their objec-

---

[15] De Gaulle, *Renouveau*, p. 195.
[16] For a Gaullist account of the row on European union, *see* Couve de Murville, ch. 9 (pp. 347 *et seq.*). Fouchet's own disappointingly sparse account is in Part IV of Christian Fouchet, *Au Service du Général de Gaulle* (henceforth, Fouchet).

tion to Britain's admission to the proposed Union of States. By then, de Gaulle's concept of Europe was clear beyond all doubt: he was against a federal Europe; and he wanted a confederal Union of States only if the British were kept out. He hammered home the confederal idea in his press conferences of 15 May 1962, with such force that five MRP ministers who had joined his government less than a month earlier announced their resignations.

Keeping England out, then, was one of the major preoccupations of General de Gaulle. His treatment of Macmillan in this context was unfeeling to the point of cruelty; although the Prime Minister cannot be exempted from blame for the dismal outcome of his European endeavours. Having hesitated too long, he tried to persuade the EEC to merge into a Free Trade Area in which it would have lost its original purpose; then launched the little Free Trade Area (EFTA) before at last applying to join the Common Market, and even then on terms that suggested an inadequate appreciation of what the European movement was all about.

The relationship between de Gaulle and Macmillan makes an interesting study. On Macmillan's side, it was tinged with sentiment because of wartime memories. Though himself capable of dissimulation, he was reluctant to see that de Gaulle might be deceiving him. On de Gaulle's side, there was little sentiment: he found pleasure in Macmillan's company, but remained unconvinced that the Prime Minister was a "European", either in the Monnet sense or even in his own. Although Macmillan never understood this until it was too late, it was really impossible for him to win against de Gaulle. Throughout, he clung to the illusion that if de Gaulle's objections on specific issues, such as agriculture or defence, could be met, there would be nothing to stop Britain joining the Common Market.[17] To him, negotiations were a means to an end, and implied good will on both sides, especially between allies. But de Gaulle was not a man who negotiated: his proposals were on a "take it or leave it" basis.

The truth was that de Gaulle did not want Britain "in" Europe. It was going to be difficult enough to impose French leadership on Germany; he could not hope to impose it on Britain as well. Macmillan wrongly thought that the similarity between his concept of Europe and de Gaulle's would facilitate agreement. But de Gaulle thought of Britain as America's "Trojan horse" in Europe. The only way Macmillan could have called the bluff would have been to sever the special relationship with the United States or, at all events, declare his readiness to pursue a

17 Newhouse, p. 234.

555

"European" defence policy, that is, a Gaullist one, independent of the United States. He could not do this; but even if he had been able to, de Gaulle would have found some other pretext to keep Britain out.

In the amicable atmosphere of Macmillan's first meeting with de Gaulle after his return to power, in Paris on 29 June 1958, this was not immediately apparent. And yet, unwittingly, Macmillan had started off on the wrong foot, by exclaiming (according to de Gaulle): "The common market is the continental blockade. Britain doesn't accept it."[18] An exchange of letters on the European Free Trade Area followed, in which de Gaulle's tone was polite but evasive.[19] At this stage, de Gaulle had still not made it absolutely clear to Macmillan that he thought the Free Trade Area would simply mean the dissolution of the EEC. Before long, however, the French view was disclosed to Reginald Maudling who was conducting the negotiations with the Six. It would be quite wrong to blame the subsequent collapse of the negotiations at the end of 1958 entirely on de Gaulle, who merely brought the issue to a head: the fact is that the Six, individually and as a whole, saw the absurdity of the Free Trade Area proposals, which would have given Britain the advantage of participation in the European market without the discipline of a common tariff in trade with the outside world.

A fairly lengthy pause followed, during which Macmillan resigned himself to seeking British membership of the EEC, and, not without difficulty, "sold" the idea to the Conservative party. On 31 July 1961 he announced that Britain sought to adhere to the treaty of Rome, a decision which de Gaulle later recorded in these words:

> ... In the middle of 1961, the English launch a new offensive. Having failed, from the outside, to prevent the birth of the Community they now plan to paralyse it from within.[20]

In de Gaulle's eyes, to ask for special concessions for Commonwealth agricultural products would mean the end of the Common Market as it was conceived. The negotiations which Edward Heath conducted in Brussels were characterised as an attempt to "square the circle". But as France's partners in the EEC were not strong enough to state the obvious, de Gaulle resolved to do so himself, in no uncertain terms. The timing, however, was important. He needed a pretext that would enable him to affirm that Britain was not truly converted to the European idea, and he found it in the Nassau conference at the end of 1962.

Meantime, relations between the two men had continued on their

---

[18] De Gaulle, *Renouveau*, p. 199.   [19] Macmillan, *Storm*, pp. 449–52.
[20] De Gaulle, *Renouveau*, p. 200.

amicably ambiguous course. From 5 to 8 April 1960 President de Gaulle made a State visit to London. It was early enough in the game for the general public to be unaware that de Gaulle was consciously working against British interests, and he received a rousing welcome from the populace, which commendably wanted to show that it remembered the one Frenchman who, when all seemed lost, had decided to fight on in Britain's darkest and noblest hour. The highlight of the visit was de Gaulle's moving address to both Houses of Parliament, impeccably delivered in his grandiloquent French, and, as usual, without notes. But for all the grandeur of the ceremonial, the occasion was of no political consequence.

More significant were de Gaulle's three meetings with Macmillan: at Birch Grove (Macmillan's Sussex home) during the weekend beginning on Friday, 24 November 1961; at the Château de Champs on 2 and 3 June 1962; and at Rambouillet on 15 and 16 December 1962. (An earlier meeting at Rambouillet in January 1961 was of less importance in the European context, Macmillan not having yet decided to seek membership of the EEC.) At Birch Grove, Macmillan suggested that the chance to bring Britain into Europe in 1962 should be taken, for if it were not, it might not recur.

In reply de Gaulle expressed the fear that the United Kingdom and the Commonwealth would dissolve Europe in the Atlantic. He concluded soothingly, however, that in the end all the problems would be solved.[21]

By the time of the further Rambouillet meeting, at the end of 1962, de Gaulle had lost all patience with the protracted attempts to "square the circle" at Brussels. He had met Macmillan again, at the Château de Champs in June, and had ignored the Prime Minister's astonishing offer to place Britain's nuclear arm at Europe's disposal.[22] The Rambouillet meeting took place shortly after the great Soviet–American nuclear confrontation in the Caribbean. There was some talk about Britain's independent nuclear deterrent, which Macmillan said he intended to preserve. The Americans had lately abandoned work on the costly Skybolt missile, which was supposed to be supplied to Britain, and the British were going to ask for an alternative. De Gaulle is said to have evoked the possibility of Anglo-French collaboration on the Blue Streak missile – a British project which had been abandoned, as the American Skybolt had been, after a succession of costly testing failures. According to French accounts of the talks, de Gaulle was actually

[21] Newhouse, pp. 145–6; for further matter, see also pp. 205–12.
[22] See above, p. 544.

proposing the revival of the Blue Streak programme, with French participation, as an alternative to any missile the Americans might be prepared to supply to the British. But his proposal, if that is what it was, was vaguely worded, and Macmillan did not respond to it; just as, the previous June, de Gaulle had not responded to Macmillan's own defence offer.

On Europe, no progress was made. Macmillan played into de Gaulle's hands by observing that if Britain were kept out of Europe's political organisation, she could no longer play her traditional role of maintaining an equilibrium – apparently unaware that this was just what de Gaulle was afraid of. The general, at last, unveiled his true thoughts. If Britain joined the EEC, he said, its character would be changed. Smaller European countries would also join and France's position would be diminished. The Common Market would be dissolved in an Atlantic trading system. As it stood, it suited France's needs, especially in her relations with Germany. He doubted whether Britain could meet the requirements of membership, as France conceived them.

Indignantly, Macmillan asked why, if de Gaulle had a fundamental objection to Britain's membership, he had not stated it fourteen months earlier, when Britain first applied to join the EEC. But at that moment, the Foreign Secretary, Lord Home, changed the subject.

From this unsatisfactory encounter, Macmillan went on to a highly technical summit meeting with President Kennedy at Nassau, from 18 to 21 December. Practising concealment in his turn, Macmillan did not even hint that his recent talks with de Gaulle had gone badly. He asked for American Polaris sea-to-ground missiles; and Kennedy, fearing that a refusal would lead to an Anglo-French nuclear deal, agreed. In return, Macmillan and his advisers endorsed the American project for a multilateral nuclear force (MLF) – a NATO fleet of Polaris-armed ships or submarines, with crews of mixed nationalities and mutual vetoes on the use of the nuclear weapons. From Nassau, Kennedy wrote to de Gaulle offering France, too, Polaris missiles and a share in the MLF.

Macmillan returned in triumph to London; and Kennedy, not displeased by the meeting in the Bahamas, wrongly supposed that he had found a way of bringing France back into active membership of NATO, and possibly even of persuading de Gaulle to abandon France's own nuclear programme. Both men were about to be traumatically disabused.

De Gaulle could have chosen the gentler course of writing to the Prime Minister and president and apprising them of his intentions. But to have done this would have been to have thrown away his chance of one of his greatest *coups de théâtre* to date in a career that had not lacked for drama. His chosen stage was the Elysée Palace, where the journalists assembled on 14 January 1963 to hear his words. He dropped two major bombshells, and a minor one. He closed the door on Britain's application to join the EEC, and he rejected the multilateral nuclear force and Kennedy's offer of Polaris missiles; for good measure, he gave advance notice that France was not interested in any treaty to ban nuclear tests.

The brutality of his No to Macmillan was slightly mitigated by an eloquent tribute to Britain's contribution to the world, and to the courage, resolution and solidity of her people, which had saved the free world; and by an offer of association between Britain and the Common Market and continued Franco-British cooperation in such projects as the supersonic airliner Concorde. Indeed, he did not actually use the word "no", but merely led his listeners to the inescapable negative conclusion inherent in his arguments about the insularity and originality of the British, and their desire to remake the community in their own image after having tried to prevent it from getting off the ground.

The message was clear enough. And its natural consequence followed, when instructions reached the French delegation in Brussels to propose a suspension of the negotiations on British entry. This duly happened on 29 January.

De Gaulle's dismissal of MLF and Polaris was equally incisive and logical. He praised the United States for its services to the freedom of the world by protecting Europe with its strategic nuclear arm. But, he reasoned, the Cuba missile crisis had shown that in a nuclear confrontation involving its vital interests, the U.S. would not consult its allies. France must therefore stick to her plans for building her own atomic striking force: even if it were much smaller than existing ones, it would still have a deterrent effect. As for MLF, while France would presumably have the right in a crisis to withdraw her components, this would be a complicated and time-consuming process that would produce paralysis just when action was needed. The offer of Polaris missiles was unpractical, for different reasons. Since France lacked launching submarines and nuclear warheads they would be useless to her; and by the time she had such things, Polaris would be obsolete.

De Gaulle's statement on test ban arrangements flowed naturally from his rejection of the Bahamas offer. France, he said, had absolutely no objection to a suspension of nuclear tests by the super-powers. But any such suspension was not in any sense a form of disarmament.[23]

---

[23] This was an indirect allusion to the UN disarmament talks that had begun in Geneva on 14 March 1962, without French participation.

If the time ever came when nuclear armaments stocks were destroyed, France would be delighted to join in the destruction. In the meantime, nothing could stop her from procuring her own weapons.

De Gaulle's cold war against the Americans – or, as David Schoenbrun termed it, with "uncivil war" – was punctuated by courteous personal contacts with American leaders. In Eisenhower's case, these came as near to warmth as de Gaulle was capable of feeling towards an "Anglo-Saxon". When Schoenbrun submitted to the American president the interesting chapter he had written on the "uncivil" war,[24] Eisenhower asked him to make it clear that his personal relations with de Gaulle were always good, even when their public disagreements were at their height. He said: "You know, de Gaulle and I got along fine personally. . . . Of course, he and I were never Charles and Ike – never – not like with Winston, for example. Winston and I – why, we were just as warm, personal friends as we could be under the circumstances. De Gaulle never was that. He never had time, for one thing, and, for another, he's rather remote and I think he believes that his position requires it. He tries to create this feeling of a remoteness, of mystery – or you might say mystique."

The people of Paris, spurred by grateful wartime memories and natural sympathy for an unusually warm personality, gave President Eisenhower an unforgettable welcome when he made his State visit there in September 1959. Perhaps more surprisingly, the people of Washington, New York and other cities reciprocated with equal enthusiasm when de Gaulle returned the visit between 22 and 29 April 1960. The welcome was the more striking for the fact that the general's visit to Canada, which he had just completed, was cold and unenthusiastic (though this cannot be deduced from his own account of it in *Mémoires d'Espoir*).[25] The delirium of the crowds, on the east coast, in San Francisco and in deepest New Orleans, and the repeated press tributes to this majestic survivor of the wartime Big Four, regenerated the old man. Nothing of consequence, however, was achieved in de Gaulle's conversations with Eisenhower and his officials. He spares a few words of praise for Richard Nixon, in whom he found "one of those frank and firm personalities on whom one feels one could count for great matters, if it fell to him, one day, to be responsible for them in the first rank". Thereafter, Nixon, whether in or out of office, was to visit the Elysée from time to time, and de Gaulle always reserved a friendly and attentive

---

[24] In Schoenbrun, *Lives*, see pp. 319–20.
[25] Newhouse, pp. 103–6; De Gaulle, *Renouveau*, pp. 250–9.

welcome for the man who was yet to be president of the United States. When President Nixon visited de Gaulle officially at the end of February 1969, the two men were already old friends, in a sense that was never true of relations with Kennedy or Johnson.[26]

President Kennedy, who was faced with major crises in Laos and Cuba shortly after his assumption of office at the beginning of 1961, did not really come to grips with European problems until his visit to Paris at the end of May 1961. Despite the great difference in age between the youthful president (forty-four) and the general (seventy), the unfeigned admiration of the younger man for the older, and the impressive self-confidence and intelligence of John F. Kennedy, were a sufficient basis for relations of mutual esteem. More than this, however, would have been needed to restore amity to the state-to-state relations of France and the United States.

The realities were in de Gaulle's refusal to help Kennedy in the Congo and Laos, and in Kennedy's initial refusal to regard France, even led by de Gaulle, as any more important than other allies, including West Germany.[27] During their Paris talks, Kennedy disclosed that he envisaged building up American power in Vietnam, then in its embryonic stages, to create a bastion against Soviet influence. But instead of the approval he had hoped for, he drew a homily from de Gaulle, which he records in the following prophetic terms:

> For you, intervention in that region will be an endless process. From the moment when nations are awakened, no foreign authority, whatever the means at its disposal, has any chance of imposing itself. You will soon find this out for yourselves. For if you find rulers on the spot who consent to obey you, out of self-interest, the peoples do not give their consent and, for that matter, do not appeal to you. The ideology you invoke will make no difference. What is more, the masses will confuse it with your will to power. That is why, the more you commit yourselves over there against Communism, the more the Communists will appear as the champions of national independence, the more help they will get, not least from their own despair. We French have already experienced this. You Americans wanted, only yesterday, to take our places in Indo-China. Now you want to succeed us to rekindle a war which we have ended. I predict that you will get bogged down step by step in a bottomless military and political quagmire, despite the losses and the expenditure you may dispense. What you, we and others must do in that unhappy Asia, is not to take

---

[26] Private information.　　　　　[27] *See above*, pp. 542–3.

the place of states on their own soil, but provide them with the wherewithal to emerge from misery and humiliation which, there as elsewhere, are the causes of totalitarian regimes. I tell you this in the name of our West.[28]

Time was soon to show that these gloomy words were without influence.

It is not possible to understand the next phase of Gaullian policy without a further look at de Gaulle's vague but persistent pan-European aspirations. During the war, Charles de Gaulle had turned with relief and hope towards Russia, to seek support and compensation for his continuing disappointments with the Anglo-Saxons. Stalin, too, had disappointments in store for him; but by and large, since de Gaulle was in no sense a rival, he had given the general at least the illusion of solidarity. The outcome had been the signing in Moscow of the Franco-Soviet treaty of alliance in December 1944. This did not, of course, stop Stalin from trying to deny de Gaulle's right to join in the ceremonial acceptance of Germany's surrender, or a share of German territory to occupy.

De Gaulle's subsequent ambition to reach an understanding with Moscow, and preside over a pan-European reconciliation, had nothing whatever to do with ideology. It was due solely to de Gaulle's interpretation of geopolitical facts, and to his obsessive, almost pathological, desire to terminate American influence in Europe. His lack of interest in ideology amounted almost to a blind spot: having decided, once and for all, that only historic national ambitions and actual military and political power counted, he was unwilling or incapable of seeing the use made of ideology, even after the Sino-Soviet split, in the service of great power policies. It is typical of him that during the Rally of the French People period, his chosen epithet for the French Communists was "the separatists". That they were, at that time, Moscow's instrument, was something he could grasp. That Moscow could, however, spread its influence by preaching the overthrow of "capitalism" in a doctrinal form acceptable to non-Russians all over the world, was not a notion that attracted de Gaulle's interest. It could also be said that he found ideology inconvenient, because it interfered with his grand design: if he had accepted ideology, then France and America would have been natural allies, not enemies, and there could be no *rapprochement* between western and eastern Europe.

[28] De Gaulle, *Renouveau*, pp. 268–9.

This did not imply any admiration on his part for the Soviet system. He was always ready to denounce it as a tyranny but uninterested in the proposition that its totalitarian character stemmed from its Marxist basis. In a television speech on 2 October 1961, for instance, he referred to "a Europe balanced between the Atlantic and the Urals, once totalitarian imperialism has ceased to deploy its ambitions". With curious optimism, by the scale of his own life-span, he looked forward to the time when "the domineering ambitions of an obsolete ideology" should cease.[29] Perhaps the most explicit of de Gaulle's expressions of his contempt for ideological concepts came in this passage from his press conference of 29 July 1963, in reply to a question about the ideological break between China and the Soviet Union:

> . . . The break? On what ideology? Since I was born, Communist ideology has been personified by many people. There was the period of Lenin, Trotsky, Stalin, whom I knew personally, of Beria, Malenkov, Khrushchev, Tito, Nagy, and of Mao Tse-tung. I know as many trustees of the Communist ideology as there are fathers of Europe, and that makes quite a number. Each one of these trustees, in his turn, condemns, excommunicates, crushes and sometimes kills the others. In any case, he firmly combats the cult of the others' personalities. . . . The standard of ideology in reality does no more than cover ambitions.[30]

The ferocity of de Gaulle's denunciations of Communist regimes, especially Russia's, was invariable; and so was the intransigence with which he opposed any deal by the western powers with Moscow. The paradox implicit in the contrast between this attitude and his own desire for an understanding with Moscow is, however, apparent, not real. To denounce totalitarian regimes while hoping for a *rapprochement* with the greatest of them was consistent with de Gaulle's view that relations between states are determined by national interests, not ideologies. As for his opposition to any Western compromise with Moscow, the important point is that he was against such a deal only if it was made by the western alliance, led by the United States. It did not extend to a hypothetical deal made by France independently of her allies.

Against this background, de Gaulle's actions, at least between 1959 and 1966, are not illogical. De Gaulle was rock-like when the Paris summit collapsed in May 1960 in the face of Khrushchev's insistence on humiliating Eisenhower over the U.2 affair. When Khrushchev,

[29] Speech in Bonn, 4 September 1962.   [30] De Gaulle, *Discours*, Vol. IV, p. 125.

accompanied by his Foreign minister, Gromyko, and his ballistic missiles expert, Marshal Malinovsky, called at the Elysée on 15 May, it was with threatening intent. "I know," Khrushchev stormed, "that France has nothing to do with American provocations. But she is the ally of the United States, which has forces on her territory. Without looking for trouble on our side, what terrible things could hit her!"

Roughly, de Gaulle retorted that it was vain to predict what would happen in the event of a conflict and that he had already, twice in his lifetime, seen a state defeated that had started a war and was certain of victory. "It is not," he added, "to talk of war that I convoked the conference in Paris, but to seek to ensure peace."[31]

There was panic in the western camp when Khrushchev maintained his refusal to proceed with the conference unless Eisenhower publicly apologised, and followed up with earthy invectives at a press conference for 500 journalists. Macmillan, contemplating the ruins of his own efforts, and fearing world war, called for appeasing gestures, and Eisenhower was inclined to agree. De Gaulle, however, stood firm, and was later thanked for it by the Prime Minister, the president and Dr Adenauer (who was hovering in the wings).

The general showed similar firmness on other critical occasions. Alarmed by Khrushchev's truculent attitude at the Vienna summit, President Kennedy deduced that a grave crisis was on the way. He was sure of it when the Soviet leader followed up with two speeches in which he threatened to conclude a separate peace with East Germany and recognise her sovereignty over the entire territory between the Oder–Neisse border and the eastern boundary of the Federal Republic. When Kennedy, in a letter to de Gaulle, expressed his apprehensions and proposed negotiations on Germany with the Soviet Union, the general replied on 6 July, to say: "In the event of a crisis provoked by the Soviets, only an attitude of firmness and solidarity, assumed and affirmed in time by America, England and France, could prevent evil consequences. . . . It is only after a long period of international *détente* – which depends on Moscow alone – that we might negotiate with Russia on the German question as a whole." And he took a similar line in a television speech on the 12th.

It was the same again at the time of the Caribbean missile crisis in October 1962. Kennedy sent the former secretary of State, Dean Acheson, to Paris with a letter from the president and the air reconnaissance photographs of Soviet missiles and installations on Cuba. Having read the letter, but before looking at the pictures, de Gaulle

[31] De Gaulle, *Renouveau*, p. 261; for further matter, *see also* pp. 272, and 237 *et seq.*

said to Acheson: "If there is a war, I will be with you. But there will be no war."

Such firmness was genuine, and perfectly in character even if it masked a dread that the Americans and Russians might reach an understanding à deux, and frustrate de Gaulle's grand design. In the meantime, he pursued his own overtures whenever opportunity presented itself. In a significant sense, the first of these, after his return to power, was the invitation to Khrushchev to visit France. The Soviet leader, bubbling with bonhomie, arrived in Paris on 23 March 1960, accompanied by his wife, their son, two daughters and son-in-law. After the public ceremonies and a lengthy provincial tour, he settled down to two days of talks with de Gaulle, at the Elysée and Rambouillet.

The hard core of the discussion was, of course, Berlin. Khrushchev had proposed that the remnants of the post-war occupation arrangements should be dismantled, and West Berlin turned into a free city. Unless a peace treaty were concluded between the two German republics, Russia would unilaterally sign a treaty with East Germany. The western authorities would evacuate West Berlin, which would then make its own arrangements with the sovereign German Democratic Republic.

Icily, de Gaulle told Khrushchev that his threats did not impress him very much. Nobody could stop him from signing a "treaty" with East Germany, but it would amount to no more than a piece of paper he would be addressing to himself. The German problem would remain entire. If there was any interference with western troops and this led to war, it would be entirely Khrushchev's fault. He went on:

But you shout at the top of your voice of peaceful co-existence, you heap blame on Stalin retrospectively at home, you were Eisenhower's guest three months ago and today you are mine. If you don't want war, don't take the road that leads to it. . . .

We must seek the solution, not by erecting monolithic blocs, face to face, but on the contrary by starting work in turn on détente, entente and cooperation within the framework of our continent. We shall thus create, between Europeans, from the Atlantic to the Urals, relations, links, an atmosphere which will, firstly, remove the virulence from German problems, including that of Berlin, next will lead the Federal Republic and your Republic of the East to draw together and join up, and finally will hold the Germanic whole bound in a Europe of peace and progress where it will be able to make a fresh start.

Mollified, Khrushchev said he was ready to wait up to two years before going ahead with a German treaty.

There were more exchanges, on predictable lines, about nuclear weapons, disarmament and the Third World. On 1 April de Gaulle had the satisfaction of giving his guest the news that the second French atomic device had just been successfully detonated on the Sahara. On the 3rd, Khrushchev and his suite took their leave. Although nothing concrete had been accomplished, de Gaulle had the feeling that "something important has happened, in depth, in the centuries-old relations of Russia and France".

De Gaulle himself set out on his journeys to England, Canada and the United States. As John Newhouse points out, the most significant event of his American trip was probably his speech at the National Press Club in Washington, where he praised Khrushchev and called attention to a passage in his war memoirs saying there was no conflict of interest between France and Russia and it was natural for the two to be allied.[32]

Three weeks later, the abortive summit in Paris temporarily dashed de Gaulle's hopes for a separate understanding with the Russians, but his long-term intentions remained unshaken.

Against this background, it is clear that his proposal for a tripartite Atlantic directorate was no more than a spectacular diversionary ploy, designed to distract attention from his real objectives.[33] His efforts at a pan-European settlement were at first tentative; they gained strength and confidence after the end of France's Algerian embroilment in March 1962. Thereafter, de Gaulle became progressively bolder, multiplying the signs of anti-Americanism and general ill-will towards the Anglo-Saxons and members of the alliance that supported them; ploughing a neutralist path in the Third World; gradually withdrawing from NATO. All this, taken as a whole, seemed designed to impress the Russians with his readiness to free France of American shackles and strengthen her credentials as Russia's natural "interlocutor" in a general European settlement. Since, however, he took care to dissimulate his real intentions, and to continue in a desultory way to play the tripartite card, it was a long time before his allies could bring themselves to see that he was turning into an enemy, not a friend.[34]

[32] Newhouse, p. 106.
[33] Schoenbrun, Lives, p. 316, takes the view, with which I disagree, that Eisenhower's rejection of the tripartite directorate is "the real explanation of de Gaulle's foreign policy". The facts do not support this theory.
[34] This interpretation of Gaullist policy, to which I myself began to subscribe in 1962, was advanced by René Courtin in the remarkable short work to which reference has been made; it found powerful support in De Carmoy's Part II. See also Newhouse, chapters 9 and 10.

With occasional exceptions – some technical agreements and de Gaulle's support of Kennedy in the Caribbean missile crisis – France's relations with her allies deteriorated steadily during 1962. The press conference of 14 January 1963 was the natural climax of the process. Now de Gaulle's cards were, more or less, on the table; though nobody could yet predict with any certainty how far he would be prepared to go in his search for "independence". Kennedy's cards, too, were on the table. On 4 July 1962, in an important speech in Philadelphia, he had launched his own "grand design", for an interdependent Atlantic Community based on equality between the European and North American partners. McNamara's multilateral nuclear force proposals were a natural corollary to the Atlantic Community. Neither stood the slightest chance of acceptance by de Gaulle, since they clashed diametrically with his own Grand Design and force de frappe.

On 29 January 1963 the Soviet ambassador in Paris, Sergei Vinogradov, called at the Elysée to see the president. That was the day on which France forced her partners in Brussels to break off negotiations with the British. De Gaulle had invited him as early as 1 January,[35] and it must be assumed that he had already made up his mind by then about the veto on Britain and the refusal of the Polaris missile. Indeed, it is likely that he had prepared the ground as early as 26 October 1962, when a tête-à-tête talk with President Kekkonen of Finland gave him a chance to "pick the brains" of a man singularly well placed to know how to deal with the Russians, and better informed than most on the state of mind of the Soviet leaders.

On 2 January – the day after the invitation to Vinogradov – a French spokesman told the press that de Gaulle had sent Kennedy a note saying he was "studying" the Polaris offer. But this means little. In the light of the press conference of the 14th, the point of the spokesman's news on the 2nd, and of personal reassurances about Britain's application given to Heath by Couve de Murville as late as the 11th, was the same: to deceive public opinion and secure maximum dramatic effect on the 14th.

The fact that the invitation to Vinogradov went out on the 1st is another indication that by then de Gaulle had decided on his course of action and a timetable, and wanted to waste no time in furthering his Grand Design at the Russian end. If so, it soon became plain that the attempt misfired. De Gaulle was in too great a hurry for the Russians. Vinogradov, who knew de Gaulle fairly well and had been shrewd enough to keep in touch with him during his time in the political

---

[35] Courtin, pp. 23 et seq., pp. 81 et seq.

wilderness, was not ill-disposed towards him. But he found the general's current views puzzling, to say the least. Questioned on 21 December 1962, at a dinner in his honour at the Foreign Press Association in Paris, the ambassador had said: "I have heard the formula: Europe from the Atlantic to the Urals. But, until now, I have not understood what it means. . . . Nobody has explained it to us."

There is no published account of the de Gaulle–Vinogradov conversation of 29 January, but on 5 February – time enough for instructions to be received from Moscow – the Soviet embassy issued a coldly worded communiqué denying French press reports that the visit had taken place at the ambassador's request. The communiqué went on to say that the ambassador had expressed Soviet views on international questions, which he would have expressed to the Foreign ministry if he had not been invited to the Elysée.

This was one sign that the Kremlin was not interested in de Gaulle's overtures. Another came two days later, on the 7th, when de Gaulle cancelled a television programme, long arranged, on the battle of Stalingrad, on the grounds that it contained an attack against the Franco-German treaty.

Despite the apparent Soviet snub and his immediate reaction to it, de Gaulle pressed on with his long-term plans. On 21 June 1963 his government announced – apparently without previously consulting Bonn, as laid down in the Franco-German treaty – that the French naval forces in the Atlantic would not be available to NATO in the event of war.

By now thoroughly alarmed, Kennedy and Macmillan agreed in July to make a further attempt to bring the French back into line by offering de Gaulle nuclear materials and technical data.[36] It was hoped, in this way, to persuade him to sign the test ban treaty, the negotiations for which were then in their concluding stages. A precise offer of tripartite discussions to that end was made. But these hopes, modest though they were, were dashed when General de Gaulle declared at his press conference on 29 July that he had no intention of signing the Moscow treaty. Asked whether he would accept an Anglo-American offer of nuclear armaments, he replied: "You know, one does not give France's signature on a series of hypotheses of which none, until now, has even begun to be executed." On the same occasion, de Gaulle denounced the proposed Atlantic Community – Kennedy's Grand Design – as another form of "integration".

Although it was now clearly too late to matter, President Kennedy

[36] Private information.

publicly declared on 1 August that France was now a nuclear power in terms of the Atomic Energy Act, and therefore eligible to receive significant nuclear data. *But de Gaulle was not interested in becoming a nuclear power with foreign aid.* The test ban treaty was signed in Moscow on 5 August; and France duly refused to sign it.

Chapter 4 ✤ The Pressure Mounts

The assassination of President Kennedy at Dallas, Texas, on 22 November 1963 interrupted de Gaulle's anti-American progress. On the 24th he flew to Washington for the State funeral, and there met President Lyndon Johnson for the first time. Johnson pressed him to come to the States for a conference, and misunderstood de Gaulle's ambiguous reply as an acceptance. Gleefully, he told American State governors that the meeting was on, and the news leaked out. There was an immediate French denial, and once again, an American president's relations with de Gaulle had got off to a bad start.[1] Not that better personal relations would have made any difference to the general's plans.

Now de Gaulle moved into a territory on which the Americans were particularly sensitive: China. Towards the end of 1963 de Gaulle had sent the former premier, Edgar Faure, to Peking on a semi-official journey of information and he had come back deeply impressed by the Communist regime's achievements. The real purpose of the trip, however, was to find out whether the Chinese would agree to an exchange of ambassadors. On 27 January 1964 France announced the opening of diplomatic relations with Peking. Until then, America and most of her allies (with Britain as a notable exception) recognised only the Nationalist government on Formosa. On the 31st at his press conference de Gaulle explained his reasons. With his customary tribute to those about to suffer, he praised Marshal Chiang Kai-shek's courage and character. But France had to take account of realities, notably the fact that in Asia nothing of importance could happen without involving China.

There was, in itself, of course, nothing untoward in French recognition of a regime which Britain had recognised as early as 1950. But the

[1] Schoenbrun, *Lives*, pp. 310–11.

act of recognition in 1964 was of wider significance: it must be seen as part of the general policy of asserting French independence as a world power, and doing things calculated to displease Washington.[2]

In the same spirit, de Gaulle set off on 15 March to Mexico on a State visit. In this back garden of the United States he made several speeches calling for closer links between France and Mexico. When a message reached him inviting him to drop in on President Johnson on his return trip, he annoyed the White House by proposing instead a meeting on the French island of Martinique.[3] There was no meeting. Sticking to his schedule, de Gaulle returned to Paris on the 23rd, after stops at Guadeloupe and Martinique.

Physically, the Mexican trip had been particularly gruelling for de Gaulle, who had developed prostate trouble and was under constant medical care. Old age, the condition he dreaded above all others, was upon him. Back in Paris, he learned from Professor Aboulker, a distinguished specialist, that an operation could not now be long deferred. Was he, then, to be proved mortal like lesser men? Presidential elections were not much more than a year away. Was this sign of ageing frailty a gift to rivals for his republican throne?

And what if he should die? Even on the assumption that the relatively banal operation merely incapacitated him for a brief period, somebody would have to run the affairs of State; and it could only be, he recognised, his Prime Minister, Georges Pompidou. There must be no public panic. De Gaulle's immediate family were told he was about to go into hospital; as were two or three of the closest associates; and Pompidou himself. The public would learn only after the event. To this end, the general's forthcoming trip to Picardy was cancelled, but official spokesmen hinted that the reason was the possibility of peasant demonstrations.

On 16 April General de Gaulle made a defiant speech rejecting dependence on the American deterrent, and asserted France's right to a role in Africa, Asia and Latin America. In the most striking indication to date of his trend towards neutralism, he spoke of "the two hegemonies" that were trying to divide the world. He was at his aggressive best: his radio and television audience of millions could not have guessed that he was due to enter hospital the following day.

Still on the 16th, he drafted a political testament and placed it in a wax-sealed envelope, to be handed to Pompidou, who was instructed to

[2] Ironically, the Chinese Communist embassy in Paris was to play a part – though not an easy one to assess precisely – in subversive activities that contributed to the riots of May 1968, which almost brought de Gaulle's rule to an end.
[3] Schoenbrun, *Lives*, p. 311.

open it only in the event of the president's death.[4] Should he not survive the surgeon's knife, he told André Malraux and Gaston Palewski, the Prime Minister would take his place. In the meantime, he was authorised to preside over cabinet meetings. It was characteristic of de Gaulle that he did not bother to inform Gaston Monnerville who, as president of the Senate, was designated under the constitution of the Fifth Republic to be the interim head of State in the event of an unforeseen vacancy. In common with the commoners, Monnerville learned of the operation seven hours after it had happened. It was, of course, successful and after a few days' rest in a private room at the Cochin hospital, the general was back at the Elysée, where one of his first acts was to recover the "testament" in its sealed envelope.

De Gaulle was recovering. The great game of world politics could go on. That April, at the ministerial council meeting of the South-East Asia Treaty Organisation (SEATO), the French delegation argued in favour of the neutralisation of South Vietnam (which the Americans were defending against Communist attack), and praised Cambodia for declining SEATO's protection. On the 27th French naval officers were withdrawn from inter-allied naval commands.

June brought de Gaulle a chance to demonstrate, if any doubts remained, that he never forgot a slight. The 6th was the twentieth anniversary of the Normandy landings of 1944, which had led to the liberation of France. Since he had not been consulted on the operations, nor had French troops taken part in the first landings, he was expected to manifest his continuing displeasure by not attending the commemoration ceremonies. But it was supposed that he would at least send his Prime Minister, Georges Pompidou, instead. It was announced, however, that neither he nor Pompidou would attend; instead both men were to take part in ceremonies on 15 August to mark the anniversary of the French landings in southern France.

Now came a shock for France's NATO partners – as they still were, at that time. The July issue of the authoritative *Revue de Défense Nationale* carried an article by the chief of the French General Staff, General Ailleret, in which he rejected the "flexible response" doctrine generally accepted, in favour of a new strategic doctrine of immediate nuclear reprisals in the event of war.

Further shocks were on the way, to be administered by de Gaulle himself, in his press conference on the 23rd. By then, it was already clear to de Gaulle that the Franco-German treaty, which he had regarded as the means of leading Germany away from dependence on

[4] Alexandre, pp. 20–2.

America, was not going to work that way. Even Adenauer had balked at the proposition that he should opt for France instead of the United States and a highly successful trip by President Kennedy to Germany in June 1963 had bolstered Bonn's resolve. In Adenauer's successor, however, de Gaulle was up against a man who had no time at all for General de Gaulle's ideas: for Dr Erhard, common sense and national interest dictated a continuing close relationship with Washington. When de Gaulle visited the chancellor on 3 and 4 July 1964, he found there was little to be hoped for from that quarter. And at his press conference, he made public his disappointment, lamenting the fact that it had not yet led to any common line of action.

Turning to Vietnam, he denounced the Americans for trying to take France's place in Indo-China, and called for the neutralisation of the whole of France's former colonies in the peninsula.

The general found time for further pinpricks in 1964. In September he kept French naval forces out of the allied Atlantic exercises. That month, he set out on a tour of Latin American republics, one purpose of which was certainly to provoke Washington, although the tone of his speeches was muted. It did not escape notice that he found time to visit six heads of State while apparently too busy to visit President Johnson.

The completeness of de Gaulle's failure to lead Bonn became apparent on 21 November, when Chancellor Erhard, in a speech at Fürth, rejected all moves to de-integrate NATO. Next day in Strasbourg, de Gaulle called on Germany to join him in creating "a European Europe, that is an independent one, powerful and influential within the world of freedom". In the same speech, he noted that the East European regimes were liberalising themselves, which encouraged hopes for a *rapprochement* of Europe as a whole.

He carried this theme further in his speech at the end of the year, in which he spoke of multiplying contacts with East European states.

In 1965 de Gaulle was, if anything, even more disagreeable towards his allies than he had been in 1964. It was as if new and ingenious ways of causing displeasure kept on occurring to him. Thus in February he extended his cold war against the Anglo-Saxons into the monetary field. Already in September 1964 the French Finance minister, Valéry Giscard d'Estaing, had drawn strong American criticism by proposing reforms of the international exchange system. For some months, a regular caller at the Elysée had been Jacques Rueff, a distinguished senior economist and financial expert, whose hostility towards the gold exchange standard that had governed international accounts since the war was well known. Now de Gaulle saw in Rueff's ideas a further weapon against the British and Americans. At his press conference on 4 February the general in turn denounced the gold exchange standard and called for a return to the pre-war gold standard.

On the 11th France unilaterally contracted out of the gold exchange standard, and de Gaulle instructed the Banque de France to convert the bulk of its holding of dollars into gold. Later that year – in September – de Gaulle forbade the bank to join other central banks in a concerted effort to support the pound sterling.

Other Gaullian surprises included a letter to the North Vietnamese leader, Ho Chi Minh, dated 8 February 1965, condemning foreign – that is, American – intervention and the extension of the war. About that time, he accepted a Soviet proposal for joint Russo-French consultations on ways to restore peace to South-East Asia; and in May France withdrew her staff officers from SEATO.

That spring de Gaulle may have thought he had fresh cause to hope that his attempted *rapprochement* with Russia might, after all, come to something. On 8 April Valery Zorin, a very senior Soviet diplomat, arrived in Paris as the new ambassador. At the farewell dinner for Vinogradov, de Gaulle alluded to the traditional friendship between France and Russia. The speech alarmed the West Germans, and Dr Adenauer, from his retirement, wrote to de Gaulle to express his concern.[5] From the 26th to the 30th, the Soviet Foreign minister, Andrei Gromyko, was in Paris on an official visit. Was de Gaulle planning a reversal of alliances? This was the question that was now being asked in the western chancelleries. It was to be revived more insistently at the end of October, when Couve de Murville went to Moscow to return Gromyko's visit.

There was no let-up. In May, France informed her allies that she would not take part in forthcoming strategic exercises. On the 4th, the French delegation at the United Nations Security Council condemned the American military intervention in the Dominican Republic – a striking act of hostility in a context of direct interest to the United States.

In June, de Gaulle decided to strike against the Six. The European Commission had tabled proposals for the financing of the common agricultural policy which were too "integrationist" for de Gaulle's case. On 30 June he ordered a six-month French boycott of all institutions of the Community. During this time France's partners were supposed to rid the EEC of some specific supranational tendencies, or face the dissolution of the common market. At the end of the six months, the

[5] Newhouse, p. 282.

French delegation returned, having gained most, though not all, of the points at issue.

As if the EEC boycott were not drama enough, de Gaulle had more in store for his second press conference of the year, which took place on 9 September 1965. For the first time, the general served notice on France's allies that France would cease to submit to "integration" within the alliance, "at the latest in 1969" – that is at the end of the twenty-year term provided in 1949 as the period that must elapse before the North Atlantic Treaty could be revised. He went on to mention the great importance France attached to "the new trend taken by our relations with Russia". Never had there been so clear a hint of an impending reversal of alliances.

In further speeches and in television interviews that autumn, de Gaulle continued to harp on the need for "independence", to denounce any subordination of France to the super-powers and to stress her friendship with Russia.[6] During this period and during the winter, French officials from time to time dropped hints, at times alarming, at others reassuring, about the general's intentions in regard to the alliance.

It was clear, to those familiar with de Gaulle's methods, that a further bombshell was on the way. His next press conference on 21 February 1966 was therefore awaited with some trepidation. Perhaps because of this, de Gaulle did not fully unveil his intentions there, reserving his surprise effect for later. He went, however, as far as it is possible to go without actually saying something. He declared that a treaty could not remain integrally valid when its object had changed, nor an alliance stay as it was when the conditions in which it had been concluded had altered. France still thought the alliance "useful to her security", but could no longer accept the "American protectorate" organised in Europe "under cover of NATO". From then on, until 4 April 1969 – the terminal date of the original treaty obligations – France would continue to modify arrangements affecting her, but of course in such a way that "these changes take place progressively and that her allies should not be suddenly thereby incommoded".

Despite this reassuring phrase, de Gaulle delivered his final blow brusquely, without prior consultations with any of France's allies, and demonstrably without consideration for their own interests. Indeed, the contrast between the quoted phrase and the general's actual actions

[6] A striking example had been the speech of 27 April 1965. *See also* the speech of 11 December 1965, and the interviews with Michel Droit on 13, 14 and 15 December (De Gaulle, *Discours*, Vol. IV).

was so stark that it may be assumed his only reason for saying what he did was to preserve, or restore, the element of surprise essential to his proposed *coup de théâtre*. In the event, on 7 March he drafted personal messages to President Johnson and other western leaders to announce that while France remained a member of the alliance, she was withdrawing from the North Atlantic Treaty Organisation. The commitment to the alliance was itself qualified, by being made subject to "events which, in the course of the next three years, might modify the fundamental elements [*données*] of relations between East and West". With this reservation, the French would be ready "in 1969 and later", as at the present, to fight with their allies should one of them be the object of an unprovoked aggression. The withdrawal from NATO, however, was sweeping. The assignment to NATO of all French armed forces in Federal Germany was terminated – though the troops themselves were to remain there. Similarly, all French officers and staff were withdrawn from integrated headquarters, and all foreign commands were to be removed from Rocquencourt near Versailles, and Fontainebleau. Finally, all France's allies were requested to remove units, installations or bases on French territory and not under French control.

The letter to President Johnson was delivered first, on the day of drafting, to the American ambassador, Charles Bohlen. The letters to Chancellor Erhard, Prime Minister Wilson, and President Giuseppe Saragat, and other allies followed. The wording of these messages, though similar, was not identical. The one to Wilson, for instance, mentioned de Gaulle's concern about being dragged into a war in South-East Asia; but the one to Johnson did not.[7]

The French president had not troubled to consult his cabinet about this momentous decision, but had informed the Prime Minister (Pompidou), the Foreign minister (Couve de Murville) and the Defence minister (Debré). Two days after the event, the Council of Ministers was summoned to give its formal approval. That day, 9 March 1966, the ministry of Information issued a communiqué which, in substance, paraphrased General de Gaulle's message to Johnson.

In a further communication to the allies dated 29 March, de Gaulle's government named two deadlines: 1 July 1966 for terminating the assignment of French personnel to allied commands; and 1 April 1967 for the departure of foreign forces and installations from France.[8]

Although something of the kind had been expected, the brutality and finality of de Gaulle's action shocked France's supposed partners.

[7] Newhouse, pp. 287–8. [8] De Carmoy, pp. 373 *et seq.*

Replying on 23 March 1966 to de Gaulle's letter of the 7th, President Johnson, with great self-restraint, argued the strategic and technological case for integration which alone would enable the alliance to function speedily and effectively in the event of a crisis.

The American government's reply to the French memorandum of the 29th recalled that France's allies had several times invited her to submit proposals for reforms, both of the treaty and of the organisation, but without result. De Gaulle's attention was drawn to the fact that France herself had joined her allies in unanimous approval of the NATO arrangements within the Ministerial Council. Moreover, the secret agreements on the establishment of American bases in France had stipulated that they should remain in force "during the validity of the North Atlantic treaty, unless the two governments should previously decide otherwise, by mutual agreement". A further agreement, concerning the communications system, was dated 6 December 1958 – that is, after de Gaulle's return to power – and provided for two years' notice of termination, in the event of disagreement.

Erhard's government replied on 3 May to the 29 March message. Pointing out that the decision to withdraw French forces in Germany from the allied command affected previous NATO decisions and the treaties governing the stationing of foreign forces on German soil, it called for fresh negotiations between France and Germany on the basis of equality and reciprocity. The Germans also complained that France had taken her decision without consulting Germany, as provided under the Franco-German treaty.

None of this, needless to say, had the slightest effect on de Gaulle, who had now done what he had wanted to do for a long time. On 18 March, France's fourteen allies published a joint statement reaffirming their support for the principle of integration within NATO and declaring their intention to strengthen the existing organisation. This, too, left the general cold, and in speeches on 13, 14 and 20 April, Pompidou energetically defended his leader's decisions.

More significant, perhaps, than western indignation was Communist approval. On 31 March, at the 23rd Congress of the Soviet Communist party, the French party leader, Waldeck Rochet, mentioned de Gaulle's name in eulogistic terms that drew applause. And on 27 April, taking advantage of the disarray within the western alliance, the Soviet Foreign minister, Gromyko, in a statement in Rome, launched the idea of a pan-European security conference.

On his side de Gaulle lost no time in making further overtures to the eastern bloc. In May he sent Couve de Murville on official visits to

Poland and Czechoslovakia; and on 21 June he himself arrived in Moscow to the grandiose reception that awaited a foreign head of State who now presented himself as a friend, no longer a foe in any but the most tenuous sense. Did he, in fact, already consider himself an "ally" of the Soviet Union? Journalists were startled to hear him refer, at Moscow University on 22 June, to "the new alliance of Russia and France". Although French spokesmen made light of this phrase, it passed unaltered into the collection of de Gaulle's speeches and messages.[9]

In 1961, when Khrushchev visited France, de Gaulle had made sure he went to the provinces as well as to Paris. Now, in 1966, the Russians made sure he went not only to European Russia and to the Ukraine, but also to the Siberian town of Novosibirsk, where he was able to see for himself that Moscow's authority did not end at the Urals. In Moscow itself he addressed the Supreme Soviet, and on the 31st, before departing, made an appearance on Soviet television, the last paragraph of which he delivered in Russian. But all this was ceremonial or public relations: what of high politics? De Gaulle gave more than he received. An important technical agreement was reached, whereby France was enabled to launch satellites and other space vehicles from Soviet launching pads and with Soviet rockets. But was this an advantage? Did it not rather tend to place the French in a state of technological dependence on the Soviet Union, of the kind it had successfully avoided with the United States? The joint Franco-Soviet declaration of 29 June 1966, however, enshrined concepts close to de Gaulle's heart: it registered the view, jointly held, that European problems should be considered in a European framework, and the hope that *détente* should lead to *entente*.

But these were words. When it came to realities, the Russians did not depart from their evident awareness that France lacked both the influence and the power to settle European problems with the Russians. The fact that it had been agreed in Moscow that there should be regular consultations on a new "hot line" between Moscow and Paris on European and other international problems, did not affect the Soviet approach. This was shown with remarkable alacrity on 8 July, with the final communiqué of the conference of ministers of the Warsaw Pact at Bucharest, which made it clear that the Soviet Union continued to recognise the existence of two blocs and knew that American views would have to be sought in any European settlement.[10]

[9] De Gaulle, *Discours*, Vol. V, p. 46.
[10] *See* De Carmoy, pp. 385–6, for a penetrating discussion of de Gaulle's policy at this stage.

De Gaulle's hostility to the western alliance and his readiness for Russia's friendship had indeed made no difference. "Europe from the Atlantic to the Urals" was make-believe, and the Russians knew it, if he did not. The general, in fact, had entered what might be termed his final eccentric phase in foreign policy. Three more years of power lay before him, although he could not know it then. He used them in the international scene, to make numerous journeys of no particular utility, to attack the Americans with increasing venom, to pick gratuitous quarrels with friendly states, to confirm France's neutralism, and, not least, to rebuff Britain in her second attempt to join the European Economic Community.

Domestic events occasionally forced themselves on the general's attention,[11] but only when they were so big that they could not be ignored. Of such were the presidential election in 1965, the student riots and general strike in 1968 and the financial crisis later that year. But by and large, foreign affairs absorbed most of the president's time and energies during his last few years in office. The following brief chronology, though by no means a complete chronicle of all he did or said in international relations after his Russian trip, illustrates the increasing virulence of his attitudes, their deepening unreality, and their unfailingly theatrical character.

25–6 AUGUST 1966

Violent riots marked de Gaulle's arrival on the French Somali coast, at the start of a journey that led on to Ethiopia and Cambodia. In part, these were clashes between the rival ethnic groups: the Afars and the Issas. But slogans were waved and shouted calling for the total and immediate independence of the territory. Here was a minor "storm" for the man of storms. Next day, in a speech before the Territorial Assembly at Djibouti, de Gaulle declared that brandishing banners and rioting did not alone establish the democratic will. Should the Somalis wish to sever their links with France, they could do so if a referendum showed that this was what they really wanted. He went on his way, after shouting: "Vive la côte française des Somalis! Vive la République française! Vive la France!" (The referendum was held on 19 March 1967; it showed the popular will to be that the Somali Coast should stay within the Republic, but with a new Statute.)

1 SEPTEMBER 1966

In a speech at Pnom Penh, Cambodia, de Gaulle denounced American

---

[11] These are considered in the following two chapters.

intervention in Vietnam, praised Cambodia's neutrality and declared France's intention to stay out of the conflict. The previous day, he had granted an audience to the North Vietnamese representative in the Cambodian capital.

28 OCTOBER 1966
At his press conference, the General called for the withdrawal of American forces in Vietnam, the neutralisation of South-East Asia and American recognition of Peking; defended his Atlantic policy; and complained that the West Germans, instead of applying the Franco-German treaty as agreed between the two governments, had been applying the unilateral preamble added later by the German deputies.

1–9 DECEMBER 1966
The Soviet premier, Kosygin, paid an official visit to France.

24–5 JANUARY 1967
The British Prime Minister, Harold Wilson, and his Foreign secretary, George Brown (later Lord George Brown), visited General de Gaulle.

10 MAY 1967
Britain renewed her application to join the common market.

16 MAY 1967
In a lengthy reply to a question at his press conference, de Gaulle dealt with the renewed British application. There was not, and never had been, he insisted, any question of a French veto. But he went on to enumerate the many difficulties that stood in the way of a British success. Not the least of these was Britain's special relationship with the United States. He concluded by listing three alternatives:

> That Britain should be admitted forthwith. This would fundamentally change the character of the Common Market.
> That the British and their EFTA partners should content themselves with a form of association.
> That the British should make the profound changes necessary to become true partners of the Europeans.

MAY–JUNE 1967
De Gaulle's handling of the Middle East crisis and the six-day war caused unease in his own government and in France, as well as abroad.

579

On 24 May, he proposed a four-power summit, of Britain, France, the United States and the Soviet Union. To his chagrin, London and Washington accepted, but Moscow declined. On 2 June, he declared, in advance of any hostilities, France's disapproval of any state that first took up arms. On the 16th, Kosygin passed through Paris on his way to a special United Nations meeting and de Gaulle promised French support for the Russian position. On the 18th, Mr and Mrs Wilson were guests of the de Gaulles in the Grand Trianon at Versailles, which had lately been restored. On the 21st, the day after the Wilsons' departure, and without informing his own Foreign minister, then in New York, de Gaulle's government issued a statement blaming the war in the Middle East, and much else besides, on American intervention in Vietnam. France duly supported the Soviet resolution at the UN whereas the western allies voted for a more moderate Latin American resolution, which was carried. De Gaulle is believed to have thought that relations between Moscow and Washington were now so bad as to rule out a meeting between the Soviet premier and the American president; but Kosygin and Johnson met anyway, at Glassboro.

27 JULY 1967

In an extempore speech from the balcony of the town hall in Montreal, General de Gaulle exclaimed, "*Vive le Québec libre!*" This violation of normal courtesy to the host government – in this instance, the federal administration in Ottawa – caused a storm. The Canadian cabinet, after a special session called by the Prime Minister, Lester Pearson, published a statement describing de Gaulle's remarks as "unacceptable". The general thereupon cancelled his plan to visit Ottawa and flew back directly from Montreal to Paris. Because of the change of plans, his ministers were required to meet him at Orly airport in the small hours. The "*Québec libre*" indiscretion attracted much unfavourable press criticism in France.

6–12 SEPTEMBER 1967

De Gaulle, on a State visit to Poland – where he had served as a young army officer in 1919–20 – not only endorsed Poland's western frontiers, which had been expected, but described the Silesian city of Hindenburg, renamed Zabrze by the Poles, as "the most Polish of all Polish cities". For this, he was rebuked by the West German government and press.[12]

---

[12] *France-Soir*, 12 September 1967, quoted in Newhouse, pp. 303 and 363; for further matter, *see* pp. 305–6.

NOVEMBER 1967

This was, from de Gaulle's standpoint, a theatrically fruitful month. The November issue of the *Revue de Défense Nationale* contained an important article by the chief of staff of the armed forces, General Charles Ailleret, advocating a French defence system on a world scale and covering all points of the compass (*mondial et tous azimuts*). It became known that General de Gaulle himself had inspired the article. Never had the new neutralist line been so strikingly expressed. From now on, France must be prepared to meet aggression not only from Russia but, say, from America, Germany or Britain.

That month, the British pound ran into acute difficulties, and devaluation was announced on the 18th. In the secret talks that preceded the decision, all the major countries except one pledged that they would not devalue their own currencies, which would have, to that extent, nullified the devaluation of sterling. The exception was France (although the French did not, in fact, devalue at that time). Inspired and carefully timed French press leaks about sterling difficulties contributed to deepen the crisis.

On the 27th, de Gaulle called another press conference. What sensations did he still hold in reserve? This time, there were at least two. The more important was the general's second No to Britain's application to join the Common Market. Once again, as in May, there was a lengthy review of the phases – he listed five – of Britain's relations with the EEC. And in the end, without mention of a veto, he declared the British to be still very far from qualifying to join "Europe". Startlingly, he declared himself ready to consider creating a free trade area that would absorb the EEC. But this was to point to the "impossibility" that Britain should join the Common Market at that time, and to the incompatibility between it and the British position.

But in the following day's newspapers, the second No to Britain competed for space and headlines with a passage in which de Gaulle, referring to the six-day war, described the Jews as "an *élite* people, sure of itself and dominating". Had de Gaulle turned anti-semitic? Certainly there had never been any sign of it, and there had always been Jews among his close associates. But his remarks aroused much unfavourable comment, and provoked the sociologist of Jewish origin, Raymond Aron, to publish a book, *De Gaulle, Israël et les Juifs*, expressing his indignation at the implication that Jewish Frenchmen were not to be regarded as French in the full sense.

1968

In terms of international affairs, de Gaulle had now almost, though not quite, run out of sensations. At home, 1968 was a traumatic year for him, for it was dominated by the spring disorders that almost brought his regime down. It was typical of the general's foreign euphoria that he was in Rumania when the crisis broke out and that he shortened his stay by only a few hours to return to Paris.

While events threw discredit on his regime – despite the subsequent triumph of the Gaullists in general elections – the year marked the utter collapse of de Gaulle's foreign policy. For on 21 August, massive forces of the Soviet Union and other Warsaw Pact countries invaded Czecho-slovakia. With this reaffirmation of Soviet power and demonstration of the continuing identity of Soviet ideology and policy, de Gaulle's pan-European vision lay in ruins. In his frustration, de Gaulle caused his government to issue a statement, in two sentences, tracing the Soviet action back to "the policy of blocs that was imposed in Europe by the effect of the Yalta agreements". This curious rationalisation carried no conviction and got a bad press.

At his press conference on 9 September 1968, de Gaulle condemned "the events of which Czechoslovakia has just been the theatre and the victim within the Communist bloc . . . notably because they are absurd in regard to the prospects for European *détente*". He could scarcely have approved the invasion in the light of his own record (which he recalled) of standing up to Stalin over recognition of the Soviet-sponsored Polish government; but his choice of reason was revealing. Was it the Soviet policy that was "absurd", or his own? The Russian invasion was logically consistent with Moscow's desire to maintain its hegemony over eastern Europe. It was surely de Gaulle's policy of seeking a deal with Russia that was "absurd" in the light of that hegemony. In his heart of hearts, de Gaulle probably recognised this; but as he could not do so publicly, he went on acting his pre-scripted part.

Indeed, on 31 December, in his New Year's Eve message, he made no mention of Czechoslovakia in a careful enumeration of world problems in which France was able to "act efficaciously to facilitate a solution". These were: *détente*; the war in Vietnam; the Arab–Israeli dispute; the entry of the Chinese People's Republic into the United Nations; autonomy for "the French people of Canada"; and self-determination for "valiant Biafra".

This was not the first time de Gaulle had mentioned Biafra in public. At his September press conference he had criticised the federations that were a legacy of the colonial system, in Canada, Rhodesia, Malaysia,

Cyprus and Nigeria. "Why," he asked, "should the Ibos, who in general are Christians, who live in the south in a certain way, who have their own language, depend on another ethnic fraction of the Federation?" He spoke at a time when the Nigerian civil war had already lasted fourteen months. The great power alignment on the issue was curious: Britain and America supported the Nigerian government, but so did Russia; France alone supported the secessionist government of Biafra, and, as de Gaulle said, had helped it. She had not, however, recognised it, because "she thinks that the management of Africa is, in the first place, the business of the Africans"; but some African governments had granted recognition and France had not ruled it out.

De Gaulle was alluding to the fact that two of the French-speaking countries – Ivory Coast and Gabon – had recognised Biafra, along with Tanzania and Zambia. What he did not say was that the Ivory Coast and Gabon had been strongly encouraged by Paris to give recognition, largely because of French oil interests in the area; and that French arms and munitions had been reaching the Biafrans through those two countries. Not that economic interests alone would have determined de Gaulle's decision to recognise the losers in the Nigerian war. Colonel Ojukwu and his secessionists had won his immediate sympathy. To Jacques Foccart, secretary-general at the Elysée for African and Malagasy Affairs, he is said to have exclaimed, "A brave little people! Foccart, we should try to do something to help them."[13] The general's reasons for this attitude were complex. The "brave little people" reaction was probably spontaneous; but it was one that was more likely to occur to him when those concerned were in actual or potential revolt against English-speaking Canadians or British-supported Nigerians than, say, when Bretons clamoured for greater autonomy. That French oil interests also had motives for supporting the Ibos was an additional reason for de Gaulle to do so. But the decisive reason was undoubtedly the chance to show that France was playing a role independently of the "Anglo-Saxons".

One of the sequels to the May disorders and the expensive social settlement of trade union claims was a flight from the franc. Both in Paris and in other capitals, devaluation was considered inevitable. The general, however, had not quite lost his talent for doing the unexpected. The stability of the franc was, for him, a point of honour and one of the aspects that distinguished the Fifth Republic from its predecessors. At his

[13] Georges Chaffard, in the third of a penetrating series of three articles on Foccart, "L'Homme des affaires secrètes", in Le Nouvel Observateur, 3 November 1969.

cabinet meeting on 13 November 1968 he declared: "To accept devaluation would be the worst absurdity that could be." He authorised his spokesman, Joël le Theule, to quote this remark: it undoubtedly reflected his real thinking. The situation, however, was apparently even worse than he had supposed, and a long letter from Jacques Rueff that day emphasised the fact.[14] Some days of Gaullian gloom followed, during which the general dropped hints of blame on Georges Pompidou for allowing the events of May to get out of hand. He did nothing to discourage press speculation about devaluation. Indeed precise forecasts of the percentage of the impending change (9.785 per cent, wrote Le Monde) appeared – probably inspired not by the Elysée but by the Prime Minister's office.[15] All the men he consulted, with one exception, advised in favour of devaluation. The exception was Jeanneney, the minister of State in charge of "participation", who reminded him that what was "absurd" yesterday could not be reasonable today, and argued that a decision to maintain the parity of the franc would end the crisis of confidence that was undermining it. De Gaulle decided, then, to listen to Jeanneney (who had told him what he wanted to hear) and to ignore the advice of Rueff and his senior ministers and officials. There was a further reason for his obstinacy: Britain had devalued sterling in November 1967, and it would have been intolerable to him to have done the same a year later. On 24 November 1968, in a national television broadcast, he confirmed that there would be no devaluation. As he had guessed, the psychological shock was immediate; and, together with the reintroduction of exchange controls, was sufficient to stem the flight from the franc, at least for the time being.

There was only one more "voluntary" sensation in the foreign field: the announcement on 6 January 1969 of a French general embargo on all arms deliveries to Israel. Government spokesmen manfully defended this decision by reference to de Gaulle's resentment against Israel for having compromised world peace. But there was more to it than that. On 27 December, two Palestinian Arabs had attacked an Israeli El Al airliner at Athens airport. In reprisal, Israel sent a special commando next day to Beirut airport, where the Israelis destroyed thirteen Lebanese civil aircraft on the ground before returning safely to their country.

The Israeli retaliation threw de Gaulle into a rage. That the Israelis

[14] Alexandre, pp. 300 et seq. See also Viansson-Ponté, Republique, Vol. II, pp. 591 et seq.
[15] John Newhouse (Anglo-Saxons, p. 327) is, I think, mistaken when he says these forecasts may have been inspired "from either the Elysée or the Prime Minister's office"; and when he surmises that de Gaulle had decided against devaluation possibly a week before announcing his decision.

should have acted the way they did towards a former French protectorate, towards which France still felt protective, was a "criminal insult"
– the words that were frequently on his lips during the next few days.
On 3 January, the government informed the Israeli embassy that no
more arms would be forthcoming from France. That night three naval
launches under construction at Cherbourg and previously destined for
Israel took to sea on test and "disappeared". It soon became known that
they had been seized by order of the Israeli secret service. This was too
much: de Gaulle's rage exploded. He dictated a ferocious statement to
Le Theule and announced his arms embargo, which, it turned out,
extended even to material already paid for by the Israeli government.
Whatever de Gaulle's sentimental concern for Lebanon – which indeed
had been made to pay for Palestinian deeds or misdeeds over which she
had no control – the connection between the arms ban and America's
normal military support of Israel was evident.

Some relatively pallid gestures followed. Between 17 and 20 February,
the first international "conférence de la francophonie" took place at
Niamey, the capital of Niger. A Canadian delegate was there. That
French-speaking countries should meet was not, in itself, a startling event,
or a particularly Gaullian one: the event was merely an extension into
the post-colonial era of France's celebrated mission civilisatrice. But
"francophonie", in common with "latinité" – much invoked at the
time of de Gaulle's Latin American trip – was yet another device for
extending France's influence; and as such, had the general's reign continued, it might not have been negligible.

Just before the Niger meeting, a meeting in London of the Western
European Union – the initially military organisation set up in 1955 and
consisting of the European Six plus Britain – gave de Gaulle a chance of
another boycott. The meeting had been called, for 14 February 1969,
on the initiative of the British Foreign secretary, Michael Stewart, to
discuss developments in the Middle East. That the British, at that time,
thought of the Western European Union as a possible way of concerting
its foreign policy with that of the EEC powers, is true, and de Gaulle was
not the man to tolerate such "Trojan horse" tactics. Not only did the
French government boycott the London meeting, but it threatened to
withdraw from the WEU altogether, unless "regular" procedures were
observed. On the 17th, indeed, the French let it be known that they
would not take part in WEU activities until further notice.

The last of the foreign sensations broke that February; and turned
out to be a damp squib. This was the so-called "Soames affair".
Its connection with the WEU row was intimate. It began in secrecy and

ended in inspired leaks on both sides of the Channel and a fury of mutual recriminations.

The new British ambassador to Paris, Christopher Soames, had been trying to see General de Gaulle, and a *tête-à-tête* lunch was arranged, to take place at the Elysée on 4 February. Soames, a Conservative politician, had been appointed by a Labour government for a number of reasons: his "European" approach, his command of French, and not least the fact that he was Sir Winston Churchill's son-in-law. Leading Gaullists in Paris privately commented at the time that the Churchill connection was bad psychology as de Gaulle had no wish to be reminded of his wartime dependence on Britain.[16] Whatever the force of this objection, de Gaulle decided to "use" the ambassador for an entirely new approach to Britain. Although the approach was novel in one sense, it was consistent with the general's public reflections at his press conference of 27 November 1967 about his readiness to consider a free trade area that would absorb the European Common Market. This was essentially the idea de Gaulle now developed in conversation with Soames. He – the general – had taken no part in the creation of the EEC and had no particular faith in it. He was sure that if Britain and other countries joined, the Community would no longer be the same. This was not necessarily undesirable, since he believed the Community would change, and he would like to see it evolve into a looser form of free trade area with arrangements by each country to exchange agricultural products. He would be quite prepared to discuss with Britain what should take the place of the Common Market, and, as a first step, he would welcome political discussion between Britain and France.

He himself would actually prefer a larger European economic associ-ation, with a smaller inner council of a European political association comprising France, Germany, Italy and Britain. But before going any further, it was necessary to establish whether France and Britain could really harmonise their political thinking. He therefore sought talks, which should be secret, between the two countries, on economic, monetary, political and defence questions aimed at resolving their differ-ences. It would be appropriate, he suggested, for Britain to make an initial request for such talks, which he would then welcome.

This was heady talk for the ambassador on his first meeting with de Gaulle. Whether it could lead to anything was, of course, for the British government to find out. On the face of it, it was hard to say what prospects the general's proposal opened, since he had preceded it with a familiar speech on the need for European countries to be

16 Private information.

independent of America. Only France, he declared, had achieved this independence, and the other European countries, against their present inclinations, would have to do the same: once Europe had become truly independent there would be no need for NATO "as such, with its American dominance and command structure".

For Soames, then, the first thing was to get a full and authoritative report of the conversation back to the Foreign Office in London. He drafted his report, then submitted it to French officials, who passed it on to de Gaulle, who, in turn, approved it as a fair account. This, at all events, was what Michael Stewart said in his statement to the House of Commons on 24 February 1969, when the row had broken.

According to Harold Wilson's account of what happened next, there was an immediate divergence of views between himself as Prime Minister and the Foreign Office officials on the significance of de Gaulle's proposal.[17] He was inclined to play down its importance. De Gaulle had said much the same thing to him when they had met in January 1967. As for the proposal for bilateral talks, he was prepared to take it as a friendly gesture, "subject to our ensuring that they were not used to divide us in either defence or economic affairs from our partners in EFTA and our prospective partners in EEC". The Foreign Office, on the other hand, feared a trap. Why, otherwise, did the general suggest that the initiative should come from the British side? Was this not so that he could turn to France's EEC partners and tell them the British were trying to sabotage the Community?

Wilson was about to go to Bonn for talks with the German chancellor, Dr Kurt Kiesinger. The question was whether he should keep quiet about de Gaulle's initiative, or mention it; and if he was to mention it, whether he should merely disclose that de Gaulle was proposing bilateral talks, or give details of the lunch-time proposal. As Wilson puts it, the Foreign Office put strong pressure on him to tell all: thus he would discredit the French with their EEC partners, and gain credit for himself, for loyalty to the Six. The Prime Minister, however, found this "little Lord Fauntleroy" role distasteful. He decided to mention the approach but withhold the details. But when he reached the chancellor's office on 12 February, and asked for the Foreign Office briefing on the Soames–de Gaulle encounter, instead of being given the "brief and anodyne note I had been expecting" he was handed "the full works". Furious, but finding concealment difficult, he then told Kiesinger exactly what had happened.

The Anglo-German talks ended with a joint declaration on European

[17] Harold Wilson, *The Labour Government 1964–1970* (1971), pp. 610 *et seq.*

policy, which gave much pleasure to the British, since it included a joint pledge to further British entry into the EEC. The declaration correspondingly displeased the French; but their fury was really aroused when reports of what Wilson had told Kiesinger filtered back to Paris. Towards the end of the week the French newspapers were given the Elysée version of the lunch-time meeting, together with encouragement to attack the British – especially Soames – for bad faith and inaccurate reporting. Thereupon, as happens in such affairs, the Foreign Office leaked their own account to the British press. A formal French protest was delivered on the 24th. The French decision to boycott the WEU meeting in London must have been made before the Soames affair leak, but the fact that it was not called off may be significant; for though the French disapproved of Britain's attempts to use the WEU as a political back door into Europe, it is unlikely that they would have made a public fuss about WEU if Anglo-French talks were thought to be on the way.

The effects of Wilson's disclosures to Kiesinger were measurable: Anglo-French relations immediately dropped to their lowest point since the first de Gaulle veto in 1963: and the usefulness of Soames as ambassador was reduced to virtually nil, at least for the time being. Christopher Soames, who had merely done his job, was conscious of declining usefulness and wished to resign, but he was dissuaded by the Prime Minister. As it happened, de Gaulle himself was to resign only a few weeks later, so the harm done was not lasting.

What would have happened if Wilson had not told Kiesinger what he knew? The answer can only be conjectural. The Foreign Office's fear of a trap was understandable, in the light of de Gaulle's consistently anti-British actions of the past six years or so. But it is unlikely, in retrospect, that de Gaulle intended to lay a trap (although he would not have hesitated to do so, in certain circumstances). The fact is that his entire pan-European policy had collapsed, and that he was making no particular progress in Europe itself. Since he could not bear either frustration or inaction in foreign policy, the most probable explanation of his approach to Soames was that he really did want to try an entirely new line. Since he continued to postulate "independence" from America as the basis for any further progress, it is improbable that it would have led to anything anyway. The British fear – which Stewart expressed in the House of Commons debate – that Franco-British talks could not have been concealed from other interested parties, was probably well-founded. But little harm would have come of a British request for further clarification of de Gaulle's intentions.

The argument cannot, of course, be resolved satisfactorily. On 15

March, de Gaulle took the unusual step of authorising a Quai d'Orsay spokesman to give the press a very full summary of the conversations he had had on the 13th and 14th with the West German chancellor, Dr Kiesinger.[18] From this summary, much of it in direct quotation, it appears that de Gaulle complained that the British had turned the substance of his talk with Soames "upside down". He had simply wanted to discuss the idea of a wider grouping in Europe, and was now ready to discuss it with Kiesinger.

Kiesinger listened, as he always did when de Gaulle spoke, with deferential attention. Unlike Erhard, he was as "Gaullist" as a German can be; and the Quai d'Orsay account of the talks recorded him as echoing de Gaulle's views on the need for *détente* and the end of the "Soviet threat" in Europe. Kiesinger did, however, express a mild reservation about Britain's exclusion from the European community.

The West German chancellor was, in fact, no more able than Adenauer or Erhard had been to resolve the dilemmas implicit in Franco-German relations during de Gaulle's tenure of power. De Gaulle, indeed, had not stopped at putting partial blame on the Germans for the events in Czechoslovakia in 1968, for having gone too far in the search for a *détente* by granting generous economic aid to the Dubcek government. As John Newhouse put it, "the price of harmony with de Gaulle was now too great for any German government, however warmly disposed".[19]

In Bonn, as in London, in the spring of 1969 the dominant concern had, in any case, ceased to be with de Gaulle, who was not expected to stay in power beyond the end of his current term, expiring in 1972. But the old man had yet another surprise in store: he would shortly announce that his continuance in office depended on the result of a referendum. And, on losing it, he would retire, as he had said he would.

[18] *Paris-Presse l'Intransigeant*, 16–17 March 1969.   [19] *Newhouse*, p. 331.

Chapter 5 ⚜ The Roots of Discontent

Neither General de Gaulle nor his Prime Minister, Georges Pompidou, had the slightest premonition of the social turmoil that was to shake the Fifth Republic in the spring of 1968. The storm struck after several years of peace, prosperity and expansion. It was the outcome of an accumulation of largely unsuspected pressures. To that extent, it was the natural, if unexpected, climax to everything Charles de Gaulle had done, or failed to do, especially at home, in ten years of power.

Throughout his life, de Gaulle had been more interested in foreign policy than domestic affairs. His study of French history was essentially that of France's position in the world. Economic prosperity and financial stability were seen primarily as essential preconditions for a policy of grandeur abroad. Both would be the natural consequences of strong and purposeful government, itself made possible by a constitution that strengthened the central power at the expense of the elected legislators.

But in the last analysis, domestic affairs are always more important than foreign, except at times of national crisis. In his later years of power de Gaulle's obsessive interest in his foreign policy, even after it had become clear that it had not the slightest chance of success, weakened his power at home. It had become too evident to too many ordinary people that in his pursuit of dreams of grandeur, de Gaulle had little or no interest in the France ordinary people had to live in. It was a curiously elementary political truth for a great contemporary master of power to neglect. And this neglect was his undoing.

By temperament, as so many writers have noted, de Gaulle was a monarch. The Parisian satirical paper, Le Canard Enchaîné, recognised the fact by running an elegantly witty feature, "La Cour", written in the French of the seventeenth century – in which the general was portrayed as if he were Louis XIV. He himself was careful not to refer to himself in public as a king – since he had often claimed to be the defender, saviour or restorer of the Republic; but in private, he declared

590

that the president of the Republic must have a monarchic character, and described the presidency as an "elective monarchy". He is even said to have toyed with the idea that he should be succeeded by the Bourbon Pretender to the throne of France, the Comte de Paris, whom he is thought to have treated with respect because of his ancestry rather than his achievements.[1]

Although de Gaulle never wavered in his conviction that all the power of the State should initially and ultimately flow from the president, the Gaullist constitution in its original form provided that he should be elected by indirect suffrage. This was, indeed, what he had proposed in his speech at Bayeux in 1946. In 1958 he could easily have had himself elected by direct suffrage: the majority would have been overwhelming. The fear of charges of Bonapartism held him back; to have proclaimed that this was his intention might have frightened many voters into opposing the constitution as a whole at the referendum in September; moreover, the results of direct voting in Algeria and some places in French Africa could not be precisely predicted.[2]

Four years later, having settled the Algerian problem, tasted the disadvantages of the original concept, and seen that some of the dangers that had loomed large in 1958 – such as that of a Communist resurgence – now looked less threatening, he decided to have himself directly chosen by the people. The 1958 constitution was in some senses ambiguous. It defined the primary functions of the president as the defence of the constitution and "arbitration"; it made the Prime Minister responsible for the work of the government; yet it clearly subordinated the Prime Minister to the president through the latter's right of appointment and dismissal. But de Gaulle, by temperament as well as circumstances, was from the start more than an arbiter: he was the policy-maker. He always thought it derogatory that he should derive his own power from a college of obscure "notables", and in time, provided for his own direct election by the people. Nor could he, in practice, treat all political parties (including the Gaullists) as equally insignificant. Clearly, it was important to the swift despatch of business that the Gaullist party should be strong; and therefore, that the older parties should be further weakened: they had already been discredited by the failure of the Fourth Republic. By making the direct election of the president a public issue he placed the older parties in the embarrassing position of appearing to oppose the will of the people if they opposed his proposal.

[1] De Gaulle, L'Effort, p. 19; Tournoux, Tragédie, pp. 477–8.
[2] For an analysis of the evolving Gaullist presidential system, *see* Williams and Harrison, ch. 10.

These, then, were the real reasons for the change. But the reason he gave publicly, in his televised speech of 20 September 1962, was that his successors, not enjoying national confidence to the degree that he did in 1958, would need the explicit support of the electorate. Some of his enemies jumped to the conclusion that he would not seek re-election after his current term; but they were soon disabused. To this general reason was added a specific one: there had been attempts against his life (the latest, which was almost successful, had been on 22 August 1962) and it was all the more necessary to ensure that he left behind him a solid Republic, which implied solidity at the top. To sum up: the change was deemed not only necessary but urgent. The country listened to him, and by three-fifths of the votes cast gave him what he wanted on 28 October. Thereafter, the claim that France had become an elective monarchy had substance.

The two most characteristic reigning devices of the Gaullian elective monarchy were the press conference and the referendum. Each had its theatrical element; or, more precisely, the press conferences were ritual and theatre, the referenda dramas of suspense. While there is no universally accepted standard of presentation in press conferences, it is normal for politicians not to know the questions beforehand. De Gaulle did not operate that way. He called a press conference when he had things to say; and the questions were worked out beforehand to meet his need, approved, and allocated among selected journalists. This does not mean that de Gaulle never answered unpremeditated questions or never gave extempore answers. But most of the questions were "planted" and the vocal statement of them was a formality. Unwelcome questions were parried by one of the general's sardonic witticisms.[3]

His astonishing memory served him well on these occasions, as in the briefer solo performances before the television cameras. It is misleading, however, to suppose that de Gaulle wrote his text, then memorised it. For so prolific a wielder of words, he had never found composition easy. He would write slowly and painfully, crossing out many words, making fresh starts; and because it took so long and he read each sentence through many times, it stuck in his capacious mind.[4] It was his habit, in any case, to spend two hours alone in his office every day, cut off from the outside world and with only the inter-ministerial telephone connected. During this period, only the most urgent news would justify an interruption. Thus, meditating and writing in solitude, he would master his words.

---

[3] De Gaulle, *Renouveau*, pp. 303–4.
[4] This description of de Gaulle's working methods was given to me by the left-wing Gaullist and Companion of the Liberation, Louis Vallon.

For de Gaulle, the advent of television was both a marvellous opportunity and an additional servitude. In public, he had never used notes; but in the days of radio, he had read his speeches in the studio. Now, to make the best use of this "means without equal"[5] and to preserve his public image, he had to be word-perfect, and rehearsed to the last gesture and inflection. Apart from the press conferences, however, the television appearances were pre-recorded: this gave him a chance to achieve perfection some hours before his audiences saw him.

But the press conferences were the most important of his public appearances. The ritual side of it was made manifest by the attendance of his ministers as well as high officials of the Elysée and dignitaries of Paris. In all, with the representatives of the French and world press, about a thousand people were gathered in the great *salle des fêtes* to hear the great man, rising respectfully to their feet on the moment of his entry at 3 p.m. The main Paris newspaper then reproduced the text of his answers verbatim, as the news was flashed around the world. For all the intimacy of the television cameras and the presence of the president in millions of homes, the personal touch was lacking. De Gaulle tried to supply it by frequent journeys to every corner of France. He records that in his first four years in office he made no fewer than nineteen provincial journeys, each of four or five days, visiting sixty-seven departments. Everywhere, apart from the notables, the general insisted on the "crowd baths" from which he drew renewed vigour, shaking hands by the thousand and patting the heads of children. For these occasions, he had perfected a speech-making technique in striking contrast to his greater utterances, the secret of which lay in frank use of the banal and platitudinous. Tournoux has collected some representative examples.[6] Not all are translatable. Here are two that are:

"I salute Fécamp, a seaport which wants to stay that way, and shall." (July 1960)

"With all the meat, wheat, wine, shoes, dresses and presses that are made at Chalonnes, I really wonder how we could eat, drink, be shod, be clothed and press wine if there were no Chalonnes. Fortunately, there is Chalonnes." (May 1965)

The referendum, as de Gaulle used it, was a way of demonstrating popular support and drawing strength from it, of dealing directly with the people instead of going through tiresome intermediaries such as deputies, and of reducing complex issues to simple terms of Yes or No. There were five during his ten-year reign. Only the first, on the

[5] De Gaulle, *Renouveau*, p. 301.
[6] Tournoux, *Tragédie*, pp. 419–20; *see also* pp. 484–5.

constitution of 1958, was in the true sense a plebiscite. He himself distinguished, at least in private, between his exercise of full powers and a dictatorship. A dictator, he explained, had himself plebiscited once, and that was the end: *he* was always ready to account for his actions. Of the other four referenda, three took place in two years – 1961 and 1962 – after which there was an interval of nearly seven years before the final and unsuccessful one. The second and third were on Algeria. The 1961 one, held on 8 January, was on self-determination for Algeria and yielded a Yes majority of 75 per cent (since only 76 per cent of registered voters turned out, the actual majority was only 55.6 per cent, about 11 per cent less than the 1958 figure). In April 1962, however, when the issue was whether or not Algeria was to be independent, the Yes majority of votes cast rose to 91 per cent (mainly because the Communists dared not vote against peace), or 65 per cent of the whole electorate. The fourth referendum (the second in 1962) was the one on whether the president should be elected by universal suffrage. The issue was controversial and brought more than 77 per cent of the voters to the polls on 28 October. Measured as a percentage of the total electorate, de Gaulle's majority – 46.4 per cent – was the smallest yet; and the Noes, at 28.8 per cent, by far the highest. The fifth referendum came nearly seven years later and its failure caused de Gaulle's retirement.

In the meantime, he had measured his popularity by the test of universal suffrage once only, in the presidential elections of December 1965, with disappointing results that may account for his reluctance, thereafter, to hold another referendum. From the beginning, de Gaulle had treated the forthcoming elections with regal indifference, as though the result was a foregone conclusion. And indeed the disarray of the opposition appeared to justify his attitude. The Socialist mayor of Marseilles, Gaston Defferre, had made a brave and initially successful attempt to launch himself as the candidate of the centre-left, but foundered on the reluctance of the established parties to dilute their identity, and withdrew from the race in June 1965. That spring, the public opinion polls showed approval for the general at 60 per cent, with disapproval at only 27 per cent. Once Defferre had withdrawn, the only rival candidate in sight was the right-wing lawyer, Jean-Louis Tixier-Vignancour.

During the last three or four months of the year, however, the outlook was transformed – in de Gaulle's disfavour. On 9 September, François Mitterrand presented himself as a candidate of the left; and on 19 October, Jean Lecanuet announced his candidacy on behalf of the centre-right. Each man was accounted "handsome", and both made skilful use of television – a State-controlled medium until then practically monopolised by de Gaulle and the Gaullists. In six weeks, the general's opinion poll rating fell by more than 20 per cent. When polling took place on 5 December, de Gaulle's share of the vote was only slightly less than 44 per cent. He was, of course, well ahead of the runner-up, Mitterrand (just over 32 per cent) and Lecanuet (just under 16 per cent), with minor candidates making up the 100. But having failed to achieve an absolute majority, he faced the humiliation of a second ballot. That he still enjoyed mass support was evident; but his claim to stand for a united France could not now be sustained.

Shaken in his self-confidence, de Gaulle seriously considered retiring, but not, it is said, for more than an hour: it was unthinkable for him to retire on a defeat.[7] At the second ballot, on the 19th, de Gaulle was duly re-elected president of the Republic, this time with a majority of 54.5 per cent of the votes cast. Mitterrand's showing, however, had been astonishingly strong, and in a straight fight his share of the vote went up from 32.2 to 45.5 per cent. Shrewdly, the left-wing candidate had declared that he would be happy if he could hold de Gaulle to less than half of the registered voters. And he did, for with abstentions, de Gaulle's share of the electorate was only 44.8 per cent (compared with Mitterrand's 37.3). The old man was still in power, but no longer with the unquestioned support of the majority.

To rule, as distinct from reigning, de Gaulle relied, not only, or even primarily, on the delegation of government to his Prime Minister of the moment, but on the able team of technocrats constituting the *cabinet* at the Elysée Palace.[8] The Elysée secretariat, in fact, amounted to an invisible government; and though its members were appointed by de Gaulle (as was the Prime Minister) and could be dismissed at his whim, they wielded considerable power. This was especially true of the secretary-general and of certain individuals, the most important of whom was Jacques Foccart. There were three secretaries-general during de Gaulle's decade: de Courcel (later ambassador in London), Burin des Roziers (later ambassador in Rome) and Bernard Tricot. The last two in particular wielded great power and on a number of occasions got the better of the argument in clashes with the Prime Minister.[9] Foccart was the most mysterious of the great Gaullists. Formerly the secretary-

---

[7] Schoenbrun, *Lives*, p. 341.
[8] The way the Elysée team worked is described in I, 1, which incorporates material first published in an article, "The System at the Elysée", in *Encounter*, October 1965. The article was written after lengthy interviewing of some of the leading high officials in the Presidential Palace.
[9] Viansson-Ponté, *République*, Vol. I, pp. 141–2.

general of the Rally of the French People, he was unconditionally faithful, in some respects the general's closest confidant, and quite the most discreet. His official job at the Elysée was initially "secretary-general for the Community", but when the Community broke up, as it soon did, the post was re-styled "secretary-general for African and Malagasy Affairs". That he performed these duties is not in doubt. But he also had others: the coordination and "digesting" of intelligence, and the general supervision and analysis of the Gaullist movement. There was a controversial duality about these functions. The State had its own intelligence and security organisations, such as the Service de Documentation et Contre-Espionnage (SDECE – a rough equivalent of the American Central Intelligence Agency and Britain's Secret Intelligence Service or MI6) and the Sûreté Nationale, an important branch of which was the Direction de la Surveillance du Territoire (DST – corresponding roughly to Britain's MI5 or America's Federal Bureau of Investigation).

To what extent did Foccart's secret functions overlap with these organs of the State? The answer, inevitably, was not very clear, and ill-intentioned rumour attributed much undercover work to Foccart, often without foundation. The other half of his secret attributions, however, was even more controversial, since it involved keeping an eye on, and if necessary defending, the Gaullist movement, which was not, in any constitutional sense, an organ of the State. In a way, Foccart was a kind of ultimate recourse in a crisis of survival of Gaullism. But he was not the only one: Roger Frey, minister of the Interior during several crucial years, was another. It was not always easy to discover where Foccart's action ended, and Frey's began. For instance, when the Fifth Republic was threatened by the riots of May and June 1968, committees for the Defence of the Republic were set up by the Gaullists. According to one authority, they were created "under the inspiration" of Foccart;[10] but they were organised by Roger Frey.[11]

The readiness to use extra-legal methods, and if judged necessary to do violence to the constitution, was a characteristic of de Gaulle's Republic and of what Jacques Soustelle termed "neo-Gaullism" – the Gaullist leadership and movement during the Fifth Republic. While the OAS terrorist phase lasted, Frey's ministry of the Interior sent strong-arm gangs of "parallel police", known as les Barbouzes, to Algeria – and later to foreign countries where OAS leaders had taken refuge – to meet terror with terror, and "no holds barred". The most notorious exploit of this parallel force was the kidnapping, by men dressed in

[10] Williams and Harrison, p. 384.
[11] Jean Charlot, Le Gaullisme (henceforth, Charlot, Gaullisme), p. 177.

German police uniforms, of Colonel (or ex-Colonel) Antoine Argoud, one of the main OAS leaders, in Munich in 1962. Argoud was later gaoled for life.

Soustelle himself, although never directly involved in acts of violence, was harried from capital to capital for seven years. By request of the French Sûreté, his luggage was searched by Italian police and his Belgian flat raided. The group he had founded after leaving de Gaulle's government, the Renouveau national, was banned under a 1936 law prohibiting "private armed militias", although its members were not armed. He was even expelled, under government pressure, from the non-political Commission des Sciences humaines of the Centre national de la Recherche scientifique.[12]

De Gaulle affected a remote distaste for such goings-on. His reaction to the so-called "Ben Barka affair" was characteristic. A left-wing Moroccan politician, Mehdi Ben Barka, was condemned to death *in absentia* in November 1963. Two years later he disappeared in Paris and it was later established that he had been abducted and murdered on orders of the Moroccan security services, but with the connivance of individuals in the French police. The affair soon became a major political scandal in France, to a degree that made it impossible for de Gaulle to ignore it entirely. He therefore had the matter raised at his press conference on 21 February 1966. It was, he said, a "vulgar and secondary" business, which had been blown up out of all proportion by political enemies ready to take advantage of the readiness of readers of James Bond and other thrillers to believe anything that was said about the *Barbouzes* as a way of discrediting the State.

Some changes in the personnel and organisation of the secret services had already been made by de Gaulle and he referred to these as evidence that the "honour of the ship" (of State) was in good hands.

Throughout his reign, however, de Gaulle showed what can only be called a contempt for the law – both the ordinary law as it affects individuals, and the fundamental law that was his own constitution. Certainly he came to power at a time of emergency: at such times, the State's right to defend itself by exceptional measures is widely conceded; full advantage was taken of the indulgence towards the arbitrary that prevails at times of emergency.

Before de Gaulle's change of line on Algeria, the main victims of arbitrary "justice" were the Algerian FLN and its French supporters. Later, it was the OAS and supporters of "French Algeria". In the first phase, torture had become a standard interrogation procedure; yet it was

[12] Soustelle, *Gaullisme*, pp. 249 *et seq.*

virtually impossible to bring perpetrators to justice. The ministry of the Interior suppressed an enquiry after the bodies of seventy Algerians had been found in the Seine in October 1961.

Outraged by the release of French activist defendants in the "barricades" trial in 1960, de Gaulle decided, after the generals' revolt the following April, to set up a Higher Military Tribunal composed of generals and civilian judges picked by himself, with limited rights for the accused, and no appeal. When the court condemned Jouhaud to death but spared his chief, Salan, de Gaulle dissolved it and replaced it by a Military Court of Justice, with more extensive powers. Named as its first president, General de Larminat – one of the original Gaullist officers – could not face the implications of his new charge, and committed suicide. After this bad start, the court went on to try six men, two of whom were sentenced to death and one of whom was actually executed. A sensational development interrupted the course of special justice: the Council of State declared the Military Court of Justice illegal. A government communiqué criticised this decision as "an incitement to subversion"; but de Gaulle pardoned the condemned man who had not been executed, the other being beyond mercy. This pardon, of course, implied that the legality of the sentence was reaffirmed, despite the State Council's decision.

After the general elections in November 1962, Pompidou's new government created a new State Security Court with more restricted powers than the military court, and with right of appeal. At the same time, however, the ordinance of 1 June 1962 creating the military court – which the Council of State had declared illegal – was *retrospectively* reactivated. The effect of this extraordinary measure was to validate the sentences which the Council of State's decision had made illegal. Thereupon, the authors of the attempt on de Gaulle's life at Petit Clamart were brought to trial under the revived Military Court of Justice.[13]

One of the most curious of the regime's judicial initiatives was the trial of the well-known author, Alfred Fabre-Luce, in November and December 1963. A supporter of Vichy during the German occupation, Fabre-Luce remained determinedly anti-Gaullist, unlike many who switched their allegiance from Pétain to de Gaulle. In 1962, he published

---

[13] Williams and Harrison, ch. 13; and Soustelle, *Gaullisme*, Part II, 2. Williams and Harrison argue (p. 266) that the Petit Clamart defendants were tried before the revived Military Court of Justice instead of the new State Security Court "from which they could have appealed". But as the State Security Court did not officially come into existence until February 1963 and did not try a case until March, there was therefore no possibility of choosing between them – unless of course, de Gaulle had waited two or three months.

a devastating satire on the general, under the title of *Haute-Cour*,[14] in which de Gaulle was pictured as being brought to trial for alleged breaches of the law and constitution. In December 1962 all unsold copies of the book were confiscated and Fabre-Luce and his publisher were brought to trial on a charge of insulting the head of State. For this traditional offence, they were fined the equivalent of £105, and the court ordered the confiscated books to be destroyed. The publisher (Julliard) later published the transcript of the trial, with an ironical preface by Fabre-Luce, in which he pointed out that the prosecution, in its eagerness to convict him, had quoted only the unflattering passages from his book; thus the fact that the book also contained complimentary passages was being concealed from many Frenchmen.

The Fabre-Luce trial raised interesting issues, for the respect traditionally due to the chief of State was not normally extended to the policy-makers and executants of policy; yet de Gaulle, unlike the politically neutral presidents of the Third and Fourth Republics, was also the policy-maker, and quite often the direct executant of his own policies. Was it appropriate, then, that he should be spared criticism in his political capacity? The court had upheld his right to immunity; but the great majority of France's intellectuals, whether of the right or the left, disputed the verdict.

The cavalier or capricious administration of justice under de Gaulle's Republic was matched by the president's arbitrary use of his tailor-made constitution. The making and unmaking of special tribunals, and the flounting of the Council of State's rulings, have been mentioned. But there were many other examples. The most striking concern the president's own functions, the use of Article 16, and the referendum procedure. We have noted some ambiguities in the constitution. Throughout his reign, however, de Gaulle chose to respect only certain articles and to ignore others. One of those consistently ignored was Article 20, which declared that: "The government decides and directs the policy of the nation." So plain was it from the start that the president alone was going to do this that Article 20 might as well not have existed. In case anybody had missed the point, de Gaulle declared at his press conference of 31 January 1964 that there could be no "dyarchy at the top", and went on to claim that "it must of course be understood that the indivisible authority of the State is entrusted entirely to the president by the people which has elected him, that there exists none

---

[14] An English translation was published in 1963 under the title of *The Trial of Charles de Gaulle* (Methuen), with an Introduction by Dorothy Pickles.

other, whether ministerial, civil, military or judicial, that is not conferred and maintained by him". This was not what the constitution said: it was what de Gaulle said. It may be noted, in passing, that at that time the president had not yet been elected by "the people".

His use of Article 16 was equally controversial, by the light of the text, although consistent with his own interpretation of his powers. He invoked it in 1961 after the four generals had announced their dissidence in Algeria. Under the constitution, the president could take "the measures required by the circumstances" in the event of "a serious and immediate threat to the institutions of the Republic, the independence of the nation, the integrity of its territory or the fulfilment of its international obligations", and if "the regular functioning of the constitutional public authorities has been interrupted". Soustelle argues[15] that none of these conditions existed, but it is hard to dispute that the institutions of the Republic, at least, were temporarily in danger. Article 16, however, went on to say that the "measures must be inspired by the desire to ensure to the constitutional public authorities, with the minimum of delay, the means of fulfilling their functions".

Since the "regular functioning of the constitutional public authorities" had not, in fact, been interrupted, even by a day, it was difficult to define the "minimum of delay" that was supposed to elapse before the "means of fulfilling their functions" should be restored. Moreover, the generals' rebellion collapsed in four days. Article 16 nevertheless remained in force for five months – until 30 September 1961; and a "state of emergency" prevailed – perhaps justifiably, in view of the OAS terrorism in metropolitan France – until 31 May 1963.[16] Thus, for about two years, de Gaulle had the power to act as he saw fit. That this power was used to meet exceptional circumstances is hard to dispute; but it is equally certain that it was abused, not merely to bring perpetrators of violence to justice, but also to persecute politicians, like Soustelle, who disagreed with de Gaulle's Algerian policy and were trying to fight it – in Soustelle's case, by means which he has consistently claimed were always within the law.

The president's use of the referendum as an instrument of rule was also strictly extra-constitutional. The procedure for calling a referendum was laid down in Articles 11 and 89, which also defined the issues that might be referred to the people. Article 11 gave the president the power,

15 In *Gaullisme*, pp. 209–10.
16 Technically, the "state of emergency" was introduced on 22 April 1961 under the act of 3 April providing for special powers to deal with such situations as Algeria. Article 16 was invoked to prolong the *état d'urgence*, but the emergency went on after Article 16 had ceased to be applied.

600

"on the proposal of the government during parliamentary sessions, or on the joint proposal of the two Assemblies", to submit to a referendum any bill "dealing with the organisation of the public authorities, approving a Community agreement or authorising the ratification of a treaty which, although not in conflict with the constitution would affect the working of institutions". Article 89 dealt with amendments to the constitution and laid down that the amending bill to be submitted to referendum must first have been passed by both houses of Parliament, in identical terms. Clearly, it seems, the constitutional amendments proposed in 1962 and 1968 should have been submitted under Article 89. In both cases, however, de Gaulle decided not to invoke that article, because the bills would have required the assent of parliament: he had nothing to fear from the Assembly, but did not trust the Senate. He therefore invoked Article 11, on the ground that "the organisation of the public authorities" self-evidently comprised the constitution itself.[17] The Council of State, however, ruled his action unconstitutional in both instances. But de Gaulle was not a man to be diverted by a "technicality", and simply ignored the Council.

Similarly, he paid little attention to Article 8, which stipulates that the president could terminate the term of office of the Prime Minister "on the presentation by the Prime Minister of the resignation of the government". This was too slow for de Gaulle: when he wanted a new Prime Minister, he simply dismissed the old. True, the Prime Ministers invariably regularised the situation by formally resigning.

De Gaulle's only answer to those who dared to remonstrate with him was the argument that Article 3 had overriding powers since it stated that "National sovereignty belongs to the people, who exercise it through their representatives and by way of referendum". If pressed, he would exclaim: "I'm not going to let France die through respect for juridicalism". When Pierre Sudreau, having resigned as minister of Education over the 1962 referendum, drew de Gaulle's attention to the dangerous precedent he was establishing for his successors, he exclaimed: "Come, come, Sudreau, nobody else will ever have the nerve to do what I'm doing."[18]

In the unfinished second volume of *Mémoires d'Espoir*, de Gaulle records the chorus of disapproval that greeted his handling of the 1962 referendum, and makes this astonishing comment:

> I must say that the obstinacy of the parties in interpreting the constitution in such a way that the people would be denied a right that belongs to it seems to me the more arbitrary in that I am myself the

[17] De Gaulle, *L'Effort*, pp. 38–40.   [18] Tournoux, *Tragédie*, pp. 431–2, 437.

principal inspirer of the new institutions and that it is really the limit to pretend to contradict me on their meaning.[19]

De Gaulle's quarrel with the Senate stemmed mainly from the leading part played by its president, Gaston Monnerville, in opposing de Gaulle's decision to by-pass the upper house – and indeed parliament as a whole – in the 1962 referendum. The coloured politician, who had done much to facilitate de Gaulle's return to power in 1958, could not stomach this violation of the constitution and said so. De Gaulle retaliated by cutting Monnerville out of the Elysée's guest list.

Such arbitrariness – in lieu of "arbitration" – was of course challenged, but it was largely tolerated at times of crisis – that is, at times when "the man of storms" showed himself naturally to best advantage. But once the Algerian war was over, and the OAS had been smashed, the crises were too often visibly of the general's own making. So long as France appeared to be getting away with de Gaulle's foreign policy, he could get away with illegality. But during the last phase of eccentricity, there were signs of popular impatience with the old man. The presidential election of 1965 ought to have come as a warning, but de Gaulle, hurt and humiliated though he was at having to face a run-off ballot, soon recovered and went on as though there had been no warning. His "Québec libre" indiscretion went further than the average Frenchman likes his leaders to take him: de Gaulle had failed to exercise that *sens inné de la mesure* which the French like to think of as their special characteristic.

It was de Gaulle's conduct of home affairs, however, that was crucial to his acceptability as a national leader. "France," he exclaimed on 12 July 1961, "has married her century." His audience knew exactly what he meant. Antiquated structures and attitudes had retarded France's adaptation to modern methods and technology. Now, he was telling the French people, France was catching up with the most advanced nations. This was true, although the process had begun before his return to power: the expansiveness inherent in Jean Monnet's Planning Commission, and the competitiveness forced on French industry by adherence to the common market, had between them started it. By 1954 economic growth had reached 5.5 per cent; by 1967, France's Gross National Product *per capita* stood at $2,210 – ahead of Belgium ($2,050), West Germany ($2,030), the United Kingdom ($1,980), and Holland ($1,810). Strikingly, from the standpoint of national vitality, the birth rate had started soaring (though here again, the process began in 1946,

[19] De Gaulle, *L'Effort*, pp. 40–1.

after de Gaulle had left power), so that France's population, which had so long stagnated, rose from 40.5 million in 1946 to more than 50 million in 1968.[20] Inevitably, the proportion of young people to the rest of the population grew, so that by 1966, 34 per cent of the French were under twenty. With this growth came fresh problems in education and a "generation gap" in attitudes that was one of the causes of the explosion of 1968. That year, the University of Paris had 154,000 students, whereas it had only 65,000 in 1955. By 1969 – the year of de Gaulle's retirement – there were 643,000 university students in France; but in 1939, there had been only 122,000. One of the Elysée's ablest technical counsellors, Jacques Narbonne, had forecast in 1963 in a note to de Gaulle that there would be an explosion in 1968.[21] His reasons for this forecast comprised not only the rapid growth of the university population, but the increasing tendency to take universities for granted and not bother with examinations. As he showed, 70 to 75 per cent of students, male and female, did not graduate. Narbonne was right, but nobody listened to him.

For four years, Narbonne had tried unsuccessfully to persuade Christian Fouchet, then minister of Education, to introduce reforms: "orientation" in secondary education, and selection in higher. He continued to try when Alain Peyrefitte succeeded Fouchet in September 1967; but shortly after, he was transferred to the Council of State from the Elysée. Peyrefitte himself, one of de Gaulle's younger ministers (forty-two on appointment), was bright and ambitious, but not exactly master in his own house. The powerful secretary-general at the ministry, Pierre Laurent, disagreed with him from the first. Peyrefitte wanted decentralisation, autonomy for individual universities, meetings with students, and so forth; Laurent wanted authoritarian centralisation and no consultations. The responsibility for education was further complicated by the veto power of the Finance minister, Michel Debré; and by Pompidou's personal interest in education as a former teacher, and his disinclination to change anything.

Not only were numbers and accommodation real problems, together with the relevance of courses to career needs and the standard of exams; but sexual liberty on the campuses in an increasingly permissive age became a major issue. Student associations were clamouring for it. De Gaulle found the subject embarrassing. Peyrefitte was ready to do something about it but was caught between conflicting pressures. In the

[20] *See* Williams and Harrison, ch. 1.
[21] Tournoux, *Mai*, p. 43; Claude Paillat, *Archives Secrètes, 1968–9* (henceforth, Paillat, *Archives*), pp. 24 *et seq.*

end, he drew up a plan, providing that boys, whether of age or not, could receive visitors in their rooms up to 11 p.m.; that young women having reached their majority could do as they pleased, and that visits to the rooms of girls below age could take place only with the consent of parents. He had called a meeting to discuss his plan on 22 February 1968, but the young revolutionaries demonstrated against it on the 13th.

Relations between the student bodies and the government were strained, or worse, from the birth of the Fifth Republic. De Gaulle told the Union nationale des Etudiants français (UNEF) in 1959 that they should mind their own business, when it had complained that higher education was being neglected in that year's budget.[22] In 1960, when the government revised the system of deferments from military service, UNEF, which had not been consulted, threatened to refer the matter to the Council of State. The scheme was withdrawn and redrafted. In 1961, after a long period of UNEF activities in support of opponents of the Algerian war, the government set up a rival student body, the Fédération nationale des Etudiants de France (FNEF). The new body was of course strongly in favour of French Algeria – a fact that soon caused official embarrassment. Subsidies to UNEF were withdrawn and transferred to FNEF. Reconciliation of a kind came in 1967, when subsidies to UNEF were restored. By this time, UNEF was losing interest in politics, and simultaneously losing membership to extremist groups. The "war" between the government and the students, followed by an uneasy peace when it was too late, was yet another contributory cause of the explosion of 1968; at a time when the problems of higher education were reaching crisis point, the failure of communication was almost complete. De Gaulle and his team did not really know what was going on.

Yet it would be wrong to accuse de Gaulle of indifference to education. Himself a former army teacher, he continued to think of himself, both out of power and back again, as "one who tried to teach".[23] On 6 March 1959 he raised the school leaving age from fourteen to sixteen; and in 1963, as a complement to the lycées, "colleges of secondary education" were created, in which courses adapted to different aptitudes were offered. But his proposals for "orientation" and "selection", designed to reduce the frightening wastage of students failing to graduate, fell on the deaf ears of the teaching profession, whom the general blamed bitterly for their resistance to his ideas. For, as he saw it, there was an imperative necessity for guidance on the part of the teachers; whereas the prevailing

---

[22] Williams and Harrison, p. 323.
[23] De Gaulle, L'Effort, p. 170.

feeling on their side was in favour of "democratisation" – that is, of equality and camaraderie between them and their charges.

That there was a measure of obstructionism from the teachers is clear. On one point, however, the teachers were right. The Fouchet-Aigrain reform, based on the orientation and selection programme, was applied in such a way that students were forced to switch from one curriculum to another, while their choice of disciplines was restricted in that, in certain cases, their former qualifications were invalid. Professor Raymond Aron cites the example of a graduate in psychology being barred from taking a master's degree in sociology.[24] This kind of anomaly, which the great majority of deans of faculties had pointed out to the ministry, had a traumatic effect on many students.

This was only one instance of the widening gap between the State and le pays réel in the Gaullian republic. The gap was not, however, due to any neglect on de Gaulle's part of economic and financial problems. In Mémoires d'Espoir, he defends himself energetically against the reiterated reproach that he did neglect such problems, dismissing it as "derisory". Far from it, he declares, he devoted "a good half" of his working time to them.[25] These were not, however, problems in which he could pretend to any expertise in his own right. But in the end, selecting between the sometimes contradictory advice of his specialists, it was he who took the big decisions, in this domain as in every other.

The inherited economic burden was as daunting as the political legacy. His first minister of Economics and Finance, Antoine Pinay, told him the worst as soon as he was back in power. For 1958, there was going to be a deficit of 1,200 milliard francs; the external debt exceeded $3,000 million, half of which was due for repayment within a year; imports were running at 75 per cent more than exports, despite the 20 per cent devaluation of 1957;[26] reserves were down to $630 million, or enough to pay for five weeks' imports; and the last sources of credit had been tapped.

De Gaulle had chosen Pinay, as he frankly admits, because the presence at his side of "this eminent personage, well-known for his common sense, esteemed for his character, popular for his devotion to the public interest", would strengthen confidence and help avert the threatening catastrophe. On Pinay's proposal, de Gaulle launched a national loan on

[24] Raymond Aron, La Révolution introuvable, pp. 61–2.
[25] De Gaulle, Renouveau, p. 140.
[26] Theoretically, this was a device to stimulate French exports by making them cheaper to foreign importers, while discouraging imports into France. Officially, there was no devaluation, as the rate of exchange was maintained.

13 June 1958. It was as spectacularly successful as the one that had helped France's immediate post-war recovery thirteen years earlier: 324 milliard francs were subscribed; and 150 tons of gold, worth $170 million, were handed in to the Banque de France. Capital that had been invested abroad began to return.

Civil service increments were deferred; the price of wheat, which had been linked on a rising basis to the 1957 price index, was reduced, and the retail prices of many commodities were cut; company taxes were raised and a surcharge added to the prices of luxury goods. These measures had the effect of slowing down the inflationary prices rise, reducing home consumption and stimulating exports.

Against Pinay's initial objections, de Gaulle created – on 30 December 1958 – a financial commission composed of representatives of official bodies, banking and industry, under the chairmanship of the well-known expert, Jacques Rueff. On 8 December, the commission submitted its liberalisation plan to de Gaulle and Pinay. It was a bold and imaginative package: inflation was to be halted, the currency stabilised, and commerce freed. The anti-inflationary measures were drastic. Civil service pay increases were to stay within 4 per cent; State subsidies to nationalised industries and social security were cut; company taxes were further raised, as were excise duties on wine, alcohol and tobacco; gas, electricity and transport charges were raised 15 per cent, and coal 10 per cent, while postal charges went up by 16 per cent. There was, however, a 4 per cent increase on the minimum wage, family allowances were to rise by 10 per cent over six months, and old age pensions by an immediate 5,200 francs a month. Against this came a mean proposal that was to make the government deeply unpopular in some quarters: during 1959 pensions to able-bodied war veterans were to be suspended.

De Gaulle, who was aware (but did not like to be reminded of the fact) that the war veterans organisations had played an important part in his return to power, habitually sought out the bemedalled old soldiers on his frequent tours of the provinces, to exchange reminiscences of Verdun and military captivity. But they never failed, during 1959, to ask him when they were going to get their pensions back. Throughout the year, his ministers kept on reminding him of it; but he held out to the last in this decision which (writes Viansson-Ponté) "for some, would long bear witness to a cold indifference, a lack of heart, an unnecessary cruelty".[27]

For the currency, the Rueff Commission prescribed a devaluation of 17.5 per cent, plus the ingenious device of knocking off two noughts at the end of figures in francs, so that 100 old francs became one new franc.

[27] Viansson-Ponté, *République*, Vol. I, p. 215.

This new and "heavy" franc powerfully contributed to public confidence in France's money (although most French people continued to reckon in *anciens francs*).

As for foreign trade, little less than a revolution was now proposed. After generations of stifling protectionism, 90 per cent of exchanges with Europe were freed and 50 per cent of those with the dollar zone.

The Rueff package was hard for Pinay to swallow, and quite impossible for Guy Mollet and the two other Socialist ministers. Pinay had opposed further devaluation and increased taxes; it was hard for him to approve them now. But the general persuaded him to stay. He could not do the same with the Socialists, who thought too many of the new burdens would fall on the poor, without enough State direction to compensate. All three resigned with the creation, on 8 January 1959, of the new Republic.

The Rueff programme pleased nobody, but worked. The Patronat complained about the higher taxes and wanted compensatory cuts in public expenditure; the smaller businesses feared exposure to European competition; the shopkeepers feared cuts in purchasing power; the trade unions said living standards were being cut; and the farming associations said the new wheat price was discriminatory. All, or most of, the objectors were wrong, however. The rate of inflation was halved, gold and dollars flowed into France's coffers, GNP rose by 3 per cent in the second half of 1959, by 7.9 per cent in 1960, 4.6 per cent in 1961, and 6.8 per cent in 1962. Industrial growth reached 5.4 per cent in this period, and agricultural 5 per cent. Short and medium foreign debts were repaid, and gold and dollar reserves soared to more than $4,000 million in 1962. Despite a gentle inflation of 3.5 per cent a year, living standards rose by 4 per cent a year. Both private savings and the investment rate rose spectacularly.

Economic planning complemented Rueff's drastic medicine. The inherited Third Plan (1958–61) was scrapped and replaced by an interim plan providing for a 5.5 per cent growth in GNP. The Fourth Plan, covering the four years from 1962 to 1965, inclusively, aimed at a global economic growth rate of 24 per cent. During the period of the interim plan, there was a spectacular growth in national energy production, with natural gas from the Lacq installations, petrol and gas from the Sahara, atomic power stations at Marcoule and Chinon. The Centre for Space Studies was opened at Brétigny, and was soon to produce the first French satellites. Some 4,000 kilometres of electrified rail were laid, motorway construction made a long-delayed start, new airports were built and old ones modernised. Housing, long a black spot in France, began to make up for lost time, with 300,000 dwellings constructed each year. More vital for the future was the allocation to investment of 75,000 million new francs in the budgets between 1958 and 1962.

The static French society of small businesses, small shopkeepers and smallholders was on the move. In four years, mergers reduced the number of industrial concerns by 5,000; where there had been eight super-markets and 1,500 self-service shops in 1958, there were 207 and 4,000 respectively in 1962. In tens and soon in hundreds of thousands, peasants were leaving the countryside for the towns. The Law of Agricultural Orientation in 1960 and a further law in 1962 speeded the process, rationalised agriculture and helped the efficient. In four years, the number of farms fell from 2,200,000 to 1,900,000, while the value of farm output rose from 32,000 million to 42,000 million new francs.

Since all this represented success, and Antoine Pinay was the minister of Finance and Economics (as the post had been renamed in 1959), the former Prime Minister ought to have been pleased. But he could not work for long under General de Gaulle. Not himself a Gaullist, although he had gone to Colombey to persuade the general to return, he could not stomach the president's arbitrary methods, his anti-Americanism, his suspicion of the British and above all his hostility towards NATO. He objected to learning about foreign policy from the newspapers and, in the name of cabinet solidarity, to be asked to approve the general's discussions without prior discussion in the ministerial council. Nor was he afraid to say what he thought, aloud and in the presence of his col-leagues and de Gaulle himself. There were tense scenes over the with-drawal of the French Mediterranean fleet from NATO, and especially after the general's speech of 3 November 1959, in which he denounced integration within the alliance. "We can't afford to defend ourselves alone," he exclaimed in cabinet. De Gaulle closed the meeting and left without the usual handshakes.[28] On 13 January 1960 Pinay resigned, to be succeeded by Wilfrid Baumgartner.

Pinay's resignation was not the only sign of discontent during the early years of expansion. There was a social price.[29] The miners struck for a week in December 1961 in the condemned mine of Decazeville, and the following September started a stay-in stoppage that lasted five months. On 1 March 1963, the mining unions decreed a general strike. The government decided on strong-arm measures and persuaded de Gaulle to sign a decree conscripting the miners. The strike went on, however,

[28] Tournoux, *Tragédie*, pp. 314–24; Viansson-Ponté, *République*, Vol. I, pp. 201–6.
[29] A good account of social conditions in France during the Fifth Republic is in John Ardagh, *The New French Revolution*, which is to the Fifth Republic what Herbert Lüthy's *La France à " Heure de son Clocher* was to the Fourth.

and after a month the government backed down, conceding most of the strikers' claims. This was perhaps de Gaulle's worst domestic setback. In July that year, lightning strikes paralysed the transport system in Paris. This time the government won: with public approval, it steered a bill into law requiring five days' notice of strikes in the public sector. There were clashes with the dairy producers in 1963 over the price of milk, leading in the summer of 1964 to a prolonged milk strike. In mid-October, however, the farmers called off the strike.

In total, these disturbances did not mean that the Fifth Republic's record was any worse than the Fourth's: they were roughly comparable. But the record negated the social theories of Gaullism, first enunciated during the Second World War, then elaborated during the RPF days. In their euphoria, the Gaullists claimed to have found the answer to Karl Marx and the end of the class struggle. The magic formula was the "association of capital and labour", sometimes called "participation". The terms "association" and "participation" were, of course, ambiguous. Did they imply profit-sharing, or workers' share in management? At times one meaning, at times another, at times both, had been read into the concept. It was one of de Gaulle's master-ideas, but he did not pursue it with the single-minded concentration he devoted to the *force de frappe* or the withdrawal of France from NATO. Indeed, he himself did not define what he meant by "participation" with any clarity until after the explosion of 1968. He gave lengthy answers to questions about it from his television interviewer, Michel Droit, on 7 June 1968, and at his press conference of 9 September that year. It emerged that he meant both profit-sharing and the right of the workers to make managerial suggestions (although this right should not extend to control: that was for the managers, just as there could be only one captain for the ship of State).[30]

In 1945, on the proposal of the left-wing Gaullist, René Capitant, de Gaulle had created "works committees" (*comités d'entreprise*), but little had come of them. On his return to power, he had not forgotten this earlier aspiration, amidst all his other preoccupations; and on 7 January 1959 – on the eve of his move to the Elysée – an ordinance instituted the *intéressement* of the workers – literally, giving them a (financial) interest in the affairs of the company employing them. When the months passed and Debré's government did nothing about implementing the ordinance, de Gaulle lost patience and called for

---

[30] Actually, de Gaulle's 1968 statements did not really add much to what the 1967 measures (*see below*, pp. 610–11) had already revealed about participation; but in 1968, it was the general himself speaking his mind.

immediate action. The outcome was the decree of 9 August 1959, organising the application of the earlier decision. But there was little enthusiasm for the scheme, either among the workers or in management, and six years later, only 6,000 of the 25,000 firms affected had set up committees.[31]

Gaullist opinion was, in fact, deeply divided on the whole issue: neither of de Gaulle's first two premiers, Debré and Pompidou, was at all enthusiastic. Support came mainly from left-wing Gaullists, such as Capitant and Louis Vallon. De Gaulle himself kept coming back to his idea, however nebulous or unpractical it was thought to be. A commission de l'Intéressement set up by Debré in 1960 produced a bill which died in parliament. In 1965, after months of negotiations with the employers and unions, the left-wing Gaullist minister of Labour, Gilbert Grandval, drafted a mild bill to strengthen works committees, which ran into fierce Patronat opposition but was finally carried after 128 amendments. When the government introduced a further bill proposing tax concessions to companies and their shareholders, Louis Vallon, then the *rapporteur-général* of the National Assembly's Finance Committee, introduced an amendment committing the government to a further bill to guarantee the right of the workers to share in growing profits. The amendment was carried.

The Patronat feared this to be the end of capitalism and its relations with the government deteriorated sharply. One of the three main trade union organisations, the Confédération française démocratique des Travailleurs (essentially the former Catholic trade unionists under a non-religious name) agreed, on the whole, with the bosses; but the Communist-controlled Confédération générale du Travail thought the whole thing was a capitalist plot, and the socialist Force ouvrière feared it would lead to company-controlled unions. A further committee decided in 1966 that the Vallon amendment would be difficult to implement, and recommended a voluntary scheme. Distant thunder greeted this finding, from the South Pacific, where de Gaulle on his travels sent orders to prepare further proposals. The Vallon amendment was dropped, provoking furious accusations from the interested party and from Capitant. Yet another ordinance, in August 1967, provided for some profit-sharing (in the form of a bonus to be frozen for five years) and some consultation (but not much) – and only in firms with more than 100 workers and a profit of at least 10 per cent on capital. Even this very

[31] Williams and Harrison, p. 303. The whole problem is discussed there: pp. 302 *et seq.* *See also* Viasson-Ponté (*République*, Vol. I, pp. 221–2; and Louis Vallon, *L'Anti de Gaulle* (henceforth, Vallon), *passim.*

diluted *intéressement* foundered on the indifference of the unions and the obstruction of the employers. Broadly speaking, nothing had come of "association" by the time of the 1968 explosion.

In the absence of meaningful participation, parliament might normally have been expected to bridge the gap between the government and the governed. But although Debré – an admirer of the British system – had thought of the new constitution as parliamentary, de Gaulle's contempt for parliamentarians, including his own followers, was not conducive to parliamentary health. Yet, paradoxically, the parliaments of the Fifth Republic were the first in France to produce a strong and stable majority. The Gaullist party[32] dominated the Assembly produced by the 1968 election – as, with the help of Giscard d'Estaing's Independent Republicans, it had dominated the chambers elected in 1958, 1962 and 1967. Although it had an absolute majority in only the second and fourth (268 and 346 seats respectively), its control was unchallenged even in 1958 (206) and in 1967 (242). The older parties had supposed the 1958 success to be a flash-in-the-pan attributable to the Algerian crisis and the general's charisma, and destined to vanish once the crisis had been resolved. The disparateness of the Gaullists, who ranged all the way from far left to extreme right, appeared to support this expectation. Yet the prophets proved mistaken.

While the stability implicit in the Gaullist majority spared the French public the unseemly spectacle of constantly shifting combinations and short-lived governments, it did not mean strength. The president could dissolve the Assembly at any time after the lapse of one year from the last dissolution. Parliament sat for less than half the year, and had no control over the expenditure of public money. Moreover, the advice of the referendum – a direct appeal to the people – further weakened parliament; and when many parliamentarians challenged de Gaulle over the propriety of the 1962 referendum, he soon showed them who was master.

The Gaullists, as the party in power (if it could be called that), accepted or condoned parliamentary debasement; and de Gaulle's hard-won success in the 1965 presidential elections showed that a considerable body of opinion in the country was dissatisfied with his style of government.

In this spectrum of opinion, the part played by the French Communist

---

[32] The Gaullists, as a party, have had several changes of name, the latest of which, at the time of writing, was the Union des Démocrates pour la République (UDR). Their first name in 1958 was the Union pour la nouvelle République (UNR), and the second, Union démocratique pour la Cinquième République (UD5). The left-wing Gaullists have their own group, Union démocratique du Travail (UDT).

party was a peculiar one. The most rigidly Stalinist of the western Communist parties and – after Italy's – the largest, the French party sat like an undigested lump on the French body politic. In the late 1940s, its power to call massive strikes for political ends at Moscow's behest was formidable. Between 1946 and 1965, however, its real – as distinct from claimed – membership had declined from more than 800,000 to under 270,000; yet its voting pull in elections continued to be measured in millions. As late as 1956, the party had polled 5,600,000 votes. But the return of de Gaulle and the advent of the Gaullist party dealt the Communists a powerful, though not a mortal, blow. In the 1958 elections only 3,900,000 electors voted Communist; even this reduced but still imposing figure was not reflected in the composition of the Assembly, for only ten Communist deputies were returned, compared with 150 in the last Assembly of the Fourth Republic. From this low watermark, the party rose again to poll five million votes in 1967 and achieve seventy-three seats.

The party's attitude towards de Gaulle was ambivalent, as was his towards them. He had denounced the Communists as "separatists" during the RPF period, but they had served in his government. They suffered electorally from his return, and in later years his attempts at a special relationship with Moscow took the wind out of their sails. His anti-Americanism, his war on NATO, his European policy – which weakened the EEC – his recognition of the Oder–Neisse line: all these served Moscow's ends, and therefore the French Communists. It was hard, then, for the French Communist party to criticise de Gaulle's foreign policy. De Gaulle himself, discounting ideology, attacked them in the 1940s and 1950s to the extent that they were ready to carry out Moscow's orders at a time of peril for western Europe and when his best hope for returning to power seemed to lie in presenting himself as the saviour of the nation. They were also, in a lasting sense, his only serious rivals for popular support and by far the best organised. They constituted a power, and as such he respected them.

The Sino-Soviet split appeared to confirm de Gaulle's view of the unimportance of ideology. At the same time, the French party's continued readiness to support Soviet objectives diminished sharply in importance, since de Gaulle, too, was now pursuing similar objectives. For all these reasons, or rationalisations, de Gaulle decided that the Communists had ceased to be a danger, in a subversive sense. His attitude towards them amounted to a kind of historical pessimism. He believed that the success of Communism was inevitable. His foreign policy mirrored this belief, or resignation. His manoeuvres, his attempts to shift alliances, his practice of geopolitics, all had as their guiding principle the desire to keep France within the Communist mainstream which, he was convinced, was going to carry the world with it. In this unexpected sense, the left-wing Gaullists were not mistaken in claiming a special affinity with him. He thought of them as the instrument that would bring socialisation to France, as the one way, in his eyes, of avoiding communisation. A private remark of his made towards the end of 1961 was symptomatic: "I myself shall bring Communism to France," he said, "to avoid Soviet Communism and its totalitarianism."[33]

From the Fourth Republic, de Gaulle had inherited a network of special services, some of them linked with private bodies, the object of which was the containment of Communist subversion. In this context a clear distinction was made between Marxism and Leninism. Marxism, as a philosophy, was in no sense illegal; but Leninism, in the sense of organising the masses as a disciplined body with ultimately revolutionary intent, had to be watched.

De Gaulle broke this anti-subversive apparatus. His pretext for acting was the admittedly dangerous turn in the activities of the army's Fifth Bureau (for psychological war) in Algiers. The first visible sign of a change of policy was the dissolution of all the Fifth Bureaux in France, whose orientation was mainly concerned with countering Leninist subversion.

There was a complementary change in French activities abroad. The Fourth Republic, by agreement with neighbouring countries, had helped to set up international information services to counter Communist subversion. From 1963, under de Gaulle's orders, France withdrew from such organisations. Because of the semi-secret nature of these activities, the French public had no inkling of what had happened.

All these moves coincided with de Gaulle's secret attempt to persuade the Germans to drop Washington by offering them a limited share in France's nuclear air force.[34] So thorough was this demolition that when President Pompidou and his premier, Chaban-Delmas, reverted to an anti-Communist line after de Gaulle's departure, they had to turn to private bodies for the factual material of their speeches.

Although these secret decisions were presumably not known to the Communist party, it could not help being aware of diminishing

---

[33] I have this remark from the mouth of the high-ranking member of de Gaulle's staff who heard the general utter it. Some people have dismissed it as a *boutade*; but it probably reflected de Gaulle's real feelings.

[34] *See above*, p. 551. De Gaulle's decision to build an independent nuclear deterrent provoked traumatic heart-searchings among many French servicemen, including some of the highest rank. In consequence, some of these resigned. (Private information.)

hostility on the part of the authorities. In these circumstances, the party was not, in any real sense, among de Gaulle's enemies when the explosion came in May 1968. In any event, as was soon to become apparent, the French Communists had lost whatever taste they might have had for violent revolution; in which, indeed, they were again demonstrating their loyalty to Moscow, for the Soviet line now envisaged the "constitutional road to power" for such parties as the French and the Italian.

If the vast Communist party had lost the taste for violence, this was not true of a number of smaller revolutionary groups. Some, like the Trotskyists and anarchists, had existed for a long time in one form or another. Others had sprung up because Moscow's "revisionist" policies offended individual Communists, who opted for Peking in the great Sino-Soviet dispute. Others still were entirely new bodies, formed by young people who wanted revolution but for whom the Communist party held no attraction. Most of these groups were small: hence they were known as *groupuscules*. But their fervour and fanaticism compensated for their minuteness. Although the *groupuscules* were often mutually at loggerheads, they were united on the proposition that something drastic had to be done about French society. It happened that de Gaulle was in power when the accumulated pressure of numbers and the lateness or inadequacy of reforms made the explosion inevitable. But it could have been any other government: the explosion would still have happened. For most of these young people, de Gaulle was an irrelevance, as well as an anachronism. They wanted to overthrow the government, and it happened to be his.

One of the most active of the little groups was the "Movement of 22 March" – so named because on that day in 1968 seven hundred students at the new university of Nanterre outside Paris had seized the administrative building.[35] Their leader was a young man of German–Jewish origin called Daniel Cohn-Bendit. Another important group was the JCR (Jeunesses communistes révolutionnaires), founded in 1966 by dissidents from the orthodox Union des Etudiants communistes (UEC), who turned to Trotskyism under the leadership of a young Sorbonne junior lecturer, Alain Krivine, aged twenty-seven. There were, too, a number of Maoist groups: the Union de la Jeunesse marxiste-léniniste (UJCML), the Cercles marxistes-léninistes (CML) and the Parti communiste marxiste-léniniste. Their importance lay less in numbers, for they were tiny, but in their access to Chinese funds, generously purveyed through the 3,000-strong Belgian Maoist party. One more revolutionary

[35] For a full description of the *groupuscules*, see Paillat, *Archives*, pp. 51 *et seq*.

group deserves mention: the Fédération des Etudiants révolutionnaires (FER), which, like the JCR, called itself Trotskyist; though the two were on bad terms. All these groups would broadly own to the description of "left-wing". But there was a right-wing student group, too, with a taste for violence. Named "Occident" and born in 1964 and 1965, it was led by militant former supporters of Algérie française. Although the members of Occident were not among the revolutionaries in May and June 1968, their activities over the preceding months had had the kind of effect on the left-wing militants that a red rag has upon a bull.

As in other western countries during the 1960s, America's intervention in Vietnam provided a rallying cry among the student revolutionaries. But if Vietnam had not existed, other causes would have been found. There were, moreover, genuine grievances, already mentioned. And for two main reasons these grievances were felt most acutely among the students of sociology. One reason was a material one: no more than 20 per cent of the "sociologists" achieved "Pass" marks in their finals, and very few of the 20 per cent were able to find jobs related to their studies. The other reason was inherent in the nature of the discipline: students of sociology study society – and frequently, given their youth and idealism, they do not like what they see.

By common consent, however, the students alone, however fanatical, however brilliantly led, could not have caused the explosion of 1968 if they had not been joined or supported by large numbers of discontented adults. On the social side, conditions had sharply deteriorated during 1967. It was not that the total figure of unemployed was dramatic, if compared with the years of the great depression: early in 1968 it stood at about 450,000. But the rate of increase had been rising sharply and there was an air of panic in industry. Too many factories were closing or going on short days. On 26 January 1968, there was a massive demonstration, turning to violence, at Fougères, a shoe and textile centre in the north-west. That day, thousands of workers at the Renault works outside Caen marched on the town. Violent riots followed. In the Rhône valley and in the northern coal mines, that month, there were massive workers' demonstrations. At the end of the month, the Messageries Maritimes shipping line personnel began a strike, and at Rochefort the workers of Sud-Aviation staged a demonstration.

No awareness of the mounting discontent could be detected in General de Gaulle's speech on the last day of 1967. He saluted 1968 "with serenity" and "satisfaction" because everything gave him to suppose that it was going to be a successful year – a year, moreover, in which the intéressement of the workers was "going to mark an important stage towards a new social order". It was this remoteness from real life that would cause tens of thousands to throw restraint to the wind in the coming spring.

Chapter 6 ✤ Storm and Aftermath

On 15 March 1968, in an article that has since become famous, Pierre Viansson-Ponté, political editor of *Le Monde*, expressed the view that France was "bored". Six days later, Pompidou addressed the Gaullist Union of Youth for Progress. He lamented the lack of combativity in the youth of the day. "It's up to youth to call everything in question, and up to the older ones to put things right again."[1] He was soon to be proved wrong on the first count and, on the second, to be given plenty to attend to.

There was a fundamental clash between the president and his premier on the whole social question.[2] De Gaulle meant what he had said at the end of the year about creating a "new social order". From time to time, through the years when one project after another was launched but came to nothing, he would come back to it. He had kept himself closely informed about the discussions of a study group organised by René Capitant and Louis Vallon after the 1962 elections. About that time, an important little book by Bloch-Lainé – an economist, *inspecteur des finances* and head of the national savings organisation, the Caisse des Dépots – was published, entitled *Pour une Réforme de l'Entreprise*. It was essentially an attempt to examine how the workers could be given an "interest" in the companies that employed them. De Gaulle read the book with attention, complimented its author in public, and had long talks with him in private.

Pompidou looked on at all this celebration with deep scepticism. He blocked all the proposals of the Capitant-Vallon group and gave Vallon an angry dressing down for introducing the amendment bearing his name. He persuaded de Gaulle to defer his social plans, on the grounds that they were incompatible with economic expansion since

[1] Paillat, *Archives*, p. 83.　　　　[2] Alexandre, pp. 202 *et seq.*

616

they would upset the Patronat and he had enough trouble with the unions already without alienating the bosses as well.

But in this spring of 1968, de Gaulle was unwilling to wait any longer. On 25 April 1968, he invited the left-wing philosopher, writer and "resister", David Rousset, to the Elysée and said: "We must condemn capitalism, capitalist society. We must condemn it explicitly. We must condemn totalitarian Communism. We must find a new way: participation."[3]

It was too late. The workers were restless; the students were in ferment; the plotters were at work. On 5 January 1968, an article by Georges Marchais in the Communist daily, L'Humanité, alleged that the Maoist groups in France had received several hundred million francs from Peking. This alarm was shared, for different reasons, by the French secret services. In February, the SDECE reported that meetings were taking place in Brussels and Hamburg between the European Maoist leaders, with the object of promoting agitation in the French universities. Funds were abundant, and the Cubans as well as the Chinese were "in" on the act.[4] The internal security service, DST, agreed, but said the climax was timed for October.

It was later than the secret services, or the premier, or the president thought. It was probably, as events turned out, later even than the revolutionary student groups thought. For events suddenly acquired a momentum of their own. On 21 April, fist-fights broke out between left-wing and right-wing students at the Sorbonne, during an extraordinary meeting of the ailing UNEF. The "non-political" president, Perraud, resigned, and was replaced provisionally by one of the revolutionaries, Jacques Sauvageot. Similar incidents took place at Nanterre on the 23rd and at Toulouse on the 25th. Next day, at Nanterre, Cohn-Bendit addressed 900 students in inflammatory terms. On the 27th, a Saturday, police ransacked Cohn-Bendit's flat and interrogated him for twelve hours: he was released on the personal intervention of the Prime Minister.

That Sunday, Trotskyist and Maoist students invaded an exhibition in support of South Vietnam, organised by a former member of the OAS, and pretty thoroughly wrecked the premises. Next day, Occident issued a communiqué threatening a week of reprisals against "the Bolshevik vermin" and announcing an attack on Nanterre. On 2 May the dean announced the suspension of lectures until calm had returned. That day,

[3] ibid. p. 216. De Gaulle's habit of saying different things to different men should be remembered. This remark is not really incompatible with the reflections on Communism mentioned above, pp. 612–13.
[4] Paillat, Archives, p. 89.

the office of a group affiliated to the UNEF at the Sorbonne was destroyed by fire – probably (it was thought) started by Occident.

That day, too (and incredibly), Georges Pompidou and his Foreign minister, Couve de Murville, left Paris on an official visit to Iran and Afghanistan. The Prime Minister was displeased at the turn of events, but calm. The minister of the Interior (and former minister of Education), Christian Fouchet, had strongly advised Pompidou not to go,[5] but the premier was not going to let disorderly students decide where he should be. With de Gaulle's agreement, he had left Louis Joxe, the minister of Justice (and another ex-minister of Education), in charge at Matignon. To Joxe, to Peyrefitte (the then minister of Education) and to Fouchet, he said before leaving that they were to show the utmost firmness in the face of student demands. The revolutionary student leaders were to be summoned to appear before the disciplinary committee of the university on 6 May. This, it was thought, would enable the ministry of the Interior to order the deportation of Cohn-Bendit, who had not yet qualified for French naturalisation.

In his majestic solitude at the Elysée, de Gaulle paid relatively little attention to the growing disorders – although he did tell Fouchet that it was time to put a stop to what was going on at Nanterre.[6] His mind was on higher things, such as his own forthcoming journey to Rumania, and – a triumph for Gaullian policy – the big news that the North Vietnamese and the Americans were ready to meet in preliminary peace talks in Paris. The talks were to begin on 13 May, the tenth anniversary of the events that had brought him back to power.

The news of the forthcoming talks was published on the 3rd. That day, George Marchais, in another article in L'Humanité, denounced the leftists as "false revolutionaries" and sons of the bourgeoisie whose only real aim was to get control of their fathers' factories and run them for the benefit of capitalism. Still on 3 May, the Paris police occupied the Sorbonne while a revolutionary meeting was in progress, and arrested as many young people as they could fit into their prison vans. In the Latin Quarter, other revolutionaries started pulling up the paving stones – an action without which no revolution in Paris would be complete. One of the stones hit a policeman full in the face.

On the 6th, a number of young revolutionaries were gaoled, and there were more incidents in the Latin Quarter. Cohn-Bendit, who had not been arrested, appeared with his friends before the university's disciplin-

[5] ibid. p. 97. Fouchet (p. 219) merely records that he "suggested" to the Prime Minister that he should defer his trip.
[6] Fouchet, p. 220.

ary committee, which decided to suspend him for one year. Was this enough to have him deported? Three days later, the board of the university decided that it was not. That evening, however, serious riots took place in two districts of Paris, Denfert-Rochereau and St Germain-des-Prés. Nearly six hundred police or students were hurt, and 422 arrests made.

Echoes of agitation were coming in from many provincial towns: from Grenoble, Bordeaux, Clermont-Ferrand, Montpellier, Aix-en-Provence, Caen, Rouen, Strasbourg, Toulouse, Nantes and Dijon. There was no question, then, of a capital monopoly.

On the morning of the 7th, General de Gaulle received a parliamentary group and told them: "It is not possible to allow the opponents of the university to install themselves inside the university. It is not possible to tolerate violence in the streets, which has never been the way to start a dialogue."

Violence, however, was happening anyway. At Denfert-Rochereau thousands of students were gathering. Aware that they would be clashing with the police before the day was out, some were wearing helmets. As they marched through the Latin Quarter, their numbers swelled to about thirty thousand. Fouchet had ordered all bridges across the Seine to be blocked, on the grounds that the State was on the right bank and must be protected. Unaccountably, the Pont de la Concorde had been left unguarded. The demonstrators poured across it, but their objective was not the Elysée. At 10 p.m. the students and the many young workers who had joined them reached the Arc de Triomphe. The clashes lasted several hours.

Next day – a Wednesday – the minister of Education made a speech in the Assembly. Some found it conciliatory, for he had foreshadowed the resumption of lectures; others thought it ambiguous, for he had mentioned the need for order. Cohn-Bendit and his Movement of 22 March found it hostile, and decided on a giant demonstration on the 10th, to call for the immediate release of the arrested students.

In Iran first, then in Afghanistan, Pompidou was enjoying the local folklore, the scenery and the eastern pomp. News reached him from Paris, by telephone and by cable. But the messages were brief and the lines bad. He had no real idea of the gravity of the situation.

In Paris the ministers were beginning to panic. From Kabul, Pompidou had cabled Joxe to stand firm. Joxe, Peyrefitte and Fouchet all agreed that, whatever the provocation, the police should not fire on the demonstrators. Negotiations with the students should begin and a precise offer should be made: the classes to be resumed and the arrested students to be freed; the police to evacuate the Sorbonne, but a police control at the gates to ensure that only students needing to attend lectures should enter.

General de Gaulle personally telephoned Fouchet to say that whatever happened the students were to be kept out of the Sorbonne.[7] At 8 p.m., ten thousand demonstrators marched to the Santé prison to demand the release of the prisoners. Two hours later the revolutionaries decided to "occupy" the Latin Quarter. Joined by secondary school children, they spent the next few hours ripping up more paving stones and erecting barricades. By order of the prefect of police, 500 members of the riot squads – Compagnies Républicaines de Sécurité (CRS) – stood by, waiting for the order to attack. It was issued at 2 a.m. Down came the shields, and up the batons. The gas masks were on, for the "slow charge" had begun with the throwing of dozens of tear-gas bombs. On the opposing side, students were setting fire to parked cars, which exploded with spectacular effect. Sirens blaring, the ambulances started arriving. At 5.30 a.m. Cohn-Bendit called on the demonstrators to disperse.

The news reached Joxe at the Hôtel Matignon, and he took the difficult decision to have the president of the Republic wakened. Had he not done so, the general would have learnt of the disorders on the 8 a.m. news. De Gaulle immediately summoned him to the Elysée, together with Fouchet and the minister of the Armed Forces, Messmer. It was 6 a.m. and Fouchet was apologetic: "I'm afraid I haven't shaved, *mon général*."

The general was not in a conciliatory mood. His main concern was to enquire just what units of the army might be available, from the provinces or Germany.

Perhaps the gravest news was that the Communist-controlled CGT trade unions, together with those of the CFDT and the UNEF students, had called a general strike for the 13th. There was to be a huge demonstration of solidarity between the workers and students that day. This about-turn on the part of the Communists was apparent rather than real. The CGT leader, Georges Séguy, had little sympathy with the students, and none at all with those of them who had set fire to parked cars: the workers owned cars, too, and it took them two years of work to pay them off. But he was afraid of being outflanked on the left, and the alleged brutalities of the police were a good cause for solidarity. One thing the Communists insisted on, however: the demonstration would be orderly. No violence; no anarchy.

On the afternoon of the 11th, de Gaulle saw in turn Joxe, Fouchet, the director of the Sûreté Nationale, Maurice Grimaud, the rector of the

[7] ibid. p. 235.

Sorbonne, Dr Roche, and Peyrefitte. The first three urged him to put an end to an "absurd escalation", by freeing the students, withdrawing the police from the Sorbonne and resuming classes.

"No, no and again no!" exclaimed de Gaulle. "We're not capitulating before the rioters. The State does not back down."

Peyrefitte and the rector, however, convinced him that the time had come for conciliation, on condition that demonstrators were kept out of the university and order maintained.

Sun-tanned, smiling and invincibly self-confident, the Prime Minister returned from Afghanistan at 7.15 that evening. At eight he held a meeting at the Matignon with Joxe, Peyrefitte, Fouchet, Messmer and other ministers. "Luckily, I wasn't here when all this was going on," he said. "That makes it easier for me to deal with it."

Before landing, he went on, he had prepared a statement. He was going to announce the reopening of the university and the resumption of classes. What about those in prison, asked Peyrefitte? They would be freed, said Pompidou.

Joxe was sceptical: he had spent hours trying to get de Gaulle to make concessions. Peyrefitte, who had succeeded where Joxe had failed, also had doubts, and thought the Prime Minister would have to make concessions. But Pompidou brushed all objections aside. "Let's not bother with fag-ends," he said.

And at 9 p.m., after a snack, he called on the president at the Elysée. In no time, he had talked de Gaulle round to his way of thinking, or rather, de Gaulle had decided to leave the decision to Pompidou. Later, André Malraux was to quote the general as saying: "You're the Prime Minister. The ball's in your court. If you win – good, France will win with you. If you lose, it'll be too bad for you."

Another thing happened that 11 May. The hitherto docile team of reporters at French radio and television issued a communiqué complaining that the film of the clashes of the last evening had been banned. They threatened collectively to suspend all broadcasting if prevented from reporting current events.[8]

For some months, Pompidou had been gaining in authority and asserting himself increasingly in the conduct of affairs. Gone were the days of unquestioning deference to the general's views. Although de Gaulle had never gone so far as to commit himself to naming the former director of Rothschild's Bank as his successor, many people – not least Pompidou – were taking it for granted. Besides, de Gaulle had dropped many hints of

---

[8] In his book, Fouchet charges the press and television with exacerbating the situation by exaggerated reporting (ibid. pp. 243–6).

his particular favour, the most telling of which had been the suggestion that Pompidou should "show yourself more", make himself known to the great French public – a suggestion to which Pompidou had responded with exuberant enthusiasm.

Now, as the crisis deepened, Pompidou took over direct control of most of the major functions of government. He forbade Joxe, Gorse, Fouchet, Debré and others to make public speeches without his express permission. At 11.15 p.m. on the 11th, his features composed in the requisite blend of gravity and humanity, Pompidou announced his conciliatory measures on millions of little screens.

"Gaullist power has been forced to step back," was the Communist party's reaction.

Some were comforted by the premier's magnanimity, others aghast at his pusillanimity. Hardest hit was the police union, which issued a communiqué complaining that the Prime Minister's statement constituted a recognition that the students were in the right and an absolute disavowal of the police action ordered by the government itself.

On the 12th Peyrefitte resigned, for reasons that remained obscure at the time, although he later explained that he thought Pompidou's concessions would play into the hands of the extremists. In this, events were to show that he was not wrong. Pompidou refused to accept his resignation; but having taken the minister's powers unto himself, along with Justice, Finance, the Interior and Information, it made little difference.

For the general, 13 May was an unsatisfactory birthday. True, the sandwichmen were out in force, wishing him a happy birthday. But so were hundreds of thousands of strikers, students and other demonstrators, with banners unfurled, proclaiming: "Ten years is too much", or "Workers and students together! The authorities are on the retreat. Let us bring them down!" "De Gaulle to the archives! De Gaulle to the convent!" shouted irreverent demonstrators. That evening, the revolutionaries reoccupied the Sorbonne, where they settled down to prolonged and euphoric discussions on the new society they were about to create.

At Nantes and Lyon, at Strasbourg and Marseilles, Toulouse and Rennes, too, crowds gathered to demonstrate against the regime. Tellingly, Gaston Defferre, who had nearly opposed de Gaulle in the presidential elections of 1965, declared at Nîmes: "Between the two ballots of the presidential election, de Gaulle asked us to choose between him and chaos. Today, alas, we have de Gaulle *and* chaos at the same time."

General de Gaulle was due to leave Paris within a few hours on his

State visit to Rumania. Should he go as arranged, or cancel the trip? Fouchet strongly advised cancellation: "The French people would not understand, *mon général.*" Pompidou advised him to go: "The worst is over. If you did not go, the French people would think the whole thing was still going on."

De Gaulle listened to his Prime Minister. He reassured himself with the thought that after all, Rumania was only four hours away by air. At Orly, on the 14th, the president instructed Gorce to announce that he would address the nation on the 24th.

On arrival at Baneasa airport near Bucharest, de Gaulle made his usual speech on reaching a foreign country, with the habitual friendly paragraph in the host's language. That evening a telephone call from Paris gave him further disagreeable news. The Sud-Aviation works at Nantes had been seized by the workers. In a morose mood, but without showing it, he attended a reception and made a speech in reply to the toast in his honour proposed by the Rumanian premier, Nicolae Ceausescu.

On the 15th his main engagement was to make a speech at the Great National Assembly of the Rumanian Socialist Republic. That day, too, the news was bad. The students were one thing: now the movement of pay claims and seizures of factories was spreading rapidly. The general's humour continued to darken. But it all seemed distant and relatively unimportant. Here he was in Rumania, making international history; or so he fancied. That evening, while the French workers were seizing their factories, he was telling the Rumanians about France's new policy of Atlantic independence, of the renewal of friendship with Russia and of Rumania's part in the forthcoming unity of Europe.

The Rumanians, aware of the news from France, were on the look-out for tell-tale signs of worry or embarrassment on the part of their distinguished visitor. But they need not have bothered: de Gaulle was too old a hand and too consummate an actor to show anything but a relaxed and smiling face. On the 16th and 17th, while he visited the more peaceful factories of Craiova, and the towns of Slatina, Pitesti, Tirgoviste and Ploesti, cables from Debré, Roger Frey and Fouchet implored him to come home. Urgent telephone calls supplemented these pleas. De Gaulle remained calm. The only indication he gave that things were not as normal as they might have been was in conversation with Ceausescu, when he complimented the Rumanian leader – with a barely perceptible note of envy – on the country's special university entrance examination.

In Paris, the revolutionaries were turning nastier. Groups of them took it in turns to telephone the members of the board of the University of Paris at all hours of the day and night, with threats or insults.[9] Surrounded by their own filth, the occupants of the Sorbonne chalked revolutionary graffiti on the walls and listened to speeches from Alain Geismar, "Danny the Red" (as Cohn-Bendit was known, as much for his red hair as for his politics), and other young revolutionaries. For good measure, the Odéon theatre was seized, to the chagrin of the minister of Culture, André Malraux.

On the evening of the 17th, Pompidou had a long telephone conversation with the president. It was de Gaulle who had booked the call. The Prime Minister told him there was no need for him to break off his Rumanian visit. De Gaulle agreed to come back on the appointed day – the 18th – but said he had decided to shorten his stay by some hours.

Before leaving on the 18th de Gaulle made an unflappably erudite speech on cultural links between France and Rumania, at the University of Bucharest, and a television farewell, ending as he had begun with a few words in Rumanian.

At 10.30 p.m. the assembled ministers greeted their returning master at Orly. The smiles of welcome were frozen. De Gaulle's mood was black and sardonic. "So, Malraux, they've taken your Odéon?" and to the the minister of Education: "What about your students – still the *chienlit*?"[10]

After the jests, the show of authority: "We're going to take all this in hand, and we're going to settle the problems as we always have settled them. We shall appeal to the French people."

The royal "we" was apt. Back at the Elysée, de Gaulle found a letter from the Comte de Paris, the substance of which was a confidence that only he, the general, could extricate France from the grave circumstances in which she found herself.[11]

Just before midnight de Gaulle received Pompidou and various ministers. Accounts differ on the identity of those present and whether the president saw them separately or together, but all agree on one point: he was in a furious temper and roundly trounced his team for letting matters get out of hand. The remonstrations went on in further sessions

---

[9] Tournoux, in *Mai*, pp. 100–2, reproduces the list of names, addresses and telephone numbers used by the *provocateurs*.

[10] This remark was much quoted in the Paris press, and abroad, and its meaning was hotly debated. The polite dictionary definitions of *"chienlit"* are: a carnival masque, a masquerade, a disguise. But the word, if spelt "chie-en-lit", means – lightly expurgated – "excrete in the bed". This was undoubtedly the meaning de Gaulle had in mind.

[11] Tournoux, *Mai*, pp. 105–7.

next day – a Sunday. There is little doubt that Pompidou was the main target of these presidential reproaches, although it is not clear whether he was given a private wigging, or, allusively, a public one. According to one account,[12] the Prime Minister offered his resignation, which the president refused, saying: "This is not the moment". But he had already, it seems, made up his mind that the premier would have to go. Pompidou had misled de Gaulle about the situation, either deliberately (for his own political ends – to shine in de Gaulle's absence?) or by misjudging it: either way, it was time he went.

That Sunday, the general again used the inelegant word *"chienlit"*, he said: "Reforms, yes. *Chienlit*, no." The phrase was much quoted, after the usual ministerial indiscretions.

Paralysis was creeping over France. Séguy had said the time was not ripe for a general strike, but already half a million workers were out, and 100 factories were occupied. Fewer trains were running and many planes were grounded; the mail was becoming irregular.

On 21 May the president received Averell Harriman, head of the American delegation at the Vietnam talks, and Xuan Thuy of North Vietnam. The visitors found him distant and depressed. That day, the president chaired a meeting of the Council of Ministers and approved an Amnesty Bill. In the Assembly a two-day debate on an opposition motion of censure was starting: it was not carried. Gaullist speakers and rumour-mongers spread the tale that the Communist party was plotting an insurrection. The Communist leader, Waldeck Rochet, warned individual Gaullists, including de Gaulle's brother-in-law, Jacques Vendroux, chairman of the Assembly's Foreign Affairs committee, not to spread such falsehoods – as indeed they were. He pressed members of Mitterrand's Left Federation to "desolidarise" themselves from Cohn-Bendit and his friends. He had already dismissed the young student leader with the contemptuous phrase: "Cohn-Bendit? Never heard of him:" (a remark also attributed to the CGT boss, Georges Séguy). And when Jacques Sauvageot led a band of demonstrators to the striking workers of the Renault factory outside Paris, he was given the cold shoulder.

On the 23rd de Gaulle chaired another cabinet meeting. This was one of his better days. He made a resolute speech, analysing the challenge of technological civilisation from the standpoint of those who suffered from it: the students and workers. Chances had been lost and public order had suffered. It must be restored. And he revealed his plan: he was going to announce a referendum on "participation", and stake his future on it. A heated discussion followed, largely on whether there

[12] Alexandre, p. 224.

should also be general elections. The Prime Minister was against, and de Gaulle sided with him.

By the time de Gaulle spoke on the 24th, more than eight million workers were on strike. The television journalists were among them, and only news bulletins and pre-recorded music programmes were on the air. In the streets of Paris uncollected refuse was reaching mountainous heights.

Always in the past, in days of crisis, de Gaulle had brandished his ultimate weapon: the radio or television speech. Always it had worked: it had caused the collapse of the barricades in 1960, and of the generals' defiance in 1961. Always he had waited until the situation seemed irretrievable, and the magic of his words and his manner had retrieved it. This time, too, he had waited: longer than ever before, partly because he had said it was to be on the 24th and that was when it was going to be; partly, as he said later, because he wanted the censure vote in parliament to be defeated first.

"Everybody understands, of course," said the old man when he did speak, "the meaning of current events, in the universities and in society. All the signs can be discerned that show the necessity for a mutation of our society, and everything indicates that this mutation must involve a more extensive participation of all in the running and the results of activities that concern them directly." The French people would have to solve its own problems, and the cost of failure was civil war, adventures and usurpations. He was about to submit to the whole people a bill to provide for the country's renovation. The vote would take place in June. If the majority said No, "it goes without saying that I shall not carry on". But a massive Yes would enable him to rid France of obsolete structures and inject her with new blood.

For the first time, the Gaullian magic failed. Within an hour of the speech, thousands of students were locked in violent clashes with the riot police. From all over the country came reports that de Gaulle's words had fallen flat. The Gaullists were dejected; the opposition, unexpectedly elated.

De Gaulle himself went through three phases: incomprehension, anger and despair. Whenever, in the past, he had asked for a blank cheque, it had been forthcoming. Why not this time? It was like a torrent, he told his associates: there was nothing to catch hold of. The whole country was falling to bits. Then anger: "The French are cattle. Just cattle." And military epithets flowed in profusion.

The phase of deep depression set in, during which, as he later told his television interviewer, Michel Droit, he seriously thought of laying down the burden.[13] He was seventy-seven: was this not a forgivable wish to have?

By now, during the weekend of 25 and 26 May, the Gaullists were afraid to importune him. With one exception, he was left utterly alone at the Elysée. The exception was a distinguished visitor, who had come to the palace on the Sunday, in secret, by an unobtrusive door. It was Couve de Murville, and the chief of State told him – to Couve's intense discomfort – that he would be the next Prime Minister.

Pompidou was active. During the whole of that weekend, in thirty hours of acrimonious discussions, the Prime Minister presided over a conference of employers and workers in the ministry of Social Affairs, in the rue de Grenelle. When it was over, at 7 a.m. on Monday, 27 May, agreement was reached. The price was unprecedentedly high: wage increases up to 35 per cent. Fortunately, the country's gold reserves also stood high. At 8 a.m. Pompidou at last went to bed. He was up at ten, with the serenity of a job accomplished. To the general stupefaction, however, the strikes went on. At Billancourt, 12,000 Renault workers met, discussed the Grenelle terms, and unanimously decided to continue the struggle. The Communist leaders, Benoît Frachon and Georges Séguy, who were there, were booed. From other factories similar news was coming in.

The general was tired. There seemed no way out. In Paris all was confusion, and the inchoate flood of news made sleep difficult. He was tired; but he was not beaten. From the 28th on, his analytical faculties intact for all his weariness, he was on the alert for the tell-tale crack, the point of weakness in the massed legions of his apparent enemies. He thought he had spotted it, and its name was Fear: the desperate fear of millions of ordinary Frenchmen. Fear of chaos, yes; but deeper still, fear that out of the chaos would come a new order, which could only be that of Communism. On the 27th Pompidou had expressed his conviction that the Communist party would not depart from legality. This seemed indeed probable. But it was a flimsy basis for confidence. De Gaulle, for his part, discounted it. Besides, events might force the hand of the Communist leaders: they could not be denied a share of power if the Fifth Republic collapsed totally; and they would be the strongest element

[13] Viansson-Ponté, in *République*, Vol. II, pp. 524 *et seq.*, argues that de Gaulle's phase of discouragement was brief, lasting only two days or so from his return from Rumania on 18 May, that he planned his disappearing trick between the 20th and the 26th, and that he feigned discouragement thereafter to deceive his own followers, the better to bring off his surprise effect. But all that is speculation; I prefer to assume that the failure of his speech on the 24th provoked a genuine discouragement, which he rapidly overcame.

in any coalition of forces that took over. If the others tried to keep them out, they would strike first. And they might well strike first if the Gaullist Service d'Action civique tried to save the Republic. Equally, if the anarchists, Trotskyists and Maoists tried to "go it alone" by over-running the Elysée and the Matignon, or merely the Hôtel de Ville to set up a commune on the 1871 model, the Communists might find the temptation of power irresistible: in such circumstances, a doctrinal attachment to "legality" might easily be discarded.

At all events, the fear of Communism, or its bogey, was an exploitable factor in the situation. But it was vague. All that was lacking was something – some event, some action, some word – that would crystallise the fear. De Gaulle waited.

On the afternoon of the 27th, during the most sombre cabinet session any of the participants had ever attended, the UNEF called a mass meeting at Charléty stadium, south of the Latin Quarter. News of its progress reached the ministers during the session. De Gaulle said: "Charléty, that's all over. . . . It's the last time. . . . No more marches."

The draft text of the proposed referendum bill was shown to the president. It provided for "the participation of the workers in pro-fessional responsibilities, at all levels of the economy". De Gaulle approved the draft, with minor changes, and it was sent to the State Council; which rejected it as unconstitutional (as it had turned down his referendum proposals in 1962). But the rejection went unnoticed in the turmoil of sensational news. And in any case, the project was a dead letter, for events forced de Gaulle to abandon it. On 27 May, however, the decision was that the referendum would be held on 16 June.

Monday 28 May brought the general the opportunity he was looking for. Two prominent men, among others, were seeking ways of turning the situation to their political advantage. Both were men of the left, but there the resemblance ended. One was Pierre Mendès France, the other François Mitterrand. Mendès France was the only statesman in the country, apart from de Gaulle, with credible claims to being a "providential man". He had "saved" France in 1954 from the con-sequences of her Indo-China folly. Like de Gaulle, though his aura was paler, he was financially incorruptible and a solitary and uncom-promising figure. A former Radical, he had joined the small Parti Socialiste unifié on its foundation in 1960, but had played next to no part in its activities thereafter, to the extent of fighting the 1962 election as an independent. Mendès France was an intransigent opponent of Communism and of any electoral or parliamentary alliance with the Communist party. He had no mass following, but his intellectual influence as a radical reformer was immense; in the main, in the late 1960s, it was exercised through the "technocratic" membership of certain of the many political clubs that sprang up during this period, largely supplanting the discredited old parties.

Mitterrand's prestige was of quite a different order. A brilliant debater (although he had got the worst of a public debate with Pompidou), he had polled more than 10.5 million votes in the second ballot of the presidential elections in 1965. This did not give him the aura of a providential man: unlike Mendès France, he was not regarded as a man of inflexible principle, and unlike Mendès France he was willing to work with the Communists. Indeed, his Left Federation (Fédération de la Gauche démocrate et socialiste) had an electoral arrangement with the Communist party in 1965, and his huge popular vote included that of Communist supporters.

During the days of revolutionary euphoria, Mendès France demonstrated that he was the only prominent politician who could go into the Latin Quarter and its heart, the Sorbonne, without fear of physical consequences. He made it clear, indeed, that he was *persona grata* with the revolutionaries, although he himself was not one. This demonstration probably irked Mitterrand. At any rate, it spurred him to do something on his own, for fear of being outflanked on the non-Communist left. So on Tuesday 28 May at midday, he called a press conference at the Continental Hotel – a symbolic choice, for it was there, on 19 May 1958, that General de Gaulle had called a celebrated conference that preceded his return to power. Mitterrand now achieved a sensation in his own right, for he announced that in the event of a No to de Gaulle on 16 June, he would be willing to form a provisional government. Cautiously, he remarked that Mendès France might legitimately be entrusted with a provisional premiership. In answer to a question about the presidency Mitterrand, who had argued in favour of an early dissolution followed by presidential elections, declared that he himself would be a candidate.

This was all de Gaulle needed: the event he was waiting for, although he could not guess the form it would take. Mitterrand, the man who had made an electoral alliance with the Communist party in 1965, was proposing himself as either the provisional Prime Minister or the permanent president, or both. The threat of a Communist take-over was becoming precise instead of vague.

Now de Gaulle knew what to do. While he slept, or lay awake, the dying 28 May brought another sensation, this time with a touch of light relief. Cohn-Bendit, who had been deported and had returned to

Germany, turned up at the Sorbonne at midnight. He had dyed his flaming hair black and eluded the frontier control. Now the regime was not merely powerless, but a laughing stock.

De Gaulle was about to produce the most stunning *coup de théâtre*, without exception, in his extraordinary career. The impact of his secret plan was bound to be sensational, for it was first to be preceded by a minor coup that could only be taken to mean the opposite of his intention.

The Council of Ministers had been arranged, as usual, for 10 a.m. At 9.15, the secretary to the cabinet, Jean Donnedieu de Vabres, telephoned Pompidou: "The general asks me to inform you that he is going to Colombey for twenty-four hours. The council meeting is deferred until tomorrow at 3 p.m."

There was no explanation. (Nor, as it became clear in time, was it the general's intention that there should be a fully explicit one.) Tortured by unspoken questions, the Prime Minister telephoned Bernard Tricot, the secretary-general to the presidency, to request an audience with the general. Tricot promised to ring back. When Pompidou's telephone rang at 11 a.m., however, it was not Tricot but the general himself – a rare occurrence. "I need to be face to face with myself," said de Gaulle. "I also need to get some sleep. I don't seem to get any here. I shall be back tomorrow at 3 p.m."

Pompidou could not conceal his apprehension, lest the general should not return.

"No, there's no reason for that," said de Gaulle in a tired voice. "In any case, there is the future. And you are on the side of the future. There may be adventures ahead. It's not all that dramatic. I intend to come back. There's no reason for you to worry."

And the general, who had already decided on Pompidou's successor, spoke an unusual "good-bye": "I embrace you." Later, Pompidou would have cause to wonder whether this was the kiss of Judas.

The news broke with sensational effect. The world's newspapers mostly assumed that this was the end and proclaimed their belief that it was in their boldest headlines. The chancelleries were agog. The NATO powers worried about the French hinterland, should the Communist party come to power. Soviet commentators declared, reassuringly, that the hour of the revolution had *not* come. French Communist sources claimed, with verisimilitude, that the Americans and Russians had reached a diplomatic understanding: America recognised Czechoslovakia (which had been gripped by the euphoria of "libertarian" Communism for some weeks) as firmly in the Soviet zone of influence; and Russia recognised France as in America's influence.

These considerations were almost certainly not uppermost in de Gaulle's mind that morning. More relevant to the situation were the assurances he had had from Messmer, the minister of the Armed Forces, that everything was ready for an armed emergency. Shock troops guarded the gates of the city of Paris. And the Town Hall was covered by a powerful force of CRS. Thus far, Pompidou, Messmer and Fouchet had stuck to their initial determination to refrain from firing on the revolutionaries. But they would not hesitate if the *enragés*, or the *contestataires*, as they were currently known, should misguidedly march on the Hôtel Matignon or the Elysée Palace. There was a good chance that de Gaulle would find his official residence as he had left it, the following day.

That was the first sensation. The second came a few hours later, and eclipsed the first. In a panic, Tricot turned up at the Matignon at about 2 p.m. "The general," he announced to the astounded ministers, "has disappeared. He has not arrived at Colombey."

The news was stunning. For two hours, Pompidou lived with his anguish, as did his ministers, each with his public and private speculations. Where was the general, if not at Colombey? Had he gone out of his mind? What were the chances of his returning? At 4 p.m. the minister of the Armed Forces telephoned to say that the president's helicopter, having landed at the military airport of Saint-Dizier, near Chaumont, had taken off again, and had now landed at Baden-Baden, in West Germany.

The relief was vast, but the questions remained unanswered. Indeed this latest instalment provoked further ones. Why had the general gone to Germany? Was he going to stay there? At 5 p.m. the second of these questions at least was answered, when the general himself telephoned Pompidou from Colombey, to say: "I am at La Boisserie. I shall come back tomorrow. I'll see you before the Council of Ministers."

Meanwhile, wild rumours were circulating in Paris and elsewhere. The wildest was that de Gaulle had gone to East Germany or Czechoslovakia to meet Kosygin. More plausible was the supposition that he had gone to see General Massu, ruthless hero of the battle of Algiers and now the commander-in-chief of the French forces in Germany, to find out under what conditions the army would be prepared to defend the Fifth Republic. The rumours went on to name Massu's main condition: the release of Salan, still in gaol for his earlier dissidence.[14]

---

[14] This rumour was the hardest to die, for on 15 June, Salan and other OAS leaders were in fact released on amnesty. But there was no substance in tales of a deal at Baden-Baden, for the decision to free Salan had been taken at Easter.

Uncertainty still reigned, and each interested party reacted to it in his own way. The Gaullist rank-and-file were in a state of trauma. On the 27th, they were calling for mass support for the general. On the 29th, assuming he had deserted them, they were switching their support and loyalty to the man who, in most people's eyes, was bearing the brunt of the crisis, without faltering and without panicking: Georges Pompidou. The defenders of the Gaullist order, Foccart and Frey, had been organising new teams of armed men, each with his firearms permit legally issued. Essentially the old Service d'Action civique, re-organised, the new militias were called Comités pour la Défense de la République (CDR). Their creation was announced on 23 May 1968. Their first secretary-general, Godefrain, was soon replaced by Yves Lancien. It had been decided that the CDR, with as many rank-and-file Gaullists and ordinary supporters of the general, would parade on the Place de la Concorde on 30 May, as an answer to the mass demonstrations of the students and workers.[15] A Gaullist deputy, Pierre-Charles Krieg, was in charge of the organisation under the minister of State, Roger Frey, but on the eve, the 29th, Krieg was still unaware that de Gaulle would be back in Paris the following day, and he feared the parade would flop.

Nor could Pompidou be certain the general would come back, although he had not disclosed this uncertainty when de Gaulle had telephoned. He, too, had a contingency plan. Just in case the general stayed away, he took the precaution of alerting Edouard Sablier, head of television news, to send the necessary technical equipment to the Matignon, with technicians, to stand by for an important announcement. This, however, he never made.

Then there were Mendès France and Mitterrand. In their ignorance of the general's plans, and on the assumption that his disappearance meant that he would not return, the two men held a council of war. With them were other Socialists, including Guy Mollet, René Billères and Gaston Defferre. At 9.10 p.m. a decision was announced: Mendès France declared his readiness to become provisional premier, in the name of the united left. It was almost as if the other "providential man" had fallen into a trap laid by de Gaulle. At all events, this announcement was to mark the political suicide of this potentially great statesman and the self-destruction of the non-Communist left.

A further event took place on that crowded day. A vast concourse of demonstrators – not students but followers of the Communist party – marched from the Place de la Bastille to Saint-Lazare station. The lowest

[15] Charlot, Gaullisme, p. 177.

estimate was 200,000, the highest half a million. That day, throughout France, ten million workers were idle.

The general, on his side, had had an interesting thirty-six hours. Having decided what to do on the 28th, and knowing that secrecy was the *sine qua non* of success, he had resolved to keep his plan entirely concealed from the government. Only servicemen were to know, and under orders to keep the plan to themselves. The one exception – an unavoidable one – was Seydoux, the French ambassador in Bonn, for protocol required that the German government should be informed of the chief of State's proposed brief visit to Baden-Baden. Seydoux was therefore instructed to notify the German chancellor, Kiesinger. But Seydoux's own instructions were not, as is normal, conveyed through the Quai d'Orsay, but from French army headquarters, through the French military *attaché* in Bonn; and the ambassador was instructed not to report the matter to his minister, Couve de Murville, or to mention it to anybody but Kiesinger.[16]

Seydoux played his part. And so did the tiny circle of confidants: General Fourquet, chief of the General Staff of National Defence; General Lalande, head of de Gaulle's military household; and naval captain Flohic, the President's aide-de-camp. Neither Pompidou nor Fouchet, both of whom the general saw on the 28th, was given the faintest inkling of his plans.

The president left the Elysée in his special Citroën, accompanied by his wife and Captain Flohic. Their usual luggage was augmented by three suitcases containing State documents. On arrival at Issy-les-Moulineaux, the presidential party transferred to waiting Alouette III helicopters. The pilots knew where they were heading, but not de Gaulle's travelling companions, who thought they were going to Colombey. The landing at Saint-Dizier caused stupefaction. There, the helicopters refuelled and de Gaulle made several telephone calls – not, assuredly, with his ministers; but conceivably with Fourquet, Massu (to announce his arrival) and to one of his ultimate defenders, Foccart. De Gaulle then went on to Baden-Baden; his wife, Captain Flohic, a doctor and a security bodyguard went to Colombey to await the general's arrival.

At Baden-Baden, de Gaulle conferred with Massu. There has been no full account of what was said, but it is certain that de Gaulle did not, as was rumoured at the time, ask for assurances of loyalty and support. The time of doubts in the army was past; the doubters and enemies were in prison or in exile. Massu may have wavered, but he had stayed loyal to the general, and had been rewarded with the five stars of a full general

16 Paillat, *Archives*, p. 215.

(which meant, of course, that he comfortably outranked Charles de Gaulle). What is more probable is that de Gaulle and Massu discussed contingency plans for emergency action. Tournoux, whose reconstruction of the general's reasoning has an authentic ring, reckons that de Gaulle's real motive was to avoid, at all costs, any repetition of 1940. The State and the legitimacy of power were under threat. In the last resort, he represented both. Therefore, wherever he went, legitimacy went too. If the Elysée were overrun in his absence, he would set up the State in the eastern front, with the bulk of the French army to back it. If it were not, he would return and smash the revolutionary movement.[17]

That evening, Captain Flohic dined with Madame de Gaulle and the general. After the meal, the general invited the younger man to walk with him in the gardens of La Boisserie. Astonished, the ADC heard a monologue, at the end of which, de Gaulle turned to him and said with a smile: "You may go to bed now, Flohic. I now know what I'm going to tell them."[18]

Flohic had been listening to an informal rehearsal of de Gaulle's speech of 30 May. That morning, one thing at least was clear: the revolutionaries had not pressed their advantage, and the Fifth Republic was still alive. The general could go back to Paris.

He arrived at the Elysée at 12.25, and saw Pompidou at 2.30. The latter wished to resign, but de Gaulle cut him short by dealing with his own position. "I shall not go," he announced. "I have a mandate, I shall fulfil it." It was obvious, he agreed, that a referendum could not now be held. Instead, he would dissolve parliament and call general elections.[19] During the cabinet meeting that followed, de Gaulle paid a lengthy tribute to "this courageous man" (the Prime Minister), and told the ministers what he intended to say to the nation; but left his intentions ambiguous, as regards Pompidou's continued stay in office.

At 4.30 he was in front of the microphones – not of the television cameras, however, the entire service having broken down. The lassitude of 24 May was entirely missing. Instead, the tones of a reinvigorated man, of the incomparable leader that he was, reverberated in millions of homes and in the Palais-Bourbon, where the deputies hung on his words.

Being the custodian of national and republican sovereignty, I have envisaged, for the past twenty-four hours, all eventualities, without

[17] Tournoux, *Mai*, pp. 295–301.   [18] Paillat, *Archives*, p. 221.
[19] On the evening of 28 May, before General de Gaulle's disappearance, Christian Fouchet had been summoned to the Elysée, apparently more as a friend than a minister. Early on the 29th he wrote to the president, advising him to scrap the referendum plans and call general elections (Fouchet, pp. 261–2).

exception, that might allow me to maintain it. I have taken my decisions.

In present circumstances, I shall not retire. I have a mandate from the people, I shall fulfil it.

I shall not change the Prime Minister, whose valour, solidity, capacity, merit the homage of all. . . . I dissolve the National Assembly this day.

He would defer the proposed referendum. The legislative elections would take place, as provided under the constitution – unless the entire French people were to be gagged by groups long organised to that end and "by a party that is a totalitarian enterprise". There followed a remarkable passage:

Everywhere and straight away, civic action must be organised. This must be done to first aid the government, then locally the prefects, who will have become, or become once more, commissioners of the Republic, in their task which consists of ensuring as far as possible the welfare of the population and to prevent subversion at all times and in all places.

France, indeed, is threatened by dictatorship [which could only be that of] totalitarian communism. . . .

Eh bien! Non! The Republic shall not abdicate.

Everything that needed to be said had been packed into a tense four and a half minutes. He had appealed to the sovereign people. He had agitated the Communist threat. He had praised Pompidou. Above all, perhaps, he had appealed to the strong-arm men of Gaullism to come out into the streets and show their strength. And there was the striking reference to "commissioners of the Republic" – which to Gaullists and students of contemporary history was a dramatic reminder of the decree of 6 July 1944, specifying that after the liberation, the commissioners of the Republic were to take all measures to administer the territory, re-establish Republican legality and satisfy the needs of the population. There were therefore three elements of force in de Gaulle's plans: two of them legitimate, the third dubious. The legitimate ones were the army and the gendarmerie, at the service of the prefects; the other was the Gaullist Service d'Action civique, lately renamed the CDR.

This time the general's verbal magic did work. The reassertion of his charisma was absolute. In the Palais-Bourbon the deputies spontaneously burst into the Marseillaise. And in the Place de la Concorde, the largest crowd of all since the beginning of the crisis started gathering. By 6 p.m.

it had reached about a million – at least twice as large as the biggest mustered by the Communists. It was a Gaullist crowd, the crowd of the enthusiasts and the faithful; it was also the crowd of the ordinary people who had been afraid and now had courage. The good bourgeois of Paris were there, and their sons. The former paratroops of French Algeria and the veterans of Indo-China or Korea, deputies, veterans of North Africa and of the First World War, Companions of the Liberation, and not a few students from Nanterre who had not been followers of Cohn-Bendit but had been afraid to say so; workers; Africans; gaily dressed young women; respectable dowagers. It was a flood, and soon it engulfed the whole of the vast Champs-Elysées.

De Gaulle had triumphed, against all odds.

His victory was at once sweeping and pyrrhic. Sweeping, because within weeks the Gaullists were back in power with the biggest majority in French parliamentary history; and pyrrhic too, because the financial cost of the social settlement and de Gaulle's loss of prestige combined to bring him down less than a year later.

The immediate concern after the traumatic *événements* was to win the elections. It was Pompidou's concern, above all, but it was de Gaulle's too, for even though he did not accord elections a fraction of the weight of a referendum, it was essential to demonstrate that his government had popular support. Only thus could the deeply damaged authority of the State be restored. Tired though he was after his sleepless weeks, Pompidou personally supervised all the arrangements: the financial side, the choice of candidates, the campaigning, especially on television. But for the first time, de Gaulle himself wanted a hand in many things, insisting, for instance, on scrutinising the list of candidates before final approval.[20]

The general was waiting for the best opportunity for replacing his Prime Minister. In private, he blamed Pompidou heavily for allowing the situation to get out of hand. His royal diagnosis was that the turning point was the fatal decision to allow the Sorbonne to be taken over. Thereafter, the students felt they could get away with anything; and the workers were not slow to compete. As for Pompidou's handling of the crisis as it developed, he dismissed it with these cutting words: "I quite agree, Pompidou fought well in May. Like M. Seguin's goat.[21] Until the 29th. But I was the one who killed the wolf, on 30 May."

[20] Alexandre, pp. 250 et seq.
[21] An illusion, instantly recognisable to anyone who has done his primary schooling in France, to Alphonse Daudet's tale, *La Chèvre de M. Seguin*, in *Lettres de mon Moulin*: M. Seguin's goat, having broken loose to taste freedom, fought the wicked wolf all night, but in the morning the wolf ate her anyway.

For the time being, however, Pompidou must be publicly supported, and retain the private illusion of support as well.

The general's public support was, however, merely implicit in the fact that it was Pompidou, while still in office, who was fighting the elections. De Gaulle made no mention of him in his speech of 30 May, nor even in his lengthy television interview with Michel Droit on 7 June, in which he gave his own analysis of the events of May.

The first ballot in the general elections took place on 23 June. The turnout reached 80 per cent, and the Gaullist poll was 46 per cent – yielding a majority of landslide proportions. The Gaullist vote had increased by 1,700,000 since 1967, and all other parties had suffered; the Communists lost 600,000 votes, and the Left Federation nearly as many. In the final Assembly, after the second ballot a week later, the Gaullists held 346 seats, against 117 for all other parties combined.

Naturally enough, the results were generally considered a personal triumph for Georges Pompidou. In the Gaullist euphoria of the moment, de Gaulle – who had broken the revolution and saved the careers of his followers – was almost forgotten. From the Presidential Palace, he viewed with disapproval, even anger, the spectacle of Pompidou, the man he had picked from obscurity to give him a political career, receiving the homage of his followers as the self-evident heir to presidential power. The general, however, retained a certain affection for the ex-school-teacher from Auvergne, who had helped him over the financial difficulties of political "exile" and handled so many difficult affairs discreetly and well. His mind was made up, but he thought, in the present triumphant circumstances, that it would be better for Pompidou to resign than to be dismissed; and incidentally, for once, in accordance with Article 8 of the constitution. Between the two ballots, Pompidou again spoke of his "extreme lassitude" and offered his resignation. The general, elated by the election returns, said: "We'll come back to that."

On 1 June, the day after the second ballot, the president again summoned the Prime Minister to the Elysée. After mutual felicitations about the electoral victory, the general accompanied his visitor to the door, and asked: "Well, what about you? What have you decided?"

Pompidou expressed his desire for a rest. He thought it would be politically useful to have a change of government after the storms of spring. De Gaulle disagreed: it would look like a defeat in the hour of victory.

When Pompidou insisted, de Gaulle advised him to think it over for two days. "I still need you," he is reported to have said.

Constitutionally very tough, Pompidou could have overcome his "lassitude" with a brief respite. But he had his own political ambitions to think of. The whole problem hinged on the general's intentions, which were no easier to guess now than ever before. Was he going to stay till the end of his term in 1972? If he was, Pompidou's friends told him, he had better stay in office, difficult though the problems now in prospect looked. If, however, de Gaulle was planning to quit six months or a year hence, then Pompidou would be well advised to resign. This would give him a good rest, leaving his successor to cope with all the difficulties, and he could hope to come back as president of the Republic before the public had had time to forget him.

Pompidou himself thought it unlikely that the general would stay till the end. The likelihood surely was that he would retire the following spring, full of glory, and preside from afar over the difficult transitional period of *l'après-Gaullisme*. He was in the frame of mind induced by this assumption when he and his wife, Claude, were the guests of the de Gaulles at dinner on Thursday, 4 June. Over coffee Pompidou reminded the general that he needed a rest. He confirmed his wish to resign in a brief letter which he had delivered by hand to the Elysée.

This was the occasion General de Gaulle had been hoping for. But it was characteristic of him to throw further doubts in the minds of his team. In telephonic conversation with Foccart, Pompidou learned with surprised dismay that the general had not yet made up his mind about the next Prime Minister, but that it could well be Pierre Messmer who, for seven years, had been an irreproachable minister of the Armed Forces. Pompidou could scarcely believe his ears: after de Gaulle's secret meeting with General Massu, Gaullism would begin to look like a militarist movement. And Gaullism was, after all, Pompidou's business. His advisers and his family all counselled him to withdraw his resignation. He slept on this advice. It was now Saturday morning, and Pompidou telephoned Bernard Tricot at the Elysée with a message for the president: all things considered, he wished to remain at the disposal of the chief of State and was ready to continue in office.

Later that morning, Tricot returned the call, to say that it was too late: the general had already made other arrangements. His choice was not Messmer but Couve de Murville, who had been appointed Prime Minister the night before, after dinner.

Forgetting that he himself had wished to resign, Pompidou was now deeply hurt; and offended by the general's impersonal procedure. The years of loyal and devoted service had, in the end, counted for nothing, and de Gaulle had not even bothered to let him know in person what had been decided. Henceforth Pompidou, who had been Prime Minister for six and a half years – longer than any other Frenchman for four generations[22] – was just a deputy. There had been some talk of his being made president of the Assembly – that is, speaker; but he would not hear of this visible demotion. In the end, the Gaullist deputies elected him their honorary president – a position of some political utility, which he accepted.

The official letters marking the end of Pompidou's premiership were exchanged on 10 July. Pompidou's contained a voluntary contradiction that provoked many comments; de Gaulle's was almost fulsome in its tributes to the outgoing head of government:

Mon Général,
You were good enough to let me know your intention, now that the National Assembly elected on 23 and 30 June is about to meet, of nominating a new government.

I have the honour, in consequence, and in conformity with the provisions of Article 8 of the constitution, of presenting the resignation of the government.

I ask you to accept, *mon Général,* assurances of my deep respect.

Georges Pompidou

My dear friend,
Measuring the full weight of your burdens at the head of government during six years and three months, I feel I must meet your request not to be, once again, named Prime Minister.

The regret I feel is the deeper in that, in the considerable work accomplished by the public powers in all domains, in the course of your tenure, your actions have been exceptionally effective and never ceased to meet in full what I expected of you and of the members of the government you led. This was true, in particular, during the grave crisis the country has been through in May and June last. This was, in any case, the judgment of the French people on this subject, as it has shown through the last elections.

Wherever you may be, I want you to know, my dear friend, that I mean to keep particularly close relations with you. I hope, finally, that you will hold yourself ready to accomplish any mission and assume any mandate that might one day be entrusted to you by the nation.

Please believe, my dear Prime Minister, in my sentiments of faithful and devoted friendship.

Charles de Gaulle

[22] This was the way de Gaulle put it at his press conference on 9 September 1968.

The commentators did not fail to point to the first sentence in Pompidou's letter, which made it clear that de Gaulle had decided he should go; whereas the second sentence paid lip service to the provision in Article 8 of the constitution that the initiative of resigning should come from the head of government. In the eyes of the political world in Paris, and in his own, Pompidou had been "sacked".

Cold, glum and self-effacing, Couve de Murville presented a striking contrast with his predecessor, who was warm, cheerful and – once he had acquired the habit – had a taste for the limelight. A Protestant and a former *inspecteur des finances,* the new Prime Minister was a man of few words and a tendency to ponderousness. Once, a senior man from the French embassy in London telephoned Couve de Murville at the Quai d'Orsay and put a question to him. The silence that followed was so prolonged that the diplomat feared the line had been cut. Anxiously, he inquired: "*Monsieur le Ministre,* are you there?" After a further lengthy pause, the Foreign minister said: "I'm thinking. . . ."[23]

Although de Gaulle was by nature incapable of disinteresting himself in foreign affairs, it was clear, even to him, that his grand design had collapsed with the occupation of Czechoslovakia by the Warsaw Pact powers in August 1968. And the events of May had brought home to him the extent of his neglect of domestic affairs. He therefore turned with renewed vigour to the idea of "participation". His condemnation of Russia at his press conference of 9 September as "absurd in regard to the prospects of European *détente*" was his indirect farewell to "Europe from the Atlantic to the Urals". Henceforth, he was obsessed with the idea of bringing about a social transformation in France that would stand as his crowning achievement, the glorious last chapter of his career. But he was no more successful in this domestic aspiration than in his foreign dream.

In Couve's government were two men with a particular interest in the general's project. One was the new minister of Justice, René Capitant – political arch-enemy of Pompidou. The other, Jean-Marcel Jeanneney, who, as minister of State, was specifically charged by General de Gaulle early in July with drawing up a precise plan of reform. There had to be participation everywhere – in commerce and industry, in the regions of France, the institutions and the universities. Jeanneney, a competent servant of the State but a more conventional man than the general, proposed to sound out parliamentarians of all tendencies, study constitutional texts and write a report. The general swept this approach aside with impatience: "I want to make haste," he said. "In Parliament,

23 Private source.

things would drag on for months or years. We'd be carried away with a flood of amendments. And at the end of the day, nothing would be left of the reform."[24]

No, said de Gaulle: here, above all else, was a theme for a referendum. The French people themselves must give their approval to participation. Only then could it be carried out. Now de Gaulle had stopped even hinting at retirement to his most intimate companions or his family. If more than 60 per cent voted for him in the next referendum, he might even see his mandate through. He would retire only in the event of a lower percentage. From then on, he mentioned participation at least once at every second meeting of the Council of Ministers.

Capitant, who thought of himself as the real originator of participation, had drawn up a plan of his own as early as 8 June 1968.[25] Although there is no evidence that it existed on paper, Capitant expounded it eloquently and with enthusiasm to a number of friends. His idea was to divide each company into three components: a production cooperative, a financial organisation, and the management. The latter would be responsible both to the shareholders and to the wage-earners' works committee. Profits would be divided on a fifty-fifty basis between capital and labour. When rumours of this plan reached businessmen, they were appalled and began to wonder whether they had jumped from the frying pan of *contestation* into the fire of participatory Communism. But their fears were groundless, for nothing came of the Capitant plan.

The legacy of May weighed heavily on the new government. The two matters of special concern were education and the economy. After the long summer holidays, the children and young men and women would shortly be returning to their classes. Would they be doing so in peace, and if so how long would their quietude last? De Gaulle's guiding lines were clear: on the one hand, sweeping reforms of the school and university systems, incorporating many concessions to the *contestataires*; on the other hand, unyielding enforcement of order and discipline. Two very different men were needed for these contrasting responsibilities. For Education, de Gaulle picked a former premier under the Fourth Republic, Edgar Faure, who was the minister of Agriculture in the Pompidou government. For the Interior, his choice was Raymond Marcellin, a tough operator who made uncompromising speeches and soon showed he meant what he said. Any students still occupying part of university buildings were evicted, and some were arrested. All the *groupuscules* of Maoist, anarchist or Trotskyist inspiration that had played so large a part

[24] Alexandre, pp. 264–5.
[25] Paillat, *Archives*, pp. 460–1.

in the disorders were banned. With evident approval, de Gaulle started saying: "Now I've got the real Fouché."[26]

Edgar Faure, of all men of the Fourth Republic, was the one who had best adapted himself to Gaullism. He had made a long visit to China on de Gaulle's behalf and his report had convinced the president of the need to recognise the Chinese People's Republic. By common consent one of the cleverest living politicians, he had whiled away the time while out of office by studying, and successfully sitting, for the formidable *agrégation*, when past fifty. He had wanted the Finance portfolio, but was made to understand that this key post could only go either to a Gaullist or to a less eminent personality than himself. (The post went to a young planning expert, François Ortoli.) So sweeping were the reforms proposed by Faure that they ran into apparently immovable opposition from the more conservative Gaullists. Compulsory Latin was to be abolished during the first two years of secondary education; there was to be a careful selection process, in the hope of reducing the appalling failure rate; and political discussion was to be allowed in the universities.[27] Presenting his bill at a Gaullist congress at La Baule, Faure drew upon himself the hostility of the militants who regarded 30 May as their victory over the young revolutionaries and thought his proposals were a capitulation. As a man of the Fourth Republic, moreover, he was generally *persona non grata* with the Gaullist rank-and-file. An important critic, Robert Poujade (secretary-general of the party), now defended him, however, and Faure's persuasive eloquence moved his audience to consent to postpone their verdict. On 10 September, at a private meeting with General de Gaulle, he secured support at the summit. Despite much initial opposition in both houses of parliament, the Faure Bill became law in early November. Although watered down in some particulars, it made many concessions to the students and to liberal opinion.[28]

This personal triumph coincided with a massive flight from the franc and the financial crisis which everybody supposed could be met only by devaluing the franc, but which de Gaulle resolved in his own way by vetoing devaluation and restoring confidence at one stroke – at least for the time being.

Pompidou watched these events with the sour frustration of the non-participant. He had spent a miserable summer at Carnac, in Brittany.

[26] A double allusion: to Joseph Fouché (1759–1820), ruthless police chief under the French Revolution and Napoleon I; and to Christian Fouchet, the minister of the Interior during the May disorders.
[27] Williams and Harrison, pp. 326 *et seq.*
[28] Viansson-Ponté, *République*, Vol II, pp. 582–3.

Time was when he and his wife would have gone to Saint-Tropez; but de Gaulle had had occasion to warn him against his wife's Bohemian acquaintances on the Riviera, and he had heeded the warning. Back in Paris, he took over a vast apartment in the Boulevard de Latour-Maubourg, made available to him by his protégé, Marcellin, the minister of the Interior. There, in the *ennui* of petty parliamentary business, he waited impatiently for any sign of those "particularly close relations" which President de Gaulle's public letter of 10 July had foreshadowed.

The weeks went by. In mid-September, along with Debré (now the Foreign minister) and other prominent Gaullists, Pompidou attended the meeting at La Baule at which Edgar Faure explained his educational reforms. He received an ovation, and declared: "Our group expects also to participate." This was a mistake. His presence, his evident popularity, and his remark were reported to de Gaulle who let it be known that he thought it lamentable that the Gaullists should publicly criticise a plan which had his support. The following week, when the Gaullists met again, this time at the Palais-Bourbon in Paris, to have a further look at the Faure proposals, Pompidou wisely stayed away.

At last at the end of September and four days before the parliamentary debate on the Faure Bill, Pompidou was invited to dinner at the Elysée. There he made the agreeable discovery that, if appearances were any guide, he was still regarded as the monarch's *dauphin*. There was an encouraging reference to the former Prime Minister's "national destiny". In a fatherly way, de Gaulle advised Pompidou to get away from the unhealthy atmosphere of political intrigue at the Palais-Bourbon. Better by far that he should travel abroad and make himself known. The general even drew up a tentative itinerary: Yugoslavia, Italy, Great Britain and the United States. Events were to make the Yugoslav trip impossible. But that night, Pompidou could not know this. He had had a satisfying evening, although he knew the general too well not to wonder what surprises might be in store for him.

France had lacked a political scandal since the Ben Barka affair in 1965. Now the Delon–Markovic affair broke. On 1 November 1968 de Gaulle, who had gone to Colombey for solitude and contemplation, was disturbed by an important visitor, Bernard Tricot. The secretary-general at the Elysée, after apologising for his intrusion, invited de Gaulle to cast his eye over a police dossier he had brought with him. With his usual distaste for this kind of news, de Gaulle read about the murder of one Stefan Markovic, a young Yugoslav who had been bodyguard to Alain Delon, the film star. There was an unpleasant detail in this sordid story,

643

to which Tricot wanted to draw de Gaulle's attention: the name of Pompidou occurred in the report. Allegations were made that Mme Pompidou had been on good terms with the Delons.

"Who knows about this?" asked de Gaulle.

"The minister of Justice, the minister of the Interior. And of course M. Couve de Murville."

"And Pompidou?"

Tricot's answer was that the ex-premier was resting at his property in Auvergne.

On the Monday, de Gaulle convoked the three ministers to the Elysée. The minister of Justice, René Capitant – Pompidou's arch-enemy – expressed the view that the allegations were probably a form of blackmail. But, he added, the Pompidous may have had undesirable acquaintances in artistic circles. He thought the best way of avoiding serious political consequences was that justice should take its course.

De Gaulle agreed. Pompidou's friend, Marcellin, asked who was going to tell the ex-premier. The president indicated Couve de Murville as the hierarchically logical person. Couve – a silent man – said nothing.

It later turned out that he had done nothing either. Thus it was that during the next three weeks, everybody knew about the "Pompidou scandal", except Pompidou. When he did learn what was being said, he was deeply depressed; and distressed at the general's apparent indifference to calumnies at the expense of the man who had served him faithfully for more than twenty years. After nursing his resentment for some time, while the rumours and discoveries of alleged documents mounted, Pompidou decided that from now on, he would play his own game. The general had no further call on his loyalty.

What call did he, Pompidou, have on the loyalty of his own friends and ex-colleagues? Many of them dropped out during this trying period. But his former rival, Michel Debré, expressed his sympathy, both in person and in the form of long letters. Even more surprisingly, Valéry Giscard d'Estaing assured Pompidou of his support and indignation. The two men had been on bad terms since Pompidou had dropped Giscard from his cabinet in the reshuffle of January 1966. The young and brilliant Giscard d'Estaing – himself potentially of presidential stature – was the leader of a conservative Gaullist group, and, as an Atlanticist, out of sympathy with Gaullian policy. Good-humouredly, he consoled Pompidou: "I know what it's like to be sacked."

Yet another foul-weather friend was Jacques Chaban-Delmas, the president of the Assembly, who hoped to become premier with Pompidou as president. This, of course, is exactly what did happen.

The affair rumbled on, as such obscure scandals do. The press would not leave it alone. Towards the end of November, Pompidou wrote to de Gaulle asking for an audience. The general replied immediately and the visit took place in secrecy, Pompidou entering by a side door. The former Prime Minister poured out his grievances: nobody had defended him, at the Matignon, at the ministry of Justice, even at the Elysée. The president demurred: "I never doubted you, Pompidou," he said; and promised to speed up the judicial process, so that Pompidou's name could be cleared.

But René Capitant fell seriously ill shortly after; Jeanneney, taking over the ministry of Justice on an interim basis, called to see Pompidou and expressed his sympathy. The minister of State, however, was too engrossed in his studies and preparations for the referendum to pay much attention to the Markovic affair.

In December, Pompidou made another clandestine visit to the Elysée, this time bringing some of the obviously faked documents that were being planted in newspaper offices. The president expressed his sympathetic concern, but discounted any suggestion of a political plot. For him, it was quite simple: the journalists were fabricating the whole thing to boost their papers' circulations and discredit the regime. Disconsolately, Pompidou realised that nobody, from the president down, was going to do anything to help him. He decided, therefore, to come out of his shell. For three weeks or so, he called meetings of prominent Gaullists, gave interviews to selected journalists, and demonstrated that he was more closely in contact with the political life of the capital than the silent man who had succeeded him at the Hôtel Matignon. This unusual activity was duly reported to de Gaulle, who said – not "off the record": "They tell me my Prime Minister doesn't exist. I prefer him to the last one who exists a bit too much."

Dropping his initial plan to visit Yugoslavia – for fear of satirical comments on the Markovic affair – Pompidou now prepared to go to Rome. Although he was no longer in office, it was obvious that his visit would have a semi-official character. Bernard Tricot himself supervised the arrangements, and on Thursday 9 January 1969, Pompidou called on the president of the Republic. Amiability itself, de Gaulle gave Pompidou a sweeping analysis of current problems – Israel, education and the referendum.

On arrival in Rome on the 15th, Pompidou immediately declared that he was not just a tourist and would report to the government and the president on his return. Two days later he invited the French correspondents to a press conference. For years he had side-stepped or stonewalled questions about his future ambitions. This time, he played the ball straight. "It is no mystery to anyone," he said, "that I shall be a candidate for the presidency." He did not declare his remark to be either "off the record" or "not for attribution".

Banner headlines in Paris were the consequence. On reading them, de Gaulle was furious. "It's incomprehensible," he declared to Tricot, and went on: "It really is a bit much. If I don't want to complete my term, it's up to me alone to announce it." For the next few days, the president's mood alternated between extreme anger and deep depression. "Look at me," he would say, "I'm not dead. Even if Pompidou would like me to be. . . . I'll never see him again."

At the next meeting of the Council of Ministers, de Gaulle sat down without a word and began to scribble on a sheet of paper, with the usual erasures and corrections. It was the draft of a *communiqué*, which read:

> In accomplishing the national task that falls to me, I was, on 19 December 1965, re-elected President of the Republic for seven years by the French people. I have the duty and the intention to fulfil this mandate until its term.

But a last battle lay ahead – the battle of the referendum. Perhaps de Gaulle already knew that he would lose it.

Chapter 7 ✤ Exit and Death

In his visionary plan for a radical reorganisation of French society, General de Gaulle had few supporters. Capitant was one; Jeanneney another; Edgar Faure; and, in a distant way, André Malraux. Within the government, that was about as far as it went. The other ministers or high officials were either hostile (though afraid to say so) or sceptical. Their scepticism or hostility took the form of delaying tactics.

Jeanneney, who was in charge of the arrangements, was in favour of an early referendum, preferably in November 1968, while the prestige of de Gaulle's victory of 30 May and of the Gaullist electoral landslide were still fresh. He explained to de Gaulle that the minimum time for preparations was two months:[1] two weeks to consult parliament; ten days to a fortnight for the Council of State to study the draft bill; the rest for the preparation of the final draft; the printing of the questions to be put before the voters, in thirty million copies; and the campaign.

Couve de Murville, notably unenthusiastic, would have preferred a much later date, say Christmas 1969. This would have given him time to deal with the urgent problems of education and finance. Roger Frey, the former minister of the Interior and now minister of State charged with relations with parliament, was dilatory; and so was another Gaullist of long standing, the gigantic Olivier Guichard, now minister of Social Affairs. Frey thought the political climate was still too disturbed for a referendum. Guichard was in favour of regional reorganisation, but saw no reason why it should not be done through normal legislation. He proposed that all the notables of France should be consulted on the subject, together with thousands of others with a special interest in, or knowledge of, regional problems. The effect of this was a further delay of several weeks. De Gaulle, anxious though he was for speed, agreed that thoroughness was important. He did not want his reform to fail for lack of proper preparation.

Regional reform was, however, only one side of de Gaulle's proposals. The other was reform of the Senate. He was right in pointing out that the present Senate was anachronistic. Owing to movements of population, some senators represented 3,000 people and others a hundred times that number. But he wanted to go further, and bring into the upper house representatives of "economic, social and cultural activities" – thus borrowing a leaf from the corporativist theories of Mussolini. This, too, was "participation".

Ever since Gaston Monnerville's challenge to de Gaulle on the propriety of the 1962 referendum on the election of the president of the Republic, the Senate had been, as it were, beyond the Gaullian pale. But the 1968 general elections had brought an amiable MRP politician, Alain Poher, to office as president of the Senate, in succession to Monnerville. The resumption of cordial relations was solemnised by a visit of Poher and his office to the Elysée, in mid-October.

At this stage, bearing in mind the suggestions or criticisms of the Gaullists, the general had approved the following timetable for his referendum: debate in the Assembly at the beginning of November; publication of the texts in the *Journal Officiel* on 20 December; voting in mid-January 1969.

The financial crisis in November upset these plans. Tricot urged him

[1] Alexandre, p. 278.

to go ahead as planned, turning to advantage the psychological shock of his refusal to devalue the franc. Jeanneney strongly supported the secretary-general. All the other ministers, with the Prime Minister in the lead, tried to dissuade him, pleading that the political outlook was too uncertain for a major vote of confidence in the chief of State. De Gaulle himself was tired and depressed. For the first time his visitors noticed blank periods of inattention. Too many pressing problems clamoured for attention. He allowed Couve de Murville to persuade him that a post-ponement was desirable.

The sensations of January 1969 restored the old man's combative spirit. His anger with Pompidou was a stimulant. Even more so was his ban on arms deliveries to Israel. Once again, he had captured the world's head-lines: the fact that he had made many new enemies in France seemed to escape him, or leave him indifferent.

At the end of January de Gaulle went to perhaps the most troubled province of his Republican kingdom: Brittany. Although an area of Gaullist electoral strength, Brittany was troubled by neglect, backward-ness and the linguistic imperialism of French; and in consequence, by local nationalism which took a terroristic form. In March 1966 and July 1967 the extremists had set off bombs. In January 1968 the extreme autonomist group, the Front de Libération de la Bretagne (FLB), began systematic attacks on State buildings and installations. Some thirty incidents occurred during the year. In October 1968, however, when the president's forthcoming tour was first announced, the FLB issued a communiqué stating that its activities would be suspended during the visit. More outrages occurred before the end of the year and in January, but some fifty people were arrested and the terrorist organisation was largely destroyed before de Gaulle's tour started.

His first engagements were at Rennes on 31 January 1969. At the end of his tour, on 2 February, he made an important speech at Quimper, at which he outlined his referendum proposals and declared that Brittany would not be left behind in the "immense transformation" that awaited France. The referendum, he revealed, would take place in the spring, but he did not name a precise date.

With increasing energy and eloquence, the general was trying to communicate his enthusiasm to his immediate followers. The whole of French society, he would say, was to be revolutionised. This was to be his great and original legacy to history and to France. Decolonisation, to be sure, was a job well done. But it was inevitable, and others – the English, for instance – had ploughed the same furrow. As for his reform of institutions, it was important, but institutions were worth no more than the men who ran them, and the French would remain what they always were, with their inconstancy and love of political change. The fundamentally conservative society of France must, however, be completely changed and that was the purpose of his "revolution".

He was sad and angry at his failure to disperse the scepticism or pessimism of those around him. Nobody wanted participation, not even the workers, for the *raison d'être* of trade unionism was *contestation*. Couve de Murville was against it; and as for Pompidou (who had said to the journalist Michel Droit that "between ourselves, the general is just dreaming"), his opposition had been made plain.[2]

None of this shook the general's resolve. A middle way must be found, between East and West, between "totalitarian and outmoded" Marxism, and "inhuman" capitalism; and he would show it.

Capitant urged him on: "*Mon Général*, don't be afraid of entering into an open conflict with the industrialists. The capitalists will fight you: so much the better. Their opposition will unfreeze popular opinion and bring it round to your ideas. You will lean on the left-wing mass of the French. True Gaullism will begin."[3]

De Gaulle saw his reform of the regions and of the Senate as only the first stage of his gigantic design, to be followed by yet another referendum to introduce participation in industry and elsewhere.

On 19 February, the Council of Ministers decided that the referendum would take place on 27 April. The government would formally propose the necessary measures to the president on 3 April, when parliament was to reassemble for its spring session. Next day, the text of the Reform Bill would be published; and the official referendum campaign, which would include provision for broadcasts for and against, would open on 14 April.

No sooner had he forced the issue and announced precise dates than the general was assailed by fresh doubts. Was this the right time? Was he going to win? He even went so far as to ask Debré and Marcellin if they could think of ways of not having a referendum after all. But nothing constructive emerged. For better, for worse, the general was stuck with his own plan.

The Markovic affair, meanwhile, after appearing to die down sprang into vicious life again when Alexander Markovic, brother of the murdered man, claimed that Stefan had been a guest of the Delons and

[2] ibid. p. 323.
[3] The argument that participation was "true Gaullism" runs through Louis Vallon's polemical denunciation of Pompidou, *L'Anti de Gaulle*. It could, of course, be counter-argued that since participation never happened, there was never such a thing as Gaullism.

had sat at the same table as the Pompidous. Lawyers defending one Marcantoni, arrested in connection with the "affair", demanded that M. and Mme Pompidou should be called as witnesses. This unfortunate news was carried on the national radio station, France-Inter, provoking a furious outburst from Pompidou and a communiqué from his office:

> The former Prime Minister of General de Gaulle, and Madame Pompidou know nothing of the causes and circumstances of this *fait divers*.

Alerted, de Gaulle judged that the political consequences of the affair remained disagreeable, and sought to put an end to the gossip in two ways: the minister of Justice would publish an exonerating communiqué, and the Pompidous would be invited to dinner at the Elysée.

By all accounts, the dinner was glacial. Apart from M. and Mme Pompidou, the only other guests were M. and Mme Debré. The Foreign minister, who was developing influenza, had a high temperature and made his excuses before coffee. The general was distant and Mme de Gaulle embarrassed. Mme Pompidou had nothing to say and her husband kept a close eye on her in case she should make a scene. Courses were served and removed with great despatch. According to the admittedly ill-intentioned right-wing magazine, *Minute*,[4] when Mme de Gaulle and Mme Pompidou were alone, they discussed fashion. Claude Pompidou remarked that she never felt older than the dresses she wore, to which Yvonne de Gaulle retorted that she preferred women to have dresses that suited their age.

When de Gaulle and Pompidou entered, the general was saying he had never felt better and might even stand for re-election in 1972. That way, Pompidou could take over in 1979, when he would still be only sixty-eight. Yvonne de Gaulle: "And you, my dear, will be barely sixty. When the time comes I shall recommend my dressmaker to you. You see, you will be happy with him."

Whether or not this was precisely what was said, Pompidou later told his friends, "That dinner did no good at all. Absolutely none." What he did not know was that this was the last time he would meet de Gaulle.

Social storms were looming ahead. On 11 March a general strike paralysed much of the country. Depressed, the ministers wanted de Gaulle to give up his whole project, but the signs of trouble merely stirred fresh

---

4 No. 362. of 20–26 March 1969.

resolve in the general; for this, he argued, was the way to transform society so that strikes should come to seem unnecessary. A minor hitch in the plan came on the 17th, when the Council of State, as on previous occasions, criticised the text of the Reform Bill and expressed the opinion that the use of a referendum to reform the Senate was unconstitutional. Next day, however, Jeanneney rejected this view: the referendum would go ahead.

An important point remained to be settled. Were the electors to be asked to answer Yes or No to two separate questions – one on the regions, the other on the Senate – or to the whole package? The balance of advice was that the two problems, being different, should be answered separately. But de Gaulle waved this argument aside. Both reforms, as he saw it, were necessary to his revolutionary plan; if one were accepted and the other rejected, he would not be able to carry on. Once again, he was going to make the whole thing an issue of confidence. An announcement on 19 March declared that he regarded the referendum as a "question of confidence that is being put to the French people". He was to broadcast before the opening of the official campaign, probably on 10 April.

For this crucial explanation de Gaulle chose to be interviewed at length by Michel Droit. Replying to a question about the Council of State's opinion that the referendum would be unconstitutional, de Gaulle castigated "professionals of politics, who cannot resign themselves to seeing the people exercising its sovereignty above intermediaries", and "certain jurists who have stayed with the law as it was at a time when this eminently democratic practice did not exist in our institutions". For such people, the referendum appeared as unfortunate and abnormal. But he was proposing to reform the constitution, and Article 11 allowed him to do this since it provided for a referendum on any bill concerning the organisation of public powers: "And what is a constitution if it is not precisely the organisation of the public powers?"

It was necessary to decentralise economic planning and give back to the provinces of France the character of which they had been deprived by the French Revolution. The reform of the Senate, too, was necessary, to give "French economic and social categories" the right to participate in the preparation of the laws.

Michel Droit remarked that he had used the word "participation" several times and asked him to define it. The general replied that this was the year when workers would begin to participate in the profits of enterprises; when the universities were being reformed on the basis of participation by professors and students; when it was hoped that parliament would approve a law providing for workers' participation in management; and when, finally, the country was being asked to approve a territorial reorganisation and a reform of the Senate, both based on participation.

In answers to further questions, de Gaulle explained that the two reforms were intimately linked in his plans: they constituted a whole. There would therefore be only one answer, a Yes or a No to the whole of his proposals for reform, despite their complexity. If the French people gave him their confidence by a massive Yes vote, he would be powerfully encouraged in his work. But if they did not – "perchance" – he would not stay a moment longer.

With these words, de Gaulle's challenge was made public. His bets were laid, irrevocably. His future would depend on the vote of 27 April.

Convinced that de Gaulle would lose, Pompidou began to make soundings. For soon, he was sure, he would be able to present himself as candidate for the presidency of the Republic.

The text of the Reform Bill, when published, was seen to be a huge and indigestible mass. There were sixty-eight articles which provided for the amendment, replacement or abrogation of twenty-three of the eighty-nine articles of the existing constitution. Was it logical, the press and public asked, for this vast and complicated document to be submitted to a single vote of Yes or No? The public opinion polls were depressing. On 24 April Figaro published the latest: it showed that 53 per cent of electors intended to vote No; and 47 per cent Yes.

Next day, de Gaulle was convinced that the polls were not mistaken. His long reign was coming to an end. He went through the formality of recording a vibrant appeal to the French people, which ended with the words: "Frenchwomen, Frenchmen, in what is going to become of France, never will the decision of each one of you have weighed so heavily!" Anticipating the verdict, however, he wrote out the text of his resignation statement, which he presented, in a sealed envelope, to Couve de Murville. The Prime Minister was to keep the envelope in his pocket for two days, and to release it only on the general's personal authority, some time in the night of Sunday to Monday.

When the results came in, they confirmed the predictions of the pollsters: 10,901,753 had voted Yes, and 12,007,102 had said No. The respective percentages were 47.58 affirmative and 52.41 negative. At 11 p.m. Bernard Tricot telephoned the general at Colombey. Was the statement to be published? Yes, said the general.

At midnight the world knew for certain what few people could doubt. The general's last official statement was laconic. It merely said:

I am ceasing to exercise my functions as president of the Republic. This decision takes effect today at midday.

Charles de Gaulle was back in the desert.

Why did de Gaulle do it? There was no actual need for him to expose himself to a public rejection from the people over whom he had reigned for ten stormy years. Had it not been for his contempt for the parliamentary process, he could have used the huge Gaullist majority to steer his proposals through. And if the texts had been unduly mangled in the process, he could then have made an issue of it with greater chances of success.

In April 1969, however, de Gaulle was in his seventy-ninth year. He had confided to his friends and family that he needed six years to write the memoirs of his years in power. In these circumstances, he was more than usually impatient with the normal processes and with the advice of the jurists. His hubris, more overwhelming than ever with advancing age, drove him on. Had he won, he would probably not, despite his threats, have stayed to complete his second term. His son, Rear-Admiral Philippe de Gaulle, has revealed that in the event of victory, he had intended to announce his retirement on 22 November 1969 – his seventy-ninth birthday.[5] When Philippe pointed out that this would be a bad time for a presidential election, the general said he might defer his announcement till his usual end of the year message. In any case, he wanted to be in retirement before his eightieth birthday, to avoid the fate of Marshal Pétain. When the signs multiplied that the referendum would bring defeat, he persisted in his course in an atmosphere of Götterdämmerung. His taste for the theatrical had never left him: he preferred a spectacular failure, followed by immediate retirement, to a duller exit brought about by the passage of time. There was indeed something characteristically heroic about his choice. At least he had dared to attempt the impossible. Like a mountaineer defeated by an unconquerable peak, his political suicide was on the grand scale.

To his chagrin, the French people greeted the news of his departure with a calm remarkably close to indifference. Their interest, intense and urgent, was concentrated on the problem of the transfer of power under the constitution. At noon on 28 April Alain Poher, in his capacity as president of the Senate, took over as interim president of the Republic. De Gaulle's ministers stayed at their posts – all except René Capitant,

---

[5] Television interview on 18 June 1971, thirty-first anniversary of de Gaulle's call from London (Figaro, 19–20 June 1971).

who stated that he refused to serve under Poher even as acting president. Jeanneney took over as acting minister of Justice, as he had done once before when Capitant was ill. With the grudging cooperation of the rest (Debré declining to use more than monosyllables when communicating with the temporary chief of State), Poher provided administration of a sort for France. His only sensational act was to dismiss Jacques Foccart as secretary-general for African and Malagasy Affairs. Foccart, apparently anticipating dismissal, had removed all evidence of his secret activities to Gaullist headquarters at the Rue de Solférino. For the "African and Malagasy" side of his former job, he enjoyed facilities provided by the Embassy of the Ivory Coast. De Gaulle's staff had indeed removed all the Elysée files, to Poher's indignation; and there was a theoretically dangerous delay of some days in briefing the acting president – who was, ex-officio, the temporary commander-in-chief – in the procedure for use of France's nuclear striking force.

Nursing his sorrows, de Gaulle stayed silent. Within forty-eight hours of the president's departure, Georges Pompidou announced his candidacy in the forthcoming presidential elections. Although he did not consult the Gaullists, he did write to General de Gaulle, in effect to ask not for the old man's blessing so much as his non-intervention. He was careful not to use the words "succession" or "successor", for how often had de Gaulle declared, in the third person singular he affected when referring to himself as a historical figure: "De Gaulle n'a pas de successeur"? Instead, Pompidou declared his determination to ensure the survival of Gaullism. Surprisingly, for some, de Gaulle replied immediately, sending his reply by the man who had brought Pompidou's letter, Xavier de la Chevalerie, the outgoing president's directeur de cabinet. The general gave his approval to Pompidou's candidacy, declared that he would in no way interfere in the campaign and (as a reminder that he never forgot slights) expressed the fear that Pompidou's Rome declaration might be held against him.[6]

One by one, General de Gaulle received his closest aides. Tricot and Foccart lunched at Colombey; so did la Chevalerie and General Lalande. Captain Flohic stayed on for a few weeks as aide-de-camp, before taking command of the Jeanne d'Arc. A cook, a maid, and his chauffeur, Fontenil, now constituted his staff. He declined the pension to which he was entitled as a former president. He was not, and never would be, interested in money. Besides, he had enough to live on, from his royalties and a farm he owned in the north of France.

One thing only he accepted from the State: a small pied-à-terre in the

6 Alexandre, pp. 384–6.

Avenue de Breteuil put at his disposal by the ministry of the Armed Forces. In it was a small office with wall tapestry in raw silk, and a mahogany desk. A voluminous mail reached him from all over France; to some of it, he replied by hand.

The general had one last surprise in reserve. He decided not to embarrass Pompidou by staying in France during the presidential election. In the greatest secrecy, Xavier de la Chevalerie, as a last service to him made arrangements for the de Gaulles to spend a holiday in Ireland. Couve de Murville provided them with a special aircraft, a Mystère 20, which landed at Saint-Dizier air base in the early hours of Saturday, 10 May. Its pilot had orders to await the arrival of a Very Important Person − identity unstated − and take him to an unspecified destination.[7]

The modest Heron Cove Hotel at Sneem, in the south-west, had been booked, entire, for a month, but the owner was not told who the guests would be. During the morning, the Irish Foreign ministry sent a lorry to Heron Cove to deliver a king-size bed − the only possible clue in a meticulously planned secret operation. At 10.50 the Mystère 20 landed at Cork airport and disgorged its mystery cargo. The Prime Minister of the Irish Republic, John Lynch, was there to greet ex-President de Gaulle.

At Heron Cove, de Gaulle had an ocean view. He had sometimes spoken of his Irish forbears, and in a curious way felt at home in his new solitude. Pictures of the giant figure, with his self-effacing wife, walking in the Irish countryside, were published in the world's press.

The acting president, Alain Poher, with the round, good-natured appearance of the typical average Frenchman, and with his own dignity, had emerged as a surprisingly popular figure in France. At one stage, the public opinion polls even showed him well ahead of Pompidou in popular favour. When it came to the first ballot on 1 June, however, Pompidou came comfortably top of the poll, with 43.96 per cent of the votes cast in metropolitan France. Indeed, his share of the total vote was greater than de Gaulle's of the first ballot in 1965. Poher came next, with 23.42 per cent. The Communist candidate, Jacques Duclos, was third, and three other candidates (including the Trotskyist ex-student leader, Alain Krivine) polled much lower percentages.

Although the Heron Cove Hotel had been booked for a month, de Gaulle felt restless, and on 23 May moved to Cashel Bay, in the north, where his staff arranged a direct telephone link between the hotel and Paris, via the local post office. On Sunday, 1 June, while the French electors were voting, de Gaulle read a book by Yves Courrière on the

[7] Jacques Chapus, *Mourir à Colombey*, pp. 86 *et seq.* (henceforth, Chapus).

Algerian war, *Le Temps des Léopards*. Next morning, he wrote a complimentary letter to the author.[8]

On the 4th, Bernard Tricot went to Cashel Bay to see the general. It was quite like old times: Tricot and de Gaulle analysed the election figures at some length. The frustration of his voluntary removal from the scene of action caused fresh restlessness, and after Tricot's visit, de Gaulle and his party moved south again, to stay as the guests of Mrs Beatrice Grosvenor, niece of the earl of Kenmare. There, in a small farmhouse in the grounds, he awaited the results of the second presidential ballot on the 15th. Pompidou was duly elected president of the Republic, with more than eleven million votes – 58.21 per cent of the total, but only 37.5 per cent of the entire electorate, abstentions being high. Poher polled nearly eight million votes: a sign of the size of that segment of the population which disliked the Fifth Republic.

De Gaulle had gone to bed before learning the final figures, the result being already a foregone conclusion. He was, it seems, curiously detached about events in France, now that they had taken their course. As a duty of citizenship, however, he cabled the new president the following morning, in a message entirely bare of hidden meanings:

> For all national and personal reasons, I send you my very cordial congratulations.

Now de Gaulle wanted to go home, but one further scruple kept him in Ireland: the desire to avoid any kind of demonstrations on 18 June, anniversary of his London call to action in 1940. On the 17th, de Gaulle paid a courtesy visit to the Irish president, Eamonn de Valera, who had dissolved the Dail on 21 May, so that the Irish general election campaign roughly coincided with the presidential campaign in France. The de Gaulles spent that night in a wing of the Irish Presidential Palace, and the day of the 18th at the French embassy, where he decorated the ambassador, Emmanuel d'Harcourt – a Companion of the Liberation – with the cravat of a commander of the Legion of Honour.

Back at Colombey on 19 June 1969, General de Gaulle settled down to his *Mémoires d'Espoir*.

To help him, the Quai d'Orsay provided him with a team of researchers, headed by Pierre-Louis Blanc. From that point forward, de Gaulle devoted most of his time to the construction of his last literary monument. From time to time, he wrote to old friends, or rather, answered their letters. There were very few visitors to Colombey. De Gaulle had let it be known that he would not see anybody actually in office. On

[8] ibid. pp. 94–5.

20 June, President Pompidou had chosen Jacques Chaban-Delmas as Prime Minister, thus fulfilling the latter's complacent prediction. The new cabinet did not include André Malraux, Louis Joxe or Couve de Murville; and these did visit de Gaulle. Another caller was the durable Jacques Foccart who, on 26 June, had been reappointed as secretary-general for African and Malagasy Affairs, though he was no longer attached to the Elysée.

The left-wing Gaullist, René Capitant, had been dropped from the government, and so had Edgar Faure, the outgoing minister of Education: clearly, "participation" was dead. Worse, the "traitor", Giscard d'Estaing, had been brought back as Finance minister. With Michel Debré as Defence minister and Marcellin for the Interior, Pompidou had not forgotten the men who had stood by him during the Markovic affair.

The men of the left, Capitant and Vallon, did not like what they saw: Gaullism, as they conceived it, was being betrayed. To mark the point, Vallon wrote his anathema of Pompidou, L'Anti de Gaulle. The allusion to Antichrist was not lost, and the little book became a bestseller. As early as 6 May 1969, an association was formed, under the name Présence du Gaullisme, to defend "a certain idea of France developed by General de Gaulle and to defend, in that spirit, a policy of national independence, of administrative modernisation, of economic and social reforms in the framework of the Fifth Republic".[9] Its original joint chairmen were Michel Debré, Louis Joxe and Pierre Messmer, with the left-wing journalist Roger Stéphane as secretary-general. A parallel organisation to operate within parliament was set up on 2 July 1969, under the name of Présence et Action du Gaullisme. The twenty-five deputies who joined it included Vallon and the general's brother-in-law, Jacques Vendroux. By creating this group, its members were, in effect, serving notice on Pompidou not to deviate from the straight and narrow path of Gaullian Gaullism.

The bill for the spilling of public treasure in the spring of 1968 was at last paid, now that the general had gone, on 10 August 1969, when the franc was devalued by 12.5 per cent. The general's reactions to this fall from heroism were not recorded.

Despite his continued silence, the giant shadow cast from Colombey continued to awe his "successors". Would he intervene again in politics? There were many, in the autumn and winter of 1969 to 1970, who answered the question with an affirmative. Had Pompidou moved too

[9] Since de Gaulle's death, the association has become Présence et Action du Gaullisme en veilleuse (indicating reduced activity), operating from 5 Rue de Solférino.

fast in foreign policy, for instance by immediately opening the gates of Europe to the British, it was argued that de Gaulle could bring his government down by simply calling a press conference to criticise the president. A stir was caused, a ripple of apprehension for some, a thrill of anticipation for others, towards the end of September with the news that from October, the general would start using his *pied-à-terre* in the Avenue de Breteuil. But there was no cause for the alarm of the "traitors" or the elation of the faithful. The general did come in occasionally, but not to interfere in politics. His brother-in-law, however, kept on saying that there was only one test of fidelity to Gaullism: it consisted of asking oneself every morning what the general would have done.

Charles de Gaulle had not given up his taste for foreign travel. On 3 June 1970, accompanied by his wife and a considerable retinue including the research team from the Quai d'Orsay, he travelled to Spain. Fulfilling an old desire which political taboos had excluded during his years of power, he dined at the Pardo Palace, outside Madrid, on the 8th, with General Franco, whose mastery of the art of staying in command he had long admired. But during most of his stay in Spain, in various towns between 3 and 27 June, he read and revised the typescript of his new memoirs, volume I.

In the end, however, the second memorial remained uncompleted. The first volume, *Le Renouveau*, covering the years 1958–62, was published in 1970, and immediately became a bestseller. But only two untitled chapters of the second, *L'Effort*, were finished. A letter to Pierre-Louis Blanc, in de Gaulle's handwriting, specified that it was to have run to seven chapters, of which two would be political, two economic and social, two would deal with foreign affairs, with a philosophical final one. In this last chapter, de Gaulle planned to give his judgment on France, Europe and the world. There was to have been a third volume, *Le Terme*, dealing with events from 1966 to 1969.

Death came suddenly, of a heart attack, on 9 November 1970. He would have been eighty years old a fortnight later. There had been no sign of illness or indisposition, and on the day of his death he had worked, as usual, on his memoirs.

The news was carried first to the mayor of Colombey-les-Deux-Eglises. President Pompidou learned of it next morning at 8.30, and at noon he broadcast the following message to the French people:

Frenchmen, Frenchwomen:
General de Gaulle is dead. France is widowed. In 1940, General de

Gaulle saved our honour. In 1944 he led us to liberation and victory. In 1958 he saved us from the threat of civil war. To present-day France, he gave her institutions, her independence, her place in the world.

In this hour of mourning for the nation, let us bow respectfully before the grief of Madame de Gaulle, her children and grandchildren. Let us take stock of the duties which gratitude imposes on us. Let us promise France not to be unworthy of the lessons which have been given to us; and may de Gaulle live eternally in the national soul.

On 10 November the general's wishes concerning his funeral were released by the Elysée. They were of long standing, but had never been modified. They were, in fact, contained in a letter dated 16 January 1952, which General de Gaulle had handed to Pompidou at the time, in a sealed envelope to be opened only after his death. The time had now come. The letter said:

I desire my funeral to take place at Colombey-les-Deux-Eglises. If I die elsewhere my body must be taken home without any public ceremony whatever.

My grave shall be that in which my daughter Anne lies and where, one day, my wife will also rest. Inscription: Charles de Gaulle (1890–). Nothing else.

The ceremony shall be arranged by my son, my daughter, my daughter-in-law, assisted by members of my personal staff, in an extremely simple manner. I do not wish for a State funeral. No president, no ministers, no parliamentary delegations, no representatives of public bodies. Only the armed forces may take part officially, as such, but their participation must be on a very modest scale, without bands or fanfares or trumpet-calls.

No oration shall be pronounced, either at the church or elsewhere. No funeral oration in parliament. No places reserved during the ceremony except for my family, my comrades who are members of the Order of Liberation, the municipal council of Colombey. The men and women of France may, if they wish, do my memory the honour of accompanying my body to its last resting place. But it is in silence that I wish it to be taken there.

I declare that I refuse in advance any distinction, promotion, dignity, citation, decoration whether French or foreign. If any whatsoever were conferred upon me, it would be in violation of my last wishes.

When de Gaulle had written these lines, he had merely once been the head of a provisional government, and his decade of power lay hidden in the future. But the request of the man in the wilderness was met eighteen years after he had made it. The day of his funeral – 12 November 1970 – was observed throughout metropolitan and overseas France as a day of national mourning. Neither ministers nor parliamentarians were present, but several Companions of the Liberation who had been ministers attended the service in the village church and the interment at the local churchyard. They included General Billotte, Christian Fouchet and Bernard Tricot. Some forty thousand men and women from all parts of France came to Colombey that day.

On the 11th, President Pompidou, Michel Debré, Couve de Murville and Jacques Chaban-Delmas had called at Colombey, in their private capacities, to express their condolences to Yvonne de Gaulle and her family.

There was pomp, too, but in Paris. During the morning of 12 November, before the burial at Colombey, Cardinal Marty, archbishop of Paris, celebrated a solemn Requiem Mass for General de Gaulle at the cathedral of Notre-Dame. A glittering congregation had come from all over the world. President Pompidou was there, of course, and so were the Prince of Wales (representing Queen Elizabeth II), the British Prime Minister, Edward Heath, and three former Prime Ministers – Harold Wilson, Harold Macmillan and Lord Avon (Sir Anthony Eden); President Podgorny of the Soviet Union; President Nixon of the United States; the Shah of Iran; the Emperor of Ethiopia; and many other heads of State. Old feuds forgotten, the secretary-general of NATO, Manlio Brosio, was there to pay his tribute to the man who had tried so hard to destroy the alliance.

Cold rain poured down on the hundreds of thousands of Parisians who marched up the Champs-Elysées that day to stand in silent tribute at the Arc de Triomphe, where, twenty-six years earlier, had stood their liberator. Next day, the Council of the City of Paris decided that the Place de l'Etoile, where the Arc de Triomphe stands, should be renamed the Place Charles de Gaulle. This was not a citation or a decoration, but the nearest approach to a "dignity" that could be thought of, to be conferred on the leader who had declined all honours.

Part VII ❧ De Gaulle in History

Chapter 1 ✤ Man and Showman

The fame of de Gaulle outstrips his achievements. Those most susceptible to the charisma of his name find this impossible to concede; but the facts speak for themselves. As a soldier, he displayed courage and tactical skill, but was denied a chance to make a bid for strategic greatness. As a writer, his stature stands far higher; but as an orator, his words, for all his diligence, were flawed by absurdities of thought and style. As a statesman, his career was made in two distinct and widely separated phases. During the first, the moral and symbolic grandeur of the man and of his initial gesture was undeniable; but his influence on world events was negligible, and on domestic ones limited. During the second phase, he displayed, in an extreme degree amounting to genius, the skills and dissimulative wiles of a master of political power. His actual achievements were also considerable, but relatively disappointing – not least to himself – if measured by the scale of his grandiose ambitions; and, in the foreign sphere especially, largely negative.

In one sphere, however, he stood supreme, or at all events among the greatest of his time: as a performer. His sense of theatre, his timing, his oratory of dominance and authority, were incomparable. He was a peerless showman and myth-maker. For all those things, and for his towering persona, inflexible will and intransigent character, his impact on the contemporary scene was overwhelming.

A man like de Gaulle is born only rarely, although the twentieth century has been rich in this respect. Jean-Raymond Tournoux calls such men – who transcend normal human capacities and ambitions – "holy monsters". Strictly speaking, each one is unique, and to mention de Gaulle in the company of Winston Churchill, Mao Tse-tung, Adolf Hitler and Francisco Franco does not imply that they are similar except to the extent that each was exceptional. Whether essentially good, or evil, cruel or benign, everything such men undertake far exceeds the scale of the puny average.

De Gaulle's inflexible character was the basic clue to his career; and in turn, it fed on his career further to strengthen its own elements.

663

There was a human, that is, an ordinary, side to de Gaulle's character, which was best shown by his fierce attachment to his defective daughter Anne. And he was, by virtue of upbringing, a civilised man, who answered letters, even from strangers, with exquisite courtesy and – as so many authors learned to their gratified surprise – appeared to read books sent to him. Against this, he was capable of using the coarsest language – of the kind usually identified with the barrack square – and tended to lapse into it at times of stress.

His intransigence sometimes took the form of stubbornness, and his memory – which was exceptional by nature and which he kept constantly trained – was at the service of his rancour, so that he had an unforgiving recollection of slights and a calculated forgetfulness of favours. He owed so much to Churchill, without whose support there could not have been a Free French movement; but apart from occasional tributes in his memoirs, he showed no gratitude towards the Prime Minister. He dismissed specific favours, such as Churchill's defence of French interests at Yalta; and lingered on slights, such as the subordination of Free French interests to British and allied strategic requirements in the Levant. He never forgave the Allies for leaving him out of the planning for the Normandy landings, and marked the fact years later by refusing to attend anniversary celebrations.

There was some justification for his life-long resentment of Roosevelt's consistent belittlement of his work. But he cannot be exonerated from the charge that he allowed his personal feelings to influence his national policy to an excessive degree.

He was not a magnanimous man; or rather, he was magnanimous only in the form of suitable comments in his memoirs, but not in actions in real life. Though less ruthless than, say, Franco towards his enemies, in the mass (such as the Germans, or the Algerians), he was less forgiving towards followers who had turned against him (such as Jacques Soustelle).

Apart from his inflexibility, the most remarkable element in his character was an apocalyptic or cataclysmic vision of the world and of his role in it. It could only be, in his eyes, a Messianic one. During his years in the wilderness, he was continually prophesying calamitous events and offering himself as a saviour. When the "call" finally came, in 1958, his speeches and messages established a parallel between the situation of the country at that time and in 1940. This was straining the facts, since there was really no comparison between the two situations in terms of national survival; but the point made was that he, de Gaulle, was saving France in 1958, as he had saved her in 1940. During the decade of power that followed, he had to face a number of real crises, in the sense of armed challenges to his authority. It was in such situations that he felt at home, as the "man of storms", and probably no other Frenchman then living could have overcome these challenges, as he did, for instance, in January 1960 and April 1961, by sheer force of personality.

De Gaulle, however, could not live without drama, and when short of a natural crisis, would create one, the better to deal with it. It was thus with his two vetoes on Britain's application to join the European Common Market, or with his blows to military integration within NATO, culminating in his decision, in March 1966, to withdraw all French forces from the organisation.

Paradoxically, while de Gaulle revelled in drama, with himself at the centre of the stage, he seemed to aspire to something approaching total immobility in the politics of lesser mortals. It is reasonable to ascribe this aspiration to his soldierly love of order and discipline. His abhorrence of the party system reflected his contempt for the tiresome habit of politicians, especially French ones, of holding different opinions, and even of changing their minds.

The general's ego was of suitably gigantic proportions. To get over the fact that he was invariably the centre of any speech or any occasion, or any piece of writing, he developed two serviceable devices. One was to attribute views and sentiments to La France; and the other was to refer to General de Gaulle in the third person – a form he reserved when talking of his own work as that of a figure in history. With his egocentric view of events, he was apt, after his return to power, to ignore the intervening twelve years as a non-existent period (except when attacking his predecessors in power) or to dismiss some of the remarkable achievements of the Fourth Republic (especially in economic matters) as of absolutely no account. Thus when visiting provincial towns in 1958, he would remark on the way they were beginning to recover from the war, as though it were still 1946.

With the ego and the sense of doom, followed by salvation, went an "all-or-nothing" attitude. The country could either have him on his own terms – that is, unconditionally and without asking him for a programme – or, in effect, stew in its own juice. In that event, as he said more than once, he would return to his sorrow and his solitude. His fondness for the referendum, in preference to elections, as a technique of power, reflected this fundamental approach.

History will not necessarily treat de Gaulle with a respect to match the adulation of the unconditional Gaullists. The purpose of this concluding section is to attempt an interim assessment, in the present state of knowledge.

In this attempt, I shall set myself, and try to answer, some hypothetical questions, such as:

What would have happened to France and the world if de Gaulle had died in battle in the spring of 1939? Or peacefully in 1947 or 1957? Or by the assassin's bullet in August 1962?

Would de Gaulle's reputation stand higher, or lower, had he retired, say, in 1965 (on completing his first term of presidential office)?

Would de Gaulle have achieved more than he actually did, if he had not resigned in January 1946, or if he had been called back to power in 1955 instead of 1958?

It may be objected that from the standpoint of serious history, such questions are no more than a game. That there is an element of diversion in the exercise, I would not deny. But games can be serious: the serious intent of this one is that it offers perhaps the best way of testing the validity of Gaullist myths.

Chapter 2 ⚜ Soldier and Writer

De Gaulle's career in the army need not detain us long. His claims to fame and greatness rest overwhelmingly upon his civilian achievements. Yet his military antecedents were an inseparable part of his personality and therefore transcend in importance the relatively minor distinction he won on the field of battle. He had become a soldier because that was the best way he knew of serving France, and he was serious in his belief that the army was the soul of his country. In a mystical sense, his service in the army was a form of identification with Mother France.

Although his rank as a two-star *général de brigade* was never confirmed, and although he was twice condemned to death *in absentia* by the *de facto* government of France (whose legality he did not recognise), he continued to call himself "General" de Gaulle throughout his life and he expected others to address him as "*Mon Général*", and not as "*M. le Président*", still less as plain "*Monsieur*" de Gaulle. In this, he presented a contrast to General Eisenhower, for instance, who had achieved five-star rank, but who, in his later civilian career, suffered himself to be addressed as "President Eisenhower" and even as "Mr" Eisenhower.

On the other hand, de Gaulle disdained to have himself promoted, as he would doubtless, if so minded, have found ways of doing, either as president of the provisional government of the Republic, or as president of the Republic during his second tenure of power. He judged, correctly, that his patriotic role in 1940 gave him an authority that transcended the official hierarchy, and it was without any sense of incongruity that he accepted the fealty of General Catroux in 1940 and the submission of General Massu in 1960. Both men outranked him; both accepted his authority. Those who rejected it – the four rebel generals in 1961 – were brought to heel in a famous televised speech by General de Gaulle, who donned his uniform of a junior general for the occasion.

As an explanation of de Gaulle's personality, as a symbolic device in his assertion of power, then, the fact that he was a soldier is important. But it was relatively unimportant *per se*. Its relevance is political, not military. At Saint-Cyr and after, Charles de Gaulle annoyed more of his superiors than he impressed. This is the fate of rebels and innovators. He was challenging a stagnant organisation, immobilised by the orthodoxy of 1918 and refractory to new ideas. To challenge the Establishment is not, normally, the best road to promotion. Those who resented his incursions into military theory made sure he remained a captain far longer than he would have done if he had been merely deferential.

Through no fault of his own, de Gaulle spent most of the First World War in captivity, and was appointed to Reynaud's government after brief tactical successes that showed what he might have been capable of achieving if the French army and State had not been on the verge of collapse. It was, however, the disaster that gave de Gaulle a chance to make history, and it was his brief tenure of political office that gave him the tenuous credentials without which he might not have gained a hearing in wartime London. If he had died in battle at Laon-Montcornet in 1940, his name as a soldier would not have merited inclusion in the reference books. At most, a minor cult might have sprung up around the memory of the man who had had the foresight to press on his superiors the notion that France needed a mechanised army.

As a writer, even in 1939, de Gaulle's claims to fame stood higher than his claims as a soldier. To evaluate the intrinsic merits of de Gaulle's earlier works, however, some effort must be made to separate the writings, as such, from the later historical associations of their author's name. The exercise is worth attempting. By common consent, *Le Fil de l'Epée* is the most important of de Gaulle's earlier works; in some senses, the most important of all his works – in much the same way that Niccolò Machiavelli's *The Prince* is more important than the *Florentine Histories*. But is *Le Fil de l'Epée* important for what it is and says – as a piece of political thinking and as literature – or because it was written by a man who so clearly proceeded to apply in practice the principles stated therein? If de Gaulle had died in 1939, without achieving political fame, would *Le Fil de l'Epée* still be read today, and continue to be read by future generations, as *The Prince* has been, is, and will be? Or does it belong to the rare category of books of no great merit that will always be read because they are prophetic of their authors' subsequent careers, in other words, in the category of Hitler's *Mein Kampf* or Gamal Abdel Nasser's *The Philosophy of the Revolution*?

These questions are of more than academic interest, and it is possible to pose them in the case of the earlier works as it is not in that of the later *Mémoires de Guerre* and *Mémoires d'Espoir*, which chronicled de Gaulle's career and would not have been written if he had not had one.

Le Fil de l'Epée is in certain respects an unsatisfactory work, in that its original framework of three lectures delivered by the author in the 1920s remains clearly visible through the subsequent expansion and embellishments. It is peppered with erudite historical allusions, not all of which illuminate the highly concentrated thought. The style is concise and noble. The three lectures have turned into five essays, plus a foreword. The least interesting essays are the first ("Of Action in War") and last ("The Politician and the Soldier"); the fourth ("Of Doctrine") attacks the costly preconceived notions of general staffs during the First World War, and praises de Gaulle's protector at that time, Marshal Pétain, for his insistence on overwhelming fire power. The most arresting chapters, in the 1970s, are the intervening ones, "Of Character" and "Of Prestige", which express de Gaulle's philosophy of leadership with a precision made the more striking by his own behaviour in his periods of public life. In scattered passages throughout the work will be found all de Gaulle's master-ideas: the exaltation of force; the solitude, grandeur and aloofness of the true leader; the need for boldness, mystery and, at times, silence; disdain for lesser mortals; surprise and cunning in attack; the sadness and loneliness of the great man. He writes about the need to "organise" surprise, "by the dissimulation of preparations, but also under cover of a thick veil of deceit". "Cunning," he goes on, "must be used to make people believe that one is where one is not, that one wants that which one does not want." And, still in the interests of surprise, he advocates deceiving those in one's own camp and "wilfully misleading the very people one is thinking of using".

Those who listened to the young major saying these things in 1927 thought, when they were not simply bewildered, that he was referring exclusively to military matters; and so he was, but his later concept of political action remained military, and the passages just quoted might have been written to describe General de Gaulle's handling of the Algerian situation between 1958 and 1962.

Two more passages are still more directly prophetic. In one, he advocates selective disobedience in the higher interest by subordinates in receipt of misguided orders: an anticipated apologia for his own stand in June 1940. In the other passage, he refers to "men who are successful in everything and are acclaimed [who] suddenly reject the burden": a fairly precise forecast of his own behaviour in January 1946.

To answer my own question: even if de Gaulle had not gone on to do what he did, *Le Fil de l'Epée* would still be worth reading. But the author's career was admittedly, in a sense, a completion of his written work, which added a new dimension to it. It is surely significant that virtually nobody read this little book for some twenty-five years, until it was rediscovered about 1959, when it became virtually compulsory reading for those, including foreign diplomats, with a professional interest in de Gaulle as a statesman.

As Alfred Fabre-Luce rightly observed (in *Le Couronnement du Prince*), Machiavelli was only a writer advising a prince, whereas de Gaulle was the prince himself with a pen in his hand. The comparison between the two is inevitable. It is a deserved compliment to de Gaulle as writer and philosopher, that his name should be bracketed with Machiavelli's, but the comparison is not entirely to his advantage. He lacks the absolute candour and clarity, the Tuscan vigour, of the Florentine. Machiavelli was utterly down to earth, realistic and uncluttered by morality: hence, cynical. De Gaulle, too, is cynical; but his realism is heavily laced with romanticism and mysticism. With the wisdom of hindsight, *Le Fil de l'Epée* can be seen as the perfect introduction to an autobiography.

Of the other early works – *La Discorde chez l'Ennemi*, *Vers l'Armée de Métier*, and *La France et son Armée* – I have nothing to add to what has already been said in the narrative chapters. If his reputation depended on these works alone, de Gaulle would be recorded as an interesting but minor military historian, with a verbal gift; and (in *Vers l'Armée de Métier*) as an original and prescient thinker, though not a true innovator, as his followers and hagiographers would have it.

His lasting literary monument is the three volumes of war memoirs:

L'Appel, L'Unité, and *Le Salut.* Written with concentrated care during de Gaulle's years in the political wilderness, they are, on the whole, accurate, though marred by occasional factual errors and inconsistencies. A more serious criticism is that, in common with most memorialists but to a greater degree than most, de Gaulle selects the facts and interprets them to his own advantage. It might almost be said that what flatters de Gaulle is history, and the rest, insignificant. His grasp of world strategy, which is masterly, is a redeeming feature, but it is frequently necessary to remind oneself that most of the events which the author describes in almost epic terms – his endless wartime clashes with Churchill and Roosevelt, for example – were on a tiny scale and quite marginal to the story of the war. From time to time, indeed, de Gaulle recognises the fact and laments it. It is a useful corrective to compare his accounts of Anglo-French events with Churchill's.

The style of the memoirs has been much praised, and on the whole rightly. There is much in them that is felicitous: the opening paragraph of *L'Appel,* for instance, with its lyrical description of France; the striking pen-portraits of wartime leaders, especially Churchill and Stalin; and the Caesarian simplicity with which the author dismissed President Lebrun: "As head of State he lacked two things: that of being a head; that of having a State."

For all their shortcomings and deliberate omissions, the war memoirs will always stand as a major source for the events of the time; and as a literary work of high merit.

It is part of the tragedy of de Gaulle's career that he did not allow himself enough time to complete his second set of reminiscences, *Mémoires d'Espoir.* It has been alleged that the portions that were published are inferior to the *Mémoires de Guerre,* but I do not share this view. Admittedly, the standard of accuracy is lower, doubtless owing to the old man's haste to complete his work before dying; in which he failed. But in other respects, the later memoirs sustain the quality of the earlier ones, and perhaps surpass it. There is a still greater concision. The portraits of statesmen are as striking: Kennedy and Eisenhower, Macmillan and Adenauer, live in his descriptions. The superb arrogance of the concluding passage in the first volume (*Le Renouveau*) in which de Gaulle catalogues the successes (but not the failures) of his four years in power, challenges comparison with anything he ever wrote, ending with this short paragraph:

> On the slope which France is climbing, my mission is always to guide her towards the heights, while all the voices from below call on her

ceaselessly to come down again. Having once more chosen to listen to me, she has pulled herself out of her stagnation and has just completed the phase of renewal. But from henceforth, exactly as before, I have no other goal to show her than the crest, no other road but that of effort.

De Gaulle lived to finish only two chapters of the second volume (*L'Effort*), and we know, from a letter he wrote to his research assistant, Pierre-Louis Blanc, that there would have been five more, including one in which he intended to express his personal judgment on the situation in France, Europe and the world. That this last chapter was never written is a great loss to students of contemporary history. De Gaulle left no outline of the third and last volume, which was to have been called *Le Terme* (1966–9).

The general had reckoned he would need six years to complete his second set of memoirs, but when he settled down to them, he worked faster than he had expected. Had he retired in 1966, at the end of his first seven-year term, it is likely that he would have finished his work. In that event, he would have avoided the extravagances and failures of his last few years in power. His stature as a statesman would have stood higher; and he would have rounded off his career as a writer. His obstinacy and vanity were thus detrimental to his place in history.

De Gaulle's speeches and statements, which have been published in a collected edition of five volumes, must be considered as part of his literary output, but separately. Some of the items were improvised; most were carefully written and revised, with an evident awareness of and desire for permanence. Though often stirring, and usually eloquent, they are less resistant to the passage of time, in terms of literary quality, than the books. One of de Gaulle's detractors, Jean-François Revel, devoted a witty but rather pedantic little book (*Le Style du Général*) to a sweeping destruction of the general's reputation as a stylist, mainly on the basis of the speeches and statements of May 1958 to June 1959.

On technical grounds, it is difficult to dispute Revel's contentions. He quotes, in great abundance, instances of tortured syntax, bad grammar, mixed metaphors, perverse use of archaicisms, and unpardonable alternations of high-flown and familiar language. He uses de Gaulle's words to denounce the pretentious and "all-or-nothing" aspects of the general's character. His book is a useful corrective to the uncritical adulation heaped on de Gaulle's literary style. But he falls into the alternative pitfall of unrelieved disparagement. That there were absurdities, solecisms and obscurities in de Gaulle's words is beyond doubt. But there were also magnificent and impressive passages.

The obscurities, in particular, deserve comment. There are undoubtedly far more of them in the speeches than in the writings. Some were due to the vagueness of his concepts, especially in the field of European integration: it remained impossible, to the end, to know just what de Gaulle meant by "Europe from the Atlantic to the Urals". But many other obscurities were deliberate. The dissimulative wiles of warrior and statesman, which de Gaulle had praised in *Le Fil de l'Epée*, required carefully contrived verbal ambiguity. In his Algerian policy, in particular, it was often vitally important to him that he should appear to be all things to all men. And he must be credited with a kind of genius in the formulation of noncommittal generalities.

Chapter 3 ✤ Politician and Statesman

It was Charles de Gaulle himself who invented the myth of Gaullism. And it was the willingness of his followers to accept it (as the unconditionals did) or say they did (as with the opportunists) that turned Gaullism into a movement. In its undiluted form, the myth comprises the following main propositions:

De Gaulle saved the honour of France, and also France herself; indeed France and de Gaulle were essentially synonymous.

The Vichy government was illegal because Pétain signed an armistice with the Nazis, capitulating instead of fighting on, giving away more than half the national territory and thereafter collaborating with the enemy.

The appeal of 18 June 1940 conferred "legitimacy" upon de Gaulle; thereafter, he remained the custodian and guardian of national legitimacy, even when out of office; indeed, he "incarnated" legitimacy.

It was de Gaulle who restored the French Republic and France's greatness.

Together, these propositions constituted the articles of a creed and the essence of a *mystique*. To argue with mystics, to contest tenets of a faith, are thankless tasks. Those outside the faith, however, need feel no compulsion to accept such assertions unquestioningly. Myths, if widely accepted, become political facts. The Gaullist myth was a political fact. It is possible to concede that it had some value to the Allied cause during the war, by providing a rallying cry for Frenchmen and women who were minded to fight on and were in search of leadership. Certainly, the myth was enormously useful to the Gaullists themselves in 1958 and at critical moments thereafter to the general himself. But the independent historian is entitled to enquire into the factual basis, if any, of the articles of the Gaullist creed.

The Gaullists have been extraordinarily successful in creating a climate of opinion in which it is clearly bad form to question de Gaulle's claims. Unadorned, the facts are cruel to his legend. Far from incarnating France in 1940, de Gaulle represented nobody but himself. France was defeated and the French were demoralised. Very few of them wanted to fight on; the great majority turned with relief to Marshal Pétain, for comfort in their sorrows, for guidance in their trials, and as the one man who might conceivably mitigate the horrors of partial occupation.

It may be admitted that a nation is greater than the sum of its citizens; but the greater entity is inconceivable without its human components. De Gaulle venerated France but despised, or at least was disappointed in, the French people, who failed to live up to his "certain idea" of the motherland. The distinction, however, is a mystical one by rational criteria. De Gaulle never "was" France; and he was unrepresentative of the French people in 1940. On the other hand, he was very widely recognised as a national leader in 1944 and 1945; and many people were disposed to see him as a saviour in 1958. At other times – and most notably in 1965 when the electorate failed to give him an absolute majority in the first round of the presidential elections, and in 1968 when revolution burst upon his unsuspecting administration – his popular support fell well short of an absolute majority, let alone an overwhelming one. (The sweeping Gaullist majority at the elections that followed the events of May 1968 reflected the citizenry's relief after recent fears; it was a tribute to Pompidou, who had weathered the storm, rather than to de Gaulle himself.) As with ordinary politicians, de Gaulle's popular support fluctuated according to events. What "France" would have done, if she had had the vote, is unknown and unknowable; as for the French, they were sometimes glad to have de Gaulle; but not at all times, or for ever.

The "illegality" of the Vichy regime is an indispensable corollary to the myth of de Gaulle's permanent "legitimacy"; and just as unfounded.

The issue here is not whether Pétain's government was good or bad, well advised or misguided, but whether or not it was *legal*. That it was – at least initially – legal seems to me beyond argument: on 10 July 1940 – admittedly in an atmosphere of apprehension and under the pressure of Laval's intimidating oratory – the French National Assembly voted itself out of existence (by 569 votes to 80, with 17 abstentions) and gave Pétain full powers to revise the constitution. The counter-argument that the French electorate was never given an opportunity to satisfy the laws of July 1940 which created the Vichy regime and that it was therefore illegal, does not affect its initial legality at the time when de Gaulle rebelled against it.

Since de Gaulle and his followers denied the legality of the Vichy regime, it was logically necessary for them to set up a government and a State of their own. This they did, by stages that have been described in this book. The operation was highly successful, but was quite without a legal basis; though it was eventually ratified by the French people after the liberation of France.

Nor was there any more substance in the Gaullian argument that Vichy acted under duress and could therefore not be considered a sovereign government. True, the writ of Vichy ran over only a portion of France, and later not even over that; but in the first phase, at least, it gave proof on a number of occasions of independence of German control. But for that matter, since we are comparing rival claims to legality and legitimacy, could de Gaulle's Free French movement claim convincingly that it was a sovereign entity? At its inception, it was entirely dependent on British good will and money. When the Royal Navy bombed and partially destroyed the French fleet at Mers-el-Kébir in July 1940, de Gaulle had no option but to accept the accomplished fact.

Despite such facts, de Gaulle and his movement declared all Vichy's laws null and void. Since Vichy ended up on the defeated side, de Gaulle could get away with this. More surprisingly, however, he apparently held the view that the twelve years of the Fourth Republic were also, in a Gaullian sense, illegitimate. This is the only inference that can be drawn from his claim in January 1960, when rebuking the Algiers insurgents, that he had incarnated "national legitimacy" for the past twenty years. If this claim was intended to be taken seriously – and it was made with some solemnity – then it follows that the constitutionally legal Fourth Republic, which was in power during twelve of those years, could not be regarded as legitimate.

Since only an unconditional Gaullist would accept the truth of this claim, it must be placed where it belongs, among the tenets of the Gaullist mystique. It is of a piece with another curious assertion in the famous statement de Gaulle made on 15 May 1958, when all France was wondering whether he would emerge from his retirement to solve the crisis that was to bring down the Fourth Republic: "Once before, the country, in the depths of its being, gave me its trust to lead it, in its entirety, to salvation."

This was pure fantasy. The country did not give de Gaulle its trust, and certainly not in its entirety, because it had no idea who he was at the time of his appeal of 18 June 1940. Admittedly, the situation changed in de Gaulle's favour during the next four years, but this was due very largely to the fact that the war situation had changed in favour of de Gaulle's Anglo-Saxon allies.

Having discarded those elements in Gaullism that most clearly are mythical, we are left with the claims that de Gaulle saved France's honour, and restored the French Republic and France's greatness. These claims must be taken more seriously, though no less critically examined. Not much time need be expended in speculating on what would have happened if General Weygand or General Noguès (the commander-in-chief in North Africa) had responded to the messages de Gaulle sent them from London on 20 and 24 June 1940, respectively, suggesting to each in turn that he should lead the French resistance. Neither did; and it is quite possible that if either of them had, de Gaulle's forceful personality might still have brought him effective control of the Free French movement. Admiral Muselier, who outranked de Gaulle, tried to oust him from the leadership, and failed. General Catroux, who also outranked him, simply accepted de Gaulle as the man who had launched the Resistance and, by virtue of his gesture, was the logical leader.

No one can deprive de Gaulle of the credit for having done what he did. It was, as he wrote himself, an adventure. The fact that his mythical claims were unfounded adds to, not detracts from, his having pulled off his great gamble. To the British in particular, who stood alone at the time, the presence of a French military man who rejected surrender was of great emotional and symbolic significance. The attitude of the French people was bound to be more complex. Pétain was at that time a far greater public figure than de Gaulle. Many of those who had turned to the old man for comfort and leadership clung to the illusion that there must be a secret deal between the two; especially on learning, as many did, of the close relationship that had once prevailed between them. When it became clear that there was no substance in this supposition, many remained reluctant to discard the marshal in favour of this distant and unknown figure whose voice they occasionally heard on the radio.

In time, many ordinary Frenchmen and women went into the Resistance, and most, but by no means all, came to acknowledge de Gaulle's leadership. For them, at least, de Gaulle's initially lonely stand came to mean French honour.

So much must be said on the positive side. But there is a negative side as well. In its nature, the Gaullist myth was profoundly divisive; for it presented the choice before all Frenchmen and women in artificially Manichaean terms. One was either for de Gaulle or against; one was either a Gaullist or a traitor; a good Frenchman or a bad. Most ordinary people in France, however, had difficulty in seeing the situation in such simple terms. It was not given to all of them to escape to London, or later, to North Africa, to continue or resume the fight. For most of them, the problem was that of keeping alive with an enemy in occupation of part, and later the whole of, the national territory. Besides, there were more ways than one of serving one's country. To serve in the Free French forces was one way. Though more glamorous than staying at home, was it necessarily more heroic? The German presence was the daily reality. Somebody had to try to provide wartime France with a government and deal with the Germans: were all who helped in this task automatically traitors?

It was from this treacherous No Man's Land of morality that the Gaullist myth seemed most dubious. By the logic of Gaullism, however, the Vichy regime, as such, was a treasonable enterprise, and all who served Vichy were, a priori, guilty of collaboration with the enemy. This indeed was the inescapable consequence of de Gaulle's decision to create a "State" of Free France and claim sovereignty for it. It was open to de Gaulle to be the leader of all Frenchmen and women who wished to continue the fight without making his controversial political claims. This was what Muselier would have preferred to do, and it was Giraud's approach, too. For these men, especially the second, the only thing that mattered was victory; and that meant working closely with the allies – while clearly stating areas of authority reserved to the French, but without attempting to pre-empt political power in France. This would have been the less divisive course. In effect, it was what Jean Monnet recommended to de Gaulle in his letter of 23 June 1940, in which he declared that it would be a great mistake to try to set up in England an organisation that might appear in France as an authority created abroad under England's "protection". Instead, he advocated the creation of a non-political committee to help any French volunteers to join the British forces.

De Gaulle, however, subordinated all else to the myth of his own legitimacy, the effect of which was to divide the French people into two categories: those who could claim to be Gaullists in 1944, who were honourable citizens; and those who had remained loyal to the marshal who, if they were not traitors or collaborators, were at the very least inferior citizens with a burden of opprobrium.

In terms of realism, he was on particularly weak ground in denying legitimacy to the Pétain government for having signed an armistice with the Germans. The French forces had been utterly defeated and demoralised. By signing an armistice, Pétain kept part of France from falling under direct and immediate German control and gave himself a bargaining instrument when it came to German claims on North Africa that violated the terms of the truce. Whether there would have been any real military advantage to the Allied cause in removing the French government to North Africa to continue the fight is at least debatable. That there would have been a moral advantage in it is probable; paradoxically, if this had happened – and the general said this was his hope – there would have been no need for his own glorious rebellion.

There were military, as well as political and moral, consequences to de Gaulle's initial decision. The most serious was that de Gaulle was more concerned to discredit Vichy, pitting French against French, than to fight the Germans. The discovery that this was indeed his attitude deeply shocked General Odic and others who had sought to join the Free French the better to fight the enemy.

These things need to be said. But there is much to be said on the Gaullist side as well. With his "purity" and his utter intransigence in defence of France's interests and his own, de Gaulle provided millions of Frenchmen and women with a model of patriotism to look up to after the humiliation of defeat and occupation. To this extent, he did "restore French honour" and set France on the road to the recovery of national self-respect. When one recalls the tenuous original basis of his movement, this was a great achievement; and it is unlikely that it would have happened without a myth of some sort. But it was flawed by the divisiveness inherent in his claims, by the dubious legality of the purge over which he presided, and by his inability to control the massacre of Frenchmen and women, not all of them collaborators, after the Liberation.

De Gaulle's claims to have restored the Republic and France's greatness also call for scrutiny. At this point, one of the hypothetical questions suggested earlier may be useful. What would have happened to France and the world if de Gaulle had died in battle in the spring of 1939? To ask this question is to draw attention to the fact that de Gaulle had remarkably little influence on the course of events during the Second World War. Militarily, the Free French contribution to the Allied war effort was negligible, until Giraud, having created his American-armed army, lost control of it to de Gaulle.

Although de Gaulle, by sheer obstinacy or intransigence, got the better of Churchill in nearly all their clashes of will, he was kept out of the Allied planning for the Normandy operations that were to liberate France. Had there been no de Gaulle, Giraud would have escaped when he did and gone to North Africa when he did. He would probably have led his forces to victory. Paris would have been liberated at the prescribed time, and the last German soldier would have been driven out of France on the known date.

De Gaulle's political, as distinct from military, role in the liberation was nevertheless of the first importance. Had he not been there, the Americans would have gone ahead with their plans for a temporary military government, with its liberation currency. France, in effect, would have been occupied, however benevolently, by the Allies, who would have attempted to preside over the restoration of the French Republic. But de Gaulle's presence doomed these plans to failure. As soon as he appeared on French soil, he asserted his authority. He re-established the State in Paris and gradually, in the face of appalling difficulties and challenges, extended its writ throughout France.

In a very real sense, then, de Gaulle did restore the Republic. Moreover, he must be given high credit for resisting any temptation he may have felt to set up a personal dictatorship. There is little doubt that he could have done so, either in 1944–5, or in 1958–9. But he dismissed the possibility, and instead aimed at the higher prize of an authoritarian "Republican monarchy" with himself as the elective monarch. This, too, was a great achievement.

The claim to have restored France's greatness is more contestable. De Gaulle was obsessed by France's historic position as a great power and by what he considered her prescriptive right to be one again. He was, however, kept out of the Big Four conference at Yalta, which dealt with matters, such as the shape of post-war Europe, in which France was vitally interested. He managed to be represented at the ceremony ratifying Germany's surrender, and (with Churchill's help, which inspired no gratitude) secured for France an occupation zone in Germany. But he was excluded from the Potsdam conference in July 1945, and therefore had no say in the practical arrangements for Germany and eastern Europe, and – humiliatingly – for French Indo-China. And nobody paid any attention to his plan for the dismemberment of Germany and her reversion to a confederation of princely States. For all his persistence, then, it cannot be said that de Gaulle secured great power status for France, except in the relatively formal question of permanent membership of the United Nations Security Council, with the great power's right of veto. His conduct of French foreign policy during his second period of power deserves separate treatment.

Let us not leave the wartime period without a further look at de Gaulle's political role. Throughout the war, his motivation was less concerned with the need to make common cause with his allies in the interests of victory over Germany, than with the creation and consolidation of an alternative French polity that would prevent the men of Vichy or the politicians of the Third Republic from staying in, or returning to, power after the war. If military victory had been his principal aim, he would have avoided the unseemly squabbles by which he sought to make Churchill "understand" that he was dealing with the living incarnation of a great power; he would have cooperated wholeheartedly in the Allied war effort; he would have effaced himself when Giraud came on to the scene. But to have done these things would have been incompatible with his own myth of identification with the motherland, and with his soaring political ambitions. In a more cooperative and self-effacing frame of mind, he would have won Roosevelt's trust; and the history of post-war France and Europe would have been different.

Not that de Gaulle alone can be blamed for poor relations with the American president. In his dealings with de Gaulle, Roosevelt showed himself singularly obtuse and blind to the future. In the early stages, this blindness was at least excusable. But from the time of de Gaulle's victory over Giraud in Algiers, it was obvious that post-war France, at least in the initial stages, was going to be dominated by de Gaulle. There was therefore nothing to be gained by continuing to snub him and attempting to by-pass him in the administration of liberated France.

Politically, de Gaulle's wartime masterpiece was undoubtedly his advent to power in Algiers against the heaviest odds. But he failed to derive the fullest advantage from this victory. In the end, the parties of the Resistance overrode de Gaulle by ignoring his constitutional views, and the general was faced with a return to the party politics he abhorred and held responsible for France's decadence and the military disaster of 1940. He had won and lost in quick succession. And he resigned in a huff, convinced that another national crisis would soon result in his recall – a miscalculation that marred his claims to prescience.

*   *   *

Let us turn now to de Gaulle's second period in power. In retrospect, his two undeniable achievements were the constitution of the Fifth Republic, which proved itself when power was transferred to his successor in 1969; and the Algerian settlement, under which France's North African departments achieved independence, not without bloodshed, but at all events without a civil war in France. To these should be added the peaceful decolonisation of French-ruled Africa in conditions ensuring a continuance of French influence (although decolonisation had begun under the Fourth Republic with the *loi-cadre,* and de Gaulle's "Community" was short-lived).

Everything he did was replete with paradox. The constitution had been tailor-made to his needs; yet he frequently abused it, overriding verdicts of illegality by the Council of State. But there was much to be said for his view that France could no longer allow herself the luxury of the political free-for-all that had prevailed under the Third and Fourth Republics. Although it is still too early to say whether the constitution of the Fifth Republic has given France long-term political stability, it did put at least a temporary halt to the regime of short-lived governments and shifting parliamentary majorities. In the hands of a head of State more respectful of its textual limitations than de Gaulle was, it could prove durable. An unexpected outcome of Gaullian constitution-making was, incidentally, the emergence of the Gaullists as a powerful, conservative ruling party.

Similarly, the Algerian settlement, through all its stages, was a study in paradox. It is certain that de Gaulle had no intention, at the outset, of conferring independence on Algeria. His hope was to persuade the Moslem rebels to accept self-rule in association with France. It is conceivable that he would have achieved this, had he been called back to power two or three years earlier. But by the time the call came, there were no moderates left among French politicians. That indeed was why he was called back. In the end, he found himself doing what he had hoped to avoid; giving the Algerians the one thing – independence – the politicised French army had trusted him to avoid. Nor, in the end, did he do all that could have been done to safeguard the position of the *pieds-noirs,* who deserted Algeria *en masse* to settle in metropolitan France. Still, on the whole, it was a politically masterly performance, marred only by his impatience to shed a burden which, as he saw it, stood between him and his dream of restoring France's greatness in the world. It was far from perfect; but nobody else could have done as well.

It is hard, on the other hand, to find anything to praise in the substance, as distinct from the presentation, of General de Gaulle's foreign policy. Its underlying premises were false, its assumptions illusory, and its consequences divisive and even disastrous for the West as a whole and for France in particular. The most persistent of de Gaulle's illusions (or delusions?) was the notion that France could do a deal with Russia. He had first toyed with this idea, which never ceased to fascinate him, during the war, when he sought (and to a limited extent secured) Soviet support for the Free French movement to improve his bargaining position vis-à-vis the "Anglo-Saxons". At the end of 1944 he signed a treaty with Stalin; having made a show of resistance to the Soviet dictator's demand for French recognition of the Russian-sponsored Lublin committee, he nevertheless sent Christian Fouchet as a representative to the committee, thereby conferring *de facto* recognition on the Polish Communists who, under protection of the Red Army, were about to set up their satellite regime in Warsaw.

This was one of two main advantages secured by Stalin for the minimal price of his signature on the treaty document. The other was de Gaulle's decision – on the eve of his departure to Moscow and as advance payment for the pact he wanted – to allow the French Communist leader, Maurice Thorez, to return to Paris from his Moscow exile. From de Gaulle's point of view, the return of Thorez, and Communist participation in his government, constituted a necessary price for relative domestic peace: he would rather have the Communists with him than against him. It was left to de Gaulle's successors to discover the impossibility of working with a subversive group which, at that time, was at Moscow's orders.

The Franco-Soviet treaty was supposed to mark France's re-entry into the ranks of the great powers, but turned out to be still-born. In May 1955, little interest was aroused when the Soviet presidium unilaterally denounced it. In the intervening years, history had by-passed de Gaulle. The Marshall Plan had helped to restore the economies of France and other West European countries; NATO had helped to contain the Soviet military threat; the Geneva conference of 1954 had ended the Indo-China war. Other people had dealt with the crises – the "storms" – which de Gaulle had hoped would bring him back to power. In vain had he denounced the Communists, whom he had introduced into the French government, as "separatists", and the menace of Soviet Communism, with whose leader he had signed a treaty. The treaty of Rome would shortly be signed, and nothing he could do or say would stop it.

It is fascinating, though fruitless, to speculate on the possible turn of events if de Gaulle had stayed in power in 1946 instead of resigning. The cards in his hands would have been no different from those at the disposal of the weak ministries of the Fourth Republic. France would still have needed Marshall Aid, and his touchy nationalism and anti-Americanism might well have induced the Americans to give less than was needed. He would probably have had to get rid of the Communist ministers and have seen for himself that the military threat to France and the rest of western Europe now came not from Germany but from Russia. The Atlantic treaty would still have been necessary, and if he had stuck out against an integrated command dominated by the United States, no amount of Gaullian eloquence could have compensated for the resulting weakness of the alliance. He would have tried to hold on to Indo-China, but it is doubtful whether he would have been more successful than other Prime Ministers. He had failed even to acknowledge Emperor Bao Dai's personal appeal for independence. Would he not have been tempted to make a deal with Ho Chi Minh, in the hope of keeping a Communist Vietnam linked in some way with France? This, after all, was what the French negotiator, Jean Sainteny, had hoped for, and de Gaulle later listened to his advice. Yet it was de Gaulle who had sent the utterly intransigent Admiral d'Argenlieu to Saigon as high commissioner.

The futility of such speculations lies in the fact that de Gaulle was, in any event, determined not to play the parliamentary game. And since he was not, he would have been even less well equipped to govern than the successive premiers who at least tried to secure a parliamentary majority. He walked out of the system because it was not the system he wanted. Had he stayed on, it would not have been for long, for he would have lost his majority and would not have been willing to lead a parliamentary opposition.

A more fruitful line of speculation arises from the supposition that he might have been called back to power, say, in 1955 after the fall of the Mendès France government. The year is well chosen: Indo-China lost, the Algerian war begun, Tunisia and Morocco on the road to independence, the first practical stirrings of the European movement manifesting themselves. From de Gaulle's standpoint, 1955 would have been a good year for a come-back. It is just possible that he would have reached an Algerian settlement on more favourable terms than he was able to secure in 1962, with a self-ruled Algeria in association with France and possibly with the two other countries of the French-speaking Maghreb. He would never have signed the treaty of Rome as it now stands; he would either have killed the European movement, or led it in a more confederal direction, without any concessions to supranationality. The Anglo-French Suez expedition would not have been called off, and Nasser would have been brought down, creating an entirely new situation in the Near East. In world politics, he would have been free three or four years earlier than was in fact the case to seek an understanding with Russia. He would have been no more successful than he was in real life, but he would have done his worst to the Atlantic alliance earlier and the damage would probably have been still graver.

Events, however, did not happen quite that way. When de Gaulle did come back in 1958, he was faced with the further accomplished fact of the treaty of Rome. It was not the text he would have liked, but it had one pleasing feature: the veto implicit in the rules of unanimity; and he made good use of it to get France's way in most disputed issues, and to keep Britain out of the European Economic Community. Nor were the French always or necessarily in the wrong. They were within their rights, for instance, in insisting that the common market in agriculture should proceed apace with the common market in industry. Nor was he entirely mistaken in his assertions that Britain was not "ready" to join the EEC. Shortly after his return to power, the British negotiations with the Six aimed at merging the EEC into a wider Free Trade Area had collapsed, as they were bound to, given the naïvety of the Macmillan government's assumption that the Six would welcome what each of them rightly considered to be either an attempt to destroy the common market, or an application to join the club without paying the dues.

Given good will, however, Britain's subsequent application to join the EEC could have succeeded, as it did when negotiations were resumed after de Gaulle's retirement. But there was no good will on de Gaulle's side. He was not interested in the original supranational objectives of the European movement. He meant to use the EEC as an instrument in his foreign policy: as a means of detaching Germany from dependence on America, and turning "Europe" into a third force able to deal directly with the Soviet bloc independently of the United States. Had Britain been admitted into the EEC, any French hopes of dominating the Community would have been frustrated; and in any case, de Gaulle regarded Britain as America's Trojan horse because of the special relationship which gave the British access to American nuclear technology that was not available to the French.

Perhaps the best verdict on de Gaulle's European policy was written by David Schoenbrun in his *The Three Lives of Charles de Gaulle* (p. 317):

Only one man could conceivably have been elected the first president of the United States of Europe: Charles de Gaulle. But de Gaulle was a Frenchman, wholly a Frenchman and nothing but a Frenchman;

because of that he was, in the final analysis, nothing more than a Frenchman.

But de Gaulle's European policy was no more than a facet of a world policy in which the other elements were NATO, Germany and Russia. His motivation was complex. Personal resentment against the Americans, and to a lesser degree the British, for wartime slights, certainly played a part. So did his passionate and mystical vision of France, and his identification with her; and his overwhelming personal ambition for a major role in contemporary history. But in addition there was what can only be described as a pervasive historical pessimism. He rejected supra-national Europe not only because it offended his French nationalism but because he was convinced the national sentiments of other EEC members would also, in the final analysis, make the whole thing unworkable. And he sought a deal with Russia not only because this was an ambition worthy of him, but because he was convinced that the Americans would not stay in Europe indefinitely anyway and the day of their departure might as well be speeded, so that Europe (under his leadership) should stand on its own feet and face its responsibilities. Similarly, while rejecting ideologies as relatively unimportant, he was convinced that Communism, in one form or another, would impose itself on Europe, and sought to give France his own brand of it, based on "participation", to pre-empt its imposition from the outside. It is probable that in de Gaulle's mind participation, so conceived, would have been comple-mentary to a deal with Russia, as part of his grand design for France and the world.

In the end, none of his objectives was achieved. He kept Britain out of the Common Market, but was powerless to keep her out once death had removed him. He established an ascendancy over Chancellor Adenauer and signed a treaty with him; but the treaty was still-born, as the Franco-Soviet treaty had been. He took France out of NATO, gravely weakening the alliance and compromising France's own security. He duly made his overtures to Moscow, but was spurned. He challenged the two world currencies – the dollar and the pound – and the whole Bretton Woods system in the name of gold; but in the end was powerless to prevent the devaluation of the franc that closely followed his second retirement from public affairs. A dismal record.

What, then, of home affairs? The constitution was a positive legacy. Participation never got off the ground. But in countless public speeches, de Gaulle consistently disregarded the record of the Fourth Republic and claimed the credit for France's rapid modernisation and soaring output and living standards. That France's recovery continued under his rule cannot be denied; but it was under the Fourth Republic that a start had been made. And in the end, the revolutionary explosion of May 1968 – which de Gaulle had not foreseen – nullified much of the economic gains and financial stability previously achieved.

Let us return to our speculative game. How would de Gaulle's reputation stand if he had died in 1947, 1957 or 1962? Death in 1947, on the eve of the creation of the Rally of the French People, would have left de Gaulle's wartime reputation untarnished; but would have deprived the world of his war memoirs. If he had died shortly after launching the RPF, the final memory would have been of something ghastly reminiscent of Fascist excesses. A slightly better year would have been 1957, which would have spared the world the disadvantages of de Gaulle's foreign policy; but only two volumes of the war memoirs would have seen the light. A better date by far would have been August 1962. Had de Gaulle's assassins found their mark (as later he half wished they had), he would have gone down at the height of his power and fame, having rid France of her Algerian burden, and not having had time to inflict more than slight damage on the Atlantic alliance.

But he survived the assassin's bullets, as he had survived his Great War wounds and all the hazards of an adventurous life. Thereafter, the choice of a time for exit was in his hands and he made a poor choice. He had taken office as president of the Republic in January 1959, for a term of seven years. Had he announced his impending retirement in 1965, he would have picked the best year of all, in terms of his place in history. Not that 1965, as such, was a good year for Charles de Gaulle. But had he announced his retirement then, he would have avoided the humiliation of his failure to keep the presidency on the first ballot. Although he had lost some of his popularity, the French people had not yet altogether wearied of his performance on the international scene. The most damaging of his foreign eccentricities or wilful acts of destruction – his cry of "Vive le Québec libre", his break with NATO – were still in the future and would therefore not have happened. The world would have been spared such actions; and he would have been spared the débâcle of 1968, and the last and unnecessary humiliation of the lost referendum of April 1969. Not least, he would have given himself time to finish his second set of memoirs, to the world's enrichment and the enhancement of his renown.

But he did not retire when the going was good; and the reason why he did not is the reason why, in the final analysis, he cannot be ranked with the greatest of his country's statesmen. With the Algerian settlement only three years behind him, he had re-entered the great game of world politics and was enjoying it too much to opt out. Although it should already have been clear to him that his German policy had failed and that his Russian policy had no chance of success, he was in search of further laurels; as if those he had collected until then were not enough. In other words, he did not know when to stop – a characteristic he shared with Napoleon III.

Charles de Gaulle had many of the attributes of the statesman: the character, the intelligence and the charisma. Between his first and second periods of power, he had even taught himself patience. He was an outstanding technician of power. It was his tragedy that his opportunities came relatively late in life and at a time when it was no longer possible for France to play the role he expected of her. Three centuries earlier, Cardinal Richelieu had set himself three goals and, with a will and ruthless drive comparable with de Gaulle's, had achieved them: he had broken the Protestants, smashed the challenge of the feudal nobles, and transferred the fulcrum of European power from the house of Austria to the Bourbon court in Paris. After the great French Revolution, Napoleon had conquered most of Europe and given France a new system of laws before meeting his Waterloo.

Those were careers of the sort de Gaulle would have liked to emulate. In the 1920s and 1930s, a spectacular and destructive career would have been open to a French politician, as it was open to Mussolini in Italy and Hitler in Germany. But de Gaulle, to his credit, deliberately spurned the opportunities for dictatorship that came his way at the end of the war. He was not a sanguinary man, although ready to send collaborators and rebels to their deaths. It was not his fault that he was born in the wrong century for a career of the scope of Richelieu or Napoleon I. But it *was* his fault to have behaved as if he were living in a previous century. With his great gifts and his prestige, he could have led Europe and France as part of Europe to unity and prosperity, and consolidated the West's defences in partnership with America. Instead, he chose to make repeated gestures of petulance and defiance that weakened the West without compensatory advantages for France. It was a sad end to the great adventure of 1940.

Bibliographical Note

Bibliographical Note

The Gaullist Association in Paris, in a list drawn up in October 1969, catalogued 215 works on General de Gaulle in French alone; and to these should be added its lists of works in English, German, Italian and other languages. Nor did the flow stop in 1969. Much of this production is, however, polemical, satirical, vituperative or hagiographic; relatively little of it is of more than ephemeral or specialist interest. The following annotated list, arranged chapter by chapter and roughly in order of appearance, includes the books I drew upon while writing my own work. It shculd not be regarded as in any sense exhaustive; nor does the omission of a book necessarily mean that I consider it to be without value.

PART I: THE ENIGMA OF DE GAULLE
1. The Man
This impressionistic picture is not based on published sources. My description of the workings of the Elysée staff was the outcome of personal enquiry at the Palace and paraphrases the account of it I wrote for *Encounter* (October 1965).

2. Historical Prologue
Of the many books on modern French history now available, by far the most useful, in my view, is Gordon Wright, *France in Modern Times* (John Murray, 1962; henceforth, Wright), which deals systematically with events and economic, social and cultural trends, with excellent reasoned bibliographies for each section. The period covered is 1760 to 1960.

Less useful, but rich in wit and insights, is D. W. Brogan, *The Development of Modern France 1870–1959* (Hamish Hamilton, 1967).

In this chapter and for all historical background, indispensable tools of trade are the entries on French history in the *Encyclopaedia Britannica* (1955 and 1967), the *Grand Larousse Encyclopédique* (10 vols, Paris 1969), and *An Encyclopaedia of World History* (ed. William L. Langer, Harrap, 1948 and subsequent editions).

PART II: HISTORIAN AND THINKER (1890–1939)
1. Pupil of the Jesuits (1890–1909)
The hagiographies are unavoidable when chronicling the early period. The

best is Georges Cattaui, *L'Homme et son Destin* (Fayard, 1960; henceforth, Cattaui, which contains, among other things, a useful genealogy of de Gaulle's ancestors. Other sources:

Pierre Galante, *Le Général* (Presses de la Cité, 1968; henceforth, Galante). English translation: *The General* by Pierre Galante with Jack Miller (Frewin, 1969). Anecdotal, superficial and not always accurate; but readable and, alas, indispensable.

Jean-Raymond Tournoux, *Pétain et de Gaulle* (Plon, 1964; henceforth, Tournoux, *Pétain*). Perhaps the best book of an indefatigable researcher and collector of Gaulliana whose works are invaluable sources which no historian of the period will be able to ignore. Rather breathless in style and occasionally facile in judgment, but compulsively readable and often profound in psychological insight.

Charles de Gaulle, *La France et son Armée* (Plon, 1938, 1965; henceforth, De Gaulle, *France*; English translation: *France and her Army* translated by F. L. Nash, Hutchinson 1940). Originally written under Pétain's orders when de Gaulle was an officer on his staff. Its publication under de Gaulle's name without the Marshal's consent led to the rift between them. Not the best of de Gaulle's works, but the best passages have an epic quality.

2. The Young Officer (1909–1918)

Paul-Marie de la Gorce, *De Gaulle entre Deux Mondes* (Fayard, 1964; henceforth, Gorce). By far the fullest of the French biographies, and the best for historical background. Written with the General's cooperation, it omits anything likely to cause offence.

De Gaulle, *France*.

Pierre Hassner, in *Interplay* (New York, vol. 1, no. 7, February, 1968). Draws a parallel between Maurras and de Gaulle.

Gaston Bonheur, *Charles de Gaulle* (Gallimard, 1946, 1958; henceforth, Bonheur). Another early hagiography.

Jean Lacouture, *De Gaulle* (Seuil, 1965, 1969; Eng. tr. by Francis K. Price, Hutchinson, 1950; henceforth, Lacouture, *De Gaulle*). Short but penetrating essay; perhaps the best book in French on de Gaulle. My references are to the 1965 French edition.

Lucien Nachin, *Charles de Gaulle, Général de France* (Colbert, 1944; henceforth, Nachin). The first of the hagiographies; sometimes nauseous but an indispensable primary source, by a close friend of the young de Gaulle.

Cattaui.

Wright.

Tournoux, *Pétain*.

3. The Historian (1919–1924)

Bonheur.

Nachin.

Gorce.

Galante.

Lacouture, *De Gaulle.*

Tournoux, *Pétain.*

Charles de Gaulle, *La Discorde chez l'Ennemi* (Berger-Levrault, 1924). De Gaulle's first published work.

4. *Pétain's Protégé* (1924–1932)

Wright.

Tournaux, *Pétain*

Capitaine de Gaulle, "Rôle historique des places françaises", *Revue militaire française*, no. 5, 1 Dec. 1925 (Berger-Lévrault).

Cattaui.

Nachin.

De Gaulle, *Le Fil de l'Epée* (Berger-Lévrault, 1932; Eng. tr. Faber, 1960, *The Edge of the Sword*, Union Générale d'Editions, 1962; henceforth, De Gaulle, *L'Epée*). Expanded from three lectures. Short, but a key work. References are to 1962 edition.

Admiral of the Fleet Lord Fisher, *Memories* (Hodder and Stoughton, 1919).

Bonheur.

Galante.

5. *A Prophet Ignored* (1932–1939)

Gorce.

Tournoux, *Pétain.*

Lacouture, *De Gaulle.*

Bonheur.

Nachin.

Charles de Gaulle, *Vers l'Armée de Métier* (Berger-Lévrault, 1934; Les Lettres Françaises, Beirut, 1942; Eng. tr. *The Army of the Future*, Hutchinson, 1940; my references are to the 1942 French edition). De Gaulle's semi-prophetic advocacy of a professional and mechanised army for France.

Alistair Horne, *To Lose a Battle* (Macmillan, 1969; henceforth, *Horne*). An outstanding reconstruction of the Battle of France and the causes of France's defeat.

Cattaui.

De Gaulle, *Mémoires de Guerre*: Vol. 1, *L'Appel*, 1940–42 (Plon, 1954; Engl. tr. *Call to Honour 1940–42* translated by J. Griffin, Collins, 1955; henceforth, De Gaulle, *L'Appel*). First volume of de Gaulle's literary masterpiece; an indispensable primary source, despite some inaccuracies and an egocentric view of history. References are to 1954 French edition.

Horne.

Brian Crozier, *Franco: a Biographical History* (Eyre & Spottiswoode, 1967; henceforth, Crozier, *Franco*).

BIBLIOGRAPHICAL NOTE

PART III: FREE FRANCE (1939–1945)

1. *The Defeat* (1939–1940)

Gorce.

De Gaulle, *L'Appel.*

J. Benoist-Méchin, *Soixante Jours qui Ebranlèrent l'Occident*: Vol. 1, *La Bataille de Nord*; Vol. 2, *La Bataille de France* (Albin Michel, 1956; henceforth, Benoist-Méchin I). A prominent Vichy figure's remarkably objective reconstruction of events.

Horne.

Winston S. Churchill, *The Second World War*: Vol. 1, *The Gathering Storm* (Cassell, 1948; henceforth, Churchill, Vol. 1). This splendid work, markedly less egocentric than de Gaulle's war memoirs, provides a useful corrective to the latter.

Nachin.

Tournoux, *Pétain.*

Major-General Sir Edward Spears, *Assignment to Catastrophe*: Vol. 1, *Prelude to Dunkirk*; Vol. 11, *The Fall of France* Heinemann, 1954; henceforth, Spears). Lively, well-written memoirs of Churchill's bilingual personal emissary to de Gaulle, who later considered him a spy and broke with him.

Max Beloff, *The Intellectual in Politics and other essays* (Weidenfeld and Nicolson, 1970).

Crozier, *Franco.*

Bonheur.

Cattaui.

2. *The Challenge*

De Gaulle, *L'Appel.*

Churchill, Vol. 1.

Robert Aron, *Histoire de Vichy* (Fayard, 1954; henceforth, Rob. Aron, *Vichy*; Eng. tr. Robert Aron and Georgette Elgey, *The Vichy Regime 1940–44* trans. by H. Hare, abridged, Putnam 1958). The first of a historian's detailed and admirable trilogy on a dark period of French history.

Churchill, Vol. 11: *Their Finest Hour* (Cassell, 1949).

Henri Michel, *Histoire de la France Libre* (Presses Universitaires de France, 1967; henceforth, Michel, *France Libre*). Useful concise guide through the intricacies of the Free French movement, by the official French historian of the Second World War.

3. *The Free French*

Henri Amouroux, *Le 18 Juin 1940* (Fayard 1964; henceforth Amouroux). The events of one day.

Colonel Passy (A. E. V. Dewavrin), *Souvenirs*, Vol. 1 Raoul Solar, 1947; henceforth, Passy, Vol. 1). Lively, ironical memoirs of the first head of de Gaulle's secret services.

692

4. Divided They Fall
De Gaulle, *L'Appel.*

Jacques Soustelle, *Envers et Contre Tout*, Vol. I, *De Londres à Alger* (Laffont, 1947; henceforth, Soustelle, *Envers*, Vol. I. The enthusiastic memoirs of an ardent Gaullist.

Michel, *France Libre.*

Robert Mengin, *No Laurels for de Gaulle* (Michael Joseph, 1966; in French, *De Gaulle à Londres par un Français Libre*. Table Ronde, 1965; henceforth, Mengin). A free Frenchman who repudiated de Gaulle's authority. References are to English version.

Passy, Vol. I.

Vice-Admiral Muselier, *De Gaulle contre le Gaullisme* (Du Chêne, 1946; henceforth, Muselier). Carefully documented memoirs of de Gaulle's defeated rival for power.

The Lacy Papers (henceforth *Lacy*: see Sources and Acknowledgements). An important primary source.

5. De Gaulle versus his Allies: 1
De Gaulle, *L'Appel.*
Wright.
Michel, *France Libre.*
Journal Officiel de la France Libre (London, 1941).
Churchill, Vol. III: *The Grand Alliance* (Cassell, 1950).
Gorce.
Tournoux, *Pétain.*
Rob. Aron, *Vichy.*

De Gaulle, *Discours et Messages*, Vol. I: *Pendant la Guerre, June 1940–Jan. 1946* (Plon, 1970; hencefoth, De Gaulle, *Discours*, Vol. I). First volume of the approved texts of de Gaulle's speeches and announcements, carefully annotated by the historian François Goguel, but occasionally marred by significant omissions or changes, some of which I have been able to point out.

6. *De Gaulle versus his Allies: 2*
De Gaulle, *L'Appel.*
Lacy.
Muselier.

The Odic memoirs (see Sources and Acknowledgements). A minor source, married by the author's petulance, but a useful corrective to the standard view of de Gaulle's "legitimacy". The essence of Odic's case is quoted in Kenneth Pendar, *Adventure in Diplomacy: the Emergence of General de Gaulle in North Africa* (Cassell, 1966).

Churchill, Vol. III.

Robert E. Sherwood, *The White House Papers of Harry L. Hopkins*, Vol. I Sept. 1939–Jan. 1942 (Eyre & Spottiswoode, 1948; henceforth, Sherwood,

Hopkins). An important source, especially for de Gaulle's relations with Roosevelt.

A. L. Funk, *Charles de Gaulle: the Crucial Years, 1943–44* (Oklahoma Uni. Press, 1959; henceforth, Funk). A scholarly study.

De Gaulle, L'Unité 1942–44: Vol. II of the war memories (Plon, 1956; Eng. tr. *Unity 1942–44* trans. by Richard Howard, Weidenfeld & Nicolson 1959).

Soustelle, *Envers*, Vol. I.

Muselier.

Lacy.

Gorce.

7. *Roosevelt in the Ascendant*

De Gaulle, *L'Appel*.

De Gaulle, *L'Unité*.

Tournoux, *Pétain*.

Galante.

Churchill, Vol. IV: *The Hinge of Fate* (Cassell, 1951).

Michel, *France Libre*.

Funk.

Fleet Admiral William D. Leahy, *I Was There* (Gollancz, 1950; henceforth, Leahy). The author was Roosevelt's ambassador to Vichy.

8. *"Torch" and After*

De Gaulle, *L'Unité*.

Claude Paillat, *L'Echiquier d'Alger*, Vol. I: *Avantage à Vichy* (Robert Laffont, 1966; henceforth, Paillat, *L'Echiquier*, Vol. I). A painstaking but lively reconstruction of events by a French journalist.

Robert Murphy, *Diplomat Among Warriors* (Doubleday, New York, 1964; henceforth, Murphy). Well-written memoirs by Roosevelt's special envoy in North Africa, who was a *bête noire* of de Gaulle's.

Churchill, Vol. IV.

Dwight D. Eisenhower, *Crusade in Europe* (Heinemann, 1949; henceforth, Eisenhower, *Crusade*). Occasionally corrects de Gaulle's one-sided account of events.

Sherwood, *Hopkins*.

Funk.

9. *Casablanca*

Samuel I. Rosenman, comp., *Public Papers and Addresses of Franklin Delano Roosevelt*, 1943; henceforth, Rosenman. The whole compilation runs to 13 volumes (Vols 1–5, Random House, New York; Vols 6–9 Macmillan, London; Vols 10–13, Harper Bros., New York).

Churchill, Vol. IV.

Murphy.

Funk.

Paillat *L'Echiquier*, Vol. II: *De Gaulle Joue et Gagne* (Robert Laffont, 1967).

De Gaulle, *L'Unité*.

Cordell Hull, *The Memoirs of Cordell Hull*, Vols. I and II (Hodder & Stoughton, 1948; henceforth, Hull). The reminiscences of Roosevelt's Secretary of State.

Sherwood, *Hopkins*, Vol. II.

Elliott Roosevelt, *As He Saw It* (Duell, Sloan & Pearce, 1946). The President's son reminisces.

Eisenhower, *Crusade*.

Harold Macmillan, *The Blast of War, 1939–45* (Macmillan, 1967; henceforth, Macmillan, *War*). During part of the period covered. Macmillan was Britain's Minister of State in North Africa.

De Gaulle, *Discours*, Vol. I.

Galante (typically, for an apocryphal anecdote).

10. *Algiers*

Macmillan, *War*.

Paillat, *L'Echiquier*, Vol. II.

De Gaulle, *L'Unité*.

Eisenhower, *Crusade*.

Marcel Peyrouton, *Du Service Public à la Prison Commune* (Paris, 1950). One of Vichy's high officials chronicles his fall from grace.

General Catroux, *Dans la Bataille de la Méditerranée* (Julliard, 1949). Literate memoirs of the first top-ranking military man to join de Gaulle.

Churchill, Vol. IV.

Leahy.

11. *The Resistance*

M. R. D. Foot, *History of the Second World War: SOE in France* (H.M. Stationery Office, 1968; henceforth, Foot). A splendid, illuminating history of the British secret operations in France.

Passy, *Souvenirs*, Vol. II (Raoul Solar, 1948).

Henri Michel, *Histoire de la Résistance en France* (Presses Universitaires, 1969; henceforth, Michel, *Résistance*). A concise guide; not invariably accurate.

De Gaulle, *L'Appel*.

12. *Roots of the Fourth Republic*

De Gaulle, *L'Unité*.

Gorce.

Michel, *Résistance*.

Henri Michel, *Les Courants de Pensée de la Résistance* (Presses Universitaires, 1962; henceforth, Michel, *Courants*). Monumentally detailed; illuminating but inaccurately indexed.

De Gaulle, *Discours*, Vol. I.

Passy, Vol. II.

Edouard Daladier, *Réponse aux Chefs Communistes* (Paris, CTP, 1946). Self-disculpatory memoir by one of the "men of Munich".

De Gaulle, *L'Appel*.

Foot.

13. *The Agony of France*

Rob. Aron, *Vichy*.

Paillat, *L'Echiquier*, Vol. II.

De Gaulle, *L'Unité*.

Dorothy Pickles, *France between the Republics* (Love and Malcomson, 1946). A scholarly interim assessment.

Yves Maxime Danan, *La Vie Politique à Alger de 1940 à 1944* (Librairie Générale de Droit et de Jurisprudence, 1963). A thesis, rich in details.

De Gaulle, *Discours*, Vol. I.

A. W. DePorte, *De Gaulle's Foreign Policy 1944–46* (Harvard, 1946; henceforth, DePorte). An intelligent and scholarly assessment.

PART IV: THE LIBERATION AND AFTER (1944–1946)

1. *Jostling for Position*

De Gaulle, *L'Unité*.

Churchill, Vol. V: *Closing the Ring* (Cassell, 1952).

E. H. Cookridge, *Inside SOE* (Arthur Barker, 1966). Anecdotal; no challenger to Foot.

Galante.

Eisenhower, *Crusade*.

De Gaulle, *Discours*, Vol. I.

Robert Aron, *Histoire de la Libération de la France* (Fayard, 1959; henceforth, Rob. Aron, *Libération*; Eng. tr. in two vols., *De Gaulle Before Paris*, Putnam, 1963; *De Gaulle Triumphant*, Putnam, 1964). Continues the same author's *Vichy*, maintaining his high standard of sober objectivity.

Leahy.

Hull, Vol. II.

Funk.

Rosenman.

Churchill, Vol. VI: *Triumph and Tragedy* (Cassell, 1954).

2. *De Gaulle's Parisian Triumph*

De Gaulle, *L'Unité*.

Churchill, Vol. VI.

Churchill, Vol. V.

Michel, *Résistance*.

Rob. Aron, *Libération*.

Soustelle, *Envers*, Vol. II: *D'Alger à Paris* (Laffont, 1950).

Rob Aron, *Vichy*.

De Gaulle, *Discours*, Vol. I.

Eisenhower, *Crusade*.

Alfred Fabre-Luce, *The Trial of Charles de Gaulle* (Methuen, 1963; henceforth, Fabre-Luce, *Trial*). My references are to Antonia White's English translation of *Haute-Cour* (Julliard, 1962), with a useful introduction by Dorothy Pickles, and in appendices, the text of de Gaulle's condemnation to death *in absentia*, and the full text of the Constitution of the Fifth Republic, translated by William Pickles. This wickedly witty satirical work by a prominent Vichy supporter was banned in France, and the edition seized by the police; it was later published in Switzerland (Editions "J.F.G.", Lausanne, 1963).

3. Trial of Strength

De Gaulle, *Salut: Le Salut*, Vol. III of the war memoirs (Plon, 1959; Eng. tr. *Salvation 1944–46*, trans. by Richard Howard, Weidenfeld & Nicolson, 1960).

Robert Aron, *Histoire de l'Epuration*, Vol. I: *De l'indulgence aux Massacres*, Nov. 1942–Sept. 1944 (Fayard, 1967; henceforth, Rob. Aron, *Epuration*, Vol. I). This history of the purges of collaborators in France continues the same author's *Vichy* and *Libération*, without any slackening of standards or interest.

Gorce.

Lacouture, *De Gaulle*.

Rob. Aron, *Libération*.

4. Foreign Disappointments

De Gualle, *Salut*.

Churchill, Vol. VI.

DePorte.

Sherwood, *Hopkins*, Vol. II.

5. International Discords

Rob. Aron, *Libération*.

De Gaulle, *Salut*.

Eisenhower, *Crusade*.

Chester Wilmot, *The Struggle for Europe* (Collins, 1952).

Crozier, *Franco*.

Brian Crozier, *The Rebels; A Study of Post-war Insurrections* (Chatto & Windus, 1960; henceforth, Crozier, *Rebels*).

Churchill, Vol. VI.

Philippe Devillers, *Histoire du Viêt-Nam de 1940 à 1942* (Seuil, 1952). A detailed account.

Aidan Crawley, *De Gaulle* (Collins, 1969; henceforth, *Crawley*). Intelligent study, marred by inaccuracies.

De Gaulle, *Discours*, Vol. I.

6. Vichy on Trial

De Gaulle, *Salut*.

Rob. Aron, *Epuration*, Vol. II: *Des Prisons clandestines aux tribunaux d'exception*, Sept. 1944–June 1949 (Fayard, 1969).

Alexander Werth, *France 1940–1955* (Hale, 1956; henceforth, Werth, *France*). A leftish account, sometimes valuable for its "feel" of places and events.

Jacques Isorni, *Pétain a Sauvé la France* (Paris, 1965). Pétain's lawyer defends his memory.

Louis Noguère, *Le véritable Procès du Maréchal Pétain* (Fayard, 1955). The author, who succeeded Mongibeaux as President of the High Court, assembles the documents on which the evidence for and against Pétain should have rested.

Peter Novick, *The Resistance versus Vichy: the Purge of Collaborators in Liberated France* (Chatto & Windus, 1968). Useful, especially for its lists of sentenced people.

René Rémond, *La Droite en France de la 1ère Restauration à la Ve République* (Aubier, 1963). A scholarly study.

Tournoux, *Pétain*.

7. *The Patient Stirs*

Werth, *France*.

De Gaulle, *Salut*.

Jacques Fauvet, *La IVème République* (Fayard, 1959; henceforth, Fauvet, *IVème*). A concise, sober account by the former political editor (later Editor-in-Chief) of *Le Monde*.

Ronald Matthews, *The Death of the Fourth Republic* (Eyre & Spottiswoode, 1954). A foreign eyewitness account.

Galante.

8. *De Gaulle Steps Down*

De Gaulle, *Salut*.

De Gaulle, *Discours*, Vol. I.

Fauvet, *IVème*.

PART V: THE FOURTH REPUBLIC (1946–1958)

1. *Birth and Challenge*

Jean-Raymond Tournoux, *La Tragédie du Général* (Plon, 1967); henceforth, Tournoux, *Tragédie*). A rich and original presentation, with interesting documentary material.

Crawley.

Fauvet, *IVème*.

Philip Williams, Politics in Post-war France (Longmans, 1954; henceforth, Williams). A scholarly handbook and guide.

Gorce.

Edward Ashcroft, *De Gaulle* (Odhams, 1962). An English admirer's pioneering biography.

De Gaulle, *Discours*, Vol. II: *Dans L'Attente*, Feb 1946–Apr. 1958 (Plon, 1970).

Jean Sainteny, *Histoire d'une Paix Manquée: Indochine 1945–47* (Amiot Dumont, 1954). Fascinating account, by a principal participant, of the French negotiations with Ho Chi Minh.

Claude Paillat, *Vingt Ans qui Déchirèrent la France*, Vol. I: *Le Guêpier* (Laffont, 1969). Excellent account of France's colonial troubles.

Dorothy Pickles, *French Politics: The First Years of the Fourth Republic* (Royal Institute of International Affairs, 1953; henceforth, Pickles, *French Politics*). A preliminary assessment.

Jacques Soustelle, *Vingt-huit Ans de Gaullisme* (Table Ronde, 1968; henceforth, Soustelle, *Gaullisme*). Though polemical and self-disculpatory, this is an important book, by a former follower who broke with de Gaulle.

2. *Triumph and Collapse*

Alexander Werth, *De Gaulle* (Penguin, 1967; henceforth, Werth, *De Gaulle*). Facile and superficial.

Pickles, *French Politics*.

Gorce.

Soustelle, *Gaullisme*.

De Gaulle, *Discours*, Vol. II.

Tournoux, *Tragédie*.

Fauvet, *IVème*.

Williams.

Guy de Carmoy, *Les Politiques Etrangères de la France 1944–66* (Table Ronde, 1967; henceforth, De Carmoy; Eng. tr. *Foreign Policies of France 1944–1968* trans. by E. P. Halpherin, Chicago University Press, 1970). An erudite and devastating analysis.

Lacouture, *De Gaulle*.

3. *In the Wilderness*

Tournoux, *Tragédie*.

Galante.

Lacouture, *De Gaulle*.

Philippe Alexandre, *Le Duel De Gaulle-Pompidou* (Grasset, 1970; henceforth, Alexandre). Occasionally inventive, but useful, if selectively used.

Gorce.

Fauvet, *IVème*.

General Henri Navarre, *Agonie de l'Indochine* (Plon, 1956) and Jean Laniel, *Le Drame Indochinois* (Plon, 1957): the mutual accusations of public figures for what happened at Dien Bien Phu.

Roger Massip, *De Gaulle et l'Europe* (Flammarion, 1963) and Lord Gladwyn, *De Gaulle's Europe* (Secker & Warburg, 1969) contain useful material.

Brian Crozier, *The Masters of Power* (Eyre & Spottiswoode, 1969; henceforth, Crozier, *Power*). Chapters on de Gaulle and the Army in Algeria Also, Crozier, "The General's Generals" (*Encounter*, April 1960).

M. and S. Bromberger, *Les 13 Complots du 13 Mai* (Fayard, 1959); J.-R. Tournoux, *Secrets d'Etat* (Plon, 1960; henceforth, Tournoux, *Secrets*); and Dominique Pado, *13 Mai: Histoire secrète d'une révolution* (Editions de Paris, 1958; henceforth Pado) are among the many books claiming to give the "inside" story of the events that brought de Gaulle back to power. Of these, Tournoux, *Secrets* is the best. There is an excellent summary of these events in Pierre Viansson-Ponté, *Histoire de la République Gaullienne*, Vol. I: *La fin d'une époque*, May 1958–July 1962 (Fayard, 1970; henceforth, Viansson-Ponté, *République*, Vol. I), an excellent work of contemporary history by a leading French journalist, who, when he started writing the book, was the political editor of *Le Monde*. Jacques Massu, *La Vraie Bataille d'Alger* (Plon, 1971). Startlingly frank memoirs, for instance about torture by French Army.

Fauvet, *IVème*.

Soustelle, *Gaullisme*.

De Gaulle, *Mémoires d'Espoir*, Vol. I: *Le Renouveau*, 1958–62 (Plon, 1970; henceforth, De Gaulle, *Renouveau*). The first volume of de Gaulle's second set of memoirs, which was to have run to three volumes. Only two chapters of the second volume (*L'Effort*) were complete at the time of his death in November 1970. (Eng. tr. *Memoirs of Hope: Renewal 1958–62; Endeavour 1962–* trans. by Terence Kilmartin, Weidenfeld & Nicolson, 1971.)

The Economist's confidential bulletin, *Foreign Report*, carried some interesting material during this period.

Gorce.

De Gaulle, *Mémoires d'Espoir*, Vol. II: *L'Effort*, 1962– (Plon, 1971; henceforth, De Gaulle, *L'Effort*).

PART VI: THE FIFTH REPUBLIC

1. *De Gaulle Breaks the Opposition* (1958–1962)

De Gaulle, *Renouveau*.

De Gaulle, *Discours*, Vol. II.

Viansson-Ponté, *République*, Vol. I.

Soustelle, *Gaullisme*.

Tournoux, *Tragédie*.

Maurice Allais, *L'Algérie d'Evian* (L'Espirit Nouveau, 1962; henceforth Allais). A Sorbonne Professor's impassioned denunciation of de Gaulle's Algerian Policy.

De Gaulle, *Discours*, Vol. III: *Avec le Renouveau, May 1958–July 1962* (Plon, 1970).

De Gaulle, *L'Effort*.

Jean Lacouture, *Cinq Hommes et la France* (Seuil, 1961; henceforth, Lacouture, *Cinq Hommes*). An interesting study of France's relations with five colonial independence leaders: Ho Chi Minh, Habib Bourguiba, Mohammed V, Ferhat Abbas and Sékou Touré.

Pierre Avril, *Le Régime Politique de la Ve République* (Droit et Jurisprudence, 1964).

Dorothy Pickles, *The Fifth French Republic* (Methuen, 1962; henceforth,
Pickles, *Fifth Republic*). A scholarly guide, which includes the translation of
the Constitution by her husband, William Pickles, that also appears in *Fabre-
Luce, Trial*.

Philip Williams and Martin Harrison in D. H. E. Butler, ed., *Elections
Abroad* (Macmillan, 1959).

Jacques Soustelle, *L'Espérance Trahie* (L'Alma, 1962; henceforth, Soustelle
Espérance). Soustelle's first work after his break with de Gaulle.

Gorce.

Brian Crozier and Gerard Mansell, "France and Algeria" in *International
Affairs*, London (Vol. 36, No. 3, July 1960).

Jacques Fauvet and Jean Planchais, *La Fronde des Généraux* (Fayard, 1959).
The best account of the affair of the generals.

Robert Buchard, *Organisation de l'Armée Secrète*, Vols I and II (Albin
Michel, 1963; henceforth, Buchard). Some picturesque details.

Dorothy Pickles, *Algeria and France: From Colonialism to Cooperation*
(Methuen, 1963). A balanced study.

Crozier, *Power*.

Brian Crozier, *The Morning After* (Methuen, 1963). Includes story of the
FLN–OAS negotiations.

2. The Atlantic Directorate Affair

Tournoux, *Tragédie*.

De Gaulle, *Renouveau*.

Harold Macmillan, *Riding the Storm, 1956–59* (Macmillan, 1971; henceforth, Macmillan, *Storm*). Covers the first years of Macmillan's premiership.

David F. Schoenbrun, *The Three Lives of Charles de Gaulle* (Hamish
Hamilton, 1966; henceforth, Schoenbrun, *Lives*). Informative on de Gaulle's
relations with President Eisenhower.

George W. Ball, *The Discipline of Power* (Bodley Head, 1968; henceforth,
Ball). Useful on Franco-American relations and NATO problems.

John Newhouse, *De Gaulle and the Anglo-Saxons* (André Deutsch, 1970;
henceforth, Newhouse). A brilliant study, with much material that was new
at the time.

Crozier, *Power*. For the Berlin crisis of 1958–9.

De Carmoy.

Maurice Couve de Murville, *Une Politique Etrangère 1958–69* (Plon, 1971;
henceforth, Couve de Murville). A dull but useful memoir by the obedient
executant of the General's foreign policy.

Interview with Lord Gladwyn, formerly Britain's ambassador in Paris, in
Le Figaro, 9 November 1971.

Anthony Hartley, *Gaullism: the Rise and Fall of a Political Movement*

(Outerbridge & Dienstfrey, New York, 1971; henceforth, Hartley, *Gaullism*). A penetrating and exhaustive study of the ideas and organisation of the Gaullist movement.

3. Europe and the World
Philip Williams and Martin Harrison, *Politics and Society in de Gaulle's Republic* (Longman, 1971; henceforth, Williams and Harrison). A scholarly sequel to the earlier *Williams*.

J.-R. Tournoux, *Le Mois de Mai du Général* (Plon, 1969; henceforth, Tournoux, *Mai*). Quoted here for one of de Gaulle's sayings.

René Courtin, *L'Europe de l'Atlantique à l'Oural* (L'Esprit Nouveau, 1963; henceforth Courtin). A far-sighted little work.

De Carmoy.

Newhouse.

De Gaulle, *Discours*, Vol. III.

Alfred Grosser, *La IVe République et sa Politique Extérieure* (Armand Colin, 1969). A wide-ranging study.

Couve de Murville.

Christian Fouchet, *Au Service du Général de Gaulle* (Plon, 1971). Important because Fouchet was Minister of the Interior at the time of the May disorders, but curiously reticent.

De Gaulle, *Renouveau*.

Macmillan, *Storm*.

4. The Pressure Mounts
Schoenbrun, *Lives*.

Alexandre.

De Gaulle, *Discours*, Vol. IV: *Pour L'Effort*, Aug. 1962–Dec. 1965 (Plon, 1970).

De Carmoy.

De Gaulle, *Discours*, Vol. V: *Vers le Terme*, Jan. 1966–Apr. 1969 (Plon, 1970).

Raymond Aron, *De Gaulle, Israël et les Juifs* (Plon, 1968). An unusually impassioned work by a normally calm commentator.

Georges Chaffard, three articles on Foccart, "L'Homme des Affaires Secrètes", in *Le Nouvel Observateur*, Oct.–Nov. 1969.

Harold Wilson, *The Labour Government 1964–1970* (1971). Primarily, for his account of "the Soames affair".

5. The Roots of Discontent
De Gaulle, *L'Effort*.
Williams and Harrison.
De Gaulle, *Renouveau*.
Tournoux, *Tragédie*.
Schoenbrun, *Lives*.

Viansson-Ponté, *République*, Vol. I.

Jean Charlot, *Le Gaullisme* (Armand Colin, 1970; henceforth, Charlot). One of several useful studies by a French academic.

Pierre Viansson-Ponté, *Les Gaullistes: Rituel et Annuaire* (Seuil, 1963). Useful and witty profiles of leading Gaullists.

Soustelle, *Gaullisme*.

Tournoux, *Mai* (mentioned in VI, 2). One of the two most durable and authentic journalistic reconstructions of the events of May 1968. The other is Claude Paillat. *Archives Secrètes, 1968–69* (Denoël, 1969; henceforth, Paillat, *Archives*).

Raymond Aron, *La Révolution Introuvable* (Fayard, 1968). A university view of the 1968 disorders.

John Ardagh, *The New French Revolution* (Secker & Warburg, 1968). A wide-ranging study of French social change during the Fifth Republic.

Louis Vallon, *L'Anti de Gaulle* (Seuil, 1969; henceforth, Vallon). A left-wing Gaullist's anti-Pompidou diatribe.

6. Storm and Aftermath

Paillat, *Archives*.

Alexandre.

Tournoux, *Mai*.

Viansson-Ponté, *République*, Vol. II: *Le Temps des Orphelins*, Aug. 1962–Apr. 1969 (Fayard, 1971). See above, under VI, 1.

Daniel Singer, *Prelude to Revolution: France in May 1968* (Cape, 1970). The author hoped the revolutionaries would win in 1968 and thinks they will next time.

Charlot.

Williams and Harrison.

7. Exit and Death

Alexandre

Vallon.

Jacques Chapus, *Mourir à Colombey* (Table Ronde, 1971). Useful, but not always accurate, account of the last months of de Gaulle's life.

PART VII: DE GAULLE IN HISTORY

This concluding assessment is different in character from the narrative sections of this book, and sources are correspondingly less important. Reference is made, however, to the following three books:

Jean-François Revel, *Le Style du Général: essai sur Charles de Gaulle*, May 1958–June 1959 (Julliard, 1959). A pedantic but valuable dissection, in the form of a classical dialogue, of de Gaulle's literary style, with special reference to his speeches after returning to power.

Alfred Fabre-Luce, *Le Couronnement du Prince* (Table Ronde, 1964). Fabre-Luce's works are too intelligent and carefully written to be dismissed as mere anti-Gaullist fulminations. This one examines aspects of the Gaullist myth.

Schoenbrun, *Lives*. I quote from this Francophile American writer's disillusioned verdict on de Gaulle as a nationalist who failed to seize his European chance of greatness.

Other books that should be considered as a corrective to Gaullophile literature include:

Newhouse, *Anglo-Saxons*.

Hartley, *Gaullism*.

A. Fabre-Luce, *Le Plus Illustre des Français* (Julliard, 1960). This author's nearest approach to a "straight" biography of de Gaulle.

A. Fabre-Luce, *The Trial of Charles de Gaulle*. See above, under IV, 2. Purports to be the verbatim account of a fictitious trial of de Gaulle, set in the future, on State charges. Real and fictitious witnesses are called; the trial ends without a verdict.

A. Fabre-Luce, *L'Anniversaire* (Fayard, 1971). Timed to coincide with, and counter, the flood of Gaullist panegyrics on the first anniversary of the General's death. Less successful than earlier works.

Eugène Mannoni, *Moi, Général de Gaulle* (Seuil, 1964). A short, sceptical biography, and a well-written one.

The following works also deserve to be consulted:

André Malraux, *Antimémoires* (Gallimard, 1967; Eng. tr. by J. Kilmartin, Penguin, 1970) and *Les Chênes qu'on Abat* (Gallimard, 1971; Eng. tr. *Fallen Oaks*, translated by I. Clephane, Hamish Hamilton, 1972). In both works, but especially the second and shorter, the outsize ego of the bearer of one of the most inflated reputations of the age stands between the book and the reader, impeding communication.

Robert Aron, *Charles de Gaulle* (Perrin, 1964). Markedly inferior to the same author's histories.

Emmanuel d'Astier, *Les Grands* (Gallimard, 1961). A left-wing Resistance leader's profiles of de Gaulle and others.

François Mauriac, *De Gaulle* (Grasset, 1964). Perhaps the most sycophantic of the hagiographies, written as an apologia by one who rallied late.

Françoise Parturier, *Marianne m'a dit* (Nouvelles Editions de Paris, 1963). A trifle, but worth reading for its light, frothy, very Parisian treatment.

Edmond Jouve, *Le Général de Gaulle et la Construction de l'Europe, 1940–1966*. Vols I and II (Librairie Générale de Droit et de Jurisprudence, 1967). A monumental and authoritative compilation.

L'Année Politique. This standard work of reference has undergone changes of name and publisher. The one consulted most was *L'Année Politique: Revue chronologique des principaux faits politiques, diplomatiques, économiques et sociaux de la France et de la co-opération franco-africaine du 25 août au 31 décembre 1945* (Le Grand Siècle, 1946). From 1952, it was published by Presses Universitaires de France; and since 1963, its title has been *L'Année politique, économique, sociale et diplomatique en France*.

704

Index

Abadie, Dr, 230, 257
Abbas, Ferhat, 503, 508
Abbeville, action at, 95
Abetz, Otto, 152, 263, 394
Acheson, Dean, 564–5
Acre, 159, 161
Action française, 50, 60, 67, 248
Adenauer, Konrad, 521, 549, 554, 564, 573;
meets de Gaulle at Colombey, 520, 527–
528, 550; effect of de Gaulle's Atlantic
policy on, 526–8, 550; meeting at Bad
Kreuznach, 528–9; reaction to de
Gaulle's views on Polish frontier, 550–
551; signs treaty of cooperation with
France, 552, 684
Africa: de Gaulle's wartime campaigns
in, and visits to, 124–33, 149–53, 171,
185–9, 198ff; post-war policies towards,
451, 481, 483, 570, 578, 582–3, 680; 1958
tour of, 488–91, 493; see also Algeria
and separate countries by name
Ailleret, General Charles, 571, 581
Alexander, A. V., 98, 168, 177
Alexander, General Sir Harold (later
Field-Marshal Earl Alexander of Tunis),
193–4, 223, 225, 288
Algeria, de Gaulle's plans (1940) for fighting on in, 96, 99, 102, 105; bombardment of Mers-el-Kébir, 117–19; "Torch"
landings, 199–201; outbreaks of violence (1945), 356–7
Algerian war: start of, 447; early stages,
448; Sakhiet raid, 448; analysis of different factions, 454–60; demonstrations
and riots of 1958, 460, 462–3, 464,
468; Committee of Public Safety proclaimed, 463; Salan invokes de Gaulle,
465; Soustelle arrives in Algiers, 469
de Gaulle's summing up of the situation, 482–3; first visit and statement
of policy, 485–7; Committee of Public
Safety calls for integration and support
of de Gaulle, 487; de Gaulle's further
visits, 487, 491; announces Constantine Plan, 495; Moslems set up provisional government, 495; de Gaulle de-

crees restoration of civil government
and replaces Salan by Challe, 500; exercises clemency towards Moslem leaders,
501
municipal elections, 503; FLN offers to
negotiate, 503; de Gaulle visits army
and offers eventual self-determination,
503–4; replaces Massu by Crépin, 505;
further insurrection (1960), de Gaulle
threatens force, civil opposition col-
lapses, 506; de Gaulle visits army, 507;
meets FLN leaders, 508; speaks of Algerian Republic, 509–10; visits Algeria for
the last time, 510; referendum on self-
determination, 510–11
army revolt (1961), 511–12; state of
emergency proclaimed, 512; de Gaulle's
television appeal, 513; rebellion col-
lapses, 514; OAS campaign of attrition
begins, 516; Evian talks and agreement,
518; settlement assessed, 680
Algiers, 116, 195, 253; events leading up
to de Gaulle's arrival in 1943, 198–206,
217–22; de Gaulle arrives, 222–3; first
meetings, 224–5; disagreements with
Giraud over Peyrouton's resignation,
226–8; removal of Vichy men, 228;
French Committee of National Liberation set up, 228–31; de Gaulle meets
Eisenhower, 232; compromise agreement between de Gaulle and Giraud,
234–5; Consultative Assembly of the
Resistance meets, 256; provisional
government set up, 256–7; retirement of
Giraud, 258; work of government under
de Gaulle, 264ff., 276ff.; Roosevelt's
proposed meeting turned down, 347–
348; for subsequent events, see Algerian
war.
Alibert, Raphael, 114–15
Allard, General Jacques, 461, 487, 500
Allied Military Government, Occupied
Territories (AMGOT), 278; issue of
"French" currency, 282, 285–6
Alphand, Hervé, 120, 529, 543
Alsace (and Lorraine), 21, 28, 42, 349–51

America: position in Second World War, 83, 124, 147; dealings with Vichy, 151, 153, 170–72, 179; offered African bases by de Gaulle, 156, 171; wartime relations with Free French, 171–2, 188–9, 196, 285; and Saint-Pierre and Miquelon, 173–6, 189; and New Caledonia, 190; strategy in Algiers, 195, 198, 202, 206; support of Giraud, 196–7, 205, 233–4; attitude to French over "Torch", 199–201

    signs Atlantic treaty, 431; attitude to de Gaulle's Atlantic policy, 520ff., 576

    de Gaulle's visits to, 288–94, 362–3, 536, 566–7, 569

    de Gaulle's attitude to, 58, 450, 548–9; his growing anti-Americanism, 560–61, 566, 568–9, 682, 684

    see also Eisenhower; Kennedy; Roosevelt

Antoine ("Fontaine"), 137–8, 140

Anvil, Operation, 295–7, 302

Argenlieu, Admiral Thierry d': in Free French, 117, 122, 133, 146n, 167, 190, 210, 313; as high commissioner in Indo-China, 365, 408–13, 682

Argoud, Colonel Antoine, 511, 514, 597

Armengaud, General, 87n

Arnold, General H. H., 289, 362

Aron, Raymond, 135, 426

Arras, 25–7

Arrighi, Pascal, 472

Astier de la Vigerie, Emmanuel d', 190, 196, 201, 256, 320; in the Resistance, 241–5

——, General Francois d', 204

——, Henri d', 204–5

Auboyneau, Captain, later Admiral Philippe, 177, 461, 474

Auburtin, Jean, 67–8, 70, 77

Auchinleck, General Sir Claude (later Field-Marshal), 159, 165, 181, 185

Auriol, Vincent, 394–5, 412, 414, 417–18, 430, 438–9, 475, 477

Baden-Baden, 631, 633

Bad Kreuznach, 528–9

Bainville, Jacques, 29

Bao Dai, Emperor, 363–4, 366, 409–10, 414n, 682

Barka, Mehdi Ben, 597

Barthou, Louis, 60

Bastien-Thiry, Colonel Jean-Marie, 517–518

Baudouin, Paul, 90, 103–4

Bayeux: de Gaulle's 1944 visit to, 286–287; his 1946 speech attacking Fourth Republic, 402–5, 484, 491, 591

Beaverbrook, Lord, 103, 278

Beeley, Sir Harold, 448

Beirut: de Gaulle's army service in, 54–5; wartime visits to, 161–3, 179, 192; scene of disorders in 1945, 358; Israeli commando raid on, 584

Belgium, 58, 129, 421, 554; vulnerability to German attack, 63, 69, 87, 91; invaded, 91–5; surrender of, 95; von Rundstedt's offensive in, 349

Ben Bella, Ahmed, 501, 504, 508

Beneš, Eduard, 274

Bergeret, General, 210–11, 228

Berlin: blockade and airlift, 431; threatened by Khrushchev, 528–9, 539, 550, 565

Bermuda, de Gaulle proposes summit meeting at, 538–9

Bertaux, Pierre, 324–5

Bessborough, Lord, 167–8

Béthouart, General, 293

Bevin, Ernest, 281, 283, 367, 424

Biafra, 582–3

Bidault, Georges, 249, 362, 367, 391, 394, 403, 406, 412, 424, 432, 446, 457, 462; in the Resistance, 241; chairman of CNR, 255; at the liberation of Paris, 310–11, 313; appointed foreign minister, 320; at Moscow meetings, 334, 336, 340–41; forms MRP, 378; becomes prime minister, 404; foreign minister under Ramadier, 414; signs Marshall Plan, 429–30; proposes Atlantic treaty, 431; fails to form government (1958), 460; sends letter of support to de Gaulle, 464, 473; makes inflammatory speeches in Algeria, 504; views on EDC, 522n

    his opinion of de Gaulle, 344, 400, 458

Biddle, Daniel, 173

Billotte, Colonel, later General Pierre, 181, 201, 223, 234, 240, 244, 281–2, 660

Billoux, François, 257, 265, 302, 320, 414–15

Bir-Hakim, French action at, 187–8, 192

Bizerta, 200, 223, 487, 515

Blaizot, General, 355

Blanc, Pierre-Louis, 656, 658, 671

Bloch-Lainé, François, Pour une Réforme de l'Entreprise, 616

Blum, Léon, 78–9, 88–9, 135, 250–51, 378; views on mechanised army, 68–9; forms Popular Front, 71; meets de Gaulle, 72–74; in prison at Riom, 249, 388; refuses office under de Gaulle, 388; is prime minister for one month (1946), 406, 412, 415; makes unsuccessful bid for power, 427–8; on a "Third Force", 428

    his opinion of de Gaulle, 72–3, 387

Bogomolov, 180–82, 194, 274–6, 334

Boislambert, Hettier de, 120, 127, 210, 277, 285
Boissieu, Alain de, 401
Boisson, Vichy Governor General, later High Commissioner, 126, 210–11, 219, 224–5, 228, 230–31, 233–4, 278–9
Bollaert, Emile, 254, 413
Bonapartism, de Gaulle accused of, 390, 433, 591
Bonnet, Henri, 230, 257, 320
Bonneval, Colonel Gaston de, 461, 465
Bordeaux, government moves to, 102–5, 108
Boris, Georges, 121, 134
Boudhors, Colonel, 30
Boulanger, General Georges, 11–12
Boumendjel, Ali, 508
Bourdelle, Maurice, 443
Bourgès-Maunoury, Maurice, 299n, 314, 447, 497
Bourguiba, President Habib, 447–8, 514–515
Bradley, General Omar, 316, 352
Brazzaville, 127, 489; de Gaulle's wartime visits to, 131, 150–53, 159, 171; publication of 1940 manifesto denouncing Vichy, 133; speech of 1944, 269
Briand, Aristide, 42–3
Briare, 100–02
Bridoux, General, 37
Britain: *for a large number of references, see* Churchill; Macmillan
    before Second World War, 42–3, 70–72, 78–9, 83; declares war, 84; in "phoney" war, 84–6; and Norwegian campaign, 86–7; after Dunkirk, 96–8; de Gaulle's first days in, 109–11; work of Secret Service, 121–2, 236–7, 240, 245, 323; propaganda to France from, 135; and Muselier affairs, 140–41, 167–8, 177–178; and Syrian campaign, 152–65; and Saint-Pierre and Miquelon, 174–7; and North African campaign, 181, 195, 207, 223; at "Torch" landings, 199–201; on French zone in Germany, 329, 332, 345, 362; at Dumbarton Oaks conference, 334, 347; in Burma, 355; in Indo-China, 365–6; at Paris conference, 367; and Suez expedition, 452; and EEC, 554–67 *passim*, 581, 665; economic difficulties in, 581; and Soames affair, 586–9
British Broadcasting Corporation (BBC), 135, 166, 200, 203, 308
Brittany, de Gaulle's 1969 tour of, 648
Brodowski, General von, 301
Broizat, Colonel, 511, 514
Brossolette, Pierre, 243–5, 251
Brouillet, René, 485

Bruneval, de Gaulle's speech at, 416–17, 422
Brussels: de Gaulle's visit to, 367; treaty of, 430
Bulganin, Marshal, 447
Bureau Central de Renseignements et d'Action (BCRA), 121n, 238–9, 245, 251
Burin des Roziers, Etienne, 7–8, 595
Byrnes, James, 362, 367

Caccia, Sir Harold, 526, 529
Cadogan, Sir Alexander, 103, 220
Caffery, Jefferson, 344, 346–7, 362, 424
Cagoule and Cagoulards, 59–60, 76, 136, 248
Cairo: de Gaulle in, 149–51, 155–8, 160–62, 165, 192; Churchill in, 193; Big Three conference in, 274
Cambodia, 410, 571, 578
Cameroun, 126–7, 129, 171, 494n
Canada: and Saint-Pierre affair, 173ff; de Gaulle's visits to, 294, 560, 580; reaction to "Québec libre" speech, 580
Capitant, René, 202, 438, 610, 616, 644–5, 646, 657; minister of education under de Gaulle, 257, 320; sets up Gaullist Union, 405; proposes works committees, 609; minister of justice under Couve de Murville, 640; his plan for participation, 641; refuses office under Poher, 653–4
Casablanca conference, 207–17, 220
Casey, Sir Richard (Lord), 192–3
Cassin, René, 133–4, 146n, 147, 179, 234, 385, 491; joins Free French, 120–21; negotiates Churchill-de Gaulle agreement, 122
Catroux, General Georges, 133, 139, 153, 181, 191, 210, 212–13, 219, 667, 675; prisoner-of-war with de Gaulle, 31–2; governor-general of Indo-China, 112–13, 125, 354; offered North African post by de Gaulle, 127; meets de Gaulle at Fort Lamy, 131; in Cairo, 131, 149–50; his part in Syrian campaign, 154–5, 157–60, 162–4; in Algiers, 217, 220, 223–4, 228, 230; threatens to resign, 227; proposes plan over leadership, 231; minister for Moslem affairs under de Gaulle, 257, 320; ambassador in Moscow, 383
Centre of Higher Military Studies, 73–4
Cercle Fustel de Coulanges, 50, 67
Chaban-Delmas, Jacques, 299n, 405–6, 445, 467, 469, 496, 541; at the liberation of Paris, 303, 306–7, 313; sends Delbecque to Algiers, 456; becomes president of Assembly, 497–9; and *domaine réservé*, 546; signs Colomb-Béchar protocol, 551n; as premier, 613, 644, 657, 660
Challe, General Maurice, 470, 501, 503–5,

Challe, General Maurice – contd
516; appointed commander-in-chief in Algeria, 500; his part in army revolt, 511–14
Chamberlain, Neville, 72, 78–9, 83, 89, 91
Chassin, General Lionel-Max, 456–7
Châteaubriant episode, 260
Chautemps, Camille, 78, 90, 113, 190
Chauvin, Captain, 44, 49
Cherrière, General, 456–8
Chevigné, Colonel Pierre, 286, 467
Chiang Kai-shek, Generalissimo, 274n, 291, 569
China, 548–9, 570n, 582, 642; as one of Big Four, 291–2, 334, 347; civil war in, 361; policy towards North Vietnam, 364–365; breaks with Russia, 563, 612, 614; France opens diplomatic relations with, 569
Choltitz, General von, 305–7, 309
Churchill, Sir Winston, 32, 86–7, 120, 131–132, 147, 153, 166, 178, 195, 201, 219–222, 234, 240, 279–80, 287, 294, 331, 334, 351, 442, 446, 545, 560, 663, 670, 678–9; becomes prime minister, 91; first meeting with de Gaulle, 98–9; at Briare and Tours, 100–04; and offer of union with France, 106–7
first wartime meetings with de Gaulle, 110–11; "finest hour" speech, 111; and destruction of French fleet, 117–18; reaches formal agreement with de Gaulle, 122–4; and Dakar expedition, 127–30; and Muselier affairs, 142–3, 168; supports de Gaulle over Somaliland, 149–150; attitude to Syria, 154–5, 161, 164; and North African campaign, 159, 181
defends de Gaulle against American opposition, 175–6, 189; defers to Roosevelt's views, 184–5, 205, 278, 282, 330; and Madagascar, 186–7, 194; crisis with de Gaulle over the Levant, 192–4; and Operation Torch, 200; views on Darlan, 202–3; at Casablanca conference, 207ff.; invites de Gaulle to Casablanca, 209–10; talks with de Gaulle, 211, 214–15; meets de Gaulle and Giraud in Algiers, 229–30; refuses to recognise French National Liberation Committee at Tehran, 274–5; illness and convalescence at Marrakesh, 278; and D-day landings, 281, 283; anger with de Gaulle over Eisenhower proclamation, 284; attitude to Operation Anvil, 295
supports French claim to occupation zone in Germany, 329, 345; proposes recognition of de Gaulle's government, 330; visits Paris and Rheims, 332–333; suggests tripartite agreement with France and Russia, 337–8; at Yalta, 343, 345; attitude to independence in the Levant, 358–60; defeated in general election, 361; congratulates de Gaulle on election, 391–2; "iron curtain" letter and Fulton speech, 420
his opinion of de Gaulle, 104, 110, 184
de Gaulle's opinion of Churchill, 98, 361, 664
Clark, General Mark, 199, 202, 288
Clemenceau, Georges, 29, 41–2
Cochet, General, 277, 299
Cohn-Bendit, Daniel, 614, 617–20, 624–5, 629–30
Colin, 140–43
Colomb-Béchar protocol, 551n
Colombey-les-deux-Eglises, 5, 399, 405, 441, 444, 465, 467; de Gaulle buys la Boisserie, 76; returns after the war to, 401–402; receives secret visit from Ramadier at, 417, 422; meeting with Adenauer at, 520, 527; in final retirement, 654, 656–8; death, 658; and funeral, 660
Combat (Resistance group), 202, 224, 241–2
Combault, Georges, 134
Comert, Pierre, 134
Comité d'Action socialiste (CAS), 249
Comités pour la Défense de la République (CDR), 632, 635
Communists, French, 302, 310, 342, 377–8, 382, 400, 405, 423, 428, 464, 466, 562, 681; in Popular Front, 71; wholesale arrests of (1939), 85–6; in Resistance, 241, 243, 252–253, 255, 299n, 300, 314, 319, 322–3; relations with Nazis, 251–2; alliance with Free French, 253–4; in Consultative Assembly, 256; attitude to National Liberation Committee, 257; their part in the liberation of Paris, 303, 307; lose trial of strength with de Gaulle, 325–8; in Algeria, 357, 510; and returning prisoners, 383; call for single-chamber constitution, 388; in 1945 elections, 390–91; join de Gaulle's government, 392–3; in 1946 elections, 404, 406; in Ramadier's government, 415; foment industrial unrest, 421–2, 425, 427, 432; in opposition to de Gaulle (1947), 426; their part in Grenoble disorders, 431; in 1948–9 elections, 433–4; in 1951 elections, 437; support withdrawal from NATO, 576; general position in Fifth Republic, 611–613; and 1968 riots, 614, 620, 622, 627–630, 632; in 1968 elections, 637
Conakry, 489–91
Confédération française démocratique des Travailleurs (CFDT), 610, 620
Confédération générale du Travail (CGT), 24, 78–9, 252–3, 421, 432, 477, 610, 620

Congo, Belgian (Zaïre), 539–41, 543, 561
Congo, French, 126–7, 171, 489, 494n
Connally, Tom, 289, 334
Conseil National de la Résistance (CNR), 245, 247, 255, 306, 309–13, 315
Constantine, 486, 495
—— Plan, 495, 500, 509
Cooper, Alfred Duff, 116, 119, 276, 278–80, 285
Corbin, Charles, 98, 100–6
Cornut-Gentille, Bernard, 484, 490n, 505–506
Corsica, 242, 253, 472–3
Coty, René, 460–61, 463–4, 474–5, 484, 498–9, 501; elected president, 446; appeals to de Gaulle to take office, 476–7
Coulet, François, 286, 303
Courcel, Geoffroy de, 98, 105, 108, 110, 120, 281, 595
Cournarie, Pierre, 230, 234
Couve de Murville, Maurice, 288, 657, 660; in Algiers, 219, 230, 257; as foreign minister, 484, 528, 535, 541, 554, 567, 573, 575–6, 618; succeeds Pompidou as prime minister, 627, 638, 640, 644, 647–9, 652, 655
Crépin, General Jean, 505–6
Croix de Feu movement, 60, 248
Cuba, 543, 559, 561, 564, 567
Cunningham, Admiral John, 118, 128, 130, 151, 297
Czechoslovakia, 79, 424–5, 429–30, 577, 582, 589, 640

Dakar, 118, 132, 191, 291; Allied expedition against, 126–31, 140, 142, 144n, 200; de Gaulle's 1958 visit to, 489, 491
Daladier, Edouard, 73, 75, 387, 466, 497; as prime minister in 1934, 59–60; advocates Maginot strategy, 68; becomes prime minister in 1938, 78; and Munich agreement, 78–9; arrests communist leaders, 79; sends troops to Finnish front, 86; resigns as premier and becomes defence minister under Reynaud, 89; opposes Reynaud's offer to de Gaulle, 90; testifies at Pétain's trial, 373
Damascus: de Gaulle's wartime visits to, 158, 161, 192; scene of fighting in 1945, 358–9
Daniel-Rops, 77
Darlan, Admiral, 106, 140, 153, 162–3, 195, 197, 213, 261; his pledge to Churchill at Briare, 102; and Massilia plan, 113, 115; his anti-British feelings, 115, 151 201; his part in setting up Vichy state, 114, 146; becomes foreign minister, 151; his

agreements with the Germans, 152, 154, 156, 172
  present in Algiers during "Torch" landings, 199; orders cease-fire and assumes authority in N. Africa, 199; treats with Americans and is disavowed by Pétain, 202; becomes high commissioner, 202; Churchill's reaction to deal with Americans, 202–3; de Gaulle's reaction, 202, 204; is assassinated, 204; consequences of this, 205–6
Darnand, Joseph, 261, 263, 265, 304, 373
Déat, Marcel, 69, 262–3, 304, 370
Dèbes, Colonel, 411
Debré, Michel, 307, 393, 426, 459n, 482, 496, 498, 510n, 519, 528, 575, 622–3, 643–4, 649–50, 657, 660; his character, 455; foretells de Gaulle's return to power, 460; urges Soustelle to go to Algiers, 469; drafts constitution of Fifth Republic, 484, 488, 491–493; is chosen as prime minister by de Gaulle, 499; his attitude to Algeria, 505; his broadcast on Algerian revolt, 514; finance minister under Pompidou, 603; his attitude to "participation", 609–11
Decoux, Admiral Jean, 144, 354
Defferre, Gaston, 249, 594, 622, 632
Dejean, Maurice, 120, 146n, 167–8, 179, 182, 194, 336, 341, 402
Delbecque, Léon, 456–72 passim, 496–7
Delestraint, General, 254
Delon, Alain, 643–4, 649
Deloncle, Eugène, 76, 248
Delouvrier, Paul, 500, 505–6
Denquin, Madame, 34–5
Dentz, General, 153–62 passim, 370
Devers, General, 350–53
Dewavrin, Captain, later Colonel, see Passy
Dien Bien Phu, 408, 413–14, 446, 453
Diethelm, André, 146n, 169, 194, 230, 238–9, 257, 320
Dinant, de Gaulle in action at, 30
Direction de la Surveillance du Territoire (DST), 596, 617
Direction Générale des Services spéciaux (DGSS), 258
Djibouti, 149–51, 153, 185, 578
Doriot, Jacques, 60, 248, 262
Douala, 127, 129, 130
Douaumont, de Gaulle taken prisoner at, 30
Doumenc, General, 64, 92
Doumergue, Gaston, 60, 67
Dreyfus affair, 12, 17, 19–21, 25n, 28, 61
Droit, Michel, 609, 626, 637, 649, 651–2
Duchet, Roger, 458
Duclos, Jacques, 326–7, 428, 477, 655

Dufieux, General, 38, 88, 95
Dufour affair, 278n
Dulac, General, 474
Dulles, John Foster, 450, 523–4, 526, 529–532
Dumbarton Oaks conference on United Nations, 334, 347, 360
Dunkirk, 94–6

Eboué, Félix, 126–7, 131, 133, 212
Ecole Supérieure de Guerre: de Gaulle as student at, 36–9; as lecturer at, 44–9
Eden, Sir Anthony (Lord Avon), 101, 158, 163, 168, 188, 192, 194–5, 200, 202–3, 208–9, 222, 229n, 281, 286, 330, 332, 522n, 660; first meeting with de Gaulle, 98; his part in Muselier affair, 140–44; gives de Gaulle information on Vichy, 156; meeting with de Gaulle over Saint-Pierre, 175–7; over Madagascar, 186–7; asks de Gaulle to accept Giraud's leadership, 220; seeks agreement with de Gaulle on recognition of his government, 285, 287; his views on French zone in Germany, 345; at Geneva summit, 447
Eisenhower, President (General) Dwight D., 189, 203, 205, 208, 220, 233, 293, 303, 309–10, 330, 529–30, 549, 566n, 666–7, 670; in command of "Torch", 199–201; provisionally endorses deal with Darlan, 202, 204; brings Peyrouton to Algiers, 226; invites Giraud and de Gaulle to confer, 232; is given full powers in France by Roosevelt, 277, 282; his D-day proclamation, 283–4; asks de Gaulle to visit Roosevelt, 285; asks for French troops in Italy, 296; opposes attack on Paris, 302, 305; orders French advance, 308; lends American troops for march-past, 315–16; transfers military command to French, 316; transfers civil authority, 331; attitude to defence of Strasbourg, 349–51, 417
   at Bermuda and Geneva summits, 446–447; receives de Gaulle's memorandum on Atlantic directorate, 521, 524–6; his reply, 527; his 1959 visit to Paris, 531–2, 560; talks with de Gaulle on proposed summit and other matters, 532–3; verdict on talks, 533–4; suggests limited tripartism at Rambouillet talks, 534–5; effect of U.2 incident and collapse of Paris summit on, 536, 563–4; his reply to de Gaulle's new proposals on tripartism, 537–8; agrees to Big Three summit but criticises French foreign policy, 539–540
   his opinion of de Gaulle, 216, 232,

277, 560; de Gaulle's opinion of Eisenhower, 232, 277, 351, 531, 560
El Alamein, 192, 194, 207
Ely, General Paul, 414n, 461–3, 470, 485–6, 503, 511
Entente Cordiale, 28, 42, 83
Eon, General, 201
Epinal, de Gaulle's speech at, 405
Erhard, Dr Ludwig, 528, 572, 575–6, 589
Estéva, Admiral, 370
Estienne, General Jean-Baptiste, 39, 46, 64
Ethiopia, 70, 149, 185, 578
European Defence Community (EDC), 446–447, 449–50, 522n
European Economic Community (EEC), 549, 552, 567, 589, 602, 684; France signs treaty of Rome, 447; de Gaulle's view of France's position in, 521, 541, 553; British policy towards, 527, 535, 542, 544, 579, 587–8; abortive negotiations on free trade area, 528, 541, 556, 683; de Gaulle's opposition to British entry, 549, 553, 555–6, 558–9, 578–9, 581, 665, 683; de Gaulle threatens French withdrawal over agricultural policy, 554, 683; "Fouchet Plan" put forward, 554–5; de Gaulle orders French boycott of, 573–4; de Gaulle's later thoughts on free trade area, 581, 586
European Free Trade Area (EFTA), 555, 579, 587; see also European Economic Community
Evian, talks and agreement at, 518

Fabre-Luce, Alfred, 598–9, 669
Fascism, de Gaulle accused of, 58, 134, 171, 227–8, 419–20, 429, 433
Fashoda, 21
Faure, Edgar, 234, 497, 646, 657; as prime minister, 438, 447; visits China, 569, 642; introduces reforms in education, 641–3
Fédération de la Gauche démocrate et socialiste, 629
Fédération des Etudiants révolutionnaires (FER), 615
Fédération nationale des Etudiants de France (FNEF), 604
Fenard, Admiral, 280–81, 285
Ferry, Jules, 28–9
Finland, 85–7
Fisher, Lord, quoted by de Gaulle, 48
Flandin, Pierre-Etienne, 146, 248, 261, 278–9
Flohic, Captain, 633–4, 654
Flouret, Marcel, 310, 313
Foccart, Jacques, 7, 458, 461, 471, 490n, 583, 595–6, 632–3, 638, 654, 657
Fort Lamy, 127, 130–31

Fouchet, Christian, 603, 642n, 660; and Lublin committee, 339, 341, 681; drafts plan for Europe, 554; as minister of the interior during 1968 riots, 618–23, 631, 633, 634n

Fourquet, General, 633

Frachon, Benoît, 326, 627

Franco, General Francisco, 4, 51, 94, 266, 356n, 373, 658, 663–4

Francs-Tireurs et partisans français (FTP), 299n, 315, 326

Franc-Tireur (Resistance group), 241

Frénay, Captain Henri, 201, 241, 244, 257, 320, 378, 383

Frey, Roger, 458, 460, 482, 496, 506, 623, 632, 647; his use of radio propaganda from Algiers, 471–2; organises defence committees, 596

Friedberg detention camp, 31

Front de Libération de la Bretagne (FLB), 648

Front de Libération Nationale (FLN), 454, 457, 462, 468, 482–3, 495, 500–04, 507–11, 516, 518, 529, 597

Front national (Resistance group), 241–2, 253

Front national français (Algerian faction), 505

Gabon, 126–7, 132, 494n, 583

Gaillard, Félix, 447–8, 456, 458, 460, 462, 522n; delegates powers in Algeria to Salan and Massu, 463

Gamelin, General Maurice, 73, 83, 85n, 87n, 90; opposes de Gaulle, 74–5; replaced by Weygand, 94–5

Gardes, Colonel Jean, 511, 514

Garreau, Roger, 182, 341

Gauche, Colonel, 88n

Gaulle, Anne de (daughter), 10, 76, 183, 255, 401, 659, 664; birth, 52; trust set up for, 442; death, 443

——, Charles de (uncle), 18–19

Gaulle, Charles André Joseph Marie de

LIFE

Up to the fall of France

birth, 19; boyhood and schooldays, 22–3; accepted for Saint-Cyr, 25; preliminary service at Arras, 25; at Saint-Cyr: second-lieutenant, 26; further service at Arras, 26–8; first meeting with Pétain, 27; lieutenant, 27; war service on Belgian front, 29–30; wounded three times: captain, 30; taken prisoner, 31; in captivity, 31–2; released, 32

in Polish army, 33–6; marries Yvonne Vendroux, 35; lecturer at Special Military School, 36; studies at Ecole Supérieure de Guerre, 37; conflict with principal over tactics, 37–8; controversy over his grading, 38–9; posted to Mayence, 39; appointed to Pétain's personal staff, 44; lectures at Ecole de Guerre and Sorbonne, 46–50; major, 50; posted to Trier, 50–54; and Near East, 54–5; publishes Le Fil de l'Epée, 56; transferred to Defence secretariat, 57–9, 61; lieutenant-colonel, 74; publishes Vers l'Armée de Métier, 62; meets Reynaud, 67; and Blum, 72–3; struck off promotions list, 74; at Centre for Higher Military Studies, 74; colonel, 75; meets Giraud, 75; posted to Alsace and Lorraine, 75–6, 87, 90; buys property at Colombey, 76; breaks with Pétain over dedication to La France et son Armée, 77–8

1940: writes memorandum on mechanised warfare, 88; summoned by Reynaud, 91; in action at Laon and Abbeville, 92–95; general, 93; meets Weygand, 95–6, 97, 99; appointed under-secretary for war, 96; first meeting with Churchill in London, 98; at Briare, 100–02; at Tours, 103–4; reaction to plan for Anglo-French union, 106; second visit to London, 106–8; final departure for England, 109

Victory and retirement

broadcasts to France, 110–12; sentenced to death in France, 112; Free French recognised by Britain, 116; recruits volunteers, 116–17; reaction to Mers-el-Kébir, 118–19; puts Passy in charge of intelligence, 121; signs agreement with Churchill, 122–4; takes part in Dakar expedition, 129–30; visits Africa, 130–32; issues Brazzaville manifesto, 133; sets up Defence Council, 133; his part in first Muselier affair, 137–44; sets up Free French State, 146; visits Cairo and Africa, 149–51; various disagreements with British over campaign in Syria, 152–165, 166; forms National Committee: trouble with Muselier, 166–9; clashes with Odic, 169–70; makes first contacts with America, 170–73; liberates Saint-Pierre and Miquelon, 174–6; has fresh trouble with Muselier, 177–8; makes contact with Russia, 178–82; in dispute with Britain over Madagascar, 185–7; receives limited recognition from America, 189; creates "Fighting French", 191; fresh disputes with Britain over Syria and Madagascar, 192–5

his relations with Giraud in Algiers, 196–8, 205–7; and "Torch" landings,

Gaulle, Charles de – *contd*
200–01; objects to Darlan's appointment, 202–4; at Casablanca, 210–16; meets Giraud, 210; first meeting with Roosevelt, 211; invited to Algiers by Giraud, 219, 221; urged to accept Giraud's leadership, 220; is acclaimed in Algiers, 222–4; disagrees with Giraud over Vichy officials, 225–8; forms Committee of National Liberation, 228; meets Churchill and Eisenhower, 229–30, 232; accepts compromise plan giving him powers over Committee, 234–5

his relations with the Resistance, 235–6, 239, 244; appoints Moulin as delegate-general, 243, 246–7; attitude of Socialists to, 249–51; message to Resistance, 250; opinion of Communists, 253–254; appoints Parodi as delegate-general, 255; as president of Consultative Assembly, 256, 267, 378–9; delivers ultimatum to Giraud, 258; attitude to Pucheu's trial, 264–5; makes speech at Brazzaville on African independence, 269

is ignored by Allies over Italian armistice and summit meetings, 273–4; disagrees with Russians over Polish government, 275; objects to Eisenhower's political powers in France, 277; meets Churchill at Marrakesh, 278–9; at Eisenhower's D-day HQ, 281–3; and AMGOT currency, 282, 285; objects to Eisenhower's proclamation, 283; broadcasts to French people, 284–5; visits Normandy, 287; visits Washington and Canada, 288–94; disagrees with Allies over use of French forces, 296–7; creates FFI, 299; prepares for advance on Paris, 305, 307; meets Leclerc at Rambouillet, 308; arrives in Paris, 309; meets Resistance leaders, 310–11; heads procession to Notre Dame, 313–14; dissolves Resistance and FFI, 314–15; receives message from Pétain, 316–17; tours provinces, 319, 323–5; sets up government, 320; subdues Communist opposition, 325; pardons Thorez, 326; government receives recognition from Allies, 331; meets Churchill in France, 332–3; is invited to join European Advisory Commission, 333; visits Stalin in Moscow, 326–8, 334–341; signs treaty with Russia, 341; is excluded from Yalta, 342–6; is invited to join Control Commission for Germany and to U.N. conference, 346–7; refuses to meet Roosevelt at Algiers, 347

his attitude to defence of Strasbourg, 349–51; and attack on Stuttgart, 351–4; and Japanese *coup* in Indo-China, 354–

355; quells disorders in Algiers, 357; fresh trouble with British in Levant, 358–60; meets Truman in Washington, 362–3; ignores Bao Dai's appeal, 363–4; sends Leclerc to Indo-China, 365

attitude to trials of Vichy leaders, 368–74; and 1945 Budget, 379–82; and returning prisoners, 383–4; makes proposals for new constitution, 388–90; endorsed by referendum, 391; elected prime minister, 391–2; resigns, 394–5

In retirement: the Fourth Republic
returns to Colombey, 401; attacks constitution at Bayeux, 402–3; speech at Epinal, 405; views on Indo-China, 408, 435–6; is consulted by Leclerc, 412–13; foretells return at Bruneval, 416–17; receives secret visit from Ramadier, 417–18

announces formation of RPF, 418, 421; his campaigning, 422–4; welcomes, then criticises, Marshall Plan, 424; attacks Communists, 426; his first speech on "participation", 428–9; attacks London proposals on European security, 430; is involved in Grenoble riots, 431–2; his reactions to 1949 elections, 434; praises MacArthur, 436; his reactions to 1951 elections, 437–8; advises Soustelle on premiership, 438–9; loses interest in RPF, 440

begins war memoirs, 441; creates Fondation Anne de Gaulle, 442; at his daughter's death, 443; publishes *Mémoires de Guerre*, 444

meets Delbecque, 456, 458; expresses views on North Africa, 459–60; announces readiness to take office, 466; gives press conference, 468, 470–71; meets Pflimlin, 473; issues appeal for peace in Algeria, 474; meets parliamentary chairmen and President Coty, 475–476; is backed by Socialists, 477; is voted into office, 478

In power: the Fifth Republic
forms first cabinet, 484–5; works on new constitution, 491–4; referendum in favour, 494; agrees to stand for president, 498; is elected, 499; takes office, 501

first visits to Algeria, 485–7; tour of Equatorial Africa, 489–91; announces Constantine Plan for Algeria, 495; removes Salan from power, 500; exercises clemency in Algeria, 501; tours military zones, 503; offers Algeria self-determination, 504; dismisses Massu, 505; threatens force, 506; tours army posts, 507; meets FLN, 508–9; speaks of

"Algerian Republic", 509–10; holds referendum on self-determination, 510; meets challenge of army revolt, 512–14, 519; deals with Bizerta blockade, 515–516; assassination attempts on, 516–518

meetings with Adenauer, 520, 527–9, 550–52; with Macmillan, 522–3; with Dulles, 523–4, 529–30, 530–31; sends memorandum on Atlantic policy to Eisenhower and Macmillan, 520–21; removes Mediterranean fleet from NATO control, 530; talks with Eisenhower about atomic weapons, 532–4; announces French deterrent, 534; talks with Eisenhower and Macmillan at Rambouillet, 534–6; at Paris summit, 536, 563–4; his further proposals on tripartism, 536–7; and Congo crisis, 539–40; receives Kennedy in Paris, 543; various meetings with Macmillan, 544, 555–8; signs treaty with Germany, 552–553; threatens French withdrawal from EEC, 554; pays State visit to London, 557; vetoes Britain's application to EEC, 559; rejects MLF and test ban treaty, 559, 568–9; visits America, 560, 566; warns Kennedy on Vietnam, 561–2; talks with Khrushchev and Vinogradov, 565–6, 567–8

at Kennedy's funeral, 569; recognises Communist China, 569; pays State visit to Mexico, 570; is operated on for prostate trouble, 571; meets Erhard, 572; calls for return to gold standard, 573; withdraws from SEATO, 573; orders boycott of EEC, 573–4; announces withdrawal from NATO, 574–6; pays State visit to Russia, 577; makes "Québec libre" speech, 580; pays State visit to Poland, 580; rejects Britain's second application to EEC, 581; supports Biafra, 582–3; refuses to devalue the franc, 584; announces embargo on arms for Israel, 584–5; boycotts WEU, 585; and "Soames affair", 586–8

in presidential elections of 1965, 594–595; reaction to Ben Barka affair, 597; attitude to student reforms, 603–4; sets up financial commission under Rueff, 606; receives setback over miners' strike, 608–9; and "participation", 609–11, 617, 640–41

attitude to 1968 riots, 618–21; pays State visit to Rumania, 623–4; holds cabinet meetings on riot situation, 624–625; broadcasts, 626; approves draft on referendum, 628; announces retreat to Colombey, 630; consults army chiefs in Germany, 631, 633–4; dissolves parliament, 635; popular demonstration in his favour, 636; accepts Pompidou's resignation, 638–9; appoints Couve de Murville, 638; forms new cabinet, 641; and Markovic affair, 643–5, 650; tours Brittany, 648; gives TV interview, 651–652; is defeated in referendum, 652; resigns, 653; his holiday in Ireland, 655–656; resumes work on memoirs, 656; his holiday in Spain, 658; death, 658; funeral, 660

PERSONALITY

Outward appearance, 3, 26, 36, 72, 75, 101, 121, 442, 470

Character, 663–6, 686; aloofness, 10, 26, 36, 183; conceit and determination, 31, 36, 38, 48, 73, 119, 184, 401; contempt for inferiors, 5–6, 9, 53, 73, 394, 399, 414, 611, 626, 673

Family life, 10, 183, 255, 385, 401–2, 442–3

Literary tastes, 22–3, 25, 55, 442, 616

Methods of government, 6–9, 385–6, 592–5

OPINIONS AND POLICIES

France as a nation, 29, 41, 50, 109, 133, 169, 196, 235–6, 267, 292, 311, 321–2, 351, 423, 466, 546–7, 602, 670–71, 673, 677–8

Resistance movement, 236, 247, 265, 314–15, 379

Vichy administration, 133, 169, 267, 319, 368ff., 674, 677

Domestic affairs

Army and defence: concepts of leadership and discipline, 5, 46–9, 56, 58, 668; theories on mechanised arms, 31, 37, 45, 62–5, 87–9, 91, 667; nuclear policy, 521, 532–4, 549, 559–60, 568–9

Economics, 322, 382, 384, 573, 584, 605–606, 648

Justice and the law, 266–7, 319, 369, 517–18, 519, 597–9

Politics: the Communists, 253–4, 316, 327–8, 423, 426–7, 612–13, 681; constitutional reform, 388, 390, 393–4, 402–403, 405, 417–18, 433n, 437, 496–7; the role of the president, 386–7, 403, 492, 499, 591; use of the referendum, 437, 477, 492–3, 592, 647, 651, 665; arbitrary use of the constitution, 475–6, 599–602

Social reform, 228, 250, 268, 377–8, 604, 613, 626, 647; "participation", 377–8, 429, 437, 609, 617, 625, 628, 649, 651–2

Foreign affairs

Africa, 131, 149, 269, 363, 451, 459–60, 487, 488–91, 578, 582–3

Algiers and Algeria, 211, 217, 225, 459–

Gaulle, Charles de – *contd*
460, 482–8 *passim*, 495, 501–2, 504, 506–10, 680
America, 172, 202, 279, 282, 288, 292, 423–4, 438, 450, 452, 529, 566, 573
Atlantic alliance, 434–5, 450, 520ff., 574–5
Britain, 98, 118, 124, 150, 156, 164, 187, 452, 555–9, 579, 581, 586–8, 683
Europe, 268, 275, 292, 334, 346, 362–3, 367–8, 449–50, 547–8, 683–4; the EEC, 541, 553ff., 573–4
Germany, 40–41, 73, 293, 331, 352–3, 362–3, 367, 430, 438, 527–8, 548–53, 565, 572, 589, 613
Indo-China, 291, 363, 365, 408–9, 412–13, 435–6, 561–2, 572, 579
Levant, the, 55, 154–64 *passim*, 191–2, 359, 363
Russia, 178–82, 336, 341–2, 426, 523, 532–3, 549, 562–5, 577, 582, 681, 684
United Nations, the, 360–61, 451, 540
LITERARY WORKS
Discorde chez l'Ennemi, La, 31–2, 39–41, 49, 67, 669
Discours et Messages, 444, 547n
Fil de l'Epée, Le, 5, 26, 47–9, 56, 61, 77, 183, 668–9, 672
France et son Armée, La, 12, 24–5, 77–8, 96, 669
Mémoires de Guerre, 441–4, 547, 668, 669–70
Mémoires d'Espoir, 458, 481n, 483n, 521n, 601–2, 605, 656, 658, 668, 670–671
Vers l'Armée de Métier, 62–5, 88, 669
Other works (published and unpublished), 23, 34, 44–5, 49, 57–8, 62, 88–9
For verdict on de Gaulle's position and achievements, see 3–5, 9, 663–end
Gaulle, Elisabeth de (daughter), 51, 183, 255, 401, 442
——, Henri de (father), 18–21, 21n, 22, 250
——, Jacques de (brother), 22, 256
——, Jeanne de (mother), 18–19
——, Joséphine de (grandmother), 17–18
——, Jules de (uncle), 18
——, Julien-Philippe de (grandfather), 17
——, Marie-Agnès de (sister), 22, 255
——, Philippe de (son), 36–7, 183, 255, 309, 401, 653
——, Pierre de (brother), 22, 256
——, Xavier de (brother), 19, 22, 255
——, Yvonne de (wife), 51, 140, 183, 255, 442–3, 633–4, 659–60; courtship and marriage, 34–5; life at Colombey, 401–2; and Madame Pompidou, 650
Geneva, summit meeting at, 447, 681
Gensoul, Admiral, 118

George VI, King, 122, 144, 222
Georges, General, 92–3, 210, 212, 257, 278–279; supports Giraud, 228, 231; appointed commissioner of State, 230
Georges-Picot, 37
Germany: before and during First World War, 29–30; de Gaulle's imprisonment in, 31–2; his views on, in *La Discorde chez l'Ennemi*, 31–2; under Versailles treaty, 41–3, 51–3, 69; Hitler's rise to power in, 59, 69; and concept of Blitzkrieg, 64–5; reoccupies Rhineland, 70; and Munich agreement, 78–9; invades Poland, 79
during Second World War: events leading to fall of France, 84ff., 99; relations with Vichy, 114, 132, 145, 152, 156, 179, 199; alliance with Italy and Japan, 144; North African campaign, 151, 158, 185, 187, 188; invasion of Russia, 165, 178, 207, 252; invasion of unoccupied France, 199, 201–2, 245, 261; treatment of France, 199, 201–2, 245, 251–2, 261; attacked by FFI, 300–302; and liberation of Paris, 303–6, 309, 314; Ardennes offensive, 349–50; battle for Stuttgart, 352–4; capitulation of Berlin, 355; final surrender of, 356, 678
occupation of: planned, 345–6, 678; carried out, 362
de Gaulle's policy towards, 367, 430, 449, 521, 548–51, 554–5, 572, 678–9; de Gaulle's visits to, 528, 554, 572; Britain's policy towards, 541–2, 587–8
attitude towards Atlantic directorate, 525–8; relations with France, 552–3, 571–2, 576, 579, 588–9, 684; threatened by Khrushchev, 564–6; de Gaulle's secret visit to French army in, 631, 633
Gerow, General, 307, 313
Ghent agreement, 103–5
Giacobbi, Paul, 257, 320, 380, 426
Giap, General Vo Nguyen, 224, 365, 407, 412, 435, 454
Gibraltar, 192, 199
Giraud, General Henri, 75–6, 135, 195–6, 200–01, 203–4, 217, 222, 225, 230, 256–7, 278, 282, 288–9, 296, 298, 394, 545, 678–679; escapes to unoccupied France, 196–197; his letter to Pétain, 197; his support by and relations with Americans, 196, 198, 202, 218, 279; spurns de Gaulle's overtures, 197–8; his military plans, 198; flies to Algiers, 199; is appointed C.-in-C., 202; and high commissioner, 205; at first refuses and then agrees to meet de Gaulle, 205, 207
meets de Gaulle and Allied leaders at Casablanca, 208–16; receives advice

from Monnet, 218; praises de Gaulle, 219; makes proposals to National Committee, 220; invites de Gaulle to Algiers, 221; first meetings with de Gaulle, 223–4; and Peyrouton incident, 226–8; comes to agreement over men of Vichy and Committee of National Liberation, 228–9; has trouble with Committee, 231–2; visits Washington, 233–4; and Boisson crisis, 233; remains C.-in-C. under compromise plan, 234–5; arms Corsican maquis, 241–2, 253; is persuaded to retire, 258; and execution of Pucheu, 264–5
  character, 197, 206, 219
Giscard d'Estaing, Valéry, 572, 611, 644, 657
Godard, Colonel, 511, 514
Godfroy, Admiral, 118, 126
Gouin, Félix, 249, 391, 400, 412
Gouvernement provisoire de la République Algérienne (GPRA), 495
Grandval, Gilbert, 610
Greece, 144, 151, 153, 420
Grenier, Fernand, 253, 257, 265, 302, 320
Grenoble, riots at, 431–3
Gromyko, Andrei, 564, 573, 576
Guderian, General Heinz, 64–5, 70, 100
Guichard, Olivier, 445, 458, 461, 471, 647
Guillaumat, General Pierre, 54, 484–5, 503, 506–7
Guinea, 529; de Gaulle's visit to, 489–91; votes for independence, 494

Hadj, Messali, 501, 504
Haile Selassie, Emperor, 185, 660
Haiphong, 366, 408, 410–12
Halder, General Franz, 84
Halifax, Lord, 103, 106, 122, 156, 158
Hallstein, Walter, 554
Hanoi, 407, 410–12
Harriman, Averell, 192, 339, 625
Hautecloque, Captain de, see Leclerc
Heath, Edward, 556, 567, 660
Henriot, Philippe, 263, 314
Hering, General, 46–7
Herriot, Edouard, 44, 104, 305, 387, 414, 438; writes to de Gaulle from prison, 248; released by Laval, 304; declines to serve under de Gaulle, 389; disagrees with de Gaulle over military awards, 394
Herter, Christian, 535–6, 541
Heydrich, Reinhard, 262
Higher Council of National Defence, 57–9, 61
Himmler, Heinrich, 355–6
Hitler, Adolf, 65, 72, 83, 144, 151–2, 179, 306, 349, 663, 668, 686; his rise to power, 59, 62; denounces Versailles treaty, 69–70; and Munich agreement, 78–9; meets Pétain and Laval, 132 145; dies, 355
Ho Chi Minh, 363, 366, 412, 414n, 573, 682; forms provisional government after Japanese surrender, 364–5; proclaims republic, 365; and uprising against the French, 406–7; signs provisional agreement with France, 409; at Fontainebleau talks, 410–11
  his opinion of de Gaulle, 413
Holland, 91–2, 554
Holz, Lieutenant-Colonel, 260
Hopkins, Harry, 190, 212, 218, 343–5, 347
Houphouët-Boigny, Félix, 484, 491, 493
Hull, Cordell, 171–6 passim, 188–9, 218n, 273, 288, 290
Huntziger, General, 97, 100

Indo-China, 28, 270, 384, 415, 421, 424, 445, 447, 453, 561, 678, 681; Vichy concessions to Japan and Siam in, 125, 144–5; American attitude to, 293, 363, 408–9; British and Chinese occupation of, under Potsdam terms, 363, 365–6; Ho Chi Minh's activity in North Vietnam, 364–5; de Gaulle sends d'Argenlieu, Leclerc and Sainteny to, 365, 682
  events leading to outbreak of war: Leclerc pacifies the south, 409; Sainteny and Ho Chi Minh sign provisional agreement, 409; d'Argenlieu proclaims Republic of Cochinchina, 410; Fontainebleau talks, 410–11; French blockade of Haiphong and action against Vietminh, 411; French bombardment of Haiphong, 408, 411
  outbreak of war: massacre at Hanoi, 406–7, 412; Leclerc declines post of high commissioner after consulting de Gaulle, 412–13; Bollaert appointed, 413; evacuation of Caobang, 435; Navarre replaces de Lattre, 446; French defeat at Dien Bien Phu, 446; lessons of war, 454
  de Gaulle's views on: at the time, 409, 413–14, 435–6; after the event, 408
  see also Cambodia; Laos; Vietnam
Ingolstadt camp, 31
Iraq, 151, 154, 524
—— Petroleum Company, 192
Irish Republic, de Gaulle's holiday in, 655–6
Irwin, Major-General N. M. S., 129–30
Ismay, General Sir Hastings, 101, 181, 281
Isorni, Jacques, 371–2
Israel, 579, 582, 584–5, 648

Italy, 70, 71, 99, 144, 273–4, 334, 421
Ivory Coast, 489, 494n, 583

Jacquinot, Louis, 256, 320, 484–5, 491
Janot, Raymond, 491
Japan, 171, 186, 355, 361, 365; forms alliance with Axis, 144; occupies Indo-China, 144–5; and Pearl Harbour, 185; *coup* in Indo-China, 354; surrenders after Hiroshima, 364
Jeanneney, Jules, 104, 319–20, 378, 389, 640, 645, 649, 654; and 1969 referendum, 646, 651
Jeanson, Francis, 509
Jebb, Sir Gladwyn (Lord Gladwyn), 540, 544n
Jeunesses communistes révolutionnaires (JCR), 614–15
Jews: deportation of, from France, 262; de Gaulle's views on the, 581
Jodl, General Alfred, 84, 356
Johnson, President Lyndon B., 569–80 *passim*
Jouhaud, General Edmond, 457, 461, 474, 519, 598; his part in army revolt, 511–512, 514
Joxe, Louis, 234, 385, 657; in Algeria, 512, 514; as minister of justice during 1968 riots, 618–22
Juin, Marshal Alphonse, 26, 288, 316, 334, 362, 409; appointed chief of general staff by de Gaulle, 298; at liberation of Paris, 310, 313; breaks with de Gaulle over Algeria, 506, 510

Keitel, Field-Marshal Wilhelm, 84, 356
Keller, General, 89
Kennedy, President John F., 545, 572, 670; receives de Gaulle's memorandum on tripartism, 542; corresponds with de Gaulle on various subjects, 543, 564; and multilateral nuclear force, 552, 559; at Nassau summit, 558; visits Paris, 561; propounds plan for Atlantic Community, 567–8; de Gaulle attends funeral of, 569
de Gaulle's verdict on, 543, 561–2
Kérillis, Henri de, 136
Khrushchev, Nikita, 530, 532, 534, 543; his Berlin policy, 528–9, 539, 550, 565–6; at Paris summit, 536, 563–4; at Vienna summit, 564; visits France, 565–6
Kiesinger, Dr Kurt, 587–9, 633
King, Admiral Ernest J., 189, 289, 362
King, Mackenzie, 294
Koenig, General Marie-Pierre, 117, 132, 277, 280, 371; at Bir-Hakim, 188; takes command of FFI, 299–300; his part in the

liberation of Paris, 303, 305–7, 313; signs agreement with Eisenhower, 310; made military governor of Paris, 315
Korea, 420, 435, 445
Kosygin, Andrei, 579–80
Krieg, Pierre-Charles, 632
Krim, Belkacem, 518–19
Krivine, Alain, 614, 655

Labarthe, André, 135–6, 138, 166–8, 177–178
la Baume, de, 132
Laborde, Admiral de, 201–2
Lacheroy, Colonel Jean, 454–5, 511, 514
la Chevalerie, Xavier de, 654–5
Lacoste, Robert, 320, 382, 457, 459, 462, 464
Lagaillarde, Pierre, 462, 472, 550–6, 509
Lakhdar, Si, 508–9
Lalande, General, 633, 654
Lampson, Sir Miles (Lord Killearn), 157–8
Laniel, Joseph, 446, 497
Laon, action at, 92, 667
Laos, 410, 541, 543, 561
la Porte du Theil, General de, 76
Larminat, General de, 125–33 *passim*, 156, 223; commits suicide, 598
la Rocque, Colonel de, 60, 248
Laroque, Pierre, 286
Lattre de Tassigny, General Jean de, 76, 99, 298, 302, 371; and defence of Strasbourg, 349–51; takes Stuttgart, 352; signs German surrender document, 356; killed in Indo-China, 445
Laurent, Augustin, 320, 389
——, Jean, 309
——, Pierre, 603
Laval, Pierre, 4, 90, 114–15, 226, 265, 335–336, 372, 394, 674; as prime minister of France, 57, 59; meets Hitler and von Ribbentrop, 145; dismissed by Pétain, 145; enters into relations with Germans, 146; as Vichy prime minister, 197, 261; his collaborationist policies and methods, 259–60, 262–3; and deportation of Jews, 262; his unsuccessful plan to treat with Allies, 304–5; as witness at Pétain's trial, 373; his trial and execution, 374
character and appearance, 115; de Gaulle's verdict on, 304
Leahy, Admiral William D., 153, 171–2, 190–91, 200, 205, 244, 289, 293, 363
Lebanon: 1941 campaign for independence of, 154–65 *passim*, 166; Franco-British dispute over, 191–4, 278n; scene of disturbances in 1945, 357–60; civil war in (1958), 523–4; Israeli raid on, 584–5

Lebrun, President Albert, 87, 89, 108, 114–115, 119; de Gaulle's verdict on, 670

Lecanuet, Jean, 594–5

Leclerc, General Philippe de Hauteclocque, 121n, 194, 316, 355, 451; his part in de Gaulle's expedition to West Africa, 127, 130, 132; appointed to Defence Council, 133; his successes against Italians, 150; designated to head French advance on Paris, 298–9, 306, 308; in Normandy, 302, 305–6; makes contact with Resistance, 307; reaches Paris and accepts German surrender, 309; meeting with de Gaulle, 309–10; at victory parade, 313; signs Japanese surrender document, 365; sent to Indo-China, 365–6, 408; his views on Indo-China and disagreement with d'Argenlieu, 409; restores order in the south, 409; resigns his command, 410; asked by Blum to resume command, 412; consults de Gaulle, 412–13; declines offer, 413

Legentilhomme, General, 126, 146n, 149–150, 153, 167, 195, 201, 257

Léger, Alexis, 190

Légion française des Combattants, 261

Lejeune, Max, 484–6

Lemaigre-Dubreuil, Jacques, 198, 202, 204, 218n

Leopoldville, 131, 133

Lepercq, Aimé, 320, 380

Le Trocquer, André, 256–7 277, 310, 313, 320, 404, 475–6

Levant, the, 112–13, 125–6, 151, 181, 185; see also Lebanon; Syria

Lévy, J.-P., 241, 244

Libération (Resistance group), 241

Lille, 18–19

Linarès, Colonel de, 224

Lloyd, Lord, 126–7

Lloyd, Selwyn, 526, 530, 535, 538

London: de Gaulle's first visits to, 98–9, 105–8; 109; his wartime stays in, 120ff., 141, 165ff., 183ff., 220–2, 239, 243–4, 250, 281–2, 284–6, 287; post-war conferences in, 361, 367, 430; de Gaulle's State visit to, 557

Lorillot, General, 470, 473

Loustaunau-Lacau, 37

Lublin committee, 332ff., 346, 681

Lu Han, General, 366

Luizet, 308, 310, 313

Lyttelton, Oliver (Lord Chandos), 159–63

MacArthur, General Douglas, 436

Macmillan, Harold, 274, 296–7, 521n, 529–530, 539–41, 545, 551n, 559, 568, 660, 670; his part in Casablanca conference,
207, 210, 214, 218–21; meets de Gaulle in Algiers, 225; and Peyrouton affair, 228; and Boisson, 233; leaves Africa for Italy, 276

talks with de Gaulle on NATO and nuclear power, 522–3; receives de Gaulle's memorandum on Atlantic directorate, 521, 524; his reactions, 525–527; meets Adenauer, 528, Eisenhower's letter to, 532–4; at Rambouillet talks on tripartism, 534–5; puts forward proposals on consultation, 536; his reaction to French and American counter-proposals, 537–8; his further meetings with de Gaulle on tripartism and nuclear arms, 542, 544, 557–8; visits Moscow, 550–51; at Nassau summit with Kennedy, 558; at Paris summit, 564

first talks with de Gaulle on EEC, 541–2, 544; his views on Europe conflict with de Gaulle's, 553, 555, 683; announces wish to sign treaty of Rome, 556; meets de Gaulle in Sussex and France, 557; and de Gaulle's objection to British entry, 558–9

de Gaulle's opinion of, 276

McNamara, Robert, 545, 567

Madagascar, 201, 494n; British occupation of, and de Gaulle's reaction to this, 185–187, 191, 193–5; insurrection in, 415, 421; de Gaulle's visit to, 489

Maginot Line, 45, 67–9, 85, 87

Maisky, Ivan, 179

Malraux, André, 392, 425, 438–9, 571, 621, 646, 657; and RPF, 420, 422–3, 431; as minister of culture, 484, 624

Mandel, Georges, 104, 113–16

Mao Tse-tung, 454, 663

Marcellin, Raymond, 641, 643–4, 649, 657

Marchais, Georges, 617–18

Marchal, Colonel, 254, 299n

Margerie, Roland de, 98, 103, 108

Marie, André, 430–31

Marin, Louis, 241, 247, 389

Markovic affair, 643–5, 649–50, 657

Marly, 399, 439

Marrakesh: de Gaulle meets Churchill at, 278

Marrane, Georges, 311, 499

Marseilles, 263, 429

Marshall, General George C., 189, 285, 289, 362, 430; announces Marshall Plan, 423; de Gaulle's verdict on, 436

Marshall Plan: announced, 423; de Gaulle's views on, 424; Soviet bloc's rejection of, 424–5; France signs agreement under, 429; French Communists' attempted sabotage of, 432; effects of, 434, 681–2

Martel, Robert, 456
Martin, Dr, 456
Marty, André, 257, 302
Massigli, René, 194, 220, 223, 228, 230, 257, 273, 280n, 285, 296, 319–20
Massilia incident, 113–15
Massu, General Jacques, 461, 469, 491, 667; declares support for de Gaulle, 459; announces Committee of Public Safety, 463; sends telegram to de Gaulle, 464; appointed prefect by de Gaulle, 487; resigns from Committee of Public Safety, 495; gives interview to German paper, 504–5; dismissed from office, 505; as C.-in-C. in Germany, 631; secret meeting with de Gaulle, 633–4, 638
Matter, General, 50
Mauclère, 126–7
Maudling, Reginald, 556
Maurin, General, 68, 74
Maurras, Charles, 25n, 60, 67, 75, 248
Mayence, de Gaulle's army service at, 39
Mayer, Daniel, 249, 404
——, Colonel Emile, 61–2, 72, 78
——, René, 230, 320, 440, 446
Meffre, Captain ("Howard"), 136, 139–43
Melun, 508–9
Mendès France, Pierre, 113, 248, 256, 384, 408n, 409n, 477, 497; as minister of national economy, 320; and 1945 Budget, 379–80; resigns over austerity programme, 381–2; as prime minister, 446–7; votes against de Gaulle's investiture, 478; attitude to 1968 riots, 628–9, 632
Mengin, Robert, 135n, 136
Menthon, François de, 249, 256, 378, 389, 393
Mercier, Colonel, 33, 36
Mers-el-Kébir, bombardment of, 117–19, 124, 144n, 674
Mesnil-les-Hurlus, de Gaulle wounded at, 30
Messmer, Pierre, 507, 620, 622, 631, 638, 657
Metz, 75–6, 79, 196
Mexico, 570
Michelet, Edmond, 459, 496, 505
Mihailovich, General Drazha, 274, 337
Mikolajczyk, 275, 332, 339
Millerand, President, 44
Mittelhauser, General, 112–13, 125
Mitterrand, François, 378, 478, 594–5, 625, 628–9, 632
Moch, Jules, 381, 428; as minister of the interior, 432, 469–74 passim
Mohammed ben Youssef, 446–7
Mollet, Guy, 632; as prime minister, 447; appeals to de Gaulle to return, 467, 471–

477 passim; as minister of state, 484, 487, 491; resigns, 607
Molotov, Vyacheslav, 182, 335–41, 367, 424
Mongibeaux, 370, 372n
Monnerville, Gaston, 475–6, 478, 499, 571, 602, 647
Monnet, Jean: in London at outbreak of war, 98, 105–6; declines to serve under de Gaulle, 115, 120, 190, 676; sent to Algiers by Roosevelt to advise Giraud, 218–19; decides to help de Gaulle, 219; meets de Gaulle, 225; on Committee of National Liberation, 228–9, 232; in provisional government, 257; as head of economic mission in USA, 320, 363; heads Planning Commission in France, 421, 602; and Europe, 553
Montalembert, Henriette de, 401
Montcornet, action at, 93, 667
Montgomery, General Sir Bernard (Viscount Montgomery of Alamein), 193–194, 207, 286–7, 352, 359n
Montreal, 294, 580
Mordant, General, 354–5
Moret, Captain, 143, 167, 177
Morice, André, 457–8
Morlière, General, 411
Mornet, 370
Morocco, 29, 357n, 451; "Torch" landings in, 199; post-war repression in, 445–7; comes to agreement with de Gaulle, 487; and Ben Barka affair, 597; see also Casablanca
Morton, Major Desmond, 106, 167–8, 195
Moscow: de Gaulle's 1944 visit to, 326–8, 334–42; Churchill in, 330–32; 1947 conference in, 420–21; de Gaulle's State visit to, 577
Mostaganem, de Gaulle's speech at, 486–7
Moulin, Jean: joins de Gaulle in London, 242, 246; de Gaulle's delegate to Resistance, 221, 243–4, 246, 299n; chairman of CNR, 222, 245, 247; capture and death, 245, 246, 254
Mouvement national algérien (MNA), 501–2
Mouvement républicain populaire (MRP): foundation of, 249, 378; calls for single-chamber constitution, 388; Communist attack on, 391; in 1945 elections, 391; joins government, 392; its position in Fourth Republic, 400; in June 1946 elections, 404; Gaullists' campaign against, 405; in November 1946 elections, 406; its opposition to RPF, 426; in 1947 municipal elections, 427; its opposition to de Gaulle's confederal ideas, 555

Movement of 22 March, 614, 619
Moyrand, Colonel, 37–8
Multilateral nuclear force (MLF), 558–9, 567
Munich agreement, 78–9, 83
Murphy, Robert, 171, 206, 218, 228, 274, 448, 529; sends Giraud offer of American support, 198–9; negotiates with Darlan, 202; at Casablanca, 207–16 passim; introduces de Gaulle to Roosevelt, 211; meets de Gaulle in Algiers, 225; and Boisson affair, 233–4; transferred to Italy, 276
Muselier, Admiral, 133–4, 136, 143–4, 146n, 675–6; joins de Gaulle in London, 117, 121; appointed head of naval forces, 137; resentment of de Gaulle's leadership, 137–8, 166; joins campaign against Antoine, 138; disagrees with de Gaulle about staff appointments, 139; sets up naval security service, 140; accused of making contact with Vichy and arrested, 140; de Gaulle's ultimatum over his release, 141; is released, 142

proposes himself as chairman of executive committee, 166–7, 180; tries to withdraw navy from de Gaulle's control, 168; gives way under British persuasion, 169; his part in Saint-Pierre and Miquelon expedition, 173–6; storm over his resignation, 177–8; severs connection with de Gaulle, 178; with Giraud in Algiers, 227
Mussolini, Benito, 70, 78, 99, 144, 355, 686
Mutter, André, 467

Nachin, Captain Lucien, 45, 50, 52–3, 55, 61
Nanterre, 614, 617–18
Napoleon III, 10–11, 686
Narbonne, Jacques, 603
Nassau, summit at, 556, 558–9
Nasser, Gamal Abdel, 452, 668, 682–3
Navarre, General Henri, 446
New Caledonia, 190, 494n
Niamey, 585
Niger, 494n, 585
Nigeria, 583
Nixon, Richard M., 532, 560–61, 660
Noguès, General, 116, 120, 133, 210–11, 213–14, 219, 224–5, 228, 675; de Gaulle offers to serve under, 111–12; and Massilia incident, 113; accepts armistice, 125; resists "Torch" landings, 199; transfers powers to Darlan, 202; removed from office, 228
Nordling, Raoul, 307
——, Rolf, 309

North Atlantic Treaty Organisation (NATO), 435, 447, 529, 531, 535–7, 541, 544, 549, 552, 681; de Gaulle's policy towards, 450, 521–4, 530, 533–4, 538, 540, 587, 609; in his memorandum, 524–526; Macmillan's policy towards, 527, 542; de Gaulle withdraws Mediterranean fleet from, 530, 608; Eisenhower's policy towards, 532–3, 538; and Kennedy's, 545, 558, 576; further stages in French withdrawal from, 566, 568, 574; German policy towards, 572, 576; final French withdrawal from, 575, 665, 684–5
Norway, 86–7, 89
Nuclear weapons and power, 521–71 passim, 613

Occident (student group), 615, 617–18
Odend'hal, Admiral, 137
Odic, General, 169–70, 216, 224, 677
Olié, General Jean, 512, 514
Oradour-sur-Glane, 263, 301
Oran, 486, 510
Orengo, Charles, 443
Organisation de l'armée secrète (OAS), 445, 483, 509, 596–7, 631n; behind revolt in Algeria, 510ff.; its campaign of attrition in France, 516–18, 600
Organisation for European Economic Co-operation (OEEC), 424
Ortiz, Joseph, 505–6
Ortoli, Captain, 177, 238–9
Oubangui-Chari (Central African Republic), 126–7, 131, 489, 494n

Painlevé, Paul, 54, 56
Palewski, Gaston, 67–8, 120, 153, 185, 210, 223, 281, 288, 334, 362, 385, 571
Panama Canal Company, 12
Parant, Major, 127, 132
Paris, 102–3, 678; declared an open city, 99; liberation of, 303ff.; Churchill's visit to, 332; food shortage in, 375; abortive summit meeting in, 536, 563–4, 556; Kennedy's visit to, 561; Khrushchev's earlier visit to, 565–6
Paris, Comte de, 591, 624
Parodi, Alexandre: as de Gaulle's delegate with the Resistance, 255; his part in the liberation of Paris, 303–13 passim; appointed minister of labour, 320
Parti Socialiste unifié, 628
Passy, Colonel, 121, 137, 167, 236–7, 240, 246, 251, 258n, 316, 318n, 406; joins Free French, 117; first meeting with de Gaulle, 121; sets up intelligence net-

Passy, Colonel – *contd*
work inside France, 121–2, 238; accused of being Cagoulard, 136; his relations with Muselier, 138–40, 142–3; takes over non-military intelligence, 238–9; relations with internal Resistance, 242–245

Patch, General Alexander, 302, 314, 349, 352–3

Patti, Major, 365

Payen, Fernand, 372

Peake, Charles, 177, 184, 187, 284

Pearl Harbour, 170, 173, 185

Péguy, Charles, 20–22, 25, 81

Peladon, 224

Pétain, Marshal Philippe, 4, 49–50, 56, 59, 68, 90, 104, 113–14, 126, 132, 152, 153, 156, 170–71, 263, 304, 668, 677; first meeting with de Gaulle, 27; confers "posthumous" decoration on de Gaulle, 30–31; acts in de Gaulle's favour in his army career, 38–9, 46–8, 53–4; appoints de Gaulle to his personal staff, 44–5; as war minister in 1934, 63, 66–7; breaks with de Gaulle over dedication to *La France et son Armée*, 76–8; as vice-premier to Reynaud, in favour of capitulation, 94–6, 103; at Briare, 101–2; last meeting with de Gaulle, 105

forms government, 108; asks for armistice, 110; is made head of State, 119; his popularity with French people, 119, 132, 145, 259, 261, 673, 675; meets Hitler, 132, 145; dismisses Laval, 145; sets up Vichy State, 146, 674; his relations with Giraud, 197, 213; with Darlan, 202, 261; policy towards Germans, 260–61; final plea to de Gaulle, 316; surrender, 355, 371; trial, 370, 372–4; imprisonment and death, 373, 434n

his opinion of de Gaulle, 373

Petit, General, 180, 459

Peyrefitte, Alain, 603–4, 618–19, 621–2

Peyrouton, Marcel, 112, 210–11, 219, 224–225, 233, 278–9; resigns, 221, 226–8

Pflimlin, Pierre: as "last card" prime minister, 460–72 *passim*; meets de Gaulle, 473; reaction to de Gaulle's statement on Algeria, 474; resigns, 474; as minister of State under de Gaulle, 484, 491

Philip, André, 134, 191, 196, 204, 223, 228, 230, 239, 244, 251, 256, 381

Picot, Colonel, 52

Pieds-noirs, 455, 457, 485

Pilsudski, Marshal, 34, 36

Pinay, Antoine, 473; as prime minister, 440, 445; as minister of finance under de Gaulle, 484, 605–6; resigns over NATO, 608

Pineau, Christian, 243, 250, 322, 377, 389, 477

Pius XII, Pope, 288

Pleven, René, 127, 146n, 147, 193–4, 201, 230, 256, 392, 520; joins Free French, 120–21; his mission in Washington, 156, 171–3; as minister for colonies, 320; as minister for finance: 1945 Budget, 379–382; his recovery plan, 384; prime minister for a day, 460–61

Poch-Pastor, Baron, 309

Poher, Alain, 647, 653–6

Poincaré, Raymond, 29, 42–4, 57

Poland, 32, 276, 347, 550, 577; de Gaulle's army service in, 33–6; invasion of, 79, 83–4, 87; Bank of France and Polish gold, 129, 275; its frontiers redrawn after the war, 332, 335–7, 346; and Lublin Committee, 338–42, 681; de Gaulle's State visit to, 580

Polaris missiles, 558–9, 567

Pompidou, Madame Claude, 644, 650

Pompidou, Georges, 477, 598, 635, 642–3, 645, 649, 660, 673; assists de Gaulle financially and over publication of memoirs, 443; as de Gaulle's *directeur de cabinet*, 491, 500; as prime minister, 519, 570–71, 575–6, 590; his conservative views, 603, 610, 613, 616; travels in Iran and Afghanistan, 618–19; faces 1968 riots, 621–4, 626–7, 630–34; his preliminary offer to resign, 625, 634, 637, supervises election campaign, 636; is praised in public and blamed in private by de Gaulle, 584, 625, 634, 637; de Gaulle accepts resignation of, 638–40; implicated in Markovic affair, 644–5, 650; announces future candidacy for presidency, 646; his last meeting with de Gaulle, 650; wins presidential election, 654–6; forms cabinet, 657; broadcasts on de Gaulle's death, 658–9

Popular Front, 71–2, 78–9, 247–8, 391, 400

Potsdam conference, 329, 361, 365, 549, 678

Présence et Action du Gaullisme, 657

Puaux, 112–13, 125, 230

Pucheu, Pierre, 261, 264–5, 319

Quebec, 332; de Gaulle's speech in, 294, 580, 602, 685

Queuille, Henri, 248, 256, 318n, 320, 446; as prime minister, 431, 433–4

Quimper, 102–3, 648

Quinton, René: *Maxims on War*, 55

Radical Socialist party, 71–2, 89, 248, 389, 391, 427, 437

Radio-Diffusion-Télévision Française (RTF), 493, 531, 621, 626–7

Ramadier, Paul, 389, 427, 477, 497; as prime minister, 412–15; makes secret visit to Colombey, 417–18, 422; dismisses Communists, 421

Rashid Ali, 151–2

Rassemblement des Gauches Républicaines (RGR), 406

Rassemblement du Peuple Français (RPF), 435–6, 439, 445, 448, 596, 609, 612, 685; founded by de Gaulle, 418–19; its aims and methods analysed, 419–21, 426, 428; early successes of, 422; its membership analysed, 425–6, 429; in 1947 municipal elections, 427; and Grenoble riots, 431–432; in 1949 senate elections, 433–4; in 1951 elections, 437–8; de Gaulle loses interest in, 440

Rembertow camp, 33

Rémy, Colonel, 422, 425, 434n

Renault works, unrest at, 421, 615, 625

Renouveau national, 597

Républicains sociaux, 456, 496

Resistance movement, French, 188, 240, 386; contacts with Passy's Intelligence Service, 121–2, 237–9, 242, 246; leaders make contact with de Gaulle, 190, 243–244, 250; relations betwen Giraud and, 210, 218, 241–2, 253, 257–8; formation of CNR, 257–8; its support for de Gaulle, 221, 225, 235; National Liberation Committee gives de Gaulle command of, 233; critical attitude of, to de Gaulle, 235, 244–5

different groupings in, 236, 241, 247–249; Franco-British conflict of views over, 236–7, 240; British contacts with, 237, 263; Communists in, 237, 241, 243–257 *passim*, 300–07 *passim*, 319, 323–8; Diethelm's political control of, 238–9; de Gaulle appoints Moulin delegate-general with, 243–4; de Gaulle's message to, 250; de Gaulle appoints Parodi delegate-general with, 255; Bidault becomes chairman of CNR, 255; de Gaulle sets up Consultative Assembly with Resistance members, 256–7; DGSS set up under Soustelle, 258

in action against Nazis, 260, 261, 263; formation of *maquis*, 263; attitude of CNR to Pucheu trial, 265; work of Consultative Assembly, 266–7, 278–9, 387; clashes between de Gaulle and, 267; de Gaulle creates FFI, 299; insurrection in preparation for D-day, 300–01; attack on Vercors redoubt, 301–2; support of Anvil landings, 302; insurrection in Paris, 303, 306–7, 309; CNR meets de Gaulle in Paris, 310-11; at march-past, 313–14; de Gaulle dissolves CNR and FFI, 315

illegal tribunals of, 318; in de Gaulle's government, 320; de Gaulle's control of, in provinces, 323–5; represented in High Court juries, 369–70

Revel, Jean-François, 671

Revers, General, 299n

Reynaud, Paul, 71, 79, 85, 88, 98–9, 387, 667; meets de Gaulle, 67; supports his views on armoured corps, 68–70; de Gaulle offers to serve under, 78; becomes prime minister, 89; is prevented from offering post to de Gaulle, 90; de Gaulle's letter to, 90–91; sends for Pétain, 94; appoints de Gaulle under-secretary for war, 96; sends de Gaulle to London, 97; at Briare, 100, 102; at Tours, 103–4; agrees to go to Algiers, 105; and proposal for union with Britain, 106–8; resigns office, 108; is witness at Pétain's trial, 373; promised post of speaker by de Gaulle, but withdraws, 498

de Gaulle's opinion of, 68

Ribbentrop, Joachim von, 145, 152

Robert, Admiral, 173–4, 176

Rol-Tanguy, Colonel, 309

Rommel, Field-Marshal Erwin, 151, 158–9, 165, 188, 192, 207, 287

Roosevelt, Elliott, 208

Roosevelt, President Franklin D., 153, 185, 189–91, 195, 200–01, 206, 207, 220, 229, 233, 281, 283, 284n, 287, 295–6, 332–3, 342, 408, 664, 670; his policy towards Vichy, 170–71; his antipathy towards and mistrust of de Gaulle, 170–71, 173, 184, 195–6, 205, 212, 273, 330, 343, 679; offers lend-lease to Free French, 172; and Saint-Pierre affair, 175–6; supports Giraud in Africa, 196, 279, 545; relations with Darlan, 202-4; at Casablanca, 208ff.; meets de Gaulle, 211–12, 215–16; sends Monnet to Algiers, 218; and Boisson affair, 231–4, 278–9; his post-war policy, 273–5; instructs Eisenhower to take full powers in France, 277; and AMGOT, 278, 282; sends indirect invitations to de Gaulle, 279–80; talks with de Gaulle in Washington, 288–94; orders attack on Paris to be delayed, 305; praises de Gaulle in State of the Union message, 343; sends Hopkins to Paris, 344; at Yalta, 345–6; invites France to conference on United Nations, 347; asks de Gaulle to meet him at Algiers, 347, 362; dies, 348

Rostand, Edmond, 22, 26, 35

Rougeron, Colonel: *Air Lessons of the Spanish War*, 89n
Roure, Rémy, 31, 74
Rousset, David, 617
Rozoy, General, 141–2
Rueff, Jacques, 572, 584, 606–7
Ruhr, the, 43, 331, 363, 367, 376, 430
Rumania, 144, 618, 623–4
Rundstedt, Field-Marshal Karl von, 349–350
Russia, 28, 32–4, 71, 240n, 291, 333, 420, 423, 430, 516, 526, 530, 550, 567–8, 580, 582, 630; signs pact with Hitler, 83, 252, 276; invades Poland, 84; invades Finland, 85–6; is invaded by Germany, 158, 178, 252; receives Allied support, 178–80, 182; recognises de Gaulle and Free French, 179, 194; de Gaulle offers troops to, 181; post-war policy of, 273–4; and Polish gold, 275; de Gaulle's 1944 visit to, 326–8, 334–42; relations with French Communists, 327–8, 342, 425–6, 612; Churchill's visit to, 332; policy towards Poland, 332, 336–40, 342; signs treaty with de Gaulle, 341, 562, 681; policy at Yalta, 345–6; at 1945 Paris conference, 367; and Marshall Plan, 424–5; and Berlin blockade, 431; de Gaulle's later policy towards, 521n, 523, 533, 548, 562, 573–4, 683–4, 686; American policy towards, 532, 564, 580; at Paris summit, 536, 563–4, 566; breaks with China, 563, 612, 614; at earlier Paris talks on Berlin, 565–6; State visit of de Gaulle to, 577–8

Saar, the, 331, 363, 367, 376, 430
Sabattier, General, 355
Saigon, 411–12, 682
Saint-Cloud, 473, 475
Saint-Cyr, 23, 24–6, 36–7, 667
Sainteny, Jean, 365, 409–12, 682
Saint-Phalle, Alexander de, 309
Saint-Pierre and Miquelon, 173–6, 494n
Sakhiet-Sidi-Youssef, raid on, 448, 453, 515, 522n
Salah, Si, 508–9
Salan, General Raoul, 5, 462, 472–4, 485–486, 631; influenced by Gaullist propaganda, 456; sends telegrams to General Ely, 461, 463; shouts "*Vive de Gaulle!*", 465–6; arrests ultras, 468; meets Soustelle, 469; appointed de Gaulle's delegate-general, 487; averts general strike, 495; demoted to inspector-general, 500; removed from Algeria, 509; takes part in army revolt, 511–12, 514; arrested and imprisoned, 519, 598

San Francisco, 348, 360
Sauckel, 262–3
Sauvageot, Jacques, 617, 625
Schuman, Robert, 415, 417, 428, 430, 432, 446, 553
Schumann, Maurice, 77, 135, 404, 406, 459–60
Séguy, Georges, 620, 625, 627
Senegal, 489, 494n; *see also* Dakar
Senghor, Léopold, 492–3
Sérigny, Alain de, 460, 506
Serreules, Lieut., 137–8
Service d'Action civïque, 628, 632, 635
Service de Documentation et Contre-Espionage (SDECE), 596, 617
Service d'Ordre Légionnaire (SOL), 261–263
Service obligatoire du Travail (SOT), 263
Seydoux, Roger, 633
Smith, General Bedell, 232, 283, 285, 296–7
Smuts, Field-Marshal Jan, 281
Soames, Sir Christopher, 585–9
Socialist party, French, 71, 135, 239, 322, 400, 471; in Resistance, 249; attitude to de Gaulle and Free French, 249–50; reconstruction of, 251; on CNR, 378; calls for single-chamber constitution, 388; in 1945 elections, 391; forms part of de Gaulle's administration, 392; calls for defence cuts, 393; in 1946 elections, 404, 406; nationalisation proposals of, 415; in 1947 municipal elections, 427; in 1951 elections, 437; attitude to de Gaulle's declaration of 15 May, 466–7; withholds support from de Gaulle, 475
Somaliland, French, 126, 149, 152, 494n, 578
Soong, T. V., 366
Sorbonne: de Gaulle's lectures at, 50; and 1968 riots, 617–24 *passim*, 630, 636
Sosnkowski, General, 274, 276
Soustelle, Jacques, 120, 134, 136, 142, 219n, 253, 394, 447, 463–4, 482, 486, 498, 546, 596, 600, 664; as de Gaulle's commissioner for information, 191, 240; put in charge of DGSS, 258; in de Gaulle's first administration, 392; his part in founding RPF, 419, 422, 425; disagrees with de Gaulle over accepting premiership, 438–440; and de Gaulle's memoirs, 444; works for de Gaulle's return to power, 455–60 *passim*; advocates integration of Algeria, 456, 502; receives popular acclaim in Algiers, 469; supports Corsican insurrection, 472; in de Gaulle's cabinet, 485; directs radio propaganda, 493; opposes de Gaulle's acts of clemency in Algeria, 501; further opposition to de Gaulle, 505; is removed from office, 506;

harried by police during OAS campaign, 597

South-East Asia Treaty Organisation (SEATO), 536, 543, 571, 573

Spain, 4, 72, 425, 509, 658

Spears, Major-General Sir Edward, 104–5, 110, 129, 191, 442n; at Briare and Tours, 101, 103; accompanies de Gaulle to England, 108–9; and Muselier affair, 141–2; accompanies de Gaulle to Cairo, 147; at Cairo, 152; at treaty negotiations in Levant, 163–5
    his first impressions of de Gaulle, 101

Special Operations Executive (SOE), 237, 242, 323

Spellman, Cardinal, 220

Stalin, Josef, 207, 326, 333, 343, 361, 421, 670; signs pact with Hitler, 83, 85, 178; on Darlan, 204; policy towards Czechoslovakia, 274; and Poland, 274–5, 332; relations with and attitude to Thorez, 327–8, 425; against French zone in Germany, 329; meets de Gaulle in Moscow, 334–42; signs treaty with de Gaulle, 341, 562, 681; at Yalta, 345–6; his post-war imperialism, 420; rejects Marshall Plan, 424
    de Gaulle's description of, 355

Stark, Admiral, 189, 201

Stavisky scandal, 60

Stéphane, Roger, 459, 657

Stewart, Michael, 585, 587–8

Strasbourg, 349–51, 417, 418, 572

Stulpnagel, General von, 260, 305–6

Stuttgart, battle for, 352–3

Sudreau, Pierre, 601

Suez expedition, 452, 522, 682

Suhard, Mgr, 314

Susini, Jean-Jacques, 482, 505–6, 509, 518–19

Sweida, 162

Syria, 166; agreement between Nazis and Vichy over, 152; disagreement between de Gaulle and Britain over campaign in, 152–4; de Gaulle's declaration of independence for, 154, 156; invaded by joint Allied force, 155; surrender terms drafted by de Gaulle, 157; and accepted by Vichy, 158; Free French excluded at signing of armistice, 159; continued Franco-British dispute over armistice, 159–61; agreement reached on paper, 161; disagreement continues in the field, 162–163; incident at Sweida, 162–3; de Gaulle's limited success over recruitment of Vichy troops, 164–5; fresh disagreement with Britain over elections in, 191–4; scene of disturbances in 1945, 356, 358–9; final evacuation of troops from, 360

Tanguy-Prigent, François, 320, 382

Tchad, 126–7, 130–31, 153, 171, 489, 494n

Tehran conference, 274

Teitgen, Pierre-Henri, 241, 249, 320, 374, 378, 389, 404, 417

Terrenoire, Louis, 459, 507

Thibault, René, 441

Third Force, 422, 424, 427, 429, 432, 434; Blum first suggests idea of, 428

Thomazo, Colonel Jean, 468

Thorez, Maurice, 257, 319, 395, 417, 425; deserts from army and goes to Moscow, 86, 251; given free pardon by de Gaulle, 326, 681; returns to France, 327; discussed by Stalin and de Gaulle, 327–8; importance of, for de Gaulle, 342, 681; claims principal post in de Gaulle's cabinet, 392; Socialist opposition to, 404; makes unsuccessful bid for premiership, 406

Tillon, Charles, 320, 326

Tito, Marshal, 274, 346, 429

Tixier, Adrien: as de Gaulle's representative in Washington, 173, 188–90, 204, 206; as commissioner for labour in provisional government, 230, 256; as minister of interior, 318n, 320, 399

Tobruk, 149, 151, 185, 188

Tollet, André, 306, 310

Torch, Operation, 199 ff.

Touré, Sékou, 489–91, 494

Tournoux, Jean-Raymond, 439–40

Tours, 103–4

Tricot, Bernard, 508, 595, 630, 638, 643–6, 647–8, 652, 654, 656, 660

Trier, de Gaulle's army service at, 50–54

Truman, President Harry S., 348, 353, 362–3, 402, 421, 435–6

Tugny, Captain de, 26

Tukhachevsky, Marshal, 31, 33

Tunisia, 357n, 445, 451; Allied campaign in, 221, 223; Bourguiba returns to, 447; and Sakhiet raid, 448, 453; agreement between de Gaulle and, 487; Algerian terrorists in, 495; takes action against French in Bizerta, 514–16

Union de la Jeunesse marxiste-léninists (UJCML), 614

Union Démocratique et Socialiste de la Résistance (UDSR), 378

Union des Etudiants communistes (UEC), 614

Union nationale des Etudiants français (UNEF), 604, 617–18, 620, 628

Union pour la nouvelle République (UNR), 496–7, 611n

United Nations, 448, 529, 534, 559n, 573, 580, 679; discussed at Yalta, 346; set up at San Francisco conference, 347, 360–361; Russian boycott of, 435; and Congo crisis, 539, 541, 543
de Gaulle's attitude to, 361, 451

Vallon, Louis, 239, 251, 426, 429, 483, 610, 616, 649n, 657
Valluy, General Jean, 410–12
Vansittart, Sir Robert (later Lord), 105
Vendroux, Jacques, 35, 405, 419, 625, 657–658
——, Madame, 35
Vercors, Resistance in, 301–2
Verdilhac, General, 159–60
Versailles: treaty of, 41–3, 65, 70; meeting at, 351
Vichy administration, 118, 119, 146, 172, 672; set up, 145–6; breaks with Britain, 124; influence in Indo-China, 125, 144–145; in Africa, 126–7, 129–30, 149; supposed contacts with Muselier, 140, 142–143; influence in Levant, 151–2, 156; General Odic and, 169–70; American relations with, 151, 153, 170–72, 179; Giraud and, 197, 213; French support of, analysed, 247–8, 673, 675; relations with Nazis, 252, 260–63; France's condition under, 259–60; laws declared null and void by de Gaulle, 266–7, 674; trials of leading figures in, 368ff., 434n; legality of, 673–4, 676–7
Viénot, Pierre, 280, 284–5, 287, 320
Vietminh, 407, 409–13, 446, 454
Vietnam, 615, 618, 682; Kennedy's policy for, 561; French attitude to American intervention in, 561–2, 571–3, 579–580, 582; see also Indo-China
Vinh Sanh, Prince (Duy Tan), 366
Vinogradov, Sergei, 567–8
Vishinsky, Andrei, 276

Waldeck-Rochet, 576, 625
Wangenbourg, de Gaulle's army service at, 76, 87, 89–90
Warsaw, 33–4, 275, 337
Washington, de Gaulle's visits to, 288ff., 362–3, 566, 569
Wavell, Field-Marshal Lord, 126, 150–59 passim
Welles, Sumner, 172, 188, 206
Western European Union, 585, 588
Weygand, General Maxime, 34, 63n, 105, 126, 133, 170, 172, 198, 675; opposes de Gaulle's military theories, 74, 94; is appointed C-in-C., 94; his defeatist outlook, 95, 99, 103–4; seeks, but does not take, de Gaulle's advice, 96; de Gaulle's efforts to get rid of, 97, 100; declares Paris an open city, 99; invites Churchill to Briare, 100; at Briare meeting, 101–2; de Gaulle's last appeals to, 112, 149; persuades Pétain to limit collaboration, 156, 171; as witness at Pétain's trial, 373
Wilbur, General William H., 214
Wilson, Daniel, 12
——, Edwin, 276, 296–7
——, Harold, 575 579–80, 587–8, 660
——, Field-Marshal Sir Henry Maitland, 159–63, 165, 288, 297
Winant, John, 188, 220

Yahia, Mohammed Ben, 508
Yalta conference, 329, 342–7, 360–61, 545, 549, 582, 664, 678
Ybarnégaray, Jean, 105
Yeo-Thomas, 245
Yugoslavia, 151, 337, 346–7, 429

Zbrucz, de Gaulle's defence at river, 34
Zeller, General André, 511–12, 514
Zhdanov, Andrei, 425, 432